Special Places to Stay

Fourteenth edition
Copyright © 2015 Alastair Sawday
Publishing Co. Ltd
Published in 2015
ISBN-13: 978-1-906136-71-0

Alastair Sawday Publishing Co. Ltd,
Merchants House, Wapping Road,
Bristol BS1 4RW, UK
Tel: +44 (0)117 204 7801
Email: info@sawdays.co.uk
Web: www.sawdays.co.uk

The Globe Pequot Press,
P. O. Box 480, Guilford,
Connecticut 06437, USA
Tel: +1 203 458 4500
Email: info@globepequot.com
Web: www.globepequot.com

Series Editor Alastair Sawday
Editorial Patrick Henry, Gwen Vonthron
Editorial Assistants Stephanie Clement,
Jennie Coulson, Florence Sivell, Louise Phipps,
Samantha Wiltshire, George Eaton
Production Coordinators Lianka Varga,
Sarah Frost Mellor
Senior Picture Editor Alec Studerus
Picture Editor Ben Mounsey
Writing Jo Boissevain, Nicola Crosse, Carmen
Cox, Wendy Ogden, Ann Cooke-Yarborough,
Monica Guy, Helen Pickles, Lucy Cowie
Inspections Diana Harris-Sawday,
Elizabeth Yates, Georgina Gabriel,
Ann Cooke-Yarborough, Jill Coyle, Lynn Kirk,
Judith Lott, Isabelle Browne, Nicky Hilyer,
Annaliza Davis, Caroline Renouf,
Rosie Jackson, Jo Wilds, Suzie Immediato,
Patricia Shears, Nicky de Bouille,
Helen Woods, June Bibby, Nikki Varney
*Thank you to those people who did an inspection
or two.*
Marketing & PR +44 (0)117 204 7801
And thanks to Ann Cooke-Yarborough and
Annie Shillito for their invaluable support.

*We have made every effort to ensure the accuracy of the
information in this book at the time of going to press.
However, we cannot accept any responsibility for any
loss, injury or inconvenience resulting from the use of
information contained therein.*

Production: PagebyPage Co. Ltd.
Maps: Maidenhead Cartographic Services
Printing: Advent Print Group, Andover
Distribution: Travel Alliance, Bath
diane@popoutmaps.com

Alastair

# Sawday's

Special Places
to Stay

# French
Bed & Breakfast

# 4    Contents

As ever, our new places are delightful. There is the little Château Lalinde, with soft stone walls, overhanging the Dordogne river. Imagine breakfast on the terrace. Then we have Marie-Alpaix's handsome Basque house with wooden timbers, white walls and stupendous view up to the Pyrénées. It has family portraits, fine furniture, modern and antique art, books – and is flooded with light. In the La Maison d'à Côté, Arlette does shabby-chic as only a Frenchwoman can. Stone stairs spiral up to an apartment of lofty 19th-century rooms – gorgeous. L'Observance, within the old walls of Avignon, has been part of a monastery, a barracks and a factory. How much sheer personality can you take? Les 3 Officiers, at the other end of France, in Meuse, is a manor house by the church – run by the delightful Frederick.

This is our 21st year – and over 30 of the B&Bs in this edition have been with us since the beginning in 1994! These entries are highlighted with a stamp. We have new places from every corner of France, and the arrival of low-cost flights has persuaded more young urbanites to do B&B, often with real panache. So the 'scene' is buzzing.

The inexorable rise of Booking.com, airbnb and others has underlined our role: providing our followers a trusted guide to the most special places. And if half the houses in France are riding the B&B bandwagon, then perspective is needed: they can't all be wonderful. We are plugging a serious gap.

Well, if that paragraph doesn't seduce you, what will? These places are remarkable. We select them because we like them, and then we tell you why. Be it a very simple cottage or farmhouse, or a splendid castle – we don't mind what they are, as long as they are Special.

The British don't need reminding how very beautiful France is, but they do need to be reminded to book earlier. Our house owners are frustrated to have to turn away so many Sawday visitors, whom they love having, because they have booked late. Please get cracking, and let us know how you fare.

*Alastair Sawday*

Photo left: Tom Germain
Photo right: Clos Marcamps, entry 466

It's simple. There are no rules, no boxes to tick. We choose places that we like and are fiercely subjective in our choices. We also recognise that one person's idea of special is not necessarily someone else's so there is a huge variety of places, and prices, in the book. Those who are familiar with our Special Places series know that we look for comfort, originality, authenticity, and reject the insincere, the anonymous and the banal. The way guests are treated comes as high on our list as the setting, the architecture, the atmosphere and the food.

## Inspections

We visit every place in the guide to get a feel for how both house and owner tick. We don't take a clipboard and we don't have a list of what is acceptable and what is not. Instead, we chat for an hour or so with the owner and look round – closely (it involves bouncing on

beds, looking at linen, testing taps). It's all very informal but it gives us an excellent idea of who would enjoy staying there and our aim is to match places and guests. If the visit happens to be the last of the day, we may stay the night. Once in the book, properties are re-inspected every three to four years so that we can keep things fresh and accurate.

## Feedback

In between inspections we rely on feedback from our army of readers, as well as from staff members who are encouraged to visit properties across the series. This feedback is invaluable to us and we always follow up on comments.

So do tell us whether your stay has been a joy or not, if the atmosphere was great or stuffy, the owners and staff cheery or bored. The accuracy of the book depends on what you, and our inspectors, tell us. A lot of the new entries in each edition are recommended by our readers, so keep telling us about new places you've discovered too. Please use the forms on our website at www.sawdays.co.uk.

However, please do not tell us if the bedside light was broken, or the shower head was scummy. Tell the owner, immediately, and get them to do something about it. Most owners are more than happy to correct problems and will bend over backwards to help. Far better than bottling it up and then writing to us a week later!

## Subscriptions

Owners pay to appear on our pages. Their fee goes towards the high costs of inspecting and writing, of developing our website and producing an all-colour book. We only include places that we like and find special for one reason or another, so it is never possible for anyone to buy their way onto these pages. Nor is it possible for an owner to write their own description. We will say if the bedrooms are small, or if a main road is near. We do our best to avoid misleading people and keep up our reputation for reliability.

## Disclaimer

We make no claims to pure objectivity in choosing these places. They are here simply because we like them. Our opinions and tastes are ours alone and this book is a statement of them; we hope you will share them. We have done our utmost to get our facts right but apologise unreservedly for any mistakes that may have crept in.

You should know that we don't check such things as fire regulations, swimming pool security or any other laws with which owners of properties receiving paying guests should comply. This is the responsibility of the owners.

Do remember that the information in this book is a snapshot in time and may have changed since we published it; do call ahead to avoid being disappointed.

Photo: Maison Numéro Neuf, entry 559

### Finding the right place for you

All these places are special in one way or another. All have been visited and then written about honestly so that you can decide for yourselves which will suit you. Those of you who swear by Sawday's books trust our write-ups precisely because we don't have a blanket standard; we include places simply because we like them. But we all have different priorities, so do read the descriptions carefully and pick out the places where you will be comfortable. If something is particularly important to you then check when you book: a simple question or two can avoid misunderstandings.

### Maps

Each property is flagged with its entry number on the maps at the front. These maps are a great starting point for planning your trip, but please don't use them as anything other than a general guide – use a decent road map for real navigation. Most places will send you detailed instructions once you have booked your stay.

### Symbols

Below each entry you will see some symbols; they are explained at the very back of the book. They are based on the information given to us by the owners. However, things do change: bikes may be under repair or a new pool may have been put in. Please use the symbols as a guide rather than an absolute statement of fact and double-check anything that is important to you – owners occasionally bend their own rules, so it's worth asking if you may take your child or dog even if they don't have the symbol.

Children – The symbol shows places which are happy to accept children of all ages. This does not mean that they will necessarily have cots, high chairs, etc. If an owner welcomes children but only those above a certain age, we have put in these details, too. These houses do not have the child symbol, but even these folk may accept your

Photo: ELIEL, entry 137

younger child if you are the only guests. Many who say no to children do so not because they don't like them but because they may have a steep stair, an unfenced pond or they find balancing the needs of mixed age groups too challenging.

Pets – Our 🐕 symbol shows places which are happy to accept pets. It means they can sleep in the bedroom with you, but not necessarily on the bed. Be realistic about your pet – if it is nervous or excitable or doesn't like the company of other dogs, people, chickens, or children, then say so.

Owners' pets – The 🐈 symbol is given when the owners have their own pet on the premises. It may not be a cat! But it is there to warn you that you may be greeted by a dog, serenaded by a parrot, or indeed sat upon by a cat.

## B&B Awards

We've chosen B&Bs that we think deserve a special mention. Our categories are:

• Favourite newcomers
• Old favourites
• One of a kind
• Most praised breakfast

More details are given on pages 17-21, and all the award winners have a stamp on their entry.

## First edition veterans

Over 30 entries have been with us since 1994. Amazing! We've highlighted these entries with a stamp, so do look out for them.

Photo: Le Châtaignier, entry 408

## Communicating with owners

As we say below, owners are living their own lives in their own homes and, ideally, receiving guests as friends – who happen to pay them something when they leave. This is why travellers choose to stay at B&Bs rather than anonymous hotels. It is also why the owners have every right to expect to be treated like friends not machines. Yet, in the 'century of information', they are reporting more and more cases of enquirers who never reply to emails, guests who book and simply don't turn up: no email, no telephone call, no explanation, let alone an apology. It isn't for lack of the means to do it, it's because they just don't think. Let's stem the tide of thoughtlessness and keep our owners in business.

Our owners are proud of the regions in which they live and are invaluable sources of knowledge about their local areas, which they love to share. Many of our owners comment that guests who only stayed one night, en route to elsewhere, wished that they had stayed longer to explore. Guests too, having arrived and stayed for one night, have also said that they wished they had booked for longer. So do consider stopping for more than one night where you might otherwise be 'travelling through'.

## Types of places

Some places have rooms in annexes or stables, barns or garden 'wings', some of which feel part of the house, some of which don't. If you have a strong

preference for being in the throng or for being apart, check those details. Consider your surroundings, too: rambling châteaux may be cooler than you are used to; city places and working farms may be noisy at times; and that peacock or cockerel we mention may disturb you. Some owners give you a front door key so you may come and go as you please; others like to have the house empty between, say, 10am and 4pm. Remember that B&Bs are people's homes, not hotels.

Do expect:
• a genuine personal welcome
• a willingness to go the extra mile
• a degree of informality, even family-life chaos, i.e. a fascinating glimpse of a French way of life

Don't necessarily expect:
• a lock on your bedroom door
• gin and tonic at 2am
• your room cleaned, bed made and towels changed every day
• a private table at breakfast
• access to house and garden during the day
• an immediate response to your booking enquiry

## Rooms

Bedrooms – We tell you if a room is a single, double, twin/double (i.e. with zip and link beds), suite (a room with space for seating or two rooms sharing a bathroom), family room (a double bed + single beds), or triple (three single beds). If 'antique beds' sound seductively

authentic, remember they are liable to be antique sizes too (190cm long, doubles 140cm wide); if in doubt, ask, or book a twin room (usually larger). Owners can often juggle beds or bedrooms, so talk to them about what you need before you book. It is rare to be given your own room key in a B&B and your room won't necessarily have a television.

Bathrooms – Most bedrooms in this book have an en suite bath or shower room; we only mention bathroom details when they do not. So, you may have a 'separate' bathroom (yours alone but not in your room) or a shared bathroom. Under certain entries we mention that two rooms share a bathroom and are 'let to same party only'. Please do not assume this means you must be a group of friends to apply; it simply means that if you book one of these rooms you will not be sharing a bathroom with strangers. For

simplicity we may refer to 'bath'. This doesn't necessarily mean it has no shower; it could mean a shower only. If these things are important to you, please check when booking.

Sitting rooms – Most B&B owners offer guests the family sitting room to share, or they provide a sitting room specially for guests.

## Meals
Unless we say otherwise, breakfast is included. This will usually be a good continental breakfast – traditionally fresh baguette or pain de campagne with apricot jam and a bowl of coffee, but brioche, crêpes, croissants, and homemade cake may all be on offer too. Some owners are fairly unbending about breakfast times, others are happy just to wait until you want it, or even bring it to you in bed.

Apart from breakfast, no meals should be expected unless you have arranged them in advance. Many places offer their guests a table d'hôtes dinner – the same food for all and absolutely must be booked ahead – but it will not be available every night. (We have indicated the distance to the nearest restaurant when dinner isn't offered; but be aware that rural restaurants stop taking orders at 9pm and often close at least one day a week.) Often, the meal is shared with other guests at a communal table. These dinners are sometimes hosted by Monsieur or Madame or both and are usually a wonderful opportunity to get to know your hosts and to make new friends among the other guests. Meal prices are quoted per person, although children will usually eat for less. Ask your hosts about reduced meal rates if you're travelling with little ones.

When wine is included this can mean a range of things, from a standard quarter-litre carafe per person to a barrel of table wine; from a decent bottle of local wine to an excellent estate wine.

## Summer kitchens

Well before the ubiquitous barbecue came upon us, the French had come up with a daring idea for their places of summer residence: a minimal kitchen outside, half in the garden, and not doing 'proper' cooking. A summer kitchen is at ground level and partially open to the elements; generally under an overhang or in an adapted outbuilding, it typically contains a couple of bottled-gas burners or hotplates, a mini-refrigerator and a source of water; also crockery and cutlery. These facilities are for family and/or hosted garden meals and some owners who don't do table d'hôtes will allow guests to use the summer kitchen and picnic in their garden.

## Prices and minimum stays

Most entries give a price PER ROOM with breakfast for two people. If this is not the case, we generally say so. The price range covers a one-night stay in the cheapest room in low season to the most expensive in high season. Some owners charge more at certain times (during festivals, for example) and some charge less for stays of more than one or two nights. Some owners ask for a two-night minimum stay and we mention this where possible.

Prices quoted are those given to us for 2015 onwards but are not guaranteed, so do double-check when booking.

Taxe de séjour is a small tax that local councils can levy on all paying visitors; it is rarely included in the quoted price and you may find your bill increased by €0.50–€2 per person per day to cover this.

## Public holidays

As well as the usual public holidays which we take in the UK, the French also celebrate on various other dates. It is likely that B&Bs will be booked up well in

Photo: Château La Touanne, entry 347

advance around these days, so do plan ahead if you are going to be travelling then.

1 January – New Year's Day
Easter Monday
1 May – May Day or Labour Day
8 May – Victory 1945 Day
Ascension Thursday and Whit Monday
14 July – Bastille Day
15 August – Assumption of the Blessed Virgin Mary
1 November – All Saints' Day
11 November – Armistice 1918 Day
25 December – Christmas

### Booking and cancellation

Do be clear about the room booked and the price for B&B and for meals. It is essential to book well ahead for July and August, and wise for other months. If you practise the last-minuting habit which seems to be spreading, you deprive yourself of choice and make life harder for your hosts. Owners may send you a booking form or contrat de location (tenancy contract) which must be filled in and returned, and commits both sides. Requests for deposits vary; some are non-refundable, some owners may charge you for the whole of the booked stay in advance.

Some cancellation policies are more stringent than others. It is also worth noting that some owners will take this deposit directly from your credit/debit card without contacting you to discuss it. So ask them to explain their cancellation policy clearly before booking so you

understand exactly where you stand; it may well avoid a nasty surprise.

Remember that the UK is one hour behind France and people can be upset by telephone enquiries coming through late in their evening.

### Payment

Cash is usually the easiest way to pay. Virtually all ATMs in France take Visa and MasterCard. Some owners take credit cards but not all. If they do, we have given them the appropriate symbol. (Check that your particular card is acceptable.) Euro travellers' cheques will usually be accepted; other currency cheques are unpopular because of commission charges.

### Tipping

Owners do not expect tips. If you have been treated with extraordinary kindness, write to them, or leave a small gift. Please tell us, too – we love to hear, and we do record, all feedback.

### Arrivals and departures

Say roughly what time you will arrive (normally after 4pm), as most hosts like to welcome you personally. Be on time if you have booked dinner; if, despite best efforts, you are delayed, phone to give warning.

### Closed

When given in months this means the whole of the month(s) stated. So, 'Closed: November–March' means closed from 1 November to 31 March.

INSPECTED & SELECTED

Sawday's

FRENCH B&B
AWARDS

2015/16

## Sawday's French B&B Awards 2015/16

We've chosen 12 absolute corkers for our first ever set of French B&B winners. Every place in the book is special but these 12 have been selected because they stand out in their particular category.

**Award categories:**

Favourite newcomers

Old favourites

One of a kind

Most praised breakfast

**La Vieille Ferme**     Entry 726
Samoëns, Rhône Valley – Alps

## Favourite newcomers

**La Maison d'à Côté**     Entry 84
Pontarlier, Franche Comté

Discovering a Special Place is always exciting. We delight in meeting new B&B owners and helping them reach likeminded people who want to stay in B&Bs that offer an authentic French experience. We've highlighted all the new ones throughout the guide and here is a selection of our favourites:

**L'Observance**     Entry 766
Avignon, Provence – Alps – Riviera

**Moulin de Fresquet**     Entry 585
Gramat, Midi – Pyrénées

INSPECTED & SELECTED
*Sawday's*
FRENCH B&B
AWARDS
2015/16

**Château d'Alteville**     Entry 71
Dieuze, Lorraine

# Old favourites

We wanted to celebrate all that is best about our most loyal owners, some of whom have been with us since the very first edition of French Bed and Breakfast in 1994. It's their boundless good humour and kindness that makes for an unforgettable stay in these fantastic B&Bs. Our Old favourites are:

**Maison Coutin**     Entry 736
Peisey Nancroix, Rhône Valley – Alps

**Les Mazures**       Entry 37
Beaumetz, Picardy

# One of a kind

Sawday's has always celebrated individuality, generosity of spirit and a sense of fun. These inspiring B&Bs stand out this year. An architect-designed eco house, a sun-drenched Indian styled house on the French Riviera and a charmingly rustic home celebrating Slow Food and conviviality. We hope you enjoy them as much as we do.

**Bastide Valmasque**       Entry 826
Biot, Provence – Alps – Riviera

**Mas St Joseph**       Entry 752
Châteauneuf Val St Donat,
Provence – Alps – Riviera

www.sawdays.co.uk/fbbawards

**La Ferme de Kerscuntec**   Entry 275
Combrit, Brittany

**Château de la Prade**     Entry 687
Bram, Languedoc – Roussillon

# Most praised breakfast

A good breakfast is a must! Our French owners source the very best local ingredients for their continental breakfasts. They race to their local boulangerie to collect freshly baked, crusty bread every morning, and serve it with homemade jams and strong French coffee. Here are our most praised French breakfasts:

**Talvern**              Entry 278
Landévant, Brittany

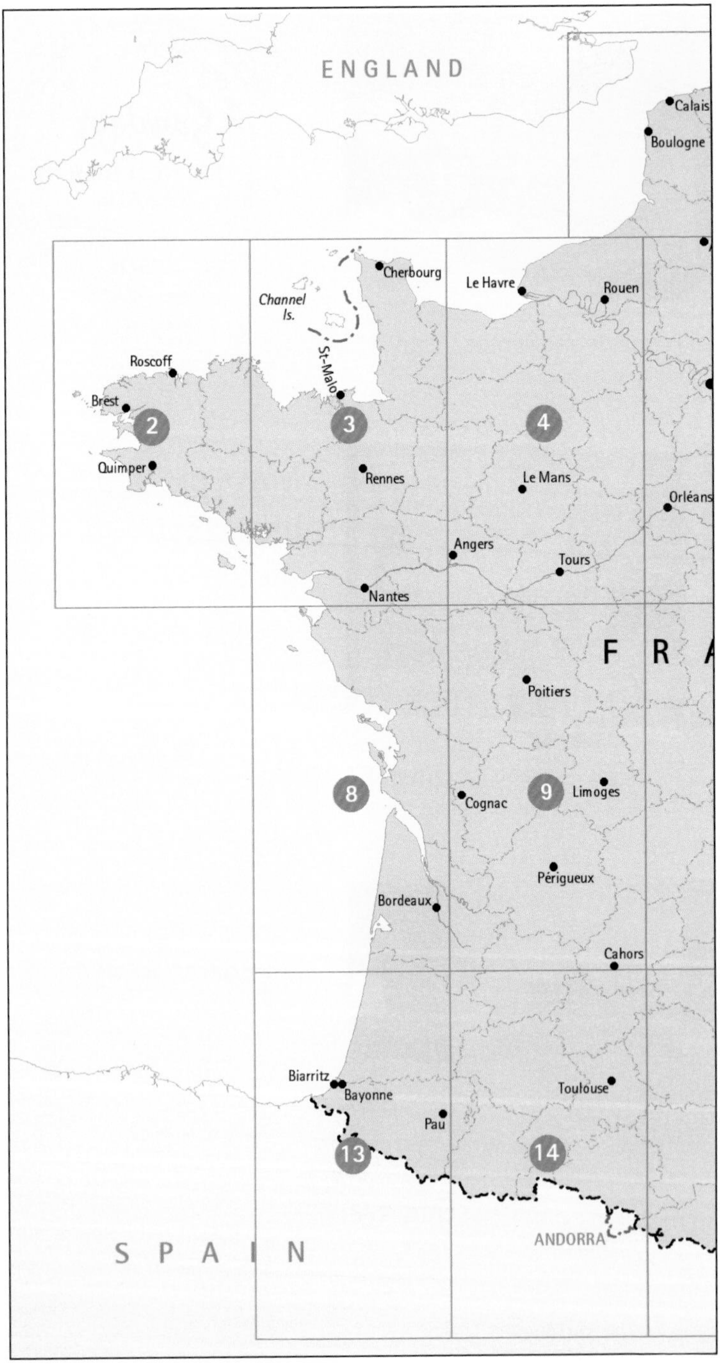
ENGLAND
Calais
Boulogne
Cherbourg
Le Havre
Rouen
Channel Is.
St-Malo
Roscoff
Brest
2
3
4
Quimper
Rennes
Le Mans
Orléans
Angers
Tours
Nantes
F R A
Poitiers
8
9
Limoges
Cognac
Périgueux
Bordeaux
Cahors
Biarritz
Bayonne
Toulouse
Pau
13
14
ANDORRA
S P A I N

# Map 1

25

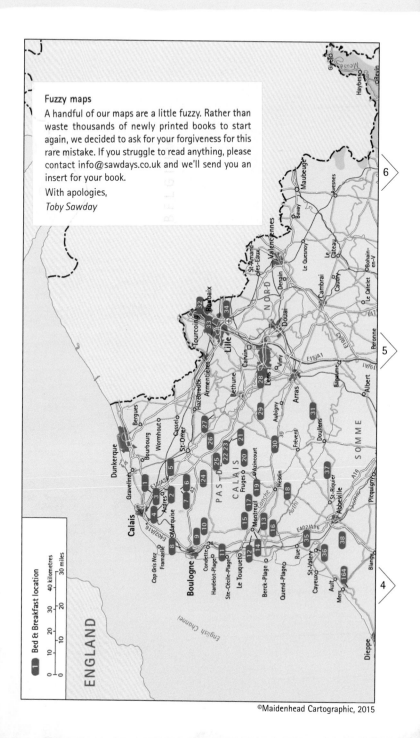

**Fuzzy maps**

A handful of our maps are a little fuzzy. Rather than waste thousands of newly printed books to start again, we decided to ask for your forgiveness for this rare mistake. If you struggle to read anything, please contact info@sawdays.co.uk and we'll send you an insert for your book.

With apologies,

*Toby Sawday*

Bed & Breakfast location

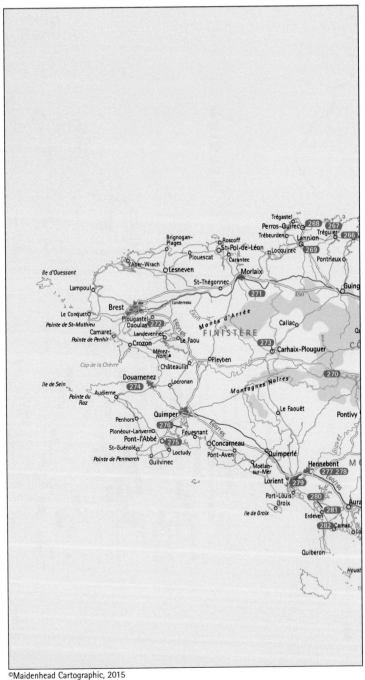

# Map 3

27

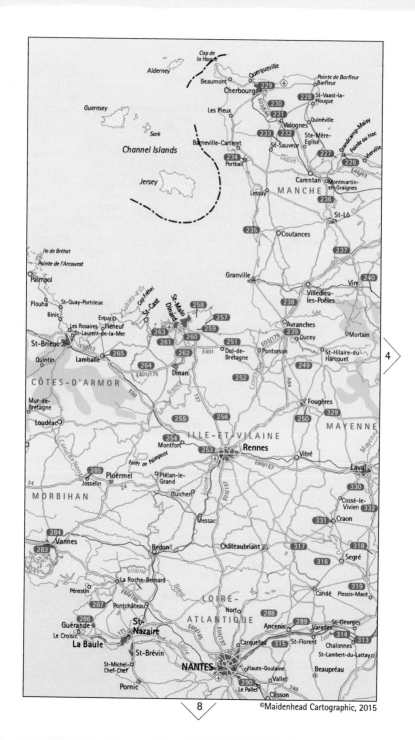

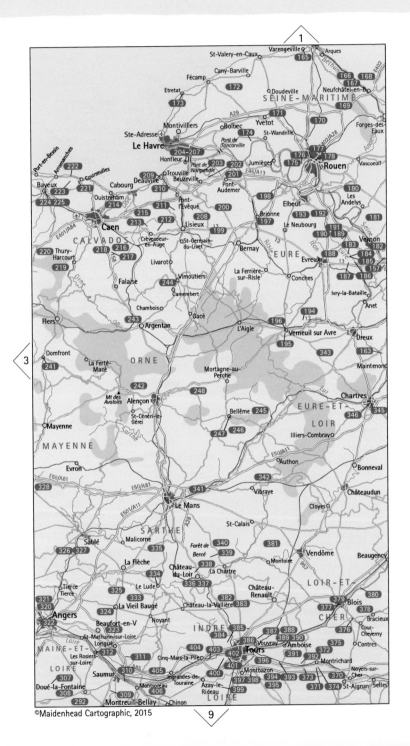

©Maidenhead Cartographic, 2015

# Map 5

29

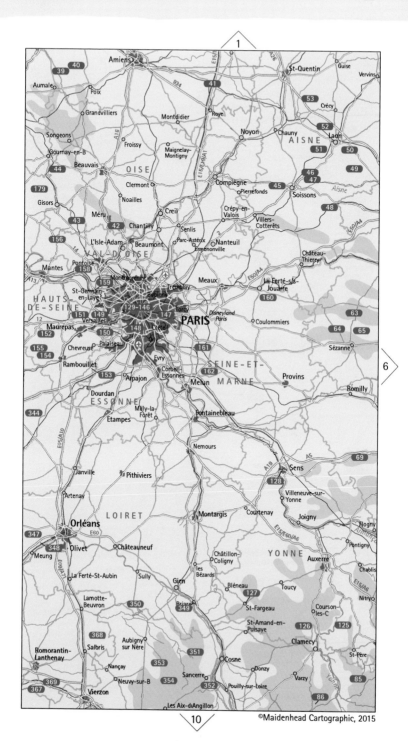

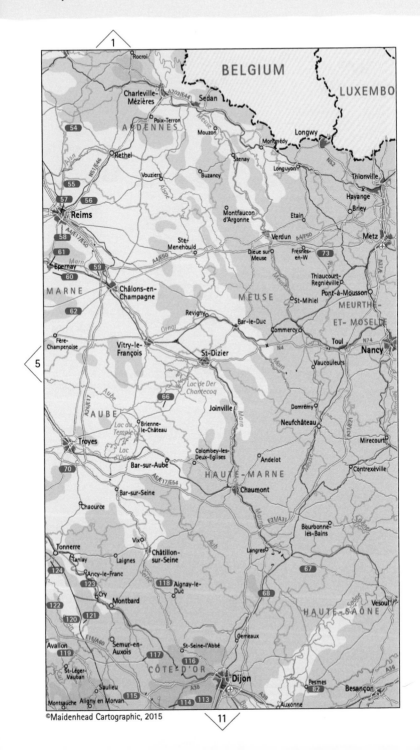

Map 7                                                                31

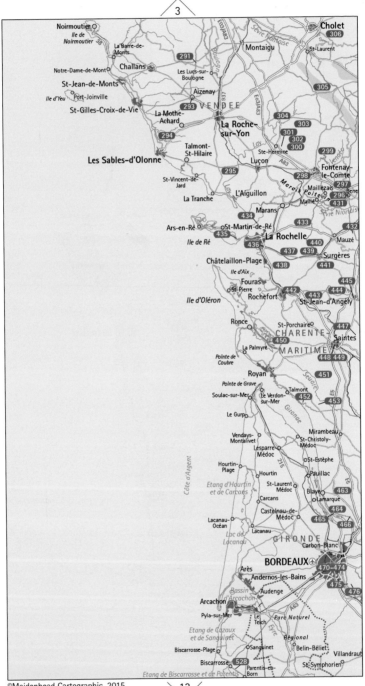

# Map 9

33

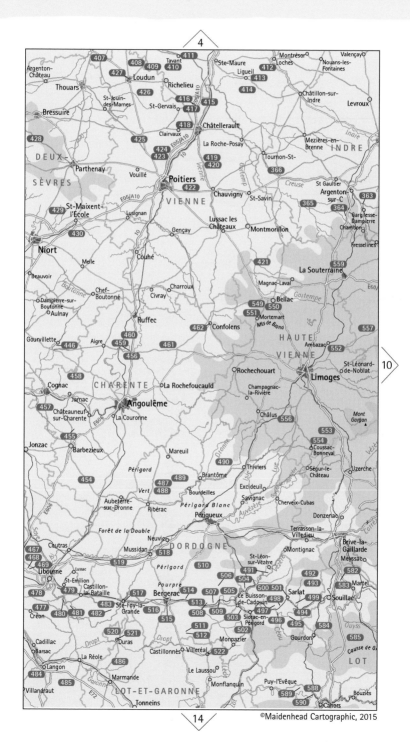

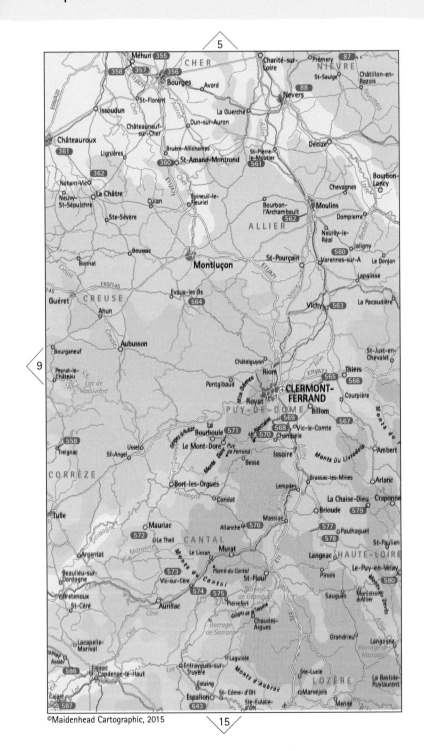

©Maidenhead Cartographic, 2015

# Map 11

35

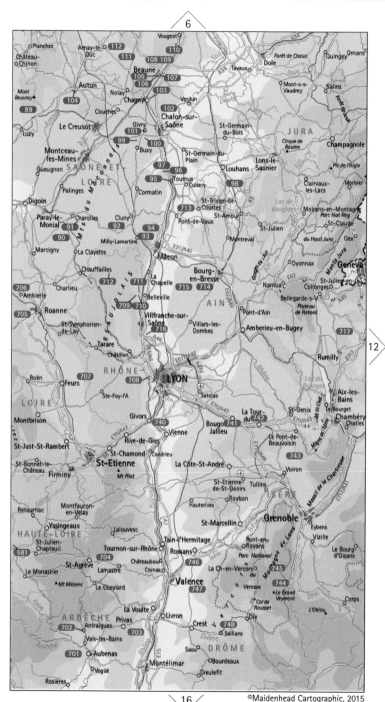

DOUBS

Mouthier
Morteau
Montbenoît
84
Pontarlier
Cluse de
Joux
Mont d'Or
Chaux-
Neuve
Les Hôpitaux-Neufs

7

SWITZERLAND

Lausanne

E25/E62
Lac Léman (Lake Geneva)

Evian
Thonon
719
Sciez   718   720
Abondance
Geneva
721  722
Morzine
723
724  725
726
Bonneville
Cluses
727
728
Argentière
HAUTE   Chamonix
SAVOIE   729   Servoz   Chamonix–Mont-Blanc
Annecy   Sallanches   Le Fayet
Thônes   Combloux   Mont Blanc
11   730   Chaîne des Aravis   731   Megève
St-   Lac   Flumet   Les
Jorioz   d'Annecy   Contamines
Ugine

Albertville   Roignais
Conflans   Bourg-St-Maurice
736   Aime   738
732   SAVOIE   737
734   735   Mt Pourri
Aiguebelle   739
733   Moûtiers   Val-d'Isère
Grande
Casse
Parc National   Bonneval
Massif de la Vanoise   de la Vanoise
St-Jean-de-Maurienne   Bessans
La Chambre   Lanslebourg
Avrieux
Modane   ITALY
Valloire

La Grave
Le Monêtier-les-Bains
La Meije
Massif des Écrins   Chantemerle   Montgenèvre
Mt Pelvoux   Briançon
Parc National
des Écrins   Abriès
Parc Nat Rég
Château-Queyras
Queyras
Vieux   du Queyras
Chaillol   751   Guillestre
HAUTES ALPES   Vars
Les Claux
Gap   Embrun
Barrage de
Serre-Ponçon

# Map 13

37

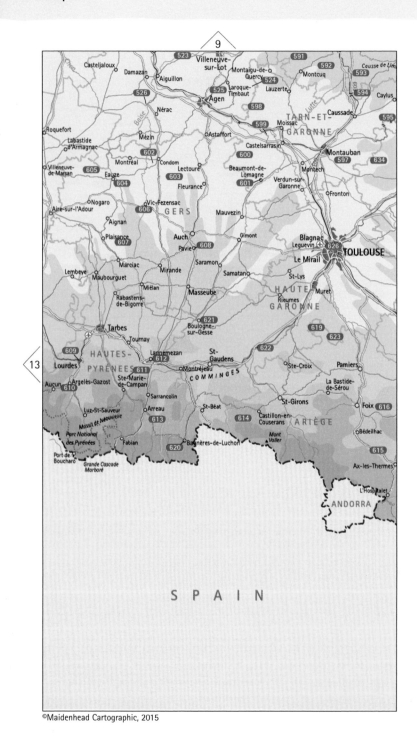

Map 15                                                                    39

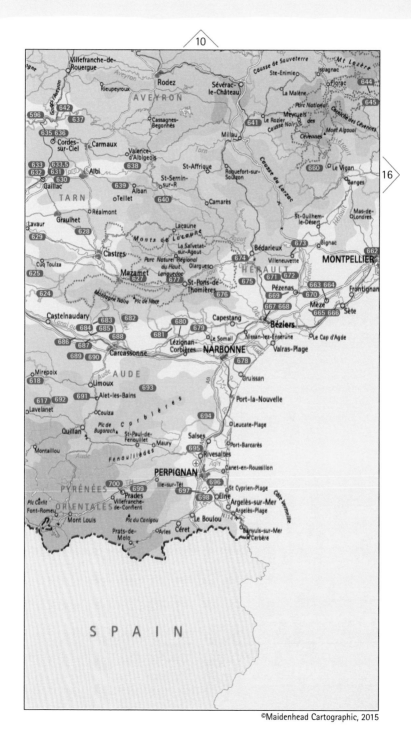

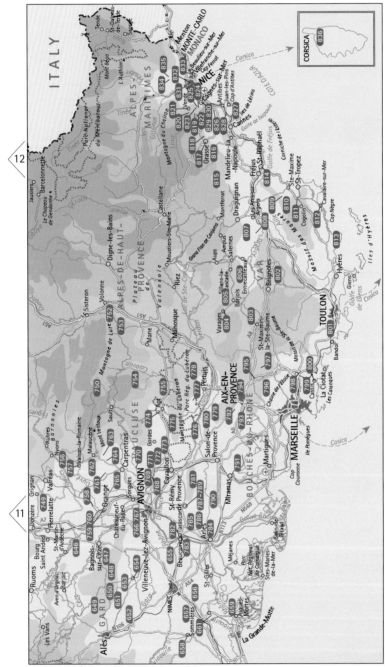

# The North • Picardy

Photo: ©iStock.com/A_Lein

## Ardres Bridge Cottage

A canal-side setting among rolling agricultural plains, usefully close to Calais. The gardens are peaceful and the owners offer friendly table d'hôtes. The ground-floor bedroom gives onto the flowery borders, the other has its own little balcony overlooking the pond, where farmyard fowl frolic; its shower room is downstairs. Both are country cosy and comfortable with floral bed linen and wooden furniture; bathrooms are among the best. You share the young and charming owners' sitting room: long and spacious with a big fire and plenty of squishy sofas; and you breakfast round a farmhouse table. Utterly touching and authentic.

## Les Fuchsias

This unusual Victorian townhouse has a pleasingly mixed-up feel with its gingerbread cutouts, variegated roofs and lovely copsy garden of woodland thrown against lawns and fields. Monsieur is chatty (in English), charming and informative; Madame is quieter but very attentive and tends her house, cats and guests with loving care. Guests have their own cosy, colourful sitting and breakfast rooms (it's a short walk to a nearby a brasserie for simple meals). Attractive bedrooms have pretty duvets, fresh modern furnishings, wicker armchairs, antique samplers; the family room and the attic suite are particularly inviting.

| Rooms | 1 double: €50.<br>1 triple with separate shower:<br>€50-€60.<br>Extra bed €10 per person per night. |
|---|---|
| Meals | Dinner with wine, €20. |
| Closed | Rarely. |

| Rooms | 1 twin sharing separate wc: €53-€60.<br>1 suite for 2-4: €55-€100.<br>1 family room for 2-4 sharing wc:<br>€53-€100. Dogs & cats €5. |
|---|---|
| Meals | Brasserie within walking distance.<br>Restaurants 2km. |
| Closed | Rarely. |

**Laurent Blanquart**
Ardres Bridge Cottage,
678 rue du Fort Bâtard,
62610 Pont d'Ardres
Pas-de-Calais
Tel       +33 (0)3 21 96 63 92
Mobile    +33 (0)6 82 02 13 47
Email     blanquart.laurent@gmail.com
Web       www.ardres-bridge-cottage.com

**Bernadette Balloy**
Les Fuchsias,
292 rue du Général de St Just,
62610 Bois en Ardres
Pas-de-Calais
Tel       +33 (0)3 21 82 05 25
Email     lesfuchsias@aol.com
Web       www.lesfuchsias-ardres.fr

Entry 1   Map 1

Entry 2   Map 1

### Les Draps d'Or

It's been an inn since 1640 and Hilary, well integrated here, fits the tradition: vivacious, elegant and English, she enjoys receiving guests. The guest wing has its own (digicode) entrance straight off the street – you are as independent as you like. Up the narrow staircase to tidy, wood-floored rooms: blue, yellow and green; fresh, spotless and bright. The triple sports red ethnic weave curtains and a powder-blue frieze. All give onto the cobbled street but few cars pass at night. Ardres is a delightful little town and the 'Cloths of Gold' is a handy stopover on the way to Calais. *Extra triple room available, sharing bathroom with another room (let to same party only).*

### Villa Héloïse

An endearing place with an owner to match. Chatty hard-working Marie-Christine does everything herself in her pretty red brick home; she's even built a treehouse in the garden. Stay in the family suite in the main house, a wonderland of plants and collected items old and new, or the independent wooden-decked apartment; this comes without a sitting room, but Madame has buckets of personality to make up for this, and you can dine out on that high decked terrace. Evergreens and shrubs provide the backdrop, agricultural fields surround you, Calais and Belgium are under 30 minutes away. Wander the dunes, cycle, fish.

| | | | |
|---|---|---|---|
| Rooms | 2 doubles: €70-€75.<br>1 triple with separate private shower room & shared wc: €75-€110.<br>Singles €70. | Rooms | 1 family suite for 2-4: €55-€90.<br>1 apartment for 2 with kitchenette: €60. |
| Meals | Restaurants within walking distance. | Meals | Dinner with wine, €25. |
| Closed | Christmas/New Year. | Closed | Rarely. |

**Hilary Mackay**
Les Draps d'Or,
152 rue Lambert d'Ardres,
62610 Ardres
Pas-de-Calais

Tel     +33 (0)3 21 82 20 44
Mobile  +33 (0)6 24 40 58 01
Email   hilary@drapsdor.com
Web     www.drapsdor.com

**Marie-Christine Debriel**
Villa Héloïse,
683 rue de l'Église,
62340 Andres
Pas-de-Calais

Tel     +33 (0)3 21 35 15 01
Mobile  +33 (0)6 87 12 51 02
Email   marie-christine.debriel@wanadoo.fr
Web     www.villaheloise.net

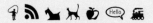

Entry 3   Map 1

Entry 4   Map 1

## La Bohême

Extrovert, excitable Sonia enjoys music, painting, cooking for and chatting with guests. Like oysters or Marmite, some love it, some loathe it. Timeworn beams, dark floors, solid country furniture and knick-knackery galore: it's 'French rustique'. The garden-view room under the eaves is prettily done in red Jouy; in an outbuilding, the plain white and grey attic room with its big bathroom is great for a family (watch the stairs). The overgrown garden bursts with life and secret corners. This is lovely walking and pony-trekking country: if you'd like to trade car for horse, riding can be organised nearby.

## Le Manoir

The trompe l'œil and frescoed friezes are lavish, from the dining panelling to the staircase 'marble'. In spite of being known in the village as Le Château it's not really big but, with the original details intact, it is a historian's delight. All four guest rooms (one a two-bedroom family suite, another an elegant tribute to Africa) have been remodelled and beautifully refurbished, combining spectacular antiques with modern fabrics. The bathrooms are luxurious and the garden views, to box parterre and trees, are soothing. Welcoming Sylvie and Pierre offer you a delicious dinner, and a living room just for guests.

| | |
|---|---|
| Rooms | 2 doubles: €60–€65. |
| | Extra bed €30 per person per night. |
| | Pets €10. |
| Meals | Dinner with wine, €26. |
| Closed | Rarely. |

| | |
|---|---|
| Rooms | 3 doubles: €75. |
| | 1 suite for 4: €110. |
| Meals | Dinner with wine, €28–€40. |
| Closed | Rarely. |

**Sonia Benoît**
La Bohême,
1947 rue de la Grasse Payelle,
62370 Zutkerque
Pas-de-Calais
Tel +33 (0)3 21 35 70 25
Mobile +33 (0)6 16 18 71 22
Email sonia-benoit-la-boheme@wanadoo.fr
Web perso.wanadoo.fr/sonia-la-boheme

**Sylvie & Pierre Bréemersch**
Le Manoir,
40 route de Licques,
62890 Bonningues lès Ardres
Pas-de-Calais
Tel +33 (0)3 21 82 69 05
Email pierre.breemersch@wanadoo.fr
Web www.lemanoirdebonningues.com

Entry 5   Map 1

Entry 6   Map 1

## La Ferme de Beaupré

These lovely gentle people will take you happily into their gorgeous old house at the end of the tree-lined drive and ply you with fine home-grown organic food (ah, those breakfast jams). Lut, from Belgium, is a gracious and unpretentiously warm music teacher and mother of two boys who speaks English; Jean-Michel takes over when she is away. Perfect, peaceful bedrooms (one in taupes, off-whites, toile de Jouy and a tiny room off with a bed for a child, the other modern red, white, rattan and wood). You have sole use of the living room; the garden bursts with peonies, lupins, roses and cherries. An adorable, very special place.

## La Villa Sainte Claire

Friendly Catherine lends you bikes – so pedal off to Wimereux, a sweet seaside town a mile down the road. Then return to a 18th-century house in the lee of a village church, its long elegant façade distinguished by tall white windows perfectly beshuttered. Fresh, spacious and uncluttered is the guest bedroom, with views to a beautiful front garden, and it's a treat to stroll the rambling grounds, dotted with statues, punctuated by topiary. Wake to fresh local croissants and organic homemade jams; set off for the markets and shops of Boulogne… and a lovely lunch in the historic old town. The coastline is wild and wonderful. *Cot available.*

| | |
|---|---|
| Rooms | 1 double: €68–€75.<br>1 family room for 2-4: €68–€125.<br>Singles €67–€77.<br>Dinner, B&B €59–€62 per person.<br>Extra bed/sofabed €20–€25 per person per night. |
| Meals | Dinner with wine, €25. |
| Closed | Christmas. |

| | |
|---|---|
| Rooms | 1 double (extra room available for 2 children): €95. |
| Meals | Restaurant within walking distance. |
| Closed | Rarely. |

**Lut & Jean-Michel Louf-Degrauwe**
La Ferme de Beaupré,
129 rue de Licques,
62890 Bonningues lès Ardres
Pas-de-Calais

Tel      +33 (0)3 21 35 14 44
Email   lut.degrauwe@nordnet.fr
Web    www.lafermedebeaupre.com

**Catherine Debatte**
La Villa Sainte Claire,
11 rue du Presbytère,
62126 Wimille
Pas-de-Calais

Tel       +33 (0)3 21 91 99 58
Mobile   +33 (0)6 16 70 84 26
Email    contact@villa-sainte-claire.fr
Web     www.villa-sainte-claire.fr

Entry 7   Map 1

Entry 8   Map 1

## Le Clos d'Esch

The golden stone of the oldest farmhouse in the village is now fronted by a large glass sunroom, and flowers flourish in the lower garden where two new houses stand. Discreetly friendly and obliging, new owners Olivier and Véronique (this was her pioneering parents' B&B) serve delicious breakfasts and for dinner there's a great little place five minutes away. One traditional-style bedroom is in an outbuilding overlooking courtyard and wooded hills; the triple has a wrought-iron bed with a leopard-skin cover and its own patio overlooking the garden; all are pristine, and there's a cosy sitting room too. Good value.

## Le Clos de Tournes

Tranquil meadows, pastoral bliss: a metaphor for your calm, smiling, fishmonger hosts. Caroline grew up with B&B: her parents were pioneers, she loves it. The fine old farmhouse, with pale façade and garden dotted by shady fruit trees, is an immaculate B&B retreat, while the outbuildings house two busy gîtes. The adventurous bedrooms are a surprise after the classic French dining room (long table, high upholstered chairs). Urban-chic in deep red and mustard; one is swathed in rich oriental toile de Jouy, the other in intensely patterned wallpaper and billowing taffeta. Caroline is graceful and sociable.

| Rooms | 1 double, 2 twins: €54–€63. |
| | 1 triple: €79. |
| Meals | Auberges within walking distance. |
| Closed | Rarely. |

FIRST
EDITION
VETERAN

| Rooms | 1 double, 1 twin: €62. |
| | Extra bed €20 per person per night. |
| Meals | Dinner with wine, €35 (not Fri). |
| | Restaurant 2km. |
| Closed | Rarely. |

Véronique Boussemaere
& Olivier Chartaux
Le Clos d'Esch,
62360 Echinghen
Pas-de-Calais
Tel +33 (0)3 21 91 14 34
Mobile +33 (0)6 89 04 72 78
Email veronique.boussemaere@wanadoo.fr
Web www.leclosdesch.fr

Caroline Boussemaere
Le Clos de Tournes,
1810 route de Tournes,
62360 Echinghen
Pas-de-Calais
Tel +33 (0)3 91 90 48 78
Mobile +33 (0)6 07 09 21 14
Email reservation@leclosdetournes.com
Web www.leclosdetournes.com

Entry 9   Map 1

Entry 10   Map 1

## Le Moulin

No more milling at the moulin, but the lake is serene and it's a treat to throw open a window and watch the ducks. All is warmly inviting at this big reassuring millhouse built in 1855 – a classically French B&B with a dark leather chesterfield and voluptuous modern baroque furniture in the sitting/dining room, and delicious breakfasts at a long elegant table. Bedrooms are pretty, one with silver-grey scatter cushions, another in tones of mauve and white; corridors have been revamped in warm colours. Christine is gentle, charming, welcoming – and you are a spade's throw from the local sandy beach.

## Le Pré Rainette

Relax with beautiful colours around you – turquoise, striking purples, soft Egyptian reds – and admire the abundance of old wood found in brocantes and used throughout to soften the interiors. 'Violette' is a perfect family room or spacious for a couple; 'Hortense' and 'Lilas' share a super modern shower room; 'La Petite Maison' has huge windows overlooking a small lake. Anne-Marie and Christophe, intelligent, helpful hosts, built the long red-roofed house in 2003, and named it 'tree frog prairie' after the quietly croaking wildlife. Have a go at rowing, use the pool, borrow bikes, or use the beach hut at Le Touquet – bliss.

| Rooms | 2 doubles: €60–€75. Singles €60. |
|---|---|
| Meals | Restaurants 5km. |
| Closed | Rarely. |

| Rooms | 1 suite for 2-4; 1 suite for 2-4 sharing bathroom: €120–€210. 1 cottage for 2-4 sharing bathroom: €150–€230. |
|---|---|
| Meals | Restaurants 3km. |
| Closed | 11 November – 15 March (open Christmas & New Year). |

**Christine Lécaille**
Le Moulin,
40 rue du Centre,
62187 Dannes
Pas-de-Calais

| Tel | +33 (0)3 21 33 74 74 |
| Mobile | +33 (0)6 62 27 60 33 |
| Email | christine.lecaille@free.fr |
| Web | www.au-moulin.com |

**Anne-Marie de Gastines**
Le Pré Rainette,
1515 Grande Rue,
62170 Sorrus
Pas-de-Calais

| Mobile | +33 (0)6 48 18 90 83 |
| Email | prerainette@hotmail.fr |
| Web | www.prerainette.com |

Entry 11   Map 1

Entry 12   Map 1

## St Justin

A short walk from Montreuil's lovely town square, this may not have the prettiest setting (edge-of-town road noise morn and eve) but it's perfect for those wanting to see a bit of French urban life. Inside all is cosy and homely in that very French way; our favourite bedroom has 19th-century coloured glass doors onto a balcony overlooking garden and townscape. Weather permitting, Madame Gobert serves a great breakfast on the crazy-paving terrace in their charming garden; smiley Monsieur is a sociable soul; and river valleys, beaches and ancient ramparts beckon. All this just across the Channel, and great value too.

## L'Art du Temps

In one of the tallest houses on Montreuil's square, reached down an obscure alley, is a wonderful chambres d'hôtes run by an engaging family. Peaceful new guest quarters lie off a slim secret courtyard at the back: two bedrooms and a sitting room, plush, cosy and contemporary with all mod cons (and umbrellas!). Handsome shower rooms sport organic soaps, the courtyard bursts with greenery, and breakfast is served by the wood-burner in the owners' part of the house: fresh fruit salad with agave syrup, breads, brioche and homemade jams. Stroll to the city ramparts for soaring views, visit the elegant boulevards of Le Touquet. *Parking available.*

| Rooms | 1 double: €63. |
| --- | --- |
| | 1 suite for 4 sharing shower room & wc: €115. |
| | Singles €57. |
| | Extra bed/sofabed €15 per person per night. |
| Meals | Restaurant 700m. |
| Closed | Rarely. |

| Rooms | 2 doubles each with separate shower: €95. |
| --- | --- |
| | Singles €70. |
| Meals | Restaurants within walking distance. |
| Closed | Rarely. |

| | |
| --- | --- |
| | Élisabeth Gobert |
| | St Justin, |
| | 203 rue de Paris, |
| | Montreuil sur Mer, |
| | 62170 Écuires |
| | Pas-de-Calais |
| Tel | +33 (0)3 21 05 49 03 |
| Mobile | +33 (0)6 09 56 29 30 |
| Email | elisabeth.gobert@gmail.com |

| | |
| --- | --- |
| | David & Elisabeth Louchez |
| | L'Art du Temps, |
| | 22 rue du Thorin, |
| | Montreuil sur Mer, |
| | 62170 Montreuil |
| | Pas-de-Calais |
| Mobile | +33 (0)6 48 76 32 94 |
| Email | lartdutempsmontreuil@gmail.com |
| Web | www.lartdutemps-montreuil.net |

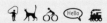

### Le Vert Bois

Ancient peace, delightful people, fields as far as the eye can see. And it's majestic for a farm – handsome house, outbuildings and courtyard are immaculately preserved. Étienne, Véronique and their family grow cereals, keep cows and look after guests – charmingly – in a converted farm building. Upstairs are a fresh cosy double and a pretty twin; ceilings slope, walls are spotless, bedcovers quilted, shower rooms small and newly fitted. Breakfasts, we're told, are lovely. The fine old town of Montreuil is just three kilometres away for restaurants and "astonishing points of view". Near Calais but feels like the heart of France.

### Ferme du Saule

Readers have called Le Saule "a little treasure". And we know that the Trunnets' smiles are genuine, their converted outbuilding handsome and perfectly finished (down to mosquito nets on windows), the ground-floor rooms solidly traditional, the beds excellent, the dayroom proud of its beautiful armoire, and you get your own little table for breakfast. Monsieur and his son are only too happy to show you the flax production process (it's fascinating); young Madame looks after her three little ones and cares beautifully for guests. Proclaimed "the best cowshed I've ever stayed in" by one happy guest.

| Rooms | 1 double, 1 twin: €65–€85. |
| --- | --- |
| Meals | Restaurants in town. |
| Closed | Rarely. |

| Rooms | 2 doubles: €60. |
| --- | --- |
| | 1 suite for 4–5: €85–€100. |
| | 2 family rooms for 3: €70. |
| | Singles €50. |
| | Extra bed/sofabed €15 per person per night. |
| Meals | Restaurants 6km. |
| Closed | Rarely. |

| | Étienne & Véronique Bernard |
| --- | --- |
| | Le Vert Bois, |
| | 62170 Neuville sous Montreuil |
| | Pas-de-Calais |
| Tel | +33 (0)3 21 06 09 41 |
| Mobile | +33 (0)6 08 74 79 43 |
| Email | etienne.bernard6@wanadoo.fr |
| Web | www.gite-montreuilsurmer.com |

| | Trunnet Family |
| --- | --- |
| | Ferme du Saule, |
| | 20 rue de l'Église, |
| | 62170 Brimeux |
| | Pas-de-Calais |
| Tel | +33 (0)3 21 06 01 28 |
| Email | fotrunnet@wanadoo.fr |
| Web | www.ferme-du-saule.com |

Entry 15   Map 1

Entry 16   Map 1

## Un Matin dans les Bois

He bakes delicious brioche, she adores birds and will take you to the marches, there are cats, dogs, ducks and plans for horses, and young Archie to make friends with you. The house, concealed in woods with rolling hill views, dates from the 15th century. Bedrooms, scattered between barn, stables and pigeonnier, are inspired, one with a wall of glass, another with a bedhead of silver birch trunks; beds are big, deep, sumptuous. There's a restaurant to walk to and a guest kitchen in a rustic-chic extension. Swing in the tree chairs, swim a lap in the pool, wander the woods with a lantern from your room. Utterly magical. *Min. stay: 2 nights in high season.*

## Ferme Prévost de Courmière

In the old, old farmhouse — 1680 is inscribed in flint on the façade — are comfort and peace in great measure. With the house restoration behind them, your hospitable hosts (good English speakers both) have turned their stylish attention to the transformation of the courtyard and delightful peony-studded garden and have happily embarked on B&B. Bedrooms are pure, fresh, new and extremely charming, bathrooms are spotless, breakfast is a moveable feast, and dinner celebrates the most delicious Flemish dishes, served at a large table in a light, lofty room. Superb all round.

| Rooms | 3 doubles: €120–€130. |
|---|---|
| | 1 family suite for 4: €120–€230. |
| Meals | Guest kitchen. Restaurants 3km. |
| Closed | Rarely. |

| Rooms | 2 doubles with sitting room: €60–€70. |
|---|---|
| | 1 suite for 4: €75–€115. |
| | 1 family room for 4: €75–€95. |
| | Extra bed €20 per person per night. |
| Meals | Dinner with wine, €30. |
| Closed | Rarely. |

**M & Mme Dubrulle**
Un Matin dans les Bois,
100 Impasse le Fresnoy,
62990 Loison sur Créquoise
Pas-de-Calais

| Mobile | +33 (0)6 52 89 55 56 |
| Email | info@unmatindanslesbois.com |
| Web | www.unmatindanslesbois.com |

**Annie Lombardet**
Ferme Prévost de Courmière,
510 rue de Crécy,
62140 Capelle lès Hesdin
Pas-de-Calais

| Tel | +33 (0)3 21 81 16 04 |
| Mobile | +33 (0)6 08 28 21 66 |
| Email | ferme-prevost-de-courmiere@wanadoo.fr |
| Web | www.ferme-prevost-de-courmiere.fr |

Entry 17    Map 1

Entry 18    Map 1

### La Gacogne

Enter a 1750 arched orangery (the tower) filled with a very long table, an open fire and 101 curiosities. Alongside teddies are chain-mail bodices, longbows, crossbows and similar armoured reminders of nearby Agincourt (Azincourt). It is a treat to be received in this most colourful and eccentric of parlours for hearty continental breakfasts (the seed cake is delicious!), hosted by motherly Marie-José and knightly Patrick who've lived here for years. Small bedrooms in the outbuilding are farmhouse simple with heavy-draped medieval touches, a lush garden melts into a conifer copse and your hosts are utterly charming.

| Rooms | 2 doubles: €70. |
| | 1 family room for 3: €80. |
| Meals | Restaurant 1km. |
| Closed | Rarely. |

Patrick & Marie-José Fenet
La Gacogne,
62310 Azincourt
Pas-de-Calais
Tel    +33 (0)3 21 04 45 61
Email  fenetgeoffroy@aol.com
Web    www.gacogne.com

Entry 19   Map 1

### Maison de Plumes

Deep in the agricultural fields of the Seven Valleys, this rural place is urban in its way — funky interiors are the handiwork of Vanessa who also makes her own perfumes and scented candles. Bedrooms are sensationally lavish: ostrich feathers frame a four-poster in one, the air shimmers with turquoise in another, and 'Parokeet' is suave and handsome; each bathroom harmonises perfectly. Richard serves breakfast eggs from their own hens on elegant white china and five-course gourmet meals by arrangement; enjoy a glass of bubbly beforehand. Country walks and fishing are nearby, battlefields and coast not much further.

| Rooms | 3 doubles, 1 twin/double: €99–€119. |
| | 1 suite for 2: €149. |
| Meals | Dinner, 5 courses, €38 |
| | (Mon, Weds, Fri & Sat). |
| | Wine €12. |
| Closed | Rarely. |

Richard & Vanessa
Rhoades-Brown
Maison de Plumes,
73 rue d'Aire,
62134 Heuchin
Pas-de-Calais
Tel    +33 (0)3 21 41 47 85
Email  enquire@maisondeplumes.com
Web    www.maisondeplumes.com

Entry 20   Map 1

### La Pommeraie

This proud, upright, formal-French house has the most relaxing of owners: friendly, intelligent and on hand to help. Farmer's daughter Béatrice was a teacher, her husband cultivates 400 acres of land. All is stylish, elegant and immaculate, from the black marble fireplace in the living room to the finely decorated bedrooms: tall windows, great beds, designer basins and walls in taupe and dove-grey. There's lots to love: a big garden for active children, bikes to borrow, local boat rides through the marshes, and beautiful breakfasts to start the day, served on embroidered linen.

### Ferme de la Vallée

This is a real farm, so don't expect pretty-pretty – but Madame is a character and her welcome is top class. Readers return, for the authentic atmosphere and the delicious food. Amazing how much space lies behind the simple frontage of this street-side farmhouse; every little corner is crammed with 40 years' worth of collecting: porcelain, plates, jugs, crystal decanter stoppers, baskets, collectable plastics... the list is long. Come for comfy beds, spacious dayroom areas, billiards, table football (a vintage table) and games. It's intrinsically French despite the eccentricities, and Madame is a delight.

| | |
|---|---|
| Rooms | 1 double, 1 twin/double: €65. |
| | 1 family room for 2-3: €85-€100. |
| | Extra bed €15 per person per night. |
| Meals | Restaurants 7km. |
| Closed | Rarely. |

| | |
|---|---|
| Rooms | 1 double: €53. |
| | 1 suite for 4: €80. |
| | 1 triple: €63. |
| | Singles €53-€80. |
| | Extra bed/sofabed €15 per person |
| | per night. |
| Meals | Dinner with wine, €23. |
| Closed | Never. |

**Béatrice Desbuquois**
La Pommeraie,
52 rue d'Hesdin,
62960 Westrehem
Pas-de-Calais
Tel    +33 (0)3 21 26 17 48
Mobile +33 (0)6 70 45 23 24
Email  beatricedesbuquois@gmail.com
Web    www.lapommeraie.onlc.fr

**Brigitte de Saint Laurent**
Ferme de la Vallée,
13 rue Neuve,
62190 Auchy au Bois
Pas-de-Calais
Tel   +33 (0)3 21 25 80 09
Email brigitte.de-saint-laurent@wanadoo.fr
Web   www.lafermedelavallee.com

Entry 21   Map 1

Entry 22   Map 1

## Les Cohettes

A winning team: Gina, her son Richard and his wife Fanny care deeply that everyone be happy, and do brilliant table d'hôtes. A full house makes quite a crowd and when B&B and gîte guests come together there can be a dozen at table. But the big garden opens its arms to all and has some comforting mature trees under which guests may link up for summer pétanque. Dark beams have been painted pale, furniture has been sanded and smudge-finished. Pretty and cosy bedrooms – in the long low farmhouse attic – are colour-coded, while the chalet studio is snug with its own little patio. The garden is peaceful and readers love it all.

## La Coulonnière

Geneviève is the immaculate gardener, Dominique, ex timber importer (now 'adjoint' to the mayor) has a limitless knowledge of the Pas-de-Calais. Both love having guests. In this new-but-traditional very French house your hexagonal bedroom in conservatory style has windows that line up east to west – catch the sun all day. 'Tout confort' here: electronically controlled shutters, a hydromassage shower with innumerable settings, 300 channels on TV, even night lights to guide you to the loo. Best of all, your own decked terrace opening to the peaceful garden. Breakfasts are top-notch: your generous hosts give you only the best.

| Rooms | 3 doubles, 1 twin: €58-€60. |
|---|---|
| | 1 family room for 4-5: €55-€91. |
| | 1 garden studio for 2: €60. |
| | Singles €50. |
| Meals | Dinner with wine, €25. |
| | Guest kitchen. |
| Closed | Rarely. |

| Rooms | 1 double: €110. |
|---|---|
| | Singles €100. |
| Meals | Restaurant 1.5km. |
| Closed | Rarely. |

**Gina Bulot**
Les Cohettes,
28 rue de Pernes,
62190 Auchy au Bois
Pas-de-Calais

| | |
|---|---|
| Tel | +33 (0)3 21 02 09 47 |
| Mobile | +33 (0)6 07 06 65 42 |
| Email | ginabulot@gmail.com |
| Web | www.chambresdhotes-chezgina.com |

**Dominique & Geneviève Ottevaere**
La Coulonnière,
26 La Place,
Hameau de Cantemerle,
62380 Wismes, Pas-de-Calais

| | |
|---|---|
| Tel | +33 (0)3 21 39 91 51 |
| Mobile | +33 (0)6 85 32 71 24 |
| Email | la-coulonniere@orange.fr |
| Web | www.la-coulonniere.fr |

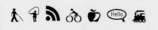

Entry 23   Map 1

Entry 24   Map 1

## Les Dornes

Table d'hôtes round the convivial table is the inspiration behind this B&B — which, being perfectionists, this couple do so well. Dinner, locally sourced, sounds delicious, while vegetables come from an immaculate potager. The interiors of their new but traditional village house are equally manicured: the L-shaped living room; the bedrooms, colour-themed and French-cosy, two on the ground floor, their tiles topped by rugs, two under the eaves with honey-coloured boards; all large and super-comfortable. Historic St Omer is a must — for music and markets, bric-a-brac and breweries. Tremendous value.

| Rooms | 3 doubles, 1 twin: €65. |
|---|---|
| Meals | Dinner with wine, €25 (not Sundays). |
| Closed | Rarely. |

**Jaqueline & Gilles Blondel**
Les Dornes,
520 rue des Deux Upen,
Upen d'Aval,
62129 Delettes, Pas-de-Calais

| Tel | +33 (0)3 21 95 87 09 |
| Mobile | +33 (0)6 88 82 55 96 |
| Email | lesdornes@lesdornes.com |
| Web | www.lesdornes.com |

Entry 25  Map 1

## Château de Moulin le Comte

A beautiful wooden floor in the 'green' bedroom and the black and white tiled hall are original touches still on show in this small château, renovated recently and completely by the Van der Elsts. Your Belgian hosts — father, mother, son — are serious about succeeding in their new venture and you will excuse the wonderfully kitsch china chihuahuas when you are relaxing in one of their spacious rooms; expect textured wallpapers and smart showers. Dinner in the elegant green and gold dining room might feature local watercress, colourful St Omer cauliflowers or veal with mustard, cooked by multilingual Francis.

| Rooms | 4 twin/doubles: €99-€139. |
|---|---|
| | 1 family room for 4: €119-€159. |
| | Singles €79-€99. |
| | Dinner, B&B €108-€177 per person. |
| | Extra bed/sofabed €20 per person per night. |
| Meals | Dinner €15-€20; 5 courses, €27; 5 courses with wine, €49. |
| | Restaurant 1.5km. |
| Closed | Rarely. |

**Francis Van der Elst**
Château de Moulin le Comte,
44 rue Principale,
Moulin le Comte,
62120 Aire sur la Lys, Pas-de-Calais

| Tel | +33 (0)3 21 88 48 38 |
| Mobile | +33 (0)6 24 21 08 91 |
| Email | info@chateaudemoulinlecomte.com |
| Web | www.chateaudemoulinlecomte.com |

Entry 26  Map 1

## La Peylouse Manoir

A wildly entertaining place to stay. Your hospitable, knowledgeable hosts live in a tall, grey and red mansion done in a madly eclectic mix of styles amid landscaped gardens full of ancient exotic trees. Intriguing military links too, from arms manufacture for the Sun King (the bullet workshop is still in the grounds) to barracks for the Royal Welch Fusiliers. Bedrooms range from cosy 19th-century boudoir to heavenly Art Deco to New York studio-style; all are excellent, all have views over the spectacular grounds; breakfast is classic continental. The canal marina is a stroll away: you could arrive by boat. *Self-catering available in 4 rooms in annexe.*

| Rooms | 2 doubles: €80–€160. |
| | 1 suite for 2, 1 suite for 4: €80–€160. |
| | Extra bed €25 per person per night. |
| Meals | Restaurant 2km. |
| Closed | Rarely. |

Luce Rousseau
La Peylouse Manoir,
Parc et Jardins de la Peylouse,
23 rue du 8 mai 1945,
62350 St Venant
Pas-de-Calais
Tel      +33 (0)3 21 26 92 02
Email    contact@lapeylouse.fr
Web      www.lapeylouse.fr

Entry 27   Map 1

## Ferme du Moulin

Terraced houses in front, a perfect little farmyard behind, the kindest of hosts within – it's a privilege to meet such splendid people, retired farmers of old-fashioned simple good manners, he silently earthy, she comfortably maternal, delighting in her short travels and guests' conversation. Their modest, authentically timeworn French farmers' house is stuffed with collections of bric-a-brac and their genuine chambres d'hôtes are family-furnished, floral-papered, draped with all sorts and conditions of crochet; the loo is across the landing. Breakfasts are good and you are perfectly placed for those battlefields.

| Rooms | 1 double with separate |
| | bath/shower & sharing wc: €48. |
| | 1 triple with separate bath/shower |
| | & sharing wc: €48–€58. |
| Meals | Restaurants within walking |
| | distance. |
| Closed | Rarely. |

Madame Agnès Dupont
Ferme du Moulin,
58 rue du Quatre Septembre,
62800 Liévin
Pas-de-Calais
Tel      +33 (0)3 21 44 65 91
Mobile   +33 (0)6 81 04 46 96

Entry 28   Map 1

## La Maison de Campagne

Everyone loves it here: wine and conversation flow, and dinners are authentic and delicious. After years as a school librarian, Jacqueline threw herself into encouraging local tourism: a member of many associations and generous to a fault, she loves taking guests on walks and visits; Pierre is active in the village, too. Many drive straight past this area – take the chance to get to know it better with people who belong. You enter through the conservatory and every window looks onto flowers and meadows. The two-bedroom suite, plus cot, is simple but welcoming. Take a train to Paris for the day!

## Le Loubarré

The period of each piece shows on its face, so you expect the elegantly coffered ceilings, the deeply carved woodwork, the vast Louis XIII dresser... but nothing prepares you for the neo-gothic stone fireplace! The rooms in the stables, some up, some down, are pretty and spotless, each with good fabrics, some antiques, a neat shower room, and you can use the comfortable family sitting room. Madame loves telling tales of the house and its contents, and has two dogs, a few goats and four donkeys (a weekend car-racing track in the valley, though). Both your hosts work constantly on their beloved house.

| Rooms | 1 family suite for 4: €80. |
| | Children under 5 stay free. |
| Meals | Dinner €25. Wine €6–€12. |
| Closed | Rarely. |

| Rooms | 1 double, 2 twins: €58. |
| Meals | Guest kitchen. Restaurants within walking distance. |
| Closed | Rarely. |

Jacqueline Guillemant
La Maison de Campagne,
6 rue de l'Europe,
62127 Magnicourt en Comte
Pas-de-Calais
Tel        +33 (0)3 21 41 51 00
Email      jguillemant@gmail.com
Web        www.lamaisondecampagne.com

Marie-Christine & Philippe Vion
Le Loubarré,
550 rue des Montifaux,
62130 Gauchin Verloingt
Pas-de-Calais
Tel        +33 (0)3 21 03 05 05
Email      mcvion.loubarre@wanadoo.fr
Web        www.loubarre.com

Entry 29   Map 1

Entry 30   Map 1

## The North

### Château de Saulty

The re-lifted stately face looks finer than ever in its great park and apple orchards (15 varieties); it is a truly lovely setting. Inside, a warm, embracing country house with a panelled breakfast room, an amazing, museum-worthy, multi-tiled gents cloakroom and, up the wide old stairs, quietly luxurious bedrooms, some huge, furnished with printed fabrics and period pieces. Be charmed by wooden floors and plain walls in sunny tones, perhaps an old fireplace or a mirrored armoire. Quiet and intelligent, Sylvie is a natural at making guests feel at home.

| | |
|---|---|
| Rooms | 1 double: €70. |
| | 1 family room for 4: €100. |
| | 2 triples: €80. |
| Meals | Restaurants 16km. |
| Closed | January. |

FIRST
EDITION
VETERAN

Emmanuel & Sylvie Dalle
Château de Saulty,
82 rue de la Gare,
62158 Saulty
Pas-de-Calais

| | |
|---|---|
| Tel | +33 (0)3 21 48 24 76 |
| Email | chateaudesaulty@nordnet.fr |
| Web | www.chateaudesaulty.com |

Entry 31   Map 1

## The North

### Le Jardin d'Alix

A quiet, elegant residential quarter – but hop on the tram and in 20 minutes you're in the historic centre of Lille. Alexandra's light, airy house, tucked away from the road, was built a mere half century ago by a well-known local church architect. Use your host's sitting room during the day; note the passage leading to the bedrooms has an internet post, and books galore, for the evening. Bedrooms, small and attractive, give onto the gorgeous garden – Alexandra's passion – and are hung with her paintings. Breakfast on homemade bread and jams served on fine porcelain in a spotless high-tech kitchen. *Short breaks available.*

| | |
|---|---|
| Rooms | 1 double: €70. |
| | 1 suite for 2: €85-€100. |
| Meals | Restaurants 3 minutes by tram. |
| Closed | Rarely. |

Alexandra Hudson
Le Jardin d'Alix,
45 bis av de la Marne,
59200 Tourcoing
Nord

| | |
|---|---|
| Tel | +33 (0)3 20 36 72 08 |
| Email | alexandra.hudson@ymail.com |
| Web | www.lejardindalix.com |

Entry 32   Map 1

## Château de Courcelette

From the small-town back street, enter unexpected 18th-century elegance – pilasters, panelling, marble, medallions – then a beautiful brick and cobble terrace to an acre of superb walled garden: bliss so near Lille, and the oldest château left standing in the area. Your hosts will enchant you with their courtesy and deep love for Courcelette, their energy in preserving its classical forms, their care for your comfort; Madame bubbles and chats, Monsieur charms quietly. Pale bedrooms with original doors and handsome antiques set the tone for this quietly luxurious and civilised house. One of the best.

| Rooms | 2 doubles, 1 twin/double: €99. |
| | 1 suite for 4: €149. |
| Meals | Dinner with wine, €35. |
| | Guest kitchen. |
| Closed | Rarely. |

Catherine & Philippe Brame
Château de Courcelette,
17 rue César Parent,
59390 Lannoy
Nord

| Tel | +33 (0)3 20 75 45 67 |
| Mobile | +33 (0)6 62 45 45 67 |
| Email | dormir@chateaulannoy.com |
| Web | www.chateau-de-courcelette.com |

Entry 33   Map 1

## Ferme de la Noyelle

Five minutes from Belgium... the 17th-century archway leads into a lovely old courtyard full of flowers, on a farm where Dominique and Nelly breed hens, geese, rabbits and cows; the moment you arrive you'll forget the shopping outlets nearby. Very basic guest bedrooms are in the old stables and are done up in new-pine cottagey style, with jolly colour matches and wide showers. There's no sitting room but a small communal kitchen for guests; the breakfasts are simple but delicious; and the dinners – guests tell us – are fabulous. There's also a restaurant in another wing, open at weekends.

| Rooms | 1 double, 1 twin: €55–€65. |
| | 1 family room for 4: €95. |
| | 1 triple: €75–€85. |
| Meals | Dinner with wine, €20. |
| | Guest kitchen. |
| Closed | Rarely. |

Dominique & Nelly Pollet
Ferme de la Noyelle,
832 rue Pasteur,
59262 Sainghin en Mélantois
Nord

| Tel | +33 (0)3 20 41 29 82 |
| Mobile | +33 (0)6 74 85 61 79 |
| Email | dnpollet@orange.fr |
| Web | www.fermedelanoyelle.fr |

Entry 34   Map 1

### La Tour Blanche

In grand French style, stable your steeds in fine boxes beneath the immensely tall sheltering trees, swirl up the staircase to superb rooms, each a symphony in fabric and colour – red or blue, green or white – with good beds on polished floors and a gentle view of the little church: all is handsome, sober and serene. And bathrooms are brand new. Your active, intelligent young hosts happily share their generous family house and big garden with guests, two children and half a dozen horses. There are games to play, bikes to hire, Amiens to visit and the shimmering Somme estuary to walk you into bird heaven.

### Château du Romerel

Set in parkland in the middle of the town with views over the bay, this classic 19th-century villa exudes quiet privilege. Graciously furnished rooms include two chandeliered salons – lavish with curtains and deep sofas – and a polished dining room for elegant breakfasts with fruits from the orchard. Dinners, too. Light-flooded bedrooms are country-house-luxurious with soft colours, thick carpets and fine antiques. Most have bay views. Go seal-spotting or cycling; visit Abbeville and Amiens. Sit by the pool or drift amongst the garden's ancient trees and discover its secret bowers. Amélie takes delicious care of you.

| Rooms | 2 doubles: €110–€120. |
| | 1 suite for 5: €190–€235. |
| | 1 family room for 3: €130–€145. |
| | Singles €95–€100. |
| | Extra bed/sofabed €20–€25 per person per night. |
| Meals | Dinner with wine, €40. |
| | Guest kitchen. |
| Closed | Rarely. |

| Rooms | 3 doubles: £183–£223. |
| | 1 triple: £243–£263. |
| Meals | Dinner €35. |
| | Restaurant within walking distance. |
| Closed | Rarely. |

**Hélène & Benoît Legru-Plancq**
La Tour Blanche,
10 rue de la Ville,
80120 Forest Montiers
Somme
Tel       +33 (0)3 22 23 69 13
Mobile    +33 (0)6 88 61 31 62
Email     helene.legru-plancq@wanadoo.fr
Web       www.latourblanche.net

**Amélie Bordier**
Château du Romerel,
15 quai du Romerel,
80230 Saint-Valery sur Somme
Somme
Tel       +33 (0)3 22 23 68 70
Email     info@chateaudenoyelles.com

# Picardy

## Les Mazures

An architect-designed eco house, whose beauty lies in its simplicity. And the garden is glorious, a blaze of colour and form: rock, Japanese and wild flower, carefully gauged scent and colour combos to attract bees, butterflies and other such beasties. Bright white bedrooms have their own entrance and are immaculate, paired with sparkling bathrooms. At the heart, an airy open-plan living room that guests share with owners Peter and Vincent whose nationalities (English and French) are reflected in their cooking – tasty regional and British. Birdwatching, markets and WWI cemeteries are nearby. Fresh, peaceful, convivial.

| | |
|---|---|
| Rooms | 2 doubles, 1 twin: €62. Singles €59. |
| Meals | Dinner with wine, €20. Restaurant 4km. |
| Closed | Rarely. |

One of a kind

Peter Clark
Les Mazures,
2b rue de la Prairie,
80370 Beaumetz
Somme
Tel    +33 (0)3 22 32 80 52
Email    info@lesmazures.com
Web    www.lesmazures.com

Entry 37    Map 1

# Picardy

## Château de Béhen

Surrounded by wooded parkland, the handsome château started life as a holiday house. In the 1950s the Cuveliers moved in, adding paddocks, a pond for swans and a deeply traditional décor. Big bedrooms come with solid oak floors and rugs, and French flourishes. Two-tone panelling graces the first-floor rooms, those above have sloping ceilings and a beam or two; bathrooms are hotel-perfect with double basins of mottled marble. Delicious dinner is at one lively table (or a single one if preferred). Saddle up and enjoy a guided trek – for a day or even two. Fun friendly people, donkeys to stroke and 15 horses to ride.

| | |
|---|---|
| Rooms | 2 doubles, 1 twin: €125-€213. 1 suite for 2: €180-€202. 2 family rooms for 4: €185-€244. |
| Meals | Dinner with wine, from €43. |
| Closed | Rarely. |

Cuvelier Family
Château de Béhen,
8 rue du Château,
80870 Béhen
Somme
Tel    +33 (0)3 22 31 58 30
Email    norbert-andre@cuvelier.com
Web    www.chateau-de-behen.com

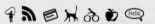

Entry 38    Map 1

## Picardy

### 3 rue d'Inval

Imposing and old-fashioned – in the best possible sense. You soon relax into the homely atmosphere created by your calm, hospitable, country hosts – the first in the Somme to open their house for B&B. Aart keeps honey, cider and calvados in the vaulted cellars and tends the serried tulips and dahlias and the gloriously billowing shrubs; Dorette was mayor for 24 years. Her big uncluttered bedrooms (smaller on the second floor) are comfortable, modern shower rooms are big enough for a third bed, and the panelled dining room is a proper setting for a good breakfast. A great place to stay, with fishing on the lake.

| Rooms | 1 double: €65. |
| | 3 triples sharing wc: €52–€75. |
| | Singles €30–€40. |
| Meals | Kitchen available. |
| | Restaurants 12km. |
| Closed | Rarely. |

**Dorette & Aart Onder de Linden**
3 rue d'Inval,
80430 Le Mazis
Somme
Tel    +33 (0)3 22 25 90 88
Mobile   +33 (0)6 33 96 52 70
Email   onderdelinden@wanadoo.fr
Web   www.lemazis.com

Entry 39   Map 5

## Picardy

### Les Chambres d'Aumont

In the grounds of a stately 18th-century château, a cleverly converted outbuilding with four peaceful rooms overlooking the garden and stables. Where grain and wood were once stored, guests now find light, smartly furnished bedrooms with coir floors and luxurious en suites. Breakfast in the vast, bright communal room is a pleasure… Feast on homemade Mirabelle jam, local cake, cheese and charcuteries. It's wonderfully calm and rural, and you could happily pass the day dozing under an apple tree, but there's plenty to see in this lovely part of Picardy – Amiens Cathedral is a half hour drive and the Somme battlefields are close. *Parking available.*

| Rooms | 3 doubles: €92. |
| | 1 family room for 4: €110–€130. |
| Meals | Restaurant 10km. |
| Closed | Rarely. |

**Stephanie Danzel d'Aumont**
Les Chambres d'Aumont,
Le Château,
2 rue d'Hornoy,
80640 Aumont
Somme
Tel   +33 (0)3 22 90 67 16
Email   stephanie@chambresdaumont.fr
Web   www.chambresdaumont.fr

Entry 40   Map 5

# Picardy

## Château d'Omiécourt

On a working estate, Omiécourt is a proudly grand 19th-century château and elegant family house (the Thézys have four teenage children), with tall slender windows and some really old trees. Friendly if formal, communicative and smiling, your hosts have worked hugely to restore their inheritance and create gracious French château guest rooms, each with an ornate fireplace, each named for a different period. In an outbuilding near the two pools is a neat apartment for self-caterers; there's a 'boutique', too, of pretty things. A house of goodwill where you will be very comfortable.

| | |
|---|---|
| Rooms | 3 doubles: €153–€156. 1 suite for 3: €165–€195. 1 family suite for 4 with kitchen (separate building): €195. Extra bed €30 per person per night. |
| Meals | Restaurants 12km. |
| Closed | Rarely. |

**Dominique & Véronique de Thézy**
Château d'Omiécourt,
80320 Omiécourt
Somme

| | |
|---|---|
| Tel | +33 (0)3 22 83 01 75 |
| Email | contact@chateau-omiecourt.com |
| Web | www.chateau-omiecourt.com |

Entry 41   Map 5

# Picardy

## Le Château de Fosseuse

Your tall windows look over the great park fading away to wooded hillside (with railway); beneath your feet are 16th-century bricks. A monumental staircase ushers you up to big, canopied, glorious-viewed bedrooms that are château-worthy but not posh; behind the panelling of one is a secret staircase. Your hosts are a fascinating, cultured marriage of exquisite French manners and Irish warmth who labour on to save their family home and genuinely enjoy sharing it. Antique rugs line the hall's walls; gumboots for guests (all sizes) wait by the door; Michelin stars are a very short drive.

| | |
|---|---|
| Rooms | 1 double: €90. 1 family room for 2-4: €110–€170. 1 triple: €90–€115. |
| Meals | Restaurant 5km. |
| Closed | Christmas. |

**Shirley & Jean-Louis Marro**
Le Château de Fosseuse,
60540 Fosseuse
Oise

| | |
|---|---|
| Tel | +33 (0)3 44 08 47 66 |
| Email | chateau.fosseuse@orange.fr |
| Web | www.chateau-de-fosseuse.com |

Entry 42   Map 5

Picardy

## Le Clos

The sprucest of farmhouses, whitewashed and Normandy-beamed, sits in its lush secret garden, reached via a door in the wall. Indoors, you find a remarkably fresh, open-plan and modernised interior, with a comfortable sitting room to share. Your bedroom above the garage is spacious, neat, uncluttered and warm; the bedding is the best, the shower room spotless and modern with coloured towels. Dine with your informative hosts by the old farm fireplace on *tarte aux pommes du jardin*. Philippe, the chef, receives much praise. Chantal, a retired teacher, keeps you gentle company. A peaceful spot, close to Paris.

Picardy

## Les Chambres de l'Abbaye

Chloé and her artist husband have the most unusual, delightful house in a village with a fine Cistercian abbey. You are free to roam a series of beautiful rooms downstairs, read a book in the pale blue formal salon, admire Jean-François' striking, exciting pictures (though sadly illness is making it harder for him). The family suite is on the first floor, the two others higher up; all are fresh, and immaculate. You should eat well: much is homemade, including walnut wine and liqueur from their own trees. Walk it off round the partly unmanicured garden with its summerhouse and pond. It's a fascinating house and a pleasure to stay.

| Rooms | 2 family rooms for 2-3: €60-€72. |
|---|---|
| Meals | Dinner with wine, €27. |
| Closed | 3 weeks in winter. |

| Rooms | 2 doubles: €95-€100. |
|---|---|
| | 1 family suite for 3: €100-€125. |
| | Extra bed/sofabed €25 per person per night. |
| Meals | Dinner with wine & coffee, €29. |
| Closed | Christmas. |

Philippe & Chantal Vermeire
Le Clos,
3 rue du Chêne Noir,
60240 Fay les Étangs
Oise
Tel     +33 (0)3 44 49 92 38
Email   philippe.vermeire@wanadoo.fr
Web     www.leclosdefay.com

Chloé Comte
Les Chambres de l'Abbaye,
2 rue Michel Greuet,
60850 St Germer de Fly
Oise
Tel      +33 (0)3 44 81 98 38
Mobile   +33 (0)6 09 27 75 41
Email    comte.resa@free.fr
Web      www.chambres-abbaye.com

Entry 43   Map 5

Entry 44   Map 5

# Picardy

## Domaine de Montaigu

Languid and pleasant gardens – pillows of lavender, dripping wisteria – hem in the large fountain'd courtyard, and neat pathways lead to stone terraces embracing the hill: welcome to this 18th-century wine domain. Gardening is one of the enthusiasms of new owner Claire (along with horses and champagne). She and Philippe love their B&B life and offer you cosy comfortable bedrooms decorated in traditional French style, three pretty with toile de Jouy. There are two sitting rooms, one large, one snug, a swimming pool for summer and a big convivial table for breakfasts of pastries and homemade jams.

| Rooms | 2 doubles: €80–€95. 1 family room for 3, 1 family room for 5: €80–€130. Extra bed/sofabed €25 per person per night. |
|---|---|
| Meals | Restaurant 5km. |
| Closed | Rarely. |

Philippe de Coster
Domaine de Montaigu,
16 rue de Montaigu,
02290 Ambleny
Aisne

| Tel | +33 (0)3 23 74 06 62 |
| Email | info@domainedemontaigu.com |
| Web | www.domainedemontaigu.com |

Entry 45  Map 5

# Picardy

## La Quincy

The old family home, faded and weary, timeless and romantic, is well loved and lived in by this charming, natural and quietly elegant couple. Corridors cluttered with books, magazines and traces of family life lead to an octagonal tower, its great double room and child's room across the landing imaginatively set in the space. A handsome antique bed on a fine polished floor, charming chintz, erratic plumbing and two parkland views will enchant you. Shrubs hug the feet of the delicious 'troubadour' château, the garden slips into meadow, summer breakfast and dinner (good wine, book ahead) are in the orangery. Special.

| Rooms | 1 family room for 3: €70. Pets €8. |
|---|---|
| Meals | Dinner with wine, €25. |
| Closed | Rarely. |

Jacques & Marie-Catherine
Cornu-Langy
La Quincy,
02880 Nanteuil la Fosse
Aisne

| Tel | +33 (0)3 23 54 67 76 |
| Mobile | +33 (0)7 86 99 37 95 |
| Email | la.quincy@yahoo.fr |

Entry 46  Map 5

## Picardy

### Verdonne

At the end of a long winding lane is kind Camille's jolly family home with hens, goats, cats, pétanque and a potager. Four rustic guest rooms are filled with bric-a-brac finds: handmade shelving and ingenious craftsmanship bring a quirky charm; a claw-foot bath is angled to give stupendous valley views while you soak. At one end of the shared salon is the dining area for home-cooked suppers; at the other are a sofa and easy chairs around the open fire. There's table tennis in the barn and games for children — families will love it. Medieval Laon is close by, as is Soissons, with its notable 12th-century cathedral.

| Rooms | 1 double with sofabed, 3 twin/doubles: €80–€90. Extra bed €30 per person per night. Child's bed (6-13 years) €20. €10 discount for stays of 2 nights or more. |
|---|---|
| Meals | Charcuterie dinner, €15. Dinner, 5 courses, €28. Wine €7–€35. Restaurants 10km. |
| Closed | Rarely. |

**Camille Hériard Dubreuil**
Verdonne,
02880 Chivres Val
Aisne

| Tel | +33 (0)3 23 72 38 57 |
| Email | casa@verdonne.org |
| Web | www.verdonne.org |

Entry 47   Map 5

## Picardy

### Ferme de Ressons

Ressons is home to a warm, dynamic, intelligent couple who, after a hard day's work running this big farm (Jean-Paul) or being an architect (Valérie) and tending three children, will ply you in apparently leisurely fashion with champagne, excellent dinner and conversation; they also hunt. The deeply carved Henri III furniture is an admirable family heirloom; bedrooms (two en suite) are colour-coordinated, views roll for miles and sharing facilities seems easy. A house of comfort and relaxed good manners (smoking is in the study only), whose decoration and accessories reflect the owners' travels.

| Rooms | 2 doubles; 1 twin sharing bath & 2 wcs; 1 double, 1 twin sharing wc: €55–€80. |
|---|---|
| Meals | Dinner €19. Wine €14; champagne €18. |
| Closed | Rarely. |

**Valérie & Jean-Paul Ferry**
Ferme de Ressons,
02220 Mont St Martin
Aisne

| Tel | +33 (0)3 23 74 71 00 |
| Mobile | +33 (0)6 80 74 17 01 |
| Email | ferryressons@orange.fr |

Entry 48   Map 5

# Picardy

## La Grange

Hidden down lanes, behind an undulating wall, glimpsed through wrought-iron gates, is this big converted barn; Tony and Thierry have been looking after guests, with great pleasure, for years. Rambling gardens and a bountiful vegetable plot run down to wide open pasture. Under the high glass atrium of the breakfast room lies the heart of the house with wood-burner, piano and windows opening to undulating views, while peaceful and immaculate bedrooms hop from fabric-swathed opulence to a more simple country elegance. Hosted dinners are convivial and delicious; Reims, rich in history and gastronomy, is under an hour.

| Rooms | 2 doubles: €63–€72. |
| | 1 apartment for 4: €140. |
| | Singles €63. |
| | Dinner, B&B €29 per person. |
| | Extra bed/sofabed €24 per person per night. |
| Meals | Dinner, 4 courses with wine, €29. |
| | Restaurant 10km. |
| Closed | Rarely. |

Tony Bridier & Thierry Charbit
La Grange,
6 impasse des Prés,
02160 Cuiry les Chaudardes
Aisne

| Tel | +33 (0)3 23 25 82 42 |
| Email | lagrangecuiry@orange.fr |
| Web | www.lagrangecuiry.fr |

Entry 49   Map 5

---

# Picardy

## Le Clos

Genuine country hospitality and warmth are yours in the big old house. Madame is kindly and direct; Monsieur is the communicator (mainly in French), knows his local history and loves the hunting horn. His 300-year-old family house is cosily unposh: floral curtains, French-papered walls, original wainscotting, funny old prints in bedrooms, comforting clutter in the vast living room, posters in the corridors. The master bedroom is superb, others are simple and fine; one has a ship's shower room, all look onto green pastures. And there's a pretty lake for picnics across the narrow road.

| Rooms | 2 doubles, 1 twin: €50–€60. |
| | 1 suite for 5: €60–€120. |
| | Extra bed €20 per person per night. |
| Meals | Dinner with wine, €22.50. |
| | Restaurant in village. |
| Closed | Mid-October to mid-March, except by arrangement. |

FIRST
EDITION
VETERAN

Michel & Monique Simonnot
Le Clos,
02860 Chérêt
Aisne

| Tel | +33 (0)3 23 24 80 64 |
| Email | leclos.cheret@club-internet.fr |
| Web | www.lecloscheret.com |

Entry 50   Map 5

### Domaine de l'Étang

The village on one side, the expansive estate on the other, the 18th-century wine-grower's house in between. There's a civilised mood: Monsieur so well-mannered and breakfast served with silver and fine china in the comfortably elegant guest dining room. Wake to church-spire and rooftop views in rooms with soft comfort where, under sloping ceilings, French toile de Jouy is as inviting as English chintz (your hosts spent two years in England). Bathrooms are frilled and pretty. Shrubs hug the hem of the house, a pool is sunk into the lawn behind and Laon trumpets one of France's first Gothic cathedrals.

| | |
|---|---|
| Rooms | 2 doubles, 1 twin: €60–€80. |
| Meals | Restaurants 6km. |
| Closed | Rarely. |

|  |  |
|---|---|
| | Patrick Woillez |
| | Domaine de l'Étang, |
| | 2 rue St Martin, |
| | 02000 Mons en Laonnois |
| | Aisne |
| Tel | +33 (0)3 23 24 44 52 |
| Mobile | +33 (0)6 26 62 36 41 |
| Email | gitemons@sfr.fr |
| Web | www.domainedeletang.fr |

Entry 51  Map 5

### Les Cernailles

Come for Emmanuelle's vibrant personality, and to be transported back to 18th-century elegance: This is an amazing example of how to renovate without using anything new. A few of the 27 metres of panelling that Emmanuelle – who has a passion for antiques – bought at a château auction dress the walls of the guest quarters, floors are reclaimed brick, stone or timber, and each piece of furniture tells a tale. Wonky Delft tiles decorate the bathrooms, moss and period porcelain and silver decorate the breakfast table. The lovely walled garden simply begs for a crinoline, though the two fine 'grey ghost' dogs might seem out of scale.

| | |
|---|---|
| Rooms | 2 doubles: €85. |
| Meals | Café in village, restaurants 8km. |
| Closed | Rarely. |

|  |  |
|---|---|
| | Emmanuelle Simphal |
| | Les Cernailles, |
| | 33 av d'Île de France, |
| | 02870 Vivaise |
| | Aisne |
| Tel | +33 (0)3 23 22 97 33 |
| Email | lescernailles@hotmail.fr |

Entry 52  Map 5

# Picardy

## La Commanderie

Up here on the hill, not easy to find, is a Templar hamlet and a millennium of history: an enclosed farmyard, a ruined medieval chapel framing the sunrise, a tithe barn with leaping oak timbers – and this modern house. José-Marie, an unhurried grandmother of generous spirit, loves the history, harvests her orchards and vegetables, and welcomes genuinely. Bedrooms are in plain, dated farm style but open the window and you fall into the view that soars away on all sides of the hill, even to Laon cathedral. Homely, authentic and simple, with lived-in plumbing and great value – most readers love it.

| | |
|---|---|
| Rooms | 1 double: €50-€55.<br>2 family rooms for 4: €60-€70. |
| Meals | Dinner with wine, €18.<br>Restaurants 10km. |
| Closed | Last week of October – February,<br>except by arrangement. |

José-Marie Carette
La Commanderie,
Catillon du Temple,
02270 Nouvion & Catillon
Aisne

| | |
|---|---|
| Tel | +33 (0)3 23 56 51 28 |
| Mobile | +33 (0)6 82 33 22 64 |
| Email | carette.jm@wanadoo.fr |
| Web | www.gite-templier-laon.com |

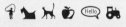

Entry 53   Map 5

Photo: iStock.com/federicofoto

# Champagne – Ardenne

## Champagne – Ardenne

### Le Presbytère de Sévigny

You'll love your hosts: Jatin, attentive and hands-on; Laurence, easy, serene and a good cook (try her nougat ice cream!). The wing of their 19th-century presbytery, once used for christenings and confirmations, has become a plush and pretty gîte, with bedrooms that can be rented individually. Extremely cosy and comfortable, they come in fashionable muted colours or in Asian style; mattresses are deep and firm, and garnished with square French pillows. Downstairs are the sitting and dining rooms, elegant and cool. The village is remote with a 13th-century church; beyond are the vineyards of Champagne. *Cot available.*

### La Grange Champenoise

Twenty minutes from Reims, this giant limestone barn has been rebuilt to create five flawless suites (new kingsize mattresses, top toiletries) and a handsome breakfast room and sitting room besides. Oak floors are impeccable, colours are ivory and cream, and bedrooms open onto a huge sunny courtyard with a low hedging trim. Enjoy an excellent French breakfast served at a convivial table with white dining chairs. Gently spoken Florent farms the estate, friendly unassuming Emmanuelle makes the pastries, and if you order champagne it arrives on a silver platter.

| Rooms | 3 doubles: €85–€95. |
|---|---|
| | 1 triple: €95–€110. |
| | Children under 6 stay free. |
| Meals | Dinner, 3 courses with wine, €30. |
| | Restaurants 11km. |
| Closed | Rarely. |

| Rooms | 4 doubles: €80–€160. |
|---|---|
| | 1 family room for 4: €120–€160. |
| | Extra bed 35€ per person per night. |
| | Cot available €15. |
| Meals | Restaurant 7km. |
| Closed | Late December to early March. |

**Laurence & Jatin Janray**
Le Presbytère de Sévigny,
7 rue du Cabas,
08220 Sévigny-Waleppe
Ardennes

| Tel | +33 (0)3 24 72 26 31 |
|---|---|
| Email | info@lepresbyteredesevigny.com |
| Web | www.lepresbyteredesevigny.com |

**Florent & Emmanuelle Guillaume**
La Grange Champenoise,
Rue du 151 R.I.,
51110 Auménancourt
Marne

| Tel | +33 (0)3 26 97 54 21 |
|---|---|
| Mobile | +33 (0)6 21 61 62 52 |
| Email | contact@lagrangechampenoise.com |
| Web | www.lagrangechampenoise.com |

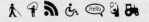

### La Closerie des Sacres

An easy drive from Reims, these former stables have changed radically. Large, cool downstairs areas – the mangers and tethering rings remain – are pale-tiled with dark leather sofas, games and books, an open fire, a glass-topped dining table, wrought-iron chairs. And you can do your own cooking in the fully fitted kitchen. Bedrooms are solid oak-floored, draped and prettily coloured with well-dressed beds, cushions, teddy bears, electric blinds and jacuzzi baths. The Jactats have farmed here for generations and tell of the rebuilding of their village in 1925. Take time to talk, and play boules in the sheltered garden.

| Rooms | 1 double: €94.<br>1 suite for 5: €120–€180.<br>1 triple: €94–€115.<br>Singles €78–€100. |
|---|---|
| Meals | Guest kitchen. Restaurants 2km. |
| Closed | Rarely. |

**Sandrine & Laurent Jactat**
La Closerie des Sacres,
7 rue Chefossez,
51110 Lavannes
Marne

| Tel | +33 (0)3 26 02 05 05 |
| Email | contact@closerie-des-sacres.com |
| Web | www.closerie-des-sacres.com |

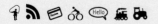

Entry 56   Map 6

### La Demeure des Sacres

A privileged spot for a privileged mansion. Reims Cathedral is 150 yards away: you can see it from the balcony of the Suite Royale. All the rooms are 'royale' here: suave, spacious, voluptuous, and the quietest facing the garden. Courteous Céline cares for house, family and guests and offers an elegant breakfast buffet of homemade cookies, crêpes and jams in the classical dining room (at one table, or several – you choose), or on the terrace on summer days, overlooking lawn, roses, shrubs and swings. You get minibars, safes, superb bathrooms, snow-white linen… and a sweeping Art Deco day room. *Parking available.*

| Rooms | 2 twin/doubles with separate shower & wc: €145.<br>1 suite for 2-4, 1 suite for 2-5: €220–€245.<br>Extra bed/sofabed available €30.<br>Child's bed (2-12 years) €20.<br>Cot €30. |
|---|---|
| Meals | Restaurants within walking distance. |
| Closed | Rarely. |

**Céline Songy**
La Demeure des Sacres,
29 rue Libergier,
51100 Reims
Marne

| Tel | +33 (0)3 26 91 03 00 |
| Mobile | +33 (0)6 79 06 80 68 |
| Email | contact@la-demeure-des-sacres.com |
| Web | www.la-demeure-des-sacres.com |

Entry 57   Map 6

### Domaine Ployez-Jacquemart

The grand old mansion sits in green serene gardens near the outskirts of a small champagne village; Ployez-Jacquemart is an exceptional domain whose fizz ranges from buttery-rich to fruity-fresh. Courteous staff (who live off site) serve breakfast at one big table, and show you to suites decorated in impeccable French style. Ask for one that faces the vineyards ('Nature', distinguished by its gentle colours and polished boards, is on the first floor, 'Savane' and 'Provence' are on the second). The communal spaces are chic, the gardens are elegant, the breakfasts are delicious and you can wander at will.
*Minimum stay: 2 nights at weekends.*

### Château de Juvigny

Oozing old-world charm, this handsome 1705 château wraps you in its warmth. The family have occupied one wing for 200 years and, thanks to Brigitte, it has a wonderfully easy-going elegance. There are chandeliers, polished floorboards, wainscotting and antiques, old-fashioned bathrooms, cracked floor tiles, rustic outbuildings. Bedrooms, in the old servants' quarters, are informally stylish with marble fireplaces, pretty bedcovers and views over the park, the formal gardens and the lake. You breakfast, colourfully, beneath a vast (and deteriorated!) portrait of an ancestor. Charming, unfussy country comfort.

| | |
|---|---|
| Rooms | 3 doubles, 1 twin: €135–€145. 1 family room for 4: €200–€210. |
| Meals | Gourmet dinner, €135 per person (min. 6). Restaurants 10km. |
| Closed | Rarely. |

| | |
|---|---|
| Rooms | 3 doubles, 1 twin: €95–€150. 1 suite for 4: €150–€200. Extra bed €25 per person per night. |
| Meals | Restaurant 10km. |
| Closed | Mid-December to mid-March, except by arrangement. |

|  | **Laurence Ployez** |
|---|---|
| | Domaine Ployez-Jacquemart, |
| | 8 rue Astoin, |
| | 51500 Ludes |
| | Marne |
| Tel | +33 (0)3 26 61 11 87 |
| Email | contact@ployez-jacquemart.fr |
| Web | www.ployez-jacquemart.fr |

|  | **Brigitte Caubère d'Alinval** |
|---|---|
| | Château de Juvigny, |
| | 8 av du Château, |
| | 51150 Juvigny |
| | Marne |
| Mobile | +33 (0)6 78 99 69 40 |
| Email | information@chateaudejuvigny.com |
| Web | www.chateaudejuvigny.com |

### Chez Eric & Sylvie

An immensely informal and friendly house plumb in the land of champagne. All is comfortable and homely with roaring log fires, vintage treasures and retro style; the garden is flowery, rambling and terraced. Bedrooms, one with a small balcony and views of the vines, have well-dressed beds and polished boards and breakfast is a generous affair, with exotic fruits, homemade cake, pots and pots of homemade jams, fresh bread and pastries – served in the large living room with garden and front-gate views. An easy drive to surrounding vineyards and Epernay; while Reims, with its Gothic cathedral, champagne houses and cellar visits, is 25 kilometres away.

| Rooms | 2 twin/doubles: €85. |
| | 1 family room for 4: €85-€115. |
| Meals | Restaurants nearby. |
| Closed | Rarely. |

**Anne Charbonnier**
Chez Éric & Sylvie,
189 rue Ferdinand Moret,
51530 Cramant
Marne

| Tel | +33 (0)3 26 57 95 34 |
| Mobile | +33 (0)6 73 59 56 82 |
| Email | alafluteenchantee@hotmail.fr |
| Web | www.a-la-flute-enchantee.fr |

Entry 60   Map 6

### Les Petits Prés

In a peaceful walled garden in Epernay is a 19th-century 'maison bourgeoise'. Pass the owners' kitchen and there is your gîte… a neat kitchen and big bathroom downstairs and, up the narrow stair, two bedrooms and a sitting room. All is stylish, contemporary, charming, full of light, and you can lunch on your own barbecue terrace. Kind Madame brings you fresh baguette and pastries each morning, and you do the rest. The train whisks you to Paris in just over an hour and as for the bubbly stuff, it's everywhere – from the 'grandes maisons' on Épernay's Avenue de Champagne to the tiniest producers. Take the house bikes!

| Rooms | 1 apartment for 4 with kitchen: |
| | €150-€190. |
| | Extra bed €10 per person per night.. |
| Meals | Restaurants within walking distance. |
| Closed | Rarely. |

**Sylvie Robinet**
Les Petits Prés,
32 rue des Petits Prés,
51200 Epernay
Marne

| Tel | +33 (0)3 26 59 34 08 |
| Mobile | +33 (0)6 37 55 82 79 |
| Email | sylvie.robinet@wanadoo.fr |

Entry 61   Map 6

## Au Pré du Moulin

The big 1789 farmhouse deep in the country has been in the Coulmier family for two generations. Luckily, one half of the main house has been given over to guests; an interconnecting suite (poppy-print wallpaper, wooden floors) provides family-sized space to match a child-friendly garden. Elsewhere, rooms are French 'rustic chic' to a tee; white lacquered bedsteads and cornflower-blue floral details in one, stylish dark wood and Burgundian limestone with tiny black cabochons in another. Valérie and Didier are lovely, friendly and knowledgeable hosts and will share delicious organic home-grown fare with you.

## Ferme de Bannay

The deep-country house in the pretty village brims with new chintz and old beams. Bedrooms dressed in ivory and white have quilted bedcovers and scatter cushions; sprays of artificial flowers brighten nooks and crannies; and there's a bathroom behind a curtain. Little English is spoken but the welcome is so endearing, the generosity so genuine, the food so delicious, that communication is easy. Just a few cows on the farm now, and the odd tractor passing, but the vegetable garden is handsome and much of the produce ends up on your (delightfully antique) plate.

| Rooms | 1 double: €70. |
| | 1 suite for 4: €100. |
| | 1 triple: €70-€85. |
| | Extra bed/sofabed €15 per person per night. |
| Meals | Dinner with wine, €25. |
| Closed | Christmas/New Year. |

| Rooms | 1 suite for 2-3 with kitchen: €77-€119. |
| | 1 triple: €66-€84. |
| | 1 quadruple: €66-€102. |
| Meals | Dinner with wine, €36; with champagne €55. |
| Closed | Rarely. |

FIRST
EDITION
VETERAN

|  | Valérie & Didier Coulmier |
| | Au Pré du Moulin, |
| | 4 rue du Moulin, |
| | 51130 Clamanges |
| | Marne |
| Tel | +33 (0)3 26 64 50 16 |
| Email | reservation@aupredumoulin.fr |
| Web | www.aupredumoulin.fr |

|  | Muguette & Jean-Pierre Curfs |
| | Ferme de Bannay, |
| | 1 rue du Petit Moulin, |
| | 51270 Bannay |
| | Marne |
| Tel | +33 (0)3 26 52 80 49 |
| Email | leschambresdemuguette@orange.fr |

## Champagne – Ardenne

### La Ferme de Désiré

A quietly talkative, personable hostess and her young daughter welcome you to this majestic 17th-century family farm. Through the huge arch is a gravelled courtyard enclosed by immaculate outbuildings and a farmhouse; potted palms add an exotic touch. In the converted stables, guests have a living room with original mangers, a log fire and kitchen, then steep stairs up to two simply decorated, carpeted, roof-lit rooms. This is a deeply rural area with farmland reaching as far as the eye can see, close to the vineyards of Champagne. *Minimum stay: 2 nights on bank holiday weekends.*

## Champagne – Ardenne

### Auprès de l'Eglise

New Zealanders Michael and Glenis do excellent table d'hôtes and love sharing their restored 19th-century house full of surprises: some walls are unadorned but for the mason's scribbles. The upstairs suite is separated by a fabulous wall of bookcases and an attic stair, the ground floor has a French country feel. Another big, cleverly designed room leads off the courtyard where you sit in the shade of birch trees and dine (and enjoy a champagne aperitif). Oyes church has no chiming clocks: you'll sleep deeply here. Plenty of fun and funky brocante yet the comforts are modern. Charming Sézanne is a 20-minute drive.

| | |
|---|---|
| Rooms | 2 doubles, 2 twins: €70-€75. Extra bed/sofabed €29 per person per night. |
| Meals | Guest kitchen. Restaurant 10km. |
| Closed | Rarely. |

| | |
|---|---|
| Rooms | 2 suites for 2-4: €90-€150. Singles €75. Extra bed/sofabed €20 per person per night. |
| Meals | Dinner with wine, €35. Child €10. |
| Closed | Rarely. |

|  | Anne Boutour |
|---|---|
| | La Ferme de Désiré, |
| | 51210 Le Gault Soigny |
| | Marne |
| Mobile | +33 (0)6 26 68 14 10 |
| Email | domaine_de_desire@yahoo.fr |
| Web | www.ferme-desire.com |

|  | Glenis Foster |
|---|---|
| | Auprès de l'Église, |
| | 2 rue de l'Église, |
| | 51120 Oyes |
| | Marne |
| Tel | +33 (0)3 26 80 62 39 |
| Mobile | +44 (0)7808 905233 |
| Email | titusprod@me.com |
| Web | www.champagnevilla.com |

## Domaine de Boulancourt

This large and splendid farmhouse is irresistible. For fishermen there's a river, for birdwatchers a fine park full of wildlife (come for the cranes in spring or autumn); for architecture buffs, the half-timbered churches are among the 100 most beautiful attractions in France. Bedrooms are comfortable and handsome; afternoon tea is served by the piano in an elegant panelled salon; dinner, possibly home-raised boar, duck or carp, is eaten at one or several tables but not with your delightful hosts who live in another wing and prefer to concentrate on their cooking!

## Le Relais du Puits

Regular guests of Michel and Évelyne in their tiny medieval village in Champagne will find this charming couple in a 'new' 200-year-old home. Just three rooms now, all reflecting Évelyne's quirky humour: snow-white 'Romantic', chic 'Belle-Époque', extravagant 'Medieval' with a gothic, dark orange décor, daggers and tapestries. Bathrooms are gorgeous, the garden large, and dinners – Évelyne's cider chicken, Michel's chocolate mousse – fabulous value. After 18 years your hosts know just what guests want, whether it's free internet, a roaring fire in the sitting room, or bicycles for the surrounding forests and country lanes.

| Rooms | 2 doubles, 1 twin: €75–€85. 1 suite for 2: €85. 1 single: €65–€75. Extra bed €20 per person per night. |
| --- | --- |
| Meals | Dinner with wine, €30. |
| Closed | December to mid-March. |

FIRST
EDITION
VETERAN

| Rooms | 1 double; 1 twin with separate bath: €72. 1 triple: €82–€125. Extra bed €20 per person per night. Cot €12. |
| --- | --- |
| Meals | Dinner with wine, €18. Children under 10, €10. Children under 3 eat free. Restaurant 8km. |
| Closed | Rarely. |

Philippe & Christine Viel–Cazal
Domaine de Boulancourt,
Le Désert,
52220 Longeville sur la Laines
Haute-Marne
Tel     +33 (0)3 25 04 60 18
Mobile  +33 (0)6 33 18 84 92
Email   dom.boulancourt@wanadoo.fr
Web     www.domaine-de-boulancourt.com

Évelyne & Michel Poope
Le Relais du Puits,
15 rue Augustin Massin,
52500 Pressigny
Haute-Marne
Tel    +33 (0)3 25 88 80 50
Email  e.m.poope@orange.fr
Web    www.le-relais-du-puits.com/

## Château de Prauthoy

This 17th-century château is one of the most beautiful guest houses in France. It hides in the middle of a small town surrounded by parkland that's full of surprises (19th-century caves, a wild wood, noble trees – a children's paradise). It's grand but homely, and fun; you can play the piano in the sitting room, and relax in summer by the heated pool. Behind the stunning façade is a faded grandeur and bedrooms airy and large, all decorated in a mix of French classical and Asian influence. Kanha, the gracious lady of the house, is Cambodian, and delicious breakfasts are served at elegant tables in a charming sun room with a glorious view.

## Domaine du Moulin d'Eguebaude

A delightful mill – and trout farm. The secluded old buildings in the lush riverside setting are home to a fish restaurant, several guest rooms and 50 tons of live fish. Delicious breakfast and dinner are shared with your enthusiastic hosts, who started the business 40 years ago; groups come for speciality lunches, anglers come to fish. Bedrooms under the eaves are compact, small-windowed, simply furnished, decorated in rustic or granny style, the larger annexe rooms are more motel-ish. Lots of space for children, and good English spoken. More guest house than B&B.

| | |
|---|---|
| Rooms | 3 doubles: €138–€156. |
| | 1 suite for 3 (joins with one double to form suite for 5), 1 suite for 4: €175–€225. |
| Meals | Dinner €29–€39 (min. 4). |
| | Wine €17–€150. |
| | Restaurants 2-minute walk. |
| Closed | Mid-December to mid-January. |

| | |
|---|---|
| Rooms | 2 doubles, 1 twin: €75–€80. |
| | 2 family rooms for 4: €108–€124. |
| | 1 triple: €85. |
| | Extra bed/sofabed €14–€22 per person per night. |
| Meals | Dinner with wine, €28. |
| | Guest kitchen. |
| Closed | Christmas/New Year & occasionally. |

**Frédéric Mailfait**
Château de Prauthoy,
22 Grande Rue,
52190 Prauthoy
Haute-Marne

| | |
|---|---|
| Tel | +33 (0)3 25 90 54 25 |
| Email | info@chateaudeprauthoy.com |
| Web | www.chateaudeprauthoy.com |

**Alexandre & Sandrine Mesley**
Domaine du Moulin d'Eguebaude,
36 rue Pierre Brossolette,
10190 Estissac
Aube

| | |
|---|---|
| Tel | +33 (0)3 25 40 42 18 |
| Email | eguebaude@aol.com |
| Web | www.moulineguebaude.jimdo.com |

## A L'Aube Bleue

Madame is a collector of intriguing finds (including the Peugeot 203). Her two family-friendly garden-facing bedrooms make good use of compact space: one has the double bed on the mezzanine floor and children sleep below; the other, pretty in pale colours, sleeps three. The disabled access room is larger, also simply furnished, with a baldequin bed. You breakfast at one big table next to the kitchen. Do arrange a meal in the sheltered outdoor dining area, too; it's fun and hung with agricultural bits and bobs, and the food will be good. All in a quiet village, in open country 18km south of medieval Troyes.

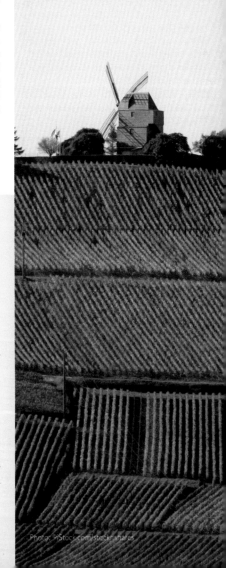

| | |
|---|---|
| Rooms | 1 double: €63. |
| | 1 family room for 4: €95. |
| | 1 triple: €80. Singles €53–€95. |
| | Dinner, B&B €25 extra per person. |
| | Extra bed/sofabed €18 per person per night. |
| Meals | Dinner with wine & coffee, €25. |
| | Children over 5, €9. |
| | Children under 5, €6. |
| Closed | Rarely. |

| | |
|---|---|
| | **Christine Degois** |
| | A L'Aube Bleue, |
| | 6 rue du Viard, |
| | 10320 Assenay |
| | Aube |
| Tel | +33 (0)3 25 40 29 58 |
| Mobile | +33 (0)6 85 10 43 50 |
| Email | contact@chambres-hotes-aube-bleue.fr |
| Web | www.chambres-hotes-aube-bleue.fr |

Entry 70   Map 6

Photo: iStock.com/anzeletti

Lorraine • Alsace • Franche Comté

# Lorraine

## Château d'Alteville

A genuine eco-friendly family château (several generations run the estate) in a privileged setting: wake to a chorus of birds. Bedrooms are deliciously *vieille France*; bathrooms are functional and adequate. The real style lies in the utterly French salon and the dining room – reached through halls, past library and billiards – where dinners are enjoyed by candlelight in the company of your charming hosts. David, a committed environmentalist, cooks local produce with skill, Agnieszka joyfully deals with two lovely children and fills the place with flowers. The lake on the doorstep is a marvel of peace and birdlife.

| Rooms | 4 doubles, 1 twin: €91. |
| --- | --- |
| Meals | Dinner €31–€38.50. Wine €5–€15. |
| Closed | Rarely. |

FIRST EDITION VETERAN

AWARD WINNER

Old favourite

**David Barthélémy**
Château d'Alteville,
Tarquimpol,
57260 Dieuze
Moselle
Tel        +33 (0)3 87 05 46 63
Mobile   +33 (0)6 72 07 56 05
Email     chateau.alteville@free.fr

Entry 71   Map 7

# Lorraine

## 51 rue Lorraine

Alina came from Poland with a bundle of talents; a professional gardener, she paints, embroiders, decorates. Gérard, a retired French architect, won a prize for his brilliant conversion of this dear little 200-year-old house. Their skills and taste for contemporary and ethnic styles shine through the house, their thoughtful, artistic personalities enliven the dinner table, their environmentalist passion informs their lives. Expect gorgeous vegetarian food if you ask for it; delicious meaty things too. No sitting room but comfortable, simple, spotless bedrooms, and a lovely garden and patio for summer.

| Rooms | 1 double: €62. 1 triple: €75. |
| --- | --- |
| Meals | Dinner with wine, €23–€25. |
| Closed | Rarely. |

**Alina & Gérard Cahen**
51 rue Lorraine,
57220 Burtoncourt
Moselle
Tel       +33 (0)3 87 35 72 65
Email    ag.cahen@wanadoo.fr
Web      www.maisonlorraine.com

Entry 72   Map 7

## Lorraine

### Les 3 Officiers

The prosperous looking manor by the church (once a modest farmhouse) has become a splendid B&B. Tea in the salon with Frederick – Anglophile restorer with a great sense of humour – is civilised and fun, while dinner at the big table (homemade orange wine, local organic produce) with both hosts, and perhaps other guests, is a gorgeous feast. As for the suites, they have been designed in the spirit of the house, one à la Napoleon III, the other Louis Philippe. Towels are snowy, bed linen crisp and all is generous and bright. Wake to fruit compotes served on antique china, come home to a beautiful box-hedged garden. *Parking available.*

| Rooms | 2 doubles: €80. Singles €70. Extra bed €20 per person per night |
|---|---|
| Meals | Dinner, 3 courses with wine, €25. Children under 7, €15. Restaurant 5km. |
| Closed | Never. |

| | Frederick Metz |
|---|---|
| | Les 3 Officiers, |
| | Rue de Verdun, |
| | 55210 Woel |
| | Meuse |
| Mobile | +33 (0)6 83 30 42 62 |
| Email | les3officiers.resa@orange.fr |
| Web | www.chambres-3officiers-lorraine.com |

## Lorraine

### Auberge de la Cholotte

In a wooded valley sits a spacious pink sandstone farmhouse framed with bright blue shutters and rambling wisteria. Both the dining room with open fire and the wood-panelled restaurant are open to the public and they host regular concerts here. Angelika serves hearty local produce so stay for supper and some music. Bedrooms have a rustic chic feel, artistic colour combinations and paintings on the walls. There's much to do here: the Vosges mountains are nearby, the pilgrim's path passes the house, there are heaps of gardens, good walking and fishing. Such peace and quiet and such a friendly couple running the show.

| Rooms | 3 doubles, 1 twin, 1 family room for 3: €90–€100. |
|---|---|
| Meals | Dinner €25. Wine €18–€32. |
| Closed | Rarely. |

| | Angelika & Patrick Colin |
|---|---|
| | Auberge de la Cholotte, |
| | 44 La Cense de Saint Dié, |
| | 88600 Les Rouges Eaux |
| | Vosges |
| Tel | +33 (0)3 29 50 56 93 |
| Email | auberge@lacholotte.com |
| Web | www.lacholotte.com |

## Alsace

### Le Moulin

The thermal waters of Niederbronn have drawn visitors since Roman times, and the town, in a half moon of hills in the Northern Vosges, retains an authentic Alsatian atmosphere. Madame and Monsieur welcome you in the same spirit to their peaceful estate, where a stream-driven mill, now gîtes, sits amid ancient trees, a pool and rose walk. The elegant manor has two history-filled guest rooms, pretty in pastel and catching the morning sun, and a fire in the salon. Quietly green, your hosts run an electric car and serve home-pressed apple juice at breakfast. Roam UNESCO forests to medieval villages and ruined châteaux.

| Rooms | 1 twin/double: €90. |
| --- | --- |
| | 1 suite for 5 (bunkbeds & extra single bed in second room): €90–€130. |
| Meals | Restaurant 1km. |
| Closed | 1 January – 31 March. |

**Henri & Marianne Mellon**
Le Moulin,
44 route de Reichshoffen,
67110 Niederbronn les Bains
Bas-Rhin

| Mobile | +33 (0)6 25 43 40 40 |
| --- | --- |
| Email | marianne.mellon@gmail.com |
| Web | gite.moulin.free.fr |

Entry 75   Map 7

## Alsace

### Le Loft 13

High (eight floors up) in central Strasbourg – a warm, spacious and opulent place, with wonderful views of ancient rooftops, cathedral spires and the Vosges peaks beyond. Homemade Lebanese cheese is a breakfast speciality, though you can have a full British if you fancy. Plush, beamed bedrooms have white linen and rich colours, and the suite has a jacuzzi; three rooms have mezzanines for children. Bold paintings, rugs and artefacts complete Le Loft-scape. You're in the thrub of the city with bustling fun a stroll away: a world famous Christmas market, flea markets and, right on the doorstep, the farmers' bio-organic stalls.

| Rooms | 4 doubles, sharing 2 bathrooms (3 rooms have a mezzanine and can accommodate a family): €150–€200. |
| --- | --- |
| | 1 suite for 2: €450–€600. |
| Meals | Dinner with wine, €60 (min. 6). Restaurants within walking distance. |
| Closed | Never. |

**Tina Starke**
Le Loft 13,
13 rue de la Douane,
67000 Strasbourg
Bas-Rhin

| Tel | +33 (0)3 88 22 00 51 |
| --- | --- |
| Email | atelier13douane@gmail.com |
| Web | www.leloft13.fr |

Entry 76   Map 7

# Alsace

## 86 rue du Général de Gaulle

A real old Alsatian farmhouse in the wine-growing area where you can be in a beautiful, bustling village street one minute and your own peaceful little world the next. It is on a main road but the bedrooms are in the guest wing at the back, protected by the courtyard. Their simplicity is reflected in the price. Your friendly hosts retired from milk and wine production in order to have more time for guests; breakfast is served in the garden or in the dining room, and Paul makes a wicked eau de vie. A useful place to know at the start of the Route des Vins, and close to gorgeous, glamorous Strasbourg.

| Rooms | 3 doubles: €38–€42. |
| | Extra bed €8 per person per night. |
| Meals | Restaurants within walking distance. |
| Closed | Rarely. |

FIRST
EDITION
VETERAN

**Paul & Marie-Claire Goetz**
86 rue du Général de Gaulle,
67520 Marlenheim
Bas-Rhin
Tel      +33 (0)3 88 87 52 94
Email    goetz.paul@wanadoo.fr

# Alsace

## Maison Fleurie

Bubbling, friendly and generous, Doris has been receiving guests for years: she learnt the art at her mother's knee and will greet you with the warmest smile. Her peaceful chalet in a residential neighbourhood is a real home, surrounded by breathtaking mountain views. Both she and her husband are upholsterers so furnishings in the neat, traditional bedrooms are perfect, and strong colours combine with modernity. Guests have their own quarters, with a log fire in the breakfast room, tables laden with goodies in the morning – try the homemade organic fruit jams and Alsace cake – and geraniums cascading. Great value.

| Rooms | 2 doubles, 1 twin: €62–€78. |
| Meals | Restaurants nearby. |
| Closed | Rarely. |

FIRST
EDITION
VETERAN

**Doris Engel-Geiger**
Maison Fleurie,
19 route de Neuve Église,
Dieffenbach au Val,
67220 Villé, Bas-Rhin
Tel      +33 (0)3 88 85 60 48
Mobile   +33 (0)6 25 14 15 13
Email    contact@lamaisonfleurie.org
Web      www.lamaisonfleurie.com

# Alsace

## La Haute Grange

On the side of a hill, looking down the valley, this 19th-century farmhouse is surrounded by forests and wildflower meadows. Rural and indulging all at once, it is a place for de-stressing, with deeply comforting bedrooms, subtle and spicy colours, and the whole house filled with the smell of baking in the morning. The large sitting room has an open fireplace, an honesty bar and hundreds of books; step onto the patio and enjoy the heart-lifting views. A warm, polyglot couple, Margaret and Philippe will help you plan days of discovery. There are a great selection of restaurants less than 15 minutes away by car.

# Alsace

## Domaine Thierhurst

Your hosts are so welcoming in their sturdily luxurious house: he, quiet and courteous, runs the farm; she, dynamic and full of energy, opens her soul – and her house – to make you feel at home: this is real B&B and she loves it. She knows the delights of Alsace and nearby Germany intimately, concocts delicious breakfasts in the octagonal kitchen-diner and loves your amazement at the upstairs 'bathroom extraordinaire' with its vast rain shower. Pale, Turkish-rugged suites have all contemporary comforts, the large garden flowers generously, the jacuzzi seats six, the swimming pool is geothermally heated – dive in! *Minimum stay: 2 nights in high season.*

| | |
|---|---|
| Rooms | 3 doubles, 1 twin/double: €110–€150. Singles €80–€120. |
| Meals | Restaurants 6km. |
| Closed | Rarely. |

| | |
|---|---|
| Rooms | 1 double, 1 suite for 2: €140. |
| Meals | Guest kitchen. Restaurant 4km. |
| Closed | Never. |

| | |
|---|---|
| | **Margaret & Philippe Kalk** |
| | La Haute Grange, |
| | La Chaude Côte, |
| | 68240 Fréland |
| | Haut-Rhin |
| Tel | +33 (0)3 89 71 90 06 |
| Mobile | +33 (0)6 15 72 15 15 |
| Email | lahautegrange@aol.com |
| Web | www.lahautegrange.fr |

| | |
|---|---|
| | **Bénédicte & Jean-Jacques Kinny** |
| | Domaine Thierhurst, |
| | 68740 Nambsheim |
| | Haut-Rhin |
| Tel | +33 (0)3 89 72 56 94 |
| Mobile | +33 (0)6 07 97 28 22 |
| Email | domainekinny@gmail.com |
| Web | www.kinny.fr |

Entry 79   Map 7

Entry 80   Map 7

# Franche Comté

## Maison d'Hôtes du Parc

Appreciate the finer things in life in Emmanuel and Mark's 1860s riverside home: gourmet cuisine, gorgeous gardens, inspired design. Polished, harmonious interiors waft with shades of mushroom, raspberry and moss, with period antiques, exquisite *objets*, a harp in the vast salon, a grand piano in the library. Fine china appears at four-course dinners as you chat over tender lamb cutlets with garden thyme. Rooms and suites are cosily sumptuous, views spilling over well-tended gardens of scampering roses, manicured hedges, a summer house and potager. Beyond centennial trees is a gem: Le Corbusier's sensually spiritual chapel.

# Franche Comté

## La Maison Royale

The gaunt exterior, part of the town's 15th-century fortress, imposes – but wait. Madame – charming, cultured, a teacher of French and Spanish – and her late husband bought the vast walls and built a house within them, their pride and joy. The courtyard has small gardens and a fountain; the huge ground-floor rooms are gorgeous; artistically marvellous bedrooms have luxury bathrooms and great views: it's like sleeping in a modern palace. It could be overwhelming but Lydie is such a delightful person that it is, in fact, unforgettably moving. And you are in one of the loveliest villages in France. *Children over 5 welcome.*

| | |
|---|---|
| Rooms | 2 doubles, 1 twin: €110–€130. 1 suite for 2: €130. 1 single: €79. |
| Meals | Dinner, 4 courses, €25. Restaurants nearby. |
| Closed | Rarely. |

| | |
|---|---|
| Rooms | 4 doubles, 1 twin: €120. |
| Meals | Restaurants within walking distance. |
| Closed | 1 November – 31 March. |

| | |
|---|---|
| | **Emmanuel Georges** Maison d'Hôtes du Parc, 12-14 rue du Tram, 70250 Ronchamp Haute-Saône |
| Tel | +33 (0)3 84 63 93 43 |
| Email | leparc-egeorges@wanadoo.fr |
| Web | www.hotesduparc.com |

| | |
|---|---|
| | **Lydie Hoyet** La Maison Royale, 70140 Pesmes Haute-Saône |
| Tel | +33 (0)3 84 31 23 23 |
| Email | lydie@maisonroyalepesmes.com |
| Web | www.maisonroyalepesmes.com |

Entry 81   Map 7

Entry 82   Map 6

# Franche Comté

## La Maison de Juliette

There are three bikes to borrow and the countryside is a 500m ride away. The moment you enter the gardens of this charming edge-of-town house, built for a wealthy family in 1904, all feels peaceful and serene. Your hosts – she with perfect English – are among the warmest we know, their generosity extending from homemade brioche at breakfast to billowing whiter-than-white muslin and tip-top mattresses. Bathrooms are minimalist with an antique touch. Book in for dinner if you can. Monsieur still cooks occasionally and with great ingenuity, Madame is a vegetarian, and everyone will go home happy!

| Rooms | 2 doubles (sharing guest kitchen): €75–€85. 1 family room for 4 (2 rooms interconnect, sharing shower room): €100–€143. |
|---|---|
| Meals | Dinner, 4 courses with wine, €28. Vegetarian meals available. Restaurants 1km. |
| Closed | Rarely. |

**Françoise Gauthé**
La Maison de Juliette,
8 rue des Combes St Germain,
25700 Valentigney
Doubs

| Tel | +33 (0)3 81 91 88 19 |
| Email | maisondejuliette@orange.fr |
| Web | www.maisondejuliette.fr |

# Franche Comté

## La Maison d'à Côté

Arlette does shabby-chic as only a Frenchwoman can. Stone stairs spiral to an apartment of lofty 19th-century rooms, a gorgeous mix of vintage and contemporary. Retro cinema seats, pretty mirrors and old hat-boxes sit amongst metal-topped tables and industrial-chic lights. Polished floors, wooden shutters and panelled walls ensure a gracious tone. Choose between the quirkily elegant bedroom or the coolly contemporary one. Charming and fun, Arlette cooks brilliantly (her restaurant is nearby) serving delicious breakfasts in her sunny kitchen. In the centre of mountain-town Pontarlier, this will suit outdoors-lovers who also want style.

| Rooms | 1 double, 1 twin/double: €90 Singles €70. Extra bed/sofabed €25 per person per night. |
|---|---|
| Meals | Owner's restaurant, 50m. |
| Closed | Rarely. |

AWARD WINNER

Favourite newcomer

**Arlette Laude**
La Maison d'à Côté,
11 rue Jules Mathez,
25300 Pontarlier
Doubs

| Tel | +33 (0)3 81 38 47 18 |
| Email | arlette.laude@orange.fr |
| Web | www.lamaison-da-cote.fr |

# Burgundy

# Burgundy

## Domaine de Drémont

Views soar from this 17th-century Burgundian farmhouse in majestically rural France. The English-French owners, quietly charming green farmers of Charolais cattle, live with their young children at one end; guest quarters – characterful, comfortable – are at the other, the atmospherically high-raftered family suite waits up outside stone stairs. Chalk-white walls, aged terracotta, the odd antique... all is spotless and unfussy. Inside: a big cosy sitting room with bold-fabric walls and stone fireplace; outside: an ancient spring-fed pool for quick plunges. Mystical Vézelay is a short drive. *Minimum stay: 3 nights in high season.*

# Burgundy

## La Villa des Prés

Deep in real peace-wrapped country, this place of secluded old-style comfort and breathtaking Morvan views has new and rightly enthusiastic Dutch owners: it's gorgeous. Inside are open fires, antique beds, sympathetic period decorations, antique linen and super modern showers. Rooms are vast and there are two salons, one gloriously golden green, for lazing about in. A baronial double stair leads down to the fine garden and the ha-ha where, rather endearingly, chickens may be roaming. A base for church, château and vineyard visits – a peaceful paradise. *Minimum stay: 3 nights.*

| | |
|---|---|
| Rooms | 1 double; 1 double with separate shower: €50-€85.<br>1 family suite for 5: €65-€135. |
| Meals | Guest kitchen.<br>Restaurant 9km. |
| Closed | Rarely. |

| | |
|---|---|
| Rooms | 5 twin/doubles: €80-€105. |
| Meals | Complimentary dinner with wine for 7-night stays (Sunday only).<br>Guest kitchen. Restaurant 3km. |
| Closed | October – March. |

FIRST
EDITION
VETERAN

| | |
|---|---|
| | Ghislaine Bentley<br>Domaine de Drémont,<br>58800 Anthien<br>Nièvre |
| Tel | +33 (0)3 86 22 04 54 |
| Email | mg.bentley@wanadoo.fr |
| Web | www.dremont.fr |

| | |
|---|---|
| | Kees & Inge Stapel<br>La Villa des Prés,<br>Route de Corbigny,<br>58420 St Révérien<br>Nièvre |
| Tel | +33 (0)3 86 29 03 81 |
| Mobile | +31 (0)6 51 18 89 67 |
| Email | villa-des-pres@orange.fr |
| Web | www.villa-des-pres.com |

Entry 85   Map 5

Entry 86   Map 5

# Burgundy

## Domaine des Perrières

Make the most of seasonal farm produce and traditional French food: the visitors' book is plump with praise. Madame the farmer's wife loves cooking (delectable pastries and jams), is happy to cater for all tastes, and makes you feel at home. Wheat fields wave to the horizon, farm and cows are next door, this is 360 hectares of deepest France. Inside, in simple, straightforward rooms, all is airy and light, cheerful and double-glazed. No sitting room to share but after a day on horses or on foot (the cross-country trails are inspiring) and a long, leisurely supper, most guests retire gratefully to bed.

# Burgundy

## Château de Nyon

A pretty little château in a secluded valley in the heart of utterly unspoilt countryside. The remarkable Catherine inherited the house and has been doing B&B for 20 years. Her bedrooms, all on the first floor, echo the 18th-century character of the house. Toile de jouy is charmingly splashed across pink paper and fabrics, bathrooms have big tubs or walk-in showers, glorious views to the garden reveal an avenue of lime trees and a hornbeam maze. Friendly Madame serves a beautiful breakfast of fresh pastries and home honey. It's hard to leave this blessed setting; the nearest restaurant is ten kilometres away.

| | |
|---|---|
| Rooms | 1 twin/double: €68. |
| | 1 family room for 4: €68–€108. |
| | Singles €55. |
| | Dinner, B&B €49–€59 per person. |
| | Extra bed/sofabed €15–€20 per person per night. |
| Meals | Dinner with wine, €25. Gluten free & vegan meals available. |
| Closed | Rarely. |

| | |
|---|---|
| Rooms | 2 doubles: €65–€85. |
| | 1 family room for 4: €150. |
| | 1 single: €45. |
| Meals | Restaurant 10km. |
| Closed | Rarely. |

|  |  |
|---|---|
| | Pascale Cointe |
| | Domaine des Perrières, |
| | 58330 Crux La Ville |
| | Nièvre |
| Tel | +33 (0)3 86 58 34 93 |
| Email | pbcointe58@orange.fr |
| Web | www.chambres-charme-bourgogne.com |

|  |  |
|---|---|
| | Catherine Henry |
| | Château de Nyon, |
| | 58130 Ourouër |
| | Nièvre |
| Tel | +33 (0)3 86 58 61 12 |
| Email | chateaudenyon@gmail.com |
| Web | www.chateaudenyon.com |

Entry 87   Map 10

Entry 88   Map 10

# Burgundy

## Château de Villette

Coen and Catherine – he Dutch, she Belgian – fell in love with this little château, then had their wedding here: they love their adopted country. They've opened just five rooms to guests (the suites are twin-roomed) and one very private cottage so they can spoil you properly. And get to know you over dinner. (Though, should you prefer a romantic dinner for two, they'll understand.) Bedrooms, large, light and airy, with warm colours and polished floors, are dressed in château-style finery. Views sail out of great windows to meadows and woodland and families will love it. Beaune and the vineyards lie temptingly close.

# Burgundy

## Château de Vaulx

Vaulx was described in 1886 as "well-proportioned and elegant in its simplicity". It is as lovely now and in the most beautiful position, high on a hill with views that stretch to distant mountains. Delightful Marty will escort you to the west wing then create a delicious dinner. Expect big bedrooms full of character, a panelled drawing room with chandeliers, a huge dining room with fresh flowers, and manicured lawns and box balls tightly topiaried – stroll down the romantic avenues in dappled sunlight. In the village, a 13th-century bell tower; nearby, one of the best chocolate makers in France (monthly tastings and lessons).

| Rooms | 1 double: €145-€235. 1 family room for 2, 3 family rooms for 4: €145-€350. 1 cottage for 2 with kitchen: €245. |
|---|---|
| Meals | Dinner €48. Wine €18-€100. |
| Closed | Rarely. |

| Rooms | 2 doubles: €100-€120. 2 family rooms for 4: €145. 1 apartment for 5: €190. |
|---|---|
| Meals | Dinner €30. Wine €18. Restaurant 3km. |
| Closed | Rarely. |

**Catherine & Coen Stork**
Château de Villette,
58170 Poil
Nièvre
Tel   +33 (0)3 86 30 09 13
Email chateaudevillette@icloud.com
Web   www.chateaudevillette.eu

**Marty Freriksen**
Château de Vaulx,
71800 St Julien de Civry
Saône-et-Loire
Tel   +33 (0)3 85 70 64 03
Email marty@chateaudevaulx.com
Web   www.chateaudevaulx.com

## Burgundy

### La Tour

The terraced garden is brimful of stepping stones and flowers, ginger tabbies wend through the irises, bucolic views stretch across undulating pastures: this is a deeply rural ensemble. June, widely travelled, kind, attentive, a great reader and lover of art in all its forms, lives in a long stone farmhouse in a cluster of outbuildings that go back to 1740. The airy two-bedroom suite in its own wing has a fine stone fireplace on its ground floor; floorboards are honey-coloured, the bathroom is a treat, and scrumptious breakfasts (organic jams, eggs from the hens) are served on charming country china.

| | |
|---|---|
| Rooms | 1 family suite for 2-3: €70-€80. |
| Meals | Dinner €24. Restaurants 7km. |
| Closed | Rarely. |

**June Bibby**
La Tour,
71120 Marcilly La Guerce
Saône-et-Loire
Mobile +33 (0)6 87 59 78 29
Email bibbyjune@gmail.com
Web www.latourbandb.com

Entry 91   Map 11

## Burgundy

### La Cure

Books burst from every corner of Annick's home: each member of this charming family is an avid reader! The tall sturdy Burgundy presbytery, tucked behind the village church, is warmly furnished with delicious colours; bedrooms lie under the eaves. Low beds rest on honey-coloured boards, walls are pale, shower rooms are enticing, fabrics are simple, serene. From 'Côté Saône' the views soar — gaze on them from bed. Annick, generous, attentive, new to B&B, serves you beautiful breakfasts on pretty white china at a welcoming table decorated with garden leaves; coffee is poured from old silver, each detail delights.

| | |
|---|---|
| Rooms | 2 doubles: €70. |
| Meals | Restaurant 3km. |
| Closed | Rarely. |

**Jean & Annick Piébourg**
La Cure,
La Cure de Brandon,
71520 Brandon
Saône-et-Loire
Tel +33 (0)3 85 50 44 55
Email jean.piebourg@wibox.fr
Web www.lacuredebrandon.fr

Entry 92   Map 11

# Burgundy

## Le Tinailler d'Aléane

The lovely stones and cascading geraniums outside, the silk flowers, frilly lampshades and polished furniture inside have an old-world charm. The breakfast room is cosily stuffed with bric-a-brac, bedrooms are family-simple. Madame was a florist: she arranges her rooms as if they were bouquets, is always refreshing them and might put a paper heart on your pillow wishing you *bonne nuit*. (Ask for the larger room; the smaller feels cramped.) She doesn't refuse children but may well be happier if you arrive with a little dog under your arm! She delightedly arranges meals at restaurants and winery visits for non-French speakers.

| | |
|---|---|
| Rooms | 1 double, 1 twin: €60–€65. |
| Meals | Dinner, 4 courses with wine, €25 (winter only). Restaurants 3km. |
| Closed | Sundays in winter. |

Éliane Heinen
Le Tinailler d'Aléane,
Sommeré,
71960 La Roche Vineuse
Saône-et-Loire
Tel      +33 (0)3 85 37 80 68

# Burgundy

## Le Clos de Clessé

Set in superb gardens (mature olive trees, clipped box hedges, gravel paths, stone-edged beds, delicious roses) the old manor by the church is the life's dream of delightful Tessy and André, Cordon Bleu cooks both – don't miss dinner! Two gorgeous cottages with split-level bedrooms overlook the garden and there's a pretty, bare-beamed guest room in the main house. Natural stone, old fireplaces, terracotta tiles and flagstones worn satin-smooth offset modern fittings and antique pieces perfectly. Vineyards and châteaux galore... though the tempting and secluded pool may be as far as you'll get. *Minimum stay: 2 nights in high season. Hosts speak English, French, Dutch & German.*

| | |
|---|---|
| Rooms | 2 doubles: €100–€110. 1 suite for 4: €110–€170. Singles €95. |
| Meals | Dinner, 4 courses, €34; with wine, €39. Children under 12, €20. Restaurant 3km. |
| Closed | Rarely. |

Tessy & André Gladinez
Le Clos de Clessé,
Ruelle Ste Marie,
71260 Clessé
Saône-et-Loire
Tel      +33 (0)3 85 23 03 56
Email   info@closdeclesse.com
Web     www.closdeclesse.com

# Burgundy

## La Tour du Trésorier

Hoping for ancient? Find a 15th-century town gate in a 10th-century wall and a 17th-century tower, added by the abbey treasurer, now an intriguing mix of old beams, embossed tiles, spiral stairs and wooden doors. Original paintings, some by Thierry, grace the walls of the grand dining room. Light-filled bedrooms are just as artistic, with sculpted furniture and unusual *objets*. Outside, a jacuzzi bubbles in the orchard; century-old trees stand in the park; loungers and terraces gaze on lush countryside. Sophie and Thierry love sharing their passion for south Burgundy and fine wine: Thierry is a sommelier, his wine list is superb.

| | |
|---|---|
| Rooms | 1 double, 3 twin/doubles: €150–€170. 1 suite for 4: €190–€250. |
| Meals | Restaurants 1-4 km. |
| Closed | Rarely. |

Sophie & Thierry Lindbergh
La Tour du Trésorier,
9 place de l'Abbaye,
71700 Tournus
Saône-et-Loire

| | |
|---|---|
| Tel | +33 (0)3 85 27 00 47 |
| Email | info@tour-du-tresorier.com |
| Web | www.tour-du-tresorier.com |

Entry 95   Map 11

# Burgundy

## Le Crot Foulot

Gutsy Jan and Annie sold their prize-winning restaurant in Brussels and filled their cellar while putting the finishing touches to this handsome wine-grower's house. Golden stones outside, a clean minimalism inside: Belgians always pull this off with flair. An elegant glass and wood staircase leads to muted bedrooms with delicate pale timbers revealed and glorified. In the open kitchen you can watch Jan whip up his mussel mousse while a farmyard chicken sizzles with citrus fruits in the oven. Annie will have brought up the perfect nectar for the menu. All is well in Burgundy tonight!

| | |
|---|---|
| Rooms | 3 twin/doubles, 1 twin: €110–€140. 1 family room for 3: €168–€198. Dinner, B&B €39 extra per person. |
| Meals | Dinner €35. Wine from €15. |
| Closed | November – February. |

Annie Coeckelberghs & Jan Hostens
Le Crot Foulot,
71240 Jugy
Saône-et-Loire

| | |
|---|---|
| Tel | +33 (0)3 85 94 81 07 |
| Email | info@crotfoulot.com |
| Web | www.crotfoulot.com |

Entry 96   Map 11

# Burgundy

## Abbaye de la Ferté

A privileged spot on a handsome estate. The abbot's palace, a listed monument open to the public in summer, is all that's left of the old abbey – glimpse the vast staircase on your way to breakfast in the more intimate dining room. Bedrooms are divine: one is in the dovecote by the road with its exquisite bathroom in the loft; the other is in the gatehouse, its tub armchairs dressed in deep pink. The fabulous palace gardens have grand fountains in an English-style setting. Your young hosts make it all pleasingly eccentric and fun; they are generous, too, providing log fires, tea trays, art books, a bottle of local wine.

| | |
|---|---|
| Rooms | 2 suites for 2-4: €77-€129. |
| Meals | Dinner with wine, €32 (July/Aug only). Restaurants 10-minute drive. |
| Closed | Rarely. |

Jacques & Virginie Thénard
Abbaye de la Ferté,
71240 St Ambreuil
Saône-et-Loire

| | |
|---|---|
| Mobile | +33 (0)6 22 91 40 11 |
| Email | abbayedelaferte@aol.com |
| Web | www.abbayedelaferte.com |

Entry 97   Map 11

# Burgundy

## La Ferme de Marie-Eugénie

Glossy-mag perfection meets deep rural sleepiness. La Ferme belonged to Marie-Eugénie's grandmother and the deft renovating flair of this ex-Parisian couple (formerly in advertising) is on show everywhere, from whitewashed beams to shabby-chic leather sofas. The pretty half-timbered barn (owners live in the cottage) overlooking a big lawned garden is now a fashionable maison d'hôtes. Be charmed by light-flooded rooms, pale tiled floors and exposed limestone walls. Bedrooms are comfortable, delightful – soft colours, modern art; there's an inviting books-and-magazines salon and a slick dining-kitchen for delicious meals.

| | |
|---|---|
| Rooms | 3 doubles, 1 twin: €115-€135. Extra bed €25 per person per night. |
| Meals | Dinner €35. Wine €25-€70. Restaurants 9km. |
| Closed | Christmas. |

Marie-Eugénie Dupuy
La Ferme de Marie-Eugénie,
225 allée de Chardenoux,
71500 Bruailles
Saône-et-Loire

| | |
|---|---|
| Tel | +33 (0)3 85 74 81 84 |
| Email | info@lafermedemarieeugenie.fr |
| Web | www.lafermedemarieeugenie.fr |

Entry 98   Map 11

## Burgundy

### L'Orangerie

Enter gardens that are secluded, charming, full of colour. Light spills into the sitting room through arched vine-clad windows while cream walls and Indian rugs add to the simple elegance of this *maison de maître*. Antiques and travel are the owners' passion: a grand staircase, interesting paintings and oriental fabrics add up to a mix of styles that work beautifully. Bedrooms vary in size and have lovely seersucker linen and antique prints; bathrooms are classically tasteful. Terraced lawns lead down to the heated pool, lavish breakfasts include unusual homemade jams, and the wonderful Voie Verte cycle route runs nearby. *Minimum stay: 2 nights.*

| | |
|---|---|
| Rooms | 5 twin/doubles: €80–€110. |
| Meals | Dinner with wine, €25–€40. |
| | Restaurants 4km. |
| Closed | Mid-November to mid-March. |

**David Eades & Niels Lierow**
L'Orangerie,
20 rue des Lavoirs, Vingelles,
71390 Moroges
Saône-et-Loire
Tel   +33 (0)3 85 47 91 94
Email   info@orangerie-moroges.com
Web   www.orangerie-moroges.com

Entry 99   Map 11

## Burgundy

### Domaine de Nesvres

There are Michelin stars in Chagny, châteaux all around and the Route des Vins beyond the door; this is a great spot for a civilised holiday. In the small village of St Désert, at the end of the private driveway, you stay on a fortified farm steeped in history and owned by a lovely French couple. Outside is vast and full of rustic charm; inside is cosy and comfy. Find billiards, books, beams, a sitting room for guests (games, music, WiFi, TV), five airy bedrooms (the family room with good antiques) and Adeline's delicious food, perhaps homemade 'pain d'épices' at breakfast, and poulet de Bresse at dinner.

| | |
|---|---|
| Rooms | 1 double, 1 twin: €75–€85. |
| | 1 family room for 3, |
| | 1 family room for 4: €85–€140. |
| | 1 triple: €85–€115. |
| | Pets €5 per night. |
| Meals | Dinner with aperitif and wine, €35. |
| | Restaurants 5km. |
| Closed | Never. |

**Adeline & Michel Courcenet**
Domaine de Nesvres,
Route de Buxy,
71390 Saint Désert
Saône-et-Loire
Tel   +33 (0)3 85 47 98 93
Mobile   +33 (0)6 16 13 30 50
Email   micourcenet@aol.com
Web   www.domainedenesvres.com

Entry 100   Map 11

# Burgundy

## Manoir du Clos de Vauvry

A ceramic stove as big as two men dominates the breakfast room of this charming 17th-century royal hunting lodge. Summer breakfasts are on the terrace; dinners flourish home-grown produce. The whole place has an air of exaggeration: over-generous stairs, ingenious double windows, voluptuous ceilings, all totally French with floral wallpapers and embroidered bedcovers in magnificent bedrooms, 1930s tiled bathrooms (one whirlpool) and immaculate linen. This adorable couple knows everyone in wine growing and Marie helps you all she can. Burgundy has so much to offer, as well as superb wines. Wonderful. *Overflow rooms available.*

| | |
|---|---|
| Rooms | 1 twin: €75–€95. |
| | 1 suite for 4: €140–€160. |
| Meals | Dinner with wine, €32. |
| Closed | Rarely. |

Marie & Daniel Lacroix-Mollaret
Manoir du Clos de Vauvry,
3 rue des Faussillons,
71640 Givry Sauges
Saône-et-Loire

| | |
|---|---|
| Tel | +33 (0)3 85 44 40 83 |
| Mobile | +33 (0)6 70 92 80 94 |
| Email | daniel.mollaret@orange.fr |
| Web | www.clos-de-vauvry.com |

Entry 101   Map 11

# Burgundy

## Domaine de l'Oiseau

Peeping out from under low slanting eaves and climbing plants, the lovely 18th-century buildings frame a courtyard. This village-end setting is secluded riverside woodland; feast by the pool on valley views *and* beautiful food. Bedrooms sing with serenity and good taste: the suite, graceful and feminine, in the old bakery, the rest peacefully in the Pavilion. Each has a dressing room, a small perfect bathroom and an enchanting old *tomette* floor. Relax in the glorious beamed barn, now the guest library; sample the local fine wines in the cellar below under the guidance of your friendly, extrovert hosts. An exceptional place.

| | |
|---|---|
| Rooms | 2 twin/doubles with separate wc: €130. |
| | 1 triple with separate wc: €140–€160. |
| | 1 family suite for 2-4 with separate wc: €130–€160. |
| Meals | Dinner with wine, from €50. |
| Closed | December – March. |

Dominique & Philippe
Monnier-Pictet
Domaine de l'Oiseau,
17 rue Chariot,
71590 Gergy, Saône-et-Loire

| | |
|---|---|
| Tel | +33 (0)3 85 91 61 26 |
| Mobile | +33 (0)6 23 46 59 07 |
| Email | info@domoiseau.com |
| Web | www.domoiseau.com |

Entry 102   Map 11

## Burgundy

### La Maison Chaudenay

The new owners, a parents and daughter team, are already loving the 17th-century winepress, its well-planned cellars, functioning bread oven and fantastic (horseless) stables that surround the gracious guest house. It came complete with grand gates, superb garden and habitable outbuildings where the Mahés live: Virginie runs the B&B, Yannick knows several wine-growers… Bedrooms, pale and rich, have taste, antiques and modern bathrooms. The 100-year old sequoia gives shade, and there's a sitting room in the converted barn. Elegant restraint and enthusiasm near one of France's best restaurants – in Chagny, near Beaune.

## Burgundy

*New Entry*

### Moulin Renaudiots

Bordering the ancient Forest of Planoise and overlooking idyllic Burgundy countryside, this former water mill is a tranquil retreat. A stream babbles quietly in the background and, as the sun sets, a chorus of crickets provides accompaniment. Classic mid-century Danish furniture features throughout the five beautifully renovated en-suite rooms, while wooden floors and exposed beams give contemporary interiors a natural feel. Breakfast on homemade jam, pastries and fruit from the gorgeous gardens… Twice a week your lovely hosts offer convivial dinners too. By day, cool off in the sparkling pool then visit fascinating Autun. *Minimum stay: 2 nights in high season.*

| | |
|---|---|
| Rooms | 4 doubles: €70–€110. |
| | 1 family room for 4: €85–€130. |
| | Extra bed €20 per person per night. |
| Meals | Summer kitchen. |
| | Restaurants 3km. |
| Closed | January – March. |

| | |
|---|---|
| Rooms | 3 doubles: €135–€165. |
| | 1 family room for 2-3, |
| | 1 suite for 2-4: €145–€155. |
| | Extra beds €30 per person per night. |
| Meals | Dinner with aperitif, wine & coffee, €52 (Sat & Mon). |
| | Cold plates available Weds & Fri. |
| | Restaurants 4km. |
| Closed | November – March. |

**Yannick & Isabelle Mahé**
La Maison Chaudenay,
26 rue de Tigny,
71150 Chaudenay
Saône-et-Loire

| | |
|---|---|
| Tel | +33 (0)3 85 87 35 98 |
| Email | info@maisonchaudenay.com |
| Web | www.beaunebedandbreakfast.com |

**Trevor Morgan**
Moulin Renaudiots,
Chemin du Vieux Moulin,
71400 Autun
Saône-et-Loire

| | |
|---|---|
| Tel | +33 (0)3 85 86 97 10 |
| Email | contact@moulinrenaudiots.com |
| Web | www.moulinrenaudiots.com |

Entry 103   Map 11

Entry 104   Map 11

# Burgundy

## Les Jardins de Loïs

The owners are wine buffs and their pride and joy is their cellar. Inside this 200-year-old house every detail delights, while bedrooms, reached by a splendid exterior stair, are lavish and beautiful. Antique armoires flatter oriental rugs, Italian bathrooms are immaculate with monsoon showers, and the garden suite is housed in a private outbuilding with its own sitting room and huge bath. Breakfast and homemade jams are enjoyed in the elegant, airy dining room. Stroll Beaune's ancient cobbles, sample the fruits of the region's wine capital. Then retire with a bottle of their own fine burgundy to a gem of a half-hectare garden.

| Rooms | 3 doubles: €155. |
| | 2 suites for 2: €185–€195. |
| | Singles €155. |
| Meals | Restaurant within walking distance. |
| Closed | Christmas/New Year. |

Anne-Marie & Philippe Dufouleur
Les Jardins de Loïs,
21200 Beaune
Côte-d'Or

| Tel | +33 (0)3 80 22 41 97 |
| Mobile | +33 (0)6 73 85 11 47 |
| Email | contact@jardinsdelois.com |
| Web | www.jardinsdelois.com |

# Burgundy

## La Maison Blanche

Nadine speaks excellent English and lives two minutes away. Upon arrival she escorts you to her amazing wine cellar/ breakfast room/ salon, where coffee and tea is on tap and you help yourself to wine (pay later). Each minimalist bedroom (one with three double beds) is reached via a white-painted stair; floors are slate, colours grey and white, art is erotic and chic bathrooms lie behind partitioned walls. Breakfast is flexible and there's a designer guest kitchen should you wish to prepare a meal. As for Beaune, beneath its cobbled streets lies a fascinating maze of corridors filled with a million bottles of wine. *Minimum stay: 2 nights in high season. Ask about parking.*

| Rooms | 2 doubles: €162. |
| | 1 triple (3 doubles): €162–€364. |
| | Whole house, €1000 for 2 nights. |
| Meals | Brunch available. Guest kitchen. |
| | Restaurants nearby. |
| Closed | Rarely. |

Nadine Belissant-Reydet
La Maison Blanche,
3 rue Jules Marey,
21200 Beaune
Côte-d'Or

| Mobile | +33 (0)6 60 93 51 84 |
| Email | contact@lamaison-blanche.fr |
| Web | www.lamaison-blanche.fr |

## Burgundy

## Burgundy

### Les Planchottes

If you find yourself in the Mecca of Wine, in the very heart of old Beaune, then surely you should stay with a family of winegrowers like the Bouchards? They are charming people, passionate about food, wine and matters 'green'; Cécile's breakfasts linger long in the memory. Immaculate is the conversion of this old townhouse, once three cottages: the craftsmanship of new oak and stone, the quiet good taste of the colours, the space in the comfortable bedrooms, the ultra modern bathrooms. Chill out in the walled, lush, flowered garden (replete with pet rabbit), glimpse the vineyards on the horizon. Outstanding.

### Sous le Baldaquin

Once Yves (the perfect host) swings open the huge doors of his townhouse in the heart of Beaune, the 21st-century disappears, the serene garden tugs at your soul and peace descends. Play the count, countess or courtesan as you mount the stone stair to your small perfect cocoon, past walls and ceiling painted in pale trompe-l'œil allegory. Gracious and elegant are the aubergine and willow-green taffeta drapes and beribboned baldaquin, charming the bathroom with its ancient double-basin, beautiful the view to the rambling roses. To call this romantic is an understatement – and Yves is the nicest host.

| | |
|---|---|
| Rooms | 1 double, 1 twin: €110. Extra bed/sofabed €25 per person per night. |
| Meals | Restaurants within walking distance. |
| Closed | Mid-December to mid-February. |

| | |
|---|---|
| Rooms | 1 double: €100–€110. Extra bed €25 per person per night. |
| Meals | Restaurants within walking distance. |
| Closed | Rarely. |

**Christophe & Cécile Bouchard**
Les Planchottes,
6 rue Sylvestre Chauvelot,
21200 Beaune
Côte-d'Or
Tel     +33 (0)3 80 22 83 67
Email   lesplanchottes@voila.fr
Web     www.lesplanchottes.fr

**Yves Cantenot**
Sous le Baldaquin,
39 rue Maufoux,
21200 Beaune
Côte-d'Or
Tel      +33 (0)3 80 24 79 30
Mobile   +33 (0)6 80 17 72 51
Email    yves.cantenot@laposte.net
Web      www.souslebaldaquin.fr

# Burgundy

## Le Clos Champagne St Nicolas

Le Clos is nicely set back from the main road and Beaune is a ten-minute stroll. Built to take guests, the new wing has spanking new bedrooms, modern bits in the bathrooms and a salon overlooking the garden. Fabrics, bedding and antiques reveal Anne as a woman of taste who thinks of everything, even a guest kitchen for your morning spread of homemade jams, cake, croissants, bread, yogurt and fresh fruit. Bruno has a passion for vintage cars, especially if they're English. Knowledgeable natives and hospitable hosts, they fill you in on the sights, restaurants and vineyards over a welcoming glass of wine.

| | |
|---|---|
| Rooms | 1 double, 2 twin/doubles: €110. |
| Meals | Guest kitchen. |
| | Restaurants within walking distance. |
| Closed | Rarely. |

**Bruno & Anne Durand de Gevigney**
Le Clos Champagne St Nicolas,
114 ter route de Dijon,
21200 Beaune, Côte-d'Or

| | |
|---|---|
| Tel | +33 (0)3 80 61 24 92 |
| Mobile | +33 (0)6 61 82 39 63 |
| Email | closchamp.stnicolas@free.fr |
| Web | closchamp.stnicolas.free.fr |

Entry 109   Map 11

# Burgundy

## Les Hêtres Rouges

A pretty old Burgundian hunting lodge, 'Copper Beeches' stands in a walled garden full of ancient trees; and its village setting is a delight. There's an unexpected air of Provence inside: beautifully judged colour schemes (Madame paints), fine furniture, numerous *objets*, a tomcat or two. Your hosts extend a warm, genuine yet ungushing welcome to the weary traveller, and can organise wine tours that are perfect for you. Up a steep stair are low rooms with dark character and fine linen. Breakfast has the savour of yesteryear: yogurt, fresh bread, homemade jam, delicious coffee.

| | |
|---|---|
| Rooms | 1 twin/double, 1 twin: €90–€104. |
| | Extra bed €32 per person per night. |
| Meals | Restaurants 8km. |
| Closed | Rarely. |

**Jean-François & Christiane Bugnet**
Les Hêtres Rouges,
10 route de Nuits, Antilly,
21700 Argilly, Côte-d'Or

| | |
|---|---|
| Tel | +33 (0)3 80 62 53 98 |
| Mobile | +33 (0)6 78 47 22 29 / |
| | +33 (0)6 75 07 65 01 |
| Email | leshetresrouges@free.fr |
| Web | www.leshetresrouges.com |

Entry 110   Map 11

## Burgundy

### La Saura

For those wishing to escape to a sweet Côte d'Or village near Beaune – and some of the world's greatest wines – come here. The house and stables are charming and peaceful, the renovation is recent, the décor is delicious, the pool is a boon. Irresistible Madame smiles easily and loves her guests, gives you generous breakfasts before the log fire and big airy bedrooms with classic colours and lavish touches – and views; she also plans an enchanting guests' hideaway off the garden (for WiFi, books and games). Bed linen is antique and embroidered, towels carry the La Saura logo, paths lead into the hills. Bliss. *Min. stay: 2 nights at weekends & in high season.*

| Rooms | 1 double (main house), 3 doubles (outbuilding): €95–€110. 1 suite for 3 (outbuilding): €120–€150. Extra bed/sofabed €30–€35 per person per night. |
|---|---|
| Meals | Restaurant 2km. |
| Closed | 20 December – 14 February. |

Jocelyne-Marie Lehallé
La Saura,
Route de Beaune,
21360 Lusigny sur Ouche
Côte-d'Or

| Tel | +33 (0)3 80 20 17 46 |
| Mobile | +33 (0)6 81 29 57 42 |
| Email | la-saura@wanadoo.fr |
| Web | www.la-saura.com |

Entry 111   Map 11

## Burgundy

Burgundy

### La Monastille

Stunning flagstones in the breakfast room (where baguettes and homemade jams are served) and wooden doors that creak open to cosy rooms. In a village of 50 souls (and 2,000 cows) is La Monastille, built in 1750 as a wealthy farmhouse. Generous Madame is passionate about history, antiques, food and loves her English guests. Traditional suppers at the big table feature local meat and poultry and veg from her garden. Wines flow. Bedrooms are a soothing mix of muted walls, dark old furniture and flowery bed covers, the dear little room in the tower is reached via many steps and outside is a lovely garden. A restful place.

| Rooms | 2 doubles: €85. 2 triples: €105. Extra bed €20 per person per night. |
|---|---|
| Meals | Dinner with aperitif & wine, €35 (Fri-Mon only). Restaurant 12km. |
| Closed | Rarely. |

Françoise Moine
La Monastille,
7 rue de l'Église,
21360 Thomirey
Côte-d'Or

| Tel | +33 (0)3 80 20 00 80 |
| Email | moine.francoise@wanadoo.fr |
| Web | www.monastille.com |

Entry 112   Map 11

## Burgundy

### Les Deux Chèvres

In the heart of Gevrey Chambertin is a splendid small hotel. The décor is delectable, the artwork is special, the manageress and owners look after you with warmth and discretion. You'll find a formal salon with choice antique pieces, a sitting room and a library for relaxing and a dining room for delicious organic breakfasts. Bedrooms are serene and traditional, one on the ground floor, four more above up a lovely wood staircase. A further two lie the other side of the courtyard, their bathrooms luscious. For culture and markets there's Dijon; for wine and champagne tastings, the cellars just beneath you.

## Burgundy

### Domaine de Serrigny

Just yards from a pretty stretch of the Burgundy Canal, a fine 18th-century house with high walls and magnificent views to perfect little Châteauneuf en Auxois. Charles and Marie-Pascale are stylish, informal and huge fun; so is their house. Fabulous antiques, interesting art and textiles, space outside for children to cavort. Bedrooms are a beautiful mix of styles with something for everyone, from grand salon to zen attic, and bathrooms are bliss. Relax in the garden with its big lawn, colourful pots, decked pool and tennis court; have breakfast here or in the large open-plan sitting/dining room. Heaps of charm.

| | |
|---|---|
| Rooms | 5 doubles: €160–€210. 2 suites for 2: €250. |
| Meals | Restaurants within walking distance. |
| Closed | Rarely. |

| | |
|---|---|
| Rooms | 1 double: €98–€108. 1 suite for 2, 1 family room for 4: €122–€139. Children under 8 stay free. |
| Meals | Auberge nearby (closed Mondays). |
| Closed | Rarely. |

**Paul Thomas & Jolanta Bakaiarz**
Les Deux Chèvres,
23 rue de l'Eglise,
21220 Gevrey Chambertin
Côte-d'Or

| | |
|---|---|
| Tel | +33 (0)3 80 51 48 25 |
| Email | info@lesdeuxchevres.com |
| Web | www.lesdeuxchevres.com |

**Marie-Pascale Chaillot**
Domaine de Serrigny,
Lieu-dit "le Village",
Route Départementale,
21320 Vandenesse en Auxois, Côte-d'Or

| | |
|---|---|
| Tel | +33 (0)3 80 49 28 13 |
| Mobile | +33 (0)6 86 89 90 07 |
| Email | chaillot.mp@wanadoo.fr |
| Web | www.manoir-de-serrigny.com |

## Burgundy

### Au Rendez-vous de l'Auxois

Breakfast in summer can be in the garden – higgledy-piggledy and full of birds. If you take the family suite, you get your own view-filled terrace. Véronique and Jacques know how to make you feel at home, and both have a great sense of humour. There's table d'hôtes too (several options and prices) and they'll even drive you to and from restaurants. Their detached house lies at the end of the village next to a rather lovely lake, one of several in the region you can fish in. Bedrooms are plain, light and airy, the triple with its original beams, and you're 15 miles from the vineyards of Beaune. *Cot & highchair available. Well-behaved dogs welcome.*

| Rooms | 1 double: €60. |
| | 1 family suite for 4 with bathroom across the hall: €50-€60. |
| | 1 triple: €60-€90. |
| Meals | Dinner with wine, €18-€28. |
| | Restaurants 8km. |
| Closed | January/February. |

Véronique & Jacques Beaumier
Au Rendez-vous de l'Auxois,
Rue de l'Etang,
21320 Essey
Côte-d'Or

| Tel | +33 (0)3 80 84 19 48 |
| Mobile | +33 (0)6 33 86 93 64 |
| Email | jacques.beaumier@wanadoo.fr |
| Web | www.aurdvdelauxois.fr |

Entry 115   Map 6

## Burgundy

### Château les Roches

A judge's passion for his mistress inspired this 1900s jewel. Built way off any beaten track, 500m high, with an unobscured view over the Serein valley and the lush forests of the Morvan, the bourgeois mansion still sits quietly behind tall gates, a haven of peace in a medieval village of 300 souls. Young Tobias, who's American, and German Marco fell just as hard as the judge and have restored it remarkably. The bones were good so they added perfect furnishings to light, spacious rooms and made the bathrooms sinful. Now they run a restaurant open to the public headed by Selby, a first-class chef. It is a perfect getaway. *Self-catering available in cottage for 4.*

| Rooms | 4 doubles: €139-€179. |
| | 2 family rooms for 3: €164-€199. |
| | Singles €129-€169. |
| | Extra bed/sofabed €15-€25 per person per night. |
| Meals | Picnic lunch €19. Dinner €32. |
| | Wine from €16. |
| Closed | Rarely. |

Tobias Yang & Marco Stockmeyer
Château les Roches,
Rue de Glanot,
21320 Mont St Jean
Côte-d'Or

| Tel | +33 (0)3 80 84 32 71 |
| Email | info@lesroches-burgundy.com |
| Web | www.lesroches-burgundy.com |

Entry 116   Map 6

## Burgundy

### L'Étoile Argentée

In a courtyard where coaching horses once rested are colourful gardens where children can play. Breakfast out here on croissants and homemade jams, or sit out with a glass of wine and a book from the library. In winter, cuddle up by the wood-burner amid Monsieur's choice of antiques and paintings. South-facing bedrooms, up wide oak stairs, are elegantly decorated by Madame, an interior designer. Two have modern en suite showers but loos are shared. There are good restaurants in the village, plus a pool and tennis for summer. You can spend happy days fishing, golfing and walking in pristine countryside. *Minimum stay: 2 nights at weekends. Male dogs welcome.*

## Burgundy

### Manoir de Tarperon

Tarperon is uniquely French. An ageless charm breathes from the ancient turrets, the antiques, the paintings, the prints, the fine linen, and marvellous old parquet floors. The feel is very pleasant, of a much-loved and lived-in family home. Bedrooms with family furniture have an uncontrived, fadedly elegant décor and bathrooms are family style. The garden too is timeless, rambling, whimsical. Fly-fish on the estate (€25 a day) and book up for Soisick's table d'hôtes – three times a week, it is the very best of authentic Burgundian. *Minimum stay: 2 nights. Whole house available.*

| | |
|---|---|
| Rooms | 1 twin/double, 1 twin sharing wc; 1 twin/double with separate bath/shower room & wc: €65–€95. Extra twin room available to let with twin/double only, €50 p.n. |
| Meals | Dinner €20. Wine €12–€20. Restaurants within walking distance. |
| Closed | Rarely. |

| | |
|---|---|
| Rooms | 3 doubles, 1 twin: €78. 1 triple: €98–€108. |
| Meals | Dinner with wine, €30. |
| Closed | November – March. |

FIRST
EDITION
VETERAN

|  | Isabelle van Delft |
|---|---|
| | L'Étoile Argentée, |
| | 2 av Carnot, |
| | 21350 Vitteaux |
| | Côte-d'Or |
| Tel | +33 (0)3 80 30 70 52 |
| Email | letoileargentee@gmail.com |
| Web | www.letoileargentee.com |

|  | Soisick de Champsavin |
|---|---|
| | Manoir de Tarperon, |
| | RD901, Beaunotte, |
| | 21510 Aignay-le-Duc |
| | Côte-d'Or |
| Tel | +33 (0)3 80 93 83 74 |
| Email | manoir.de.tarperon@wanadoo.fr |
| Web | www.tarperon.fr |

## Burgundy

### Les Champs Cordois

Welcome to deepest Burgundy: pastures as far as the eye can see, sheep and Charolais cattle. The building is rambled by roses, and the garden, Dominique's pride and joy, climbs the hill. The hub of this handsome old house is its huge, slopey ceiling'd living room with friendly tables and leather sofas and chairs, and a wonderful terrace just off it. Enjoy jams from their own fruits at breakfast, and hearty dishes at dinner: genuine table d'hôtes. The big private family suite is on the ground floor, the first-floor rooms interlink, and the style is cottage cosy. Great for groups.

## Burgundy

### Maison Crème Anglaise

From a Tintin collection to Custard the dog, this gracious old house is full of surprises. Swallows nest in a medieval archway, a staircase winds up a tower and the garden falls steeply away giving unforgettable views. Sumptuous rooms are bright with flowers, bedrooms are pretty, cosy, comfy, appealing and the charming bathroom is shared. Graham and Christine, open, enthusiastic, entertaining, hands-on, go the extra mile for their guests and hold evening recitals and exhibitions for local artists in the courtyard. The garden pool is delicious, the hilltop village is historic, the peace is a balm.
*Minimum stay: 2 nights.*

| | |
|---|---|
| Rooms | 2 doubles, 2 twins (can interconnect to form 2 family suites for 4): €72–€123. 1 family suite for 2–6 with kitchen: €82–€150. Children under 3, €5. |
| Meals | Picnic €12. Dinner, 4 courses, €27. Restaurant 4 km. |
| Closed | Rarely. |

| | |
|---|---|
| Rooms | 2 doubles 1 twin all sharing bathroom: €80. |
| Meals | Buffet supper available. Catering available for special events. |
| Closed | Rarely. |

| | |
|---|---|
| | **Martine Goichon** Les Champs Cordois, 46 route de Rouvray, 89630 Bussieres Yonne |
| Tel | +33 (0)3 86 33 01 31 |
| Email | les.champs.cordois@wanadoo.fr |
| Web | www.les-champs-cordois.com |

| | |
|---|---|
| | **Graham & Christine Battye** Maison Crème Anglaise, 22 Grande Rue, 89420 Montréal Yonne |
| Tel | +33 (0)3 86 32 07 73 |
| Email | grahambattye@maisoncremeanglaise.com |
| Web | www.maisoncremeanglaise.com |

Entry 119   Map 6

Entry 120   Map 6

# Burgundy

## La Cimentelle

After an astoundingly beautiful drive you reach this handsome family house built by titans of the cement industry at the turn of the last century: now a pool sits on top of the old factory. Come for extraordinary food (both hosts are gourmet cooks), thoughtfulness, friendly chat and the loveliest rooms. Three are works of art and a touch of fun: a Murano mirror, an antique desk, pink faux-baroque wallpaper and stunning white linen curtains. Swish bathrooms shine with monogrammed towels and showers of Italian mosaic. Family suites at the top of the house are huge. Don't miss it, you'll need at least two nights.

| Rooms | 3 doubles: €90–€120. |
| | 2 family suites for 6: €170–€280. |
| Meals | Dinner with wine, €40. |
| Closed | Rarely. |

**Nathalie & Stéphane Oudot**
La Cimentelle,
4 rue de la Cimentelle,
89200 Vassy lès Avallon
Yonne

| Tel | +33 (0)3 86 31 04 85 |
| Email | lacimentelle@orange.fr |
| Web | www.lacimentelle.com |

Entry 121   Map 6

# Burgundy

## Carpe Diem

In a tranquil Burgundy village lies this handsome old farmhouse. Peek through the gate: all is verdant with vines and the garden is picnic perfect. Eat convivially on a pretty terrace or in a grand dining room with luxurious décor and a fireplace. With home-grown veg and local produce (the Charolais beef is as sweet as a nut), dinner is well worth booking. Immaculate bedrooms are romantic in toile de Jouy with pepperings of fine paintings and antiques. Ask for Chambre Diane in the main house with its big bath, or choose the beautiful stables – children will love the secret mezzanine rooms. *Min.stay: 2 nights in high season. Children over 12 welcome.*

| Rooms | 2 doubles, 1 twin/double: €95. |
| | 2 family rooms for 3: €72. |
| | Singles €64–€87. |
| Meals | Dinner with wine, €37. |
| | Restaurants 4km. |
| Closed | Rarely. |

**Patrick Cabon**
Carpe Diem,
53 Grande Rue,
89440 Massangis
Yonne

| Tel | +33 (0)3 86 33 89 32 |
| Email | carpediem.ser@gmail.com |
| Web | www.acarpediem.com |

Entry 122   Map 6

## Burgundy

### Le Petit Village

You are on the outskirts of a medieval village close to the Armançon river and this is perfect for families. Choose between the cottage or coach house. Each has attractively decorated rooms with oak beams, flagstone floors, great mattresses and good fabrics. Bathrooms are clean and modern, and there's a play barn full of toys. Breakfast is served at one convivial table – freshly baked bread and pastries or the Full Monty from Annabella's trusty Aga. She will cook you a delicious dinner too if you ask. Warm, friendly hosts, a heated pool, private gardens and a tearoom and gift shop on site make this is a jewel. Enchanting. *Minimum stay: 2 nights at weekends, 7 nights in high season. Extra bed / sofabed available.*

| Rooms | 1 double; 1 double with separate bathroom: €65–€75. 1 cottage for 4, 1 cottage for 6: €115–€130. Dinner, B&B €60–€160 per person. |
|---|---|
| Meals | Breakfast €5–€8. Dinner, 4 courses, €25. Restaurant 3km. |
| Closed | Rarely. |

**Annabella Ware**
Le Petit Village,
33 route de Genève,
89160 Fulvy
Yonne
Tel +33 (0)3 86 75 19 08
Email le-petit-village@orange.fr
Web www.le-petit-village.com

Entry 123 Map 6

## Burgundy

### Château de Béru

Château life as you'd dream it, and windows that survey vineyards for miles. Home to the Comtes de Béru since 1627, the estate includes a working vineyard. Harvested by hand, the grapes are grown naturally, mostly organically – a delectable extra as you tour the cellars. It's a place that transports you to another era, yet the choice antiques and tasselled tie-backs harmonise with contemporary backdrops: raw brickwork and pretty fabrics, fresh linens, chic bathrooms; we loved 'Havane'. Have breakfast in the sitting-dining room, by the pool, or in bed. Abbeys to visit, shops to plunder, and one of Chablis' prettiest valleys.

| Rooms | 3 doubles: €130–€150. 1 suite for 5: €220. |
|---|---|
| Meals | Dinner €30. Wine €12–€22. Restaurant 7km. |
| Closed | Rarely. |

**Laurence & Athénaïs de Béru**
Château de Béru,
32 Grande Rue,
89700 Béru
Yonne
Tel +33 (0)3 86 75 90 43
Email laurencedeberu@gmail.com
Web www.chateaudeberu.com

Entry 124 Map 6

# Burgundy

## Le Charme Merry

Their table d'hôtes says it all. Delicious dinners – simple yet fine – are served in the lofty high-raftered dining room under a hooped chandelier. This winemaker's property by the village church has been immaculately restored and furnished in modernist style: cream leather sofas by open fires and beautiful bedrooms next door (two up, two down). Be delighted by à la mode fabrics and big fat pillows, exotic orchids and limestone floors, the charming owner's photographs on perfect pale walls and bathrooms worth saving up for. Outside: gravel, grass and a serene pool. Beyond: Romanesque churches and a heavenly spa.

| | |
|---|---|
| Rooms | 4 doubles: €140–€150. |
| Meals | Dinner with aperitif, wine & coffee, €50.<br>Child €15.<br>Restaurants 13km. |
| Closed | Rarely. |

**Nicolas & Olivia Peron**
Le Charme Merry,
30 route de Compostelle,
89660 Merry sur Yonne
Yonne

| | |
|---|---|
| Tel | +33 (0)3 86 81 08 46 |
| Mobile | +33 (0)6 07 33 15 15 |
| Email | olivia.peron@gmail.com |
| Web | www.lecharmemerry.com |

Entry 125   Map 5

# Burgundy

*New Entry*

## Auberge de la Tuilerie

Surrounded by acres of woodland and pasture, a blissfully remote Burgundy farmhouse with charming rooms. Retired journalists Lee and Philippe have transformed their historic home into a mellow countryside retreat. Parquet floors and oak beams endure in light, spacious bedrooms filled with antiques; each has a sparkling modern bathroom. Lee's bountiful vegetable garden provides much of the produce for superb regional meals eaten communally. Only birdsong disturbs the deep peace, so go slow and laze by the inviting pool, explore the wild gardens, take a siesta… or head out to Vézelay hilltop village or medieval Clamecy. Wonderful.
*Minimum stay: 2 nights in high season.*

| | |
|---|---|
| Rooms | 3 doubles, 2 twin/doubles: €90.<br>Singles €70.<br>Extra bed/sofabed €20 per person per night. |
| Meals | Dinner €35.<br>Restaurant 4km. |
| Closed | Rarely. |

**Philippe Chamaillard**
Auberge de la Tuilerie,
La Tuilerie, 89480 Andryes
Yonne

| | |
|---|---|
| Mobile | +33 (0)6 76 79 26 77 |
| Email | auberge.tuilerie@gmail.com |
| Web | www.auberge-tuilerie.com |

Entry 126   Map 5

## Burgundy

## Burgundy

### Château de Saint Fargeau

A handsome, moated château with an ancient history, a swan-flecked lake and acres of rolling woodland. Four flanking towers enclose a courtyard with its own museum, while high ceilinged rooms whisk you back in time with wood panelling, buffed Versailles parquet, 18th-century printed wallpaper and soaring views. All is authentic rather than immaculate but history buffs will swoon. Breakfast regally in the pale grey panelled boudoir, explore the library and armour room, visit the museum, see owner Michel's wonderful collections, sleep in damask-covered beds, take a guided tour of the whole place. Wonderfully preserved, very special.

### La Maison d'Aviler

On each floor, eight tall windows look down on the resplendent garden that shelters Aviler from noise. At the back is the Yonne where barges peacefully ply: what a setting. The house was originally a workhouse – destitution in 18th-century France had its compensations. Your hosts were interior decorators by trade and are collectors by instinct, so expect subtle but sumptuous detail in elegantly French bedrooms. Sens has a memorable cathedral, a tempting market, and the shops and restaurants of this lovely town simply yell 'quality'.

| | | | | |
|---|---|---|---|---|
| Rooms | 1 suite for 2-4: €200-€300. Child €35. | | Rooms | 3 suites for 3: €80. Extra person €30 per night. |
| Meals | Restaurants 12km. | | Meals | Restaurants in Sens. |
| Closed | October to mid-April. | | Closed | Mid-January to mid-February. |

Noémi Brunet & Michel Guyot
Château de Saint Fargeau,
89170 St Fargeau
Yonne
Tel        +33 (0)3 86 74 05 67
Mobile     +33 (0)6 32 37 05 73
Email      saintfargeau@chateaudesaintfargeau.com
Web        www.chateau-de-st-fargeau.com

Christiane & Bernard Barré
La Maison d'Aviler,
43 quai du Petit Hameau,
89100 Sens
Yonne
Tel        +33 (0)3 86 95 49 25
Email      daviler@online.fr
Web        www.daviler.online.fr

Entry 127   Map 5

Entry 128   Map 5

# Région Parisienne

www.sawdays.co.uk/region-parisienne

## Châtelet district

You will meet a most civilised couple – Mona a bubbly, award-winning artist, Jean a quietly studious former university professor – in their very personal, gently refined apartment where original timbers divide the living room and two friendly cats proclaim the cosiness. It is beautifully done and eminently French, like a warm soft nest, with antiques, lots of greenery, interesting art. Mona loves her guests and is full of good tips: the Seine and historic Paris are at the end of the road. Your attractive, compact guest quarters are nicely private with good storage space, a new shower room, pretty quilts and lots of light. *Minimum stay: 2 nights.*

## Bonne Nuit Paris

Absolute Paris, 300-year-old timbers, crazy wonky stairs and modern comforts, independent rooms and a warm welcome, little streets, friendly markets: it's real privilege. Charming, intelligent Jean-Luc serves his honey, Denise's jams and fresh bread in their generous, rambling living room upstairs. To each room, be it ground or first floor, a colourful shower, a lot of quirk (the last word in creative basins), an appealing mix of antique woodwork and modern prints, and a sense of seclusion. Simplicity, panache and personality, attention and service: these are the hallmarks. No communal space, but a lovely peaceful courtyard.

| Rooms | 1 twin: €110. |
|---|---|
| Meals | Restaurants nearby. |
| Closed | Summer holidays. |

| Rooms | 3 doubles: €160–€210. |
|---|---|
| | 2 triples: €260–€315. |
| | Extra bed €75 per person per night. |
| Meals | Restaurants within walking distance. |
| Closed | Rarely. |

| | Mona Pierrot |
|---|---|
| | Châtelet district, |
| | 75001 Paris |
| Tel | +33 (0)1 42 36 50 65 |
| Email | pierrot-jean@orange.fr |

| | Denise & Jean-Luc Marchand |
|---|---|
| | Bonne Nuit Paris, |
| | 63 rue Charlot, Le Marais, |
| | 75003 Paris |
| Tel | +33 (0)1 42 71 83 56 |
| Email | jean.luc@bonne-nuit-paris.com |
| Web | www.bonne-nuit-paris.com |

## Notre Dame district

At the end of the street are the Seine and the glory of Notre Dame. In a grand old building (with a new lift by the 17th-century stairs), the two unaffected rooms, one above the other, look down to a little garden. The mezzanined family room has its bathroom off the landing; a simple breakfast of shop-packed items is laid here. Upstairs is the smaller room: bed in the corner, timeworn shower room and your own entrance. Madame is polyglot, active and eager to help when she is available; she leaves breakfast ready if she has to go out. She and her daughter appreciate the variety of contact guests bring. A gem in the heart of Paris. *Minimum stay: 2 nights.*

## La Maison d'Anne – Paris Historic Bed & Breakfast

Dare we say unique? A four-storey 17th-century private mansion in the shadow of Notre Dame: surely the rarest B&B in Paris. Then there's the refined welcome into a lively, educated family; the basement pool, sauna and gym; the wine-and-cheese tasting in the cellar. Your suite is off the covered ground-floor courtyard: beams tell of great age, paintings of modern taste, bathroom and kitchen of Moroccan travels. Take the ancient stairs or the lift to top-floor breakfast with Anne and masses of inside lore on hidden Paris: she is charmingly erudite, her time is a gift. Worth every centime. *Minimum stay: 3 nights. Babies & children over 6 welcome.*

| | |
|---|---|
| Rooms | 1 double (breakfast not included): €95. |
| | 1 family room for 4 with separate bath & breakfast area: €115–€140. |
| | Singles €95–€110. |
| Meals | Continental breakfast left ready if owner has to go out. |
| Closed | Rarely. |

| | |
|---|---|
| Rooms | 2 suites for 5: €270. |
| | 1 triple: €240. |
| | Extra bed €40 per person per night. |
| Meals | Kitchenette in suite. |
| | Restaurants nearby. |
| Closed | Rarely. |

| | |
|---|---|
| | **Brigitte Chatignoux** |
| | Notre Dame district, |
| | 75005 Paris |
| Tel | +33 (0)1 43 25 27 20 |
| Email | brichati@hotmail.com |

| | |
|---|---|
| | **Anne Cany** |
| | La Maison d'Anne – Paris Historic Bed & Breakfast, |
| | Latin Quarter, |
| | 75005 Paris |
| Tel | +33 (0)1 56 81 10 85 |
| Email | abaronnet@parsys.com |
| Web | www.parishistoricbnb.com |

Entry 131   Map 5

Entry 132   Map 5

### 1 rue Lamennais

Even the air feels quietly elegant. Soisick doesn't do clutter, just good things old and new: the sense of peace is palpable (nothing to do with double glazing). Her flat turns away from the rowdy Champs-Élysées towards classy St Honoré: ask this lively active lady for advice about great little restaurants – or anything Parisian. The simple generous bedroom has size and interest – an unusual inlaid table is set off by white bedcovers – and leads to a walk-in wardrobe fit for a star and a tasteful white and grey bathroom. With three windows, parquet floor and its mix of antique and modern, the living room is another charmer.

### 52 rue de Clichy

Rosemary's peaceful top-floor flat, protected from buzzing St Lazare by the building's inner garden, has an immaculate blue bedroom and bathroom, the loo just over the passage. The other room is a third-floor, chocolate and fire-red flat with kitchen: breakfast upstairs or enjoy your privacy here. Much-travelled, Rosemary will chat about her many-faceted life, serve breakfast on the pretty balcony or at the walnut table in her relaxing chiaroscuro living room, and point you to the Paris that suits your taste. Her flat is quietly elegant, her presence is competent and gentle, you will be well cared for.

| | |
|---|---|
| Rooms | 1 twin/double: €100. |
| Meals | Restaurants nearby. |
| Closed | Rarely. |

| | |
|---|---|
| Rooms | 1 twin/double with separate wc; 1 twin/double with sofabed, kitchen & separate wc: €105-€200. |
| Meals | Restaurants within walking distance. |
| Closed | Rarely. |

|  | |
|---|---|
| | **Soisick Guérineau** |
| | 1 rue Lamennais, |
| | 75008 Paris |
| Tel | +33 (0)1 40 39 04 38 |
| Email | soisick.guerineau@wanadoo.fr |

|  | |
|---|---|
| | **Rosemary Allan** |
| | 52 rue de Clichy, |
| | 75009 Paris |
| Tel | +33 (0)1 44 53 93 65 |
| Mobile | +33 (0)6 66 01 75 44 |
| Email | rosemarylouiseallan@gmail.com |
| Web | www.52Clichy.com |

## Région Parisienne

### Côté Montmartre

Walk in and touch an 1890s heart: floral inlay on the stairs, stained-glass windows behind the lift. On the top landing, a curly bench greets you. Young and quietly smiling, Isabelle leads you to her personality-filled living room, a harmony of family antiques and 20th-century design, and a gift of a view: old Paris crookedly climbing to the Sacré Cœur. Breakfast may be on the flowering balcony, perhaps with fat cat Jules. Your big white (no-smoking) bedroom off the landing with independent entrance is modern and new-bedded in peaceful rooftop seclusion; the shower room a contemporary jewel. Interesting, cultured, delightful people, too.

| Rooms | 1 double: €140–€160. |
| | Singles €130. |
| | Extra bed €30 per person per night. |
| Meals | Restaurants nearby. |
| Closed | Rarely. |

**Isabelle & Jacques Bravo**
Côté Montmartre,
11 bis rue Jean Baptiste Pigalle,
75009 Paris
Tel      +33 (0)1 43 54 33 09
Mobile   +33 (0)6 14 56 62 62
Email    isabelle.c.b@free.fr
Web      www.cotemontmartre.com

## Région Parisienne

### Les3chambres

Colour and soft comfort, family antiques and atmosphere are here in buckets thanks to Laurent's flair for interiors (he's a lighting designer) and his love of meeting people. Easy and relaxed, he is a walking encyclopaedia on Paris and serves a succulent breakfast. Storm-blue fades into bright turquoise, khaki is married to terracotta, old floorboards meet thick new carpet, gilt-framed oils hang beside good contemporary works, purple plush lifts modern sofas and brocades flatter old fauteuils. Bedrooms have splendid beds, high-tech gadgets and neat little designer shower rooms. Place and person are a delight, old Paris is at your door.

| Rooms | 3 doubles: €179–€209. |
| Meals | Restaurants within walking distance. |
| Closed | August. |

**Laurent Rougier**
Les3chambres,
14 rue Bleue, 75009 Paris
Tel      +33 (0)1 42 47 07 42
Email    contact@les3chambres-paris.com
Web      www.les3chambres-paris.com

## Région Parisienne

### ELIEL

Live like a hip Parisienne. From the Belle Époque elevator and carved cornices to the glass dining table and original art, Madame's second-floor apartment makes you feel like a true native. Parquet-floor, white-on-white panelled bedrooms are luxuriously minimal – marble, mirrors, leather – with elegant splashes of colour – perhaps an Hermès scarf or Chinese cloisonné jar. Bathrooms are elegantly stunning. Madame is glamorous, adorable and has her finger on the pulse of the city's fashion, art and eating scenes, and will advise. Breakfast on top-quality teas, preserves and pastries then explore nearby Montmartre and boho Marais.

| Rooms | 2 doubles, 1 twin (extra child's bed available): €170–€240. Singles €150–€190. |
| --- | --- |
| Meals | Restaurants within walking distance. |
| Closed | Never. |

| | Sabine |
| --- | --- |
| | ELIEL, |
| | 91 rue La Fayette, |
| | 75009 Paris |
| Mobile | +33 (0)6 70 80 51 72 |
| Email | sabine@eliel.fr |
| Web | www.eliel.fr/en/ |

Entry 137   Map 5

## Région Parisienne

### B&B Guénot

A garden! In Paris! A restful corner and quiet, well-travelled hosts who greet you after a day of cultural excitements. The architect-renovated apartment, a delight of clever design, embraces their private garden. All rooms turn towards the greenery, including your charming compact bedroom with its timber floor, large oil painting and wonderful bathroom. Once through the door that leads off the red-leather sitting room, you are in this intimate space, enjoying a lovely wide window onto bird twitter. A generous continental breakfast – and you're ready for more museum fare.

| Rooms | 1 double: €130–€140. |
| --- | --- |
| Meals | Restaurants within walking distance. |
| Closed | Rarely. |

| | Anne-Lise Valadon |
| --- | --- |
| | B&B Guénot, |
| | 4 passage Guénot, |
| | 75011 Paris |
| Tel | +33 (0)1 42 74 23 84 |
| Mobile | +33 (0)6 22 34 34 53 |
| Email | anne-lise.valadon@wanadoo.fr |
| Web | www.bb-guenot.com |

Entry 138   Map 5

## Le P'tit Gobert

Are there just two of you, romantic in Paris? 'Bleu' is a brilliantly designed miniature dream, its plant-screened terrace a huge bonus. The light, fresh, blue and white cube has all you need – clever little shower room, good mezzanine beds (up a tricky staircase), sitting space below, corner kitchen, and not a scrap more. A family, looking forward to all the city's delights? 'Rouge' is excellent value, though with less light charm. Enjoy breakfasts with your friendly, interesting hosts in their fine great modern living room upstairs. A whole group? Take the two, share the terrace and buy your own baguettes. *Minimum stay: 2 nights.*

## Un Ciel à Paris

For 30 years they brought up three children, taught primary kids, played the piano (Lyne), and cooked divinely (Philippe), unaware of hidden beauty overhead: the trompe-l'œil ceiling ('sky in Paris') was discovered by sheer chance in 2009. Warm, cocoon-like bedrooms, beautifully decorated, lightly furnished, give onto trees and a rustic house; snug stone-tiled shower rooms are perfect. Loving their life as B&B hosts in this gently elegant flat where striking modern art sets off family antiques, Philippe and Lyne will give you superb breakfast and insider tips, sharing their passions for art, opera and Paris. *Children over 8 welcome.*

| Rooms | 1 twin/double with kitchenette: €120–€150. 1 family room for 3 with kitchen: €140–€155. Singles €120–€140. Extra bed/sofabed €15 per person per night. |
| --- | --- |
| Meals | Restaurants within walking distance. |
| Closed | Rarely. |

| Rooms | 1 double: €170. 1 triple (single bed on mezzanine): €210. Extra bed €50 per person per night.. |
| --- | --- |
| Meals | Restaurants nearby. |
| Closed | Rarely. |

Carine Bordier
Le P'tit Gobert,
12 rue Gobert,
75011 Paris

| Mobile | +33 (0)6 11 70 59 72 |
| Email | carinebordier@gmail.com |
| Web | www.le-petit-gobert-paris.fr |

Lyne & Philippe Dumas
Un Ciel à Paris,
3 bd Arago,
75013 Paris

| Tel | +33 (0)1 43 36 18 46 |
| Mobile | +33 (0)6 69 73 37 26 |
| Email | contact@uncielaparis.fr |
| Web | www.uncielaparis.fr |

## Région Parisienne

### Montparnasse Edgar Quinet

Filled with books, paintings and objects from around the world, the Monbrisons' tiny flat is old, eccentric, fascinating. Christian, quintessentially French, knowledgeable about history, wine and cattle-breeding, and American Cynthia, an art lover, offer great hospitality, thoughtful conversation, a furry feline, and splendid breakfasts. They have years of generosity behind them. Their bedroom, quiet and snug, has a king-size bed and a good airy bathroom. Twice a week, the open market brings the real food of France to your street; you can visit the bars frequented by Beauvoir and Sartre, or stroll to the Luxembourg Gardens.

| Rooms | 1 twin/double: €95. |
|---|---|
| Meals | Restaurants nearby. |
| Closed | Rarely. |

**Christian & Cynthia de Monbrison**
Montparnasse Edgar Quinet,
11 bd Edgar Quinet,
75014 Paris
Tel    +33 (0)1 43 35 20 87
Email  chris.demonbrison@free.fr

Entry 141    Map 5

## Région Parisienne

### Montparnasse Maine

A little house in a quiet alley behind Montparnasse? It's not a dream and Janine, a live-wire cinema journalist who has lived in Canada, welcomes B&B guests to her pretty timber-ceilinged kitchen/diner; she's a night bird but her charming cat may accompany you over DIY breakfast, laid for you for the morning, and you can look forward to her cultural input in the evening. The big square bedroom across the book-lined hall – a pleasing mix of warm fabrics, honeycomb tiles, old chest and contemporary art – is ideally independent and has a good new pine bathroom. At the end of the lane you'll find glorious buzzy Paris. *Minimum stay: 2 nights.*

| Rooms | 1 double: €80. Singles €70. |
|---|---|
| Meals | Restaurants nearby. |
| Closed | July – September. |

**Janine Euvrard**
Montparnasse Maine,
75014 Paris
Tel    +33 (0)1 43 27 19 43
Email  janine.euvrard@orange.fr

Entry 142    Map 5

## Région Parisienne

### Les Toits de Paris

The attic-level flat, the guest room opposite and the most courteous young owners (with baby Marius) are all of a lovely piece: modest, quiet, clothed in gentle earthy colours, natural materials and discreet manners. You will feel instantly at ease in this cultured atmosphere. Across the landing, your quiet and intimate room has a super-comfy bed, a convertible sofa and a darling little writing desk beneath the sloping beams; the beautiful bathroom has everything. Walk round 'the village', discover its quirky shops, its restaurants for all tastes and budgets – then head for the riches of central Paris.

| Rooms | 1 double with single sofabed: €130. Extra bed €20 per person per night. |
|---|---|
| Meals | Restaurants nearby. |
| Closed | Rarely. |

**Matthieu & Sophie de Montenay**
Les Toits de Paris,
25 rue de l'Abbé Groult,
75015 Paris
Mobile +33 (0)6 60 57 92 05
Email resa@chambrehotesparis.fr
Web www.chambrehotesparis.fr

Entry 143  Map 5

## Région Parisienne

### 11 rue de Siam

A vivacious photographer, Anne has her eyrie up a small private stair in the upper-class peace of charming Passy. Here, she lays breakfast for you in a pretty kitchen with the perfect night-and-day Eiffel Tower view. In your elegant, atmospheric suite (where sitting and sleeping sections connect) are Asian artefacts and family antiques, a chic and fragrant bathroom, a window to the quiet white courtyard. Prints, photographs, a piano, gorgeous books on art… all superb illustrations of Anne's interests and fascinating travellers tales. And she's full of insights into what's on in Paris.

| Rooms | 1 suite for 2-3: €100-€110. Extra person €20 per night. |
|---|---|
| Meals | Restaurants within walking distance. |
| Closed | Rarely. |

**Anne de Henning**
11 rue de Siam,
75116 Paris
Tel +33 (0)1 45 04 50 06
Email dehenni@club-internet.fr

Entry 144  Map 5

## Région Parisienne

### Studio Amélie

In Montmartre village, in a quiet street between bustling boulevard and pure-white Sacré Cœur, Valérie and her architect husband offer a super-chic and ideally autonomous studio off their charming, pot-planted and cobbled courtyard with your bistro table and chairs. A bed dressed in delicate red against white walls, an antique oval dining table, a pine-and-steel gem of a corner kitchen, a generous shower, a mirror framed in red. Valérie's discreet decorative flourishes speak for her calm, positive personality and her interest in other lands. A delicious Paris hideaway you can call your own. *Minimum stay: 3 nights. Extra bed available.*

| Rooms | 1 twin/double with kitchenette: €115. €790 per week. Extra bed available. |
|---|---|
| Meals | Breakfast not included. Guest kitchen. Restaurants nearby. |
| Closed | Rarely. |

**Valérie Zuber**
Studio Amélie,
Montmartre,
75018 Paris

| Mobile | +33 (0)6 30 93 81 35 |
| Email | studiodamelie@wanadoo.fr |

Entry 145   Map 5

## Région Parisienne

### Une Chambre à Montmartre

The steep climb is worth every characterful step. Up one floor, through a garden where convivial picnics happen, up again: Claire lives at the top of a real old Montmartre house: wonky stairs, the neighbour's cat, a sense of community. The window of your room gives dramatically onto the whole of Paris; the Sacré Cœur peeks into a super-stylish bathroom; the room is not big but hugely attractive in its mix of fascinating brocante (Claire was in antiques) and clean-limbed modernity, with space for two easy chairs. Delicious breakfast comes to you on a 1950s trolley, Claire is a mine of information.

| Rooms | 1 double: €140–€160. |
|---|---|
| Meals | Restaurants within walking distance. |
| Closed | Rarely. |

**Claire Maubert**
Une Chambre à Montmartre,
18 rue Gabrielle,
75018 Paris

| Mobile | +33 (0)6 82 84 65 28 |
| Email | claire.maubert@gmail.com |
| Web | www.chambre-montmartre.com |

Entry 146   Map 5

## Région Parisienne

### Villa Mansart

Wind your way up the handsome staircase, nudge open the attic door. The guest sitting room has sunny walls and ethnic rugs. Slim, arched bedrooms are blue or vanilla-and-orange with family furniture and windows peeping over rooftops. Breakfast on fresh fruit and mini-pastries in an elegant dining room or on the terrace. Marble steps, rescued from a local demolition, sweep down to an immaculate peaceful garden curtained by trees. Bruno and Françoise are welcoming, charming and extremely helpful when it comes to route planning. Such calm, only 20 minutes from the centre of Paris.

| Rooms | 1 double: €96. |
|---|---|
| | 1 family room for 3: €96–€126. |
| | Singles €85. |
| | Extra beds €30 per night. |
| | Discounts for full-occupancy: |
| | 6 people €245, 7 people €255. |
| Meals | Restaurants nearby. |
| Closed | Rarely. |

Françoise Marcoz
Villa Mansart, 9 allée Victor Basch,
94170 Le Perreux sur Marne
Val-de-Marne
Tel    +33 (0)1 48 72 91 88
Mobile +33 (0)6 62 37 97 85
Email  villamansart@yahoo.fr
Web    www.villamansart.net

Entry 147   Map 5

## Région Parisienne

### Le Clos des Princes

Paris is 20 minutes by train, Versailles 15 by motorway. Here, behind wrought-iron gates in an elegant suburb, the French mansion sits in an exuberant town garden of pergolas, box bushes and mature trees. Your kind, attentive hosts – she an ex-English teacher, he with a passion for Sully Prudhomme – may give you the poet/philosopher's two-room first-floor suite; he lived here in 1902. Polished floorboards, pretty prints, choice antiques, decorative perfume bottles by a claw-footed tub, all dance to the 19th-century theme. Breakfast unveils gorgeous porcelain and delicious homemade muffins and jams. Outstanding. *Child's sofabed available.*

| Rooms | 1 suite for 2 with separate bath: |
|---|---|
| | €105–€120. |
| | 1 family room for 4: €95–€110. |
| Meals | Restaurant within walking distance. |
| Closed | Rarely. |

Christine & Éric Duprez
Le Clos des Princes,
60 av Jean Jaurès,
92290 Châtenay Malabry
Hauts-de-Seine
Tel    +33 (0)1 46 61 94 49
Email  ce.duprez@yahoo.com
Web    www.leclosdesprinces.com

Entry 148   Map 5

## Région Parisienne

### Villa de la Pièce d'Eau des Suisses

Ah, Versailles! The gilded grandeur of the château, the tiny backstreets of the old town, the great lake of the Swiss Guards and, in between, a discreet door opening to a rambling house warmed by cultured parents, well-mannered teenagers, friendly pets and the smell of beeswax. Bathe in books, colour and art (Laure is an accomplished artist and dress designer); a garden too. Climb two gentle floors (pictures to study at every step) to your large light room with both street and tree-lined lake views. Add unusual family furniture and a superb new biscuity shower room: this genuine family B&B is a rare privilege.

| Rooms | 1 twin/double: €140. |
| | Singles €130. |
| | Cot €40. |
| | Child under 12, €60. |
| Meals | Restaurants within walking distance. |
| Closed | Rarely. |

**Laure de St Chaffray**
Villa de la Pièce d'Eau des Suisses,
6 rue de la Quintinie,
78000 Versailles
Yvelines

| Tel | +33 (0)1 39 53 65 40 |
| Mobile | +33 (0)6 22 60 05 84 |
| Email | bedinversailles@gmail.com |
| Web | www.bedinversailles.com |

Entry 149   Map 5

## Région Parisienne

### Maison Prairie Bonheur

Deep in the Chevreuse nature park, among great woods, rolling fields and country peace, you wouldn't know that a buzzing new town is 3km away and Paris an hour by train. Anne and Jean-François are a fine team, she doing the décor and the daily caring, he in charge of maintenance and cooking (at which he excels). In this house of many chambers (they have four children), each person counts and there's room for everyone in the big bright veranda dayroom, the stone and glass terrace and the big rambling garden. Rooms are not big but pretty and well-designed. Visit the great palaces or Paris, ride or walk and return to a cosy country home.

| Rooms | 2 doubles: €85–€108. |
| | 3 family rooms for 3: €138. |
| | Singles €80–€98. |
| | Dinner, B&B €70–€87 per person. |
| | Extra bed/sofabed €33 per person per night. |
| Meals | Dinner, 3–5 courses, €25–€30. |
| | Wine from €10. |
| Closed | Rarely. |

**Anne & Jean-François Bonassies**
Maison Prairie Bonheur,
Le Village,
6 chemin des Patissiaux,
78114 Magny les Hameaux
Yvelines

| Tel | +33 (0)1 30 44 26 08 |
| Email | annebonassies@wanadoo.fr |
| Web | www.chambres-hotes-prairie-bonheur.com |

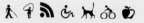

Entry 150   Map 5

# Région Parisienne

## 7 rue Gustave Courbet

In a residential area, behind a modest façade, is a generous interior where Madame's paintings stand in pleasing contrast to elegant antiques and feminine furnishings. Picture windows let the garden in and the woods rise beyond. The larger guest room is soberly classic with a big bathroom; the smaller one with skylight, books and bath across the landing is excellent value. Madame, charming and gracious, sings as well as she paints and enjoys cooking elegant regional dinners for attentive guests; she is very good company. Small and intimate with Paris Montparnasse station half an hour away by train and Versailles close by.

| Rooms | 1 double; 1 double with separate bathroom: €60-€80. |
|---|---|
| Meals | Dinner with wine, €20. |
| Closed | Rarely. |

**Hélène Castelnau**
7 rue Gustave Courbet,
Domaine des Gâtines,
78370 Plaisir
Yvelines

| Tel | +33 (0)1 30 54 05 15 |
| Email | hcastelnau@club-internet.fr |

Entry 151   Map 5

# Région Parisienne

## Cosi à la Moutière

In an 18th-century building that once housed a legendary auberge (frequented by Orson Welles and Ava Gardner, statesmen and royals) is an elegant chambres d'hôtes in a peaceful old town. Imagine white orchids and muslin, board games and books, spaciousness and light, and stylish taupe sofas before a grand fire. Dine at one table or on the wide terrace, wake to Micaela's lemon jams, muffins and clafoutis; all is delicate and delicious. Pedal off to explore Montfort-l'Amaury's cobbled streets, return to big boutique bedrooms with monsoon showers and myriad cushions – dazzling symphonies in grey, butterscotch and white.

| Rooms | 1 twin/double: €115. 1 family room for 4: €125-€160. Extra room (annexe) €60 per night. |
|---|---|
| Meals | Restaurants within walking distance. |
| Closed | Rarely. |

**Micaela Tomasino**
Cosi à la Moutière,
12 rue de la Moutière,
78490 Montfort l'Amaury
Yvelines

| Mobile | +33 (0)6 29 37 56 23 |
| Email | maisondecosi@yahoo.fr |
| Web | www.chambresdhotes-cosi.com |

Entry 152   Map 5

## Nid de Rochefort

Wander among fruit trees in Stephane's tranquil walled garden; hard to believe that Paris is just 30 minutes by train. Wake to birdsong, and fabulous views of ancient Rochefort and the forest beyond. Breakfast is a convivial delight – feast on pancakes, pastries and honey (fresh from the hives) in the elegant sitting room. Stylish, brightly painted doubles and a spacious family suite are split between the 18th-century house and a blue-shuttered cottage, or seek privacy in an extra room in the garden with its own kitchen: DIY breakfast, or sneak some from the house. Stroll to the unspoilt village for divine pastries.

## Domaine des Basses Masures

The serene and beautiful Rambouillet forest encircles this hamlet and the house is a former stables; horses still graze in the field behind. Long, low and stone-fronted, cosily draped in Virginia creeper and wisteria, it was built in 1725. Madame, hospitable and easy-going, does B&B at one end; the gîte is at the other. The B&B bedrooms, one a triple, the other with a big double bed, are friendly and charming, with pretty paintings and mirrors on the walls. Come to walk or ride, or visit the cities and sights: Versailles is 20 minutes, Paris not much further.

| | |
|---|---|
| Rooms | 3 doubles: €85–€88. |
| | 1 suite for 5: €115–€165. |
| | Garden – 1 studio for 2 with |
| | kitchenette: €150–€180. |
| | Singles €78–€105. |
| | Extra bed/sofabed €15 per person |
| | per night. |
| Meals | Restaurants nearby. |
| Closed | Rarely. |

| | |
|---|---|
| Rooms | 1 double, 1 triple: €90. |
| | Extra bed/sofabed €30 per person |
| | per night. |
| Meals | Restaurant 2km. |
| Closed | Rarely. |

| | |
|---|---|
| | **Stephane Jacquerez** |
| | Nid de Rochefort, |
| | 34 rue Guy le Rouge, |
| | 78730 Rochefort en Yvelines |
| | Yvelines |
| Tel | +33 (0)1 78 97 02 82 |
| Mobile | +33 (0)6 13 24 50 99 |
| Email | stephane.jacquerez@gmail.com |
| Web | www.lenidderochefort.fr |

| | |
|---|---|
| | **Mme Walburg de Vernisy** |
| | Domaine des Basses Masures, |
| | 13 rue des Basses Masures, |
| | 78125 Poigny la Forêt |
| | Yvelines |
| Tel | +33 (0)1 34 84 73 44 |
| Mobile | +33 (0)6 95 41 78 46 |
| Email | domainebassesmasures@gmail.com |
| Web | www.domaine-des-basses-masures.com |

Entry 153  Map 5

Entry 154  Map 5

## Région Parisienne

### La Grange de la Guesle

In a hamlet of stone houses, electronic gates glide open to an immaculate farmhouse owned by Catherine and Michel. In the barn are four bedrooms with forest views, two up (one a dreamy family room) and two down (with private terraces), all linked by a steep spiral stair. They're big and super-stylish, with monsoon showers tucked behind half-height walls. Breakfast tables are laid with homemade breads and artisan jams, restaurants are an easy drive, and the decked terrace is for all to share. In this deeply rural setting you have bikes to borrow, stables close by, and a station 4km away – set off for Paris and Versailles! *Parking available. Owners can collect guests from the station. Cot available.*

## Région Parisienne

### À l'Ombre Bleue

Let the willows weep over the village pond; you go through the high gate into a sheltered paradise. The prettiest rooms have masses of old pieces, dolls, books, pictures to intrigue you, a chirruping garden with two rescue dogs to play with and the most caring hostess to provide an exceptional brunch. Have dinner too if you can (Catherine teaches cookery and sources locally: it's delicious). The miniature garden house is a lovers' dream: tiny salon downstairs, bedroom sporting superb bath up. Fulsome towels, extras of all sorts: charming, chatty Catherine thinks of everything.

| | |
|---|---|
| Rooms | 3 doubles: €90–€110. 1 family room for 3 with sofabed: €90–€130. Extra bed/sofabed €40 per person per night. |
| Meals | Kitchenette available. Supper hamper available. Restaurants 5km. |
| Closed | Rarely. |

| | |
|---|---|
| Rooms | 1 double; 1 double with sofabed: €85–€150. Garden house – 1 suite for 2-4: €85. Singles €65–€85. |
| Meals | Dinner with wine, €25. Light supper €15. |
| Closed | Rarely. |

| | |
|---|---|
| | **Catherine Sergent** La Grange de la Guesle, 33 bis rue de la Forêt, 78125 Hermeray Yvelines |
| Tel | +33 (0)1 75 25 34 48 |
| Email | reservation@lagrangedelaguesle.fr |
| Web | www.lagrangedelaguesle.fr |

| | |
|---|---|
| | **Catherine Forget-Pépin** À l'Ombre Bleue, 22 rue de la Mare, Les Pâtis, 78125 Mittainville Yvelines |
| Tel | +33 (0)1 34 85 04 73 |
| Email | catherine@alombrebleue.fr |
| Web | www.alombrebleue.fr |

Entry 155   Map 5

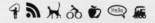

Entry 156   Map 5

## Région Parisienne

## Région Parisienne

### La Mona Guesthouse – Giverny

Blanca, a prolific artist, has Mexican panache (chat, bold colour flashes, quirky ornaments) and American friendliness. Her partner, Cathy the journalist, smiles quietly. The sheltered guest barn comes with lots of windows, white walls, Blanca-painted furniture and attention to comfort: a mixture of simplicity (hangers on hooks, shower rooms behind curtains) and luxury (fine mattresses, lovely tiling, art). The big upstairs suite thrills with Hollywood glamour. Breakfast at the kitchen table brings homemade goodies, dinners are delicious. Explore the twisty old farming village or bike out beyond.

### Les Tourelles de Thun

The neo-gothic brick pile rearing above its suburban street to peer across the Seine valley astonishes. Built by an ancestor in the 1850s as a summer residence, decorated with Corentin's father's varied and talented art, it has tall windows, big rooms – the modern salon is vast – and huge personality. Breakfast and dinner are in the 'medieval' dining room, the library is alive with books, scrolls and prints, there are armchairs and thick carpets in each big bedroom, from 'Hector'; you can spy the Eiffel Tower. Charming, informative and eager, Nathalie uses simple colour schemes and good fabrics to create warm comfort – and she loves cooking.

| | |
|---|---|
| Rooms | 2 doubles: €100-€120. 1 suite for 2-4: €140. Extra bed €25 per person per night. |
| Meals | Dinner €35. Barbecue available. Wine €12-€35. |
| Closed | Rarely. |

| | |
|---|---|
| Rooms | 3 doubles: €82-€98. 1 suite for 3 with extra bed: €112-€158. Singles €82-€98. Dinner, B&B €98 per person. |
| Meals | Dinner with wine, €30. |
| Closed | Never. |

**Blanca Villalobos**
La Mona Guesthouse – Giverny,
5 route de La Roche,
78270 Limetz Villez
Yvelines

| | |
|---|---|
| Tel | +33 (0)1 30 93 31 26 |
| Mobile | +33 (0)6 32 97 74 36 |
| Email | lamonaguesthouse@gmail.com |
| Web | www.lamonaguesthouse-giverny.com |

**Nathalie & Corentin Delhumeau**
Les Tourelles de Thun,
25 rue des Annonciades,
78250 Meulan en Yvelines
Yvelines

| | |
|---|---|
| Tel | +33 (0)1 30 22 06 72 |
| Email | contact@tourellesdethun.com |
| Web | www.chambredhotetourellesdethun.com |

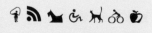

Entry 157   Map 4

Entry 158   Map 5

## Région Parisienne

### Les Colombes

On the doorstep of Paris, in the grounds of a royal château, surrounded by quiet tree-lined residential avenues, it's a trot from an atmospheric racecourse, almost on the banks of the Seine, with forest walks, good restaurants, efficient trains to and from Paris, impeccable, harmonious rooms, table d'hôtes and a deeply pretty garden to relax in. What Les Colombes lacks in old stones it makes up for in a welcome steeped in traditional hospitality – and that includes generous breakfasts, home-grown fruit and veg at dinner – and glowing antiques. Courteous, caring French hosts and great value.

| Rooms | 2 doubles, 1 twin: €80–€94. Extra bed €35 per person per night.. |
|---|---|
| Meals | Dinner with wine, €48. |
| Closed | Rarely. |

**Irène & Jacques James**
Les Colombes,
21 av Béranger,
78600 Maisons Laffitte
Yvelines

| Tel | +33 (0)1 39 62 82 48 |
|---|---|
| Mobile | +33 (0)6 71 13 51 05 |
| Email | jacques.james@orange.fr |
| Web | www.chambresdhotes-lescolombes.fr |

Entry 159   Map 5

## Région Parisienne

### Le Clos de la Rose

For seekers of garden peace, for champagne and architecture buffs (vineyards and historic Provins nearby), this gorgeous green retreat from crazed Paris – cool, quiet, stylishly homely – has been restored with fine respect for 200-year-old origins: limewash, timbers, country antiques, a gathering of books. Charming Brendan (he's Irish) and gentle, organised Véronique have a lovely family and, amazingly, time to chat over aperitifs. Bedrooms have pretty colours, antique linen and patchwork charm, the adorable cottage (with kitchen) is ideal for a longer stay. Don't miss dinner, hot or cold: you choose.

| Rooms | 2 doubles: €94–€146. 1 cottage for 3: €99–€181. Extra bed/sofabed €25 per person per night. |
|---|---|
| Meals | Breakfast €11. Dinner €29. Wine €20–€34. Champagne €32. Restaurant 10-minute drive. |
| Closed | Never. |

**Véronique & Brendan Culligan**
Le Clos de la Rose,
11 rue de la Source, L'Hermitière,
77750 St Cyr sur Morin
Seine-et-Marne

| Tel | +33 (0)1 60 44 81 04 |
|---|---|
| Mobile | +33 (0)6 82 56 10 54 |
| Email | resa@clos-de-la-rose.com |
| Web | www.clos-de-la-rose.com |

Entry 160   Map 5

# Région Parisienne

## La Briarde Medievale

Birds, trees and shrubs abound, in a high-hedged garden that avoids edge-of-village intrusion, a delight in summer with dining terrace and pale pool. Inside is equally inviting, all open-plan and on the ground floor: a cooks' kitchen, an iron-framed sofa, a small bar. Upstairs: an immaculate bed under high eaves, a rail for clothes against a dark beam, and a huge tapestry on a stippled wall of a damsel and a knight in shining armour. Natalie and Stephane, young, courteous and kind, have a passion for the Gothic so swords, helmets and candelabra abound. Breakfasts are continental and exceptional; table d'hôtes is special. *Cot available.*

| Rooms | 1 family room for 2 with separate wc & single sofabed: €70–€103. Garden – 1 family room for 4: €90–€136. |
| --- | --- |
| Meals | Dinner, 4 courses with wine, €25 (weekends only). Restaurants 5km. |
| Closed | Rarely. |

Stephane Pantaleon
La Briarde Medievale,
11 rue des Boulayes,
77610 Châtres
Seine-et-Marne

| Tel | +33 (0)1 64 40 42 07 |
| --- | --- |
| Email | labriardemedievale@gmail.com |
| Web | www.briarde-medievale.fr |

Entry 161   Map 5

# Région Parisienne

## Ferme de Vert St Père

Cereals and beets grow in wide fields and show-jumpers add elegance to the fine landscape. A generous farm courtyard surrounded by very lovely warm stone buildings encloses peace and a genuine welcome from hosts and labradors alike, here where Monsieur's family has come hunting for 200 years. Find family furniture (the 1900s ensemble is most intriguing) and planked floors in beautiful bedrooms, immaculate mod cons and a handsome guest living room where breakfast is served at a convivial table surrounded by honey polished floors and oriental-style rugs. Utter peace, a remote setting, and a Michelin-rated auberge in the village.

| Rooms | 1 family room for 3: €75–€85. 2 apartments for 4: €115–€120. |
| --- | --- |
| Meals | Restaurant in village, 1.5km. |
| Closed | Christmas. |

Philippe & Jeanne Mauban
Ferme de Vert St Père,
77390 Crisenoy
Seine-et-Marne

| Tel | +33 (0)1 64 38 83 51 |
| --- | --- |
| Mobile | +33 (0)6 71 63 31 36 |
| Email | mauban.vert@wanadoo.fr |
| Web | vert.saint.pere.free.fr |

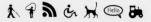

Entry 162   Map 5

### Les Chandelles

At the end of a pretty village, a converted farmhouse behind high gates. Jean-Marc teaches golf to all ages and levels, Catherine, who's been doing B&B for many years, is full of advice for visitors. They receive you with alacrity in the old beamed kitchen then send you up steep, in part slippery, barn stairs to rooms where patches of bright colour punctuate the space. Two larger rooms are designed for families and can take plenty of bods, and there's a wood-clad sitting room. Outside space extends to many acres: perfect for picnics and gatherings in the garden. Near to Versailles and so convenient for Paris.

| | |
|---|---|
| Rooms | 2 doubles: €65–€85. |
| | 2 family rooms for 4: €115–€150. |
| Meals | Kitchen available (min. stay 2 nights). |
| | Restaurants in Nogent le Roi & Maintenon. |
| Closed | Rarely. |

**Catherine & Jean-Marc Simon**
Les Chandelles,
19 rue des Sablons, Chandelles,
Villiers le Morhier
Eure-et-Loir

| | |
|---|---|
| Tel | +33 (0)2 37 82 71 59 |
| Email | info@chandelles-golf.com |
| Web | www.chandelles-golf.com |

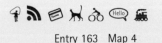

# Normandy

www.sawdays.co.uk/normandy

# Normandy

## Manoir de Beaumont

In the old hunting lodge for guests, a vast, boar- and stag's-headed dayroom with log fire and chandelier, and bedrooms above – ideal for parties. In the main house (charming, heavily wallpapered, colourful) is the handsome Jouy'd room for four. From the very lovely garden are hilltop views. Monsieur manages the Port and is a mine of local knowledge; Madame tends house, garden and guests, masterfully. Proud of their region, naturally generous, elegant, poised, they are keen to advise on explorations: nature, hiking, historical visits… Legend has it that Queen Victoria 'stopped' at this very gracious house.

| Rooms | 1 double: €53. |
| | 1 suite for 2: €65. |
| | 1 quadruple: €60-€86. |
| Meals | Restaurant 2km. |
| | Choice of restaurants 4.5km. |
| Closed | Rarely. |

Catherine & Jean-Marie
Demarquet
Manoir de Beaumont,
76260 Eu
Seine-Maritime

Tel  +33 (0)2 35 50 91 91
Email  catherine@demarquet.eu
Web  www.demarquet.eu

Entry 164  Map 1

# Normandy

## St Mare

A fresh modern house under a steep slate roof in a lush green sanctuary; it could not be more tranquil. The garden really is lovely and worth a wander – a tailored lawn, a mass of colour, huge banks of rhododendrons for which the village is renowned (three of its gardens are open to the public). Claudine runs home and B&B with effortless efficiency and gives you homemade brioches for breakfast; smiling Remi leads you to guest quarters in a freshly wood-clad house reached via stepping stones through the laurels. Bedrooms are comfortable, sunny, spotless, shining and utterly peaceful – two are big enough to lounge in. *Extra beds available.*

| Rooms | 2 suites for 4 (1 with kitchenette), |
| | 1 suite for 5: €75-€135. |
| Meals | Restaurants 20-minute walk. |
| Closed | Rarely. |

Claudine Goubet
St Mare, Route de Petites Bruyères,
1 chemin des Sablonnières,
76119 Varengeville sur Mer
Seine-Maritime

Tel  +33 (0)2 35 85 99 28
Mobile  +33 (0)6 18 92 28 20
Email  claudine.goubet@chsaintmare.com
Web  www.chsaintmare.com

Entry 165  Map 4

## Normandy

### Château Le Bourg

Silk bedspreads and scatter cushions, soaps, colognes and fresh roses... and Leonora's mix of English mahogany and French fabrics as refined as her dinners. Having finished decorating the soberly elegant bedrooms – one with boudoir touches – of her grand 19th-century mansion, she is turning her attention to the garden: it will undoubtedly delight. An intelligent hostess and fine cook, she is both entertaining and generous, handles house parties for celebrations and has a mass of books for you to browse on your return from walking the old railway line or exploring the cliffs.

| Rooms | 2 doubles: €100. |
|---|---|
| Meals | Dinner with wine, €30–€75. |
| Closed | Rarely. |

**Leonora Macleod**
Château Le Bourg,
27 Grande Rue,
76660 Bures en Bray
Seine-Maritime
Tel       +33 (0)2 35 94 09 35
Email   leonora.macleod@wanadoo.fr

## Normandy

### 23 Grand Rue

Peter loves his wines (he was in the trade), Madeleine is energetic and vivacious, both welcome you generously at their 'maison bourgeoise' on the edge of a château village. Set back from the road behind fence and clipped hedge are four cosy classically furnished bedrooms: books and fresh flowers, immaculate duvets, smart French furniture, a calvados nightcap on the landing. Shower rooms are small and beautifully tiled. There's a conservatory for breakfast, a front room for relaxing and, at a table dressed with silver, French dinners are served. Dieppe, Rouen, Honfleur: all are wonderfully close.

| Rooms | 2 doubles, 1 twin: €68. |
|---|---|
|  | 1 triple with separate bath: €80. |
| Meals | Dinner with wine, €27. |
| Closed | Rarely. |

**Peter & Madeleine Mitchell**
23 Grand Rue,
76270 Mesnières en Bray
Seine-Maritime
Tel       +33 (0)2 32 97 06 31
Email   info@23grandrue.com
Web     www.23grandrue.com

## Normandy

### Les Glycines

Close to coast and ferry, in a quiet village in undulating farmland, a wisteria-hugged, red-brick house with gregarious bilingual hosts. Inside, a sitting room with sofa, wood-burner, books, DVDs; outside, a large lawn and sweet sheltered alcove for reading and dreaming. It's intimate: just two bedrooms, one sky-lit and country-pretty, one wallowing in fine fabrics and green views; awake to fresh fruit and croissants. Jenny and Christopher, who've lived in France for ten years, point you to walks, bike rides, cheese makers, cider farms... auberge meals in Londinières and gourmet offerings in Rouen.

| Rooms | 2 doubles: €65–€70. |
|---|---|
| Meals | Restaurants 8km. |
| Closed | First 2 weeks in September. |

**Christopher & Jenny Laws**
Les Glycines,
19 rue de la Houssaye Béranger,
76270 Lucy
Seine-Maritime

| Tel | +33 (0)2 35 93 12 45 |
|---|---|
| Mobile | +33 (0)6 47 59 21 41 |
| Email | kpylaws@orange.fr |

Entry 168   Map 4

## Normandy

### Le Jardin de Muriel

Standing tall and proud – backed by a beautiful flowering garden – is a red-brick townhouse owned by a gentle and pleasant couple. Muriel is a passionate gardener and amateur artist, and her pretty watercolours and drawings decorate the walls – buy any that take your fancy! Two bedrooms with views over neighbouring houses and her treasured garden have good-size bathrooms with scrummy smellies. There's also a family cottage with a kitchen and a tiny intimate terrace, and a cosy salon furnished with a deep-pink brocade period sofa and chairs. Head for history, culture and shopping in Rouen. Delightful.

| Rooms | 1 double, 1 twin: €75. |
|---|---|
| | 1 cottage for 4: €82–€96. |
| Meals | Restaurants within walking distance. |
| Closed | Rarely. |

**Muriel & Jean-Jacques Duboc**
Le Jardin de Muriel,
23 rue Paul Lesueur,
76680 St Saëns
Seine-Maritime

| Tel | +33 (0)2 35 59 86 18 |
|---|---|
| Mobile | +33 (0)6 08 47 86 84 |
| Email | muriel7623@gmail.com |
| Web | lejardindemuriel.free.fr |

Entry 169   Map 4

### La Grange des Marettes

In pure, peaceful countryside, an impeccably renovated hay barn and luxurious small hotel. The décor is mix-and-match in contemporary style, the walls are clad in white wood, the furniture is pastel-washed and each room is different. There are big square French pillows, pristine white salad-bowl hand basins, fat duvets, and a couple of saunas to steam up in. Accomplished paintings and engravings add colour and depth and from every upper room there's a beautiful view. Look forward to buffet breakfast in the day room, served until 11; glimpse the owner's manor house through the sheltering trees. Riverside Rouen is a 20-minute drive.

### Manoir de la Rue Verte

The 300-year-old house stands in a classic, poplar-sheltered farmyard, its worn old stones and bricks, and less worn flints, bearing witness to its age — as does some timberwork inside. Otherwise it has been fairly deeply modernised, and filled with knick knacks and paddywhacks from everywhere. The long lace-clothed breakfast table before the winter fire is most welcoming, as are your retired farmer hosts. Madame was born here, has a winning smile and loves to talk (French only). Her pleasant rooms are in simple rural style; the only sounds are the occasional lowing of the herd and the shushing of the poplars.

| Rooms | 1 double: €150. |
|---|---|
| | 2 suites for 2, |
| | 2 family suites for 2-3: €150-€180. |
| | Singles €130. |
| | Dinner, B&B €75 per person. |
| | Extra bed/sofabed €30 per person per night. |
| Meals | Guest kitchen. Restaurant 3km. |
| Closed | Rarely. |

| Rooms | 1 double: €60. |
|---|---|
| | 1 family room for 4: €55-€110. |
| | 1 triple: €80. |
| Meals | Auberge 1km. Restaurant 4km. |
| Closed | Rarely. |

|  | Jacques Lernon |
|---|---|
| | La Grange des Marettes, |
| | Lieu-dit Le Bois Hébert, |
| | Les Marettes, 76690 Clères |
| | Seine-Maritime |
| Tel | +33 (0)2 35 33 24 44 |
| Mobile | +33 (0)6 84 77 21 42 |
| Email | la-grange@les-marettes.fr |
| Web | www.les-marettes.fr |

|  | Yves & Béatrice Quevilly Baret |
|---|---|
| | Manoir de la Rue Verte, |
| | 21 rue Verte, |
| | 76970 Flamanville |
| | Seine-Maritime |
| Tel | +33 (0)2 35 96 81 27 |
| Mobile | +33 (0)6 24 33 54 26 |

Entry 170   Map 4

Entry 171   Map 4

## Le Clos du Vivier

The lush garden shelters bees, bantams, sleek cats and a phenomenal variety of shrubs and flowering plants. Monsieur is retired and he looks after all this while Madame tends to their guests, with respect for everyone's privacy; Madame also offers guidance on hiking, and there's tennis and fishing nearby. She is an intelligent, active and graceful person, her bedrooms, some under sloping ceilings, are cosily colourful, her bathrooms big and luxurious, her breakfast richly varied. After a jaunt, you can read their books, relax among their lovely antiques or make tea in their breakfast room. The cliffs at Étretat are 20 minutes away.

## Jardin Gorbeau – Étretat Guesthouse & Spa

The ingredients of a super seaside holiday in Normandy: a cosy 1820s black-and-white mansion steps from the beach, feast-like breakfasts, leafy walled garden, big showers for sloshing off sea salt, sauna, jacuzzi... Arizona-born Jon's art collections add personality to sober French or floral décor; a cinema room is good for quiet nights. Best bedrooms are Cosette in the main house with a secret study behind wardrobe doors, and cool Laigle in the garden house, a loft suite with coastal views. Étretat's white cliffs mirror Dover's and the GR21 cuts through this pretty town of seafood restaurants, galleries and sunsets. *Minimum stay: 2 nights at weekends.*

| | |
|---|---|
| Rooms | 1 twin/double: €120. |
| | 1 suite for 5: €150–€170. |
| | 1 triple: €120–€140. |
| Meals | Restaurants in Valmont, 1km. |
| Closed | Rarely. |

| | |
|---|---|
| Rooms | 3 doubles: €89–€159. |
| | 2 suites for 2: €109–€185. |
| | 1 quadruple: €129–€189. |
| Meals | Dinner €39. |
| Closed | Mid-November to mid-December. |

**Dominique Cachera-Gréverie**
Le Clos du Vivier,
4 chemin du Vivier,
76540 Valmont
Seine-Maritime

| | |
|---|---|
| Tel | +33 (0)2 35 29 90 95 |
| Email | le.clos.du.vivier@wanadoo.fr |
| Web | www.le-clos-du-vivier.com |

**Jon Cooper**
Jardin Gorbeau –
Étretat Guesthouse & Spa,
27 rue Adolphe Boissaye,
76790 Étretat
Seine-Maritime

| | |
|---|---|
| Tel | +33 (0)2 35 27 16 72 |
| Email | info@gorbeau.com |
| Web | www.gorbeau.com |

## Mille Roses

Poised on a hillside gazing south over the Seine, this proud red-brick mansion was once home to opera tenor Placide Poultier. Now Patsy welcomes you in; a teacher and guide, she is well versed in local history and happy to share the local secrets over a light breakfast. At the top of the house are two modern, simple twin bedrooms and a sitting room where you can browse a guide book over a cup of tea; bathrooms are separate but private and everything is spotless. Outside, a huge copper beech and blue cedar sprinkle shade into a lush, sloping garden where a barbecue and hammock promise lazy summer afternoons.

| Rooms | 2 twins sharing living area with separate bath/shower rooms: €80–€90. |
|---|---|
| Meals | Restaurant nearby. |
| Closed | March – May & October/November. |

|  | **Patsy Musto** |
|---|---|
|  | Mille Roses, 9 rue Jean Le Gaffric, |
|  | 76490 Villequier, Seine-Maritime |
| Tel | +33 (0)2 32 70 44 32 / |
|  | +44 (0)1527 873645 |
| Mobile | +33 (0)6 48 85 92 19 / |
|  | +44 (0)7768 886407 |
| Email | patsy.musto8@orange.fr |
| Web | www.frenchencounters.com |

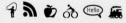

Entry 174   Map 4

---

## Le Brécy

Jérôme has happy childhood holiday memories of this elegant 17th-century manor house; he and delightful Patricia moved to join grand-mère who had been living here alone for years. A long path flanked by willows leads down to the Seine: perfect for an evening stroll. One suite is on the ground floor, in classically French coral and cream, its windows opening to a walled garden; the second, equally refined, is in the attic. Breakfast is when you fancy: brioches, walnuts, fresh fruit in a pretty green-panelled room. Ask about the Abbey and walks to its gardens. A charming rural paradise just 15 minutes from Rouen Cathedral.

| Rooms | 1 suite for 2, 1 suite for 3: €94–€108. |
|---|---|
| Meals | Restaurant in village. |
| Closed | Rarely. |

|  | **Jérôme & Patricia Lanquest** |
|---|---|
|  | Le Brécy, |
|  | 72 route du Brécy, |
|  | 76840 St Martin de Boscherville |
|  | Seine-Maritime |
| Tel | +33 (0)2 35 32 00 30 |
| Mobile | +33 (0)6 62 37 24 22 |
| Email | lebrecy@gmail.com |
| Web | www.lebrecy.perso.sfr.fr |

Entry 175   Map 4

# Normandy

## Manoir de Captot

The drive curves through paddocks and pillared gates to this serene 18th-century mansion. The forest behind may ring with the stag's call, the heads and hooves of his kin line the grand staircase. The fine classic French interior is peacefully formal: a gorgeous primrose-yellow dining room with an oval mahogany table for breakfast feasts, a collection-filled drawing room, a beautiful first-floor bedroom with the right curly antiques and pink Jouy draperies. Michelle cherishes her mansion and resembles it: gentle, attentive, courteous. Giverny is near, Rouen and heaps of lovely restaurants are ten minutes away. *Children over 10 welcome. Extra double occasionally available.*

| Rooms | 1 double: €95–€110. |
| | 1 suite for 2-3: €95–€110. |
| Meals | Restaurant 900m & in Rouen, |
| | 10-minute drive. |
| Closed | Rarely. |

Michelle Desrez
Manoir de Captot,
42 route de Sahurs,
76380 Canteleu
Seine-Maritime
Tel      +33 (0)2 35 36 00 04
Email    captot76@yahoo.fr
Web      www.captot.com

Entry 176   Map 4

# Normandy

## Chambres avec Vue

The elegant black door hides a little house of treasures, curios, art and character, an easy walk (25 minutes) from the centre of Rouen. Dominique, full of energy and enthusiasm, has a flair for decoration – as her paintings, coverings and light, bright furniture declares. Oriental rugs on parquet floors, French windows to balcony and garden, bedrooms brimful of interest. Nothing standard, nothing too studied, a very personal home and leisurely breakfasts promising heavenly surprises. The house's hillside position in this residential area is equally special. Great value, great views.

| Rooms | 3 doubles: €65. |
| | Singles €45. |
| Meals | Restaurant 1km. |
| Closed | October – November. |

Dominique Gogny
Chambres avec Vue,
22 rue Hénault,
76130 Mont St Aignan – Rouen
Seine-Maritime
Tel      +33 (0)2 35 70 26 95
Mobile   +33 (0)6 62 42 26 95
Email    chambreavecvue@free.fr
Web      chambreavecvue.online.fr

Entry 177   Map 4

# Normandy

# Normandy

## Le Clos Jouvenet

From your bath you gaze upon the cathedral spire. It is a privilege to stay in these refined city surroundings, safely inside a serene walled garden above the towers of Rouen. The garden is as elegantly uncomplicated as the house and its Belgian owners, the décor classic sophisticated French to suit the gentle proportions: there are pretty pictures and prints, lots of books, handsome antique furniture and breakfast is served in the conservatory or on the terrace in warm weather. Madame is charming, Monsieur enjoys guests too, and you wake to birdsong and church bells. *Priority to two nights at weekends & high season. Children over 13 welcome.*

## La Lévrière

The garden laps at the river bank where moorhens nest; trout swim, birds chirrup, deer pop by – it's the dreamiest village setting. Madame is charming and takes everything (including escapee horses) in her stride and her young family love it when guests come to stay. Breakfast is at a grey-painted table with crimson plexiglass chairs; garden loungers are a temptation to stay. Bedrooms are across the way, two in the granary, one up, one down, the third in the immaculate coach house attic with a fine garden view. Creamy walls, sweeping floors, rafters, toile de Jouy, fresh flowers... stay a long while.

| | |
|---|---|
| Rooms | 1 double, 1 twin/double: €110–€130. |
| Meals | Restaurants within walking distance. |
| Closed | Mid-December to mid-January. |

| | |
|---|---|
| Rooms | 1 triple, 1 suite for 3, 1 suite for 4: €85. |
| Meals | Restaurant 5km. |
| Closed | Rarely. |

**Catherine de Witte**
Le Clos Jouvenet,
42 rue Hyacinthe Langlois,
76000 Rouen
Seine-Maritime

| | |
|---|---|
| Tel | +33 (0)2 35 89 80 66 |
| Mobile | +33 (0)6 62 73 80 66 |
| Email | leclosjouvenet@gmail.com |
| Web | www.leclosjouvenet.com |

**Sandrine & Pascal Gravier**
La Lévrière,
24 rue Guérard,
27140 St Denis le Ferment
Eure

| | |
|---|---|
| Tel | +33 (0)2 32 27 04 78 |
| Mobile | +33 (0)6 79 43 92 77 |
| Email | contact@normandyrooms.com |
| Web | www.normandyrooms.com |

# Normandy

## Château de Bonnemare

A Renaissance gatehouse leads to a remarkable 16th-century brique de St Jean façade as you enter the grounds of this enticing 'monument historique'. Alain and Sylvie, generous and charming, have restored two elegant ground-floor rooms in the north wing, and two with listed decoration on the first floor. Find French classical elegance, chandeliers, mouldings, deep mattresses and pleasing modern bathrooms. Breakfast in the vaulted Great Kitchen with embroidered napkins, fresh fruits and flowers, pâtisserie and homemade jams. The estate walls enclose chapel, farm, cider press, bakery, barns and 44 acres of park and woodland. Grand.

| Rooms | 1 double: €102–€135. |
| --- | --- |
| | 3 suites for 2-3: €202–€235. |
| | Singles €102–€202. |
| | Extra bed/sofabed €25 per person per night. |
| Meals | Guest kitchen. |
| | Restaurant 6km. |
| Closed | 1 December – 15 February. |

**Sylvie Vandecandelaere**
Château de Bonnemare,
990 route de Bacqueville,
27380 Radepont
Eure

| Tel | +33 (0)2 32 49 03 73 |
| --- | --- |
| Mobile | +33 (0)6 03 96 36 53 |
| Email | sarlbonnemare@nordnet.fr |
| Web | www.bonnemare.com |

Entry 180   Map 4

# Normandy

## Chambres d'hôtes de la Bucaille

In a small hamlet surrounded by 600 acres of land is a farmhouse where Sophie and her children live, and a four-square brick mansion for the guests. You'll find a breakfast room, sitting room and TV room downstairs, and five bedrooms up, with choice fabrics, period furniture and fine contemporary bathrooms. Breakfast is served on antique tablecloths and white china, and elegant wallpapers and north African rugs are scattered throughout. All feels polished, pleasing, and hospitable. Say hello to the horses, borrow the bikes, visit Richard the Lionheart's Château Gaillard; one of many historic sites.

| Rooms | 1 double, 3 twin/doubles: €80–€110. |
| --- | --- |
| | 1 apartment for 5: €90–€150. |
| Meals | Restaurant 8km. |
| Closed | Never. |

**Sophie Hamot**
Chambres d'hôtes de la Bucaille,
2 rue Jean Lucas,
27700 Guiseniers
Eure

| Tel | +33 (0)2 32 54 58 45 |
| --- | --- |
| Email | hamot.jerome@orange.fr |
| Web | www.chambres-hotes-labucaille.com |

Entry 181   Map 4

# Normandy

## La Réserve

You will like Valérie, lively mother of four, and her quietly refined house and breakfast at the big guest table you will want to stay forever. Over home-grown eggs and homemade jams, cake of the day, cheeses, charcuterie and fruit kebabs, conversations flourish, friendships bud. Outside, limewash walls stand among lavender-edged lawns and orchards, kindly Flaubert the Leonberger ambles, cows graze; inside are grey woodwork and gorgeous rooms, superb beds, handsome rugs on parquet floors, fine antiques and touches of brocante. Monet's ineffable gardens are just down the hill. *Whole house available.*

| | |
|---|---|
| Rooms | 2 doubles, 4 twin/doubles: €135–€165. Extra bed €40 per person per night. |
| Meals | Restaurants 1km. |
| Closed | November – March, except by arrangement. |

**Valérie & François Jouyet**
La Réserve,
27620 Giverny
Eure
Tel +33 (0)2 32 21 99 09
Email mlreserve@gmail.com
Web www.giverny-lareserve.com

# Normandy

## L'Aulnaie

Michel and Éliane have invested natural good taste in their restoration of this lovely 19th-century farmhouse in a particularly pretty village. Guests share a self-contained part of the house with its own dayroom and breakfast area – there's lots of space to settle in – with books, music and open fire. Bedrooms are gentle, beautiful, fresh, with Jouy-print fabrics, plain walls and honey-coloured floors. Enthusiastic, charming Éliane is an amateur painter and inspired gardener, pointing out the rich and the rare; lawns sweep down to a stream that meanders beneath high wooded cliffs. Such value!

| | |
|---|---|
| Rooms | 1 double, 1 twin: €90. |
| Meals | Restaurants 2km. |
| Closed | Rarely. |

**Éliane & Michel Philippe**
L'Aulnaie,
29 rue de l'Aulnaie,
27120 Fontaine sous Jouy
Eure
Tel +33 (0)2 32 36 89 05
Mobile +33 (0)6 03 30 55 99
Email emi.philippe@worldonline.fr

## Clos de Mondétour

Tiny church to one side, lazy river behind, views to weeping willows and majestic limes – the house oozes grace and tranquillity. Grégoire and Aude have created a calm, charming atmosphere inside: this is a family home. Lofty, light-drenched bedrooms with polished floorboards, antiques and monogrammed bed linen are beautifully refined; bathrooms are light and luxurious. The living area, with a striking tiled floor and bold colours, is a restful space in which to settle in front of a log fire – or enjoy a special breakfast among fresh flowers and family silver. Aude's horses graze in the meadow behind.

| Rooms | 1 double, 1 twin/double: €120. |
| | 1 family room for 4: €90–€150. |
| | 1 triple: €140. |
| Meals | Restaurants 2km. |
| Closed | Rarely. |

**Aude Jeanson**
Clos de Mondétour,
17 rue de la Poste,
27120 Fontaine sous Jouy
Eure

| Tel | +33 (0)2 32 36 68 79 |
| Mobile | +33 (0)6 71 13 11 57 |
| Email | aude.jeanson@closdemondetour.com |
| Web | www.closdemondetour.com |

Entry 184   Map 4

## Les Logis du Moulin

Welcome to a serene green paradise – a converted water mill and burgeoning B&B. Across deckchair'd lawns linked by meandering paths (clogs and umbrellas provided!) are two separate cottages, sober, simple, fresh and warm; total tranquillity. In the first, the main bedroom is downstairs and the single is up, leading through to a rustic-stylish shower. In the converted bread oven, bucolically on the river bank, is a family suite. Find floors of rosy terracotta, arched windows hung with muslin, pretty beds topped with quilts. In the handsome dining room, gentle Elisabeth serves a breakfast worth lingering over; and you can, until 11am. *Pets by arrangement.*

| Rooms | 1 double: €85. |
| | 1 family suite for 3 sharing shower room: €105. |
| | Singles €65–€70. |
| | Extra bed/sofabed €15 per person per night. |
| Meals | Assiette gourmande with cider, €16. Restaurant 3km. |
| Closed | Rarely. |

**Elisabeth Lamblardy**
Les Logis du Moulin,
4 rue du Moulin,
27120 Fontaine sous Jouy
Eure

| Tel | +33 (0)2 32 26 06 07 |
| Email | elisabeth.lamblardy@orange.fr |
| Web | www.leslogisdumoulin.fr |

Entry 185   Map 4

## Les Hautes Sources

Three golden farmhouses around a central lawned terrace, with views that sail over the valley to a distant church spire: an incomparable setting. Enthusiastic Amaury and Audrey arrived with their family in 2012 and give you three bedrooms in the second house and a family cottage in the third: uncluttered, gorgeous, luxurious. Imagine decorative floors, white-painted beams, muted colours and snowy linen. Wake to five homemade jams that include apple caramel, set off for Monet's beautiful Giverny, wander the lovely gardens, splash in the pool, sink into sofas by the great stone fire. You will unwind here.

## Les Granges Ménillonnes

An active farm until 1950, it sits beside a pretty garden in the prettiest countryside in the Eure valley, 20 minutes from Monet's gardens at Giverny, midway between Rouen and Paris. In converted outbuildings, big comfortable bedrooms, one with a balcony, all furnished with warm colours, honeyed floorboards and country quilts beneath a riot of beams, overlook a lily pond and loungers that beckon you to doze over a book – though excellent walking abounds. Chantal and Michel, energetic hosts, offer speciality breads and up to 15 different jams for breakfast, and run a farm shop in the village.

| | | | | |
|---|---|---|---|---|
| Rooms | 1 twin/double, 1 twin: €120-€130. 1 suite for 2: €160. 1 cottage for 5 with kitchen & living area: €150-€190. | Rooms | 2 doubles, 1 twin each with separate shower: €55-€70. 1 suite for 4, 1 suite for 7 each with separate shower: €55-€130. |
| Meals | Restaurants 3km. | Meals | Restaurant 3km. |
| Closed | Never. | Closed | Rarely. |

| | | | |
|---|---|---|---|
| | **Amaury de Tilly** | | **Michel & Chantal Marchand** |
| | Les Hautes Sources, | | Les Granges Ménillonnes, |
| | 32 rue Roederer, | | 2 rue Grand'Cour, |
| | 27120 Ménilles | | 27120 Ménilles |
| | Eure | | Eure |
| Mobile | +33 (0)6 72 84 91 89 | Mobile | +33 (0)6 70 46 87 57 |
| Email | amaury.detilly@hotmail.fr | Email | chant.mich.marchand@wanadoo.fr |
| Web | www.les-hautes-sources.fr | Web | www.lesgranges27.com |

Entry 186   Map 4

Entry 187   Map 4

## Normandy

### Clair Matin

Handsomely carved Colombian furniture, strong colours, interesting prints – not what you expect to find at a long, low, 18th-century French village homestead with a turret at each end. Your kind and very lovely Franco-Spanish hosts raised five children in South America before renovating their home. Bedrooms, not huge, are solidly comfortable, bathrooms are immaculate and there's a new games room in an outbuilding. At the huge Andean breakfast table you will enjoy fresh breads, homemade jams and good conversation. Jean-Pierre is a passionate gardener and his plantations burst with every kind of shrub and flower!

| Rooms | 1 double: €65. |
| | 1 suite for 2: €80–€110. |
| | 1 family room for 4: €65–€95. |
| Meals | Auberges 6km. |
| Closed | Rarely. |

**Jean-Pierre & Amaia Trevisani**
Clair Matin,
19 rue de l'Église,
27930 Reuilly
Eure

| Tel | +33 (0)2 32 34 71 47 |
| Email | bienvenue@clair-matin.com |
| Web | www.clair-matin.com |

## Normandy

### Manoir de la Boissière

Madame has been doing B&B for years, is well-organised and still enjoys meeting new people – and cooking tasty dinners when she's not too busy. Guest quarters, independent of the house, have pretty, traditional rooms, good bedding and excellent shower rooms. Sympathetically restored 15th-century farm buildings, carefully chosen furniture – some tenderly hand-painted – and decorative fowl on the large, lovely, willow-fringed pond add character. Near the motorway yet utterly peaceful – though courting peacocks in spring/summer may wake you.

| Rooms | 2 doubles, 1 twin; 1 double with kitchenette: €65–€75. |
| | 1 family room for 3 with kitchenette: €85. |
| Meals | Dinner with cider, €26. Guest kitchen. |
| Closed | Rarely. |

**Clotilde & Gérard Sénécal**
Manoir de la Boissière,
Hameau la Boissaye,
27490 La Croix St Leufroy
Eure

| Tel | +33 (0)2 32 67 70 85 |
| Email | chambreslaboissiere@wanadoo.fr |
| Web | www.chambres-giteslaboissiere.fr |

# Normandy

## La Londe

The big beautiful garden flows down to the river Eure – what a setting – and the old farmhouse and yesteryear buildings are as neat as new pins. Delightful Madeleine devotes herself to home and guests and bedrooms are neat, clean, pretty, sober and relaxing; the double's French windows open to the garden, the perfect small suite sits under the eaves. Expect antique lace, silver snuff boxes, a kitchen/salon for guests and very delicious breakfasts with garden views. A form of perfection in a privileged and peaceful spot: woods and water for walking, canoeing, fishing; Giverny – or Rouen – a half-hour drive.

| Rooms | 1 double: €60–€65. |
|---|---|
| | 1 suite for 3: €62–€70. |
| | Extra bed/sofabed €20 per person per night. |
| Meals | Guest kitchen. |
| | Restaurants 5km. |
| Closed | Rarely. |

**Madeleine & Bernard Gossent**
La Londe,
4 sente de l'Abreuvoir,
27400 Heudreville sur Eure
Eure

| | |
|---|---|
| Tel | +33 (0)2 32 40 36 89 |
| Mobile | +33 (0)6 89 38 36 59 |
| Email | madeleine.gossent@online.fr |
| Web | www.lalonde.online.fr |

Entry 190   Map 4

---

# Normandy

## La Ferme des Isles

Approach this sprawling 19th-century farm through a watercolour of mills, meadows and bridges… friendly French hosts await with a menagerie of four-legged friends. With vintage chairs, suspended lamps, billiards and book-filled mangers, it's perfect for fun social soirées and François's four-star dinners. Beams break up modern bedrooms – a triangular bath and a sunburst bed will astound you. Breakfast in the cavernous barn (on goat's cheese, grainy breads, garden fruits); end the day amongst fireplaces, convivial tables and chesterfields in stone-walled sitting and dining rooms. For nature lovers, couples and families – huge fun. *Cot available.*

| Rooms | 4 doubles: €95–€130. |
|---|---|
| | 1 family room for 2-3: €150–€170. |
| | Extra bed €20 per person per night. |
| Meals | Dinner, 4 courses with wine, €40. |
| | Restaurants within walking distance. |
| Closed | Rarely. |

**François & Sophie Breban**
La Ferme des Isles,
7 chemin des Isles,
27490 Autheuil Authouillet
Eure

| | |
|---|---|
| Tel | +33 (0)2 32 36 66 14 |
| Mobile | +33 (0)6 63 46 00 45 |
| Email | lafermedesisles@gmail.com |
| Web | www.lafermedesisles.com |

Entry 191   Map 4

# Normandy

## On Rue Tatin

Artistic and full of vintage character, this tall, venerable, half-timbered building (a convent for 300 years) sits on a corner in Louviers town centre, opposite the towering church of Notre Dame. Here lives Susan, award-winning cookery writer, generous and vivacious. She offers one-to-five-day cookery courses, dinner on request, and a cosy sitting room facing the front garden. Imagine twisting staircases and ancient timbers, colourful artefacts all around, books, board games and scattered kilims. Both bedrooms are spacious, the one in the attic sharing the other's turquoise bathroom – perfect for families and friends.

| Rooms | 2 doubles sharing bathroom: €90. |
|---|---|
| Meals | Dinner, 4 courses with wine, €50. Restaurant within walking distance. |
| Closed | Christmas. |

Susan Herrmann Loomis
On Rue Tatin,
1 rue Tatin,
27400 Louviers
Eure
Tel       +33 (0)2 32 25 03 98
Email    susan@susanloomis.com
Web      www.onruetatin.com

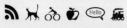

Entry 192   Map 4

# Normandy

## Au Vieux Logis

They are full of character and terribly French, this artist owner and her crooked house marked by the slings and arrows of 500 years: wonky floorboards, bathrooms among the beams, old-fashioned floral bedrooms and a sensuous garden full of old favourites: lilac and honeysuckle, luscious shrubs and fruit trees. Set in the middle of the village, the quiet old house has an atmosphere that inspires ease and rest. (Saint-Exupéry, author of the *Le Petit Prince* and a friend of Madame's father, stayed here.) Madame, a good, generous soul, was once an antique dealer so breakfast is served on old silver.

| Rooms | 2 doubles: €50. 1 triple: €50–€80. 1 quadruple: €50–€100. |
|---|---|
| Meals | Dinner €17. Wine €15. |
| Closed | Rarely. |

Annick Auzoux
Au Vieux Logis,
27370 St Didier des Bois
Eure
Tel       +33 (0)2 32 50 60 93
Email    levieuxlogis5@orange.fr
Web      www.levieuxlogis.fr

Entry 193   Map 4

## Manoir Les Perdrix

The young, hands-on owners of Les Perdrix are full of infectious enthusiasm for their enterprise: running a themed, welcoming, upmarket B&B. Food tastings, walking weekends – they can do it all! In the throes of serious restoration, the old house has an intimate dining room and cavernous reception room for tasty breakfasts and jolly dinners, and comfortable bedrooms off a winding second-floor corridor: thick duvets and pretty linen, coordinated fabrics and polished floors, shower gels and plush bathrooms. The run-around garden – great for kids – is within earshot of the road to Verneuil.

## Château de la Puisaye

A fine château which oozes 19th-century elegance (pale façade, shuttered windows) in 27 acres of rural bliss. Find large airy bedrooms with antiques, huge mantelpiece mirrors, glass-panelled doors that flood spaces with light; ivory paintwork and snowy linen create an ordered calm. Diana, a stylish cook, will prepare a light supper or dinner on request, perhaps foie gras then truffle-stuffed guinea fowl; fruit and veg come from the potager, the 19th-century greenhouse and local markets. Lounge in the book-filled library, borrow a bike and pedal the grounds; relax in the infra-red sauna among delicious aromatherapy oils.

| Rooms | 4 twin/doubles: €75-€90. |
| | 1 family room for 4: €90-€100. |
| | Singles €70. |
| | Extra bed €20 per person per night. |
| Meals | Dinner with wine, €16-€28. |
| | Restaurant 5km. |
| Closed | Rarely. |

| Rooms | 3 doubles, 1 twin: €98-€128. |
| | 1 suite for for 2-4: €138-€185. |
| Meals | Dinner €33; menu gourmand €55; |
| | Normandy platter with cider €16. |
| Closed | One week in winter. |

**Christine Vandemoortele**
Manoir Les Perdrix,
Les Marnières,
27570 Tillières sur Avre
Eure
Mobile   +33 (0)6 21 21 08 52
Email    postmaster@manoirlesperdrix.fr
Web      www.normandy-guest-house.com

**Bruno & Diana Costes**
Château de la Puisaye,
Lieu-dit La Puisaye,
27130 Verneuil sur Avre
Eure
Tel     +33 (0)2 32 58 65 35
Email   info@chateaudelapuisaye.com
Web     www.chateaudelapuisaye.com

## La Trimardière

Midway between Paris and Deauville, in the beautiful town of Verneuil-sur-Avre, is an 18th-century mansion in a neat French garden, immaculate inside and out. Glass decanters decorate the mantelpiece and swathes of pale pattern dress the windows, giving the lofty airy dining room a handsome allure; here Domitila serves perfect breakfasts at a big oval table. Bedrooms are on the top floors – smart, spacious, luxurious, traditional – with oriental rugs on satin-smooth floors, wonderful new mattresses, crisp snowy linen and bathrobes cosseted in hygienic packaging. Shops, restaurants, festivals wait outside the door.

## Manoir d'Hermos

The sedately old-French bedrooms with good antiques and satin touches in the 16th-century house (in Madame's family for 100 years) are large, light and lovely. All sit in peace by pastoral meadows, a birdy orchard and spreading lake. Béatrice is full of spontaneous smiles, puts flowers everywhere, organises big parties on a theme (not when B&B guests are here), serves good breakfasts and brunches at one table and keeps four gentle donkeys. The orchards produce cider and trees are being carefully and meticulously planted to Napoleonic plans discovered in the archives. A super place to stay, filled with interesting history.

| | |
|---|---|
| Rooms | 2 doubles, 2 twin/doubles: €110-€120. 1 suite for 4: €120-€170. Singles €95. |
| Meals | Restaurant within walking distance. |
| Closed | Rarely. |

| | |
|---|---|
| Rooms | 1 family room for 3: €72-€97. 1 quadruple: €94-€138. |
| Meals | Restaurants 2km. |
| Closed | Rarely. |

**Domitila Aranda**
La Trimardière,
366 rue Gambetta,
27130 Verneuil sur Avre
Eure
Tel       +33 (0)2 32 30 28 41
Mobile    +33 (0)6 30 50 83 08
Email     latrimardiere@orange.fr
Web       www.latrimardiere.com

**Béatrice & Patrice Noël-Windsor**
Manoir d'Hermos,
27800 St Éloi de Fourques
Eure
Tel       +33 (0)2 32 35 51 32
Mobile    +33 (0)6 11 75 51 63
Email     contact@hermos.fr
Web       www.hermos.fr

### Le Logis des Monts

The house, picturesquely timbered and behind wrought-iron gates, lies on the edge of a hamlet. The setting is rural; the garden — large, with beehives — is delightful. Here live Françoise, Jean-Pierre and an elegant Spanish greyhound, friendly hosts all. The sitting room is shared (log fireplace, overhead beams) and the immaculate bedrooms are in the guest wing, the cosiest under the eaves. After a fine breakfast served in the conservatory at flexible times, set off for Rouen, Honfleur and glamorous Deauville. Table d'hôtes is offered at weekends — don't miss it: Françoise is an excellent cook.

### Les Clématites

An enchanting *maison de maître*, one of several that housed the nimble-fingered ribbon weavers, with the bonus of fine table d'hôtes. Hidden amid the fields of the Normandy plains, it stands in a dream of a garden, overgrown here, brought to heel there, flanked by a majestic walnut and age-old pears, filled with shrub roses; the odd forgotten bench adds to the Flaubertian charm. Inside, Marie-Hélène, bright-eyed and eager, has used Jouy cloth and elegant colours to dress the country-French bedrooms that fill the first floor. These ex-Parisian hosts are courteous, considerate, truly endearing.

| | |
|---|---|
| Rooms | 2 doubles: €58. |
| | Singles €48. |
| Meals | Dinner with wine, €23. |
| | Light dinner €14 (Mon-Thurs). |
| | Restaurants 7km. |
| Closed | Rarely. |

| | |
|---|---|
| Rooms | 1 double; 1 twin: €72. |
| | 1 triple: €87. |
| Meals | Dinner, 3 courses with wine, 21€. |
| Closed | Rarely. |

Jean-Pierre & Françoise
Hannedouche
Le Logis des Monts,
26 impasse des monts nord,
27520 Theillement, Eure
Tel       +33 (0)2 32 57 25 88
Mobile    +33 (0)6 85 42 38 07
Email     lelogisdesmonts@orange.fr
Web       www.lelogisdesmonts.fr

Marie-Hélène François & Hughes
de Morchoven
Les Clématites,
Hameau de la Charterie,
27230 St Aubin de Scellon, Eure
Tel       +33 (0)2 32 45 46 52
Mobile    +33 (0)6 20 39 08 63
Email     la.charterie@orange.fr
Web       monsite.orange.fr/la.charterie

Entry 198   Map 4

Entry 199   Map 4

## Normandy

### Le Coquerel

Jean-Marc brims with ideas for your stay and love for his garden, modern art and long divine dinners with guests. He has turned the old cottage, surrounded by soft pastures, into a country gem in an exuberant garden: flowers, leafy trees, a water feature behind tall reeds. Inside, a mix of the sober, the frivolous, the cultured and the kitsch: old and modern pieces, rustic revival and leather, masses of art and brocante. Bedrooms stand out in their uncomplicated good taste, bathrooms are being revived, but it's your host who makes the place: duck in cider, lots of laughter, butterflies alighting on the table at breakfast.

| Rooms | 1 double, 1 twin: €65–€75. |
| | 2 family rooms for 4: €85–€105. |
| | 1 triple: €75–€85. |
| Meals | Dinner with wine, €28. |
| | Picnic available. |
| Closed | Rarely. |

|  |  |
| --- | --- |
| | Jean-Marc Drumel |
| | Le Coquerel, |
| | 27560 St Siméon |
| | Eure |
| Tel | +33 (0)2 32 56 56 08 |
| Email | coquerel27@nordnet.fr |
| Web | www.chambredhoteducoquerel.com |

Entry 200   Map 4

## Normandy

### Les Sources Bleues

A privileged setting on the banks of the Seine just below Rouen: once every four years the great armada comes sailing by. The garden (old trees, long grasses, the odd goat, sheep and pig) is 50m from the water's edge and there are binoculars for birdwatching. This Panda (WWF) house is for guests only: the owner lives next door. Old-fashioned bedrooms are in need of a lick of paint but have a certain charm, the family rooms are squeezed into the attic, and Monsieur, a great host, cooks beautifully if you fancy table d'hôtes – genuine Normandy style. There's a kitchen/diner for guests, and a sitting room too.

| Rooms | 2 suites for 3: €58–€70. |
| | 2 quadruples: €80. |
| Meals | Dinner €20. |
| | Wine €12–€15; cider €5. |
| | Kitchen available. |
| Closed | Rarely. |

|  |  |
| --- | --- |
| | Yves Laurent |
| | Les Sources Bleues, |
| | Le Bourg, |
| | 27500 Aizier |
| | Eure |
| Tel | +33 (0)2 32 57 26 68 |
| Mobile | +33 (0)6 80 62 84 31 |
| Web | www.les-sources-bleues.com |

Entry 201   Map 4

## Normandy

### Château de Saint Maclou la Campagne

These days, the proud brick and limestone mansion is more peaceful than in the past, yet it's every bit as deliciously luxurious. Warm British hosts welcome guests into a wood-panelled drawing room where you can admire porcelains, portraits and family photographs – and snuggle before a winter fire. Breakfast at a fine mahogany table; waft up to gorgeous bedrooms in apple green, mushroom, apricot or sunny yellow, and bathrooms that are thoroughly 21st-century. A dry moat encircles the château; beyond lie vast lawns interspersed with neat hedges, an orchard and a dovecote. A fascinating slice of history in tranquil surroundings. *Whole house available.*

| Rooms | 1 double, 3 twin/doubles: €175–€225. Extra bed/sofabed €50 per person per night. |
| Meals | Breakfast €12.50. Restaurant within walking distance. |
| Closed | Rarely. |

**Robin Gage**
Château de Saint Maclou la Campagne
352 rue Émile Desson,
27210 Saint Maclou
Eure

| Tel | +33 (0)2 32 57 26 62 |
| Mobile | +33 (0)6 75 96 87 74 |
| Email | info@chateaudesaintmaclou.com |
| Web | www.chateaudesaintmaclou.com |

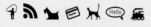

## Normandy

### Ailleurs sous les Étoiles

In an idyllic setting of orchards and pastures is a 19th-century farmhouse with two half-timbered cottages – a bucolic spot for Normandy B&B. The grounds are landscaped and large, there's a heated pool for all to share, and the only sounds you'll hear are the braying of the donkey, the odd tractor, and the birds. Denis (ex-hospitality) and Isabelle (fashion) have created two immaculate light-filled bedrooms, one in the eaves, both with tip-top bathrooms and pretty green views. Exemplary breakfast includes homemade brioche and orchard fruits. For dinner you can pop into neighbouring Beuzeville or bustling Honfleur.

| Rooms | 2 doubles: €95–€130. Singles €95–€120. Extra bed/sofabed €10 per person per night. |
| Meals | Restaurants 3.5km. |
| Closed | Rarely. |

**Isabelle & Denis Block**
Ailleurs sous les Étoiles,
616 route de l'Ermitage,
La Petite Campagne,
27210 Manneville la Raoult
Eure

| Tel | +33 (0)2 77 18 53 80 |
| Email | contact@ailleurssouslesetoiles.com |
| Web | www.ailleurssouslesetoiles.com |

## Logis Saint Léonard

A seductive little place, in delightful, painterly Honfleur. Behind the plain façade all is pretty, cosy, stylish and interesting; oriental art and rugs, unusual ceramics, contrasting fabrics. You wind up a narrow stair to the rooms; both are attractive, the top-floor one the star of the show with a rooftop terrace and port and estuary views. Shower rooms are neat and spotless. Breakfast well in the gentle L-shaped sitting/dining room with its open fire and view of the sheltered, flower-tumbling garden. Anne-Marie, whose creation this is, also runs a much-praised restaurant in town. Deauville and Trouville are close.
*Minimum stay: 2 nights.*

| Rooms | 2 doubles each with separate wc: €125–€155. Singles €125–€155. |
| --- | --- |
| Meals | Restaurants within walking distance. |
| Closed | Rarely. |

**Anne-Marie Carneiro**
Logis Saint Léonard,
39 rue St Léonard,
14600 Honfleur
Calvados

| Mobile | +33 (0)6 63 72 72 38 |
| --- | --- |
| Email | annecarneiro@aol.com |
| Web | www.logis-saint-leonard.com |

Entry 204   Map 4

## Le Clos Bourdet

Welcome to chic, charming B&B, off a residential street, in a big hilly garden high above town. Françoise ran a tea room for 25 years, Jean-Claude is a photographer whose black-and-white prints beautify elegant rooms. Tall windows pull in the light in a sitting room heaving with books, crowned by a chandelier. Wend your way up the corkscrew staircase (past a collection of vintage bird cages that catch the eye) to bedrooms with antique wicker chairs on seagrass floors and soft-raspberry walls showing off turquoise taffeta. There are monsoon showers and a big terrace view... such fun to be in historic Honfleur!
*Minimum stay: 2 nights at weekends.*

| Rooms | 4 doubles: €125–€180. 1 suite for 2: €190. Extra bed €35 per person per night. |
| --- | --- |
| Meals | Restaurants within walking distance. |
| Closed | Never. |

**Françoise Osmont**
Le Clos Bourdet,
50 rue Bourdet,
14600 Honfleur
Calvados

| Tel | +33 (0)2 31 89 49 11 |
| --- | --- |
| Mobile | +33 (0)6 07 48 99 67 |
| Email | info@leclosbourdet.com |
| Web | www.leclosbourdet.com |

Entry 205   Map 4

# Normandy

## Au Grey d'Honfleur

There's a fairytale feel to this pair of tall narrow houses in a quiet cobbled backstreet. You don't quite know what to expect but you know you're somewhere rare and special. Inside, stairs and steps in all directions link little rooms; age-old beams and sloping ceilings contrast with imaginative décor and modern luxury. Josette, a globe-trotting lawyer, knows a thing or two about what's required of a guest bedroom… Looking down over the haphazard roofs of medieval Honfleur, the miniature terraced garden and fountain, delightfully formal, add to the pleasure. Breakfasts are divine.
*Minimum stay: 2 nights.*

| Rooms | 2 doubles: €125–€160. |
|---|---|
| Meals | Restaurants within walking distance. |
| Closed | Rarely. |

**Josette Roudaut**
Au Grey d'Honfleur,
11 rue de la Bavole,
14600 Honfleur
Calvados
Mobile  +33 (0)6 85 07 50 45
Email  info@augrey-honfleur.com
Web  www.augrey-honfleur.com

# Normandy

## La Cour Ste Catherine

Through the Norman gateway into the sun-drenched courtyard; Liliane and history embrace you. The building was first a convent, then fishermen's cottages, later a *cidrerie*. Now this historic quarter is a conservation area and all has been properly restored. Breakfast viennoiseries are served in the huge beamed room where the apples were once pressed; sip a summery aperitif in the courtyard with fellow guests. Bedrooms are sunny, airy, impeccable, contemporary, one in the hayloft with its own outside stair. There's a small sitting room for guests and Honfleur at your feet; your charming hosts know the town intimately.

| Rooms | 2 doubles, 1 twin/double: €90–€110. 1 family room for 4: €170. 1 triple: €140–€170. Extra bed €30 per person per night. |
|---|---|
| Meals | Restaurants nearby. |
| Closed | Rarely. |

**Liliane & Antoine Giaglis**
La Cour Ste Catherine,
74 rue du Puits,
14600 Honfleur
Calvados
Tel  +33 (0)2 31 89 42 40
Email  coursaintecatherine@orange.fr
Web  www.coursaintecatherine.com

# Normandy

## Bergerie de la Moutonnière

Sheep still graze behind this charming old bergerie, in the grounds of your hospitable Dutch hosts' manor house. Great independence here: a rustic, open summer kitchen and super bathroom below, and a spacious suite above, tidy and homely beneath lofty rafters, with a wooden floor and colombage walls, two armchairs, a sofa and a super-comfortable bed. Colours are gentle and warm, heating comes from a wood-burning stove and children are welcome. After walking, cider-making, Trouville and golf, return to beautiful, peaceful grounds, with smart wooden dining furniture and a barbecue on request.

| Rooms | 1 suite for 2: €85–€100. |
|---|---|
| Meals | Breakfast €7.50. |
| | Summer kitchen. Restaurants 4km. |
| Closed | Rarely. |

Rudolf Walthaus
Bergerie de la Moutonnière,
Le Mesnil, 14590 Le Pin
Calvados
Tel      +33 (0)2 31 62 56 86
Email    walthaus@mac.com
Web      www.bergerienormandy.com

Entry 208   Map 4

# Normandy

## La Cerisée

In glamorous, horsey Deauville, a wee garden cottage all to yourselves: kitchen/living room downstairs, airy blond bedroom up. And now there's a peaceful, pretty bedroom in the main house too, with an alcove shower in the corner and tall French windows to a tiny balcony overlooking the street. The house is a cosy, uncomplicated and imaginative mix of new-simple and antique-reclaimed – plus Isabelle's driftwood art. She is elegantly informal and stores her raw materials on the flowery patio that you share with her. A simple treasure in Deauville – bursting with beaches, bicycle outings, markets and luscious seafood.

| Rooms | 1 cottage for 2: €130–€150. |
|---|---|
| | 1 double: €100. |
| | Extra person €20 per night. |
| Meals | Restaurants within walking distance. |
| Closed | 1 January – 28 February. |

Isabelle Quinones
La Cerisée,
15 rue du Général Leclerc,
14800 Deauville
Calvados
Tel      +33 (0)2 31 81 18 29
Mobile   +33 (0)6 83 16 51 19
Email    la.cerisee@hotmail.fr
Web      www.chambre-hotes-deauville.com

Entry 209   Map 4

# Normandy

## La Longère

There are two stars in this show: the whirlwind Fabienne who decorates everything from tables to crockery and delivers breakfast feasts (a party every morning!), and the seductively long, low, half-timbered 17th-century farmhouse. Fabienne and her as-generous husband throw open their home and sheltered garden, join you for dinner and perhaps drinks on the terrace; she also happily babysits. Smallish rooms are pretty with quilts and hand-painted furniture, tiles or polished floorboards; children will love the hideaway mezzanine in the family suite. An endearing hostess, and beaches five minutes away. *Minimum stay: 2 nights at weekends.*

| Rooms | 2 doubles: €80–€160. |
| | Wing – 1 family room for 4, |
| | 1 family room for 5: €80–€160. |
| Meals | Dinner with wine, €28. |
| | Restaurant within walking distance. |
| Closed | Rarely. |

Fabienne Fillion
La Longère,
Chemin de la Libération,
14800 Bonneville sur Touques
Calvados

| Tel | +33 (0)2 31 64 10 29 |
| Mobile | +33 (0)6 08 04 38 52 |
| Email | fafillion@wanadoo.fr |
| Web | www.lalongerenormandie.com |

# Normandy

## Clos St Hymer

A typical long and low Normandy cottage on the edge of the village, with pale green shutters and a terracotta roof. Ever-welcoming Françoise has been doing B&B for years and serves simple breakfasts with homemade jams in the kitchen/diner, or outside on the front terrace on sunny days. Simple bedrooms (one has a balcony and is large enough for an extra child's bed) are on the first floor under sloping ceilings: find plain quilted bedspreads, some vibrant colours, good views and spotless shower rooms. You're near good restaurants, sandy beaches, country markets and lush countryside; WW1 landing beaches can be visited on a day trip. *Child's bed available.*

| Rooms | 2 doubles: €80–€95. |
| Meals | Restaurants 5km. |
| Closed | January. |

Françoise Valle
Clos St Hymer,
14130 Le Torquesne
Calvados

| Tel | +33 (0)2 31 61 99 15 |
| Mobile | +33 (0)6 30 56 57 90 |
| Email | leclossthymer@wanadoo.fr |
| Web | www.leclossainthymer.com |

# Normandy

## Manoir de Cantepie

It may have a make-believe face, among the smooth green curves of racehorse country, but it is genuine early 1600s and astonishing from all sides. Inside, an astounding dining room, resplendently carved, panelled and painted, serves for tasty organic breakfasts. Bedrooms, all amazing value, have a sunny feel, and are delightful: one with white-painted beams and green toile de Jouy, another in yellows, a third with a glorious valley view. Madame, a beautiful Swedish lady, made the curtains and covers. She and her husband are well-travelled, polyglot and cultured: they make their B&B doubly special.

| | |
|---|---|
| Rooms | 3 doubles: €75. |
| Meals | Restaurant 1km. |
| Closed | Mid-November to February. |

Christine & Arnauld Gherrak
Manoir de Cantepie,
Le Cadran,
14340 Cambremer
Calvados
Tel +33 (0)2 31 62 87 27
Email c.gherrak@dbmail.com
Web www.manoir-de-cantepie.jimdo.com

Entry 212   Map 4

# Normandy

## Le Fresnay

Playfully guarded by a flock of sculpted sheep, this beautiful half-timbered manor house stands proudly in acres of pastures, orchard, woodland and garden. Courteous Italian owner Mr Fabra has created a chic, peaceful sanctuary in the Normandy countryside. Breakfast on pastries and home-produced honey; sleep in stylish terracotta-floored rooms with stone fireplaces and contemporary bathrooms. Gently wake to birdsong and the prospect of a day exploring the Cider Trail or local markets. In the evenings, read by the open fire in one of the sumptuous sitting rooms or drive to a nearby village for dinner. Bliss.

| | |
|---|---|
| Rooms | 3 doubles, 2 twin/doubles: €90–€110. |
| Meals | Restaurants 2.5km. |
| Closed | Never. |

M Fabra
Le Fresnay,
2630 chemin d'Englesqueville,
14340 Cambremer
Calvados
Mobile +33 (0)6 89 82 95 40
Email lefresnay@gmail.com

Entry 213   Map 4

# Normandy

## Château de Bénéauville

Down the plane-flanked drive to an immaculate Renaissance château in harmonious grounds. Find painted 17th-century beams in perfect condition, heads of antelope and oryx surprising the walls, a panelled library, a powder-blue dining room, and fireplaces imposing and theatrical. Here live the Augais family, with horse, hens and handsome gundogs. In big peaceful bedrooms with tall windows are chestnut floors and grey-washed beams, oriental carpets, quilted bedspreads, boudoir armchairs, deep baths (with shower attachments) and exquisite curtain tassels. Take a dip in the discreet pool; set off for culture in Caen. Marvellous.

| Rooms | 3 doubles (2 can join to form suite), 1 twin (extends into a suite): €190–€270. |
|---|---|
| Meals | Restaurants 5km. |
| Closed | 1 October – 1 June. |

**Philippe Augais**
Château de Bénéauville,
Bénéauville, 14860 Bavent
Calvados
Tel       +33 (0)2 31 72 56 49
Email     reservation@chateaudebeneauville.fr
Web       www.chateaudebeneauville.fr

Entry 214   Map 4

# Normandy

## Bed In Normandy

Your smiling hostess brings breakfast to your barn in a barrow… or to her long rustic table: an elegant feast of homemade cakes, breads, Normandy cheeses, fresh fruits and garden cherries in season. A half-timbered manor house, a beautiful décor, a deep rural setting (this was a cider farm), and verdurous grounds with a pool; the place is fabulous! As for your barn, it's a stunner: the living area and kitchen below and the bedroom snug under the rafters, with a claw-foot tub centre stage and a separate shower. Come home to sheepskin rugs, faux-fur blankets, naïf paintings, great books, and a wood-burner packed with logs.

| Rooms | 1 suite for 2-4: €140–€150. |
|---|---|
| Meals | Restaurant 4 km. |
| Closed | Rarely. |

**Marie Laure Heuzey**
Bed In Normandy,
Départementale 80,
14430 Brocottes
Calvados
Mobile    +33 (0)6 64 84 33 23
Email     bedinnormandy@orange.fr
Web       www.bedinnormandy.com

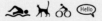

Entry 215   Map 4

Normandy

## Château du Mesnil d'O

The approach to this 18th-century château lifts the spirit. Stone pillars and tall iron gates mark the entrance: the setting is lovely. Bedrooms scented by fresh flowers are on the first floor up a staircase of white Caen stone with a wrought-iron handrail and balustrade. A landing with a view over the park is the perfect place to spread your newspaper on a lovely old table; bookshelves bursting with books line the length of one wall, family portraits line the corridors. Breakfast is taken in the dining room with painted scenes above the doors and a Louis XVI buffet displaying its collection of beautiful china plates.

| Rooms | 3 doubles: €110. |
| | 1 suite for 4: €170. |
| Meals | Restaurants within 5km. |
| Closed | Rarely. |

**Guy de Chabaneix**
Château du Mesnil d'O,
14270 Vieux Fumé
Calvados
Tel        +33 (0)2 31 20 01 47
Email      lemesnildo@wanadoo.fr
Web        www.lemesnildo.com

Entry 216   Map 4

Normandy

## Ferme de la Ruette

The gates glide open to a gravelled sweep and a tree'd lawn, with an old stone cider press to the side. Elegant, compassionate Isabelle looks after house, garden, guests – and rescue cats and horses – with warmth and charm; Philippe, a friendly GP, fills the game larder. The barn houses two bedrooms plus a delightful family suite under the rafters (up a steep private stair) and a cosy guest sitting room with a bar. Rooms have pretty striped wallpapers, seagrass floors and elegant Louis XV-style chairs, quirky *objets* on shelves and in crannies, beds dressed with white heirloom spreads. Vivacious, bustling Caen is an easy drive.

| Rooms | 2 doubles: €60–€80. |
| | 1 family suite for 4 with |
| | kitchenette: €60–€80. |
| | Extra bed €10 per person per night. |
| Meals | Restaurant 5km. |
| Closed | Rarely. |

**Isabelle & Philippe Cayé**
Ferme de la Ruette,
5 chemin Haussé,
14190 Cauvicourt
Calvados
Tel        +33 (0)2 31 78 11 82
Mobile     +33 (0)6 28 26 22 61
Email      laruette@gmail.com
Web        www.fermedelaruette.fr

Entry 217   Map 4

### Château des Riffets

Period ceilings and parkland views make Riffets a gracious château experience. Admire yourself in myriad mirrors, luxuriate in a jacuzzi, bare your chest to a supersonic shower and lie, at last, in an antique bed. The walls of the huge hall and the galleried landing are an elegant foil for tapestries, plants and austere antique pieces. Wry Monsieur was a psychologist, gentle Madame an English teacher, and a fine breakfast is served at one big table. Take a stroll in the park, hire a nearby horse or a canoe, enjoy a lap in the pool. Caen's historic treasures are a ten-minute drive, Bayeux and Mont St Michel are an hour away.

### Château La Cour

Welcome to a 13th-century castle, once owned by the Ducs d'Harcourt, full of comfort and joy. There are Lloyd Loom chairs and marble fireplaces, one bedroom has a curved stair to a lavish bathroom, the apartment is stunning and every room faces the garden. Breakfast includes home-grown fruits, homemade yogurt and eggs from the château's hens, while English china, damask and candelabra grace the dinner table. David's potager is a wonder; Lesley's cooking is delicious. The Cravens are conservationists, too; barn owls nest in the end wall and the birdwatching is fabulous. Don't miss the Normandy beaches, or Bayeux. *Children over 12 welcome.*

| | | | |
|---|---|---|---|
| Rooms | 2 doubles, 2 suites for 2: €125–€175. | Rooms | 3 doubles, 1 twin: €150. |
| Meals | Restaurant 1km. | Meals | Dinner with wine, €35–€50. |
| Closed | Rarely. | Closed | Rarely. |

FIRST
EDITION
VETERAN

**Anne-Marie & Alain Cantel**
Château des Riffets,
14680 Bretteville sur Laize
Calvados
Tel      +33 (0)2 31 23 53 21
Mobile   +33 (0)6 14 09 74 93
Email    chateau.riffets@wanadoo.fr
Web     www.chateau-des-riffets.com

**David & Lesley Craven**
Château La Cour,
14220 Culey le Patry
Calvados
Tel     +33 (0)2 31 79 19 37
Email   info@chateaulacour.com
Web    www.chateaulacour.com

Entry 218   Map 4

Entry 219   Map 4

## Normandy

### Le Gaudin

Shooting through the centre of this 18th-century farmhouse is a chimney of 4,500 bricks. Clive knows: he built it! Every feature conveys space, age and the care and creativity of your British hosts. Exposed stone walls; an old manger, now a wine rack; Denise's upholstered coffee table; a doll's house in the sunny breakfast room, and the long table at which guests gather for Clive's superb dinners. Sophisticated bedrooms, delighting in hand-sewn fabrics, are a fanfare of colours. Pilgrims to Mont St Michel once filled their bottles at the stream in the wooded grounds; many attractions are close. No wonder people return.

| Rooms | 3 doubles, 1 twin: €70–€90. |
|---|---|
| Meals | Dinner with wine, €38. |
| Closed | January – March. |

**Clive & Denise Canvin**
Le Gaudin,
Route d'Aunay,
14260 Campandré Valcongrain
Calvados
Tel   +33 (0)2 31 73 88 70
Email   legaudin14@yahoo.co.uk
Web   www.legaudin.co.uk

## Normandy

### Ferme Le Petit Val

Close to landing beaches, village markets, the Bayeux Tapestry and jolly Caen is this perfectly maintained and very French farmstead, Outside, shrubs, conifers and a profusion of flowers; inside, country comfort and handsome furniture. It's been in the family for six generations, all is immaculate and the Lesages look after you with an easy charm. Off a Frenchly wallpapered landing, with views of garden and pretty gravelled courtyard, are the two biggest and most characterful bedrooms. Expect good china and jams at breakfast's long tables, tourist brochures on the sideboard, mountain bikes to borrow.

| Rooms | 1 double: €63–€73. |
|---|---|
| | 1 family room for 3: €63–€99. |
| | Barn – 1 double, 1 twin: €63–€73. |
| | Barn – 1 family room for 3: €63–€99. |
| | Singles €59. |
| | Extra bed/sofabed €26 per person per night. |
| Meals | Restaurants 3km. |
| Closed | December – March. |

**Gérard et Anne Lesage**
Ferme Le Petit Val,
24 rue du Camp Romain,
14480 Banville
Calvados
Tel   +33 (0)2 31 37 92 18
Mobile   +33 (0)6 87 03 85 52
Email   fermelepetitval@wanadoo.fr
Web   www.ferme-le-petitval.com

# Normandy

## La Malposte

It's just plain lovely, this little group of stone buildings with a wooden footbridge over the rushing river, ancient steps, moss, trees, a fine garden with flowers and hens. The age-old converted mill is for the family, the hunting lodge (and an enchanting annexe) is for guests. Patricia's talented decoration weaves nostalgia with designer tones; the spiral stair winds to an enchanting dayroom with guest kitchen and homemade preserves (superb fig jam); sun pours into the bedroom at the top. Woods for nut-gathering, beaches nearby, table tennis and that playful stream. Your hosts are sweet and love having families.

| Rooms | Lodge – 2 doubles: €88. |
| | Lodge – 1 family room for 3, |
| | 1 family room for 4: €108–€144. |
| | 1 annexe for 4: €144. |
| Meals | Guest kitchen. Restaurants 2km. |
| Closed | Rarely. |

**Patricia & Jean-Michel Blanlot**
La Malposte,
15 rue des Moulins,
14470 Reviers
Calvados
Tel     +33 (0)2 31 37 51 29
Email   jean-michel.blanlot@wanadoo.fr
Web     www.lamalposte.com

Entry 222   Map 4

# Normandy

## Le Mas Normand

A fun place, warm and colourful, run with great charm by Mylène and Christian. They've done a fine job on their 18th-century house: old stonework and beams, super showers, a modern-rustic style, and Provençal fabrics and soaps from Mylène's native Drôme. Bedrooms are sheer delight: the sunny much-furnished double on the ground floor, the charming suite across the yard, filled with good pieces including an 'armoire de mariage'. The new family room? A delightful fisherman's caravan in the garden, with a great shower. Ducks, geese and hens roam; the beach is 300 yards. Generous and special.

| Rooms | 1 double: €80. |
| | 2 suites for 2-4: €100–€150. |
| | Extra charge for pets. |
| Meals | Restaurants nearby. |
| Closed | Rarely. |

**Christian Mériel & Mylène Gilles**
Le Mas Normand,
8 impasse de la Rivière,
14114 Ver sur Mer
Calvados
Tel     +33 (0)2 31 21 97 75
Email   lemasnormand@wanadoo.fr
Web     www.lemasnormand.com

Entry 223   Map 4

# Normandy

## Les Glycines

This lovely couple are kindness itself, she softly spoken and twinkling, he jovial, talkative, utterly French. Having retired from farming, they moved into the heart of Bayeux. You can glimpse the cathedral spires from their house, once part of the old bishop's palace. Beyond the gates and the wisteria, the door opens to a lofty beamed living room rejoicing in good antiques and a monumental fireplace; through another is the kitchen. Up the ancient stone stairs are pretty bedrooms – immaculate bedding, pastel-tiled showers – that look quietly over a pocket-handkerchief garden. Delicious breakfasts, history all around, and no need for a car.

| | |
|---|---|
| Rooms | 2 doubles: €69. |
| | 1 family room for 3: €95. |
| | Singles €59. |
| Meals | Restaurant within walking distance. |
| Closed | Rarely. |

FIRST
EDITION
VETERAN

| | |
|---|---|
| | **Louis & Annick Fauvel** |
| | Les Glycines, |
| | 13 rue aux Coqs, |
| | 14400 Bayeux |
| | Calvados |
| Tel | +33 (0)2 31 22 52 32 |
| Mobile | +33 (0)6 89 39 84 79 |
| Email | louisfauvel@orange.fr |

Entry 224   Map 4

# Normandy

## Clos de Bellefontaine

Come to be pampered and effortlessly spoiled at this elegant townhouse, a ten-minute stroll from the famous Tapestry. Bedrooms are chic and gracious with choice antiques, colours are mocha and white, floors polished parquet or seagrass. Choose the top floor for snugness and charm, the first floor for grandeur and space. With a walled garden and two handsome ground-floor salons – antiques, family photographs, help-yourself refreshments – to lounge around in, you'll not miss home. Carole's breakfasts, with homemade tarts, fruit compotes and cheeses, are the highlight of the stay.

| | |
|---|---|
| Rooms | 1 double, 1 twin: €135–€175. |
| | Extra bed/sofabed €20 per person |
| | per night. |
| Meals | Restaurants nearby. |
| Closed | Rarely. |

| | |
|---|---|
| | **Carole & Jérôme Mallet** |
| | Clos de Bellefontaine, |
| | 6 rue de Bellefontaine, |
| | 14400 Bayeux |
| | Calvados |
| Mobile | +33 (0)6 81 42 24 81 |
| Email | clos.bellefontaine@wanadoo.fr |
| Web | www.clos-bellefontaine.fr |

Entry 225   Map 4

# Normandy

### Le Château

The château dates proudly from 1580; once, Emile Zola stayed. In the yard, now restored to tremendous shape and character as a garden area for guests, an ancient arched barn houses three beamy bedrooms (admire astounding roof timbers through a trap window). Just beyond the flowering stone steps, the fourth room is in a tiny cottage. These country-elegant rooms are beautiful in Jouy and stripes, restful and private. Madame is a vibrantly warm, well-read, eco-friendly person, who speaks good English, loves having guests and can discourse at fascinating length about the Vikings, the Inuit, the Dukes of Normandy...

| Rooms | 2 doubles, 1 twin, 1 suite for 5: €70-€85. |
|---|---|
| Meals | Dinner with wine or cider, €35. Child €20. Restaurants nearby. |
| Closed | December to mid-January. |

**Dominique Bernières**
Le Château,
Chemin du Château,
14450 Grandcamp Maisy
Calvados

Tel +33 (0)2 31 22 66 22
Email dominiquebernieres@orange.fr
Web perso.wanadoo.fr/alain.marion/gbindex.html

# Normandy

### Ferme-Manoir de la Rivière

Breakfast by the massive fireplace may be oil lamp-lit on winter mornings in this 13th-century fortress of a dairy farm, with its ancient tithe barn and little watchtower. Isabelle is proud of her family home, its flagstones worn smooth with age, its high vaulted stone living-room ceiling, its second-floor rooms, one narrow with a shower in a tower, another with exposed beams and *ciel de lit* drapes. Her energy boundless, she is ever improving her rooms, gives you homemade brioche for breakfast and imaginative Norman cuisine — much supported by delightful Gérard.

| Rooms | 1 double: €65-€75. 2 triples: €65-€75. |
|---|---|
| Meals | Dinner with cider or wine, €27. |
| Closed | Rarely. |

**Gérard & Isabelle Leharivel**
Ferme-Manoir de la Rivière,
14230 Géfosse Fontenay
Calvados

Tel +33 (0)2 31 22 64 45
Mobile +33 (0)6 81 58 25 21
Email leharivel@wanadoo.fr
Web www.lemanoirdelariviere.net

# Normandy

# Normandy

## Manoir de la Fèvrerie

Your blithe, beautiful, energetic hostess is a delight, forever indulging her passion for interior decoration. Her exquisite rooms are a festival of colours, textures, antiques and embroidered linen. It's a heart-warming experience to stay in this wonderful old Normandy farmhouse where the great granite hearth is always lit and a breakfast of superb local specialities is served on elegant china; there is a richly carved 'throne' at the head of the long table. Find a deep courtyard at the entrance, a pretty garden behind; soft countryside surrounds you and Barfleur and the coast is a short drive.

## Manoir de la Fieffe

An idyllic manor, minutes from Cherbourg. Michel and Emmanuel chose this spot for its beauty and temperate climate and are developing four hectares of botanical garden; already splendid. Breakfasts on the terrace, or elegantly indoors, are a treat with the best fruit and pastries. High-ceilinged bedrooms are a delight too; homely and luxurious with garden views, soft colours, elegant embroidered headboards on big, comfortable beds, writing desks and Persian rugs on wooden floors. Bathrooms are top-stylish-notch. Research your visits under the library chandelier: a coastal walk? A local Michelin-starred restaurant?

| | |
|---|---|
| Rooms | 3 twin/doubles (children's room available in main house): €72–€80. |
| Meals | Restaurants 3km. |
| Closed | Rarely. |

| | |
|---|---|
| Rooms | 1 double: €115–€130. |
| | 1 suite for 3: €105–€120. |
| | 1 family room for 3: €98–€110. |
| Meals | Restaurants 3km. |
| Closed | Rarely. |

Marie-France Caillet
Manoir de la Fèvrerie,
4 route d'Arville,
50760 Ste Geneviève
Manche

| | |
|---|---|
| Tel | +33 (0)2 33 54 33 53 |
| Mobile | +33 (0)6 80 85 89 01 |
| Email | lafevrerie@orange.fr |
| Web | www.lafevrerie.fr |

Emmanuel de La Fonchais
Manoir de la Fieffe,
Rue Lefèvre et Toulorge,
50470 La Glacerie
Manche

| | |
|---|---|
| Tel | +33 (0)2 33 20 81 45 |
| Mobile | +33 (0)6 15 06 83 42 |
| Email | accueil@manoirdelafieffe.com |
| Web | www.manoirdelafieffe.com |

# Normandy

## Bruce Castle

Live graciously — even if it's only for a stopover (Cherbourg is 15km away). The Fontanets are a charming and amusing couple and their 1914 neo-classical mansion is full of pretty antiques. From the restrained elegance of the hall a handsome white staircase sweeps up to big, serene bedrooms with garden and woodland views; oriental rugs and crystal chandeliers add another dash of luxury. Breakfast off white porcelain with antique silver cutlery in a charming dining room then retire to the elegant 'library' overlooking the gardens. In the 20-acre grounds are the ruins of an 11th-century castle… to stay here is a treat.

# Normandy

## Manoir de Bellauney

Even the smallest bathroom oozes atmosphere through its *œil de bœuf*. The youngest piece of this fascinating and venerably ancient house is over 400 years old; its predecessor stood on the site of a monastery, and the fireplace in the lovely medieval bedroom carries the coat of arms of the original owners. To furnish the rooms, your ex-farmer hosts hunted out carved *armoires de mariage*, lace canopies, footstools, and hung tapestry curtains at the windows. They share their energy enthusiastically between this wonderful house, its small dense garden, and their guests. Sheer comfort among warm old stones.

| | |
|---|---|
| Rooms | 3 doubles: €110–€130. |
| Meals | Restaurant 8km. |
| | Simple bistro 3km. |
| Closed | Rarely. |

| | |
|---|---|
| Rooms | 1 double: €70–€100. |
| | 2 suites for 2-3: €70–€120. |
| Meals | Restaurants 4km. |
| Closed | November – April. |

**Anne-Rose & Hugues Fontanet**
Bruce Castle,
13 rue du Castel,
50700 Brix
Manche

| | |
|---|---|
| Tel | +33 (0)2 33 41 99 62 |
| Mobile | +33 (0)6 72 95 74 23 |
| Email | bruce-castle@orange.fr |
| Web | www.bruce-castle.com |

**Christiane & Jacques
Allix-Desfauteaux**
Manoir de Bellauney,
50700 Tamerville
Manche

| | |
|---|---|
| Tel | +33 (0)2 33 40 10 62 |
| Email | bellauney@wanadoo.fr |
| Web | www.bellauney.com |

Entry 230   Map 3

Entry 231   Map 3

# Normandy

## Le Château

Gravel crunches as you sweep up to the imposing granite château on the Cherbourg peninsula. The beguiling fairytale turrets, Françoise's welcome and Bernard's collection of vintage horse-driven carriages (the whole family love horses) soon work their magic. External stone stairs lead to the red-velvet charm of the 'Chambre Château'; ancient chestnut stairs in the converted outbuilding lead to simple family rooms. In the morning, as you breakfast generously in a light-flooded, pink-panelled family dining room and sip your café au lait, you might like to nod a grateful 'merci' to Bernard's obliging Normandy cows.

| Rooms | 2 doubles (in outbuilding): €110–€120. 1 family suite for 4 (in outbuilding): €80–€150. |
| --- | --- |
| Meals | Restaurant within walking distance. |
| Closed | Rarely. |

Françoise Lucas de Vallavieille
Le Château,
50700 Flottemanville Bocage
Manche

| Tel | +33 (0)2 33 40 29 02 |
| --- | --- |
| Mobile | +33 (0)6 99 06 59 82 |
| Email | contact@chateau-flottemanville.com |
| Web | www.chateau-flottemanville.com |

Entry 232   Map 3

# Normandy

*New Entry*

## Le Petit Ruisseau

In the hamlet of Le Douit is a 350-year-old house, rather grand with its own little turret, a delicious piece of Norman history. Linda's welcome is generous and warm, and her knowledge of World War Two second to none; her father-in-law was a renowned photo journalist and his black and white photos are captivating. There are books, antiques, squishy sofas too, and a kitchen with a big old Aga. Linda loves real food so her suppers and dinners reflect the seasons and you eat under the old walnut tree in summer. All this, feather quilts, fresh flowers and deep mattresses, and a young garden backed by pastures – enchanting!

| Rooms | 1 twin/double: €70–€80. |
| --- | --- |
| Meals | Dinner with wine & coffee, €35. Light supper €17.50. Restaurants 4km. |
| Closed | Never. |

Linda Malindine
Le Petit Ruisseau,
9 chemin de L'Église,
50390 Biniville
Manche

| Tel | +33 (0)2 33 41 47 05 |
| --- | --- |
| Email | lande.la@orange.fr |
| Web | www.normandybandb.co.uk |

Entry 233   Map 3

# Normandy

## La Roque de Gouey

A fishing and sailing port and a bridge with 13 arches: a pretty place to stay. The enchanting *longère* is the home of two of our favourite owners: Madame, the same honest open character as ever and Monsieur, retired, who has time to spread his modest farmer's joviality. Your side of the house has its own entrance, dayroom and vast old fireplace where old beams and *tomettes* flourish. The bedrooms up the steepish outside stairs are small, with pretty bedcovers and antiques that are cherished, the ground-floor room is larger, and the breakfast tables sport flowery cloths. Brilliant value.

# Normandy

## Manoir de Coutainville

Secluded rooms with views over rooftops and sparkling seas are a traveller's joy. Add a cultured hostess, delectable dining and a 15th-century manoir and you have a dash of French magic. Through pale stone arches serenity awaits, genteel apéritifs ushering in five-course dinners that showcase fish and seafood. Sophie Véron provides spare wellies and captivating conversation, her fashion career informs her calm interiors – a rare mix of charm and luxury – and history resonates through every sea-view room. Downstairs in the annexe find library armchairs and a scullery kitchen. Stroll to Coutainville, watch the sailing boats.

| Rooms | 2 doubles: €57. 1 family room for 3, 1 family room for 5: €75-€110. |
| --- | --- |
| Meals | Guest kitchen. Restaurants within walking distance. |
| Closed | Rarely. |

FIRST EDITION VETERAN

Bernadette Vasselin
La Roque de Gouey,
Rue Gilles Poërier,
50580 Portbail
Manche
Tel +33 (0)2 33 04 80 27
Email vasselin.portbail@orange.fr

Entry 234 Map 3

| Rooms | Courtyard annexe – 2 doubles; 1 twin with separate shower: €160-€260. 1 suite for 2-4, 1 suite for 2-5: €240-€360. Singles €160-€260. |
| --- | --- |
| Meals | Dinner with wine, €54. |
| Closed | Rarely. |

Sophie Véron
Manoir de Coutainville,
2 rue de la Maugerie,
50230 Agon Coutainville
Manche
Tel +33 (0)2 33 47 05 90
Mobile +33 (0)6 07 55 29 77
Email sophie-veron@manoir-de-coutainville.com
Web www.manoir-de-coutainville.com

Entry 235 Map 3

Normandy

## La Vimonderie

Sigrid's big country kitchen and crackling fire are the heart of this fine 18th-century granite house and you know instantly you are sharing her home: the built-in dresser carries pretty china, her pictures and ornaments bring interest to the salon and its Normandy fireplace, and she proudly tells how she rescued the superb elm staircase. A fascinating person, for years a potter in England, she has retired to France and vegetarian happiness; she loves to cook for guests. Bedrooms have colour, unusual antiques and original beams. Five acres of garden mean plenty of space for children and grown-ups alike. Great value. *Minimum stay: 2 nights.*

| Rooms | 2 doubles: €50. |
|---|---|
| Meals | Dinner with wine, from €18. Light supper from €10. Picnics from €5. Guest kitchen. |
| Closed | January/February. |

Sigrid Hamilton
La Vimonderie,
50620 Cavigny
Manche

| Tel | +33 (0)2 33 56 01 13 |
| Mobile | +33 (0)6 59 21 48 07 |
| Email | sigrid.hamilton@googlemail.com |
| Web | www.lavimonderie.com |

Entry 236   Map 3

Normandy

## La Thiaumerie

With a wink of its green shutters, this pretty stone farmhouse welcomes you in from the Normandy countryside – to a beamed sitting room with a big fireplace and three immaculate bedrooms with cuddly duvets and kettles. All are special: pink-and-white 'Picardie' with its sofa; 'Grenier' with extra beds in the eaves; cosy 'Blue' downstairs. Michael and Sally have spent many happy years here and, over a breakfast of fresh fruit, yoghurt and yummy croissants, offer tips on restaurants, beaches, historical sites – you're close to all. Trees and flowers surround a garden room and terrace, perfect for a picnic supper of seafood and white wine. *Children over 12 welcome.*

| Rooms | 1 double; 1 double with separate bathroom: €80-€90. 1 family suite for 4: €85-€150. Singles €60-€65. |
|---|---|
| Meals | Dinner €17-€27.50. Restaurant 3km. |
| Closed | 1 November – 1 March. |

Sally Byrne
La Thiaumerie,
50420 St Louet sur Vire
Manche

| Tel | +33 (0)2 33 55 48 81 |
| Email | normandyvacation@gmail.com |
| Web | www.vacances-normandes.co.uk |

Entry 237   Map 3

# Normandy

## Manoir de la Porte

A pepperpot turret gives a medieval flourish to the sturdy, creeper-dressed 16th-century manoir. There's a Japanese bridge to the jungly island, a large and luscious garden, two bright, romantic top-floor bedrooms with old-fashioned bathrooms and a tempting sitting area; a fabulously ancient, tiled dining room with huge fireplace, a trio of tables and solid granite walls. Add ethnic rugs and a pair of curly-toed Rajasthani slippers on the stone stairs. Your friendly, chatty, ex-army hosts are great travellers. And Madame is a keen and gifted cook – championing all things local. Breakfast is typically French.

| Rooms | 2 family rooms for 3: €80–€95. |
|---|---|
| Meals | Dinner with wine, €21. |
| | Kitchen available. |
| Closed | Rarely. |

Annick & Hervé Lagadec
Manoir de la Porte,
50870 Ste Pience
Manche
Tel    +33 (0)2 33 68 13 61
Email  manoir.de.la.porte@wanadoo.fr
Web   www.manoir-de-la-porte.com

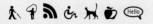

# Normandy

## 2 Le Bois de Crépi

Madame's welcome is as cheerful and bright as her bedrooms – and she loves to cook. The Gavards' immaculate 1980s house, resting in one pretty acre (lawns, roses, little footbridge over the pond) is the perfect stopover: near the autoroute yet truly tranquil. Borrow bikes and cycle the 'voie verte' to Mont St Michel or spend the day in St Malo. Then come home to friendly table d'hôtes and a great-value menu that reflects the seasons. There's a guest sitting room to retire to, with guide books, games, TV, and bedrooms under the eaves, warm, simple, characterful, with brand new beds and flowers. Bathrooms gleam.

| Rooms | 2 family rooms for 4: €53–€58. |
|---|---|
| | Singles €48. |
| | Extra bed/sofabed €12 per person per night. |
| | Under 3's free. |
| Meals | Dinner, 3 courses with wine, €20. |
| | Child €10. |
| | Restaurants 1km. |
| Closed | Rarely. |

Jean-Paul & Brigitte Gavard
2 Le Bois de Crépi,
Poilley,
50220 Ducey
Manche
Tel     +33 (0)2 33 48 34 68
Mobile  +33 (0)6 65 31 99 99
Email   jpgavard@club-internet.fr

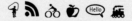

## Orchard Gîtes

At Alison's rose-covered farmhouse, wrapped in bucolic views, you feel you're staying with family – and Fudge, the friendly terrier. Breakfasts, with homemade jams, are in the kitchen; the cosy sitting-room and garden are yours to share. The small simple bedroom under the eaves is colourful and homely, with a window at floor level through which the late afternoon sun pours, and you have a view of an apricot tree. Gardener-turned-artist Alison loves sharing her local knowledge and, on request, cooks delicious suppers from her 'potager'. Simple, unshowy, with a garden of quiet places in which to dream. *Pets by arrangement.*

## Belle Vallée

Built in 1800, the tall house stands in acres of woods, pastures and landscaped gardens, with outbuildings (the owners' quarters) and cottage. Footpaths meander to a lovely walled orchard, the kitchen garden provides for table d'hôtes, the hens donate the eggs. Inside are corridors alive with books, five delightful bedrooms – vintage beds, polished floors, boudoir chairs, divine duvets – and an inviting sitting room with a log fire. In the panelled dining room, hospitable Richard and Victoria, both from the catering industry, serve French breakfasts at crisp tables. Domfront on its hill is wonderfully close.

| | |
|---|---|
| Rooms | 1 double with separate, private bathroom: €45-€50. Singles €40-€45. |
| Meals | Dinner €15. |
| Closed | Rarely. |

| | |
|---|---|
| Rooms | 3 doubles: €70-€90. 2 quadruples: €100-€120. Extra bed €15 per person per night. |
| Meals | Dinner, 4 courses with wine, €23. Restaurants 5-minute drive. |
| Closed | Never. |

| | |
|---|---|
| | **Alison Smith** Orchard Gîtes, La Foucaudiere, 61800 St Quentin les Chardonnets Orne |
| Tel | +33 (0)2 33 65 32 09 |
| Email | alisonsmith@orange.fr |
| Web | www.orchardgites.lowernormandy.com |

| | |
|---|---|
| | **Victoria & Richard Hobson-Cossey** Belle Vallée, 61700 Domfront Orne |
| Tel | +33 (0)2 33 37 05 71 |
| Email | info@belle-vallee.net |
| Web | www.belle-vallee.net |

## La Louvière

Charming hostess Isabelle says the 18th-century manor house has "une ambiance de soie": a chandelier sparkles above lace tablecloths in the dining room, pale chintz dresses elegant windows in the sunny salon. Take an aperitif on the terrace, get sporty on the tennis court, and dream in the gardens, fragrant with roses, buzzing with bees, and fecund with potager crammed with vegetables and herbs. Inside, an oak staircase curves up to the bedrooms, daintily, exquisitely romantic, decorated with fine fabrics and antiques. Everything you could want is here: a heated pool, tennis court, small fishing lake, happiness and peace.

| Rooms | 3 doubles; 1 double with separate, private bathroom: €95-€150. 1 suite for 4: €180. |
| --- | --- |
| Meals | Dinner with wine & coffee, €38. |
| Closed | Rarely. |

Isabelle & Alain Groult
La Louvière,
Le Fault,
61420 Saint Denis sur Sarthon
Orne
Tel      +33 (0)2 33 29 25 61
Email   isabelle@louviere.fr
Web     www.louviere.fr

Entry 242  Map 4

---

## Le Mesnil

There are fresh flowers everywhere and your hosts, retired farmers, offer true country hospitality. Peace is the norm, not the exception, in this deeply rural spot, racehorses graze in the pasture and you are unhesitatingly received into a warm and lively extended family. The rooms, in a converted self-contained side wing, have an appropriately rustic air with beams, old wardrobes and tiny kitchenettes. The ground-floor room has a little private garden; up steepish stairs is a second larger bedroom. Breakfast is in the family dining room, with tiled floors and a large fireplace. Children are welcome to visit the family farm next door.

| Rooms | 2 doubles each with kitchenette: €52. |
| --- | --- |
| Meals | Restaurant 5km. |
| Closed | Rarely. |

FIRST
EDITION
VETERAN

Janine & Rémy Laignel
Le Mesnil,
61200 Occagnes
Orne
Tel      +33 (0)2 33 67 11 12
Email   janineremy.laignel@orange.fr

Entry 243  Map 4

## Le Prieuré St Michel

An atmospheric time warp for a night on the St Michel pilgrim route: traditional décor in the timbered 14th-century monks' storeroom with tapestry wall covering and antiques, or the old dairy, or a converted stable; a huge 15th-century cider press for breakfast in the company of the Ulrichs' interesting choice of art; a chapel for yet more art, a tithe barn in magnificent condition for fabulous receptions, and perfectly stupendous gardens, a sort of medieval revival. Your hosts are totally devoted to their fabulous domain and its listed buildings and happy to share it with guests who appreciate its historical value.

## Country Garden

Former farm buildings make up this tiny hamlet in the beautifully unspoilt Perche. English Diane, ex interpreter and gentle, graceful hostess, has created three stylish-French bedrooms in her 18th-century barn, and serves breakfast in a big open-plan living room overlooking a garden (so pretty!) where clipped box hedges grow and views stretch to the copse-crested horizon. Her home is a gorgeous haven filled with oriental rugs, paintings and porcelain, tall candles and log fires. All feels rural, even remote, yet you are five minutes from Rémalard, a quaint market town with shops, galleries and bars. *Extra twin room available.*

| Rooms | 2 doubles, 1 twin/double: €95–€110. 2 suites for 3: €120–€130. Singles €95–€105. Extra bed/sofabed €15 per person per night. |
|---|---|
| Meals | Restaurant 4km. |
| Closed | Rarely. |

| Rooms | 1 double (sleeps 2-4): €99–€170. 1 family room for 3- 5: €145–€225. |
|---|---|
| Meals | Restaurants 5-minute drive. |
| Closed | Christmas/New Year. |

|  | **Jean-Pierre & Viviane Ulrich** Le Prieuré St Michel, 61120 Crouttes Orne |
|---|---|
| Tel | +33 (0)2 33 39 15 15 |
| Email | leprieuresaintmichel@wanadoo.fr |
| Web | www.prieure-saint-michel.com |

|  | **Diane Leroy** Country Garden, Lieu-dit La Riffetière, 61110 Dorceau Orne |
|---|---|
| Tel | +33 (0)2 33 83 56 14 |
| Email | countrygarden@hotmail.fr |
| Web | www.countrygarden.fr |

### Château de la Mouchère

Art Deco enthusiasts will happily splash out on a stay at this 18th-century château. Bold tiling, muted colours and elegant windows characterise the interior, while magnificent trees and soft parkland promise leafy strolls. Lucky dogs are treated to their own towel and biscuits on arrival – the laundry room with washing and sewing facilities is an added plus – while the sunny south-facing terrace is a birdwatcher's dream. Charming, cultured, generous Roger and Marie-Monique give you homemade jams at breakfast, the best local produce at dinner and keep parkland, gardens and outbuildings pristine.

### Hôtel de Suhard

Bellême – a famously beautiful medieval town of cobbled streets, markets and gourmet restaurants. On its square a tall, shuttered, oh-so-French mansion with a 16th-century pedigree. Interiors are gorgeously unfussy: Louis XV fireplaces, tinkling chandeliers and claw-foot baths. Two bedrooms overlook the walled garden – for breakfasts of fresh fruits and pastries – with views to the countryside; three overlook the road and the quaint town. All are divine. Run by warm Parisian owners with exceptional attention to detail, there are mushroom forays in autumn, order-in dinners on fine china, and three types of coffee for breakfast. *Minimum stay: 2 nights at weekends.*

| Rooms | 3 doubles: €110–€150. |
|---|---|
| | 2 suites for 2-4: €160–€190. |
| Meals | Dinner with wine, €30–€40. |
| | Restaurant 5km. |
| Closed | Rarely. |

| Rooms | 1 double, 2 twin/doubles: €82–€130. |
|---|---|
| | 2 suites for 2: €93–€140. |
| | Singles €83–€140. |
| | Extra bed/sofabed €30 per person per night. |
| Meals | Catered dinner available. |
| | Restaurant within walking distance. |
| Closed | Christmas/New Year. |

**Marie-Monique Huss**
Château de la Mouchère,
61130 St Cyr la Rosière
Orne
Tel       +33 (0)2 33 83 02 99
Mobile    +33 (0)6 32 35 92 66
Email     lamouchere@gmail.com
Web       www.lamouchere.com

**Josiane Lenoir**
Hôtel de Suhard,
34 rue d'Alençon,
61130 Bellême
Orne
Tel       +33 (0)2 33 83 53 47
Mobile    +33 (0)6 79 64 35 21
Email     contact@hotel-de-suhard.fr
Web       www.hotel-de-suhard.fr

Entry 246   Map 4

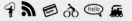

Entry 247   Map 4

# Normandy

## Les Larry

Just beyond the village of St Quentin de Blavou, this 19th-century farmhouse has long sweeping views across the valley and Norman countryside. Isobel is a bubbly Englishwoman who settled here in 2004; her Shetland and Connemara ponies keep her busy – she teaches, too – but she's still a hands-on hostess. The cosy double has a sloping roof and beams; use the second room, where the bed doubles as a divan, as your sitting room – or sit and chat with Isobel in hers. In fine weather you can breakfast on the terrace and drink in the view. Head out to the countryside for biking and hiking – the peace is divine!

| Rooms | 1 double sharing bathroom with single (let to same party only): €50. 1 single: €40. Singles €40-€45. |
|-------|------------------------------------------------------------|
| Meals | Restaurants 7km. |
| Closed | Rarely. |

Isobel Jagger
Les Larry,
61360 St Quentin de Blavou
Orne

| Tel | +33 (0)2 33 73 17 87 |
|-----|----------------------|
| Email | isobel.jagger@nordnet.fr |
| Web | www.chambresdhotesleslarry61360.com |

Photo: ©iStock.com/Dutchy

Brittany

www.sawdays.co.uk/brittany

## Brittany

### Les Touches

In rolling countryside at the end of the track is an immaculately restored 350-year-old farmhouse. The setting? Three acres of beautifully tended gardens that fall to a babbling brook. In the stone barn are three pretty bedrooms – two cosily under dark beams, the third, for families, with a secluded courtyard aglow with roses and birdsong. Owners Sue and Jerry, new to France, new to B&B, full of plans, love hosting four-course table d'hôtes at their big rustic table. Swings, trampoline and smooth rocks for playing on, an above-ground pool for splashing in, and sofas, books and small log-burner for cosy nights in. Perfect.

## Brittany

### La Foltière

The 'parc floral', magnificent from May to November and fashionably formal, dates from 1836 when the château was built. Paths meander round a huge lake, secret corners burst with camellias, old roses and banks of hydrangea, and children are welcomed with mazes, bridges, slides and surprises. The setting is magical, the architecture lovely, the rooms vast, and the feel is of a hushed and faded stately home (refurbishment happening soon). Tall-windowed bedrooms are big enough to dance in, one with an original porcelain loo, and you breakfast on homemade croissants, parma ham, cheeses and a neighbour's delicious jams.

| | |
|---|---|
| Rooms | 2 doubles: €75–€85. |
| | 1 family room for 4: €85–€121. |
| | Extra bed €18 per person per night. |
| | Cot €10. |
| Meals | Dinner, 4 courses with wine, €35. |
| | Auberge 3km. |
| Closed | Rarely. |

| | |
|---|---|
| Rooms | 4 doubles: €158. |
| | 1 suite for 2: €178. |
| Meals | Breakfast €12.50. Restaurants within walking distance. |
| Closed | 20–28 December. |

| | |
|---|---|
| | **Sue & Jerry Thomas** |
| | Les Touches, |
| | 35420 St Georges de Reintembault |
| | Ille-et-Vilaine |
| Tel | +33 (0)2 99 17 09 91 |
| Email | sue@lestouches.info |
| Web | www.lestouches.info |

| | |
|---|---|
| | **Mathias Haefeli** |
| | La Foltière, |
| | 35133 Le Châtellier |
| | Ille-et-Vilaine |
| Tel | +33 (0)2 99 95 48 32 |
| Email | parcfloral@bois-guy.fr |
| Web | www.jardin-garden.com |

# Brittany

## Le Presbytère

Inside its walled garden of flower-bordered lawns, orchards and potagers, the vast old priest's house is warm, reassuring and superbly restored. Welcome to a traditional Breton home of ancient beams, twisting staircases, family photos, panelling and ecclesiastical features. Some bathrooms are old-fashioned but each bedroom has character and space – a canopied bed, a striped wall, a garden view; two come with private outside stairs. Madame, a lovely energetic and warmly attentive person, cooks with passion – her dinners are special. A great base for touring St Malo and the bay of Mont St Michel.

| Rooms | 1 suite for 4, |
| --- | --- |
| | 2 family rooms for 4: €80–€110. |
| | 1 triple: €80–€95. |
| Meals | Dinner, 5 courses, €20–€25. |
| | Wine list €8.50–€30. |
| Closed | Rarely. |

Madeleine Stracquadanio
Le Presbytère,
35610 Vieux Viel
Ille-et-Vilaine
Tel    +33 (0)2 99 48 65 29
Email  madeleine.stracquadanio@voila.fr
Web    www.vieux-viel.com

Entry 251   Map 3

# Brittany

## Château de la Ballue

The formal gardens are listed and open to the public, a French reverie of paths and groves sprinkled with modern sculptures gazing over Mont St Michel. Baroque recitals may ring in the courtyard and Purcell odes float over marble fireplaces, antique paintings, gilded mirrors and orchids. This is no museum, however, but a family home enlivened by children. Sleep deeply in dreamy canopied beds, wake to silver cutlery and a fine continental spread in a blue-panelled breakfast room. Some bedrooms have tented 'cabinets de toilette', birds sing in the *bosquet de musique*. Baroque, family-friendly, enchanting.

| Rooms | 3 doubles: €200–€240. |
| --- | --- |
| | 1 suite for 2-4: €250–€305. |
| | 1 triple: €260–€280. |
| | Extra bed €40 per person per night. |
| Meals | Breakfast €19. |
| | Restaurants 7km. |
| Closed | Rarely. |

Marie-Françoise Mathiot-Mathon
Château de la Ballue,
35560 Bazouges la Pérouse
Ille-et-Vilaine
Tel    +33 (0)2 99 97 47 86
Email  chateau@la-ballue.com
Web    www.la-ballue.com

Entry 252   Map 3

# Brittany

### Les Demeures de Marie

This 13th-century former mansion, lovingly coaxed into modernity by the Roussels, is entirely serene with pale Farrow & Ball walls, fine fabrics and exposed beams. Matching bedrooms come with real fires, painted furniture, wall-mounted tellies; the mezzanine has its own terrace. Madame is on hand, serving aperitifs in the sitting room; outside, the private garden spa is protected from the road by the carefully tended garden. Dinner can be arranged, with sumptuous fare on the menu (beef carpaccio, smoked salmon) and the restaurants in Rennes are a short drive – as are the legendary Mont St Michel and the sparkling Emerald Coast.

# Brittany

### Château du Pin

The small château with its pretty faded shutters is now inhabited by the Josses. Modern furniture rubs shoulders with brocante finds, bookshelves burst with books and art, bold red walls brighten up the salon where breakfast is served. Up to soft-hued bedrooms, their swathes of ruched silk clasped by tassels, their beds delicious with hand-painted headboards and luxurious covers. Outside: masses of park and woodland for children to roam. A light supper is available at separate tables: a platter of smoked salmon, a hot gratin – ideal for the first night. You're within easy reach of the Emerald coast, the gulf of Morbihan, Dinard and St Malo. *Helipad available.*

| Rooms | 2 doubles: €99–€109. |
|---|---|
| | 3 suites for 2-4: €129–€149. |
| | Extra bed/sofabed €20 per person per night. |
| | Private hammam or spa €10 per person. |
| | 50% discount for under 10's. |
| Meals | Breakfast €12. Dinner €29. |
| | Restaurant 2km. |
| Closed | Never. |

Marie Roussel
Les Demeures de Marie,
Méault, 35740 Pacé
Ille-et-Vilaine

| Mobile | +33 (0)7 86 42 99 38 |
|---|---|
| Email | contact@lesdemeuresdemarie.com |
| Web | www.lesdemeuresdemarie.com |

| Rooms | 1 double, 2 twin/doubles, |
|---|---|
| | 2 family rooms for 4: €88–€163. |
| | 1 cottage for 3-4: €140. |
| | Extra person €29 per night. |
| Meals | Breakfast €14. |
| | Dinner €29. |
| | Wine €10–€30. |
| | Restaurant 5km. |
| Closed | Rarely. |

Marie France & Jean-Luc Josse
Château du Pin,
Route départementale 125,
La Veronnière,
35750 Iffendic
Ille-et-Vilaine

| Tel | +33 (0)2 99 09 34 05 |
|---|---|
| Email | josse.jeanluc@free.fr |
| Web | www.chateau-pin.fr |

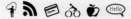

Entry 253   Map 3

Entry 254   Map 3

# Brittany

## Château du Quengo

Anne, descendant of an ancient Breton family, and Alfred, who is Swiss, are passionate about animals, gardens, music, life! They welcome you open-armed to their inimitable house: a private chapel, a bio garden, rare trees, 1800s wallpapers, a carved staircase, a mosaic'd floor. She runs willow-weaving classes and plies you with homemade delights; he builds organs; both love the slow life. Bedrooms have antique radiators and are properly old-fashioned, our favourite being the family room. No plastic anything, few mod cons, just intelligent, humorous hosts and a house steeped in atmosphere, beauty and peace.

| | |
|---|---|
| Rooms | 2 doubles, 1 suite for 5: €65–€85. |
| Meals | Guest kitchen. Restaurants 1.5km. |
| Closed | Rarely. |

**Anne & Alfred du Crest de Lorgerie**
Château du Quengo,
35850 Irodouër
Ille-et-Vilaine
Tel    +33 (0)2 99 39 81 47
Email  lequengo@hotmail.com
Web    chateauduquengo.free.fr

# Brittany

## La Lande

A delightful find only five minutes from the motorway – a pretty stone and cob longère from the 17th century. Chantal and Franck came here 14 years ago and have been lovingly restoring ever since, creating a happy balance of comfort and charm. Borrow bikes and explore the countryside (mercifully flat) or stroll the gardens and surrounding orchard. Return to a tranquil bedroom with big windows, seagrass matting, a blend of ancient and new furniture and original quirky oils by Franck's father. There's a bistro nearby but, with such well-travelled hosts, why not swap stories over a sumptuous seasonal dinner instead?

| | |
|---|---|
| Rooms | 1 double: €75. Singles €70. Extra bed/sofabed €18 per person per night. |
| Meals | Dinner, 3 courses with wine, €22. Restaurant 3km. |
| Closed | Rarely. |

**Chantal & Franck Bauvin**
La Lande,
35630 Vignoc
Ille-et-Vilaine
Tel     +33 (0)2 99 69 85 83
Mobile  +33 (0)6 31 75 74 57
Email   chantal.bauvin@orange.fr
Web     www.lalandevignoc.com

# Brittany

## La Seigneurie

In a seaside town of wide sands and blue sea hides an 18th-century house in a church-side garden: charming Madame's B&B. Across the courtyard, in stable and barn, is the sitting room: a minstrels' gallery, books, magazines, tapestries, an ornate chandelier... and smouldering embers scenting the air. Big suites in the stables are just as enchanting, one on the ground floor, another up private stairs. Fresh flowers and macaroons welcome you, antiques and silver coffee pots delight you, walls are in soft blues and greys, and breakfast arrives in wicker baskets stuffed with local and homemade treats. Seduction by the sea!

| Rooms | 1 double: €85. |
| --- | --- |
| | 3 suites for 2-5: €95-€130. |
| Meals | Shared seafood platter with wine, €29-€58. |
| | Restaurants 7km. |
| Closed | Rarely. |

Françoise Busson
La Seigneurie,
35114 St Benoit des Ondes
Ille-et-Vilaine

| Tel | +33 (0)2 99 58 62 96 |
| --- | --- |
| Mobile | +33 (0)6 72 43 06 97 |
| Email | contact@la-seigneurie-des-ondes.net |
| Web | www.la-seigneurie-des-ondes.net |

Entry 257   Map 3

# Brittany

## La Petite Ville Mallet

You can spot the sea before you arrive – at this traditional-but-new white-shuttered house on the edge of St Malo. Pet sheep and goats mow the grass and Monsieur's fruit garden spilleth over! Inside all is comforting and inviting and your retired hosts – proud descendants of the swashbuckling corsairs – are a joy to meet. Sun spills through French windows at breakfast, and elegant carpeted bedrooms have armchairs for relaxing cups of tea. Circle the ramparts of seafaring St Malo or 15th-century Dinan (small, exquisite), catch the ferry to Jersey or a boat to the isles of the Emerald Coast.

| Rooms | 1 double: €85-€90. |
| --- | --- |
| | 1 suite for 4: €140-€150. |
| | 1 triple with separate bathroom: €100-€110. |
| Meals | Restaurants 3km. |
| Closed | Never. |

Joëlle et Henri-Pierre Coquil
La Petite Ville Mallet,
Le Gué,
35400 St Malo
Ille-et-Vilaine

| Tel | +33 (0)2 99 81 75 62 |
| --- | --- |
| Email | lapetitevillemallet@orange.fr |
| Web | www.lapetitevillemallet.com |

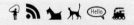

Entry 258   Map 3

# Brittany

## Malouinière des Trauchandières

This handsome manoir in big peaceful walled gardens has been lovingly restored by Claude, who speaks six languages, and equally well-travelled Agnès; both are charming and gregarious. Theirs is a fascinating house dating from 1510, with French windows opening to a south-facing terrace and a salon lined with rich oak panelling; relax by the blazing fire. Bedrooms, comfortable, traditional and up two sets of stairs, are dominated by dark ships' timbers; the port of St Malo is close, so are golden sand beaches. Breakfast is served beneath the chandelier and there's an annual garden party in the grounds. Marvellous.

| | |
|---|---|
| Rooms | 3 twin/doubles: €80-€100. |
| | 1 suite for 3: €120-€130. |
| Meals | Dinner with wine, €35. |
| | Restaurants in St Méloir, 5-minute drive. |
| Closed | Rarely. |

Agnès François
Malouinière des Trauchandières,
Albiville, St Jouan des Guérets,
35430 St Malo
Ille-et-Vilaine

Tel     +33 (0)2 99 81 38 30
Mobile  +33 (0)6 22 80 47 97
Email   agnesfrancois@hotmail.com
Web     www.les-trauchandieres.com

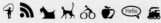

Entry 259   Map 3

# Brittany

## Les Mouettes

House and owner are imbued with the calm of a balmy summer's morning, whatever the weather, and Isabelle's talent seems to touch the very air that fills her old family home. Timeless simplicity reigns; there is nothing superfluous: simple carved pine furniture, an antique wrought-iron cot, dhurries on scrubbed plank floors, palest grey walls to reflect the ocean-borne light, harmonious gingham curtains. Starfish and pebbles keep house and little garden sea-connected, whimsical mobiles add a creative touch. The unspoilt seaside village, popular in season, is worth the trip alone.

| | |
|---|---|
| Rooms | 4 doubles, 1 twin: €60. |
| Meals | Restaurants in village. |
| Closed | Rarely. |

Isabelle Rouvrais
Les Mouettes,
17 Grande Rue,
35430 St Suliac
Ille-et-Vilaine

Tel     +33 (0)2 99 58 30 41
Email   contact@les-mouettes-saint-suliac.com
Web     www.les-mouettes-saint-suliac.com

Entry 260   Map 3

# Brittany

## Manoir du Clos Clin

Monsieur found this ancient, grand farmhouse derelict and has lavished huge attention on it. He's done it all immaculately, from re-roofing and installing geothermal underfloor heating, to creating smart, super-comfortable and historically themed bedrooms and bathrooms; the Louis XIII-style four-poster is exemplary. Formal family portraits hang in the huge living room where you can gen up on things local and play the piano. Fresh breakfasts come from the open-plan kitchen. You're on the outskirts of Pleurtuit, a couple of miles from Dinard, and can lounge peacefully in the lawned garden or pedal the cycle path to Dinan.

| Rooms | 2 doubles: €64–€160. |
| | 2 family rooms for 4: €104–€190. |
| Meals | Restaurants within walking distance. |
| Closed | Never. |

**Guy Macquart de Terline**
Manoir du Clos Clin,
Le Clos Clin, 35730 Pleurtuit
Ille-et-Vilaine

| Mobile | +33 (0)6 88 17 93 91 |
| Email | gmacquart@orange.fr |
| Web | www.en.manoirclosclin.fr |

Entry 261   Map 3

---

# Brittany

## La Vallée de la Rance

All is funky, bright and contemporary at smiling Hervé and Anne's apartments converted from a 19th-century longère and perfectly positioned on the shores of the estuary. Plenty of fun touches: a teacup light, amusing caricatures on the walls — just mind your head in the mezzanine double. Delicious breakfast served in a cheery dining room overlooking the Rance is a leisurely affair before everyone tumbles out for a swim in the pool. After crepes with Anne's famous 'caramel beurre salé', St Malo yogurts, Breton cakes and butter, you might need a bit of exercise! A wonderful, friendly spot to stay en famille.

| Rooms | 1 double: €80–€90. |
| | 2 suites for 4 with bunk beds, |
| | 2 suites for 6: €80–€165. |
| | Extra person €20 per night. |
| Meals | Dinner from €20. |
| Closed | Never. |

**Anne & Hervé Desert**
La Vallée de la Rance,
La Vallée,
22490 Plouer sur Rance
Côtes-d'Armor

| Tel | +33 (0)2 96 89 11 53 |
| Email | valleedelarance@gmail.com |
| Web | www.valleedelarance.com |

Entry 262   Map 3

# Brittany

## Le Clos St Cadreuc

Peace in a hamlet a pebble's throw from the coast, driving distance from ten golf courses (bring your clubs!) and a good stopover for St Malo. There's a welcoming atmosphere in this stone farmhouse, and colour and space in the living/dining room. The guest quarters are in the converted stables, comfortable, very French, with great walk-in showers and hotel-like extras; the bright airy family suite is super and spacious. Your warm hosts put Breton dishes on your plate and pour organic wines; between house and stables is a pretty sheltered garden, for DIY barbecues and picnics.

| Rooms | 2 doubles: €75. |
| --- | --- |
| | 1 family room for 4: €80-€135. |
| | 1 triple: €80-€100. |
| | 1 quadruple: €75. |
| Meals | Dinner with wine, €28. |
| Closed | Rarely. |

**Brigitte & Patrick Noël**
Le Clos St Cadreuc,
22650 Ploubalay
Côtes-d'Armor

| Tel | +33 (0)2 96 27 32 43 |
| --- | --- |
| Mobile | +33 (0)6 82 14 94 66 |
| Email | clos-saint-cadreuc@wanadoo.fr |
| Web | www.clos-saint-cadreuc.com |

Entry 263   Map 3

# Brittany

## Malik

Clad in red cedar, this open-plan Nordic-style house has timber and metal details and sliding glass doors, all in keeping with the woodland feel – and every detail is taken care of. Harmonious covers on excellent beds, oriental wall hangings on restful walls, monogrammed towels, lovely soaps and, across the little footbridge, private seating areas just for you. Breakfast, *un peu brunch*, deliciously Scandinavian, is served in your own little conservatory, with homemade breads and jams. Lovely people and an exquisitely serene house that seems to hug its garden to its heart. A haven on the edge of a small town.

| Rooms | 1 suite for 2, |
| --- | --- |
| | 1 suite for 4: €82-€126. |
| Meals | Restaurants within walking distance. |
| Closed | Rarely. |

**Martine & Hubert Viannay**
Malik,
Chemin de l'Étoupe,
22980 Plélan le Petit
Côtes-d'Armor

| Tel | +33 (0)2 96 27 62 71 |
| --- | --- |
| Mobile | +33 (0)6 09 92 35 21 |
| Email | malikbretagne@free.fr |
| Web | www.malik-bretagne.com |

Entry 264   Map 3

# Brittany

## Le Manoir de la Villeneuve

Embraced by rolling lawns, wooded parkland and sweeping drive, this manor house seems untouched by the 21st century. Light airy pools of calm – high ceilings, tall windows, polished boards – are furnished with a contemporary elegance while plain walls, beams and tomette floors have been allowed to glow. Beautiful bedrooms have soothing colours, pretty antiques, delicious soaps, beams in some and sloping ceilings; the suite has a vast bathroom and its own salon. Breakfast handsomely at the convivial table, then explore Dinan, St Brieuc, the coast. Return for a dip in the new summer pool. Charming Nathalie oversees all.

| Rooms | 3 doubles, |
| --- | --- |
| | 1 twin/double: €70–€115. |
| | 1 suite for 3: €120–€140. |
| | Singles €70–€140. |
| Meals | Restaurant 2km. |
| Closed | Rarely. |

Nathalie Peres
Le Manoir de la Villeneuve,
22400 Lamballe
Côtes-d'Armor

| Tel | +33 (0)2 96 50 86 32 |
| --- | --- |
| Email | manoirdelavilleneuve@wanadoo.fr |
| Web | www.chambresaumanoir.com |

Entry 265   Map 3

---

# Brittany

## Manoir de Coat Gueno

The 15th-century, country-cocooned manor house, close to fishing ports, headlands and long sandy beaches, is a treasure. Beautifully restored over decades, every detail has been considered yet Christian is not so precious that he stops the blue tits nesting in a nook in the stone work! The salon's 'lit clos' is a treat, as is the vast stone fireplace, crackling with logs in winter. Gaze from a florally furnished suite onto the lawns below, enjoy the splashing of the pool or the crack of the billiards. The games room and the charming cottage suite (with its own fire) are in the grounds, and your host is the perfect French gentleman. *Children over 7 who are able to swim welcome.*

| Rooms | 2 suites for 2-4: €110–€170. |
| --- | --- |
| | 1 cottage for 2: €100–€170. |
| Meals | Restaurants 4km. |
| Closed | September – April. |

Christian de Rouffignac
Manoir de Coat Gueno,
Coat Gueno,
22740 Pleudaniel
Côtes-d'Armor

| Tel | +33 (0)2 96 20 10 98 |
| --- | --- |
| Email | coatguen@aol.com |
| Web | mapage.noos.fr/coatgueno |

Entry 266   Map 2

# Brittany

## Kerlilou

This may be your dream, too: to leave city jobs, renovate – meticulously, lovingly, yourself, with talent and your well-loved antiques – an ancient farmhouse, then throw it open to like-minded visitors. Pascaline is happy to chat about it, and to cook organic/local dinner at the big kitchen table by the fireplace. She and Patrick are a lovely, anglophile couple, easy, cultured and humorous. Two of the pretty, airy bedrooms are on the ground floor (one through the kitchen); bathrooms have seaweed soap and candles. The setting sun streams out of a dark blue sky onto yellow rapeseed; islands and markets abound. Superb value.

| Rooms | 1 double, 1 twin/double: €67–€72. |
| | 1 family room for 4: €105. |
| | 2 triples: €85. |
| Meals | Dinner with wine, €25. |
| Closed | Rarely. |

**Pascaline & Patrick Cortopassi**
Kerlilou,
3 Calvary,
22220 Plouguiel
Côtes-d'Armor

| Tel | +33 (0)2 96 92 24 06 |
| Mobile | +33 (0)6 17 84 31 08 |
| Email | contact@kerlilou.fr |
| Web | www.kerlilou.com |

Entry 267   Map 2

# Brittany

## À la Corniche

Enter and you will see why we chose this modernised house: the ever-changing light of the great bay shimmers in through vast swathes of glass. Each guest room has its glazed veranda where you can sit and gaze at islands, coastline and sea – stunning. Marie-Clo has enlivened the interior with her patchwork and embroidery, installed a fine new wood-burner in the living space and tea trays in the rooms. It is calm, light, bright; she is attentive, warm and generous, and it's great for families. A ten-minute stroll brings you to Perros with restaurants and beaches; ideal for couples on a gentle seaside holiday.

| Rooms | 2 suites for 2: €95–€100. |
| Meals | Dinner €24. |
| | Restaurants within walking distance. |
| Closed | Rarely. |

**Marie-Clotilde Biarnès**
À la Corniche,
41 rue de la Petite Corniche,
22700 Perros Guirec
Côtes-d'Armor

| Tel | +33 (0)2 96 23 28 08 |
| Mobile | +33 (0)6 81 23 15 49 |
| Email | marieclo.biarnes@wanadoo.fr |
| Web | perso.wanadoo.fr/corniche |

Entry 268   Map 2

# Brittany

## Manoir de Kerguéréon

Such gracious hosts with a wonderful sense of humour: you feel you are at a house party; such age and history in the gloriously asymmetrical château: tower, turrets, vast fireplaces, low doors, ancestral portraits, fine furniture; such a lovely garden, Madame's own work. Up the spiral stone staircase are bedrooms with space, taste, arched doors, a lovely window seat to do your tapestry in, good bathrooms; and the great Breton breakfast can be brought up if you wish. Aperitifs among the roses, breakfast before the crackling fire; their son breeds racehorses on the estate and their daughter-in-law runs the B&B. Sheer delight.

| Rooms | 1 double, 2 twins: €100. |
| | Extra bed €30 per person per night. |
| Meals | Restaurants 7km. |
| Closed | Rarely. |

FIRST
EDITION
VETERAN

Mr & Mme de Bellefon
Manoir de Kerguéréon,
Ploubezre,
22300 Lannion
Côtes-d'Armor

| Tel | +33 (0)2 96 38 80 59 |
| Mobile | +33 (0)6 03 45 68 55 |
| Email | arnaud.debellefon@nordnet.fr |

Entry 269   Map 2

# Brittany

## Toul Bleïz

There may be badgers and wild boar on the moors but civilisation is a five-minute drive – and you breakfast when you want to in a courtyard trilled by birds. Julie offers 'painting with picnics' and Jez concocts delicious vegetarian dishes for your supper (take these 'en famille' or in private by the summerhouse). This is an enchanting Breton cottage with French windows pouring light into a snug ground-floor guest bedroom with a patchwork quilt and lace pillows, armchairs, barbecue and summerhouse kitchenette, and an outdoor deck with lavender and sweeping views – what better place for an aperitif! The village is delightful, the Abbaye de Bon Repos is near. Flexible, and great value.

| Rooms | 1 double: €65. |
| Meals | Vegetarian dinner with wine, |
| | 2 courses, €20. |
| | Picnic available. |
| | Summerhouse with kitchenette & |
| | barbecue. |
| Closed | Rarely. |

Julie & Jez Rooke
Toul Bleïz,
22570 Laniscat
Côtes-d'Armor

| Tel | +33 (0)2 96 36 98 34 |
| Mobile | +33 (0)6 88 57 75 31 |
| Email | jezrooke@hotmail.com |
| Web | www.phoneinsick.co.uk |

Entry 270   Map 2

## La Grange de Coatélan

Yolande is a smiling young grandmother of three, Charlick the most sociable workaholic you could find. They are artistic (he paints) and fun. They have beautifully renovated their old Breton weaver's house and converted other ruins into rooms for guests. Their small auberge is mostly doing table d'hôtes now – a single menu of traditional dishes – and the food is brilliant. Bedrooms under the eaves (some steep stairs) have clever layouts, colour schemes and fabrics and an imaginative use of wood. Joyful rustic elegance deep in the countryside, with animals and swings for children's delight.
*Minimum stay: 2 nights in high season.*

| | |
|---|---|
| Rooms | 2 doubles: €67-€79. |
| | 3 quadruples: €113-€122. |
| | Singles €55-€68. |
| | Extra bed/sofabed €18 per person per night. |
| Meals | Dinner €23. |
| | Wine €17-€57. |
| Closed | Christmas/New Year. |

| | |
|---|---|
| | **Charlick & Yolande de Ternay** |
| | La Grange de Coatélan |
| | 29640 Plougonven |
| | Finistère |
| Tel | +33 (0)2 98 72 60 16 |
| Email | la-grange-de-coatelan@wanadoo.fr |
| Web | www.les-gites-en-bretagne.fr |

Entry 271  Map 2

## Domaine de Moulin Mer

Bordeaux shutters against white-washed walls, graceful steps rising to the front door, attendant palm trees… Stéphane has restored this manor house to its full glory. The luxurious rooms are a masterly combination of period elegance and tasteful minimalism, the gardens a riot of shady trees – olives, palms, eucalyptus and mimosas. Across the road you can glimpse the waters of the estuary and a fine old mill. Stéphane, who used to work in Dublin, is an amusing, genial host and a collector of furniture and art. He will cook you (according to availability and his whim) an inventive dinner using fresh local produce.

| | |
|---|---|
| Rooms | 2 doubles: €80-€110. |
| | 2 suites for 2: €120-€150. |
| | Singles €80-€140. |
| Meals | Dinner €35. |
| | Wine from €10. |
| Closed | Rarely. |

| | |
|---|---|
| | **Stéphane Pécot** |
| | Domaine de Moulin Mer, |
| | 34 route de Moulin Mer, |
| | 29460 Logonna Daoulas |
| | Finistère |
| Tel | +33 (0)2 98 07 24 45 |
| Email | info@domaine-moulin-mer.com |
| Web | www.domaine-moulin-mer.com |

Entry 272  Map 2

# Brittany

## Manoir de Kerledan

Everyone loves Kerledan, its gargoyles, its sophisticated theatrical décor, its owners' enthusiasm. Peter and Penny have made it stunningly original. Sisal and unstained oak, limed walls, the odd splash of antique mirror or gilded bergère with fake leopard skin create a mood of luxury and calm; stone-floored bathrooms are delicious; candlelit, cut-glass dinners are legendary. Sit by the great dining room fire, stroll in the lovely gardens (baroque courtyard, palisade hornbeam allée, potager), lounge in antique linen in a perfect bedroom and let yourself be pampered by your hosts: arrive as strangers, leave as friends.

| Rooms | 2 doubles, 1 twin/double: €90–€115. 1 family room for 4: €110–€155. |
|---|---|
| Meals | Dinner, 2-3 courses, €23–€28. Wine from €5. |
| Closed | Mid-November to March. |

Peter & Penny Dinwiddie
Manoir de Kerledan,
Route de Kerledan,
9270 Carhaix Plouguer
Finistère
Tel      +33 (0)2 98 99 44 63
Email    kerledan@gmail.com
Web      www.kerledan.com

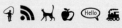

# Brittany

## Manoir de Kerdanet

Irresistible cakes, savouries, fruits and teas are served in a salon with a vast granite fireplace and logs that flicker at the first sign of cold weather. Off a country road, down an alley of trees, and there it is, a beautiful manor house 600 years old, lived in and loved by urbane hosts with a talent for making you feel instantly at home. A spiral stone staircase leads to authentic and timeless bedrooms, comfortable with crisp sheets and woollen blankets, coordinated furnishings and dark Breton antiques. Walkers and sailors will love the coast... watch out for the regattas at Douarnenez! *Self-catering available in cottage for 2.*

| Rooms | 2 doubles: €104. 1 suite for 4: €124–€184. |
|---|---|
| Meals | Restaurants 5km. |
| Closed | Mid-October to mid-May. |

Sid & Monique Nedjar
Manoir de Kerdanet,
29100 Poullan sur Mer
Finistère
Tel      +33 (0)2 98 74 59 03
Email    manoir.kerdanet@wanadoo.fr
Web      www.manoirkerdanet.com

# Brittany

## La Ferme de Kerscuntec

In the bucolic heart of the country, yet close to white sand beaches, the 17th-century cider farm has become a heavenly B&B. Elegant bedrooms are fresh and calming, one with its own decked terrace; the garden is prolific, Anne is creative and humorous, breakfasts are exceptional: wake to muffins and hedgerow jams. Tempting confections are displayed in glass jars for guests to enjoy, zinc pots are stuffed with flowers, bathrooms are for lingering in, sparkling windows frame the fields. Visit the fishing boats in Ste Marine harbour and the grand shops of Quimper, set off for the islands. Seafood restaurants abound. *Minimum stay: 2 nights.*

| Rooms | 5 doubles: €85–€140. |
| | Singles €75–€130. |
| Meals | Restaurant 2km. |
| Closed | Rarely. |

Most praised breakfast

**Anne & Bruno Porhiel**
La Ferme de Kerscuntec,
Kerscuntec, 29120 Combrit
Finistère

| Tel | +33 (0)2 98 51 90 90 |
| Mobile | +33 (0)6 86 99 78 28 |
| Email | contact@lafermedekerscuntec.fr |
| Web | www.lafermedekerscuntec.fr |

# Brittany

*New Entry*

## Château de Penfrat

You can ride or hike freely around 100 hectares of forested parkland, and watch birds on the banks of the Odet. As for the château – it's a tall handsome hunting lodge built by eccentric nobles, now owned by Patrick and Barbora. Enjoy life's simple pleasures: a good book, an easy chair, light jazz, crêpes at breakfast with chèvre frais, and an apéro before dinner (come winter) with your hosts. There's a retro feel to the salons, and a sunny feel to the bedrooms: tall windows, low beds, candlelit baths. Explore the fish markets of Quimper, the tall ships of Locronon, the artists' village of Pont-Aven. Then back for a delicious massage.

| Rooms | 1 double: €95–€110. |
| | 1 suite for 3, |
| | 1 suite for 4: €120–€180. |
| Meals | Dinner €35 (not in summer). |
| | Wine €8–€20. Restaurant 5km. |
| Closed | Never. |

**Barbora Kairyte & Patrick Viossat**
Château de Penfrat,
25 chemin de Penfrat,
29950 Gouesnach
Finistère

| Mobile | +33 (0)6 33 33 37 63 |
| Email | info@penfrat.fr |
| Web | www.penfrat.fr |

## La Longère

A stylish retreat 20 minutes from the sea — arrive as strangers, leave as friends. Elaine and Paul swapped London for a 18th-century longère surrounded by orchards and fields; then modernised in country-contemporary style. Three attic bedrooms, airy and light, come with roof windows and calming colours, spoiling showers and laundered linen. The sofa'd salon is equally inviting; comfy loungers line the pool. Chat to Elaine as she prepares your dinner, delivered with a flourish to the convivial table. Make the most of the music festivals of Lorient, and all those Brittany gardens that open in summer. *Minimum stay: 2 nights at weekends & in high season. Children over 14 welcome.*

## Talvern

Steamer trunks and leather club chairs, deep-set windows and hefty beams, a family to greet you and Patrick's great food: welcome to an escape by the sea. Patrick was a chef in Paris (note the fine potager), Christine is the talent behind the quietly original bedroom décor (hemp, seagrass, organic colours) and the farmhouse once belonged to the château. There are walks in the woods and good cycling nearby, you are well placed for Vannes and the Morbihan Gulf yet the coastal inlet is five minutes away. Separated from the road by a grassy courtyard, the wall encloses a sunny terrace on which children may play, *Pets by arrangement.*

|  |  |
|---|---|
| **STOP PRESS:** No longer doing B&B, but available as a self-catering property. Please contact the owners for prices and availability. | **Rooms** 2 doubles, 1 twin/double: €70–€79. 2 suites for 4: €123. Extra bed/sofabed €20 per person per night. |
|  | **Meals** Dinner with wine, €24. |
|  | **Closed** Rarely. |

AWARD WINNER

Most praised breakfast

**Elaine & Paul Hayden**
La Longère,
Keroallic,
56440 Languidic
Morbihan
Tel +33 (0)2 97 65 13 15
Email info@perfectplacefrance.com
Web www.perfectplacefrance.com

**Patrick Gillot**
Talvern,
56690 Landévant
Morbihan
Tel +33 (0)2 97 56 99 80
Mobile +33 (0)6 16 18 08 75
Email talvern@chambre-morbihan.com
Web www.chambre-morbihan.com

# Brittany

## La Masana

Behind the pretty, pink, unassuming façade is a peaceful retreat, so close to town you can hear the gulls in the marina. Here lives friendly, lively Madame, in the house she grew up in. The two guest rooms can interlink, while the separate entrance (and the option to take breakfast in the twin) means you don't have to be sociable! If you are, table d'hôtes is on offer – fresh fish, tarte au pomme... and jams at breakfast from home-grown fruits. The twin faces the little street, the double faces the garden – a sweet secluded space. Décor is simple, mattresses are delicious, the shower room shines.

| | |
|---|---|
| Rooms | 1 double, 1 twin sharing shower room & separate wc: €70-€80. |
| Meals | Dinner, 3 courses, €22. Restaurants 1km. |
| Closed | Rarely. |

**Annie Girouard**
La Masana,
12 rue de la Louisiane,
56100 Lorient
Morbihan
Tel     +33 (0)2 97 83 38 43
Email   annie.douaron-girouard@orange.fr
Web     www.chambres-hotes-lorient.com

Entry 279   Map 2

# Brittany

## Ker-Ysta

The old barn has been done in a lovely mix of traditional (old beams and stone walls) and modern: soft grey pleasingly married with more vibrant green, blue or purple. It's all warm and inviting with views to the big lush garden and a sense of peace. Yolande and her husband came home to Brittany for a simpler life after working hard in buzzy Paris. Quietly bubbly, she is passionate about cooking and interiors so converting an old farmhouse and its outbuildings into a B&B was the ideal plan. Breakfast and dinner (masses of fresh local fish) are at the big table in her kitchen; guests have a cosy sitting room in the barn.

| | |
|---|---|
| Rooms | 4 doubles, 1 twin: €79-€89. Extra bed €15 per person per night. |
| Meals | Dinner with wine, €29. |
| Closed | Rarely. |

**Yolande Le Gall**
Ker-Ysta,
Le Manémeur,
56410 Erdeven
Morbihan
Tel      +33 (0)2 97 55 97 20
Mobile   +33 (0)6 16 71 73 71
Email    contact@ker-ysta.fr
Web      www.ker-ysta.com

Entry 280   Map 2

# Brittany

## Kerimel

The standing stones of Carnac are minutes away, beaches, coastal pathways and golf course close by. Kerimel is a handsome group of granite farm buildings in a perfect setting among the fields. Bedrooms are simple beauties: plain walls, some panelling, patchwork bedcovers and pale curtains, old stones and beams. The dining room is cottage perfection: dried flowers hanging from beams over a wooden table, a spring fire in the vast stone fireplace, breakfasts from grand-mère that promise an organic treat each day. A gentle, generous young family with excellent English, and passionately eco minded. *Minimum stay: 2 nights in high season.*

| | |
|---|---|
| Rooms | 2 twin/doubles: €88–€98. 3 triples: €103–€113. |
| Meals | Crêpes supper available €20, with cider. Restaurants 3km. |
| Closed | March – May, October/November. |

Nicolas Malherbe
Kerimel,
56400 Ploemel
Morbihan
Tel +33 (0)2 97 56 83 53
Mobile +33 (0)6 83 40 68 56
Email chaumieres.kerimel@wanadoo.fr
Web www.chambres-kerimel.com

Entry 281  Map 2

# Brittany

## Kernivilit

Right on the quayside, with the oyster boats under your windows, a very simple but friendly address. French windows open to tiny balconies and bedrooms touch the view; catch the lovely limpid light as you drink coffee on the balcony, listening to the chug-chug of the boats, smelling the sea. Madame worked in England, Germany and the US before coming here to help François farm oysters; he'll take you out in the boats if you ask. Hospitable and generous, alert and chatty, she hangs interesting art in her rooms, lights a fire on cool days and serves a good breakfast (great breads, fine jams) on a terrace shaded by pines.

| | |
|---|---|
| Rooms | 1 apartment for 2-4 with kitchenette: €160. |
| Meals | Restaurant within walking distance. |
| Closed | November – February. |

Christine & François Gouzer
Kernivilit,
Route de Quéhan,
St Philibert,
56470 La Trinité sur Mer
Morbihan
Tel +33 (0)2 97 55 17 78
Mobile +33 (0)6 78 35 09 34
Email fgouzer@club-internet.fr

Entry 282  Map 2

### Maison de la Garenne

Ditch the car and dart down a side street to this impressively elegant townhouse – a secluded eyrie with luscious views of the public gardens and the old city ramparts. Sweep up the stairs (past Antoine and Christine's parents' quarters) to refined bedrooms each with a peaceful garden theme and views over the charming garden. Find the soft tones of the 19th century plus antiques, and the rich colours of the orient. Bathrooms are a treat – note the amusing portable bidet! Sip coffee from classy china in the breakfast salon, then stroll into Vannes to explore its historic harbour. Return home to evening sun in a cosy wee salon.

| | |
|---|---|
| Rooms | 2 doubles, 1 twin: €91–€124. 1 family suite for 2–4: €110–€168. Extra bed €13 per person per night. |
| Meals | Restaurants within walking distance. |
| Closed | Rarely. |

**Antoine & Christine Goursolas**
Maison de la Garenne,
2 rue Sébastien de Rosmadec,
56000 Vannes
Morbihan
Tel +33 (0)2 97 67 00 31
Email contact@maisondelagarenne.com
Web www.maisondelagarenne.com

Entry 283   Map 3

### Domaine de Coët Bihan

Close to beautiful, medieval Vannes, Jantine and Jacques' house lies in undulating country where horses graze and clematis clambers. Light-filled bedrooms, the most luxurious on the first floor, are crisp and comfy with pukka linen and top-class showers. Feast on crêpes before setting off for walks and climbs and, from the top of wooded summits, views over the Morbihan Gulf. Then a nap in the enclosed garden or an espresso in the tiny salon. If you're enjoying the indoor pool too much to be tempted by the local Michelin-starred restaurants (there are two), Jantine will make you a tasty platter.

| | |
|---|---|
| Rooms | 4 doubles: €90–€105. Extra bed €15 per person per night. |
| Meals | Cold platter, €12–€20. Restaurants 4km. Kitchen & barbecue available. |
| Closed | Rarely. |

**Jantine Guégan-Helder**
Domaine de Coët Bihan,
Lieu-dit Coët Bihan, Monterblanc,
56250 Vannes
Morbihan
Tel +33 (0)2 97 44 97 22
Mobile +33 (0)6 20 42 42 47
Email domainedecoetbihan@gmail.com
Web www.chambredhotes-vannes.fr

Entry 284   Map 3

# Brittany

## Le 14 St Michel

This professional B&B joins a skyline tickled by the turrets of a medieval castle. A modernised 1893 townhouse, perched on the Nantes-Brest canal, it exudes boutique hotel rather than B&B, yet keeps a family feel. There's a feeling of peace and privacy and the suite has its own floor. Spacious bedrooms come in tasteful grey with contemporary bathrooms and garden views. Fresh pancakes and homemade yogurt star at continental breakfast, served al fresco in summer; on cool evenings, enjoy aperitifs by the dining room's open fire. Arthurian legend and Merlin's tomb are a cycle away, in the mythical Brocéliande Forest.

| | |
|---|---|
| Rooms | 3 doubles, 1 twin: €65–€95. 1 suite for 4: €97–€123. Singles €65–€85. Extra bed/sofabed €26 per person per night. |
| Meals | Dinner with wine, €28. Restaurants within walking distance. |
| Closed | Christmas. |

**Viviane Le Goff**
Le 14 St Michel,
56120 Josselin
Morbihan

| | |
|---|---|
| Tel | +33 (0)2 97 22 24 24 |
| Email | contact@le14stmichel.com |
| Web | www.le14stmichel.com |

Entry 285    Map 3

iStock.com/Roberto Caucino

Western Loire

www.sawdays.co.uk/western-loire

## Le Manoir des Quatre Saisons

Jean-Philippe and his mother are attentive hosts, providing both swimming robes and drinks by the pool. Communal breakfasts are flexible, complete with eggs and cereals as well as local choices. Well-loved, lived-in rooms (some in two-storey cottages in the grounds, some with kitchens) are colourfully co-ordinated with a traditional feel (delightful Jean-Philippe has an eye for detail: stripes, patterns, French flourishes) and distant sea views. Beach, river and town are walkable but children will enjoy mucking around in the big dog-friendly garden full of secret corners. *Minimum stay: 2 nights on bank holiday weekends & in high season.*

## Château de Coët Caret

Come for a taste of life with the French country aristocracy – it's getting hard to find; the family have lived here for 13 generations. Gwénaël greets you on arrival and is on hand when needed. The château is tucked into the woods and 100 hectares of parkland with plenty of paths for wandering: serenity is guaranteed. Bedrooms are faded but comfortable; *Saumon*, under the eaves, comes with binoculars for the birds. Start the day with excellent bread, jams and coffee in the wonderful breakfast room. Gwénaël is full of tips and you are in the Brière Regional Park where water and land are inextricably mingled and wildlife abounds.

| | |
|---|---|
| Rooms | 3 doubles, 1 twin: €75–€95. |
| | 1 quadruple: €95–€105. |
| | Extra bed €20 per person per night. |
| Meals | Restaurants 1.5km. |
| Closed | Rarely. |

| | |
|---|---|
| Rooms | 3 doubles, 1 twin: €100–€115. |
| Meals | Restaurants 2-10km. |
| Closed | Rarely. |

**Jean-Philippe Meyran**
Le Manoir des Quatre Saisons,
744 bd de Lauvergnac,
44420 La Turballe
Loire-Atlantique
Tel +33 (0)2 40 11 76 16
Mobile +33 (0)6 87 33 43 86
Email jean-philippe.meyran@club-internet.fr
Web www.le-manoir-des-quatre-saisons.com

**Gwénaël de La Monneraye**
Château de Coët Caret,
44410 Herbignac
Loire-Atlantique
Tel +33 (0)2 40 91 41 20
Email coetcaret@gmail.com
Web www.coetcaret.com

Entry 286  Map 3

Entry 287  Map 3

## Western Loire

### Château de Cop-Choux

Where to start: the elegant house built just before the French Revolution (with later towers), the 18-hectare park, the pool, the rolling lawns? Or the 17 marble fireplaces and your friendly hosts? The house is full of light and bedrooms are lofty: fabric floating at tall windows, perhaps an exquisite carved bed. A river runs through the grounds, there are lakes and woods for ramblers, rare ferns for plant buffs, farm animals, even dromedaries in summer. Breakfast comes with a selection of teas in a pretty panelled room and dinner is served at separate tables. All feels calm and serene.

## Western Loire

### Loire-Séjours

"I want to ride my bicycle, I want to ride…"; Well, cycle your way along the Loire à Vélo route to this lovely spot – a double-fronted 18th-century townhouse run with love and pride by French Aline and English Andrew. They've thought of everything for the saddle-sore including secure storage and washing facilities for gear. Rooms are elegant and comfortable with good beds. The Anglo-French alliance is in full swing at breakfast when you can choose a full English or a delicious continental. Plan your day in the guests' sitting room with grand piano and parquet or the pretty, tiered garden presided over by a happy hen. *Parking available.*

| | |
|---|---|
| Rooms | 4 twin/doubles: €95–€120. |
| | 1 suite for 4: €160–€240. |
| | Dinner, B&B €191–€216 per person. |
| | Extra bed/sofabed available €20 per person per night. |
| Meals | Breakfast €8. |
| | Dinner with wine €39. |
| | Restaurants 12km. |
| Closed | Rarely. |

| | |
|---|---|
| Rooms | 3 doubles, 1 twin: €55–€70. |
| | 1 family room for 3: €60–€105. |
| Meals | Full English breakfast extra €6.50. |
| | Restaurants within walking distance. |
| Closed | Never. |

|  |  |
|---|---|
| | **Patrick Moreau** |
| | Château de Cop-Choux, |
| | 44850 Mouzeil |
| | Loire-Atlantique |
| Tel | +33 (0)2 40 97 28 52 |
| Email | chateau-cop-choux@orange.fr |
| Web | www.chateau-cop-choux.com |

|  |  |
|---|---|
| | **Andrew Treppass** |
| | Loire-Séjours, |
| | 196 rue du Général Leclerc, |
| | 44150 Ancenis |
| | Loire-Atlantique |
| Tel | +33 (0)9 64 40 47 46 |
| Email | info@loire-sejours.fr |
| Web | www.loire-sejours.com |

Entry 288    Map 3

Entry 289    Map 3

### Château de la Sébinière

Young, warm, humorous, Anne has exquisite taste, a perfectionist's eye and lovely twin daughters. The house of her dreams, this 18th-century château in its pretty park is a light, sunny and harmonious home. Walls are white or red-ochre, ceilings beamed, bathrooms a blend of old and new. There's an extravagant attention to detail – a pewter jug of old roses by a gilt mirror, a fine wicker chair on an ancient tiled floor. You have your own entrance and the run of the sitting room, log-fired in winter. There may be real hot chocolate at breakfast and, if you wish, a glass of wine on arrival. Nearby Clisson is full of charm.

### Logis de Richebonne

Monsieur's parents bought this old *logis Vendéen* when he was six. Years later, researching the history of the house, he found his family had owned it in 1670! Framed in the hall, Madame's family tree goes back to the 14th century. Both are warm, welcoming and not at all grand and the old house is full of personal touches: Madame painted the breakfast china and embroidered the beautiful tablecloths. Vast bedrooms have peaceful views and quantities of fresh and dried flowers. The suite is ideal for a family, the huge grounds hold two pretty ponds (unfenced) and a barbecue: you may picnic here. Wonderful all round.

| | |
|---|---|
| Rooms | 3 doubles: €105–€125. |
| Meals | Dinner with wine, €30. |
| Closed | Rarely. |

| | |
|---|---|
| Rooms | 2 double: €70. |
| | 1 suite for 5: €70. |
| Meals | Picnic available. |
| | Restaurant in village, 1.5km. |
| Closed | Rarely. |

**Anne Cannaferina**
Château de la Sébinière,
44330 Le Pallet
Loire-Atlantique

Tel     +33 (0)2 40 80 49 25
Mobile  +33 (0)6 17 35 45 33
Email   info@chateausebiniere.com
Web     www.chateausebiniere.com

**Alain & Françoise de Ternay**
Logis de Richebonne,
7 impasse Richebonne,
44650 Legé
Loire-Atlantique

Tel    +33 (0)2 40 04 90 41
Email  adeternay@wanadoo.fr
Web    www.logisderichebonne.com

## La Grande Maison d'Arthenay

Micaela was in the hotel trade, Sue worked at a Sussex winery, now they run an idyllic B&B on a former Saumur wine estate. The tours of their cellars and of the region are unmissable. The house dates from 1706, the potager is organic, and the outbuildings create a delicious hollyhock'd garden off which two rustic-chic bedrooms lie. The two in the house are equally lovely, one with an extra bed on the mezzanine: tuffeau walls, deep mattresses, soft beautiful colours. Start the day with a convivial breakfast (fresh figs, eggs from their hens), end it with a twice-weekly wine-tasting dinner at the big table. *Children over 16 welcome.*

## Château de la Maronnière

Friendly Marie and François have excelled in restoring their luxurious, 18th-century château. Oak parquet is warm underfoot, copper leaf chandeliers light the circular hall and a stuffed fox surprises on the spiral staircase. Many rambling acres of green-fingered Eden await; take a wildlife walk or pluck cherries by the pool. Stylish shared spaces are immaculate with a baby grand in residence: 'Le Petit Bois' has carved antique furniture; 'La Rotonde' is marble grey with unusual panelling. Textiles and trimmings are sumptuous, bath robes fluffy; throw open the shutters and the views pour in. Stroll into Aizenay – or dine here.

| | |
|---|---|
| Rooms | 3 twin/doubles, 1 suite for 4: €95-€110. |
| Meals | Dinner with wine, €50 (Sun & Mon only). |
| Closed | November – March. |

| | |
|---|---|
| Rooms | 1 double, 2 twin/doubles: €110-€120. 1 suite for 2: €195. Child bed €25. |
| Meals | Dinner with wine, €35. Restaurants within walking distance. |
| Closed | Never. |

**Micaela Frow & Sue Hunt**
La Grande Maison d'Arthenay,
Rue de la Cerisaie, Arthenay,
49700 Saumur – Le Puy Notre Dame
Loire-Atlantique
Tel     +33 (0)2 41 40 35 06
Email   resv@lagrandemaison.net
Web    www.lagrandemaison.net

**François-Xavier & Marie-Hélène d'Halluin**
Château de la Maronnière,
Route des Sables,
85190 Aizenay
Vendée
Mobile   +33 (0)6 25 02 00 55
Email    dhalluinmh@gmail.com
Web     www.chateauvendee.com

Entry 292   Map 4

Entry 293   Map 8

## Les Fermes de Terre Neuve

The setting is rural, flat, open, with fields of crops all around, the barns, sumptuously renovated, are 200 years old, and the hosts live in the big house. Ex château-owners – pictures, sconces, antiques abound! – they are a delight. There's a guest salon with a double-height ceiling, a custom-made bar for drinks and snacks, an elegant pool lined with exotics. Toiletries are by Hermès and bedrooms are luxurious ground-floor suites: vibrant wall florals for 'Dame au Camélia', a colonial four-poster for 'Kipling', a piano for 'Montgolfière' – great fun. It feels remote yet the town is close, and so is the Vendée coast.

## Le Clos du Marais

Spot egrets, herons and storks as you gaze across to the marshes beyond Jacqueline and Gil's delightful whitewashed home. At the edge of a historic village close to the Vendée coastline, this beautifully renovated longère has two elegant, light-filled rooms for guests. Cheery blue 'Hortensia' has an en suite with a roll top bath and scented stuff for pampering; romantic 'Les Dimes' has a stylish walk-in shower and its own sitting room with a pair of stylish leather armchairs. Breakfast on pastries, homemade jam and local honey in the dining room or by the heated pool; book ahead for Gil's superb three-course dinners.
*Minimum stay: 3 nights in high season.*

| | |
|---|---|
| Rooms | 2 doubles; 1 twin with sofabed: £111–£142. |
| Meals | Restaurants 2km. |
| Closed | Never. |

| | |
|---|---|
| Rooms | 2 doubles: €75–€135. Dinner, B&B €62–€70 per person. Extra bed/sofabed available €30 per person per night. |
| Meals | Dinner €30. |
| Closed | Rarely. |

| | |
|---|---|
| | **Marie France Goueffon de Vaivre** Les Fermes de Terre Neuve, Route de St Mathurin, 85340 L'Île d'Olonne Vendée |
| Tel | +33 (0)2 51 23 17 39 |
| Email | mfv@lagirardiere.com |
| Web | www.lesfermesdeterreneuve.com |

| | |
|---|---|
| | **Jacqueline Davies & Gil Darlavoix** Le Clos du Marais, 10 rue du Communal, 85540 Curzon Vendée |
| Tel | +33 (0)2 28 14 01 12 |
| Mobile | +33 (0)6 21 74 75 01 |
| Email | leclosdumarais@gmail.com |
| Web | www.leclosdumarais.com |

Entry 294   Map 8

Entry 295   Map 8

## La Marienne

A perfect blend of serene seclusion and homeliness, this 15th-century priory of warm stonework and beams has been tenderly restored. Charming Françoise dispenses homemade marmalade with advice and smiles, alongside dappled shade and poolside loungers (and open fires in winter). Airy bedrooms, clean-line bathrooms and pure décor induce total relaxation, enhanced by a jacuzzi or hammam (€10). Bedrooms share a tranquil sitting room opening onto beautiful, rustic gardens. You could punt the waterways, cycle country lanes and browse the markets – but La Marienne's hypnotic beauty will tempt you to return.

## Le Rosier Sauvage

The pretty village is known for its exquisite abbey and some of that monastic serenity pervades these rooms. We love the family room under the rafters: massive oak door, cool tiled floor, a touch of toile, a simple mix of furniture. Through the family kitchen, breakfast is at a long polished table in the old stable: linger over cake and compote; the old laundry, its huge stone tub intact, is now a sitting room. Guests can picnic in the many-flowered walled garden, overlooked by the abbey and a glorious cedar tree. Energetic Christine is as charming as her house, which is also home to her husband and twin girls.

| | | | | |
|---|---|---|---|---|
| Rooms | 3 doubles: €78–€90. 1 annexe for 4: €90–€145. | | Rooms | 1 double, 1 twin: €49–€52. 1 family room for 3, 1 family room for 4: €59–€72. Singles €42–€45. Extra bed/sofabed €10 per person per night. |
| Meals | Restaurants 10km. | | Meals | Restaurants within walking distance. |
| Closed | Rarely. | | Closed | October – April. |

Françoise Charraud
La Marienne,
14 rue de la Virée-Lesson,
85490 Benet
Vendée

Tel +33 (0)2 51 51 50 41
Mobile +33 (0)6 71 77 02 51
Email charraud.francoise@wanadoo.fr
Web www.la-marienne.com

Christine Chastain-Poupin
Le Rosier Sauvage,
1 rue de l'Abbaye,
85240 Nieul sur l'Autise
Vendée

Tel +33 (0)2 51 52 49 39
Email lerosiersauvage@gmail.com
Web www.lerosiersauvage.c.la

Entry 296   Map 8

Entry 297   Map 8

## Le Logis de la Clef de Bois

The town, a *ville d'art et d'histoire*, is one of the loveliest in the Vendée. The house stands in lushness at one end of it. Madame has an easy elegance and her home overflows with taste and glamorous touches, from the fabulous Zuber mural in the dining room to the immaculate fauteuils of the salon. Big paintings, a collection of muslin caps from Poitou, bedrooms that celebrate writers… all point to cultural leanings. 'Simenon' speaks of the Renaissance, 'Michel Ragon' is flamboyant in red and white checks, 'Rabelais' is joyful in trompe l'œil. Come down to a royally elegant breakfast and, perhaps, Madame's own cannelés.

## La Grange aux Peintres

Bernadette's paintings cover the tall stone walls of this artistic barn overlooking the Vendée's fields and forests. Beams criss-cross high above the sitting room, lime and purple chairs sit by a wood-burner and you can borrow a book from a four-metre case (with a ladder!). Read it by the blue decked pool, or on the garden terrace where you breakfast on home-baked cakes and local hams. And you sleep on snowy linen in big, harmonious bedrooms with names like Degas and Picasso. Wander into the village or whip up a picnic in the old piggery, also beautifully converted. Alain (a doctor) and Bernadette never rush you to leave.

| | |
|---|---|
| Rooms | 2 doubles, 2 family suites for 3-5: €115-€135. Extra bed €26 per person per night. |
| Meals | Barbecue & picnic available. Restaurant within walking distance. |
| Closed | Mid-September to mid-April. |

| | |
|---|---|
| Rooms | 5 doubles: €110. Singles €100. Extra bed/sofabed €25 per person per night. |
| Meals | Dinner with wine, €20 (low season only). Restaurants 1km. |
| Closed | Never. |

**Danielle Portebois**
Le Logis de la Clef de Bois,
5 rue du Département,
85200 Fontenay le Comte
Vendée

Tel      +33 (0)2 51 69 03 49
Mobile   +33 (0)6 15 41 04 31
Email    clef_de_bois@hotmail.com
Web      www.clef-de-bois.com

**Alain & Bernadettte Rouffignat**
La Grange aux Peintres,
Faîte,
85120 Vouvant
Vendée

Tel      +33 (0)2 51 52 43 97
Email    bernadette@rouffignat.eu
Web      www.lagrangeauxpeintres.fr

Entry 298   Map 8

Entry 299   Map 8

## Western Loire

### Maison des Amis

Opposite the church of sleepy La Chapelle-Thémer is a village shop turned immaculate B&B. Emma and Phil have happily opened their doors to guests and offer table d'hôtes. The sitting and dining rooms have a bright clean feel; the courtyard garden catches the sun. One guest bedroom is reached through the kitchen, the other is upstairs, each a symphony in white with walls of palest pastel. Bathrobes are soft, breakfast is delicious, and Bertie the labrador will charm you. The house is remote but the region is wonderful for cyclists and wine lovers, and the coast is under an hour.

| Rooms | 2 doubles: €60-€65. |
|---|---|
| Meals | Dinner, 4 courses, €28. |
| | Restaurants 10km. |
| Closed | Rarely. |

Philip & Emma Johnson
Maison des Amis,
13 rue de l'Église,
85210 La Chapelle-Thémer
Vendée
Tel +33 (0)2 51 28 99 48
Email philip@picalo.co.uk
Web www.abreakinfrance.com

Entry 300  Map 8

## Western Loire

### La Maison de Landerie

Annie used to have her own restaurant in Devon so whether you are outside on her little stone terrace overlooking open fields and forest or inside at her long antique table, it will be a Cordon Bleu breakfast. Multi-talented Annie could open an antique shop: her lovingly collected artefacts decorate this sweet little farmhouse like a dream from the past. The paintwork is gorgeous, the vintage linens are sumptuous, the towels are thirsty, the mattresses are from heaven. You can walk to town, pick a trail in the forest or rent a canoe and follow the lazy river Lay. Annie's dinners are renowned, even the Mayor comes to dine.

| Rooms | 2 doubles: €65. |
|---|---|
| Meals | Dinner with wine, €30. |
| Closed | Christmas. |

Annie Jory
La Maison de Landerie,
La Réorthe,
85210 Sainte Hermine
Vendée
Tel +33 (0)2 51 27 80 70
Email richard.jory@wanadoo.fr
Web www.lalanderie.com

Entry 301  Map 8

## La Frelonnière

An elegant country house in a peaceful, pastoral setting – who would not love it? The 18th-century farmhouse, complete with musket holes and open rafters, is informal and delightful. Your English/Scottish hosts are fun, friendly and intimately acquainted with France – they brought their children up here. Now they generously open their living space to guests, their serene pool and their exquisite Monet-style garden. Quietly stylish bedrooms (coir carpets, white walls, fresh flowers, silk flourishes) are divided by a sofa'd library on the landing; dinners, served three times a week, may be romantic or convivial. A gem.

## La Joulinière

Wrapped in flowers and lawns in a sleepy Vendée hamlet, this farmhouse looks a treat with its white shutters and bumpy stone. Find leafy terraces, parasols, a pool… inside, a baby grand piano in a country-pretty sitting room where soft, pale fabrics reflect floods of light. There are two cosy suites: 'Eléonore' in the old smithy, with vaulted oak ceilings and stony walls, 'Guinevere' upstairs with a four-poster draped in floaty white. Anthony and Carol, musicians, have an ear for birdsong, eye for décor and heart for B&B. It's like staying with cultured friends in the country, near Chantonnay and the beaches of western France.

| Rooms | 2 doubles: €75. |
| --- | --- |
| Meals | Dinner with wine, €35 (Fri & Sat); €20 (Sun-Thurs). |
| Closed | Rarely. |

| Rooms | 2 doubles: €65. |
| --- | --- |
| | Extra bed/sofabed €15 per person per night. |
| Meals | Restaurants 3km. |
| Closed | End-October to Easter. |

|  | Julie & Richard Deslandes |
| --- | --- |
| | La Frelonnière, |
| | 85410 La Caillère – St Hilaire du Bois |
| | Vendée |
| Tel | +33 (0)2 51 51 56 49 |
| Mobile | +33 (0)6 70 08 50 26 |
| Email | julie@lafrelonniere.fr |
| Web | www.bandbvendee.com |

|  | Carol & Anthony Langford |
| --- | --- |
| | La Joulinière, |
| | 85390 Bazoges en Pareds |
| | Vendée |
| Tel | +33 (0)2 51 50 62 23 |
| Mobile | +33 (0)7 87 28 91 23 |
| Email | anthony.langford@yahoo.fr |
| Web | www.bandbwestfrance.com |

### Domaine du Revêtison

A 19th-century farmhouse, immaculately converted into a smart B&B. Corinne speaks good English, Steve is British, they give you a family-friendly pool (with poolhouse, bar and games) and nothing is too much trouble. Best of all is Corinne's table d'hôtes at the big convivial table, Vendée style (garlicky bread, bean and lamb stew). Kitchen and dining rooms are linked, bedrooms are country-pretty, towels are white and fluffy and all is splendidly maintained. It's peaceful and remote but the historical theme park Le Puy du Fou is not too far; nor are the glam beaches of Les Sables d'Olonne. Great for sociable families. *Minimum stay: 2 nights at weekends.*

### Château de la Flocellière

You stay in the château, where bedrooms are vast, gracious and opulent, with huge windows onto the gardens and park. Overseeing all is the Vicomtesse and her meticulous eye misses nothing, from the topiary in the grounds to the maids' attire. You can lounge around in the sitting room in the gallery, play a game of billiards, admire the magnificent potager below the ruined walls, visit the library or be taken on a full tour. Splash in the heated saltwater pool in spring and summer, hobnob with your hosts during thrice-weekly tables d'hôtes. This is living at its most sedate and children are welcome providing they behave impeccably! *Minimum stay: 2 nights in high season.*

| Rooms | 1 twin: €79. |
| --- | --- |
| | 3 family rooms for 2-4: €79-€145. |
| Meals | Dinner €32. |
| | Child €15. |
| | Restaurant in town. |
| Closed | Rarely. |

| Rooms | 3 twin/doubles: €175-€235. |
| --- | --- |
| | 2 suites for 2-4: €235-€295. |
| | Singles €150-€175. |
| | Dinner, B&B €140-€170 per person. |
| | Extra bed/sofabed €30 per person per night. |
| Meals | Dinner with wine, €55. Restaurant within walking distance. |
| Closed | January/February. |

**Corinne & Steve Wilson**
Domaine du Revêtison,
85110 Chantonnay
Vendée

| Tel | +33 (0)2 51 09 63 92 |
| --- | --- |
| Mobile | +33 (0)6 18 93 79 23 |
| Email | revetison@gmail.com |
| Web | www.domainedurevetison.com |

**Vicomte & Vicomtesse Vignial**
Château de la Flocellière,
85700 La Flocellière
Vendée

| Tel | +33 (0)2 51 57 22 03 |
| --- | --- |
| Email | flocelliere.chateau@gmail.com |
| Web | www.chateaudelaflocelliere.com |

### Château de la Frogerie

It's not often you can pretend to be medieval royalty but ascending the fabulous spiral staircase to your turret bedroom presents the ideal opportunity! Overlooking glorious Loire countryside, this petite château dates back to the 15th century. Panelled walls, a moat and parquet floors create historical atmosphere but charming owner Jean-Christophe has ensured that modern comfort co-exists. Antique beds are dressed in fine linen, cosy leather armchairs surround the fireplace and there's a pool shaded by ancient walls. Breakfast like a king on pastries, milk from the local Jersey herd and honey from the château's hives. *Parking available.*

### Château du Beugnon

Run by delightful retired restaurateurs, a tranquil château where foodies can feast on creatively prepared seasonal stuff from the potager. The setting couldn't be more idyllic; a fine landscaped park shaded by plane trees surrounds the property and a resident swan glides across an ornamental lake... Antique-filled bedrooms in the château have a homely, traditional charm; lovely doubles in the converted barn have rustic stone walls and terracotta-tiled floors. All have immaculate en-suites, some with fabulous 1930s sinks. Plan a Layon Valley wine tour or visit Angers for a glimpse of the medieval Apocalypse Tapestry.

| | |
|---|---|
| Rooms | 2 doubles: €80–€114. |
| | 1 family room for 4-5: €140–€240. |
| | Singles €65–€78. |
| Meals | Restaurant 6km. |
| Closed | Rarely. |

| | |
|---|---|
| Rooms | 4 doubles: €95. |
| | 1 suite for 5: €105. |
| Meals | Dinner, with wine, €35. |
| | Restaurant 5km. |
| Closed | Never. |

| | |
|---|---|
| | **Jean-Christophe Robert** |
| | Château de la Frogerie, |
| | 49360 Maulévrier |
| | Maine-et-Loire |
| Tel | +33 (0)2 41 30 60 67 |
| Email | contact@chateau-frogerie.fr |
| Web | www.chateau-frogerie.fr |

| | |
|---|---|
| | **Jean-Yves Bauchart** |
| | Château du Beugnon, |
| | 49540 La Fosse de Tigné |
| | Maine-et-Loire |
| Tel | +33 (0)2 41 38 32 05 |
| Email | reservation@chateaudubeugnon.fr |
| Web | www.chateaudubeugnon.fr |

## Le Clos de la Brète

Most of the houses in the village are owned by winemakers still, but this one is lived in by gentle Madame. With her adorable daughter, two cats and a handful of pretty hens, she does B&B that is perfect for families. There are troglodyte villages to visit and, just up the road, a bamboo-forested zoo, the famously animal-friendly Doué la Fontaine. Beds are beautiful and brand new, eiderdowns add colour to a neutral palette and everything feels sunny and warm. Wake to homemade yogurts, breads, cakes and jams, set off for the châteaux of the Loire, return to rambling lawns, toys to share, and a stylish grey sofa in front of the fire.

| | |
|---|---|
| Rooms | 2 doubles: €65–€76. |
| | 1 suite for 5: €75–€155. |
| | Extra bed/sofabed €16–€25 per person per night. |
| Meals | Restaurants 2km. |
| Closed | Never. |

Florence Lacroix
Le Clos de la Brète,
9 rue Jean de la Brète,
Village d'Igné,
49700 Cizay la Madeleine
Maine-et-Loire

| | |
|---|---|
| Tel | +33 (0)2 41 50 46 26 |
| Email | flodelabrete@orange.fr |
| Web | www.le-clos-de-la-brete.fr/ |

Entry 308   Map 4

---

## Manoir de Boisairault

Our inspector had an *Alice Through The Looking Glass* moment as she stepped off the street, through the unremarkable gate and into the wonderful gardens – a series of secret 'rooms' – that surround this elegant, 18th-century, cloistered manor. A labyrinth of caves, typical of the region, lies below and guests sometimes dine there with Jean-Pierre and Béatrice, your cultured, interesting hosts. Pray for the camembert sprinkled with pastis, cooked in the fire's embers – it's divine. Inside are an attractive dining room and three pretty bedrooms; the ground-floor one – all Louis XV – is particularly enchanting.

| | |
|---|---|
| Rooms | 2 doubles: €125–€140. |
| | 1 family room for 4: €180–€240. |
| Meals | Dinner with wine, €35. |
| | Children under 10, €15. |
| | Restaurants 10 km. |
| Closed | Rarely. |

Jean-Pierre Delmas
Manoir de Boisairault,
8 rue de Pas d'Aubigné,
49260 Le Coudray Macouard
Maine-et-Loire

| | |
|---|---|
| Mobile | +33 (0)6 08 93 85 61 |
| Email | contact@manoir-de-boisairault.com |
| Web | www.manoir-de-boisairault.com |

Entry 309   Map 4

### Château de Beaulieu

Set back from the banks of the river Loire lies a château of character and charm, a perfect reflection of its delightful owners. The house was built in 1727 and the décor, traditional and authentic, captures the romance of that earlier age. Five bedrooms lead off an oak-beamed corridor and range from the dramatic to the cosy and intimate. Find antique armoires, ornate fireplaces, bold colours and dreamy views of the large, tree-brimmed garden – with a lovely pool and a small prospering vineyard. Snuggle down with a book from the library, try your hand at billiards, visit historic Saumur.

### Château de Salvert

This highly sculpted neo-gothic folly is home to a couple of grand aristocrats (Monsieur is delightful). The baronial hall is properly dark and spooky, the dining room and salon elegant and plush with gilt chairs and ancestors on the walls. The vast suite has two double bedrooms, a sitting area and a library in an alcove. Both rooms are well decorated with fine French pieces and modern fabrics. The pool is flower-fringed, the park is huge – wild boar roam, spring boarlets scamper – and Madame plays the piano and holds concerts. On the edge of the forest, an easy drive to Loire Valley châteaux and vineyards. *Arrival after 4pm.*

| | |
|---|---|
| Rooms | 4 doubles: €95–€120. |
| | 1 suite for 2–4: €160–€200. |
| Meals | Restaurants 1km. |
| Closed | November – April. |

| | |
|---|---|
| Rooms | 1 suite for 4: €120–€200. |
| Meals | Dinner with wine, €55. |
| Closed | Rarely. |

| | |
|---|---|
| | **Conor & Mary Coady-Maguire** |
| | Château de Beaulieu, |
| | 98 route de Montsoreau, |
| | 49400 Saumur |
| | Maine-et-Loire |
| Tel | +33 (0)2 41 50 83 52 |
| Email | info@chateaudebeaulieu.fr |
| Web | www.chateaudebeaulieu.fr |

| | |
|---|---|
| | **Monica Le Pelletier de Glatigny** |
| | Château de Salvert, |
| | Salvert, |
| | 49680 Neuillé |
| | Maine-et-Loire |
| Tel | +33 (0)2 41 52 55 89 |
| Mobile | +33 (0)6 15 12 03 11 |
| Email | info@salvert.com |
| Web | www.chateau-de-salvert.fr |

## Western Loire

### Domaine de l'Oie Rouge

Recline in bed in the quaint 'Chambre Camélia' and watch the Loire flow by. The 19th-century townhouse sits in a large peaceful garden, and Christiane runs a lovely shop selling all manner of jams, pâtés and excellent produce. One bedroom has an astonishingly ornate 1930s brown-tiled bathroom with its bath bang in the middle, another opens to the garden and trees; all the rooms are lavishly French and art-hung. Monsieur is chef, Madame hosts dinner – great fun when a number of guests are staying. Both your hosts will be happy to help you decide what to see and make the most of your stay.

## Western Loire

### La Rousselière

A hymn to peace, permanence and gentle living. The superb garden is Monsieur's pride and joy; château-like reception rooms open one into another – glass doors to glass doors, billiards to dining to sitting – like an indoor arcade; family portraits follow you everywhere; Mass is still said once a year in the chapel. But it's never over-grand. Bedrooms are highly individual with their antiques and hand-painted armoires (courtesy of an artistic sister), many bathrooms are new and Madame is the most delightful smiling hostess and a fine cook (veg, meat and eggs all home-grown). Your lovely hosts join you for an aperitif before dinner.

| Rooms | 5 doubles: €80–€100. Extra bed €19 per person per night. |
|---|---|
| Meals | Dinner with wine, €27. |
| Closed | Rarely. |

| Rooms | 2 doubles, 2 twins: €70–€100. 1 family room for 4: €150. |
|---|---|
| Meals | Dinner with wine, €30. |
| Closed | Rarely. |

**Christiane Batel**
Domaine de l'Oie Rouge,
8 rue Nationale,
49350 Les Rosiers sur Loire
Maine-et-Loire
Tel       +33 (0)2 41 53 65 65
Email   c.batel@wanadoo.fr
Web     www.domaine-oie-rouge.com

**François & Jacqueline de Béru**
La Rousselière,
49170 La Possonnière
Maine-et-Loire
Tel       +33 (0)2 41 39 13 21
Mobile  +33 (0)6 60 67 60 69
Email   larousseliere@unimedia.fr
Web     www.anjou-et-loire.com/rousseliere

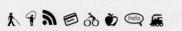

Entry 312   Map 4

Entry 313   Map 3

## Western Loire

### Loire-Charmilles

A house and garden full of surprises and a dazzling mix of styles. Chunky beams and old floors are set against slabs of slate, Japanese art and some very modern furniture. Up wooden stairs, through a low doorway (mind your head), bedrooms have huge beds, dimmer switches, antique desks with perspex chairs and ultra-chic bathrooms, one with a repro bath. The enclosed garden teems with roses, mimosa and orchids; breakfast and dinner are on the veranda on warm days or in the huge-windowed orangery; bubbly Nadia cooks on a fireplace grill; she and Jean-Pierre, son Jules and the lovely lab, make this a warm family house. *Arrival after 6pm.*

| | |
|---|---|
| Rooms | 1 double, 1 twin: €72. 6 nights, €390. Singles €69. |
| Meals | Dinner with wine, €27. Guest kitchenette. |
| Closed | Rarely. |

|  | **Nadia Leinberger** |
|---|---|
| | Loire-Charmilles, |
| | 9 rue de l'École, |
| | 49410 Le Mesnil en Vallée |
| | Maine-et-Loire |
| Tel | +33 (0)2 41 78 94 74 |
| Mobile | +33 (0)6 77 10 69 66 |
| Email | nadia@loire-charmilles.com |
| Web | www.loire-charmilles.com |

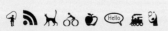

Entry 314   Map 3

## Western Loire

### Le Mésangeau

The house is long-faced, and refined; the grounds (superb) come with a fishing pond and 'aperitif gazebo'. The Migons have expertly renovated this unusual house with its barn-enclosed courtyard, two towers and covered terrace. Big, north-facing bedrooms are elegant and comfortable behind their shutters, and keep the housekeepers busy. Expect leather sofas and a suit of armour, colourful beams above antique furniture, two billiard tables, and bikes, ping-pong and drums in the barn. At dinner, French cuisine from Madame, and much entertainment from Monsieur, who collects veteran cars and plays bass guitar.

| | |
|---|---|
| Rooms | 3 doubles, 1 suite for 4, 1 suite for 5: €90–€110. |
| Meals | Dinner with wine, €35. |
| Closed | Rarely. |

|  | **Brigitte & Gérard Migon** |
|---|---|
| | Le Mésangeau, |
| | 49530 Drain |
| | Maine-et-Loire |
| Tel | +33 (0)2 40 98 21 57 |
| Email | le.mesangeau@orange.fr |
| Web | www.loire-mesangeau.com |

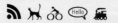

Entry 315   Map 3

## Château de Challain

Plucked from a fairy tale, this château remains true to its noble history with an understated nod to more modern times. The original features remain: sweeping staircases, vaulted ceilings, chandeliers. You may repose in the grand salons, or choose the private treatment rooms; retire to bedrooms with trompe l'oeil wallpaper and antiques alongside excellent beds and spoiling bathrooms. Dinner is served by your host Fabian in the music room (or in the atmospheric kitchen) and, despite the undeniable grandeur, a sense of warmth flows throughout. History imbibes this part of the world: Angers and the Loire are a short drive away.

## Le Moulin de l'Etang

You approach the mill alongside the grand lake: the setting is stunning. Birds trill, the brook babbles and you can breakfast on the patio in summer. Bubbly Maria loves art, food, fashion and gives you two peaceful beamed bedrooms on the lower floor (one bed in the old bread oven!). Sumptuous canopies and cushions are hand-sewn, the feel is boudoir, the bathrooms are freshly modern. Boat and fish on the lake, splash in the above-ground pool, stroll to Noëllet (25 minutes). Then it's home for a lovely French / Sicilian supper hosted at the candlelit table; or, on balmy nights, from the barbecue. Wonderful.

| | |
|---|---|
| Rooms | 5 suites for 2: €250–€350. |
| Meals | Restaurant within walking distance. |
| Closed | Rarely. |

| | |
|---|---|
| Rooms | 1 double: €95. |
| | 1 family room for 3: €120. |
| Meals | Dinner, 5 courses, €25. |
| | Wine from €10. |
| | Restaurant 3km. |
| Closed | Rarely. |

**Cynthia Nicholson**
Château de Challain,
49440 Challain la Potherie
Maine-et-Loire

| | |
|---|---|
| Tel | +33 (0)2 41 92 74 26 |
| Email | chateauchallain@aol.com |
| Web | www.chateauchallain.com |

**Maria Mizzi**
Le Moulin de l'Etang,
49520 Noëllet
Maine-et-Loire

| | |
|---|---|
| Tel | +33 (0)2 41 94 47 59 |
| Mobile | +33 (0)6 26 52 28 52 |
| Email | mariamizzi@aol.com |
| Web | www.lemoulindeletang.com |

Entry 316   Map 3

Entry 317   Map 3

## Château du Plessis Anjou

Sixteenth-century Le Plessis has been welcoming guests for years. Dinner, brought to a long table in a dining room grandly furnished with Roman Empire frescoes, might include duck with apricots, cheese, a crisp fruit tart. One bedroom is striking with oriental rugs and the bed in a deep alcove; others have lofty beamed ceilings. Children are welcome and the Renouls have two of their own, hence the playground and the trampoline, the rabbits and the goat. Madame invites children to gather breakfast's eggs, and the pool hides in the grounds; the trees are sublime. Terra Botanica is a 15-minute drive.

| Rooms | 3 doubles: €150–€180. |
| | 2 suites for 2: €220–€250. |
| Meals | Dinner €48. |
| | Wine €20–€240. |
| Closed | Rarely. |

Valérie & Laurent Renoul
Château du Plessis Anjou,
49220 La Jaille Yvon
Maine-et-Loire
Tel  +33 (0)2 41 95 12 75
Email  plessis.anjou@wanadoo.fr
Web  www.chateau-du-plessis.com

Entry 318  Map 3

## La Croix d'Étain

Frisky red squirrels decorate the stone balustrade, the wisteria is a glory in spring, and the wide swooshing river cascades over the weir. It feels like deep country yet this handsome manor has urban elegance in its very stones. Panelling, mouldings, subtly muted floor tiles bring grace; traditional French florals add softness. It looks fairly formal but sprightly Madame loves having guests and pampers them, in their own quarters, with luxury. Expect plush, lacy, flowery, carpeted bedrooms, three with river views, all with sunny bathrooms. The yacht-side setting is stunning – it could be the Riviera.

| Rooms | 1 double, 3 twin/doubles: €85–€100. |
| | Singles €75. Extra bed/sofabed €25 |
| | per person per night. |
| Meals | Dinner with wine, €30. |
| | Crêperie within walking distance. |
| Closed | Rarely. |

FIRST
EDITION
VETERAN

Jacqueline & Auguste Bahuaud
La Croix d'Étain,
2 rue de l'Écluse,
49220 Grez Neuville
Maine-et-Loire
Tel  +33 (0)2 41 95 68 49
Email  croix.etain@loire-anjou-accommodation.com
Web  www.loire-anjou-accommodation.com

Entry 319  Map 3

## Manoir du Bois de Grez

An ancient peace lingers over the fan-shaped cobbled courtyard, the old well, the little chapel: the Manoir oozes history. Your doctor host, a talented gardener, and his charming wife, much-travelled antique-hunters with imagination and flair, offer guests warm generous bedrooms (including a superb family room) hung with well-chosen oriental pieces and paintings in good strong colours that reflect the garden light. Most wonderful of all are the specimen tree'd gardens, their great grassy carpets embracing a small lake. You share a big sitting room with your lovely hosts, lots of plants and a suit of armour.

## Château de Montriou

The park will explode your senses – and once the visitors have gone home, what a treat to have it to yourselves: the lake, the famous sequoia, the waves of crocuses in spring, the centuries-old chapel with three statues of Marie. This 15th-century château has been lived in and tended by the same family for 300 years and Monsieur and Madame know exactly how to make you feel at home. A spiral stone staircase leads to properly formal bedrooms whose bold colours were design flavour of the period; wooden floors, thick rugs and antiques are only slightly younger. And the venerable library is now a guest sitting room. Special.

| Rooms | 2 doubles, 1 twin: €85–€100. |
| | 1 family room for 4: €100–€145. |
| Meals | Picnic available. |
| | Guest kitchen. |
| | Restaurant 1.5km. |
| Closed | Rarely. |

| Rooms | 2 doubles; |
| | 1 double with kitchen: €85–€130. |
| | 1 suite for 4 with kitchen: €165. |
| Meals | Restaurant 6km. |
| Closed | Rarely. |

**Marie Laure & Jean Gaël Cesbron**
Manoir du Bois de Grez,
Route de Sceaux d'Anjou,
49220 Grez Neuville
Maine-et-Loire
Tel     +33 (0)2 41 18 00 09
Mobile  +33 (0)6 22 38 14 56
Email   cesbron.boisgrez@wanadoo.fr
Web     www.boisdegrez.com

**Régis & Nicole de Loture**
Château de Montriou,
49460 Feneu
Maine-et-Loire
Tel     +33 (0)2 41 93 30 11
Email   chateau-de-montriou@wanadoo.fr
Web     www.chateau-de-montriou.com

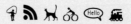

## Logis de la Roche Corbin

In the middle of old Angers, a secret, special place. Behind a high wall: a cobbled path, a climbing rose, a bunch of lettuces to keep the tortoise happy. Off this courtyard garden is your room, aglow with 18th-century charm; off a French-grey hallway, an exquisite zen-like bathroom. Breakfast is up the magnificent rough-hewn stair, in a room with a rooftop view. Behind this hugely sympathetic restoration of a 16th-century house are a generous couple, happy to collect guests from the station – Michael, an American painter with a studio over the road, and warm, charming Pascale from Paris. Free parking too. *Whole house available July/August.*

## Le Logis du Pressoir

Birdsong and sunlight filter through eau de nil shutters into your cosy 18th-century cottage on this former wine pressing estate. A chestnut-panelled haven (pretty curtains, antique furniture, pale linens, a luxurious shower) it's all the work of friendly, knowledgeable Lisa and Mark. Lush parkland conceals four gîtes, whose guests share the heated pool with you. Breakfast amidst wisteria and lavender on your private terrace, a feast of summer fruits from the orchard and pâtisserie fresh from the village minutes away. A local restaurant delivers carefree dinners, and Lisa will pack a picnic for forays into historic wine country. *Minimum stay: 2 nights.*

| Rooms | 1 double: €86. |
|---|---|
| Meals | Dinner with wine, €20–€30. |
| Closed | Rarely. |

| Rooms | 1 double: €85–€95. |
|---|---|
| | Singles €65. |
| Meals | Restaurant 10-minute walk. |
| | Picnics available. |
| Closed | December/January. |

**Michael & Pascale Rogosin**
Logis de la Roche Corbin,
3 rue de la Harpe,
49100 Angers
Maine-et-Loire

| Tel | +33 (0)2 41 86 93 70 |
|---|---|
| Mobile | +33 (0)6 14 78 37 06 |
| Email | logisdelaroche@gmail.com |
| Web | www.logisdelaroche.com |

**Lisa & Mark Wright**
Le Logis du Pressoir,
Villeneuve,
49250 Brion
Maine-et-Loire

| Tel | +33 (0)2 41 57 27 33 |
|---|---|
| Mobile | +33 (0)6 73 49 96 77 |
| Email | info@logisdupressoir.com |
| Web | www.logisdupressoir.com |

Entry 322   Map 4

Entry 323   Map 4

## Les Bouchets

It's spotless now, with all mod cons, gleaming antiques, open fires and vases of fresh flowers. The house was a ruin when the Bignons found it but they managed to save all the old timbers and stones. The result is a seductively warm cheerful house with bedrooms cosy and soft, two upstairs, one with an entrance off a garden where swings invite children to play. Passionate about food, they used to run a restaurant where Michel was chef; note the coppers in the kitchen/entrance hall, and memorabilia in the family sitting room. Géraldine, bright, friendly and organised, serves beautiful homegrown or local food and the wines of Anjou.

## La Besnardière

"Divine,"; says a happy guest. Lovely Joyce brims with knowledge about all things horticultural, cooks beautiful vegetarian and vegan food, welcomes art, yoga and meditation workshops in her meditation room and shares her fresh, tranquil, comfortable home with generosity. Beams spring everywhere in the 500-year-old farmhouse, roof and velux windows are new, and the big, book-filled and freshly decorated bedrooms are tucked under the rafters, one with steps to a courtyard below. Be charmed by log fires, a soft-pink sofa'd sitting room, a garden full of wild flowers, a donkey, goats, ducks, hens and views.

| Rooms | 1 double, 1 twin/double: €70–€75. 1 family room for 4: €120. | Rooms | 1 double, 1 triple sharing bathroom: €60. |
|---|---|---|---|
| Meals | Dinner with wine, €29. | Meals | Vegetarian or vegan dinner with wine, €20. |
| Closed | Rarely. | Closed | Rarely. |

**Michel & Géraldine Bignon**
Les Bouchets,
49150 Le Vieil Baugé
Maine-et-Loire
Tel       +33 (0)2 41 82 34 48
Mobile    +33 (0)6 71 60 66 05
Email     geraldinebignon@gmail.com
Web       www.lesbouchets.com

**Joyce Rimell**
La Besnardière,
Route de Baugé,
49150 Fougeré
Maine-et-Loire
Tel       +33 (0)2 41 90 15 20
Email     rimell.joyce@wanadoo.fr
Web       www.holiday-loire.com

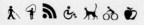

## La Maison du Roi René

The famous old auberge has become a charming B&B. Scrunch up the drive serenaded by soft roses to a lovely welcome from Madame. Part medieval, part 18th century, like the village around it, it has corners, crannies and a stunning central stone fireplace. The Valicourts – they speak four languages! – are the happy new owners of these magnificent oak doors and rosy tomette floors; bedrooms are beamed and very pleasing – one opens to the garden, three to the tower. There's a pretty paved terrace for breakfast with viennoiseries and a room of auberge proportions for a light supper of cold meats and local specialities.

| Rooms | 2 doubles, 1 suite for 2, 1 twin with sofabed: €65–€85. |
| --- | --- |
| Meals | Dinner €15.<br>Restaurant within walking distance. |
| Closed | Rarely. |

**Dominique de Valicourt**
La Maison du Roi René,
4 Grande Rue,
53290 Saint Denis d'Anjou
Mayenne
Tel   +33 (0)2 43 70 52 30
Mobile   +33 (0)6 89 37 87 12
Email   roi-rene@orange.fr
Web   www.roi-rene.fr

Entry 326   Map 4

## Le Logis du Ray

All who stay are wonderfully looked after – and we don't mean only the guests. Warm and caring, Jacques and Martine run a carriage-driving school, own four horses, three carthorses, two Shetland ponies and one Irish cob stallion, and house them in spotless pens and paddocks. Bedrooms are equally immaculate, their lovely old waxed terracotta floors setting off fine antiques and taupe and white furnishings to perfection in refined-traditional French style. The house is handsome in its historic village, your hosts are all smiles, and the area is rural and charming. Guests love the breakfasts.

| Rooms | 2 family rooms for 3: €89–€133. Singles €74. |
| --- | --- |
| Meals | Light dinner with wine, €18.<br>Restaurant in village. |
| Closed | Rarely. |

**Martine & Jacques Lefebvre**
Le Logis du Ray,
53290 Saint Denis d'Anjou
Mayenne
Tel   +33 (0)2 43 70 64 10
Email   ecoleattelageduray@orange.fr
Web   www.ecoleattelageduray.com

Entry 327   Map 4

### Domaine de la Houzardiere

Marguerite welcomes with tea and cakes; within minutes, you're part of her family. Large bedrooms in the converted barn of her 19th-century farmhouse are furnished with antiques from her grandfather's château; elegant armoires, beds and tables. Colourful quilts cover the beds, bright rugs are laid on tiled or parquet floors, original paintings hang on the walls. Windows look to woods – beckoning for walks – or the walled garden. Breakfasts – dinners, too – are served in a beautiful, spacious barn on sunny days (with kitchen for rustling up lunches); in the farmhouse kitchen on cooler days. Wonderfully, traditionally French.

### La Rouaudière

Prize-winning cows in the fields, an adorable family in the house, and a wagging farm dog. Thérèse, her farming son and husband (retired) are exceptionally engaging, relaxed people and their conversation is the heart and soul of this place. Dinners are divine, breakfasts in front of the crackling fire are estimable – delicious fresh everything and lashings of coffee. You'll find roses, pergolas, a rare magnolia and birdsong in the garden (Madame is a nature lover and keen plantswoman) and bedrooms that are straightforward, spotless and simple: plain walls, a few antiquey bits and bobs, pretty window boxes. Lovely.

| Rooms | 3 doubles, 1 twin: €59. Extra bed €18 per person per night. |
|---|---|
| Meals | Dinner with aperitif, wine & coffee, €21. Children's meals available. Restaurants within walking distance. |
| Closed | January/February. |

| Rooms | 1 double, 1 twin: €60-€63. 1 triple: €67-€87. |
|---|---|
| Meals | Dinner with wine, €25. |
| Closed | Rarely. |

**Marguerite Moenner**
Domaine de la Houzardiere,
Route de St Georges,
53170 Bazougers
Mayenne
Tel    +33 (0)2 43 02 37 16
Email    marguerite@houzardiere.com
Web    www.houzardiere.com

**Maurice & Thérèse Trihan**
La Rouaudière,
Mégaudais,
53500 Ernée
Mayenne
Tel    +33 (0)2 43 05 13 57
Email    therese-trihan@wanadoo.fr
Web    www.rouaudiere-megaudais.fr

Entry 328    Map 4

Entry 329    Map 3

### Château de la Villatte

From the village, a drive rises to the top of the butte where a 19th-century château sits in splendour. Isabelle arrived some years ago and her loving restoration knows no bounds – the fine outbuildings have just been completed – yet still she finds time to enjoy her guests. Dimensions are generous throughout and bedrooms are vast, their parquet floors strewn with rugs. Tall windows overlook the steeply sloping park and the valley below, there are marble fireplaces, paintings in gilt frames, an original claw-foot bath. Breakfast on the balcony or in the grand salon, borrow bikes, or explore the lovely tree'd grounds.

### Château de Craon

Such a close and welcoming family, whose kindness extends to include you. It's a magnificent place, with innumerable expressions of history, taste and personality, and gracious Loïk and Hélène, young grandparents, treat you like friends. A sitting room with sofas and a view of the park, an Italianate hall with sweeping stone stair, classic French bedrooms in lavender, blue, cream... an original washstand, a canopied bed, a velvet armchair. Everywhere a feast for the eyes; paintings, watercolours, antiques. Outside, 40 acres of river, meadows, lake, ice house, tennis court, pool, and a potager worth leaving home for.

| | |
|---|---|
| Rooms | 1 double, 1 twin/double (rooms interconnect to form suite): €80–€174. Singles €69–€87. Extra bed/sofabed €26 per person per night. |
| Meals | Buffet dinner €22. Wine €14–€39. Summer kitchen. |
| Closed | Rarely. |

| | |
|---|---|
| Rooms | 3 doubles, 1 twin: €100–€160. 1 suite for 2-4: €260. 1 single: €80. |
| Meals | Dinner with wine, €30. Restaurants within walking distance. |
| Closed | November – March. |

**Isabelle Charrier**
Château de la Villatte,
53970 Montigné le Brillant
Mayenne

| | |
|---|---|
| Tel | +33 (0)2 43 68 23 76 |
| Mobile | +33 (0)6 85 43 55 99 |
| Email | info@lavillatte.com |
| Web | www.lavillatte.com |

**Loïk & Hélène de Guébriant**
Château de Craon,
53400 Craon
Mayenne

| | |
|---|---|
| Tel | +33 (0)2 43 06 11 02 |
| Email | chateaudecraon@wanadoo.fr |
| Web | www.craoncastle.com |

### Le Rocher

Being the Richecours' only guests means a free run of Madame's delightful conversation (travel, history, houses, gardens, people), her intoxicating garden (pigeons and quails, specimen trees, an abundance of old roses), and the house that they have restored with such care and imagination. Character fills the big guest room above the old kitchen – 17th-century floor tiles, glowing colours, a divine bed – and the meadow sweeps down to the river where the family pedalo awaits to take you to the restaurant on the opposite bank. Elegance, warmth, originality – perfection!

| Rooms | 1 family room for 2-3: €90-€150. |
|---|---|
| Meals | Restaurants 7km. |
| Closed | Rarely. |

**Mme de Richecour**
Le Rocher,
St Germain de l'Hommel,
53200 Fromentières
Mayenne

| Tel | +33 (0)2 43 07 06 64 |
|---|---|
| Email | eva2richecour@free.fr |
| Web | www.manoirdurocher.fr |

Entry 332   Map 3

### Le Moulin de la Diversière

In a loop of a small river, a honey-coloured mill surrounded by trees, silence and willow-fringed paths leading to two cottages – yours for self-catering or B&B – that Anne and Jean-Marc have lovingly converted in tune with the setting and their green ideals. Outside: a big sloping garden, a play area for your children (and theirs), shady arbours, an above-ground pool. Inside: old tommettes and limewashed walls, cane chairs and fresh flowers, pretty kitchens and showers with pebble floors. Breakfast is brought to your door; table d'hotes is at your hosts' friendly table, by a roaring fire in winter. Special indeed.

| Rooms | 1 double: €59. |
|---|---|
| | 1 triple: €83. Connects with double to form suite: €100-€125. |
| | 1 cottage for 4: €80-€120. |
| Meals | Dinner with wine, €23. |
| Closed | Rarely. |

**Anne & Jean-Marc Le Foulgocq**
Le Moulin de la Diversière,
72800 Savigné sous le Lude
Sarthe

| Tel | +33 (0)2 43 48 09 16 |
|---|---|
| Mobile | +33 (0)6 77 44 79 95 |
| Email | contact@moulin-de-la-diversiere.com |
| Web | www.moulin-de-la-diversiere.com |

Entry 333   Map 4

# Western Loire

## 5 Grande Rue

On Le Lude's Grande Rue is a nobleman's house built around 1650, in its own walled garden, sunny and peaceful; from many of the windows you can glimpse the Château. Simon and Susan pay huge attention to detail, love having guests, offer tea, cakes or wine on arrival, and give you one of five big comfortable bedrooms upstairs. All have immaculate linen, sparkling bathrooms and original button cushions made by Susan. There's an illuminated dining terrace a wonderful salon to come home to, and long, leisurely breakfasts to wake to. Wine caves and châteaux abound, including Baugé's with its 17th-century apothecary.

| Rooms | 4 doubles, 1 twin: €70–€95. |
|---|---|
| Meals | Dinner with wine, 3 courses, €25; with cheese €27. Restaurants within walking distance. |
| Closed | Rarely. |

Simon & Susan Wachter
5 Grande Rue,
72800 Le Lude
Sarthe
Tel     +33 (0)2 43 94 92 77
Email   info@5granderue.com
Web     www.5granderue.com

# Western Loire

## Château de Montaupin

Outside, a virginia creeper has the façade in its clutches – to pretty effect! Inside, wine and conversation flow. Mme David is friendly and welcoming and adores her house, family and guests. There's a laid-back feel, a cluttered elegance, a faded decor; the atmosphere is that of a happy household. A suspended spiral staircase leads to the upper floors and the best suite is right at the top, its roof timbers exposed. Families will feel at home. Breakfasts are robust and table d'hôtes is classic French, with much produce from the garden. Be sure you try the family wines!

| Rooms | 2 doubles, 2 suites for 4, 1 triple: €75–€80. Extra person €20 per night. |
|---|---|
| Meals | Dinner with wine, €22.50. |
| Closed | Rarely. |

FIRST EDITION VETERAN

Marie David
Château de Montaupin,
Montaupin,
72330 Oizé
Sarthe
Tel      +33 (0)2 43 87 81 70
Mobile   +33 (0)6 83 56 60 40
Email    chateaudemontaupin@wanadoo.fr

## Western Loire

### Le Prieuré

Bushels of history cling to the beams and vaulted ceilings of the moated priory, snug beneath its old church. Built in the 12th, extended in the 16th, it had monks until the 20th century. Christophe loves telling the history, Marie-France does the decorating, brilliantly in keeping with the elegant old house: oriental rugs on old tiled floors, pale-painted beams over stone fireplaces, fine old paintings on plain walls, good beds under soft-coloured covers. They are attentive hosts, happy to share their vaulted dining room and pretty, peaceful garden, and the road is not an inconvenience.

| | |
|---|---|
| Rooms | 2 doubles, 1 twin: €110–€130. Singles €90–€100. |
| Meals | Restaurants nearby. |
| Closed | November – February, except by arrangement. |

**Christophe & Marie-France Calla**
Le Prieuré,
1 rue de la Gare,
72500 Dissay sous Courcillon
Sarthe
Tel        +33 (0)2 43 44 09 09
Mobile   +33 (0)6 15 77 84 48
Email     ccalla@club-internet.fr
Web       www.chateauprieure.com

Entry 336   Map 4

## Western Loire

### La Châtaigneraie

Outside is a fairy tale: mellow old stone, white shutters, green ivy, a large leafy garden, a clematis-covered well, a little wood and glimpses of the 12th-century castle round the corner; La Châtaigneraie used to be the servants' quarters. Green-eyed Michèle, modern, intelligent and interested in people, shares the hosting with Michel. The suite is made up of three pastel-hued bedrooms that look onto garden or endless fields. Stay a while and connect – with the soft hills, the woods, the streams, the châteaux. Guests can be as independent as they like and can take one, two or three rooms. Dinner is great value.

| | |
|---|---|
| Rooms | 1 suite for 2-5: €65–€120. |
| Meals | Dinner with wine, €23. Child €12. Restaurant 2km. |
| Closed | November – March. |

**Michèle Letanneux & Michel Guyon**
La Châtaigneraie,
72500 Dissay sous Courcillon
Sarthe
Tel        +33 (0)2 43 79 36 71
Mobile   +33 (0)6 16 44 45 97
Email     michelecretagne@yahoo.fr

Entry 337   Map 4

## Le Moulin Calme

Willow-fringed millponds dreamy with lilies and irises, a duck house, a rickety hump-backed bridge, create a magic waterworld that wraps you in calm. Add quietly spoken Joëlle's excellent cooking (guests return for favourite dishes) using organic produce from the garden and served by ebullient Jean-Luc in the conservatory or by the pond. Old-fashioned charm – not for Mr and Mrs Tickety-Boo! There's fishing, a heated pool and swings; children may need watching. Three exterior staircases lead to rooms in the former millhouse – homely, traditional, with views over water or wooded hills. Do remember that mills can be damp.

## Le Moulin de St Blaise

A house of surprises: mill machinery in the dining room; vast bread oven in the kitchen; fruit and vegetable plot like a Garden of Eden. Come here for fantastic fresh food (dinners, too), the sounds of water, and freedom. Huge beamed dining and sitting rooms have books, games, billiards – and space for children to play. More space on the terrace and in the meadow and garden; keep an eye on children by the river. Airy, white bedrooms have garden and vineyard views; most have smart shower rooms. Friendly owners will point you to Le Mans, a lakeside beach, châteaux. Catch fish for supper, or relax with a book and the rushing water. *Cot available.*

| | |
|---|---|
| Rooms | 2 doubles, 1 twin: €65. 2 family rooms for 3: €65–€93. Singles €54. |
| Meals | Dinner €22. Wine €9–€28. Auberge in village. |
| Closed | Christmas/New Year. |

| | |
|---|---|
| Rooms | 1 double, 2 twins, 1 family room for 3: €89–€149. Extra bed/sofabed €29–€49 per person per night. |
| Meals | Dinner with wine, €25. Restaurant 1km. |
| Closed | Rarely. |

**Joëlle & Jean-Luc Combries**
Le Moulin Calme,
Gascheau,
72500 Luceau
Sarthe
Tel    +33 (0)2 43 46 39 75
Email  moulincalme@wanadoo.fr
Web    www.lemoulincalme.com

**Elaine Love Miles**
Le Moulin de St Blaise,
72340 Chahaignes
Sarthe
Tel    +33 (0)2 43 46 78 05
Email  philelaine2007@yahoo.co.uk
Web    www.moulinstblaise.com

Entry 338    Map 4

Entry 339    Map 4

### Le Chaton Rouge

The Le Mans race track is less than ten miles; in St Pierre du Lorouer life is lived at a slower place. Opposite the church is a house that combines château grandeur with a cottagey feel – thanks to cheerful, generous, imaginative Sarah. Relax in the courtyard, climb the steps to the walled garden where the vegetable patch awaits. With luck its produce will end up on your plate: Sarah is a fabulous cook! There's a real fire for winter, an outdoor dining room for summer, and, up a sweeping stair, the bedrooms – fresh, white and uncluttered. New is a fine studio (double bed, kitchen, glass table, chandeliers) cosily in the attic. *Children over 5 welcome. Pets by arrangement.*

| Rooms | 2 doubles; 1 double with separate shower: €90–€120. 1 family suite for 2-4 with separate bathroom: €160–€200. Singles €50–€80. Dinner, B&B €65–€80 per person. Extra bed/sofabed free of charge. |
|---|---|
| Meals | Lunch €10. Dinner with wine, €25. Restaurant 20m. |
| Closed | Rarely. |

Sarah Carlisle
Le Chaton Rouge,
4 rue du Calvaire,
72150 Saint Pierre du Lorouer
Sarthe

| Tel | +33 (0)2 43 46 21 37 |
|---|---|
| Mobile | +33 (0)6 44 17 23 74 |
| Email | sarah@lechatonrouge.com |
| Web | www.lechatonrouge.com |

Entry 340   Map 4

### La Maison du Pont Romain

Cross Montfort's exquisite stone bridge to this pretty house on the banks of the river. Enter the grounds and forget the world in heavenly peace among very old trees. Gentle Madame saved it all from ruin and gives you two comfortable rooms upstairs, privately off the courtyard, both with fine armoires. The suite in the old stables (salon below, bedrooms above) has a charming late 18th-century feel. There are delicious jams at the big table for breakfast and a family salon for guests. Visit Montfort's castle and the lovely, unsung villages and vineyards of the Sarthe. For children? Forest animals at Pescheray and an aquapark in the village.

| Rooms | 2 doubles: €65–€75. 1 suite for 3-4: €65–€75. |
|---|---|
| Meals | Dinner with wine, €24. |
| Closed | Rarely. |

Chantal Paris
La Maison du Pont Romain,
26 rue de l'Église,
72450 Montfort le Gesnois
Sarthe

| Tel | +33 (0)2 43 76 13 46 |
|---|---|
| Email | chantal-paris@wanadoo.fr |
| Web | www.le-pont-romain.fr |

Entry 341   Map 4

## Maison Conti

Relaxed charm fills this regal village house, built by Louis XIV's favourite daughter near her own château and the church (no bells at night). Off a light-bathed corridor, bedrooms are limewashed in blue, yellow, green and rose with period décor, luxurious beds, superb bathrooms. Breakfasts in the dining room are scrumptious: freshly squeezed orange juice, farm fresh local yogurt, jams, delicious croissants… In summer, enjoy it on the terrace while the swallows swoop. Spend time exploring the idyllic Perche countryside, Loire Valley and Chartres, or stroll to the pretty garden. An ideal stop-over en route south.

| | |
|---|---|
| Rooms | 4 doubles: €85–€90. Extra bed €15 per person per night.. |
| Meals | Dinner, 3 courses with wine, €30. Restaurant nearby. |
| Closed | Never. |

**Richard & Nancy Harrison**
Maison Conti,
2 place de l'Église,
72320 Montmirail
Sarthe

| | |
|---|---|
| Tel | +33 (0)2 43 93 35 26 |
| Email | info@maisonconti.com |
| Web | www.maisonconti.com |

Entry 342   Map 4

Loire Valley

www.sawdays.co.uk/loire-valley

# Loire Valley

# Loire Valley

## Chambres d'Hôtes Les Champarts

This was Dagmar's country cottage until she left Paris to settle here. She left her native Germany and adopted France many moons ago. Come for compact, cosy, immaculate B&B set in a charming village. Breakfast is a feast: hot croissants, jams, smoked salmon, farm butter. The cottage garden is cherished and, if you time it right, every old wall will be covered with roses. Up the steep stairs, one bedroom is wood-panelled, the other more typical with sloping rafters; fabrics are flowered and varnished floors symmetrically rugged. Traditional, authentic, friendly, and great fun. *Extra beds available.*

## Le Moulin de Lonceux

A placid river sets ancient mill stones grinding and flour flows; ducks dip, swans preen, geese saunter; gardens are beset by roses, herbs, bantams, goats, a hammock. The mill has been ingeniously restored by this hard-working family into a home, museum, a ballroom for weddings and a B&B, wrapped around a courtyard. Sleep in stables complete with manger; a two-room loft suite; a smart Miller's Room with fireplace; a flint-walled cider press. Breakfast in the dayroom (sofa, games, candles, log fire) on fresh pastries from home-milled flour (of course). Chartres is close, Paris an easy train ride. A gem.

| | |
|---|---|
| Rooms | 1 double: €53.<br>1 suite for 2: €63. |
| Meals | Restaurants 3km. |
| Closed | Rarely. |

| | |
|---|---|
| Rooms | 3 doubles: €105-€120.<br>1 suite for 2-4: €170.<br>Extra bed/sofabed €20 per person per night. |
| Meals | Catered meals & cold tray on arrival, with wine, €15-€25.<br>Restaurant 3km. |
| Closed | Rarely. |

| | |
|---|---|
| | **Dagmar Parmentier**<br>Chambres d'Hôtes Les Champarts,<br>2 route des Champarts,<br>Blévy,<br>28170 Maillebois<br>Eure-et-Loir |
| Tel | +33 (0)2 37 48 01 21 |
| Email | leschamparts@bab-blevy.com |
| Web | www.bab-blevy.com |

| | |
|---|---|
| | **Isabelle Heitz**<br>Le Moulin de Lonceux,<br>Hameau de Lonceux,<br>28700 Oinville sous Auneau<br>Eure-et-Loir |
| Mobile | +33 (0)6 70 00 60 45 |
| Email | contact@moulin-de-lonceux.com |
| Web | www.moulin-de-lonceux.com |

## Loire Valley

### Maison JLN

Come to enjoy this gentle, charming family and the serene vibes of their old Chartrain house. Up two steep twisting spirals to the attic, through the family's little prayer room (a shell for each pilgrim who's stayed here), the sweet, peaceful bedroom feels like a chapel itself with its honey floorboards and small windows (no wardrobe). Lots of books: reminders of pilgrimage, just beneath the great cathedral. Madame artistic, friendly, offers artists a small studio to borrow; Monsieur speaks nine languages and is quietly amusing; both are interested in your travels. An unusual and special place, in a timeless town.

| Rooms | 1 twin with separate shower & wc on floor below: €55. Singles €44. Extra bed/sofabed €14 per person per night. |
|---|---|
| Meals | Restaurants nearby. |
| Closed | Rarely. |

**Jean-Loup & Nathalie Cuisiniez**
Maison JLN,
80 rue Muret,
28000 Chartres
Eure-et-Loir

| Tel | +33 (0)2 37 21 98 36 |
|---|---|
| Mobile | +33 (0)6 79 48 46 63 |
| Email | chartres.maison.jln@gmail.com |
| Web | www.chambre-hotes-chartres.com |

Entry 345   Map 4

## Loire Valley

### Maison Ailleurs

A short stroll from the glorious cathedral is the home of the former bishop. Valérie and her husband, after a life of international travel, fell for its beauty and brought it back to life. Now this young family live in the right wing and the suites are in the left, up a wide stone stair: one in the original chapel, with a modern four-poster and dramatic stripes, one overlooking the garden (idyllic, walled and full of roses), and one on the second floor, elegant in dove greys and soft yellows. Find iPod docks, Nespresso machines, flawless kitchenettes, lovely linen. Breakfasts are beautiful, the parking is a boon. *Extra bed available in suites.*

| Rooms | 1 double with kitchenette; 1 double with kitchenette & single sofabed: €129-€149. 1 suite for 2-3: €179-€224. Singles €119-€179. Extra bed/sofabed €15 per person per night. |
|---|---|
| Meals | Restaurants within walking distance. |
| Closed | Never. |

**Valérie Genique**
Maison Ailleurs,
17 rue Muret,
28000 Chartres
Eure-et-Loir

| Mobile | +33 (0)6 09 47 75 48 |
|---|---|
| Email | vg@maisonailleurs.com |
| Web | www.maisonailleurs.com |

Entry 346   Map 4

# Loire Valley

## Château La Touanne

Lush trees and elaborate gates frame the graceful façade. Nicolas and Christine's courteous informality permeates their peaceful 17th-century château. Downstairs, ancestral portraits survey antiques, gilt mirrors and fine porcelain in sitting room and salon. Breakfast in the stately dining room, where locally sourced table d'hôtes dinners are also held. Bedrooms are sumptuous: marble fireplaces, high ceilings, fine oak parquet. The terrace leads into parkland, farm, and an orchard hiding the heated pool. Stroll through meadows to explore bosky riverside paths, borrow a boat. An authentic family château, just 90 minutes from Paris.

| Rooms | 3 doubles, 1 twin/double: €120–€180. |
|---|---|
| Meals | Dinner with wine, €35. |
| Closed | Rarely. |

**Nicolas & Christine d'Aboville**
Château La Touanne,
45130 Baccon
Loiret

| Tel | +33 (0)2 38 46 51 39 |
|---|---|
| Mobile | +33 (0)6 88 76 69 89 |
| Email | chateau-latouanne@orange.fr |
| Web | www.chateau-latouanne.com |

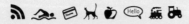

Entry 347   Map 5

---

# Loire Valley

## La Feuillaie

Monsieur's 'light and aromatic' dinners are paired with Loire Valley wines and served at Madame's beautifully dressed table. Risen gloriously from ruin, your hosts' 18th-century home hides in rambling grounds amid a duck-filled lake and 40 species of trees. Eclectic objects catch the eye in soundproofed bedrooms: a sculpted elephant, grandma's lace, ornate wallpapers, claw-foot baths. After dinner, there's billiards or cards by the fire, a piano and literally hundreds of recipe and wine books. (Inspired? They run cooking courses.) Borrow a bike and follow the Loire from this charming village to châteaux, gardens and lakes. *Cot available.*

| Rooms | 4 doubles, 1 twin/double: €148–€165. Extra bed/sofabed €35 per person per night. Children under 2, €15. |
|---|---|
| Meals | Dinner, 3 courses with aperitif, wine & coffee, €42. Restaurants 2km. |
| Closed | Rarely. |

**Véronique & Philippe Frenette**
La Feuillaie,
4 rue Basse,
45130 Saint Ay
Loiret

| Mobile | +33 (0)6 16 75 71 27 |
|---|---|
| Email | contact@lafeuillaie.com |
| Web | www.lafeuillaie.com |

Entry 348   Map 5

## Loire Valley

### Domaine de la Thiau

A large estate by the Loire, with a 19th-century house for the family, a 17th-century one for guests, and pheasants and peacocks strutting around the spacious grounds with mature trees. Your hosts – he is a busy vet, she elegantly looks after house, gîtes and you – make it feel welcoming despite the apparent grandeur. Peaceful bedrooms are carefully decorated with carved bedsteads and papered walls – extremely, Frenchly traditional. There's a Victorian-style conservatory for breakfast, furnished with a large oval table and blue velvet chairs. A wonderful address for summer. *Minimum stay: 2 nights at weekends, on bank holidays & in high season.*

## Loire Valley

### Les Vieux Guays

Looking for seclusion? This house sits in 200 acres of woods, its beautiful garden rambling down to the duck-bobbed lake. Alvaro, a tennis professional, and Sandrine returned from Chile to the family home, now merry with two youngsters. They are a poised and friendly couple easily mixing old and modern, bright and dark. Sandrine produces meals for you from an impressive professional kitchen, mostly regional dishes using local organic food. Bedrooms are high quality too: antiques, excellent new bedding, plain walls and floral fabrics. And there's a nice day room, with terrace and fireplace. Very special.

| | |
|---|---|
| Rooms | 2 doubles: €66-€86. |
| | 1 suite for 3 with kitchen: €76-€101. |
| | Child's bed €20-€30 p.p. per night. |
| Meals | Dinner with wine, €73 for 2. |
| | Restaurants 4km. |
| Closed | Rarely. |

FIRST
EDITION
VETERAN

Bénédicte François
Domaine de la Thiau,
45250 Briare
Loiret

| | |
|---|---|
| Mobile | +33 (0)6 62 43 20 92 |
| Email | info@lathiau.fr |
| Web | www.lathiau.fr |

Entry 349  Map 5

| | |
|---|---|
| Rooms | 2 doubles, 1 twin: €85. |
| | 2 family rooms for 4: €120. |
| | Singles €90-€135. |
| | Extra bed/sofabed €25 per person per night. |
| Meals | Dinner with wine, €30; |
| | Thurs-Sun only. |
| Closed | Rarely. |

Sandrine & Alvaro Martinez
Les Vieux Guays,
45620 Cerdon du Loiret
Loiret

| | |
|---|---|
| Tel | +33 (0)2 38 36 03 76 |
| Mobile | +33 (0)6 80 16 53 76 |
| Email | lvg.france@gmail.com |
| Web | www.lesvieuxguays.com |

Entry 350  Map 5

## Loire Valley

### Moulin Guillard

Just outside the village of Subligny, not far from Sancerre, is an idyllic blue-shuttered mill where flour was once produced. Now it is a fascinating B&B. Dorothée, a cultured woman who once ran a bookshop in Paris, divides her time between her exquisite garden of rare plants and her guests. She offers you a smallish, softly serene double upstairs, and an enchanting two-bedroom suite across the way, with a sitting room and a piano you may play. In summer you breakfast between the two, in an open barn overlooking the stream and Dorothée's several breeds of free-roaming hen. Dinners are superb.

| | |
|---|---|
| Rooms | 1 double, 1 suite for 4: €95. |
| Meals | Dinner €26. Wine from €18. |
| Closed | Rarely. |

**Dorothée Malinge**
Moulin Guillard,
18260 Subligny
Cher

| | |
|---|---|
| Tel | +33 (0)2 48 73 70 49 |
| Mobile | +33 (0)6 61 71 15 30 |
| Email | malinge.annig@orange.fr |

Entry 351   Map 5

## Loire Valley

### Moulin de Reigny

The family's wines – citrusy whites and fruity reds – are centre-stage here, and rightly so; three generations of Guilleraults live here. Next comes charming, courteous Geneviève's delicious Sancerrois cuisine, served hand in hand with the appropriate wines at your hosts' table, bathed in evening light from a huge arched window. She takes English lessons to be even more helpful to guests. Then you will walk the short distance through the village to the Caves du Prieuré where the little old mill now houses the peaceful B&B rooms which are utterly simple, old-fashioned and unpretentious. Lovely people, remarkable value.

| | |
|---|---|
| Rooms | 3 doubles: €55. Singles €45. Extra bed & baby cot, €25. |
| Meals | Dinner with wine, €18–€22. Restaurants 8km. |
| Closed | Rarely. |

**Geneviève Guillerault**
Moulin de Reigny,
2 rue des Fontaines,
Reigny,
18300 Crézancy en Sancerre
Cher

| | |
|---|---|
| Tel | +33 (0)2 48 79 01 74 |
| Email | jacques.guillerault@wanadoo.fr |

Entry 352   Map 5

## Loire Valley

### La Verrerie

Deep countryside, fine people, fantastic bedrooms. In a pretty outbuilding, the double, with a green iron bedhead, old tiled floor and Provençal quilt, looks onto the garden from the ground floor; the suite's twin has the same tiles underfoot, beams overhead and high wooden beds with an inviting mix of white covers and red quilts. The Count and Countess, who manage forests, farm and hunt, enjoy doing B&B; they are charming and thoroughly hospitable. If you would like to dine in, you will join them for dinner in the main house. Members of the family run a vineyard in Provence, so try their wine.

| Rooms | 2 doubles: €75-€110. |
| | 1 family suite for 2-4: €99-€145. |
| Meals | Dinner with wine, €20-€30. |
| | Guest kitchen. Restaurants 10km. |
| Closed | Rarely. |

**Étienne & Marie de Saporta**
La Verrerie,
18380 Ivoy le Pré
Cher
Tel      +33 (0)2 48 58 90 86
Email    m.desaporta@wanadoo.fr
Web      www.laverreriedivoy.com

Entry 353   Map 5

## Loire Valley

### Demeure des Tanneries

Revel in rich croissants and breads at breakfast – Monsieur was a boulanger and pâtissier, Madame loves to make jams. Dinner is just as good, accompanied by local wines – tasty miniature tartine appetisers, a goat's cheese millefeuille perhaps, a blanquette of turkey, a luscious chocolate tart. Eat in the ruby and gold salon, to a splendid mishmash of antique furniture collected by Monsieur, and polished wood floors, gilt-framed mirrors, crystal chandeliers… somehow it all works. Set off on woodland and vineyard walks, return to a heated pool. A nice friendly spot for an extended stopover as you traverse France. *Children over 8 welcome.*

| Rooms | 2 doubles: €80-€90. |
| | Extra bed €30 per person per night. |
| Meals | Dinner with aperitif €30. |
| | Wine €12. |
| | Restaurants 5km. |
| Closed | Rarely. |

**Paulette Loup**
Demeure des Tanneries,
Lieut-dit Les Billets,
30 route la Chapelotte,
18250 Henrichemont
Cher
Tel      +33 (0)2 48 26 19 54
Email    info@demeure-tanneries.com
Web      www.demeure-tanneries.com

Entry 354   Map 5

# Loire Valley

## La Grande Mouline

Ten years ago, your hosts came to raise their family in this rustic haven where the natural garden flows into woods and fields, deer roam and birdlife astounds. Jean is a kindly grandfather, proud of his efforts in converting his outbuildings for B&B. Bedrooms reflect his far-flung travels: Indian rugs, Moroccan brasses, a collection of fossils in an old chemist's cabinet, lots of old farmhouse stuff – nothing too sophisticated. Breakfast is in the main house where family life bustles. Return after contemplating Bourges to meditate in this sweet corner of God's garden or share the above-ground pool.

# Loire Valley

## Les Bonnets Rouges

Cross the garden courtyard to the ancient, peaceful coaching inn where Stendhal once laid his head. Beyond the breakfast room, where 15th-century timbers, wraparound oak panels and stone alcoves dance in mixed-up glory for breakfast amid Turkish rugs, is the staircase up. Three bedrooms, wonderfully quaint and nicely tatty, have antique beds (one a four-poster), new mattresses, hanging rails, perhaps a roll top bath. Up steeper, narrower stairs, a pretty attic double has festoons of beams and the loo behind a curtain. Your charming host, Olivier, lives just across the courtyard. Sleep among angels beneath Bourges' unsurpassed cathedral.

| Rooms | 1 family room for 4: €85. |
|---|---|
| | 2 triples: €55–€70. |
| | 1 quadruple: €85. |
| | Singles €48–€55. |
| | Extra bed/sofabed €15 per person per night. |
| Meals | Restaurant 3km. |
| Closed | Rarely. |

| Rooms | 2 doubles: €72–€80. |
|---|---|
| | 2 suites for 3-4: €80–€110. |
| | Extra bed €20 per person per night. |
| Meals | Restaurants within walking distance. |
| Closed | Rarely. |

|  | Jean Malot & Chantal Charlon |
|---|---|
| | La Grande Mouline, |
| | Bourgneuf, |
| | 18110 St Éloy de Gy |
| | Cher |
| Tel | +33 (0)2 48 25 40 44 |
| Email | jean-m4@wanadoo.fr |
| Web | pagesperso-orange.fr/lagrandemouline |

|  | Olivier Llopis |
|---|---|
| | Les Bonnets Rouges, |
| | 3 rue de la Thaumassière, |
| | 18000 Bourges |
| | Cher |
| Tel | +33 (0)2 48 65 79 92 |
| Email | bonnets-rouges@bourges.net |
| Web | bonnets-rouges.bourges.net |

Entry 355 Map 10

Entry 356 Map 10

## Loire Valley

### Domaine de l'Ermitage

Ten minutes from the delights of café-chic Bourges, this articulate husband-and-wife team run their beef and cereals farm and Menetou-Salon vineyards (tastings arranged), make their own jam and still have time for their guests. Vivacious and casually elegant, Laurence runs an intelligent, welcoming house. The big, simple yet stylishly attractive bedrooms of her 18th-century farmhouse are of pleasing proportions, one (the least grand) up a steep tower stair, the rest full of light and views over the graceful park. Guests may use the discreet pool at pre-arranged times.

| Rooms | 2 doubles, 1 twin: €73–€76. |
| | 1 triple: €104. |
| | 1 quadruple: €136. |
| Meals | Restaurants in village. |
| Closed | Rarely. |

**Laurence & Géraud de La Farge**
Domaine de l'Ermitage,
18500 Berry Bouy
Cher
Tel +33 (0)2 48 26 87 46
Mobile +33 (0)6 64 77 87 46
Email domaine-ermitage@wanadoo.fr
Web www.hotes-ermitage.com

Entry 357  Map 10

## Loire Valley

*New Entry*

### Les Aubuées

In a peaceful street overlooking lush meadows, sheltered by old walls and surrounded by trees, is an 1850s *maison de maître*, a Belle Epoque residence; the first view takes your breath away. Little Toto and Chopin wag their welcome, followed by smiling Pascale. In big bedrooms on the first floor, wood, linen, silk and cotton blend with antique pieces and a luxurious modern feel pervades. Borrow the bikes, visit Sancerre and the cathedral at Bourges, return to a secluded courtyard and a delicious pool. Breakfast, served under the Napoleonic chandelier, is divine: Pascale, warm hostess, is a skilled pastry chef.

| Rooms | 1 suite for 2, |
| | 1 family suite for 2–4: €85–€135. |
| | Singles €85. |
| Meals | Restaurant 5km. |
| Closed | Rarely. |

**Pascale & Benoît Portier**
Les Aubuées,
51 route de Montcorneau,
18500 Mehun sur Yèvre
Cher
Tel +33 (0)2 48 57 08 24
Email les.aubuees@gmail.com
Web www.lesaubuees.fr/

Entry 358  Map 10

# Loire Valley

## Domaine de la Trolière

The beautifully proportioned house in its big shady garden has been in the family for over 200 years. The sitting room is a cool blue-grey symphony, the dining room smart yellow-grey with a rare, remarkable maroon and grey marble table: breakfast is in here, dinner, sometimes en famille, always delicious, is in the big beamed kitchen. Each stylishly comfortable room has individual character and Madame has a fine eye for detail. She is charming, dynamic, casually elegant and has many cats. Visitors have poured praise: quite the most beautiful house we've ever stayed in; the evening meals were superb.

| | |
|---|---|
| Rooms | 3 doubles; 1 double with separate wc: €51–€71. Extra bed €10 per person per night. |
| Meals | Dinner with wine, €25. |
| Closed | Rarely. |

**Marie-Claude Dussert**
Domaine de la Trolière,
18200 Orval
Cher

| | |
|---|---|
| Tel | +33 (0)2 48 96 47 45 |
| Mobile | +33 (0)6 72 21 59 76 |
| Email | marie-claude.dussert@orange.fr |

Entry 360   Map 10

## Loire Valley

### Château de la Villette

More pretty 19th-century hunting lodge than grand château, la Villette sits in 40 idyllic acres of parkland, close to a huge spring-fed lake: borrow the row boat and potter. Capable, hospitable, generous Karin – dynamic gardener, fine cook – loves and cares for each inch of the place. A winding staircase leads to a beauty of a bedroom done in Biedermeier style, with a sloping ceiling and serene views; the second room too is seductive. Feather duvets will cosset you, elegant breakfasts and dinners at the convent table will delight you, and nothing is too much trouble for Karin.

## Loire Valley

### La Croix Verte

Vincent and Élisabeth's serene home lies plumb in the heart of George Sand country. Linger under lime trees in a secret courtyard garden while relishing a plentiful breakfast; enjoy a dinner of home-grown produce; get cosy in the family sitting room before an open fire. A staging post in the 12th century, La Croix Verte stands in the heart of the village but you won't hear a peep as you slumber under a hand-stitched bedcover; the two charming loft bedrooms in natural tones share sofas, books and games. Come for heaps of character, unspoilt countryside, and artist hosts (potter and painter) who are an absolute delight.

| Rooms | 1 double; 1 double with separate bathroom: €90. |
|---|---|
| Meals | Dinner with wine, €25. |
| Closed | Rarely. |

| Rooms | 2 doubles, 1 twin: €65. Singles €57. Extra bed/sofabed €25 per person per night. |
|---|---|
| Meals | Dinner with wine, €23. Restaurant 1.5km. |
| Closed | Rarely. |

Karin Verburgh
Château de la Villette,
St Août,
36120 Ardentes
Indre
Tel +33 (0)2 54 36 28 46
Web www.romantik-destinations.com

Élisabeth & Vincent Portier
La Croix Verte,
Le Bourg,
12 rue des Maîtres Sonneurs,
36400 St Chartier
Indre
Tel +33 (0)2 54 31 02 71
Email contact@veportier.com
Web www.veportier.com

Entry 361  Map 10

Entry 362  Map 10

## Loire Valley

### Le Manoir du Menoux

In the heart of a quiet village, through a formal French garden, is a pretty half-timbered house with a Normandy air. Pleasant Marie-Estelle is a straightforward lady with a quiet smile, serving breakfast around a large oak table in the dining room, or outside in summer. Sit listening to the gurgling stream down by the charming summerhouse; in chillier weather, the salons' daybeds make a comfy spot. Up the winding oak staircase are the light and luminous suite 'Diane', southern-coloured 'Manon' gazing over romantic rooftops, and 50s-feel 'Amélie'. Visit snail and chestnut fêtes, and the Lac d'Eguzon for nautical things. Lovely.

## Loire Valley

### Le Canard au Parapluie Rouge

This pretty 17th-century house has been welcoming guests for most of its history: it was once the Auberge de la Gare; the station has gone but a train occasionally shoots through the sleepy calm. Kathy, from Ohio, and Martin, from Wiltshire, are great fun and will make you feel instantly at home. Each of the sunny little bedrooms has a charm and flavour of its own and the big heavy-beamed living room opens onto an enclosed garden with a well-hidden above-ground pool. Beautiful meals are served in the elegant dining room or out under the trees. Kathy loves cooking and Martin grows the vegetables. It's all absurdly good value.

| | |
|---|---|
| Rooms | 2 doubles: €68-€78. 1 suite for 2-4: €94-€130. |
| Meals | Dinner €25. Restaurant within walking distance. |
| Closed | Last 2 weeks in December. |

| | |
|---|---|
| Rooms | 3 doubles, 1 family room for 3; 1 double with separate bathroom: €58-€85. Extra bed/sofabed €10 per person per night. |
| Meals | Dinner with wine, €26. |
| Closed | Rarely. |

Marie-Estelle Rives
Le Manoir du Menoux,
15 rue Haute,
36200 Le Menoux
Indre

| | |
|---|---|
| Tel | +33 (0)2 36 27 91 87 |
| Mobile | +33 (0)6 60 10 20 57 |
| Email | rivesme@wanadoo.fr |
| Web | www.manoirdumenoux.com |

Martin & Kathy Missen
Le Canard au Parapluie Rouge,
3 rue des Rollets,
36200 Celon
Indre

| | |
|---|---|
| Tel | +33 (0)2 54 25 30 08 |
| Email | info@lecanardbandb.com |
| Web | www.lecanardbandb.com |

## Loire Valley

### Domaine du Ris de Feu

No longer part of a defensive frontier of castles, this 15th-century manor and lake is a sanctuary swathed in lush forest. The domain is the pride and joy of Caroline, who runs it to the highest eco and ethical standards, and husband Luc. Artisan builders (still discreetly on site) have restored using natural materials and traditional craft. Your charming fruit loft, on two floors, has oval windows, oak fittings and a wood-burner; drift off upstairs under organic linen. After breakfast in the old bakery, wander and enjoy, listen to the birdlife, bathe in the lake, hire canoes or bicycles... explore this enchanted kingdom!

| | |
|---|---|
| Rooms | 1 suite for 2: €105–€125. |
| Meals | Dinner from €35 (except Saturdays). |
| Closed | Never. |

**Luc & Caroline Fontaine**
Domaine du Ris de Feu,
36370 Chalais
Indre

| | |
|---|---|
| Tel | +33 (0)2 54 37 87 73 |
| Email | contact@lerisdefeu.fr |
| Web | www.lerisdefeu.fr |

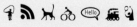

Entry 365   Map 9

## Loire Valley

### Saint Victor La Grand' Maison

The 16th-century château bursts into view from its wooded hilltop, tall turrets and ivy-clad façade towering over the river Anglin. You can saunter down here past the pool and picnic on organic pâté under a 400-year-old oak; just water, trees and birdsong. Inside, read by the fire, tinkle on the baby grand, retire to bed. Deeply comfortable rooms in warm reds, blues and pastels have museum-worthy antiques, plush fabrics, gilt portraits, book-lined walls. Hugely friendly, Madame offers tastings, courses and talks by local savants – and there are gîtes in the grounds. "Simply a delight", says our inspector, "for anybody at all."

| | |
|---|---|
| Rooms | 1 double: €120. |
| | 2 suites for 2 (can interconnect to form suite for 4): €150–€200. |
| Meals | Dinner €15–€20. |
| | Wine €8–€20. |
| | Restaurant 1.5km. |
| Closed | Christmas/New Year. |

**Marie Rouet Grandclément**
Saint Victor La Grand' Maison,
36300 Ingrandes
Indre

| | |
|---|---|
| Mobile | +33 (0)6 03 81 51 37 |
| Email | marie@saintvictorlagrandmaison.fr |
| Web | www.saintvictorlagrandmaison.fr |

Entry 366   Map 9

# Loire Valley

## Les Sequoias

Friendly and foodie is this townhouse B&B, on the quiet backstreet of a pretty market town. Here live Marie-Chantal and Colin and a charming black poodle called Pixie. The sequoias that dominate the garden give the house its name, and garden designer Colin is inspired by feng shui (book yourself into a garden design course!). Bedrooms, one yellow, two sky-blue, are spotless and new. Outside is a pool, a log cabin, a super wicker-chaired summer sitting room for guests. As for the food, it's delicious: wild-fruit jelly and viennoiserie at breakfast, generous dishes at dinner, shared with hosts and guests at one big cheerful table. *Self-catering available in suite.*

| Rooms | 2 doubles, 1 twin: €70–€75. 1 suite for 4: €180. |
| --- | --- |
| Meals | Dinner €23. Restaurants within walking distance. |
| Closed | Rarely. |

**Marie-Chantal Elliott**
Les Sequoias,
45 rue de Varennes,
36210 Chabris
Indre
Tel   +33 (0)2 54 40 15 42
Email   marie-chantal.elliott@orange.fr
Web   www.chabrisloirevalley.com

# Loire Valley

## Le Bouchot

Come not for luxury but for deep country authenticity – and to make friends with a generous, charming, free-thinking family who gave up Paris for this lush corner of France. They have restored, renovated and eco-converted a run-down farm, insulated it with hemp, wattle and daub, then added wood-burning stoves, organic breakfasts... and cats, dogs, horses, hens, donkeys. Family rooms in outbuildings round the courtyard are wood-clad with sloping ceilings, rudimentary furnishings, mix and match bed linen, the odd rug. Dinner is in the kitchen diner – or the barns when there are campers. A place for new horizons.

| Rooms | 2 family rooms for 3, 1 family room for 4, 1 family room for 5: €73–€115. |
| --- | --- |
| Meals | Dinner with wine, €25. Restaurant 2km. |
| Closed | Rarely. |

**Anne & Jean-Philippe Beau-Douëzy**
Le Bouchot,
Route de Chaon,
41300 Pierrefitte sur Sauldre
Loir-et-Cher
Tel   +33 (0)2 54 88 01 00
Mobile   +33 (0)6 71 57 61 26
Email   contact@lebouchot.net
Web   www.lebouchot.net

## Loire Valley

### La Gaucherie

A talented hostess, a beautifully restored farmhouse, a serene chic decor, a magical spot. The grassy garden leads seamlessly to woodland; there's a pond, a lovely orchard, and quiet spots for contemplation. Gentle Aurélia swapped New York for the forests of the Solonge, and loves light and simplicity. Fabulous bedrooms – and a 'restaurant' – lie in the converted stables and barn, with a wood-burning stove and red sofas; floors are terracotta or seagrass, bathrooms are mosaic'd. Rejoice in ponies and hens for the children, home-produced lamb, a lake with boat, marvellous breakfasts and a discreet, fenced pool.

| | |
|---|---|
| Rooms | 2 doubles, 1 twin/double: €65–€145. 2 suites for 4: €154–€200. Dinner, B&B €29–€34 extra per person. |
| Meals | Dinner €28. |
| Closed | Mid-January to mid-February. |

| | |
|---|---|
| | **Aurélia Curnin** |
| | La Gaucherie, |
| | Route de Méry, Dep 76, |
| | 41320 Langon |
| | Loir-et-Cher |
| Tel | +33 (0)2 54 96 42 23 |
| Mobile | +33 (0)6 88 80 45 93 |
| Email | lagaucherie@wanadoo.fr |
| Web | www.lagaucherie.com |

Entry 369　Map 5

## Loire Valley

### Le Moutier

This fine traditional townhouse hides behind vast cedars on the edge of the village. Behind its walls lie warmth, exuberance, good humour, windows flung open to let in light and fresh air, and Jean-Lou's vibrant paintings. All feels friendly and unpretentious: a den-like sitting room, a comfy leather sofa, wonderful books, an open fire. Two bedrooms are in the main house, two are accessed via the studio, heaving with paintings and brushes. All this and a charming garden, throngs of fruit trees, a few loitering hens and, best of all, table d'hôtes at which food and wine flow. B&B at its best.

| | |
|---|---|
| Rooms | 4 doubles: €75. |
| Meals | Dinner with wine, €30. |
| Closed | Rarely. |

| | |
|---|---|
| | **Martine & Jean-Lou Coursaget** |
| | Le Moutier, |
| | 13 rue de la République, |
| | 41110 Mareuil sur Cher |
| | Loir-et-Cher |
| Tel | +33 (0)2 54 75 20 48 |
| Email | lemoutier.coursaget@wanadoo.fr |
| Web | www.chambresdhotesdumoutier.com |

Entry 370　Map 4

## Loire Valley

### Le Clos de la Chesneraie

In a traditional Tourangeau home on the edge of a small town is a calm, peaceful, elegantly decorated B&B sitting in glorious gardens. In the converted barn are four guest suites, two upstairs with slopey ceilings, and two down, opening to a prettily furnished garden corner. Dahlias nod their heads outside windows, bedroom floors are seagrass and ancient terracotta, bathrooms are immaculate, and muted colours add serenity. Château-hop to your heart's delight – Chenonceau is five minutes away – then polish up for one of Béatrice's fine dinners at the big friendly table.

## Loire Valley

### Prieuré de la Chaise

A delight for the senses: stunning ancient buildings outside, Madame's decorations within. The 13th-century chapel, still used on the village feast day, and the 'new' manor house (1500s) are awash with history, 16th-century antiques, tapestries and loveliness – huge sitting and dining rooms, and a winding staircase to the tower room (with a curtained-off loo). One room has a stone fireplace, a fine rug, and limewashed beams. The setting is superb, mature trees shade the beautiful gardens, horses adorn the paddock, you are surrounded by vines; over a simple French breakfast, ask your dynamic hostess to arrange tastings.

| | |
|---|---|
| Rooms | 1 double, 1 twin (joins with triple to form family suite): €90–€110. 1 triple, 1 quadruple: €90–€130. |
| Meals | Dinner with wine, €30. Restaurant 1km. |
| Closed | Rarely. |

| | |
|---|---|
| Rooms | 2 doubles: €90. 2 suites for 3, 1 suite for 5: €130–€190. |
| Meals | Restaurants nearby. |
| Closed | Rarely. |

| | |
|---|---|
| | Béatrice Chrétien |
| | Le Clos de la Chesneraie, |
| | 107 rue Gilbert Michel, |
| | 41400 St Georges sur Cher |
| | Loir-et-Cher |
| Tel | +33 (0)2 54 32 76 89 |
| Email | leclosdelachesneraie@orange.fr |
| Web | www.leclosdelachesneraie.com |

| | |
|---|---|
| | Danièle Therizols |
| | Prieuré de la Chaise, |
| | 8 rue du Prieuré, |
| | 41400 St Georges sur Cher |
| | Loir-et-Cher |
| Tel | +33 (0)2 54 32 59 77 |
| Email | prieuredelachaise@yahoo.fr |
| Web | www.prieuredelachaise.com |

# Loire Valley

## La Roseraie de Vrigny

White shutters, beams, old stones, comfortable bedrooms, organic potager, communal breakfasts and generous hosts – quintessential Sawday's. Rosalind, musician and philosopher, and John understand what B&B is all about and treat their guests as friends; sup with them on fine French food in the candlelit dining room and you will be charmed. The garden is entrancing too, all rambling roses, contemplative spots, even a little corner that is forever Scotland (like your hosts) and a Chinese bridge across a weeping-willow'd stream. Perfectly restful and welcoming after a day contemplating the glories of Chenonceau!

# Loire Valley

## La Folie Saint Julien

On the edge of Saint Julien is a small 'maison bourgeoise', with handsome white outbuildings and charming French gardens. Here live Frédérique and Fabrice, warm-hearted Parisians who left the capital to pursue the B&B dream – and how! All is exquisite and serene and 18th century in style, from the polished limestone floors to the gilt-framed paintings and the beds dressed in fine velvet eiderdowns. Look out for the sparkling wines of Montlouis sur Loire… you can visit the vineyards and every château, including the finest, Chenonceau: it's five minutes down the road. Come home to a lap in the barn's glassy pool – sheer bliss.

| Rooms | 1 double; 1 double with separate private bathroom: €70. 1 family room for 4, 1 cottage for 2 with sofabed: €75–€115. Singles €65. Extra bed €23 per person per night. Cot €12. |
| --- | --- |
| Meals | Dinner €32. Children under 12, €18. Restaurant 1km. |
| Closed | Rarely. |

| Rooms | 2 doubles: €90–€115. 1 suite for 4: €130. 1 cottage for 2: €145. Extra bed/sofabed €25 per person per night. |
| --- | --- |
| Meals | Dinner with aperitif & wine, €30 (Fri & Sat only). Restaurants 2km. |
| Closed | Late November – March. |

**Rosalind Rawnsley**
La Roseraie de Vrigny,
3 rue du Ruisseau,
41400 St Georges sur Cher
Loir-et-Cher

| Tel | +33 (0)2 54 32 85 50 |
| Mobile | +33 (0)7 60 45 99 14 |
| Email | rosalind.rawnsley@gmail.com |
| Web | www.laroseraiedevrigny.com |

**Fabrice Gacon**
La Folie Saint Julien,
8 route de la Vallée,
41400 St Julien de Chédon
Loir-et-Cher

| Tel | +33 (0)1 46 49 01 07 |
| Mobile | +33 (0)6 75 15 60 91 |
| Email | fabrice_gacon@orange.fr |
| Web | www.lafoliesaintjulien.com |

Entry 373  Map 4

Entry 374  Map 4

# Loire Valley

## Le Cormier

Wake in the morning and sigh with pleasure at the beauty of the garden: box hedges and cottage flowers, sweet herbs, poplars and an iris-fringed pond. Then think about breakfasting on garden fruits and homemade banana bread. Californian Michael and Dutch Marie-Louise rescued this long, low farmhouse and barn from ruin; it's hard to imagine more endearing hosts. The two suites are exceedingly pretty, with creamy stone walls, overhead beams, dainty fabrics and ethnic rugs, and each has its own salon with kettle, fridge, books, magazines, logs for the fire (one has its own little kitchen). Perfect peace, and not another house in sight. *Minimum stay: 2 nights.*

| | |
|---|---|
| Rooms | 2 suites for 2; one with kitchen: €100–€110. |
| Meals | Restaurant nearby. |
| Closed | November – April. |

| | |
|---|---|
| | **Michael & Marie-Louise Harvey** |
| | Le Cormier, |
| | 41120 Sambin |
| | Loir-et-Cher |
| Tel | +33 (0)2 54 33 29 47 |
| Email | michael@lecormier.com |
| Web | www.lecormier.com |

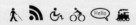

Entry 375   Map 4

# Loire Valley

*New Entry*

## La Closerie de l'Aventure

In the bucolic Loire Valley, a charming retreat with four en-suite rooms in a pretty whitewashed house and a converted stable. Surrounded by acres of woodland and pasture, shared with a menagerie of donkeys, goats and hens, it's wonderfully peaceful. Little ones can use 'Tintin's Treasure map' to find their bearings. Delightful Pascaline has ploughed energy and taste into this B&B; bedrooms are beautifully furnished with her flea market finds and a couple are painted in bold, vibrant colours. Generous breakfasts of just-laid eggs, bread and homemade jam set you up nicely for a day's Châteaux-seeing or cycling. *Minimum stay: 2 nights.*

| | |
|---|---|
| Rooms | 3 doubles, 1 twin/double: €85–€105. Extra bed €20 per person per night |
| Meals | Dinner with aperitif, wine & coffee, €35. Child €15. Supper trays available. Guest kitchen. Restaurant 5km. |
| Closed | Never. |

| | |
|---|---|
| | **Pascaline Maslard** |
| | La Closerie de l'Aventure, |
| | L'Aventure, |
| | 41700 Cheverny |
| | Loir-et-Cher |
| Mobile | +33 (0)6 99 23 07 29 |
| Email | closeriedelaventure@gmail.com |
| Web | www.chambres-dhotes-chateaux-loire.com |

Entry 376   Map 4

## Au 16 Place Saint Louis

In the cobbled streets of old Blois, bang in front of the cathedral, with the fascinating château round the corner, stands this elegant townhouse. Inside, an antique staircase twists up three floors of treasures: a retired gramophone, a grandfather clock, bright Malian paintings. The best room at the top has a Turner-worthy view over rooftops to the Loire. Philippe, who loves his old family house, provides big delicious breakfasts in the dining room or, in summer, the flower-run courtyard. Then head for the countryside – or hop in a hot air balloon and spy the châteaux from above. A dreamy place. *Minimum stay: 2 nights in high season.*

## Château de Nanteuil

Revered grand-mère's house has faded charm but no châteauesque style or opulence: a few crumbly bits outside, frescoes and trunks in the hall, antlers in the dining room, floral wallpapers, large wardrobes and marble fireplaces in the bedrooms. These are light-filled and unashamedly old-fashioned but there's soul; bathrooms are time-warp 70s; river-water murmurs below your window. Most of all, you'll enjoy Frédéric – he's refreshingly unfussy, occasionally mercurial and serves you excellent organic dinners; asparagus in season, baked fillet of perch: he really cares about food. In summer sit on the terrace by the river.

| | | | |
|---|---|---|---|
| Rooms | 1 double, 1 twin/double: €90–€100. 1 suite for 2: €120–€130. Singles €90–€120. | Rooms | 2 doubles: €75–€95. 2 family rooms for 2-4: €80. Extra person €20 per night. |
| Meals | Restaurants in town. | Meals | Dinner with wine, €30. |
| Closed | Rarely. | Closed | Rarely. |

| | |
|---|---|
| | Philippe Escoffre |
| | Au 16 Place Saint Louis, |
| | 41000 Blois |
| | Loir-et-Cher |
| Tel | +33 (0)2 54 74 13 61 |
| Mobile | +33 (0)6 09 65 94 05 |
| Email | 16placesaintlouis@orange.fr |
| Web | www.16placesaintlouis.fr |

| | |
|---|---|
| | Frédéric Théry |
| | Château de Nanteuil, |
| | 16 rue Nanteuil, Le Chiteau, |
| | 41350 Huisseau sur Cosson |
| | Loir-et-Cher |
| Tel | +33 (0)2 54 42 61 98 |
| Mobile | +33 (0)6 88 83 79 84 |
| Email | chateau.nanteuil@free.fr |
| Web | www.chateau-nanteuil.com |

Entry 377  Map 4

Entry 378  Map 4

# Loire Valley

## La Villa Médicis

Why the Italian name, the Italianate look? Queen Marie de Médicis used to take the waters here in the 17th century: the fine garden still has a hot spring and the Loire flows regally past behind the huge old trees. Muriel, a flower-loving perfectionist (artificial blooms as well as fresh), has let loose her decorative flair on the interior. It is unmistakably yet adventurously French in its splash of colours, lush fabrics and fine details. Fine antiques and brass beds grace some rooms, while the suite is a great 1930s surprise with a super-smart bathroom. You are wonderfully well looked after in this elegant and stylish house.

| Rooms | 2 twins: €69. |
| | 1 suite for 2: €99. |
| | 1 triple: €83. |
| Meals | Dinner with wine, €32. |
| Closed | November – January, except by arrangement. |

FIRST
EDITION
VETERAN

**Muriel Cabin-Saint-Marcel**
La Villa Médicis,
Macé,
41000 St Denis sur Loire
Loir-et-Cher
Tel      +33 (0)2 54 74 46 38
Email   medicis.bienvenue@wanadoo.fr
Web     www.lavillamedicis.com

Entry 379   Map 4

# Loire Valley

## Château de la Rue

This 1810 'Directoire' mansion, approached via a grand avenue of trees, is lived in and loved by adorable Madame, who has been doing B&B for years. The croissants are home baked, the fruits are from the orchard – a historic walled beauty – the bedrooms are handsome ('Mme de Ségur' the smallest, 'Cassandre' the most luxurious) and the furniture, all antique with the exception of some comfortable sofas, look as if it has been here forever. The Château de Chambord is close but, best of all, you can cycle along the river to Blois (restaurants, market, château): the Loire flows at the end of the park.

| Rooms | 3 doubles: €120–€180. |
| | 2 suites for 4: €250. |
| Meals | Dinner with wine, €39 |
| | Restaurants 2km. |
| Closed | January /February. |

**Véronique de Caix**
Château de la Rue,
41500 Cours sur Loire
Loir-et-Cher
Tel      +33 (0)2 54 46 82 47
Email   chateaudelarue@wanadoo.fr
Web     www.chateaudelarue.com

Entry 380   Map 4

## Loire Valley

### La Cave Margot

The approach is pretty, along a green open valley, the family is charming, and the house is an immaculate longère. As for the bedrooms, they are large, inviting and contemporary, with original features and superb bathrooms. Two open to gardens and terrace, the third is up an outside stair, dotted with objects from exotic travels and overlooking an ancient walnut tree. For families, couples and seekers of peace: billiards, books, a warming wood-burner for chilly nights. Table d'hôtes is great fun and dinners are delivered with enthusiasm and imagination; Nathalie grows organic vegetables for savoury crumbles and Nicolas loves his wines.

| Rooms | 1 double: €70–€80. |
| --- | --- |
| | 1 suite for 2-3, |
| | 1 suite for 2-5: €90–€95. |
| | Singles €70–€95. |
| | Extra bed/sofabed €20 per person per night. |
| Meals | Dinner with aperitif, €20–€30. |
| | Restaurant 12km. |
| Closed | Never. |

**Nathalie & Nicolas Leal**
La Cave Margot,
La Cave Margot,
41360 Lunay
Loir-et-Cher

Tel     +33 (0)2 54 72 09 53
Email   info@lacavemargot.fr
Web     www.lacavemargot.fr

Entry 381   Map 4

## Loire Valley

### 20 rue Pilate

In the lovely Loire valley where the intimate and the romantic reign, you have the little house in the garden all to yourselves: a kitchen and a bathroom downstairs, two bedrooms upstairs and a private piece of flower-filled garden for breakfasts. Or you can join your delightful hosts at the long wooden table in the cheerful kitchen where baskets hang from beams. Cultured, dynamic and a superb maker of jams, Ghislaine is involved in visiting artists and writers to this peaceful Touraine town. Be charmed by the genuine welcome, unpretentious comfort, wisteria climbing over the terrace and bird song all around.

| Rooms | 1 cottage for 4: €70–€120. |
| --- | --- |
| Meals | Dinner with wine, €30. |
| Closed | November – March. |

**Ghislaine & Gérard de Couesnongle**
20 rue Pilate,
37370 Neuvy le Roi
Indre-et-Loire

Tel     +33 (0)2 47 24 41 48
Email   ggh.coues@gmail.com

Entry 382   Map 4

## Loire Valley

### La Louisière

Simplicity, character and a marvellous welcome make La Louisière special. Madame delights in her role as hostess; Monsieur, who once rode the horse-drawn combine, tends his many roses, and his paintings of the countryside line the walls. A caring and unpretentious couple, both are active in their community. The traditional bedrooms have well-chosen colour schemes and sparkling bathrooms; touches of fun, too. Surrounded by chestnut trees, the farmhouse backs onto the gardens of the château and is wonderfully quiet. Tennis, bikes, tractors, horses to ride and an old-fashioned playground – it's bliss for children.

## Loire Valley

### Château de l'Hérissaudière

You could get used to country-house living here, French-style. Madame, charming, cultured, welcomes you as family. Wrapped in 18 acres of parkland, the manor is all light, elegance, bold paintings and fresh flowers. Relax in the sunny salon or the splendid library. Bedrooms are spacious, gracious and subtly themed, Empire perhaps, or rich Louis XV. Bathrooms have the original tiling and marble floors. Tuck into a gourmet breakfast while Madame recommends local restaurants for dinner. Ping-pong and pool are in the grounds, with wild cyclamen and giant sequoias, and the old chapel has become a summer kitchen. *Minimum stay: 2 nights at weekends & in high season. Contact owner for prices for larger numbers.*

| | |
|---|---|
| Rooms | 1 twin, 1 suite for 5, 1 triple: €55–€60. |
| Meals | Auberge 800m. |
| Closed | Rarely. |

| | |
|---|---|
| Rooms | 2 doubles: €120–€135. 3 suites for 2-5: €130–€150. |
| Meals | Summer kitchen. Restaurant 3km. |
| Closed | Rarely. |

**Michel & Andrée Campion**
La Louisière,
37360 Beaumont la Ronce
Indre-et-Loire
Tel      +33 (0)2 47 24 42 24
Mobile   +33 (0)6 78 36 64 69
Email    andree.campion@orange.fr
Web      www.louisiere.racan.org

**Claudine Detilleux**
Château de l'Hérissaudière,
37230 Pernay
Indre-et-Loire
Tel      +33 (0)2 47 55 95 28
Mobile   +33 (0)6 03 22 34 45
Email    lherissaudiere@gmail.com
Web      www.herissaudiere.com

Entry 383   Map 4

Entry 384   Map 4

## Loire Valley

### Le Grenadier

The garden of this immaculate longère in a leafy suburb of Tours overlooks rooftops and spires. Martine, hospitable and discreet, offers guests three pristine ground-floor bedrooms in a converted barn, two sharing a wide deckchair'd patio. Elegant breakfasts of viennoiseries and homemade jams are served in a delightful sunny room with modern art on pale walls. Doors open to serene lawns, mature trees, and an al fresco space under high rafters hung with a brass chandelier; you are welcome to picnic here. A peaceful spot in which to lay your head after touring the gardens and châteaux of the Loire.

| | |
|---|---|
| Rooms | 1 twin/double: €75–€95. 1 family room for 3, 1 family room for 4: €75–€115. Singles €65. |
| Meals | Restaurants 3km. |
| Closed | Never. |

Martine Butterworth
Le Grenadier,
5 rue des Patys,
37230 Fondettes
Indre-et-Loire

| | |
|---|---|
| Tel | +33 (0)2 47 42 08 32 |
| Email | martine@legrenadier.net |
| Web | www.legrenadier.net |

Entry 385   Map 4

## Loire Valley

### Les Hautes Gâtinières

Good, unpretentious, authentic B&B, high on a cliff above the Loire, gazing over village, valley and vines. Les Hautes Gâtinières may be modern imitating old, but we like it for Jacqueline's five-star hospitality. All is immaculate and meticulous within: glossy floors, smart wallpapers, French repro furniture; there are small traditional bedrooms in the attic and an excellent family suite. The garden is surprisingly large, its lawns perfect for children – and Api, the fluffy white dog. Expect giant breakfasts and a generous welcome. Great value in the châteaux-rich Loire.

| | |
|---|---|
| Rooms | 2 doubles: €64. 1 suite for 4: €109. Singles €58. Extra bed/sofabed €18 per person per night. |
| Meals | Restaurants within walking distance. |
| Closed | Rarely. |

Jacqueline Gay
Les Hautes Gâtinières,
7 chemin de Bois Soleil,
37210 Rochecorbon
Indre-et-Loire

| | |
|---|---|
| Tel | +33 (0)2 47 52 88 08 |
| Email | gatinieres@wanadoo.fr |
| Web | www.gatinieres.eu |

Entry 386   Map 4

# Loire Valley

## La Falotière

A cave suite! Hewn long ago into the rock beside a bell-topped presbytery, deliciously cool and light, it's a spacious retreat. Step from private courtyard to sitting room with big fireplace and old bread oven, smart wicker chairs, red lamps, tiled floors. Burrow through to a cushioned, red-carpeted bedroom sculpted into whitewashed rock; soak in a theatrical free-standing bath. Locals and walkers, your delightful hosts serve home-laid eggs at breakfast, enjoy sharing their lovely shady garden and this intriguing town, wedged in a gully ten minutes from Tours amid the Loire's vineyards and châteaux. Private, unique, fantastic.

| | |
|---|---|
| Rooms | 1 suite for 2: €130.<br>Cot €15. |
| Meals | Restaurant within walking distance. |
| Closed | Rarely. |

Dominique & Jean-Pierre Danderieux
La Falotière,
51 rue du Docteur Lebled,
37210 Rochecorbon
Indre-et-Loire

| | |
|---|---|
| Mobile | +33 (0)6 50 65 41 49 |
| Email | jpdanderieux@gmail.com |
| Web | www.falotiere.com |

Entry 387   Map 4

# Loire Valley

## Château de Nazelles

A charming 16th-century manor house in the centre of the village with a shady courtyard and a winding track leading to woodlands and vineyards. House and garden are an exuberant mix of formal and informal, contemporary and traditional. Steps and pathways entice you through a series of 'secret' gardens, doorways cut in high hedges offer intriguing glimpses of the Loire valley. Rooms are a delight, furnished with simple understated elegance to fully show off the character of the house, and the breakfast room is serene with a low, beamed ceiling. Great breakfasts, delightful hosts; even the pool is special.

| | |
|---|---|
| Rooms | 4 doubles: €115–€150.<br>2 suites for 4: €260–€300. |
| Meals | Summer kitchen.<br>Restaurants 3km. |
| Closed | Rarely. |

Véronique & Olivier Fructus
Château de Nazelles,
16 rue Tue-La-Soif,
37530 Nazelles
Indre-et-Loire

| | |
|---|---|
| Tel | +33 (0)2 47 30 53 79 |
| Email | contact@chateaudeperreux.fr |
| Web | www.chateau-nazelles.com |

Entry 388   Map 4

# Loire Valley

## Manoir de la Maison Blanche

The 17th-century manor sits in blissful seclusion with châteaux nearby – you're on the outskirts of Amboise and the Loire. Annick, vivacious host, gives you three fabulous, generous sized bedrooms in the converted outbuilding. One is tiled and beamed with a patio overlooking the garden, another, under the eaves with a lofty ceiling, is reached via an outside spiral stair. The garden is surprisingly big, bursting with roses and irises that may make their way to your room. Enjoy delicious breakfasts in the new conservatory, and a kitchenette and dining area for all guests to share.

| Rooms | 2 doubles: €97. |
|---|---|
| | 1 family room for 4: €125. |
| | Singles €86. |
| | Extra bed/sofabed €26 per person per night. |
| Meals | Guest kitchenette. |
| | Restaurants 30-minute walk. |
| Closed | Rarely. |

| | Annick Delécheneau |
|---|---|
| | Manoir de la Maison Blanche, |
| | 18 rue de l'Épinetterie, |
| | 37400 Amboise |
| | Indre-et-Loire |
| Tel | +33 (0)2 47 23 16 14 |
| Mobile | +33 (0)6 88 89 33 66 |
| Email | annick.delecheneau@wanadoo.fr |
| Web | www.lamaisonblanche-fr.com |

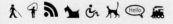

Entry 389   Map 4

# Loire Valley

## Belleroche

Faint sounds sometimes drift upwards from the embankment far below but Belleroche remains serene. Only a 15-minute walk from the centre of Amboise, this fine house stands poised and aloof in a three-hectare garden high above the Loire. Florence searched high and low for the perfect place for her B&B; having found it, she and her vet husband have devoted energy and imagination to its restoration. The exquisite bedrooms and the guest sitting room, once the old library, overlook the river. So, too, does a little 18th-century pavilion under the lime trees where Florence may serve breakfast on sunny mornings. Heaven.

| Rooms | 1 double with separate bath: €130. |
|---|---|
| | 1 suite for 4 with separate bath: €110-€170. |
| Meals | Restaurants nearby. |
| Closed | Mid-October to mid-April. |

| | Florence Janvier |
|---|---|
| | Belleroche, |
| | 1 rue du Clos de Belleroche, |
| | 37400 Amboise |
| | Indre-et-Loire |
| Tel | +33 (0)2 47 30 47 03 |
| Mobile | +33 (0)6 73 89 60 16 |
| Email | belleroche.amboise@orange.fr |
| Web | www.belleroche.net |

Entry 390   Map 4

# Loire Valley

## Château de Pintray

Instant charm at the end of the long leafy avenue. This intimate château glows with personality and peculiarity yet this is no museum-piece: delightful Anne looks after the B&B while Jean Christophe produces some of the region's best sweet and dry white wines; enjoy the tastings. Stuffed full of character, bedrooms have super comfy beds on carpeted floors and bathrooms big old roll top tubs and walk-in showers. Tuck in to a splendid breakfast at the convivial table – alongside the Guignol puppet theatre! – before setting off for the great châteaux: Chenonceau, Amboise, Villandry and Azay le Rideau, all within an hour's drive.

| Rooms | 2 doubles: €115. |
| | 1 family room for 4: €115–€165. |
| Meals | Restaurant 2km. |
| Closed | Rarely. |

Anne Ricou & Jean Christophe
Rault
Château de Pintray,
RD 283, Lussault sur Loire,
37400 Amboise
Indre-et-Loire

| Tel | +33 (0)2 47 23 22 84 |
| Email | marius.rault@wanadoo.fr |
| Web | www.chateau-de-pintray.com |

Entry 391  Map 4

# Loire Valley

*New Entry*

## La Maison de Famille

Strolling distance from the grandest château of the Loire: a traditional village house, a marvellous garden, and charming merry Madame. Breakfast is served in a pretty room filled with morning sun and dinner is on request; or a trot away, in Chenonceaux. Choose the 'Camel' bedroom with its big balcony/terrace; come as a family and stay in 'Chocolat' or 'Yellow' (on the ground floor), each with a shower. Spend the day exploring historic Loches and Chinon, or the vineyards and magical gardens of the area. Return to seats on the lawns, frogs on the lily pads, and chirping birds in the woodland. *Extra beds available in some doubles.*

| Rooms | 1 double; 2 doubles sharing wc: |
| | €60–€80. |
| | Extra bed €20 per person per night. |
| Meals | Dinner, 4 courses with aperitif, €25. |
| | Wine €10. |
| | Restaurants within walking |
| | distance. |
| Closed | Rarely. |

Yves & Cècile Rasquin
La Maison de Famille,
49 rue Dr Bretonneau,
37150 Chenonceaux
Indre-et-Loire

| Tel | +33 (0)2 47 23 53 71 |
| Email | cec.rasquin@gmail.com |
| Web | www.lamaisondefamillechenonceaux.com/ |
| | english/welcome |

Entry 392  Map 4

# Loire Valley

## Le Clos de Fontenay

Sweep up the wooded drive to the formal garden to be greeted by Madame, or one of her grown-up children brushing up their English… and know you have entered an enchanting place. The graceful château sits in wooded splendour on the banks of the Cher – and you can see it the river from the suitably châteauesque bedrooms. Breakfast well on a wisteria-shaded terrace by the pool, or in the elegant dining room where you can tuck into a rather fine dinner too. Borrow bikes (masses to see within pedalling distance), play billiards in the fab games room or just have a wander: it's the most relaxed of places. *Minimum stay: 2 nights at weekends. Cot & highchair available.*

| | |
|---|---|
| Rooms | 2 twin/doubles; 2 doubles with separate bathroom: €90-€148. Extra bed €30 per person per night. |
| Meals | Restaurants 5km. |
| Closed | Rarely. |

**Nathalie Carli**
Le Clos de Fontenay,
Château de Fontenay,
5 Fontenay, 37150 Bléré
Indre-et-Loire

| | |
|---|---|
| Tel | +33 (0)2 47 57 12 74 |
| Mobile | +33 (0)6 07 34 48 32 |
| Email | contact@leclosdefontenay.fr |
| Web | www.leclosdefontenay.com |

Entry 393   Map 4

# Loire Valley

## Manoir de Chaix

Up a quiet lane, embraced by woodland and fields, an exceedingly fine manor house with dovecot, orchard, barn, pool and flourishing potager. Warm friendly Christian, ex sommelier, welcomes you in; on Saturdays his wife (a Parisian chef!) treats you to table d'hôtes. Spacious beamed bedrooms – four reached via a stone turret stair – are full of traditional comfort, and the dining room is inviting, with blazing logs, light-flooded windows and a great big convivial table. This is the Loire and there are châteaux by the hatful: Chenonceau, Loches, Amboise, Azay le Rideau, Villandry. A great find, and good value.

| | |
|---|---|
| Rooms | 4 doubles, 2 twins: €80-€95. 1 family suite for 2-4: €120. 1 triple: €100-€112. Extra bed/sofabed €25 per person per night. |
| Meals | Dinner with wine, €30. Restaurants 5km. |
| Closed | Rarely. |

**Francis Fillon & Christian Poil**
Manoir de Chaix,
Lieu-dit Chaix,
37320 Truyes
Indre-et-Loire

| | |
|---|---|
| Tel | +33 (0)2 47 43 42 73 |
| Email | manoirdechaix@sfr.fr |
| Web | www.manoir-de-chaix.com |

Entry 394   Map 4

# Loire Valley

## Moulin de la Follaine

A smart metal gate opens to courtyard and garden beyond: Follaine is a deeply serene place. Ornamental geese adorn the lake, the tended garden has places to linger, colourful bedrooms have antique furniture, fabulous mattresses and lake views; one opens to the garden. Upstairs is a lovely light sitting room – and a guest fridge for picnics in the garden. Amazingly, the old milling machinery in the breakfast area still works – ask and Monsieur will turn it on for you; there are relics from the old hunting days, too. Your hosts, once in the hotel trade, know the area intimately and are utterly charming.

| | |
|---|---|
| Rooms | 1 double: €75–€80. |
| | 2 suites for 4: €80–€120. |
| Meals | Bar-restaurant 800m; |
| | choice of restaurants in Loches. |
| Closed | November – March. |

Danie Lignelet
Moulin de la Follaine,
2 chemin du Moulin,
37310 Azay sur Indre
Indre-et-Loire

| | |
|---|---|
| Tel | +33 (0)2 47 92 57 91 |
| Email | moulindelafollaine@wanadoo.fr |
| Web | www.moulindefollaine.com |

Entry 395  Map 4

# Loire Valley

## Le Pavillon de Vallet

Monks once lived in this beautiful house at the end of a pretty riverside hamlet. With its flowered walkways, ornamental pond, serenading frogs and meadow leading down to the river Cher, it is perfect for nature lovers. Your hosts, a delightful couple, love to share their house with visitors. He loves opera, she bakes delicious cakes served with breakfast in the large beamed dining room. The suite with boudoir, beautifully tiled en suite bathroom, parquet floor and pretty private courtyard is comfy and uncluttered. The cosy 'Bread Oven' with its sunny yellow walls and private walled garden is a real love nest. Irresistible. *Minimum stay: 2 nights. Extra bed / sofabed available.*

| | |
|---|---|
| Rooms | 1 double: €105. |
| | 1 suite for 2-3; extra single and |
| | children's bed available: €105–€135. |
| | Singles €95–€105. |
| Meals | Restaurant 1km. |
| Closed | Rarely. |

Mme Montet-Jourdran
Le Pavillon de Vallet,
4 rue de l'Aqueduc, Hameau de
Vallet, 37270 Athée sur Cher
Indre-et-Loire

| | |
|---|---|
| Tel | +33 (0)2 47 38 77 16 |
| Mobile | +33 (0)6 72 84 64 45 |
| Email | j.montet-jourdran@orange.fr |
| Web | www.pavillondevallet.com |

Entry 396  Map 4

## Loire Valley

### Les Moulins de Vontes

"Magical" say readers. Three old mills side by side on a glorious sweep of the Indre, boats for messing about in, wooden bridges to cross from one secluded bank to another, a fine view of the river from the terrace. No dinners so gather a picnic en route and your entertaining hosts will happily provide cutlery, rugs and anything else you need. The airy, elegant, uncluttered rooms are in historic style and have stunning river views (the rushing water becomes a gentle murmur at night). Bathrooms sparkle. Billiards in the sitting room, home honey for breakfast, swimming and fishing in the river, eco-aware owners. Heaven. *Minimum stay: 2 nights.*

| Rooms | 2 doubles, 1 twin: €140. |
|---|---|
| Meals | Restaurants 2.5km. |
| Closed | October – March. |

**Odile & Jean-Jacques Degail**
Les Moulins de Vontes,
37320 Esvres sur Indre
Indre-et-Loire
Tel       +33 (0)2 47 26 45 72
Mobile   +33 (0)7 78 11 87 66
Email    info@moulinsdevontes.com
Web      www.moulinsdevontes.com

Entry 397    Map 4

## Loire Valley

### La Lubinerie

Built by Elizabeth's grandfather, its typical brick-and-tile face still looking good, this neat townhouse is a spirited mixture of nostalgic and modern. Strong colours and delicate muslin, elegant mirrors and her own patchwork, and a fascinating collection of paintings, prints, old cartoons and… teapots. Elizabeth lived for years in England, collected all these things and calls her delicious rooms 'Earl Grey', 'Orange Pekoe', 'Darjeeling'. Your hosts love sharing their stories and knowledge with guests. A lovely dog, a friendly little town, a sweet cottagey garden – and, we are told, the best croissants ever.

| Rooms | 2 doubles: €71–€82. |
|---|---|
| | 1 suite for 4: €71–€144. |
| Meals | Crêperie nearby. |
| | Restaurants 3km. |
| Closed | Rarely. |

**Elizabeth Aubert-Girard**
La Lubinerie,
3 rue des Écoles,
37320 Esvres sur Indre
Indre-et-Loire
Tel       +33 (0)2 47 26 40 87
Mobile   +33 (0)6 82 89 00 95
Email    lalubinerie@orange.fr
Web      www.lalubinerie.fr

Entry 398    Map 4

# Loire Valley

## Le Châtelet

Step into a fairy tale – a medieval mini-castle with pepper-pot turrets, moat and countryside views. Grégoire's restoration – his wife inherited a derelict building – using traditional methods (oak shutters, hemp insulation) has created a medieval environment with 21st-century luxuries. Stairs spiral to a vast bedroom with terracotta tiles and oak furnishings; bath in one turret, loo in another. Breakfast on home-produce in the stone-flagged hall, a soaring space with glazed doors to the grassy terrace. Explore the Loire, return to your private stronghold. Your endearing hosts live nearby. For green views and a dip in the moat.

| | |
|---|---|
| Rooms | 1 suite for 2: €140. Singles €15. Extra bed/sofabed €15 per person per night. |
| Meals | Restaurant 5km. |
| Closed | Rarely. |

**Gregoire Le Lasseux**
Le Châtelet,
37260 Thilouze
Indre-et-Loire
Tel +33 (0)2 47 29 02 57 /
+33 (0)7 81 15 32 97
Email lechatelet@hotmail.fr

Entry 399   Map 4

# Loire Valley

## Le Château des Templiers

This attractive small château, in a peaceful green valley surrounded by woodland ten minutes from Tours, was a Knights Templar commandry. Its owner is helpful, elegant, charming Madame, who gives you a delightful sitting room with a wood-burner for cosy nights in, and brings fresh pastries and homemade jams to the long breakfast table. Each of her cool, quiet guest bedrooms (one on the ground floor) opens off a terrace that fronts the outhouse at the back. Each comes with a new parquet floor, a pretty canopied bed, a beautifully tiled bathroom, and windows onto large, sloping grounds. *Children over 12 welcome.*

| | |
|---|---|
| Rooms | 3 doubles (outbuilding), 1 twin: €110-€130. 1 triple: €110-€130. |
| Meals | Restaurants 10-minute drive. |
| Closed | December/January. |

**Cyrille Aubry Le Borgne**
Le Château des Templiers,
17 rue de la Commanderie,
37510 Ballan Miré
Indre-et-Loire
Tel +33 (0)2 47 53 94 56
Mobile +33 (0)6 25 79 81 95
Email contact@chateaudestempliers-touraine.com
Web www.chateaudestempliers-touraine.com

Entry 400   Map 4

## Loire Valley

### Château du Vau

At the end of a long bumpy drive is a house of great character run with good humour: delightful philosopher Bruno has turned his family château into a stylish refuge for travellers. Two large, light bedrooms have been redecorated with seagrass and family memorabilia round splendid brass bedsteads; others remain, very comfortably, in their traditional, distinguished garb. And then there are the beautifully crafted treehouses: oriental in the oak tree, African in the cedar, breakfast hampers delivered at the end of a rope... Dinners showcase estate produce. There's a fine pool, and a golf course bang opposite.

| Rooms | 3 doubles: €130. |
| | 1 family room for 4, 1 triple, |
| | 2 treehouses for 2: €140. |
| Meals | Dinner with wine, €42. |
| | Summer buffets in garden €26. |
| Closed | Rarely. |

**Bruno Clément**
Château du Vau,
37510 Ballan Miré
Indre-et-Loire

Tel +33 (0)2 47 67 84 04
Email info@chateau-du-vau.com
Web www.chateau-du-vau.com

Entry 401  Map 4

## Loire Valley

### Les Mazeraies

Beautifully sculpted from the same ancient cedar trees that stalked the splendid grounds 100 years ago, this thoroughly contemporary mansion on the old château foundations in the Garden of France is a real delight. Humour, intelligence and love of fine things inhabit this welcoming family and their guest wing is unostentatiously luxurious in rich fabrics, oriental and modern furniture, good pictures and lovely, scented, cedar-lined bathrooms. Ground-floor rooms have a private terrace each, upstairs ones have direct access to the roof garden. Marie-Laurence is utterly charming.

| Rooms | 1 double, 2 twin/doubles: €110. |
| | 1 suite for 3-4: €130-€150. |
| Meals | Restaurants nearby. |
| Closed | Rarely. |

**Marie-Laurence Jallet**
Les Mazeraies,
34 route des Mazeraies,
37510 Savonnières
Indre-et-Loire

Tel +33 (0)2 47 67 85 35
Email les.jallet@wanadoo.fr
Web www.lesmazeraies.com

Entry 402  Map 4

# Loire Valley

## Le Chat Courant

A handsome 18th-century family house on the river Cher just opposite Villandry and with its own lovely garden (whose birdsong drowns out occasional train noise). Bedrooms are pretty and stylish: the double in the converted cottage opens to the swimming pool, the suite in the main house has fine antique furniture. Éric – who is also a keen photographer – has created garden enchantment here with old species of apple trees, a walled vegetable garden, a wisteria-clad pergola, a formal boxed flower garden, and a semi-wild garden beyond, all surrounded by woodland and pasture where the families' horses peacefully graze. *Minimum stay: 2 nights in high season.*

| Rooms | 1 double: €75–€80. |
| | 1 family suite for 2-5: €100–€170. |
| Meals | Restaurant 5-minute drive. |
| Closed | Rarely. |

**Éric Gaudouin**
Le Chat Courant,
37510 Villandry
Indre-et-Loire

| Tel | +33 (0)2 47 50 06 94 |
| Mobile | +33 (0)6 37 83 21 78 |
| Email | info@le-chat-courant.com |
| Web | www.le-chat-courant.com |

Entry 403  Map 4

# Loire Valley

## Château de Crémille

Deep within a forest lies an elegant little château where swans glide and frogs croak. A staircase curves gracefully to peaceful and traditional bedrooms – all with family stories to tell. Glimpse deer from the room with the roof garden, or choose triple-aspect Chambre de la Tour. Aldric is your host, cook, and delightful dinner companion. Gaze at parkland views; enjoy a welcoming aperitif in the tower's salon with wood fire; feast in a chandelier'd dining room. Catch the eerie bark of stags – and enjoy forest forays when hunting season's over. Dramatic setting, a family feel – and a splendid wire-haired terrier!

| Rooms | 2 doubles: €120–€130. |
| | 1 family room for 6: €295. |
| Meals | Dinner with wine, €25–€38. |
| | Restaurant 10km. |
| Closed | November – April. |

**Aldric de La Brosse**
Château de Crémille,
37130 Mazières de Touraine
Indre-et-Loire

| Tel | +33 (0)2 47 24 00 32 |
| Email | cremille@orange.fr |
| Web | www.chateaudecremille.fr |

Entry 404  Map 4

# Loire Valley

## Le Moulin de Touvois

Delightful, good-natured, hospitable Myriam and Jean-Claude have renovated the old miller's house in a blend of styles; now stonework, beams and terracotta mix with modern furniture. The Moroccan tiled dining table looks great beside the big old stone fireplace; simple, smallish, comfortable bedrooms have carpets and crisp bedding. Best of all is the garden, with its planked bridge, orchard, swings and pool, and shady terrace by the bucolic stream. Three hens contentedly roam, horses dot the paddock, Myriam's food is wonderful and Jean-Claude has a small vineyard nearby. Brilliant value.

| Rooms | 2 doubles, 2 twin/doubles, 1 quadruple: €60-€65. Extra bed €15 per person per night. |
|---|---|
| Meals | Dinner with wine, €25. |
| Closed | Mid-November to mid-February. |

**Myriam & Jean-Claude Marchand**
Le Moulin de Touvois,
3 rue du Moulin de Touvois,
37140 Bourgueil
Indre-et-Loire

| Tel | +33 (0)2 47 97 87 70 |
| Email | info@moulindetouvois.com |
| Web | www.moulindetouvois.com |

Entry 405   Map 4

# Loire Valley

## Cheviré

Wonderful hosts, wonderful surroundings. You stay in the well-converted stable block of a traditional farmhouse on the edge of a peaceful village. Welcome to the protected wetlands between the Loire and the Vienne, all a-shimmer in the Loire's inimitable light. Pretty, uncluttered bedrooms display a happy mix of old and new and bathrooms gleam. There's space to sit and cook (dishwasher, hob, microwave) and a wood-burner to get cosy by. The meadows are full of birds and fritillaries, the treasures of Chinon await, the wines of Bourgueil and Saumur are delicious, and homemade jams abound at breakfast. Astounding value. *Extra beds available.*

| Rooms | 1 double: €48-€56. 1 triple: €52-€67. 1 quadruple: €56-€86. |
|---|---|
| Meals | Guest kitchenette. Restaurant 1km. |
| Closed | Mid-November to mid-March. |

**Marie-Françoise & Michel Chauvelin**
Cheviré,
11 rue Basse,
37420 Savigny en Véron
Indre-et-Loire

| Tel | +33 (0)2 47 58 42 49 |
| Email | chauvelin.michel@wanadoo.fr |
| Web | www.ch-hotes-chevire.fr |

Entry 406   Map 4

## Loire Valley

### Le Clos Chavigny

Views sail across pastures and grazing ponies to little Lerne's rooftops and pretty church spire. Through carriage doors you wash up at this long, shuttered, extremely attractive building, the impeccably restored wing of a 17th-century farm complex. Inside... a magnificent salon and dining room, a charming 'library' for bookish nights in, and big sophisticated bedrooms with canopied beds beneath soaring timbers and internal bathrooms. The gardens are box hedged and rose bordered, with a pool to the side, Jean-Claude is your host, Moha is your chef, and the Loire's glorious châteaux lie at your feet.

| Rooms | 3 doubles: €130-€150. |
| | 1 suite for 4: €150-€200. |
| Meals | Dinner with wine, from €40. |
| | Restaurants 10km. |
| Closed | Rarely. |

**Moha Oulad**
Le Clos Chavigny,
3 rue de la Rouillère,
37500 Lerné
Indre-et-Loire
Tel        +33 (0)2 47 93 94 72
Mobile     +33 (0)6 83 10 46 64
Email      closchavigny@gmail.com
Web        www.lecloschavigny.com

Entry 407   Map 9

## Loire Valley

### Le Châtaignier

A pretty old stone farmhouse on the edge of a hamlet, beautifully restored by Odile – and Jean-Joseph who loves his garden. With open lawns, swings, fruit trees and a vast chestnut tree – and its own blissful platform for deckchairs and views – it's a joy to spend time in; and there's a summer kitchen. The décor is cool and charming, the suites, each with a private entrance, are big and inviting. Artistic Odile, who speaks good English, presents you with a homemade lavender bag on leaving, a typical touch. Sunny, country-elegant sitting and dining rooms open to the garden, and the fields stretch for miles.

| Rooms | 1 suite for 4 (bedrooms separated |
| | by landing): €76-€126. |
| | 1 family suite for 2-4: €74-€112. |
| | Singles €57-€60. |
| | Extra bed/sofabed €19 per person |
| | per night. |
| Meals | Summer kitchen. |
| | Restaurant 3km. |
| Closed | Rarely. |

**Odile & Jean-Joseph Crescenzo**
Le Châtaignier,
16 rue du Carroi, La Roberderie,
37500 Marcay
Indre-et-Loire
Tel        +33 (0)2 47 93 97 09
Mobile     +33 (0)6 71 42 22 15
Email      info@lechataignier.com
Web        lechataignier.free.fr

Entry 408   Map 9

## Loire Valley

### Le Clos de Ligré

This elegant country house sings in a subtle harmony of traditional charm and contemporary chic under Martine's modern touch. Sponged walls, creamy beams and eye-catching fabrics breathe new life into rooms with old tiled floors and stone fireplaces, and the doubles in the attic are great, with views over the huge garden. Windows are flung open to let in the light and the stresses of city living are forgotten in cheerful, easy conversations with your hostess, who joins guests for candlelit dinners. Bookcases, baby grand, buffet breakfasts at the oval table, a barn for barbecues, a pool for the energetic... delightful.

| Rooms | 3 doubles: €110. |
|---|---|
| Meals | Dinner with wine, €35. |
| Closed | Rarely. |

Martine Descamps
Le Clos de Ligré,
Le Rouilly,
37500 Ligré
Indre-et-Loire
Tel +33 (0)2 47 93 95 59
Email mdescamps@club-internet.fr
Web www.le-clos-de-ligre.com

Entry 409   Map 9

## Loire Valley

### La Baumoderie

Anne designed interiors in Paris, Jean-François managed hotels, now they do B&B from their imaginatively restored farmhouse on the top of a hill. Lively, charming people, they serve excellent French dinners in a modern chandelier'd conservatory and give guests big rustic-elegant rooms: one cool and spacious on the ground floor (with just French windows) and a suite at the top of an outside stone stair; there's a stunning 'cabane' with a shower on the veranda. The large garden and wildflower meadow and Jeremy Fisher-like pond blend into the landscape, the small village is up the road, and peace reigns supreme.

| Rooms | 1 double with separate shower & wc: €100–€125. |
|---|---|
| | 1 suite for 2 with separate shower & wc: €135–€150. |
| Meals | Lunch or dinner €35, with wine. Restaurant 4km. |
| Closed | Rarely. |

Anne Tardits
La Baumoderie,
17 rue d'Étilly,
37220 Panzoult
Indre-et-Loire
Mobile +33 (0)6 08 78 00 73
Email anne@labaumoderie.fr
Web www.labaumoderie.fr

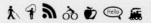

Entry 410   Map 9

## Loire Valley

### Domaine de Beauséjour

Dug into the hillside with the forest behind and a panorama of vines in front, this wine-grower's manor successfully pretends it was built in the 1800s. Venerable oak beams and stone cut by troglodyte masons create a mood of stylish rusticity. Bedrooms are charming, the suite in the main house, the other two in the romantic poolside tower. Find carved bedheads, old prints, vases of fresh and artificial flowers, elegant bathrooms. Your vivacious hostess helps her son run the family wine estate and will arrange a tasting for guests. Picnic in the conservatory or in one of the caves overlooking the valley. *Minimum stay: 2 nights.*

| Rooms | 2 doubles: €70–€90. |
| | 1 suite for 3-4: €120. |
| Meals | Restaurants 5km. |
| Closed | Rarely. |

FIRST
EDITION
VETERAN

Marie-Claude Chauveau
Domaine de Beauséjour,
37220 Panzoult
Indre-et-Loire

| Tel | +33 (0)2 47 58 64 64 |
| Mobile | +33 (0)6 86 97 03 40 |
| Email | info@domainedebeausejour.com |
| Web | www.domainedebeausejour.com |

## Loire Valley

### Le Moulin de St Jean

The restored mill in its delicious island setting is all ups and downs, nooks and crannies, big rooms and small, character and variety. Your delightful host John, a Welshman, fled a city job for a quieter life, bringing his love of Loire wines (just ask) and a fondness for entertaining with him. Assorted wallpapers, patterns, frills and furniture – and a welcome bottle of wine – make for a warm, homely feel. Plus new mattresses and good bathrooms, two sitting rooms, numerous DVDs and books, a shady garden, a heated pool – and all the fascinations of the Loire Valley.

| Rooms | 2 doubles, 1 twin: €85–€99. |
| | 1 suite for 2: €99–€110. |
| Meals | Dinner €15–€25. |
| | Wine from €10. |
| | Restaurant 8km. |
| Closed | Rarely. |

John Higginson
Le Moulin de St Jean,
St Jean St Germain,
37600 Loches
Indre-et-Loire

| Tel | +33 (0)2 47 94 70 12 |
| Email | john@lemoulinstjean.com |
| Web | www.lemoulinstjean.com |

# Loire Valley

## La Roche Berthault

Benoît and Raphaëlle have restored their 16th-century château to perfection. Find tall turrets and manicured gardens, watch the sun rise while feasting on hams, cheeses and homemade jams on one of two terraces. The other faces the setting sun, near a graceful sitting room and library. A light green and cream colour scheme suits the mansion's natural elegance, as do the antiques, original tiles and ornate headboards in three light, airy and elegant bedrooms upstairs. 'Parisienne' and 'Italienne' overlook parkland where you'll find two gîtes and a large swimming pool. Your hosts are only too happy to help you explore.

| Rooms | 2 doubles: €95–€115. |
| | 1 suite for 3: €105. |
| Meals | Cold platter with wine, €12. |
| | Restaurants 1km. |
| Closed | October – April. |

Benoît & Raphaëlle Cardon de Lichtbuer
La Roche Berthault,
37240 Ciran
Indre-et-Loire

| Tel | +33 (0)2 47 92 38 98 |
| Mobile | +33 (0)6 74 74 00 80 |
| Email | larocheberto@hotmail.com |
| Web | www.larocheberthault.fr |

Entry 413   Map 9

# Loire Valley

## Château de la Celle Guenand

In the heart of an old Touraine village, four hectares of delightful walled park and a fairytale castle that dates from 1442. It's large but not palatial, grand but not ornate, and refreshingly unstuffy. Much is being updated, everything is charming, and Stephen is putting all his energies into his new project. You get top mattresses on king-size beds, bedrooms with beautifully proportioned windows (cool conservative shades for the newest) and delicious quince jams at breakfast. After dinner: brocade sofas in faded reds, books to browse and a piano to play. All this, châteaux by the hatful, and the Brenne National Park. *Children over 6 welcome.*

| Rooms | 4 doubles: €110–€150. |
| | 1 family room for 2-5: €130–€160. |
| | Dinner, B&B €70–€85 per person. |
| Meals | Dinner with wine, €30. |
| | Restaurant in village. |
| Closed | Christmas. |

Stephen Palluel
Château de la Celle Guenand,
14 rue du Château,
37350 La Celle Guenand
Indre-et-Loire

| Tel | +33 (0)2 47 94 93 61 |
| Mobile | +33 (0)6 76 23 74 77 |
| Email | stephane@chateaucelleguenand.com |
| Web | www.chateaucelleguenand.biz |

Entry 414   Map 9

# Poitou – Charentes

www.sawdays.co.uk/poitou-charentes

## La Grenouillère

In a cluster of buildings on a residential road, a true, traditional B&B. Impossible not to be charmed by these warm, easy, good-hearted people who offer you extremely good food, flowing wine, meals on a shady terrace in summer and, always, flowers on the table. The bedroom in the converted woodshed has beams, a colourful tiled floor and a view over the huge, lush garden – rambling and delightful with a long pond and weeping willows. More rooms await in the house across the courtyard where Madame's charming mother lives (and makes delicious jam). There's even a Mongolian yurt – and a compact Loire river boat to sleep in.

## Château de la Motte

Nothing austere about this imposing, lovingly restored 15th-century castle. A wide spiral stone staircase leads to grandly high yet simply decorated rooms where family furniture, vast stone fireplaces and rich canopies, finely stitched by talented Marie-Andrée, preserve the medieval flavour; bathrooms are state of the art. The lofty, light-filled sitting room is engagingly cluttered, the elegant dining room witnesses excellent, organic home cooking and enlightened conversation with your dynamically green, cultured and charming hosts. Everyone is welcome here, families included.

| | | | |
|---|---|---|---|
| Rooms | 2 doubles: €54–€62.<br>2 triples: €50–€57.<br>1 houseboat for 2: €85–€100.<br>1 yurt for 4 with kitchen: €98. | Rooms | 1 double, 1 twin: €100–€115.<br>2 suites for 2: €145–€150.<br>1 triple: €175–€200.<br>Singles €95–€160.<br>Dinner, B&B €138–€203 per room.<br>Extra bed/sofabed €30 p.p per night. |
| Meals | Dinner, 4 courses with wine, €29. | Meals | Dinner, 4 courses with wine &<br>aperitif, €38. Children under 12, €25.<br>Children under 6 eat free. |
| Closed | Rarely. | Closed | Rarely. |

Annie & Noël Braguier
La Grenouillère,
17 rue de la Grenouillère,
86220 Dangé St Romain
Vienne
Tel     +33 (0)5 49 86 48 68
Email   lagrenouillere86@orange.fr
Web     www.lagrenouillere86.com

Jean-Marie & Marie-Andrée Bardin
Château de la Motte,
2 La Motte,
86230 Usseau
Vienne
Tel     +33 (0)5 49 85 88 25
Mobile  +33 (0)6 19 03 35 35
Email   chateau.delamotte@wanadoo.fr
Web     www.chateau-de-la-motte.net

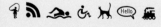

Entry 415   Map 9

Entry 416   Map 9

## Manoir de la Boulinière

Laughter echoes in this 15th-century country manor where descendants of Scottish royalty once lived. Share with Alain and Marie-Pierre the great gothic windows, the stone-flagged floors, the huge fireplaces, a living room replete with period pieces and their art collection. Alain is generous with the Loire valley's secrets, the feeling is of a lovely family home and table d'hôtes dinners burst with fresh herbs. The walled garden, too, is delightful, with giant cedar, plums, cherries, vines, a pretty gazebo. Two-room suites, up spiral stairs, revel in canopied beds, gorgeous bathrooms and a heady sense of history.

| | |
|---|---|
| Rooms | 2 family suites for 4-6: €140. Extra bed (12+ years) €60 per person per night. Under 12's, €30 per night. Under 2's free. Travel cot available. |
| Meals | Dinner €40. Children under 12, €20. 'Birthday' dinner with champagne, €50. |
| Closed | Rarely. |

Marie-Pierre & Alain Guillon-Hardyau
Manoir de la Boulinière,
7 Manoir de la Boulinière,
86230 Usseau
Vienne

Tel    +33 (0)5 49 85 07 49
Mobile    +33 (0)6 87 03 58 84
Email    manoir.bouliniere@hotmail.fr
Web    www.manoirdelabouliniere.fr

## Château de La Plante

You'll be charmed by this unpretentious stone manor looking proudly over farmland to the wooded Vienne valley. It has been in Françoise's family for ever and she and Patrick tend it with loving car, as they do their guests. Period elegance drifts through rooms where the family grew up, leaving canopied beds, parquet floors and the odd empty picture frame in bedrooms named after great-grandmothers. Serenity reigns supreme; breakfast is in the old music room, a fittingly classic cream-blue affair. Join your hosts for an aperitif on the balustraded terrace or under the spreading lime tree. If houses could sing, this one surely would.

| | |
|---|---|
| Rooms | 2 doubles, 1 twin/double: €90-€110. 1 family suite with separate wc: €140. Children's triple room €60-€80. |
| Meals | Restaurants 10-minute drive. |
| Closed | Rarely. |

Patrick & Françoise Dandurand
Château de La Plante,
86540 Thuré
Vienne

Tel    +33 (0)5 49 93 86 28
Email    patrick.dandurand@orange.fr
Web    www.chateaudelaplante.fr

### La Pocterie

A "passionate gardener" is how Martine describes herself, with a soft spot for old-fashioned roses: they ramble through the wisteria on the walls and gather in beautifully tended beds. The 'L' of the house shelters a very decent pool (alarmed) while furniture is arranged in a welcoming spot for picnics. Martine works but will see you for breakfast (in the delightful dining room or under the pretty arbour) or in the evening: she's the one with the big smile. A fresh, polished and peaceful retreat with Futuroscope minutes away. Bikes and tennis nearby, and a huge range of day trips to choose from: excellent for families.

### Les Pierres Blanches

A pretty, unpretentious house built with century-old beams, in gardens bright with perennials, mature trees and swimming pool. Madame, friendly and charming, makes her own cakes and jams at a large table in the open-plan dining room with a cheery fire in winter. You have your own sitting room with cool beige walls, beams, a red sofa and armchairs, and pottery by family members, while the large ground-floor bedroom is light and airy, prettily painted in fresh apple green and with a romantic, canopied bed; this leads to a private decked terrace with a blue table and chairs. You are near to the medieval delights of Chauvigny.

| Rooms | 1 double: €70. |
|---|---|
| | 1 triple: €80. |
| Meals | Restaurants 3km. |
| Closed | Rarely. |

| Rooms | 1 double with separate, private sitting room: €60-€70. |
|---|---|
| | Extra bed/sofabed €10 per person per night. |
| Meals | Restaurant 2km. |
| Closed | Rarely. |

**Michel & Martine Poussard**
La Pocterie,
86210 Vouneuil sur Vienne
Vienne
Tel     +33 (0)5 49 85 11 96
Mobile  +33 (0)6 76 95 49 46
Email   martinelapocterie@orange.fr
Web     lapocterie.chambres.free.fr

**Nicole Gallais-Pradal**
Les Pierres Blanches,
86210 Bonneuil Matours
Vienne
Tel     +33 (0)5 49 85 24 75
Email   les.pierres.blanches@orange.fr
Web     www.les-pierres-blanches.fr

## La Maison Verte

At the end of the pretty country lane is a lovely longère filled with tranquillity and views. Here live Mark and Monica, the most generous people, with one friendly Jack Russell and chickens running free. Step inside: to space, warmth and bonhomie. Seductive bedrooms, one in the house, two in the barn, have down duvets and pale old beams, bathrooms are white, fresh and luxurious and there are interesting pictures throughout. Doze on the terrace, play the piano, read… or set off with a champagne picnic! Return to candles and a Swedish dinner – or a barbecue on the camp fire. Heaven for city escapees.

## Logis du Château du Bois Doucet

Naturally, graciously, aristocratically French, owners and house are full of stories and eccentricity. Beautiful treasures abound: a jumble of ten French chairs, bits of ancient furniture, pictures, heirlooms, lamps in a stone-flagged salon, a properly elegant dining room, old dolls and family hunting buttons. There are statues inside and out and bedrooms with personality; the two-storey suite in the main house is fit for a cardinal. Monsieur's interests are history and his family, Madame's are art and life, and the garden is listed, a symphony in green. Feel part of family life in this delightful people- and dog-orientated house.

| Rooms | 3 doubles: €75. |
|---|---|
| Meals | Dinner with wine, from €20. Lunch from €15. Picnic available. Restaurants 4km. |
| Closed | Rarely. |

| Rooms | 1 double (in wing): €80–€90. 1 family suite for 4 (wc on ground floor), 1 family room for 4-6 (in wing): €150. |
|---|---|
| Meals | Dinner with wine, €30. |
| Closed | Rarely. |

Monica Green
La Maison Verte,
2 chemin des Vallées,
86390 Lathus St Rémy
Vienne

| Tel | +33 (0)5 49 48 96 19 |
| Email | info@lamaisonvertefrance.com |
| Web | www.lamaisonvertefrance.com |

Vicomte & Vicomtesse de
Villoutreys de Brignac
Logis du Château du Bois Doucet,
86800 Lavoux
Vienne

| Tel | +33 (0)5 49 44 20 26 |
| Mobile | +33 (0)6 75 42 79 78 |
| Email | mariediane1012@yahoo.fr |

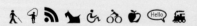

Entry 421   Map 9

Entry 422   Map 9

Poitou – Charentes

## La Roseraie

Country B&B with one foot in the town:
Neuville is a mere stroll. Warm and
generous, Heather and Michael live in an
elegant townhouse in four enclosed acres
with orchard, vegetable garden and two rows
of vines. The sitting area is cosy, the pool is
fabulous, the bedrooms are immaculate,
restful and calm: seagrass floors, white tub
chairs, a carved bedhead, a balcony here, a
patio off the garden there. Put the world to
rights over Heather's delicious dinner served
at the big table, or under the pergola in
summer: gîte and B&B guests combine.
Doves coo, Jack Russells frolic, Poitiers is the
shortest drive. *Pets by arrangement.*

| Rooms | 3 doubles: €68-€95. |
| | 2 family suites for 4-5: €120-€160. |
| Meals | Dinner with wine, €28. |
| Closed | Rarely. |

Michael & Heather Lavender
La Roseraie,
78 rue Armand Caillard,
86170 Neuville de Poitou
Vienne
Tel      +33 (0)5 49 54 16 72
Email   heather@laroseraiefrance.fr
Web     www.laroseraiefrance.fr

Entry 423   Map 9

Poitou – Charentes

## Château de Labarom

A great couple in their genuine family château
of fading grandeur; mainly 17th century, it has
a properly aged face. From the dramatic hall
up the superbly bannistered staircase, you
reach the salon gallery that runs majestically
through the house. Here you may sit, read,
dream of benevolent ghosts. Bedrooms burst
with personality and wonderful old beds.
Madame's hand-painted tiles adorn a shower,
her laughter accompanies your breakfast
(organic garden fruits and four sorts of jam);
Monsieur tends his trees, aided by Hermes
the dog – he's a fount of local wisdom. A
warm, wonderful, authentic place, and
Michelin stars five miles away.

| Rooms | 2 doubles, 1 twin: €74-€84. |
| | Child €20, in connecting room. |
| Meals | Auberge nearby. |
| | Restaurants 3-8km. |
| Closed | Rarely. |

Éric & Henriette Le Gallais
Château de Labarom,
86380 Chénéché
Vienne
Tel      +33 (0)5 49 51 24 22
Mobile  +33 (0)6 83 57 68 14
Email   labarom@labarom.com
Web     www.labarom.com

Entry 424   Map 9

## Manoir de Vilaines

An oasis in the middle of rolling fields and wooded copses is an elegantly proportioned manor farmhouse, home to a hard-working family with a great sense of hospitality. Sleep in a super-comfortable bed, wake to a delicious breakfast at the big oval table overlooking the garden's cherry tree (home-produced apple juice, local honey…). In the two end wings are the biggest family suites, and the décor is traditional in keeping with the period of the house – long drapes, calm colours, folded bathrobes on immaculate beds. Outside is the paddock where the old carthorse lives, beyond is the market town of Mirebeau. Great value.

## Domaine de Bourgville

Time slows down here. In the converted stable block of a 17th-century 'gentilhommière' the style is gentle, provincial France, in tune with the rolling countryside of forests, hamlets and hills. The first-floor bedrooms wrap you in a soft embrace of old French bedsteads and shiny seagrass, flowers, rush-seated chairs and views to garden or terrace; all is intimacy and calm. Breakfast in the airy sitting room with its comfortable, well-chosen furnishings; John is a superb cook so stay for dinner. Explore medieval Chinon, walk the trails, then return to the rambling garden. Supremely restful, truly hospitable. *Whole house available on a self-catering basis.*

| Rooms | 1 double: €65. |
|---|---|
| | 1 suite for 3: €65-€80. |
| | 1 family room for 4, |
| | 1 family room for 5: €65-€110. |
| | Singles €46-€110. |
| Meals | Restaurant 4 km. |
| Closed | Rarely. |

| Rooms | 3 doubles: €70. |
|---|---|
| | 1 single: €50-€55. |
| | Singles €50-€55. |
| Meals | Dinner with wine, €28. |
| | Restaurant in village. |
| Closed | Christmas/New Year. |

| | |
|---|---|
| | Géraldine Simonnet |
| | Manoir de Vilaines, |
| | Vilaines, |
| | 86110 Varennes |
| | Vienne |
| Tel | +33 (0)5 49 60 73 93 |
| Email | manoirdevilaines@orange.fr |
| Web | www.manoir-de-vilaines.com |

| | |
|---|---|
| | John & Glyn Ward |
| | Domaine de Bourgville, |
| | Allée de Bourgville, |
| | 86420 Mont sur Guesnes |
| | Vienne |
| Tel | +33 (0)5 49 98 74 79 |
| Mobile | +33 (0)6 61 71 92 97 |
| Email | info@vie-vienne.com |
| Web | www.vie-vienne.com |

## Poitou – Charentes

### L'Aumônerie

This old hospital priory beside the original moat (now a boulevard bringing new neighbours, garden centre included) has eight drama-packed centuries to tell. The L'Haridons have put back several original features and alongside picture windows the old stone spiral leads up to the suite (big warm sitting room, low oak door to fresh beamed bedroom with extra bed). The small ground-floor double is utterly charming; outside is a playhouse for children. Madame is well-travelled, loves old buildings and gardens and is a most interesting and considerate hostess who also has a passion for patchwork.

| Rooms | 1 double: €58–€64. |
| --- | --- |
| | 1 suite for 2-3: €60–€74. |
| | 1 family room for 2-6: €100. |
| | Children under 3 stay free. |
| Meals | Restaurants within walking distance. |
| Closed | Rarely. |

**Christiane L'Haridon**
L'Aumônerie,
3 bd Maréchal Leclerc,
86200 Loudun
Vienne

| Tel | +33 (0)5 49 22 63 86 |
| --- | --- |
| Mobile | +33 (0)6 83 58 26 18 |
| Email | chris.lharidon@wanadoo.fr |
| Web | www.l-aumonerie.biz |

Entry 427   Map 9

## Poitou – Charentes

### Chez Jasmin

The B&B spirit is alive and well in this Vendéen farmhouse encircled by dairy cows and hedgerows yet close to culture at Parthenay. Your lovely hosts are Dave, Pamela, two handsome Irish setters and an adorable black cat. Make yourself at home amongst rugs, books and big sofas, wallow in super bathrooms, sleep in charming brass beds; the upstairs room is reached via the kitchen, the other opens to the garden. Best of all is the food: gazpacho with fresh crab, pork belly with boudin, melt-in-the-mouth truffles… it's wonderful value and Dave is a professional chef. Kids should visit the extraordinary Puy du Fou (50km); fishing is a five-minute walk.
*Minimum stay: 2 nights in high season.*

| Rooms | 2 doubles: €70–€80. |
| --- | --- |
| | 2 sofabeds available for under 12's, €25 per child per night. |
| Meals | Dinner with aperitif, wine & coffee, €35. Restaurants 15km. |
| Closed | Rarely. |

**Dave & Pamela Burns**
Chez Jasmin,
Les Pouilleres,
79430 La Chapelle St Laurent
Deux Sèvres

| Tel | +33 (0)5 49 72 79 18 |
| --- | --- |
| Email | markaddy2011@gmail.com |
| Web | www.chezjasmin.com |

Entry 428   Map 9

### La Petite Bêchée

In the middle of a remote green valley, this beautifully restored building girdled by mature trees happens to be part of an alpaca farm; you are free to wander across the river and through swathes of grassland in search of a picnic spot. Josephine's welcome reflects the loved and lived-in qualities that you'll find everywhere: snuggled under beams in the sitting room, or up the oak staircase to the cosy country bedroom. Before heading off to find medieval France, enjoy breakfast on the garden terrace hung with wisteria or in the dining room… but it's all so peaceful you may decide to stay put after all. *Extra single available downstairs.*

### Bois Bourdet

A Charentaise farmhouse steeped in character, with hens in the gardens, two barns for self-catering and enchanting bedrooms for B&B guests. A family live here so it's ideal for children, with ropes, slides, swings, toys, and Monsieur a marvellous chef. There's a pool surrounded by lavender, a sitting room just for guests and a kitchen opening to a patio (with bedrooms above) and home-grown produce in the garden for every guest to enjoy. Hire a traditional punt or cycle along the canals; this is the 'Little Venice' of France, the Marais Poitevin. Handmade soaps, bikes to borrow, cookery courses to book into… Bois Bourdet is a gem.

| | |
|---|---|
| Rooms | 1 suite for 2: €85. |
| Meals | Plat du jour €12–€15. |
| | Restaurants 4km. |
| Closed | Rarely. |

| | |
|---|---|
| Rooms | 1 double, |
| | 1 family room for 3: €70–€80. |
| Meals | Guest kitchen. |
| | Dinner, 4 courses, €35. |
| | Child €15. |
| | Restaurants 6km. |
| Closed | Never. |

Josephine Colclough
La Petite Bêchée,
Le Moulin de La Bêchée,
Le Plessis,
79400 Auge
Deux Sèvres
Tel     +33 (0)5 49 75 53 19
Email  beechy.colclough@orange.fr
Web   www.rural-gites-france.com

Xavier & Stéphanie Trouillet
Bois Bourdet,
Lieu-Dit Bois Bourdet,
79800 Souvigné
Deux Sèvres
Tel     +33 (0)5 49 34 57 99
Email  info@boisbourdet.com
Web   www.boisbourdet.com

Entry 429   Map 9

Entry 430   Map 9

## Le Logis de Bellevue

You're within strolling distance of one of the prettiest towns in the Marais Poitevin. The green-shuttered lodge has been transformed by this happy, hospitable British couple into a colourful home with the guest suite on the first floor: white walled, wooden floored, clean-limbed and spotless. The garden is immaculate too, with lawns and colourful borders, croquet, table tennis and (shared with gîtes) super pool. Garden fruits make an appearance at breakfast in homemade juices and jams; clever Marylyn even makes brioche. Dinner might include goat's cheese from the area and lamb from the farmer next door. A treat.

## Le Logis d'Antan

Blue shutters against pale walls, faded terracotta roofs, gardens full of beeches, wild poppies, fruit trees and figs. Bruno and Annie have created a friendly, unpretentious atmosphere and you'll like their style – simple, country elegance. Home-cooked meals are eaten at a table seating up to 16 in a typically French dining room – or out on the veranda in good weather. Upstairs you can prepare picnics in a communal kitchen. Up here, too, are two double rooms, one with a bunk-bedded children's annexe. The rest are on the ground floor: big, traditional rooms, with their own entrances off the drive. Grab bikes and explore the country.

| | | | |
|---|---|---|---|
| Rooms | 1 family suite for 2-4: €100-€190. Singles €80-€100. | Rooms | 1 double: €73-€93. 1 suite for 4: €113. 2 family rooms for 3, 1 family room for 4-5: €73-€133. Singles €73. Extra bed/sofabed €20 per person per night. |
| Meals | Dinner with wine, €35. Child €17. Restaurants within walking distance. | Meals | Guest kitchen. Dinner with wine, €28. Restaurant 12km. |
| Closed | 1 October – 31 March. | Closed | Christmas/New Year. |

| | |
|---|---|
| | **Marylyn & Anthony Kusmirek** Le Logis de Bellevue, 55 route de Benet, 79510 Coulon Deux Sèvres |
| Tel | +33 (0)5 49 76 75 45 |
| Email | kusmirek@orange.fr |
| Web | www.lelogisdebellevue.com |

| | |
|---|---|
| | **Annie & Bruno Ragouilliaux-Di Battista** Le Logis d'Antan, 140 rue Saint-Louis, 79270 Vallans, Deux Sèvres |
| Tel | +33 (0)5 49 04 86 75 / +33 (0)5 49 32 85 05 |
| Email | info@logisdantan.com |
| Web | www.logisdantan.com |

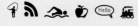

## Le Puits Sainte Claire

The family's house is the old post office on the edge of town, and the chambres d'hôtes are in the old stables. Fabienne, warm-hearted and softly spoken, loves to plan the best for guests and is an enthusiastic cook: breakfasts are delicious. Inside is so inviting: whitewashed beams, country antiques, books, games, brochures and magazines, an open fire and splashes of colour from paintings. Bedrooms face the courtyard and are upstairs – fresh, very French, very delightful. Restaurants are a walk away, but for summer there's a summer kitchen amongst the trees, all for you. Close by is a heated glass-covered pool. *Minimum stay: 2 nights.*

## Un Banc Au Soleil

Only birds and bells break the bubble around this handsome B&B, set in quiet gardens near Marsilly port. The old stables of Stephane's family home are transformed: soaring beams, elegant stone, huge terrace doors, a window to the cellar…You can slip into the pool after a day on the beach or brew a coffee and sit by the wood-burner flipping through magazines. At night, find snowy linen, original art, perhaps an antique desk or African carving. And in the morning, a homemade feast with traditional breads, tarts and more; nothing is any trouble for sweet Corinne. Hike or cycle coastal paths, golf, sail, visit historic Rochefort or La Rochelle… *Minimum stay: 2 nights in high season.*

| | |
|---|---|
| Rooms | 3 doubles: €85–€95. |
| | 1 suite for 4: €110–€150. |
| | Extra bed/sofabed €25 per person per night. |
| Meals | Summer kitchen. |
| | Restaurants within walking distance. |
| Closed | 30 October – 27 March. |

| | |
|---|---|
| Rooms | 5 doubles: €85–€118. |
| | Extra bed €28 per person per night. |
| Meals | Restaurants within walking distance. |
| Closed | Never. |

**Fabienne & David Drappeau**
Le Puits Sainte Claire,
17 Grande Rue,
17170 Courçon
Charente-Maritime
Mobile +33 (0)6 88 16 40 07
Email contact@puits-sainte-claire.com
Web www.puits-sainte-claire.com

**Stéphane & Corinne Lassegue**
Un Banc Au Soleil,
25 Quater Rue du Port,
17137 Marsilly
Charente-Maritime
Mobile +33 (0)6 24 96 82 70
Email contact@unbancausoleil.com
Web www.unbancausoleil.com

## Maison des Algues

In a residential area, behind private gates on the outskirts of Rivedoux Plage, is a single-storey hotel, whitewashed, shuttered and impeccably maintained. Nothing is too much trouble for Christian and Jocelyne, who will pick you up from the airport and insist on giving you the best: white towels for the bathroom, coloured towels for the pool, pâtisseries for tea. Bedrooms open to a wicker-chaired terrace and are roomy, restful and flooded with light. Spin off on a bike (there are ten, all free) and acquaint yourself with the island – the whitewashed houses of La Flotte, the fabulous white sands, the chic shops of St Martin. *Minimum stay: 2 nights in high season.*

## Eden Ouest

This fabulous building, built in 1745, stands in the old heart of La Rochelle. An immense amount of thought has gone into its renovation, and manager Véronique is brimming with ideas as to how they can go the extra mile. Sweep up grand stairs to a marble fireplace and muted grey walls, a long polished dining table and a rococo-esque chandelier. Bedrooms are colour coordinated right down to the paintings; most have sofabeds for children, all but one have bath tubs crafted from wood, and one bathroom's doors open to a patio and salty sea air. Tread the ancient cobbles, sample the local aperitifs, catch a boat to the marvellous Ile de Ré. *Cot & highchair available.*

| | | |
|---|---|---|
| Rooms | 3 doubles (2 rooms interconnect): €125–€215. 2 suites for 2: €125–€215. | |
| Meals | Guest kitchen. Restaurants within walking distance. | |
| Closed | Rarely. | |

| | |
|---|---|
| Rooms | 4 doubles: €125–€255. 1 suite for 2: €170–€255. Extra bed €25 per person per night. |
| Meals | Restaurants within walking distance. |
| Closed | Never. |

|  |  |
|---|---|
| | **Christian & Jocelyne Gatta–Boucard** Maison des Algues, 147 rue des Algues, 17940 Rivedoux (Île de Ré) Charente-Maritime |
| Tel | +33 (0)5 46 68 01 23 |
| Mobile | +33 (0)6 88 48 35 80 |
| Email | information@maison-des-algues.com |
| Web | www.maison-des-algues.com |

|  |  |
|---|---|
| | **Véronique Le Breton** Eden Ouest, 33 rue Thiers, 17000 La Rochelle Charente-Maritime |
| Mobile | +33 (0)6 82 62 68 97 |
| Email | contact@edenouest.com |
| Web | www.edenouest.com |

Entry 435   Map 8

Entry 436   Map 8

## A l'Ombre du Figuier

A rural idyll, wrapped in birdsong. The old farmhouse, lovingly restored and decorated, is simple and pristine; its carpeted rooms, under eaves that are polished to perfection, overlook a pretty garden where you may picnic. Your hosts are an interesting couple of anglophiles. Thoughtful, stylish Madame serves generous breakfasts of homemade jams, organic breads, cheeses and cereals under the fig tree in summer. Monsieur teaches engineering in beautiful La Rochelle; follow his suggestions and discover its lesser-known treasures. Luscious lawns are bordered by well-stocked beds. Great value.

## La Grande Barbotière

Between the fruit trees a hammock sways, breakfast is served next to a sparkling pool and sculpted chickens peck. Tucked behind gates (child-safe) in the heart of a busy village is a *maison de maître* of elegance and charm. Your hosts (she half Belgian, he from Yorkshire) have a wicked sense of humour and have created a luxurious and eclectic décor – gazelle antlers, pebbled showers, delicious French linen – for suites with private terraces. Table tennis, croquet, bicycles, toys, jasmine and, everywhere, that spirit-lifting light that you find on this cherished stretch of coastline. *Minimum stay: 2 nights. Children under 4 welcome.*

| Rooms | 1 family suite for 2-4, 1 family room for 4 (in annexe): €61-€137. |
|---|---|
| Meals | Guest kitchen. Restaurants within walking distance. Auberge 3km. |
| Closed | Rarely. |

| Rooms | 2 suites for 3: €95-€200. |
|---|---|
| Meals | Restaurants 4km. |
| Closed | Rarely. |

Marie-Christine & Jean-François Prou
A l'Ombre du Figuier,
43 rue du Marais, 17230 Longèves
Charente-Maritime
Tel        +33 (0)5 46 37 11 15
Mobile     +33 (0)6 79 35 55 12
Email      mcprou@wanadoo.fr
Web        www.alombredufiguier.com

Christopher & Jacqui McLean May
La Grande Barbotière,
10 rue du Marais Doux,
17220 St Vivien
Charente-Maritime
Tel        +33 (0)5 46 43 76 14
Mobile     +33 (0)6 43 12 11 04
Email      info@mcleanmay.com
Web        www.lagrandebarbotiere.com

## Le Clos de la Garenne

Charming owners and animals everywhere, from boxer dog to donkey to hens! Brigitte and Patrick gave up telecommunications for their dream of the country and the result is this heart-warming, small-village B&B. Avid collectors, they have decorated their roomy 16th-century house with eclectic flair, and old and new rub shoulders merrily; discover doll's house furniture and French cartoon characters, old armoires and antique treasures. Harmony breathes from walls and woodwork, your hosts are endlessly thoughtful, food is slow, exotic, organic (and delicious), and families are truly welcome.

*Minimum stay: 2 nights in high season.*

## La Villa Cécile

Stroll from the church and there is Cécile and Gérard's peaceful garden with odoriferous roses. The house's traditional Charantaise exterior belies a chic modern interior with sofas and windows opening to terraces from your own sitting and dining room: find leather, wood and glass. Big light-filled bedrooms are immaculate and luxurious, one with its own terrace and huge bath, another with a circular bed. Breakfast on the terrace is a treat – homemade everything from pancakes to yogurt, deliciously different each day. Sink into the outdoor spa pool or head off for La Rochelle.

*Minimum stay: 2 nights during summer holidays.*

| | |
|---|---|
| Rooms | 2 doubles: €75-€85. |
| | 1 suite for 6: €105-€175. |
| | 1 cottage for 5: €85-€135. |
| | Singles €65. |
| | Dinner, B&B €27 per person. |
| | Extra bed/sofabed €20 per person per night. |
| Meals | Dinner with wine, €27. |
| | Teenager €22. Child €12. |
| Closed | January/February. |

| | |
|---|---|
| Rooms | 2 doubles, 1 twin/double: €105-€145. |
| | Singles €105-€145. |
| | Sauna €20. Hot tub €10. |
| Meals | Restaurants within walking distance.. |
| Closed | Never. |

|  |  |
|---|---|
| | **Brigitte & Patrick François** |
| | Le Clos de la Garenne, |
| | 9 rue de la Garenne, |
| | 17700 Puyravault |
| | Charente-Maritime |
| Tel | +33 (0)5 46 35 47 71 |
| Email | info@closdelagarenne.com |
| Web | www.closdelagarenne.com |

|  |  |
|---|---|
| | **Cécile Thureau & Gérard Blumberg** |
| | La Villa Cécile, |
| | 1 rue de Puyravault, |
| | 17700 Vouhé |
| | Charente-Maritime |
| Tel | +33 (0)5 46 00 61 50 |
| Mobile | +33 (0)6 75 85 00 34 |
| Email | lavillacecile@orange.fr |
| Web | www.lavillacecile.fr |

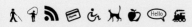

Entry 439  Map 8

Entry 440  Map 8

## Les Grands Vents

In a lovely village in the heart of cognac country, beside a sleepy road, the old farmhouse has simple limewashed walls and French country décor. New to B&B and very enthusiastic, Virginie, who has an interiors boutique in town, and Philippe, a cabinet-maker, will be changing things gradually. You have your own entrance and living room but your happy hosts want you to feel completely at home. Bedrooms, with views onto a big garden, are large, fresh and catch the morning or evening sun. There's a lush pool, turquoise water surrounded by velvet greenery – and a covered terrace for simple summer breakfasts. Good value.

| Rooms | 1 suite for 4, |
| | 1 family room for 3: €64. |
| | Extra bed €20 per person per night. |
| Meals | Restaurants in St Mard, 3km, & |
| | Surgères, 8km. |
| Closed | Rarely. |

**Virginie Truong Grandon**
Les Grands Vents,
17380 Chervettes
Charente-Maritime

| Tel | +33 (0)5 46 35 92 21 |
| Mobile | +33 (0)6 07 96 68 73 |
| Email | adaunis@orange.fr |
| Web | www.les-grands-vents.com |

Entry 441  Map 8

## Palmier Sur Cour

A handsome townhouse in the heart of the historic town with an understated, calm interior. Find period details, deep skirtings, fireplaces, cornices and a light-flooded stone staircase with iron balustrading. Three lovely lofty bedrooms are decorated in classic French style with a mix of antiques and prettily dressed beds. Catherine and Eric give you homemade breakfasts of fresh fruit salad, cakes, yogurts and jams at one big table; in summer you spill onto the terrace. Beaches and seafood beckon and the port of Rochefort (that lies within the charmed triangle of La Rochelle, Saintes and Royan) is fascinating. *Minimum stay: 2 nights.*

| Rooms | 1 double: €84–€102. |
| | 1 family room for 3, |
| | 1 family room for 4: €110–€135. |
| | Reduced rate for single occupancy. |
| Meals | Guest kitchenette. |
| | Restaurants within walking distance. |
| Closed | Rarely. |

**Catherine & Eric Malingrey**
Palmier Sur Cour,
55 rue de la République,
17300 Rochefort
Charente-Maritime

| Tel | +33 (0)5 46 89 72 55 |
| Mobile | +33 (0)6 70 76 41 91 |
| Email | contact@palmiersurcour.com |
| Web | www.palmiersurcour.com |

Entry 442  Map 8

### Chateau de Champdolent

On the edge of a village in a pastoral landscape is an 11th-century manor, an 18th-century farmhouse, and a keep, its outline majestic in the setting sun. You sleep under beams in rooms elegant and simple, the largest with its own kitchen and sitting room (designer chairs, huge sofas). Rifle through art books in the library, repair to the guard room with armchairs and immense chimney. Dinner? Enjoy Line's tarte tatin, bounty from the potager and the best foie gras in France. The place is amazing and the charming owners (he a sculptor and food producer, she a lover of philosophy) relate the history with relish. *Parking available.*

### Les Hortensias

Behind its modest, wisteria-covered mask, this 17th-century former wine-grower's house hides a charming interior – and a magnificent garden that flows through orchard to topiary, a delight in every season. Soft duck-egg colours and rich trimmings make this a warm and safe haven, light airy bedrooms are immaculate and unpretentious (one with its original stone sink, another with a pretty French pink décor), the bathrooms are luxurious, the walls burst with art and the welcome is gracious, warm and friendly. Superb value with a good restaurant a mile or so away. It's a treat to stay here.

| | |
|---|---|
| Rooms | 1 double: €80.<br>1 apartment for 2, with kitchen: €120. |
| Meals | Dinner with wine, €27.<br>Restaurants 15km. |
| Closed | Never. |

| | |
|---|---|
| Rooms | 2 doubles: €62.<br>1 triple: €69-€83.<br>Extra bed €17 per person per night. |
| Meals | Summer kitchen.<br>Restaurant in village, 1.5km. |
| Closed | Christmas/New Year. |

**Line & Dominique Cozic**
Chateau de Champdolent,
17430 Champdolent
Charente-Maritime
Tel   +33 (0)5 46 82 96 07
Email   d.cozic@gmail.com
Web   www.chateaudechampdolent.fr

**Marie-Thérèse Jacques**
Les Hortensias,
16 rue des Sablières,
17380 Archingeay
Charente-Maritime
Tel   +33 (0)5 46 97 85 70
Email   jpmt.jacques@wanadoo.fr
Web   www.chambres-hotes-hortensias.com

## Poitou – Charentes

### L'Etoile du Port

Built in 1633, this mellow-stone former cognac store is part of a terrace on the banks of the languid Butonne. Here lives Clare, full of life, with a love of people and an eye for detail: cotton buds in bathrooms, honey from the market, umbrellas by the door! All is tranquil and delightful inside, from the first-floor salon with its gorgeous grand fireplace and inviting cream sofas, to the bedrooms with their delicious pale-stone walls; there's also a tip-top guest kitchen. Atlantic beaches are a 40-minute drive, restaurants are a stroll, and a children's park and café lie on the other side of the river.

| Rooms | 3 doubles: €70-€75. |
| | 1 suite for 4: €80-€120. |
| | Singles €65-€75. Cot €10. |
| | Extra bed €20 per person per night. |
| Meals | Guest kitchen. |
| | Restaurant 10-minute walk. |
| Closed | Rarely. |

**Clare Pickering**
L'Etoile du Port,
14 quai de Bernouet,
17400 Saint Jean d'Angely
Charente-Maritime
Tel      +33 (0)5 46 32 08 93
Email   etoileduport@gmail.com
Web     www.letoileduport.com

## Poitou – Charentes

### N°1 Rue St Nicolas

In a working village where chickens peck by the road is a perfectly beautiful *maison de maître*, with a courtyard surrounded by cognac barns. Your young English hosts, relaxed and down-to-earth, give you two delicious bedrooms upstairs, and one down – a quick flit across the hall to the loo. Find big wide floorboards and fresh light colours, soft fluffy towels on vintage ladders and elegant antique finds. A chic chandelier hangs in the cosy living room, while breakfast (homemade jams on pretty white porcelain, artisan breads under a glass dome) is served by full length windows and a view to a mini-maze of immaculate topiary. *Children over 16 welcome.*

| Rooms | 2 doubles; 1 double with separate |
| | bathroom & wc: €80-€90. |
| Meals | Dinner, 4 courses with wine & |
| | coffee, €25. |
| | Supper platters available, €18. |
| | Restaurants 8km. |
| Closed | Rarely. |

**Sandra Doolan & Kevin Kelly**
N°1 Rue St Nicolas,
Rue St Nicolas,
17400 Varaize
Charente-Maritime
Tel      +33 (0)5 46 26 71 77
Email   contact@1ruestnicolas.com
Web     www.1ruestnicolas.com

## Logis de l'Astrée

Along the rustic track to a long, low nobleman's house walled behind vines, and sweet Sophie to welcome you with a glass of their wine. All is beautiful inside and flooded with light: lofty ceiling beams painted white, 17th-century terracotta looking like new. Elegant beds are topped with blankets and sheets; two rooms have kitchenettes, one opens to the garden. A stone fireplace stacked with logs dominates the irresistible salon, and home-grown grape juices join homemade jams at the table. Explore the pretty Coran valley and the river on foot or by bike, and visit historic Saintes with its amphitheatre and cathedrals. *Parking available.*

## La Rotonde

Stupendously confident, with priceless river views, this city mansion seems to ride the whole rich story of lovely old Saintes. Soft blue river light hovers into high bourgeois rooms to stroke the warm panelling, marble fireplaces, perfect parquet. Double glazing, yes, but ask for a room at the back, away from river and busy road. The Rougers love renovating and Marie-Laure, calm and talented, has her own sensitive way with classic French furnishings: feminine yet not frilly, rich yet gentle. Superb (antique) linen and bathrooms, too, breakfasts with views and always that elegance.

| | |
|---|---|
| Rooms | 2 doubles with separate wc: €110. 1 suite for 4 with separate wc: €125-€195. 1 studio for 2 with separate wc: €125. Extra bed €25 per person per night. |
| Meals | Dinner with wine, €25. Restaurants 5-minute walk. |
| Closed | November – February. |

| | |
|---|---|
| Rooms | 3 doubles, 1 twin with kitchenette, 1 family room for 4: €100. |
| Meals | Restaurants in town centre. |
| Closed | Rarely. |

| | |
|---|---|
| | **Sophie Boutinet Mangeart** Logis de l'Astrée, Le Logis, 17770 St Bris de Bois Charente-Maritime |
| Tel | +33 (0)5 46 93 44 07 |
| Email | smangeart@terre-net.fr |
| Web | www.logis-astree.fr |

| | |
|---|---|
| | **Marie-Laure Rouger** La Rotonde, 2 rue Monconseil, 17100 Saintes Charente-Maritime |
| Mobile | +33 (0)6 87 51 70 92 |
| Email | laure@laboutiquedelarotonde.com |
| Web | www.laboutiquedelarotonde.com |

## La Porte Rouge

Central, cobbled, car-free Saintes – perfect for Francophile lovers. Do arrange a meal here at one big table (herbs from the walled garden). Cooking comes high on well-travelled (American) Jim and Monique's list of passions; history and art too – their relaxed, typically French home (a hotel since the 16th-century) is full to bursting with beautiful antiques from different countries. Quiet, comfortable bedrooms on the second floor have linen from Italy, beams, white stone walls, original wood and parquet floors, and modern bathrooms with antique tubs. Take a trip on the Charente which runs through this fine town. *Cot available.*

## Le Logis du Port Paradis

Seafood is fresh from the Atlantic, the palm-ringed pool shimmers and five light-filled rooms exude your hosts' love of the sea. Clustered round a family home a short drive from Royan's sandy beaches, the nicely independent rooms and family suites have terraces, gleaming showers, ingenious headboards (sail canvas, slate, terracotta), a seaside feel. If you're lucky, Monsieur will cook – tuna carpaccio, fresh sole, gratin aux fraises – joining guests at one long table overlooking the pool; Madame may share stories of oyster farming. Plump down afterwards on cherry sofas or step out to the flower garden for fresh air and stars.

| | |
|---|---|
| Rooms | 2 doubles; 1 twin: €95–€105. 1 suite for 4: €145–€175. Singles €85–€95. Child bed €6 per night. |
| Meals | Dinner, 4 courses with aperitif, wine & coffee, €26. Child €12. Restaurant 2-minute walk. |
| Closed | Never. |

| | |
|---|---|
| Rooms | 3 doubles: €70–€75. 2 suites for 4: €92–€132. Singles €70. Extra bed/sofabed €20 per person per night. |
| Meals | Dinner with wine, €32. Restaurants 3km. |
| Closed | Rarely. |

Monique Potel
La Porte Rouge,
15 rue des Jacobins,
17100 Saintes
Charente-Maritime
Tel    +33 (0)5 46 90 46 71
Email    monique.potel@la-porte-rouge.com
Web    www.la-porte-rouge.com

Nadine Bauve
Le Logis du Port Paradis,
12 route du Port Paradis,
17600 Nieulle sur Seudre
Charente-Maritime
Tel    +33 (0)5 46 85 37 38
Mobile    +33 (0)6 09 71 64 84
Email    contact@portparadis.com
Web    www.portparadis.com

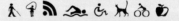

### Château de la Tillade

It's clear that Michel and Solange like people: they immediately put you at ease in their comfortable home. The château sits at the top of an avenue of lime trees; the vineyards have produced grapes for cognac and pineau for two centuries. Solange holds painting courses; her artistic flair is reflected in her love of fabrics, and the comfortable bedrooms are marvellously individual, each like a page out of Michel's memory book, steeped in family history. Meals around the family table are a delight with conversation in English or French; lavish, but without stuffiness. A rare opportunity to get to know a pair of charming French aristocrats.

### Domaine du Meunier

A lovely, friendly house built in 1893 and renovated perfectly. Find a living room with a library and a piano, a dining room and a games room. Bedrooms are calm and serene, breakfast is a feast with coddled eggs from the family's hens; dinner (twice a week in high season) is lively! The outbuildings have become gîtes, the 'Pinball Hall' hosts events, and the family live in the old mill. Stroll through the walled garden, let the children splash in the pool, doze in an antique deckchair; at high tide you can swim or sail. Views are gentle, while the nearby harbour, pretty with sailing boats, joins the port to the Gironde.

| | |
|---|---|
| Rooms | 1 twin, 3 family rooms for 3-4 (one with wc just outside room): €100-€130. Singles €100-€130. Extra bed/sofabed €25 per person per night. |
| Meals | Dinner €38. Restaurant 12km. |
| Closed | Rarely. |

| | |
|---|---|
| Rooms | 3 doubles, 2 twins: €70. |
| Meals | Dinner €25 (twice weekly in high season). Restaurants within walking distance. |
| Closed | Rarely. |

|  | |
|---|---|
| | **Vicomte & Vicomtesse Michel de Salvert** Château de la Tillade, Gémozac, 17260 Saint Simon de Pellouaille Charente-Maritime |
| Tel | +33 (0)5 46 90 00 20 |
| Email | contact@la-tillade.com |
| Web | www.la-tillade.com |

| | |
|---|---|
| | **Ariane & Coen Ter Kuile** Domaine du Meunier, 36, quai de L'Estuaire, 17120 Mortagne sur Gironde Charente-Maritime |
| Tel | +33 (0)5 46 97 75 10 |
| Email | info@domainedumeunier.com |
| Web | www.domainedumeunier.com |

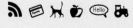

Entry 451   Map 8

Entry 452   Map 8

## Château des Salles

Behind a fine old exterior, this small château exudes light, harmony, colour and elegant informality. Sylvie runs all with passion and effortless taste, her mother's watercolours hang in the public rooms and decorate bedroom doors. At dinner, local and home-grown produce is served with class and estate wines. The well-furnished bedrooms have gentle colours and wallpapers; deliciously airy and warm. You can have breakfast in your room and Sylvie will help you plan your stay – people return again and again to this congenial, welcoming house. One guest said: "She welcomed us like family and sent us home with goodies from her vineyard".

## Le Chatelard

This is a gem of a place to stay, both grand and intimate. Béatrice inherited the exquisitely French neo-gothic château and she lovingly protects it from the worst of modernisation (though the hurricane took its toll and trees have had to be replanted). Sleep between antique linen sheets, sit in handsome old chairs and be charmed by a bedroom in a tower. The sitting room has that unusual quirk, a window over the fireplace, the dining room a panelled ceiling studded with plates. Béatrice, a teacher, and Christopher, a lecturer in philosophy, are interesting, cultured hosts who enjoy eating with their guests.

| Rooms | 1 double, 4 twin/doubles: €88–€160. |
|---|---|
| Meals | Dinner €29–€38. Wine from €15. |
| Closed | November – March. |

FIRST
EDITION
VETERAN

Sylvie Couillaud
Château des Salles,
17240 Saint Fort sur Gironde
Charente-Maritime
Tel      +33 (0)5 46 49 95 10
Email   chateaudessalles@wanadoo.fr
Web     www.chateaudessalles.com

| Rooms | 1 double; 1 double, 1 twin with separate wc: €60–€70. 1 family room for 6 with separate wc: €80–€120. Extra bed €10 per person per night. Singles €50. |
|---|---|
| Meals | Dinner with wine, €25. Restaurant 1km. |
| Closed | Rarely. |

Béatrice de Castelbajac &
Christopher Macann
Le Chatelard,
16480 Passirac
Charente
Tel      +33 (0)5 45 98 71 03
Email   c.macann@wanadoo.fr
Web     www.chateaudepassirac.jimdo.com

Entry 453    Map 8

Entry 454    Map 9

## Poitou – Charentes

### Logis des Jardins du Chaigne

Lush gardens cascade into Cognac vineyards (giant lilies, snowy roses, topiary, a lavender-lined stream, lake, tennis, a pool with bar)… a superb setting for summer concerts, a garden-loving public and this handsome brandy château. As gracious as their historic home, Béatrice and Philippe welcome you with exquisite *objets*, a gardening library, and convivial table d'hôtes with fresh herbs. Sweep upstairs to a galleried landing and luxurious bedrooms with soft linen and monogrammed towels. Wake to sunrise over vineyards and myriad pleasures: fêtes, markets, beaches, cognac and peace. *Children over 12 welcome.*

| Rooms | 2 doubles: €130–€150. |
| --- | --- |
| | 2 suites for 2: €120–€150. |
| | 1 apartment for 2: €100–€120. |
| Meals | Dinner €35. |
| | Restaurant 2km. |
| Closed | Rarely. |

**Philippe & Béatrice Marzano**
Logis des Jardins du Chaigne,
Le Chaigne,
16120 Touzac
Charente
Tel       +33 (0)5 45 62 33 92
Email   philippe.marzano@wanadoo.fr
Web     www.logisdesjardinsduchaigne.com

Entry 455   Map 9

## Poitou – Charentes

### Le Logis du Paradis

Mellow stones, chunky beams, sensuous fabrics… there's a timeless feel to the Logis, with 18th-century buildings embracing a magnificent oval courtyard. In big luxurious bedrooms you snuggle down in superbly comfortable king-size beds under white linen… and wake in anticipation of a delicious breakfast. There's a pool in the aromatic garden, books on the landings, a tea and coffee kitchen, a bar in the former distillery shared with the other guests. Sally's generous table features market-fresh local produce, fine wines, and a glass of the neighbour's superb XO Cognac to finish with. Highly professional. *Short breaks available in low season.*

| Rooms | 5 doubles sharing 2 bathrooms: |
| --- | --- |
| | €95–€125. |
| Meals | Lunch €19. |
| | Dinner €39. |
| | Wine from €12.50. |
| | Restaurant 4km. |
| Closed | Mid-January to end February. |

**Sally Brimblecombe**
Le Logis du Paradis,
La Magdeleine,
16300 Criteuil la Magdeleine
Charente
Tel       +33 (0)5 45 35 39 43
Email   sally@logisduparadis.com
Web     www.logisduparadis.com

Entry 456   Map 9

## Poitou – Charentes

### Le Chiron

The big old well-lived-in house is all chandeliers, ceiling roses and heavy dark furniture. The toile de Jouy triple has a rustic elegance, La Rose is... pink. Bathrooms are more functional than luxurious but with so much natural beauty to hand who wants to stay in anyway? Madame's regional cooking is a treat, served in a conservatory big enough for many. Genuinely welcoming, your farmer hosts stay and chat (in French, mostly!) when they can. They'll also show you the fascinating old cognac still. Big, off the beaten track and great for families (they run a campsite next door).

| Rooms | 2 doubles, 1 twin: €50. |
| | 1 family room for 4: €80. |
| | 2 triples: €50. |
| Meals | Dinner with aperitif & wine, €20. |
| Closed | Rarely. |

FIRST
EDITION
VETERAN

Micheline & Jacky Chainier
Le Chiron,
16130 Salles d'Angles
Charente
Tel       +33 (0)5 45 83 72 79
Email    mchainier@voila.fr

## Poitou – Charentes

### Le Bourg

Stone cottages, nodding hollyhocks, ducks in the lane: Mareuil epitomises rural France, and the house sits in its heart. Arrive to a sweeping drive, an immaculate pool, a grand façade and Ron and Vanessa, who have travelled the world. After a final posting in Paris they have landed in sunny Charente, and are happy. Bedrooms are bright, airy and comfortable, with cosy bathrooms; dinners, in the ample dining room, are gastronomic, cosmopolitan, entertaining and preceded by pineau de Charente. You are surrounded by sunflowers and vines and Cognac is close. Friendly, interesting, great fun.

| Rooms | 3 twin/doubles: €95. |
| Meals | Dinner with wine, from €32. |
| Closed | Rarely. |

Vanessa Bennett-Dixon
Le Bourg,
16170 Mareuil
Charente
Tel       +33 (0)5 45 66 29 75
Email    lebourg-charente@wanadoo.fr
Web      www.lebourg-charente.com

## Poitou – Charentes

## Poitou – Charentes

### La Fontaine des Arts

Along the narrow street in the charming, bustling town, through the heavy oak gates, under the ancient arch, is a cottage by the Charente with a little boat for trips up the river. Beautifully coiffed Marie-France combines the glamour of the city with the warmth of a country hostess: guests love her. Breakfast in the conservatory alongside Gérard's easel and piano, or in the courtyard by the pretty fountain pool. Décor is quintessential French: shiny gold taps, striped and flowered walls, a white dressing table. There's a shared guest kitchenette – and a surprising open-gallery bathroom in the double. One night just isn't enough.

### La Cochère

Cool off by the lush pool, listen to the clacking and cheering of summer Sundays' boules. Rebecca and David are delighted to start their new life in France as the proud protectors of this dreamlike old coach house where the long breakfast table groans with fresh compotes and croissants and the tranquil garden sparkles with lanterns at dusk. Antique iron beds wear floral quilts and pretty stone peeps through timeworn render; independent souls choose the garden room. Who wouldn't fall for this heart-warming rustic/chic blend in a sleepy farming village, once a horse-trading centre? Don't miss the fascinating Jardins Européens project.

| Rooms | 1 double, 1 twin: €69–€79. |
| --- | --- |
| | 1 triple: €75–€98. |
| | Singles €63–€73. |
| | Extra bed €24 per person per night. |
| Meals | Guest kitchenette. |
| | Restaurant within walking distance. |
| Closed | Rarely. |

| Rooms | 3 doubles, 1 twin: €65. |
| --- | --- |
| | 1 family room for 3 |
| | (May-Sept only): €65–€75. |
| | Singles €55. |
| Meals | Dinner with aperitif & wine, €25. |
| Closed | Christmas. |

**Marie-France Pagano**
La Fontaine des Arts,
13 rue du Temple,
16230 Mansle
Charente

Tel     +33 (0)5 45 69 13 56
Mobile  +33 (0)6 12 52 39 86
Email   mfpagano@wanadoo.fr
Web    www.la-fontaine-des-arts.com

**David & Rebecca Ball**
La Cochère,
4 rue des Hôtes,
16700 Salles de Villefagnan
Charente

Tel     +33 (0)5 45 30 34 60
Email   rball@fastmail.fm
Web    www.lacochere.iowners.net

## Wisteria House

A bright white table greets you, topped with books and info, and teas and coffees to the side — and Judy and Peter, full of generosity and good humour, proud of their finely restored barn. Grazing cows, farmland, more barns: the setting is green and deliciously peaceful. Tucked under the eaves, the en suite shower rooms are as fresh and charming as the bedrooms themselves, and the treats continue at table… what could be nicer than to be served a beautiful dinner under a wisteria-strewn pergola on a warm southern night? Ancient Angoulême is an easy drive, bustling market town Chasseneuil is even closer.

| Rooms | 2 doubles, 1 twin: €50. |
| --- | --- |
| | Singles €35. |
| Meals | Dinner, 4 courses with aperitif & |
| | wine, €25. |
| Closed | Rarely. |

Judy Hemsworth
Wisteria House,
La Chaume,
16450 St Laurent de Céris
Charente
Tel        +33 (0)5 45 84 07 61
Mobile   +33 (0)6 04 47 81 24
Email     pj@thewisterias.com
Web      www.thewisterias.com

---

## Le Pit

What a remote, interesting and gentle place – heaven for walkers, and for children. Pets doze by the fire, llamas munch on the hillside. Simple, floral bedrooms are in a converted outbuilding (with parking right by), the larger one overlooking the lake. Dinner is unusual (venison pâté perhaps), delicious (produce from the precious vegetable garden) and preceded by a glass of local pineau. Alex left London for French farming with a difference, capable Hélène looks after you, and there are many little corners of rustic charm and colour from which to enjoy the fascinating surroundings. Fun and hugely welcoming.

| Rooms | 1 double: €55. |
| --- | --- |
| | 1 quadruple: €55–€100. |
| Meals | Dinner with wine, €27. |
| Closed | Rarely. |

Alex & Hélène Everitt
Le Pit,
Lessac,
16500 Confolens
Charente
Tel        +33 (0)5 45 84 27 65
Mobile   +33 (0)6 30 34 14 11
Email     everitt16@aol.com
Web      www.lepit.fr

Photo: ©iStock.com/elkor

# Aquitaine

www.sawdays.co.uk/aquitaine

# Aquitaine

## Château Bavolier

The classic pale-stone building lies low among unfussy lawns and trees. Inside, the space, light and simplicity of décor are striking. Your charming talented hostess uses a restrained palette to give a floaty, dreamy quality: beige and white paint, pale-straw sisal, impressive decorations (she has finely restored some hand-painted panelling). The first bedroom is beautiful in white, gilt and black Louis XVI. The second is enormous, breathtaking, with myriad windows, play of dark and light across the huge brass bed and monochrome oils of Paris. And in each a magnificent chandelier. Amazing.

| Rooms | 2 doubles: €110-€160. |
|---|---|
| Meals | Restaurant nearby. |
| Closed | October – March. |

**Ann Roberts**
Château Bavolier,
33920 St Christoly de Blaye
Gironde

| Tel | +33 (0)5 57 42 59 74 |
|---|---|
| Email | info@chateau-bavolier.com |
| Web | www.chateau-bavolier.com |

Entry 463   Map 8

# Aquitaine

## Château de la Grave

Come for three sweeping bedrooms, two balconies with vineyard views, a stone entrance hall – and a wrought-iron terrace for a glass of the Bassereaus' own dry white semillon (their red is superb, too). They are a hard-working, caring and confident couple in an 18th-century château with too much good taste to make it sumptuous, thank heavens. It is relaxed and easy with six friendly cats, and horses in the fields. Breakfast is on the terrace, wine-tasting courses in the magnificent *salle de dégustation*. The small pool is for evening dippers rather than sun-worshippers. Good value.

| Rooms | 1 double: €85-€120. |
|---|---|
| | 1 family room for 4: €160. |
| | 1 triple: €105-€140. |
| Meals | Restaurants 2km. |
| Closed | December – March; 2 weeks in August. |

**Philippe & Valérie Bassereau**
Château de la Grave,
33710 Bourg sur Gironde
Gironde

| Tel | +33 (0)5 57 68 41 49 |
|---|---|
| Email | reservation@chateaudelagrave.com |
| Web | www.chateaudelagrave.com |

Entry 464   Map 8

## Aquitaine

### Le Castel de Camillac

Perched above vineyards and the lazy Dordogne, a perfect mini-château. Madame has restored its 18th-century spirit with passion, giving rooms delicious drama: panelled walls, vast tapestries, Turkish rugs, elegant antiques. Bedrooms, gleaming with polished wood and lush fabrics, feel like intimate family rooms while head-ducking beams and odd-shaped but sparkling bathrooms add to the charm. Breakfast in the voluptuous dining room or on the terrace, swim in the discreet circular pool, play tennis on the floodlit court, enjoy a round of billiards by the wood-burner. A rich experience, 30 minutes from Bordeaux.

| Rooms | 3 doubles: €75-€105. Extra bed €15-€20 per person per night. |
|---|---|
| Meals | Guest kitchenette. Restaurant 2km. |
| Closed | Rarely. |

Élisabeth Frape
Le Castel de Camillac,
1 Camillac,
33710 Bourg sur Gironde
Gironde
Mobile   +33 (0)6 74 31 15 85
Email    elisabeth.frape@lecasteldecamillac.com
Web     www.lecasteldecamillac.com

Entry 465   Map 8

## Aquitaine

### Clos Marcamps

A super-stylish makeover by a couple who moved here from Paris with young children. All is pale and lovely, clear and uncluttered – designed to enhance the elegant proportions of this handsome Chartreuse house. You eat, superbly and seasonally, in the main house. You sleep in beautifully compact rooms in the converted barns. All have their own entrances and are on two levels with beds upstairs. Bathrooms are sleek, with walk-in showers; one has a spa bath. Roam the grounds; there's a wow of a pool, swings and table tennis; stroll through the vines; book beauty treatments or baby-sitting, and head for Bordeaux. Smart.

| Rooms | 2 doubles: €110. 1 suite for 2-4, 1 suite for 2-5: €125-€170. |
|---|---|
| Meals | Dinner €35. Restaurant 7km. |
| Closed | Never. |

Alexandre da Gama
Clos Marcamps,
2 chemin des Carièrres,
33710 Prignac et Marcamps
Gironde
Tel     +33 (0)5 57 58 57 09
Email    contact@closmarcamps.fr
Web     www.closmarcamps.fr

Entry 466   Map 8

## Manoir d'Astrée

In the gentle folds of Bordeaux sits this 1766 house half way up a hill, with views across vineyards – swoop through electronic gates to find owner Béatrice who gives you a comfortable shared sitting room and four private-feeling bedrooms. There are three on the ground floor and one upstairs, all with a Gustavian flavour and extremely plush. Sleep peacefully in beautifully dressed beds, pad around serious bathrooms with soft robes and pebble flooring and breakfast (outside on balmy days) on local jams, honey and fresh pastries from the village baker. Splash in the pool, wander the grounds, visit vineyards, discover Perigueux. Restful. *Minimum stay: 2 nights in high season.*

| Rooms | 3 twin/doubles: €115-€140. |
|---|---|
| | 1 suite for 2-4: €140-€160. |
| | Extra bed/sofabed €30 per person |
| | per night. |
| Meals | Restaurant 2km. |
| Closed | 18 December – 28 February. |

Béatrice Rengner
Manoir d'Astrée,
Lieu-dit Pelet,
33240 Lugon et l'Île du Carnay
Gironde
Tel      +33 (0)5 57 25 24 25
Mobile   +33 (0)6 73 33 90 56
Email    contact@manoirdastree-bordeaux.com
Web      www.manoirdastree-bordeaux.com

Entry 467   Map 9

## Domaine du Freyche

From the domaine on the serene Île du Carnay, views stretch for miles across vast flood plains where deer forage silhouetted against the setting sun. Bedrooms are quirky, minimalist, zen (two baths sit side by side in one), the gardens are serene, and the Airstream caravan, decorated in sugar pink and bubblegum green (with its own bathroom) makes a stunning third billet. Makers of organic bed linen and fans of classic cars – you can hire theirs out – the warm, approachable Riperts have many strings to their bow. Take your own horse (it's been an equestrian centre for years) or sample wines in St Émilion. Superb.

| Rooms | 1 double, 1 twin/double: €100. |
|---|---|
| | 1 Airstream for 2: €100. |
| Meals | Restaurants nearby. |
| Closed | Rarely. |

Carole Ripert
Domaine du Freyche,
Lieu-dit Le Freyche,
33240 Lugon & l'Île du Carnay
Gironde
Mobile   +33 (0)6 18 03 80 37 /
         +33 (0)6 15 22 52 25
Email    contact@domainedufreyche.com
Web      www.domainedufreyche.com

Entry 468   Map 9

# Aquitaine

## Château de la Vieille Chapelle

A long, leafy lane brings you to a secluded and sumptuous estate, its backdrop sweeping vineyards and raw 12th-century stone. It's an idyllic retreat, a perfect balance of shabby and chic. Each river-view bedroom is smartly decorated with state-of-the-art wet rooms, and beds you can simply sink into. In the château's galleried dining room, the discreet Madame Mallier serves light meals or full dinners, and suggests an exclusive tour of the renowned cellars. Explore the vineyards, fish, recline, and let yourself be hypnotised by the fast-running (but unfenced) river and the beauty of glorious Bordeaux.

| | |
|---|---|
| Rooms | 3 doubles (2 in outbuildings): €85. Singles €80. Extra bed/sofabed €20 per person per night. |
| Meals | Dinner €16–€25. Wine €6.40–€35. |
| Closed | Rarely. |

**Fabienne & Frédéric Mallier**
Château de la Vieille Chapelle,
4 Chapelle, 33240 Lugon & l'Île du
Carnay, Gironde

| | |
|---|---|
| Tel | +33 (0)5 57 84 48 65 |
| Mobile | +33 (0)6 17 98 19 56 |
| Email | best-of-bordeaux-wine@ chateau-de-la-vieille-chapelle.com |
| Web | www.chateau-de-la-vieille-chapelle.com |

Entry 469   Map 9

# Aquitaine

## L'Esprit des Chartrons

A delicious vintage townhouse in chic Chartrons, metres from the Garonne quays where Bordeaux's bourgeoisie once traded: 21st-century design blends with wine-soaked history. Playful bedrooms are named after famous local writers: glamorous 'Montaigne' with bubble tub; red-brick, industrial-style 'Montesquieu'; light-filled 'Mauriac'. There are private terraces for tête-à-têtes, swish Italian bathrooms for pampering, a leafy sun terrace and a stylish stove-warmed salon for breakfast (crisp pastries, real hot chocolate). On a quiet lane, with covered parking, yet a stroll from restaurant-lined streets and World Heritage sites.

| | |
|---|---|
| Rooms | 2 doubles, 1 twin/double: €115–€155. Singles €105–€135. |
| Meals | Restaurants nearby. |
| Closed | Never. |

**Brigitte Gourlat**
L'Esprit des Chartrons,
17 bis rue Borie,
33300 Bordeaux
Gironde

| | |
|---|---|
| Tel | +33 (0)5 56 51 65 87 |
| Mobile | +33 (0)6 82 20 20 67 |
| Email | brigitte.gourlat@gmail.com |
| Web | www.lespritdeschartrons.fr |

Entry 470   Map 8

## Aquitaine

### La Villa Chaleemar

In an up-and-coming neighbourhood of the wine capital of France, near the renowned Jardin Public and the revived dockside, is a super-contemporary B&B. Impeccable Leena lives on one side of the courtyard – glass glides open to loungers and bamboo – while guests' quarters are on the other, reached via a sweeping stair. Find a limewashed dining table for organic breakfasts, leather seating before the fire and bleached bedrooms flooded with light, two with space for a slatted table and chairs. There's an entry code so your independence is guaranteed – and grand old Bordeaux lies at your feet.

| | |
|---|---|
| Rooms | 4 doubles: €90–€110. |
| Meals | Restaurant within walking distance. |
| Closed | Rarely. |

| | |
|---|---|
| | Leena Negre |
| | La Villa Chaleemar, |
| | 67 rue Mandron, |
| | 33000 Bordeaux |
| | Gironde |
| Tel | +33 (0)5 57 87 33 07 |
| Mobile | +33 (0)6 87 67 23 57 |
| Email | contact@villa-chaleemar.com |
| Web | www.villa-chaleemar.com |

Entry 471   Map 8

## Aquitaine

### L'Arène Bordeaux

Within strolling distance of the most beautiful spots in Bordeaux is this elegant townhouse in a residential street. Handsome colours and discreet décor blend with herringbone parquet, cosy shared spaces are classically furnished, and the Roman arena views are stunning. Lofty and evocatively named bedrooms ('Margaux', 'St Émilion') have sumptuous beds, accent chairs or three-piece suites, espresso machines, iPod docks and chic bathrooms in grey slate. Your friendly hosts offer wine in the garden on arrival, homemade jams at breakfast and all their best tips. Markets, antiques, boutiques, bistros and bars lie at your feet. *Minimum stay: 2 nights at weekends.*

| | |
|---|---|
| Rooms | 5 twin/doubles (2 rooms interconnect): €95–€200. |
| Meals | Restaurants within walking distance. |
| Closed | Rarely. |

| | |
|---|---|
| | Jean Marie Terroine |
| | L'Arène Bordeaux, |
| | 29 rue Émile Fourcand, |
| | 33000 Bordeaux |
| | Gironde |
| Tel | +33 (0)5 56 52 05 89 |
| Mobile | +33 (0)6 16 06 48 31 |
| Email | larenebordeaux@gmail.com |
| Web | www.larenebordeaux.com |

Entry 472   Map 8

# Aquitaine

### Ecolodge des Chartrons

A many-splendoured delight: city-centre and eco-friendly, with lovely materials and the warmth of simplicity. Your relaxed and friendly hosts have put their earth-saving principles to work, stripping the wonderful wide floorboards, insulating with cork and wool, fitting solar water heating and sun pipes to hyper-modern shower rooms, dressing beds in organic linen and blankets and providing all-organic breakfasts. At the bottom of this quiet road flows the Garonne where cafés, shops and galleries teem in converted warehouses (English wine merchants traded here 300 years ago) and a mirror fountain baffles the mind.

# Aquitaine

### 83 rue de Patay

Martine may have just one room but she's used to making guests feel welcome: she owns a restaurant in the middle of the old town. Le Loup has been serving local specialities since 1932: you will probably want to pay a visit. This old stone townhouse is a welcome retreat after days visiting the city (ten minutes by tram) or those renowned vineyards. Martine has given it a light modern touch which works well. Your cosy little bedroom is approached up a curved stone staircase and you have the floor to yourselves. It overlooks a small courtyard garden and has a desk and other pieces stencilled by a friend.

| | |
|---|---|
| Rooms | 2 doubles, 2 twin/doubles: €101–€138. 1 triple: €159–€175. |
| Meals | Restaurants within walking distance. |
| Closed | Rarely. |

| | |
|---|---|
| Rooms | 1 twin/double: €70. |
| Meals | Owner's restaurant 'Le Loup' near Cathedral. |
| Closed | Rarely. |

**Véronique Daudin**
Ecolodge des Chartrons,
23 rue Raze,
33000 Bordeaux
Gironde
Tel     +33 (0)5 56 81 49 13
Mobile  +33 (0)6 99 29 33 00
Email   veronique@ecolodgedeschartrons.com
Web     www.ecolodgedeschartrons.com

**Martine Peiffer**
83 rue de Patay,
33000 Bordeaux
Gironde
Tel     +33 (0)5 56 99 41 74
Mobile  +33 (0)6 19 81 22 81
Email   mpeifferma95@numericable.fr

Entry 473   Map 8

Entry 474   Map 8

# Aquitaine

## Château Lestange

We are full of admiration for Eric and Anne-Marie, who keep this proud old place and its vineyards afloat. The château, built in 1645 and 'modernised' after the Revolution, is full of charm, with polished wooden floors and pale panelled walls, crystal chandeliers and family furniture. The family suites are both private and capacious, one facing a sweet, formal French garden. Wake to a bountiful breakfast in a vast room before a gilded mirror, then head for Arcachon for boat trips and oysters. Or splendid old Bordeaux, a 15-minute drive – you can see the city skyline from the tranquillity of the château grounds.

| Rooms | 2 family rooms for 3: €100–€180. |
|---|---|
| Meals | Tapas with wine, €30. |
| | Restaurant in village. |
| Closed | Rarely. |

**Anne-Marie Charmet**
Château Lestange,
33360 Quinsac
Gironde
Mobile   +33 (0)6 73 00 86 19
Email    charmet@chateau-lestange.com
Web      www.chateau-lestange.com

# Aquitaine

## Domaine de l'Espelette

Take a picnic to the stream, stroll down the avenue into the village, let the children frolic, swim in the shaded pool. This long house, tucked into the hillside and overlooking the Romanesque church, dates from the 15th century. Unearth a treasure or two in the sitting room and library shared with the owners: books, magazines, paintings. Bedrooms are reassuringly chintzy, bathrooms generously marble. Madame is happy to serve breakfast until two o'clock; in such a haven she's used to guests oversleeping and the thick walls will ensure you won't hear a murmur from the grandchildren playing upstairs. *Minimum stay: 2 nights. Children over 12 welcome.*

| Rooms | 3 twin/doubles: €100–€150. |
|---|---|
| Meals | Restaurant 1.5km. |
| Closed | 15 August, December/January. |

**Silvia Prevost**
Domaine de l'Espelette,
Route de Chaumont,
33550 Haux
Gironde
Tel      +33 (0)5 56 23 37 36
Mobile   +33 (0)6 63 82 01 78
Email    contact@domainedelespelette.com
Web      www.domainedelespelette.com

# Aquitaine

## Château de Castelneau

A heavenly 14th-century château with Provençal towers. Behind: a shuttered 17th-century façade, a courtyard with outbuildings and an avenue lined with young trees. All around: hectares of vines. The de Roquefeuils are a warm, intelligent, enthusiastic couple, working their socks off to make the estate pay (and oh! the claret is delicious). Guests stay on the upper floor of one of the outbuildings, in bedrooms simple, comfortable, traditional – and there's a landing with videos for early risers. Downstairs: stone flags, rugs, books, paintings, eclectic aristocratic furnishings, and breakfasts generous and delicious. Outstanding.

| Rooms | 1 twin/double: €95. |
| --- | --- |
| | 1 suite for 3: €95–€140. |
| Meals | Kitchen & barbecue available. |
| | Restaurants 2km. |
| Closed | Rarely. |

**Loïc & Diane de Roquefeuil**
Château de Castelneau,
8 route de Breuil,
Lieu-dit Châteauneuf,
33670 Saint Léon
Gironde

| Tel | +33 (0)5 56 23 47 01 |
| --- | --- |
| Email | dianederoquefeuil@gmail.com |
| Web | www.chateaudecastelneau.com |

Entry 477   Map 9

# Aquitaine

## La Forge

Overlooking vines once worked by the blacksmith's horse is an unforgettable house. Carol fell in love with France many years ago, then married a French man, Bruno. Since when they have been opening their hearts to family and guests, serving breakfasts under the cherry trees (home honey, eggs, bread, fruits, jams), and organising cookery classes and brocante tours. The place is resplendent with modern art, family antiques, fresh flowers. Tables are laden with books, sofas demand you unwind, beds have vintage linen and the bunk bedroom is a child's dream. Down the road at the farm: hens, pool, and a wildflower meadow to roam.

| Rooms | 1 double; 1 twin/double sharing bath: €75–€85. |
| --- | --- |
| | 1 suite for 3: €95. |
| | 1 single sharing shower/bath room: €65. |
| | 1 bunk room for 4 sharing bath: €60–€120. Child's bed €30. |
| Meals | Restaurants 8km. |
| Closed | Never. |

**Carol de Montrichard Dalléas**
La Forge,
26 route du Moulin Neuf,
33750 St Quentin de Baron
Gironde

| Tel | +33 (0)5 57 24 18 54 |
| --- | --- |
| Mobile | +33 (0)6 31 85 65 20 |
| Email | whatscookinginfrance@gmail.com |
| Web | www.whatscookinginfrance.wordpress.com |

Entry 478   Map 9

## Château Claud-Bellevue

On the edge of a sleepy village, a 17th-century priory with a lych gate to the church. Mellow stone walls are lapped by groomed lawns and gravel paths; a central fountain plays; beyond are ten hectares of vines. Your hosts, new to chambres d'hôtes and full of plans, give you an effusive welcome and delicious air-conditioned rooms: gilt-edged prints on rustic walls and goosedown as soft as a cloud. The treats continue at table for Madame is cordon-bleu trained; expect cheeses, fruits, charcuterie, homemade breads, granola and conserves. Take a private tour of their own château, discover the wines of St Émilion. *Minimum stay: 2 nights.*

## Château de Courtebotte

Off a country lane a romantic 17th-century château stands in wooded grounds with glorious views to the glassy waters of the river Dordogne. Myriad charming features include open hearths and high ceilings, spotless bathrooms and lavish bedrooms; one room comes with a covered balcony, another has a four-poster and an antique commode… Breakfast on the terrace in fine weather; delicious dinners can be booked ahead. The inviting pool (unfenced) is shared with guests from the neighbouring gîte. Your hosts, friendly and delightful, know the best producers for vineyard tours – don't miss them. Stroll to shops and restaurants. *Extra bed available.*

| | |
|---|---|
| Rooms | 2 doubles, 1 twin/double: €100–€130. |
| Meals | Light dinner with wine, €22. Afternoon tea included. Restaurants 3km. |
| Closed | Rarely. |

| | |
|---|---|
| Rooms | 3 doubles, 1 twin/double: €115–€210. 1 suite for 4: €200–€290. |
| Meals | Breakfast €12. Dinner with wine €35. Restaurant 1km. |
| Closed | Mid-December to mid-January. |

| | |
|---|---|
| | Ana Bockmeulen |
| | Château Claud-Bellevue, |
| | 31 le Bourg, |
| | 33350 Belves de Castillon – |
| | St Emilion |
| | Gironde |
| Tel | +33 (0)5 57 49 48 23 |
| Email | ana@chateauclaudbellevue.com |
| Web | www.chateauclaudbellevue.com |

| | |
|---|---|
| | Isabelle Jehanno |
| | Château de Courtebotte, |
| | 1 Courtebotte, |
| | 33420 St Jean de Blaignac |
| | Gironde |
| Tel | +33 (0)5 57 84 61 61 |
| Email | contact@chateaudecourtebotte.com |
| Web | www.chateaudecourtebotte.com |

Entry 479   Map 9

Entry 480   Map 9

## Aquitaine

## Aquitaine

### Domaine de Polus

Waves of vines surround St Emilion, horses graze the field, a shaded terrace overlooks the large heated saltwater pool. The Fergusons have lovingly renovated the former chai for the sole use of guests, Alex's interior design experience producing a gorgeously stylish retreat with its own sitting room, English furniture, French fabrics and subtle paints. There's homemade cake for tea and a choice of local wines as aperitifs. The dawn-facing double has a balcony with steps to the pool, showers are luxuriously new. After self-service breakfast, you can cycle all the way to magnificent Bordeaux, or hire a canoe and explore the Dordogne River.

### La Girarde

In gentle countryside of wooded valleys near pretty Ste Foy la Grande, this smartly renovated farmhouse has its origins in the wine industry; St Émilion lives and breathes wine. You will be impeccably looked after by lovely, relaxed, fuss-free owners Trish and Mark, who give you serene rooms in classical-chic style – heated stone floors, designer fabrics, African art, touches of tartan from home. All the bedrooms, upstairs and down, have big beds and super bathrooms, and dinners are delicious. Outside: a lovely terrace, a park-like garden edged with cedars and weeping willows, a heated saltwater pool. Gorgeous!

| | |
|---|---|
| Rooms | 1 double, 1 twin: £120–£130. |
| Meals | Dinner €30. Wine from €15. Restaurants 1km. |
| Closed | Rarely. |

| | |
|---|---|
| Rooms | 2 doubles, 2 twin/doubles: €105–€120. Extra bed/sofabed €30 per person per night. |
| Meals | Dinner €27. Wine €15–€45. Child €7. |
| Closed | Rarely. |

**Alexandra & Dominic Ferguson**
Domaine de Polus,
33420 St Vincent de Pertignas,
St Émilion
Gironde

| | |
|---|---|
| Tel | +33 (0)5 57 50 22 03 |
| Mobile | +44 (0)7803 434619 |
| Email | mrsaferguson@btinternet.com |
| Web | www.depolus.blogspot.com |

**Trish Tyler**
La Girarde,
33220 St Quentin de Caplong
Gironde

| | |
|---|---|
| Tel | +33 (0)5 57 41 02 68 |
| Mobile | +33 (0)6 76 07 97 43 |
| Email | bienvenue@lagirarde.com |
| Web | www.lagirarde.com |

Entry 481   Map 9

Entry 482   Map 9

# Aquitaine

## Château de Carbonneau

Big château bedrooms bedecked in soft linens with splashes of splendid detail, a fine old bed in the 'Peony' room, huge bathrooms done with rich tiles – here is a self-assured family house where quality is fresh, history stalks and there's plenty of space for guests. Visit Wilfrid's winery and taste the talent handed down by his forebears. Jacquie, a relaxed dynamic New Zealander, provides tasty alternatives to the ubiquitous duck cuisine, has a relaxed approach to dining and has now opened a salon de thé; a dab hand at interiors, she has also cultivated a luminescent, airy guest sitting room near the orangery.

| Rooms | 2 doubles, 3 twin/doubles: €90–€145. |
|---|---|
| Meals | Dinner €30. |
| | Wine €8–€20. |
| Closed | December – February. |

Jacquie & Wilfrid Franc de Ferrière
Château de Carbonneau,
33890 Pessac sur Dordogne
Gironde

| Tel | +33 (0)5 57 47 46 46 |
| Mobile | +33 (0)6 83 30 14 35 |
| Email | carbonneau@orange.fr |
| Web | www.chateau-carbonneau.com |

Entry 483   Map 9

# Aquitaine

## Peyraguey Maison Rouge

Born and raised amid the Sauternes' vine-clothed hills and châteaux, the Belangers know Bordeaux wines intimately. Monsieur may offer a tasting on your second night in this authentic old wine-grower's house; for deeper insights, book an œnology course (min. 4). Tour châteaux, kayak down the Ciron, follow Bordeaux's wine trail past the 12 top Grands Crus Classés and St Émilion. Return to a dip in the pool, a game of ping-pong, grilled duck in the village auberge and a book by the fire in the elegant sitting room where wine scenes dot warm stone walls and champagne-coloured curtains glimmer. A genuine French vineyard stay.

| Rooms | 2 doubles, 1 twin: €75–€107. |
|---|---|
| | Extra bed €25 per person per night. |
| Meals | Restaurants 2km. |
| Closed | Rarely. |

Annick & Jean-Claude Belanger
Peyraguey Maison Rouge,
33210 Bommes Sauternes
Gironde

| Tel | +33 (0)5 57 31 07 55 |
| Email | belanger@club-internet.fr |
| Web | www.peyraguey-sauternes.com |

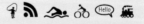

Entry 484   Map 9

# Aquitaine

## Chambres d'Hôtes Janoutic

Charming Jean-Pierre finds the finest organic produce for his table. From croissants to charcuterie, 'poulets fermier' to orchard jams (apricot, blackcurrant, redcurrant, fig), it sounds delicious. This is a well-restored old farmhouse in the hamlet of Janoutic, two miles from the motorway, a great little stopover between Bordeaux and Toulouse. We like the two bright, carpeted bedrooms upstairs best, their rustic rafters hung with tobacco leaves in memory of old farming days; all have big walk-in showers. There's more: leather sofas and a great log fire; a wild garden with an aviary and a pool for newts and birds.

| Rooms | 2 doubles: €70. |
| | 1 family room for 3: €70–€96. |
| | Extra bed €26 per person per night. |
| | Singles €60. |
| Meals | Dinner €28. |
| | Children under 12, €19. |
| Closed | Rarely. |

**Jean-Pierre Doebele**
Chambres d'Hôtes Janoutic,
2 Le Tach,
33124 Aillas
Gironde
Tel     +33 (0)5 56 65 32 58
Mobile   +33 (0)6 81 97 02 92
Email    jpdoebel@club-internet.fr
Web     www.chambresdhotesjanoutic.com

Entry 485   Map 9

# Aquitaine

## La Cigogne

Croaking frogs, prune-drying paraphernalia and a wacky springwater pool – this is rural, unstuffy, great fun. In its leafy garden, La Cigogne (the name of the nearby stream) is a typical farmhouse, inherited by Véronique and modernised by this charmingly natural couple to give simple and wonderfully individual guest rooms, each with its own vine- and rose-shaded terrace. There's a cosy sitting room for winter evenings; the huge barn, its mangers still intact, makes a comfortable retreat – with billiards – for damp summer days. Yves, a talented golfer, is happy to give you a free lesson and cycle paths pass the door.

| Rooms | 2 doubles: €65–€80. |
| Meals | Dinner with wine, €25. |
| Closed | November – March. |

**Yves & Véronique Denis**
La Cigogne,
5 le Grand Janot,
33580 Ste Gemme
Gironde
Tel     +33 (0)5 56 71 19 70
Mobile   +33 (0)6 75 93 66 32
Email    lacigogne.33@orange.fr
Web     www.chambres-lacigogne.fr

Entry 486   Map 9

## Aquitaine

### Briançon

The 14th-century walnut mill is a house full of art, riches and light, and the English garden, blessed with a burbling brook, is resplendent with rare plants. Inside, sofas wear colourful throws, boho-stylish bedrooms burst with personality and shower rooms have retro touches. Dinners at the big old country table sound enticing: wines from Michael's cellar, produce from Katie's potager, herbs scattered with studied abandon, and plenty for vegetarians. Katie and Michael, from London, have created a sophisticated yet laid-back home – and two heated, saltwater swimming pools!

| Rooms | 3 doubles; 2 twins sharing bathroom: €85–€150. |
|---|---|
| Meals | Dinner €35. Restaurant 2km. |
| Closed | December – March. |

Katie Armitage
Briançon,
24320 Verteillac
Dordogne
Tel      +33 (0)5 53 91 38 40
Email    katie@elliottarmitage.com
Web      www.elliottarmitage.com

## Aquitaine

### Pauliac

The exuberant hillside garden, full of blossom and bamboo, has gorgeous views of sunflowers and an overflowing stone plunge pool. John and Jane's talents are a restful atmosphere, great dinners, and interiors that are a brilliant marriage of cottage simplicity and sparks from African throws and contemporary paintings. Beautiful bedrooms have a separate entrance. Delightful, energetic Jane offers superb, imaginative food in the sun-splashed veranda with its all-season views, or the bright, rustic dining room with roaring log fire – and early suppers for children. Lovely people in a tranquil view-drenched spot.

| Rooms | 2 doubles, 1 twin: €60–€85. 1 suite for 4: €80–€110. |
|---|---|
| Meals | Dinner €25. Wine €10. |
| Closed | Rarely. |

Jane & John Edwards
Pauliac,
Celles,
24600 Ribérac
Dordogne
Tel      +33 (0)5 47 23 40 17
Mobile   +33 (0)6 88 13 06 27
Email    info@pauliac.fr
Web      www.pauliac.fr

# Aquitaine

## La Bastide de Chapdeuil

Keep your eyes peeled or you'll miss the tiny sign as you wind along the village lanes: La Bastide is not be missed. The 18th-century house, restored with comfort in mind, is modern, friendly and has dashes of luxury; kids and grown-ups will love the home cinema, gardens, long pool, and the al fresco dining. Bedrooms are blissful, bathrooms sumptuous, and Franck is all gentle courtesy. He and eco-minded Michaëlla offer organic whenever possible, so you breakfast on village bread, homemade jams and yogurt, and dine on Perigordin goodies such as confit and asparagus. Markets, medieval towns, abbeys – take your pick!

| Rooms | 4 doubles: €80–€95. |
| | 1 family room for 2-4: €75–€100. |
| Meals | Dinner with wine, €26. |
| | Restaurants 2km. |
| Closed | Rarely. |

**Franck & Michaëlla Pinel**
La Bastide de Chapdeuil,
La Pouze,
24320 Chapdeuil
Dordogne
Tel     +33 (0)5 53 91 25 44
Email   labastidechapdeuil@gmail.com
Web    www.labastidedechapdeuil.com

Entry 489    Map 9

---

# Aquitaine

## Château de Villars

View the château from a teak pool lounger, iced drink in hand: views swoop to forests as far as the eye can see and church bells from the village occasionally break the peace. Light pours into the neo-Gothic building, where guests drift between library, terrace-bar, sitting room, gym and massage salon. The bedrooms are immaculate; tucked between the trees the splendid summerhouse is ideal for self-caterers, as is the 18th-century village townhouse. There's a long banqueting table for breakfast, and dinner (good value) is served three days a week, with delicious homegrown veg from the garden. One welcoming retreat. *Minimum stay: 2 nights. Self-catering available: 2 cottages for 4.*

| Rooms | 5 doubles: €125–€165. |
| Meals | Dinner €32. |
| | Wine €11–€35. |
| | Restaurant 5-minute drive. |
| Closed | November to mid-April. |

**Bill Davies & Kevin Saunders**
Château de Villars,
Près de la Cure,
24530 Villars
Dordogne
Tel      +33 (0)5 53 03 41 58
Mobile   +33 (0)6 83 26 03 95
Email    chateauvillars@aol.com
Web     www.gofranceholiday.com

Entry 490    Map 9

## Auberge de Castel-Merle

High above the valley of the Vézère – with peerless views from the terrace – a stunningly atmospheric inn where a Templar castle once stood. It has been in Anita's family for generations and she and Christopher love the place. Pastel pelmets and painted flowers on the walls clothe the dining room, modest bedrooms have an uncluttered country look, there's a bright boutis quilt on every bed and small curtain'd showers. Some rooms overlook the courtyard, others the woods. Christopher is an enthusiastic truffle hunter and a wonderful cook, wild boar being one of the restaurant's specialities. Hiking in the forests is a joy. Great value.

| Rooms | 7 doubles, 1 twin: €75–€78. |
|---|---|
| Meals | Dinner €19–€30. |
| | Wine €9–€28. |
| | Restaurant closed lunchtimes. |
| | Half-board only in August. |
| Closed | 2 October – 4 April. |

Anita Castanet & Christopher Millinship
Auberge de Castel-Merle,
24290 Sergeac
Dordogne
Tel       +33 (0)5 53 50 70 08
Email   hotelcastelmerle@yahoo.fr
Web     www.hotelcastelmerle.com

## Les Charmes de Carlucet

An 18th-century house with a poignant history: Jewish families sheltered here during the Second World War. Now welcoming Anglo-French Éric and his team run the B&B, Éric juggling this with running a five-hectare estate and bringing up two children. In a vast walled garden on the edge of the village, the house has been completely renovated. Living and dining rooms are cool compositions of natural stone, white walls, pale fabrics, while pitch-ceilinged L-shaped bedrooms under the eaves have gleaming floors, spotless bath or shower rooms, and air-conditioning. Should you tire of the heated pool or new sauna, you can stroll to the clipped hedges of Eyrignac.

| Rooms | 2 doubles: €99–€119. |
|---|---|
| | Extra beds €20 per person per night. |
| Meals | Restaurant within walking distance. |
| Closed | Rarely. |

Éric Edgar
Les Charmes de Carlucet,
24590 St Crépin & Carlucet
Dordogne
Tel       +33 (0)5 53 31 22 60
Mobile  +33 (0)6 72 47 58 08
Email   lescharmes@carlucet.com
Web     www.carlucet.com

## Aux Fontaines d'Eyvigues

No wonder this happy young family loves welcoming guests: their big stone house is in a beautiful spot, hugged by wooded hills and a semi-wild flower meadow with a swimming pool. Cleverly restored and romantic for two, the bedroom has a claw-foot bath behind a head-height wall and a wood-burner by its soft purple bed. You can join in family dinners around the kitchen table – food is local but influenced by Jean-Yves' Moroccan origins – and take breakfast in the garden. Whether on foot, in a canoe, by (hired) bike or whizzing down a zipline, the northern Dordogne is a playground for couples seeking peace and adventure. *Child's bed available.*

## Les Chambres de la Voie Verte

Steps curl up and around the old stone walls and lead to four rooms, each delightful, each with its own outside entrance. Find soft purples, greens, greys, rose reds, comfortable new beds and state-of-the-art bathrooms with walk-in showers. From the top floor, views stretch over the town's Perigordian rooftops, to Château de Montfort beyond. Enjoy breakfast off white Limoges china at the long table in the house next door (and on the terrace on warm days). The friendly owners also run the bar and florist's on either side; extrovert Madame revels in her projects. The old railway track for cycling to Sarlat and Souillac is near.

| | |
|---|---|
| Rooms | 1 double: €75–€95. |
| Meals | Dinner with wine, €25. |
| | Restaurants 1km. |
| Closed | Rarely. |

| | |
|---|---|
| Rooms | 2 doubles, 2 twins: €78–€88. |
| | Extra bed €20 per person per night. |
| Meals | Restaurants in town. |
| Closed | Rarely. |

| | |
|---|---|
| | **Jean-Yves & Cathy Tomas** |
| | Aux Fontaines d'Eyvigues, |
| | Lieu-dit Eyvigues, |
| | 24590 Salignac Eyvigues |
| | Dordogne |
| Tel | +33 (0)5 53 29 04 35 |
| Mobile | +33 (0)6 72 61 33 27 |
| Email | ctomas446@gmail.com |
| Web | www.auxfontainesdeyvigues.com/figuiers1 |

| | |
|---|---|
| | **Annie Boyer** |
| | Les Chambres de la Voie Verte, |
| | 24200 Carsac Aillac |
| | Dordogne |
| Mobile | +33 (0)6 70 09 38 95 |
| Email | annie.boyer43@orange.fr |
| Web | www.chambres-de-la-voie-verte.com |

## La Guérinière

Once a charterhouse in private parkland, this big, good-looking Perigord house, on a hill facing Domme, is a tribute to the rich sober taste of the area. Inside reflects outside: the same dark timbers against pale stone. The feel is warmly authentic and the owners have redecorated the bedrooms most charmingly, gradually replacing the modern furniture with country antiques. They used to run a restaurant; now there's a big candlelit table for guests and you may find more gourmets in the beamed dining room (outsiders are occasionally allowed in). Outside: palm trees and pool. A gem.

## Manoir de la Malartrie

On the banks of the Dordogne, a beautifully restored 19th-century manor house with luxurious rooms and a cosy, beamed gîte. Surrounded by fragrant Mediterranean gardens planted with lavender and rosemary, this is an idyllic retreat for sybarites. Inside, charming Ouafaa has blended Moroccan style with Edwardian elegance. Sleep in sumptuous bedrooms furnished with antiques; eat Franco-Moroccan meals made with veg from the potager in the magnificent salon. There's a sleek pool and you can watch boats sail by as you picnic in the grounds. Explore grand châteaux or stroll to popular La Roque-Gageac for shops and restaurants. *Minimum stay: 3 nights. Heated pool available May-Oct.*

| Rooms | 2 doubles, 2 twin/doubles: €90–€105. 1 triple: €130–€140. 1 quadruple: €155–€170. |
|---|---|
| Meals | Dinner €28. Wine from €20. |
| Closed | November – March. |

| Rooms | 4 doubles: €110–€160. 1 suite for 4: €200–€260. 1 apartment for 2–4: €140–€260. Extra bed/sofabed available €30 per person per night. |
|---|---|
| Meals | Dinner with wine & appetizer, €50 (min. 8). Restaurants 5-min walk. |
| Closed | Mid-December to mid-March (except pre-booked Christmas parties). |

**Brigitte & Christophe Demassougne**
La Guérinière,
Baccas,
24250 Cénac & St Julien
Dordogne
Tel      +33 (0)5 53 29 91 97
Email    contact@la-gueriniere-dordogne.com
Web      www.la-gueriniere-dordogne.com

**Ouafaa Diebolt–Balbal**
Manoir de la Malartrie,
La Malartrie,
24220 Vezac
Dordogne
Tel      +33 (0)5 53 29 03 51
Email    lamalartrie@orange.fr
Web      www.manoir-lamalartrie.com

### Balcon en Forêt

A wine-stocked honesty bar in your room, dinner a feast of local produce, and picnics enhanced by crockery 'chic' or 'rustique': such is your hosts' attention to detail! A steep winding lane leads to a stunningly restored wine and tobacco farm, home of warm, generous, creative Sandra and Badouin. Their guest suites are remarkable: one inspired by 17th-century Dutch interior paintings, another with its own wood-burner; the bed linen is embroidered and the craftsmanship is exquisite. As for Beynac, it's medieval, beautiful and down the hill; borrow a torch and tumble down for dinner. *Minimum stay: 2 nights.*

### Le Clos des Sources

Birdsong, a frog chorus, the murmur of springs: the rest is silence in these splendid gardens, a labour of love for owner Monique, a joy for her guests, who have private access. Looking down on this happy valley is a cluster of apricot-hued limestone buildings. Rooms – sleek and contemporary, mixing dressed stone with rag-rolled walls – are in the apex of the old barn; each has its own terrace fragrant with lavender and wisteria. Walk over wobbly stone to the shabby chic salon and dining room, where breakfast is served on English bone china. For dinner, Monique plunders her garden to produce regional specialities. A delight in the Dordogne!

| | |
|---|---|
| Rooms | 3 suites for 2: €145-€175. |
| Meals | Dinner, with wine, €27. Restaurants within walking distance. |
| Closed | Rarely. |

| | |
|---|---|
| Rooms | 2 doubles: €65-€85. 1 suite for 2: €85-€105. |
| Meals | Dinner €25. Restaurants 3km. |
| Closed | Rarely. |

**Baudouin & Sandra Koerts**
Balcon en Forêt,
Tral Pech,
24220 Beynac-et-Cazenac
Dordogne
Tel     +33 (0)5 53 28 24 01
Email   bonjour@ladordogne.info
Web     www.ladordogne.info

**Monique Jourdan**
Le Clos des Sources,
Rue Les Crochets,
24200 Vitrac
Dordogne
Tel      +33 (0)5 53 29 67 93
Mobile   +33 (0)6 82 14 57 76
Email    jardinleclosdessources@yahoo.fr

Entry 497   Map 9

Entry 498   Map 9

## La Blanquette

High in the Dordogne, where private houses hide behind trees, is a friendly and immaculate B&B. The Dolman family's Perigordian house stands in seven wonderful hectares of meadow and woodland, not far from their bell tents, neat gîtes and super pool. Guest bedrooms are on the first floor, two with high pitched ceilings, all with polished oak floors, retro French furniture and spoiling bathrooms. Breakfasts include omelettes à la maison served at dapper tables, you can have lunch in pretty Carsac-Aillac or stunning Sarlat, and canoe on the Dordogne – your hosts will ferry you there and back. You can hire bikes, too. *Minimum stay: 2 nights. Children over 12 welcome.*

| Rooms | 2 doubles, 1 twin: €98–€118. Extra bed €30 per person per night. |
|---|---|
| Meals | Restaurants 1.5km. |
| Closed | Christmas, New Year. |

Nicola Dolman
La Blanquette,
Route du Cambord, Le Cambord,
24200 Sarlat la Canéda
Dordogne

| Tel | +33 (0)5 53 31 14 68 |
|---|---|
| Mobile | +33 (0)6 32 04 90 45 |
| Email | nik@la-blanquette.com |
| Web | www.la-blanquette.com |

Entry 499   Map 9

## Loge des Dames Blanches

Astonishing! High-tech design in 16th-century central Sarlat and Mary-Bel's remarkable creations: 'Les Colletines', for two, bright in Monroe red and 'Le Clos de l'Abbaye', for four, with a fabulous steel and mango wood spiral staircase. Both impress with Italian-style urban chic, Murano lights and hand-painted cement tiles in clever kitchens and power shower rooms. The elegant studio's king-size foldaway bed is concealed by a mirrored cupboard. 'Le Clos de l'Abbaye' scintillates too with designer chrome, glass and two king beds aloft between curtained, grey-painted beams. And Mary-Bel lays on everything from fine breakfasts to truffle weekends.

| Rooms | 1 house for 4 with kitchen, living area & sofabed: €190–€300. 1 studio for 2 with kitchen & living area: €110–€175. |
|---|---|
| Meals | Dinner with wine, €30. Restaurants within walking distance. |
| Closed | Never. |

Mary-Bel Lozano
Loge des Dames Blanches,
6 rue de l'Abbaye,
24200 Sarlat la Canéda
Dordogne

| Mobile | +33 (0)6 09 74 88 55 |
|---|---|
| Email | lalogedesdamesblanches@gmail.com |
| Web | www.lalogedesdamesblanches.com |

Entry 500   Map 9

## Aquitaine

### Château de Puymartin

Neither dream nor museum, Puymartin gives you the chance to act the aristocrat for a spell, and survey the day visitors from your own wing (with a smug smile). The fireplace in the tapestried baronial dining room would take a small tree, painted beams draw the eye, the carved stone staircase asks to be stroked, the furniture is authentic 17th-century Perigordian; history oozes from every corner. Bedrooms are vastly in keeping – twin four-posters, a faded ceiling painting, a loo in a turret, thick draperies. The Comtesse's son (friendly and with good English) looks after you well.

## Aquitaine

### Château de la Bourlie – Les Bories

Delicious breakfast is delivered by tractor in a basket – to your private tobacco barn on a dreamy estate. After which it's a gentle stroll to the fortified château with its 'jardin remarquable', its potager and pool. Lovely Lucy lives on site and welcomes you into a funky-urban space, all white and flooded with light from glazed barn doors at either end. Polished concrete floors run throughout, there's an Italian 50s sofa, a sleek cooking unit, a great oak table, a stunning shower, a vast lofty bedroom with a curtain-hung bed – and pallet mattresses for a couple of friends. Car-free, nature-steeped, hilltop heaven.

| | |
|---|---|
| Rooms | 1 twin: €150. |
| | 1 family room for 4: €120. |
| | Extra bed €30 per person per night. |
| Meals | Restaurant 5km. |
| Closed | November – March. |

| | |
|---|---|
| Rooms | 1 barn for 2-4: €200. |
| Meals | Private kitchenette. |
| | Restaurants 5-10km. |
| Closed | Rarely. |

| | |
|---|---|
| | **X de Montbron** |
| | Château de Puymartin, |
| | 24200 Sarlat la Canéda |
| | Dordogne |
| Mobile | +33 (0)6 33 64 01 88 |
| Email | xdemontbron@orange.fr |
| Web | www.chateau-de-puymartin.com |

| | |
|---|---|
| | **Lucy Williams** |
| | Château de la Bourlie – Les Bories, |
| | 24480 Urval |
| | Dordogne |
| Mobile | +33 (0)6 18 72 05 74 |
| Email | contact@chateaudelabourlie.com |
| Web | www.chateaudelabourlie.com/ |
| | les-bories.html |

Entry 501   Map 9

Entry 502   Map 9

# Aquitaine

## Manoir de la Brunie

An elegant village manor in a glorious setting: the views are stupendous. The owners live in Paris but the genial manager will introduce you to a fine living room full of warm bright colours overlooking a sweeping lawn (play the piano, browse the books) and excellent bedrooms. The tower suite and small double have a modern feel, the other rooms, huge and high-ceilinged, are more classical; all have subtle colours, new wood floors, space for armchairs and sofas, and good lighting. Breakfasts are fresh, bathrooms delightful… there's a heated pool shared with gîte guests, a river beach nearby, riding next door.

| Rooms | 3 doubles, 1 twin/double: €75–€110. 1 suite for 4: €125–€140. Extra bed €17 per person per night. |
|---|---|
| Meals | Dinner with wine, €27. |
| Closed | December/January. |

Joyce Villemur
Manoir de la Brunie,
La Brunie,
24220 Le Coux & Bigaroque
Dordogne
Tel    +33 (0)5 53 31 95 62
Email  manoirdelabrunie@wanadoo.fr
Web    www.manoirdelabrunie.com

Entry 503   Map 9

# Aquitaine

## Maison Olea

High in the hills, on the rustic-suburban outskirts of Le Bugue, is a hospitable house, designed and built expressly for B&B. Roses billow around the infinity pool, views pour over the valley, and children are free to roam. The house hums with people, the owners are delightful and the bedrooms, four with terraces and one on the ground floor, are filled with light and decorated with flair; big bathrooms have a Mediterranean theme. This is the Dordogne, and hosted dinners – fun affairs – flourish truffles, duck and Perigordian treats, as well as fruit and veg from the great gardens.

| Rooms | 2 twin/doubles: €75–€105. 1 family room for 3, 2 family rooms for 4: €85–€105. |
|---|---|
| Meals | Dinner with wine, €35–€38. Restaurants 3km. |
| Closed | 15 December – 15 January. |

Murielle Nardou
Maison Olea,
La Combe de Leygue,
24260 Le Bugue
Dordogne
Tel    +33 (0)5 53 08 48 93
Email  info@olea-dordogne.com
Web    www.olea-dordogne.com

Entry 504   Map 9

## Aquitaine

### Le Moulin Neuf

Robert's greeting is the first line of an ode to hospitality written in warm stone in breathtaking gardens, set to the tune of the mill stream. Immaculate rooms in the guest barn are comfortingly filled with good beds and fresh flowers, bathrooms are sheer luxury, and views sweep over the lawns. Wake up to a royal breakfast of breads, croissants, pâtisseries, homemade jams, fruits and tiny cheeses served on white tablecloths on the vine-shaded veranda. All is beautifully, lovingly tended by Robert. His two happy rescue dogs will make friends with yours; find your own special spot in the gardens. *Minimum stay: 3 nights in winter. Children over 10 welcome.*

| Rooms | 2 doubles, 1 twin/double, 1 suite for 2: €93–€97. 1 family room for 3: €123. Singles €82.60–€86.60. |
|---|---|
| Meals | Restaurant in Paunat, 1km. |
| Closed | Rarely. |

Robert Chappell
Le Moulin Neuf,
Paunat,
24510 Ste Alvère
Dordogne
Tel +33 (0)5 53 63 30 18
Email moulin-neuf@usa.net
Web www.the-moulin-neuf.com

Entry 505   Map 9

## Aquitaine

### Les Hirondelles

Carine, half-Greek, energetic, charming and fun, makes you feel welcome in the sunny kitchen of her restored farmhouse on the top of a hill. She enjoys cooking French and international dishes and makes amazing walnut jam. Simple, dim-lit, inexpensive bedrooms are in a converted barn set back from the house, each with a terrace delineated by concrete planters and the pool is far enough away not to disturb your siesta. Spend two or three nights and get to know this beautiful village and the whole area; Carine knows the best places to go. *Minimum stay: 2 nights in high season.*

| Rooms | 2 doubles: €50–€55. |
|---|---|
| Meals | Dinner, 3 courses with wine, €19. |
| Closed | November – April. |

Carine Someritis
Les Hirondelles,
Le Maine,
24510 Ste Alvère
Dordogne
Tel +33 (0)5 53 22 75 40
Email leshirondelles.carine@orange.fr
Web www.les-hirondelles-dordogne.jimdo.com

Entry 506   Map 9

## Aquitaine

### Château Lalinde

This small turreted 1269 château floating above the Dordogne river is a fairytale delight with bags of history. Easy-going Wilna is a passionate cook; enjoy continental yumminess at breakfast and traditional French with a South African twist at dinner. Classic bedrooms, all with modern bathrooms, come in varying sizes: snug with sloping ceilings (mind the steep stairs) or larger with balconies and views; one has a seating area in a turret. There's a dinky garden and pool, and a fabulous balcony terrace running the length of the house that overlooks the river. The village has a weekly market, and Bergerac and the Lascaux caves are close. *Minimum stay: 2 nights. Cot & high chair available.*

| Rooms | 5 twin/doubles: €200–€240. Children under 2 stay free. |
|---|---|
| Meals | Lunch, 3 courses, €25. Dinner, 4 courses with wine, €35. Restaurants within walking distance. |
| Closed | 1 November – 1 April. |

| | Wilna Wilkinson |
|---|---|
| | Château Lalinde, |
| | 1 rue de Verdun, |
| | 24150 Lalinde |
| | Dordogne |
| Mobile | +33 (0)6 89 38 68 22 |
| Email | twoxscotch@gmail.com |
| Web | www.chateaulalinde.com |

Entry 507   Map 9

## Aquitaine

### Maison Porte del Marty

Poised on the river, beside a bridge, gardens tumbling to the water, this is in the heart of the Dordogne. The building oozes history – Roman foundations, 10th-century chateau, merchant's house – its interior (restored by big-hearted New Zealanders, Cheri and Brian) elegant with polished floors and brocante finds. High-ceilinged bedrooms are country-house-gracious with chandeliers, mirrors and huge windows, and overlook the river (one with balcony). Breakfast on Lalinde's best pastries then cycle (bikes to hire), bargain-hunt or explore Sarlat. Come back to relax on the terrace, soothed by the sights and sounds of the river. *Minimum stay: 2 nights. Owners can collect guests from the station.*

| Rooms | 2 doubles, 1 double with separate, private bathroom: €100–€120. 1 family room for 3: €120–€160. |
|---|---|
| Meals | Restaurants within walking distance. |
| Closed | Never. |

| | Brian Hewitt |
|---|---|
| | Maison Porte del Marty, |
| | 1 rue des Martyrs, |
| | 24150 Lalinde |
| | Dordogne |
| Tel | +33 (0)5 53 57 54 06 |
| Email | brian@chambres-hote-lalinde.com |
| Web | www.chambres-hote-lalinde.com |

Entry 508   Map 9

## Aquitaine

### Le Domaine de La Millasserie

Near lovely lively Trémolat, and the Dordogne with its watery charms, is this elegant, immaculate B&B. American Byrne and Alain from Bordeaux have swapped literature and antiques for hospitality – and they do it well. Alongside their honey-hued 18th-century manor overlooking the woods, the B&B wing in traditional style houses four generous rooms. French windows open to private terraces, huge beds are dressed in toile de Jouy, gorgeous antiques glow: armoires, paintings, mirrors. Lazy breakfasts, on the terrace or by the pool, offer fresh fruits, croissants, viennoiseries, strong French coffee and good English tea.

## Aquitaine

### Manoir de Beauregard

Artist and interior designer Angela welcomes guests to her beautifully restored 17th-century house set in 40 acres of landscaped gardens with grass paths and wide views. Inside is filled with taste and passion: discover antiques, French and Italian painted furniture, and bedrooms with carved four-poster beds, embroidered linen sheets and limewashed beams. Splash in the pool in summer, warm yourself by a big log fire on chilly days with tea and homemade cakes. On Fridays, Angela may cook you a candlelit dinner using local, seasonal ingredients: duck, wild mushrooms, foie gras or truffles, with excellent Bergerac wine.

| | |
|---|---|
| Rooms | 4 doubles: €95. |
| Meals | Restaurants 5km. |
| Closed | Rarely. |

| | |
|---|---|
| Rooms | 3 doubles: €160–€180. |
| Meals | English breakfast €8. |
| | Afternoon tea €5. |
| | Dinner, 4 courses with wine, from €35. |
| | Restaurant 1.5km. |
| Closed | Never. |

**Byrne Fone & Alain Pioton**
Le Domaine de La Millasserie,
24150 Mauzac & Grand Castang
Dordogne
Tel +33 (0)5 53 57 78 01
Email lamillasserie@gmail.com
Web www.bandbfrancedordogne.com

**Angela Meunier**
Manoir de Beauregard,
Le Grand But,
24140 Clermont de Beauregard
Dordogne
Tel +33 (0)5 53 81 66 97
Email manoirbeauregard@gmail.com
Web www.manoirbeauregard.com

### Maison Campana

It's a beguiling town, a maze of streets and stone archways, and you can reach the house from church or square. The welcome is very warm – Eva is Polish and would rather speak English than French (both with a delightful accent). Up a charming twisting stair are two bedrooms on the first floor, each pale, elegant and contemporary, enlivened by touches of raspberry red. Eva, who lives close by but pops across to make breakfast, gives guests a communal kitchen and a salon with pale stone floors, cool retro leather sofas and vibrant art. Visit the Sunday market, walk to a wine château, pick a pretty café and watch the world go by. *Minimum stay: 2 nights at weekends.*

### Château Gauthié

Outside a perfect bastide village, here is château B&B run with warmth and energy. Stéphane cooks brilliantly and loves wine; Florence is enormous fun, a breath of fresh air. Restful, light-filled, traditional bedrooms have white bathrooms. An infinity pool overlooks the lake below, above it perches the rustic-modern treehouse, its balcony gazing over meadows and cows, its mother tree thrusting two branches through the floor. Solar-lit paths lead you down through the trees at night, a breakfast basket is winched up in the morning. Later... play badminton, fish in the lake, spin off on a bike, bask in the hot tub. *Minimum stay: 2 nights. Self-catering available in treehouse.*

| | |
|---|---|
| Rooms | 2 doubles: €60–€90. |
| Meals | Guest kitchen. |
| | Restaurants within walking distance. |
| Closed | Rarely. |

| | |
|---|---|
| Rooms | 3 doubles, 1 twin: €90–€115. |
| | 1 treehouse for 2: €120–€165. |
| Meals | Dinner, 4 courses with wine €40. |
| | Wine €15–€50. |
| Closed | Mid-November to March. |

|  | |
|---|---|
| | **Eva & Gary Burn** |
| | Maison Campana, |
| | 1 rue de la Paix, |
| | 24560 Issigeac |
| | Dordogne |
| Tel | +33 (0)5 53 23 79 85 |
| Mobile | +33 (0)6 38 32 83 36 |
| Email | eva.belvain@orange.fr |
| Web | www.maisoncampana-dordogne.com |

| | |
|---|---|
| | **Florence & Stéphane Desmette** |
| | Château Gauthié, |
| | 24560 Issigeac Monmarvès |
| | Dordogne |
| Tel | +33 (0)5 53 27 30 33 |
| Email | chateau.gauthie@laposte.net |
| Web | www.chateaugauthie.com |

## Aquitaine

### La Ferme de la Rivière

The busy auberge sits surrounded by fields in a hamlet near the river Dordogne. The Archer family honour tradition; he is a poultry breeder, she is an industrious (decidedly non-vegetarian) cook and the recipes for handcrafting pâtés and foie gras are their heirlooms. Readers talk of fabulous meals and delicious aperitifs. The honey stones of the building are impeccably pointed and cleaned, bedrooms are spotless (though dark), shower rooms are large and pristine and there's a delightful, very French dining room with an open fire. Good for families (a climbing frame in the garden) – and brilliant value.

| Rooms | 1 double, 1 triple: €59. |
|---|---|
| Meals | Dinner with wine, €21.50. |
| Closed | November – February. |

**Marie-Thérèse & Jean-Michel Archer**
La Ferme de la Rivière,
24520 St Agne
Dordogne
Tel +33 (0)5 53 23 22 26
Email archer.marietherese@wanadoo.fr
Web www.lafermedelariviere.com

Entry 513   Map 9

## Aquitaine

### La Rebière d'Or

The Dordogne laps sleepily alongside this renovated bijou château with its own slipway, majestic grounds and swish pool. Roam freely through living areas lavished with antiques and boudoir trinkets. Woodland and river cameo views unfold from large, comfortable Edwardian-style bedrooms where artistic charm abounds – even in the bathrooms. Breakfast on fresh fruit brochettes in the dining or piano room – or outside where peacocks parade. You're a stone's throw from the busy market town of Mouleydier and a leg stretch away from good eateries. In a suburb, a surprising haven of tranquillity – with grandeur and style in spades. *Minimum stay: 2 nights. Children over 12 welcome.*

| Rooms | 2 doubles: €125. |
|---|---|
| | Extra bed €25 per person per night. |
| Meals | Restaurant within walking distance. |
| Closed | Rarely. |

**Catherine Fournel**
La Rebière d'Or,
13 rue de la Rocade,
24520 Mouleydier
Dordogne
Tel +33 (0)5 53 58 23 05
Mobile +33 (0)6 13 77 33 83
Email catherinefournel@free.fr
Web www.rebiere-dor.com

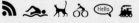

Entry 514   Map 9

## Aquitaine

### Le Relais de la Myrpe

A joy to stay on the oldest square in Bergerac, where heavily beamed houses stand cheek by jowl and locals toss boules under the plane trees as the tourists snap away. Up the wonky staircase is your small, private, studio-style living space, full of quaint comfort and Xavière's colourful brocante. She speaks excellent English, lives close by and runs a bric-a-brac shop on the ground floor. You get an unexpectedly capacious bedroom at the top overlooking the leafy square; beams abound, scatter rugs adorn the polished boards and there's a big curtained-off shower. Foie gras, truffles and wine are yours to discover. *Minimum stay: 2 nights.*

| | |
|---|---|
| Rooms | 1 double, sharing bathroom & 2 wcs with single: €55–€75. 1 single with day bed: €55–€75. €300–€400 per week. |
| Meals | Restaurants within walking distance. |
| Closed | Never. |

Xavière Simand-Lecouve
Le Relais de la Myrpe,
18 place de la Myrpe,
24100 Bergerac
Dordogne

| | |
|---|---|
| Mobile | +33 (0)6 29 18 03 84 |
| Email | xavierelamyrpe@hotmail.fr |
| Web | www.relaisdelamyrpe.com |

Entry 515  Map 9

## Aquitaine

### Logis des Baudry

Steeped in 500 years of history, the four solid wings of this distinguished château enclose a grand central courtyard where water shimmers with tiny fish. In a dining room wrapped in blue wallpaper and ribbon you'll discover that Hélène's cooking *à la grand-mère* is more than delicious, it's a reason to be here. Breakfast is among terracotta and citrus trees; bedrooms are large, traditional, framed by lofty beams, aglow with antiques and soft quilting. Views of Italianate gardens give way to more untouched countryside; pillars by the pool guide the eye to Dordogne vistas. And they are a wonderful, eco-committed couple.

| | |
|---|---|
| Rooms | 1 double, 4 twin/doubles: €128–€150. |
| Meals | Breakfast €13. Dinner €35. Wine €12–€35. |
| Closed | Rarely. |

Hélène Boulet & François Passebon
Logis des Baudry,
Château des Baudry,
24240 Monestier
Dordogne

| | |
|---|---|
| Tel | +33 (0)5 53 23 46 42 |
| Email | contact@logisdesbaudry.com |
| Web | www.logisdesbaudry.com |

Entry 516  Map 9

# Aquitaine

# Aquitaine

## Chambre d'Hôtes de La Batellerie

Luxuriate in period splendour in a 1750s riverfront mansion: tapestries, open fires, panelled walls, oriental rugs, fine antiques, chandeliers and a white gravel fountain'd courtyard. Add 21st-century luxuries: king-size beds in big beamed bedrooms, power showers, claw foot baths, and – joy of joys – a leafy indoor pool. Monsieur's 27 years as a New York chef show at breakfast, a feast of mini croissants and charcuterie; Madame, from Thailand, has thankfully put dinners on the menu. Across the river from this former wine warehouse (and later, town hall) lies a bustling market town of slate roofs and church spires. Great value for the decadence.
*Minimum stay: 2 nights in high season.*

## Le Moulin de Leymonie du Maupas

The Kieffers did the utterly successful restoration of their remote Dordogne mill themselves, their gardening past speaks softly in the herb-scented patio and the little brook trembles off past grazing horses to the valley. Inside, levels juggle with space, steep stairs rise to small rooms of huge character with stone and wood walls, rich rugs and selected antiques; loos are tiny. Your sitting room is seductive with its logs on the fire and timbers overhead. Add a relaxed, bubbly welcome, organic dinners served with crisp linen and candles, homemade bread and jams for breakfast, and you have great value.

| Rooms | 3 doubles: €100–€125. 1 family suite for 2-4: €125–€155. Singles €100–€125. Extra bed/sofabed €20–€30 per person per night. |
|---|---|
| Meals | Dinner from €15. Restaurants within walking distance. |
| Closed | Christmas, New Year. |

| Rooms | 1 double (children's room available), 1 twin: €70–€85. |
|---|---|
| Meals | Dinner €15–€20. Wine €9. |
| Closed | Rarely. |

Éric Lagrange
Chambre d'Hôtes de La Batellerie,
2 rue Onésime, Reclus,
33220 Port Ste Foy & Ponchapt
Dordogne
Tel      +33 (0)5 53 61 05 92
Mobile   +33 (0)6 16 64 35 65
Email    info@labatellerie.com
Web      www.labatellerie.com

Jacques & Ginette Kieffer
Le Moulin de Leymonie du Maupas,
24400 Issac
Dordogne
Tel      +33 (0)5 53 81 24 02
Email    jacques.kieffer2@wanadoo.fr
Web      www.moulin-leymonie.com

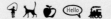

Entry 517   Map 9

Entry 518   Map 9

# Aquitaine

## The Old Bakery

A place of rest for weary Dordogne travellers, simple and green with a wood stove in the snug and full English or continental breakfast each morning. Owner Louis has opened up this old baker's building, so that the sitting room and kitchen flow into one – and out through terrace doors to the lush garden. You can wander among the fruit trees or lie in the shade of an old pine, soaking up the peace of this hamlet near the market town of Montpon Ménestérol. Artworks, vintage furniture and *objets* will keep you intrigued, and you wake on a handmade mattress to see the sun rise over the vegetable patch – beautiful. *Minimum stay: 2 nights at weekends.*

| Rooms | 1 double: €85–€95. |
|---|---|
| Meals | Dinner & picnic available. |
| Closed | Rarely. |

Lou O'Leary
The Old Bakery,
29 rue Jean Monnet,
24700 Montpon Ménestérol
Dordogne
Tel     +33 (0)5 53 82 34 59
Email    lou.oleary@yahoo.co.uk
Web     www.oldbakeryfrance.co.uk

Entry 519    Map 9

# Aquitaine

## Labarthe

At the end of a track lined with cherry trees, surrounded by vineyards and sunflowers, is a blue-shuttered house with far-reaching views; take a book to the garden and dream. There's no traffic to disturb the peace, just the odd splash from the pool which you are most welcome to share. Jeanette and Richard have taken the leap, to leave the UK for the Lot-et-Garonne and open up a B&B. Bedrooms are spotless and sweet; bathrooms are new; dinner includes local wines. Little Duras (2km) has restaurants, a bar, a market and a château on top of the hill – and if you're feeling lively you can kayak down the Dordogne.

| Rooms | 4 doubles: €60–€68. |
|---|---|
| Meals | Dinner, 3 courses with wine, €24. Vegetarian meals available. Restaurants 2km. |
| Closed | Never. |

Richard & Jeanette Hyde
Labarthe,
47120 Duras
Lot-et-Garonne
Tel     +33 (0)5 53 89 77 58
Email    Hideawayfrance@gmail.com
Web     www.hideawayfrance.co.uk

Entry 520    Map 9

### Manoir de Levignac

Walk through the hall into the handsome country kitchen and thence into the peaceful grounds: with nature reserve, views and resident donkey. Or stay and dine, beautifully, in a room with a big fireplace, pottery pieces and carved cupboard doors. In the sitting room, terracotta tiles, kilim rugs and grand piano give a comfortably artistic air. Adriana is Swiss-Italian, Jocelyn is South African; they are thoughtful and kind and do everything well. You'll have a lush bedroom with rural views, a sitting room and an immaculate bathroom. Outside, a small pine wood, a daisy-sprinkled lawn and a pool surrounded by palms.

### Domaine du Moulin de Labique

Soay sheep on the drive, ducks on the pond, goats in the greenhouse and food *à la grand-mère*. Shutters are painted with *bleu de pastel* from the Gers and the 13th-century interiors have lost none of their charm. In house and outbuildings there are chunky beams, seagrass on ancient tiles, vintage iron bedsteads, antique mirrors, and wallpapers flower-sprigged in raspberry, jade and green. Outside are old French roses and young alleys of trees, a bamboo-fringed stream, a restaurant in the stables, an exquisite pool. Wonderful hosts, the Bruxellois owners loved this place for years; now they are its best ambassadors.

| Rooms | 2 suites for 4: €70–€80. |
|---|---|
| Meals | Dinner with wine, €25. |
| Closed | Rarely. |

| Rooms | 3 doubles, 2 twins: €110–€140. |
|---|---|
| | 1 suite for 4: €199. |
| | Dinner, B&B €83–€99 per person. |
| Meals | Dinner €31. |
| | Wine €16–€30. |
| Closed | Rarely. |

Jocelyn & Adriana Cloete
Manoir de Levignac,
St Pierre sur Dropt,
47120 Duras
Lot-et-Garonne
Tel     +33 (0)5 53 83 68 11
Email   cloete@wanadoo.fr
Web     manoir.de.levignac.free.fr

Patrick & Christine Hendricx
Domaine du Moulin de Labique,
St Vivien,
47210 Villeréal
Lot-et-Garonne
Tel     +33 (0)5 53 01 63 90
Email   moulin-de-labique@wanadoo.fr
Web     www.moulin-de-labique.net

## Aquitaine

### Domaine de Rambeau

Handsome and enticing, this 18th-century manor house is perched on a hillside with views of silken wheat fields and distant valleys. But feast your eyes on the star of the show: an all-bells-and-whistles pool. Inside: an air of decadent splendour – even a knight in armour – where all is tasteful, relaxed and spacious in sitting, dining and bedrooms; just watch out for some low beams (and ask for an extra single if you need one). There's lovely artisan bread and homemade jams for breakfast, scrumptious dinners from generous owners and acres of parkland to mosey around – home to a huge and friendly black pig. *Extra bed available.*

| Rooms | 3 doubles: €120. |
| | Extra bed €20 per person per night. |
| Meals | Breakfast €10. |
| | Dinner, 3 courses with wine, €25. |
| | Restaurant 4km. |
| Closed | Rarely. |

| | Kim Reeves |
| | Domaine de Rambeau, |
| | 47260 Castelmoron sur Lot |
| | Lot-et-Garonne |
| Tel | +33 (0)5 53 79 38 43 |
| Mobile | +33 (0)6 13 95 39 52 |
| Email | reeves.kim@hotmail.fr |
| Web | www.domainederambeau.com |

Entry 523   Map 14

## Aquitaine

### Domaine de Pine

Hidden among sunflower fields is a well-proportioned and delightful hotel, an intimate haven run by charming English hosts. Convivial meals are served on fine white linen on a summer terrace with stunning panoramic views, beamy bedrooms are mostly large, light and elegant in whites and creams, and bathrooms sport fluffy robes. Springtime calls for lazing on loungers by the walled pool, happy hour is between five and six. For winter: a fitness room, a roaring fire, a candlelit supper in a blue and white dining room. Step out for music festivals and markets – or stay put and explore. Brilliant.

| Rooms | 3 doubles (2 rooms can |
| | interconnect): €99-€235. |
| | 1 suite for 4: €145-€190. |
| | Singles €79-€149. |
| | Dinner, B&B from €115 (for 1) & |
| | €180 (for 2). |
| | Extra bed/sofabed €15 p.p per night. |
| Meals | Lunch & dinner from €35. |
| | Restaurants 2-minute drive. |
| Closed | Rarely. |

| | Marcus & Cathy Becker |
| | Domaine de Pine, |
| | 47470 Blaymont |
| | Lot-et-Garonne |
| Tel | +33 (0)5 53 66 44 93 |
| Mobile | +44 (0)7831 115599 |
| Email | email@ddpine.com |
| Web | www.domainedepine.com |

Entry 524   Map 14

## Aquitaine

### Manoir Beaujoly

The medieval manor surveys fertile land rich in tales of knights and kings: a stunning hilltop setting. Horses graze, quails potter and guests gather by the pool in a ruined granary to barbecue trout from the river or duck from the market. The cool, thick-walled building wears its no-frills minimalism well: rough stone, hefty beams, a roll top bath, canvas wardrobes, ancient bullet holes... and 'open' bathrooms behind screens. There's a great fire in the monastic sitting room where delightful Dutch-German hosts serve breakfasts of cheese and charcuterie. Rampage, like those medieval Templars, across glorious 'French Tuscany'. *Minimum stay: 3 nights.*

| Rooms | 5 doubles: €100–€120. |
|---|---|
| Meals | Restaurants 4km. |
| Closed | December – March. |

**Lana Elise Siebelink Waltermann**
Manoir Beaujoly,
47340 Hautefage la Tour
Lot-et-Garonne

| Tel | +33 (0)5 53 01 52 51 |
|---|---|
| Mobile | +31 (0)6 28 12 64 76 |
| Email | be@beaujoly.com |
| Web | www.beaujoly.com |

Entry 525   Map 14

## Aquitaine

*New Entry*

### Moulin de Larroque

In a beautiful corner of the Lot-et-Garonne is an old watermill once used in the production of armagnac. Millstream and mill pond lie prettily behind; in front is a sweep of mown parkland and willows. Owned and run by a charming young couple, this small hotel is furnished in functional French style with character and comfort, and there's an indoor sauna, steam room and pool. You are near Barbaste and Nérac, so do go explore. The moulin has no communal space (bar a vast loft space for weddings and a breakfast room with smart tables) but the bedrooms, with their wooden floors and delicately patterned walls, are cosy and charming.

| Rooms | 5 doubles: €106–€137. Extra bed/sofabed €20 per person per night. |
|---|---|
| Meals | Restaurants 1.5km. |
| Closed | Rarely. |

**Béatrice & Jean-Philippe Guitton**
Moulin de Larroque,
47230 Barbaste
Lot-et-Garonne

| Tel | +33 (0)5 53 97 23 34 |
|---|---|
| Mobile | +33 (0)6 80 70 60 49 |
| Email | guitton.jean-philippe@wanadoo.fr |
| Web | www.moulin-larroque.com |

Entry 526   Map 14

Aquitaine

### Domaine de Sengresse

In the undiscovered Landes, two hours from Spain, a remote and ravishing 17th-century domaine. A solid stone house, a cathedral-like barn, an elegant pool, red squirrels in luscious acres and a 'petite maison' whose bread oven served the area's farms: such are the riches in store. A Godin stove and six-oven Aga feed today's guests in gourmet style from a wonderful array of homemade produce, the rooms are bathed in light and everything sparkles, from the luxurious bedrooms with their calming colours to the library brimful of books. More country hotel than B&B, run by the loveliest people. *House: minimum stay: 2 nights.*

### Le Domaine de l'Escuderia

Monsieur milks 100 Friesian cows, Madame breeds horses happily. Their *maison de maître* was a wreck in storm-torn woodland before they rolled up their sleeves. Now it has country-pretty rooms with iron four-posters and massage showers, a modern guest kitchen, sofas on the veranda, a bubbling hot tub... one extravagance in an eco-friendly restoration. Breakfast on farm milk and homemade flan, borrow bikes for a spin down to Lac Biscarrosse, tempt the ponies with a carrot, jog around sprawling grounds and unkempt woods – or kite-surf off Atlantic beaches, half an hour away. Country fun for all the family. *Extra beds available.*

| | |
|---|---|
| Rooms | 3 doubles, 2 twins: €115–€135. 1 house for 2–6: €100–€165. Singles €95–€125. Extra bed/sofabed €25 per person per night. |
| Meals | Dinner with wine, from €30. |
| Closed | Rarely. |

| | |
|---|---|
| Rooms | 3 doubles: €65–€140. 1 family room for 2–5: €80–€146. |
| Meals | Guest kitchen. Restaurant 3km. |
| Closed | Never. |

| | |
|---|---|
| | Michèle, Rob McLusky & Sasha Ibbotson |
| | Domaine de Sengresse, |
| | Route de Gouts, |
| | 40250 Souprosse |
| | Landes |
| Tel | +33 (0)5 58 97 78 34 |
| Email | sengresse@hotmail.fr |
| Web | www.sengresse.com |

| | |
|---|---|
| | Emmanuelle Gallouet |
| | Le Domaine de l'Escuderia, |
| | Route de Blaise, |
| | 40160 Parentis en Born |
| | Landes |
| Mobile | +33 (0)6 61 42 58 83 |
| Email | contact@lescuderia.com |
| Web | www.lescuderia.com |

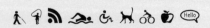

## Aquitaine

### Villa le Goëland

It is lush, lavish, inviting. Dominating the ocean, yards from the beaches of glamorous Biarritz, the only privately owned villa of its kind to have resisted commercial redevelopment has opened its arms to guests. Turrets were added in 1903; Paul's family took possession in 1934; now he and his wife, young, charming, professional, are its inspired guardians and restorers. Be ravished by oak floors, magnificent stairs, tall windows and balconies that go on for ever. Two bedrooms have terraces, beds are king-size, bathrooms are vintage or modern, breakfasts flourish sunshine and pastries. And the surfing is amazing.

| | |
|---|---|
| Rooms | 3 doubles, 1 suite for 3: €150–€270. |
| Meals | Breakfast €10 (free breakfast on presentation of a Sawday's guide). Restaurant within walking distance. |
| Closed | November – February. |

Paul & Élisabeth Daraignez
Villa le Goëland,
12 rue Grande Atalaye,
64200 Biarritz
Pyrénées-Atlantiques

| | |
|---|---|
| Tel | +33 (0)5 59 24 25 76 |
| Mobile | +33 (0)6 87 66 22 19 |
| Email | info@villagoeland.com |
| Web | www.villagoeland.com |

Entry 529   Map 13

## Aquitaine

### Bidachuna

The electronic gate clicks behind you and 29 hectares of forested peacefulness begin – with wildlife. Open wide your beautiful curtains next morning and you may see deer feeding; lift your eyes to feast on the Pyrenean foothills; trot downstairs to the earthly feast that is Basque breakfast; fall asleep to the hoot of the owl. Shyly attentive, Isabelle manages all this impeccably and keeps a refined house where everything gleams; floors are chestnut, bathrooms are marble, family antiques are perfect. Pop off to lovely St Jean de Luz for lunch or dinner, return to this manicured haven and blissful cosseting.

| | |
|---|---|
| Rooms | 2 doubles, 1 twin: €125. Singles €115. |
| Meals | Restaurant 6km. |
| Closed | Mid-November to mid-March. |

Isabelle Ormazabal
Bidachuna,
Route D3, Lieu-dit Otsanz,
64310 St Pée sur Nivelle
Pyrénées-Atlantiques

| | |
|---|---|
| Tel | +33 (0)5 59 54 56 22 |
| Email | isabelleormazabal@gmail.com |
| Web | www.bidachuna.fr |

Entry 530   Map 13

### Les Volets Bleus

High in these ancient hills stands a beautiful new farmhouse built with old Basque materials. Chic, clever Marie has made a perfect creation. The décor has been meticulously studied, a magical effect achieved. Through the double-arch door, a flagged entrance hall, then a terrace with charming rattan chairs. Up stone staircases are bedrooms in restful colours with wood or tiled floors, gilt mirrors, embroidered sheets, ancestral paintings; exquisite bathrooms have iron towel rails and aromatic oils. Marie is an accomplished gardener so retreat to her garden for a read or a swim — or lounge in the salon on deep sofas. Heaven.

### Martzukondo Etxea

On the outskirts of the village, the big house stands in privacy well below the main road, its sloping garden offering flowers and peace. The stupendous view sweeps down the valley and up to the Pyrénées, the landmark Basque mountain 'La Rhune' rising squarely ahead. This highly civilised place has myriad family portraits, fine furniture, modern and antique art, books — and light pouring in through south-facing windows. Madame, refined, well-travelled and a keen bridge player, will show you to your elegantly old-style suite and suggest visits to lovely Bayonne and ever-fashionable Biarritz for watery fun.
*Minimum stay: 2 nights.*

| | |
|---|---|
| Rooms | 2 doubles, 1 twin: €110–€170. |
| | 1 suite for 2: €140–€186. |
| Meals | Restaurants 1.5km. |
| Closed | December – February. |

| | |
|---|---|
| Rooms | 1 suite for 2, |
| | 1 suite for 4: €85–€120. |
| | Extra room €50 per night. |
| Meals | Pizzeria within walking distance. |
| Closed | Rarely. |

| | |
|---|---|
| | **Marie de Lapasse** |
| | Les Volets Bleus, |
| | Chemin Etchegaraya, |
| | 64200 Arcangues |
| | Pyrénées-Atlantiques |
| Mobile | +33 (0)6 07 69 03 85 |
| Email | maisonlesvoletsbleus@wanadoo.fr |
| Web | www.lesvoletsbleus.fr |

| | |
|---|---|
| | **Marie-Alpaix del Moral** |
| | Martzukondo Etxea, |
| | Av de la Croix de Mouguerre, |
| | 64990 Mouguerre |
| | Pyrénées-Atlantiques |
| Tel | +33 (0)5 59 42 66 07 |
| Email | alpaix64@gmail.com |
| Web | www.chambresdecharme.net |

Entry 531   Map 13

Entry 532   Map 13

# Aquitaine

## La Bergerie d'Anne-Marie

Basque houses have a charm all of their own. This one is steeped in green hills and its views are panoramic, with thrilling sightings of the sea. Bruno, once a magazine photographer in Paris, knows and loves his neck of the woods and looks after guests with aplomb; his table d'hôtes is a delight. Bedrooms have the same fabulous views, the Squirrel Room, with mirrors and Louis XVI pieces, the most pleasing to the eye. The suite is ideal for a family, with interlinking rooms and a gorgeous old bath down four stairs. Cruise the coastal road, hop into Spain, return to an aperitif on the intimate terrace.
*Minimum stay: 2 nights.*

| | |
|---|---|
| Rooms | 1 double: €110–€140. |
| | 1 suite for 3 with bathroom |
| | downstairs: €185. |
| | Pets €20. |
| Meals | Dinner with wine, €30. |
| | Restaurant 1km. |
| Closed | November. |

| | |
|---|---|
| | **Bruno Krassinine** |
| | La Bergerie d'Anne-Marie, |
| | Chemin de Goyetchea 1285, |
| | La Croix des Bouquets, |
| | 64122 Urrugne |
| | Pyrénées-Atlantiques |
| Tel | +33 (0)5 59 20 79 44 |
| Email | bkrassinine@free.fr |
| Web | www.labergeriedannemarie.venez.fr |

Entry 533   Map 13

# Aquitaine

## Domaine de Silencenia

The ideal place for discovering the Basque country. The house cornerstone, the magnificent magnolia, the towering pines were all planted on one day in 1881. A heated pool and a lake (with fountain, boat, trout and koi carp) are set in spacious parkland, and a billiard room, sauna and small gym (for a small charge) are on tap. This sensitive restoration includes a honeymoon room, a pretty pine four-poster, a desk made from wine cases and respect for the original chestnut panelling. Philippe, aided by his young wife Ruth, is proud of his 'table gourmande'. He knows about wine, too: his cellar is brilliant. Be charmed.

| | |
|---|---|
| Rooms | 3 doubles, 2 triples: €90. |
| Meals | Dinner with wine, €30. |
| Closed | Rarely. |

| | |
|---|---|
| | **Philippe Mallor** |
| | Domaine de Silencenia, |
| | 64250 Louhossoa |
| | Pyrénées-Atlantiques |
| Tel | +33 (0)5 59 93 35 60 |
| Mobile | +33 (0)6 72 63 81 66 |
| Email | domaine.de.silencenia@orange.fr |
| Web | www.domaine-silencenia.com |

Entry 534   Map 13

## Aquitaine

### Maison Marchand

A lovely face among all the lovely faces of this listed village, the 16th-century Basque farmhouse, resuscitated by delightful French/Irish owners, is run with well-organised informality. Dinners are lively; local dishes are excellent. Discreetly luxurious bedrooms (each with its own sitting area and terrace) have beams, exposed wafer bricks, thoughtful extras. Summer breakfast is on the covered terrace in the beautiful walled garden with peaceful reading spots and three friendly cats. Your hosts delight in sharing their culture of 'pelote basque', rugby, real tennis, horses… and their passion for all things Basque.
*Minimum stay: 2 nights in high season.*

## Aquitaine

### Maison Etchebehere

The house sits surrounded by rivers and streams with vast views onto woods and hills: paradise in the Basque. Step in to a lofty, light-filled, galleried space, an uplifting mix of old and new: an ancient work bench, a sleek modern kitchen, a sweeping floor of Egyptian stone. Corinne's creative eye reaches to the bedrooms above: harmonious colours, natural materials and the deepest mattresses we have ever seen. One bathroom, with rain shower and free-standing tub, is made for lingering all day in. Wake to a breakfast feast, then it's off to Bayonne, Biarritz, the charming townlets of Bidache and Espelette… and the beaches.

| | |
|---|---|
| Rooms | 2 doubles: €75–€85.<br>1 family room for 2-4: €75–€125.<br>Extra bed/sofabed €25 per person per night. |
| Meals | Dinner with wine, €25. |
| Closed | 1 November – 31 March. |

| | |
|---|---|
| Rooms | 2 doubles, 1 twin/double: €90–€110.<br>Extra bed €20 per person per night. |
| Meals | Dinner with wine, €30. |
| Closed | January – March. |

|  |  |
|---|---|
| | Valerie & Gilbert Foix<br>Maison Marchand,<br>64240 La Bastide Clairence<br>Pyrénées-Atlantiques |
| Tel | +33 (0)5 59 29 18 27 |
| Mobile | +33 (0)6 82 78 50 95 |
| Email | maison.marchand@wanadoo.fr |
| Web | pagesperso-orange.fr/<br>maison.marchand |

|  |  |
|---|---|
| | Richard Meadmore<br>Maison Etchebehere,<br>64520 Bardos<br>Pyrénées-Atlantiques |
| Tel | +33 (0)5 59 55 13 69 |
| Email | richard@meadmore.net |
| Web | www.maison-etchebehere.com/<br>index2-en.html |

Entry 535  Map 13

Entry 536  Map 13

## La Closerie du Guilhat

Through the iron gates, up the tree-lined drive to an astonishing kingdom of plants of all shapes and sizes: a hidden garden of exotica. Weave your way through rhododendrons and magnolias, bananas and bamboos to secret benches for reading and the Pyrénées as a backdrop. A delight for all ages! To this sturdy and spotless Béarn house with its solid old furniture Marie-Christine – a genuine and generous host – has added her own decorative touches. Table tennis is shared with gîte guests, dinners are delicious. The other-worldliness is restorative yet the spa town of Salies is a pedal away.

## La Bergerie

Through ancient woods and unspoilt farmland you wind your way up to little Montestrucq, to a farm half a mile from the church, steeped in ancient character. Now, in the former bergerie, are sheepskin-strewn sofas, standing timbers, a huge open fire and, upstairs, bedrooms charming and cosy… Irish bed linen, pure wool carpets, Italian walk-in showers. Cassoulets, piperades, fondues, wild boar: Didier loves his 'cuisine gourmande' and sources with gusto; Sabine is full of smiles. The house faces south, the pool is inviting, and views soar over the hills to the majestic Pyrénées.

| | |
|---|---|
| Rooms | 1 double, 1 twin: €60-€66. 1 suite for 4: €74-€88. |
| Meals | Dinner €22. Wine from €16. |
| Closed | Rarely. |

| | |
|---|---|
| Rooms | 2 doubles; 1 twin with private bathroom across hallway: €90. Extra bed/sofabed €14 per person per night. |
| Meals | Lunch €18. Dinner with wine, €31. Gastronomic dinner with wine, €39. Restaurants 10km. |
| Closed | Never. |

|  |  |
|---|---|
| | **Marie-Christine Potiron** La Closerie du Guilhat, 64270 Salies de Béarn Pyrénées-Atlantiques |
| Tel | +33 (0)5 59 38 08 80 |
| Email | guilhat@club-internet.fr |
| Web | www.closerieduguilhat.com |

|  |  |
|---|---|
| | **Sabine & Didier Meyer** La Bergerie, 2 chemin de Lhostebielh, 64300 Montestrucq Pyrénées-Atlantiques |
| Tel | +33 (0)5 59 38 63 76 |
| Mobile | +33 (0)6 14 83 53 24 |
| Email | sabine.meyer3@orange.fr |
| Web | www.sites.google.com/site/labergeriebearn |

Entry 537   Map 13

Entry 538   Map 13

## Domaine de la Carrère

Country-house grandeur! With its oak panelling, parquet floors and ancient beams this house feels solid, strong and in keeping with its illustrious past and royal connections. Built during the reign of Louis XIV, it was the village town hall before the current owners moved in. Bedrooms are classically elegant with high ceilings, carved bedheads, flamboyant drapes; bathrooms are high luxe. Quiet corners display plump sofas while the garden is lush with terraces, lawns and a dreamy pool. Historic Pau is 20 minutes away and glorious Biarritz 40; return to Fritz's fabulous dinner amid candles and cut glass.

## Château de Bouillon

A 14th-century 'donjon' restored by British couple Rory and Mini, now a charming wisteria-draped family home. The grandeur begins at the wrought-iron gates and continues to the formal gardens, retreats inside to the elegant 18th-century salon and culminates in the stately dining room, where breakfast is served beneath the ancestors. Throw open the shutters of one of the grand double bedrooms – blessed by antique beds and marble bathrooms – and breathe in the peace. Mini holds the prestigious status of 'master of wine'; you will appreciate this over a glass on the terrace, gazing towards the snow-capped Pyrénées. *Extra beds available.*

| | |
|---|---|
| Rooms | 4 doubles, 1 twin: €95–€125. |
| Meals | Dinner with wine, €35. |
| Closed | Rarely. |

| | |
|---|---|
| Rooms | 1 double, 1 twin/double: €130. |
| Meals | Dinner €25. |
| | Wine €12–€60. |
| | Restaurant 4km. |
| Closed | November – March, except by arrangement. |

Fritz Kisby & Mike Ridout
Domaine de la Carrère,
54 rue la Carrère,
64370 Arthez de Béarn
Pyrénées-Atlantiques
Tel     +33 (0)5 24 37 61 24
Mobile  +33 (0)6 32 96 34 62
Email   info@domaine-de-la-carrere.fr
Web     www.domaine-de-la-carrere.fr

Rory & Mini Constant
Château de Bouillon,
8 chemin des Berges du Luy,
64410 Bouillon
Pyrénées-Atlantiques
Tel    +33 (0)5 59 81 40 95
Email  info@chateaubedbreakfast.com
Web    www.chateaubedbreakfast.com

## Aquitaine

### Château de Baylac

The charming Darrigrands discovered their enchanting B&B in fairytale style... Wandering through remote woodland, they stumbled upon an ancient château abandoned for decades. Restoring the neglected building became a labour of love for the whole family. It is still off the beaten track, only the bucolic sounds of deer rutting and cows chewing the cud breaks the silence, but interiors are now fabulously stylish. Sleep in distinctive rooms, from playful 'Vivaldi' to the minimalist-chic of 'Perce-Neige'; all have luxurious bathrooms. Explore Béarn on horseback or from a hot air balloon; then dine beneath chandeliers.

| Rooms | 2 doubles, 3 suites for 2: €138. |
|---|---|
| Meals | Dinner with aperitif, wine & coffee, €37. Restaurants 6km. |
| Closed | Never. |

Jacqueline et Patrick Darrigrand
Château de Baylac,
64190 Bugnein
Pyrénées-Atlantiques

| Mobile | +33 (0)6 07 80 72 54 |
|---|---|
| Email | patrickdarrigrand@yahoo.fr |
| Web | www.chateaudebaylac.com |

## Aquitaine

### Domaine Lespoune

Renovated with panache in unsung Béarn, this 18th-century manor calms and charms. Easy-going and interesting, Nicole and Yves poured their hearts into its restoration: panelling, tiled and wooden floors, original doors, and added modern touches: colourwashed walls, contemporary art, walk-in showers. The ground-floor bedroom has a striking black-and-white tiled floor and a private terrace; the rooms upstairs are palely soft (one with a covered balcony). Breakfast under the spreading magnolia, spend the day fishing, return to Nicole's beautiful food — and a Navarrenx cigar in the garden.

| Rooms | 3 doubles, 1 twin: €75–€95. 1 suite for 4: €95–€105. €10 supplement for single-night stays, July/August. |
|---|---|
| Meals | Dinner with wine, €25–€38. |
| Closed | 15 November – 15 March. |

Yves & Nicole Everaert
Domaine Lespoune,
20 route de Camblong,
64190 Castetnau Camblong
Pyrénées-Atlantiques

| Tel | +33 (0)5 59 66 24 14 |
|---|---|
| Email | contact@lespoune.fr |
| Web | www.lespoune.fr |

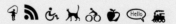

## Maison L'Aubèle

The Desbonnets transformed their grand 18th-century village house after finding it and this sleepy village in the Pyrenean foothills: both house and owners are quiet, elegant, sophisticated and full of interest. He collects precious old books, she binds them, and her furniture and florals are a feast for the eyes. As you breakfast off fine china ask what you need to know about the region, and do delve into their tempting library. The light, airy bedrooms have more interesting furniture on lovely wooden floors. 'La Rose' is very chic, 'La Verte' is large and luminous with views of the mountains and a 'waltz-in' bathroom.

| Rooms | 2 doubles: €70–€75. |
| --- | --- |
| Meals | Restaurants 4km. |
| Closed | Rarely. |

**Marie-France Desbonnet**
Maison L'Aubèle,
4 rue de la Hauti,
64190 Lay Lamidou
Pyrénées-Atlantiques
Tel      +33 (0)5 59 66 00 44
Mobile   +33 (0)6 86 22 02 76
Email    desbonnet.bmf@infonie.fr
Web      www.laubele.fr

Entry 543   Map 13

## La Bastide Estratte

In six remote hectares of woodland with Pyrenean peaks beyond, a solid slate-roofed farmhouse. Enter the wide stone arch into a beautiful balcony-fringed, flagstoned courtyard: sip a cappuccino among ornamental acers, japonicas, and box hedges as Virginia creeper winds her way over the walls. Inside, a patina of light greys, olives and ecru provides a studied canvas for polished floors, white sofas, porcelain in bookcases, fine fittings and herbal prints. Lovely, lively Chantale will help with Jurançon wine routes, excellent restaurants and fantastic walks. If it's all too cool, hop in the jacuzzi. *Minimum stay: 2 nights.*

| Rooms | 3 doubles: €85. |
| --- | --- |
| | Singles €75. |
| | Extra bed €30 per person per night. |
| Meals | Restaurants 10km. |
| Closed | Rarely. |

**Chantale Albert**
La Bastide Estratte,
Quartier St Michel, Chemin de Bas
Afittes, 64360 Lucq de Béarn
Pyrénées-Atlantiques
Tel      +33 (0)5 59 34 32 45
Mobile   +33 (0)6 22 64 16 55
Email    chantale.albert@nordnet.fr
Web      www.labastide-estratte.com

Entry 544   Map 13

Aquitaine

Aquitaine

### Château de Lamothe

An idyll of indulgence whose grandiose interior makes you feel like royalty but whose playful touches make you feel at home. Breakfast in a dining room of gilt mouldings and candelabras, then slink off to the billiard room, the home cinema, the plush aubergine salon. A lavish Designers Guild décor complements flat-screens and walk-in showers, while Pyrenean backdrops frame expansive gardens – the pool is fabulously discreet. Your charming Dutch hosts prepare evening meals of local specialities or dishes from their global travels; they'll tell you the places to go, the wines to drink. A beguiling place you'll long to return to.

### Chambres d'Hôtes Les 3 Baudets

This 17th-century manor, in sight of the Pyrénées, is a happy and beautifully run place: your hosts – French Véronique, German Werner – are old hands at hospitality. Guests stay in the cosy converted barn where evenings can be spent over Werner's lovingly prepared dinners. Each fresh, pretty bedroom has a wall of warm colour – mango orange, deep yellow. Through wrought-iron gates are leisurely gardens and a lovely pool. It's tempting to stay all day but this is spectacular hiking, skiing and canyoning country: rivers gush, hills roll, the fabulous Cirque de Lescun beckons, Lourdes and Biarritz should not be missed. *Minimum stay: 2 nights in high season.*

| | | | | |
|---|---|---|---|---|
| Rooms | 4 doubles: €225–€285. 1 family room for 4-6: €295. | | Rooms | 4 twin/doubles: €75–€85. Singles €50–€65. |
| Meals | Dinner €55. Restaurant 5km. | | Meals | Dinner €25. Wine €10–€35. |
| Closed | Rarely. | | Closed | November – January. |

Laurent Nederlof
Château de Lamothe,
64400 Moumour
Pyrénées-Atlantiques
Mobile +33 (0)6 88 28 38 61
Email laurentnederlof@gmail.com
Web www.chateau-de-lamothe.eu

Véronique & Werner Stich
Chambres d'Hôtes Les 3 Baudets,
Maison Escoubes,
64570 Issor
Pyrénées-Atlantiques
Tel +33 (0)5 59 34 41 98
Email 3baudets@wanadoo.fr
Web www.3baudets-pyrenees.com

Entry 545  Map 13

Entry 546  Map 13

## Maison Rancèsamy

Painters love this haven and respond to Isabelle's own gentle talent; she is the loveliest hostess. From terrace and pool you can see for ever into the Pyrénées – sunlit snowy in winter, all the greens in summer. Beside the 1700s farmhouse, the barn conversion shelters artistic, uncluttered, stone-walled bedrooms and incredible views. The superb dining room – Isabelle's trompe-l'œil floor, huge carved table – reflects the origins (Polish, French, South African) of this happy, relaxed couple. On balmy summer evenings, the food (book ahead) is deliciously garden-aromatic: Simon is a powerful, eco-aware gardener. Wonderful.
*Minimum stay: 2 nights in high season.*

| Rooms | 2 doubles, 1 twin: €75–€90. |
| | 2 family rooms for 4: €108–€125. |
| Meals | Dinner with wine, €32. |
| Closed | Rarely. |

**Simon & Isabelle Browne**
Maison Rancèsamy,
Quartier Rey,
64290 Lasseube
Pyrénées-Atlantiques

| Tel | +33 (0)5 59 04 26 37 |
| Email | missbrowne@wanadoo.fr |
| Web | www.missbrowne.com |

Entry 547  Map 13

## Clos Mirabel

Fifteen minutes from city lights, yet surrounded by vineyards. French-Canadian André is a retired diplomat, Ann worked in travel, Emily goes to the village school. They fell in love with Clos Mirabel five years ago, now they delightedly welcome guests. The 18th-century manor is flanked by a winery and gatehouse; the interiors are light, airy and restful, their gracious proportions enhanced by Ann's elegant eye. A spiral staircase links the Gustavian apartment's three levels, there's a pool terrace with breathtaking Pyrenean views and breakfast honey comes from André's bees. Outstanding.

| Rooms | 2 doubles: €110–€159. |
| | 1 apartment for 2-4 with kitchen: |
| | €139–€217. |
| | Extra bed €35 per person per night. |
| Meals | Restaurants 3km. |
| Closed | Rarely. |

**Ann Kenny & André Péloquin**
Clos Mirabel,
276 av des Frères Barthélémy,
Jurançon, 64110 Pau
Pyrénées-Atlantiques

| Tel | +33 (0)5 59 06 32 83 |
| Mobile | +33 (0)6 79 59 04 91 |
| Email | info@closmirabel.com |
| Web | www.closmirabel.com |

Entry 548  Map 13

Photo: iStock.com/Wierinkevitiea

# Limousin

www.sawdays.co.uk/limousin

## Limousin

### Château de la Côte

The château, in a charmed setting with immense views, has been in Madame's family since 1204. It was rebuilt in 1560, and rebuilt again two centuries later; the history is fascinating, the architecture is delightful. Bedrooms have patterned wallpapers, comfy antiques, parquet floors and paintings dotted about. 'Renaissance' is darkish but wonderfully lofty, the simple family suite is up a spiral stair, and 'Amethyst' in the annexe is airy and modern. Swim in the pool, fish on the lake, admire the roses, eat out in Mézières – then wake to a breakfast of homemade jams and local 'fromage blanc' in the dining room in the grounds.

| | |
|---|---|
| Rooms | 2 doubles: €82–€87. 1 suite for 4: €138–€145. Double & suite can be rented together, €205–€215. |
| Meals | Restaurants 4.5km. |
| Closed | Mid-October to Easter. |

Isabelle Foujols
Château de la Côte,
2 La Côte,
87330 Mézières sur Issoire
Haute-Vienne

| | |
|---|---|
| Tel | +33 (0)5 55 68 33 98 |
| Mobile | +33 (0)6 82 37 30 65 |
| Email | isafoujols@hotmail.com |
| Web | www.lechateaudelacote.com |

## Limousin

### La Flambée

You will find simple French value and a sweet, hard-working young couple in this organic smallholding. They genuinely like sharing their country fare, created from home-grown vegetables and home-reared lamb, duck, pigeon and rabbit (delicious pâtés). Myriam cares for their children, potager and guests and is redoing the rooms with fun and colour; Pierre, a builder by trade, looks after the animals and myriad house improvements. The 18th-century roadside farmhouse has characterful old wood – a great oak staircase, beams, timber framing – family clutter, fireplaces, peaceful bedrooms and a garden full of toys. *Children over 12 welcome. Extra bed available.*

| | |
|---|---|
| Rooms | 1 double: €45. 1 family room for 3, 2 family rooms for 4: €55–€65. |
| Meals | Dinner with wine, €18. |
| Closed | Rarely. |

Pierre & Myriam Morice
La Flambée,
Thoveyrat, 87300 Blond
Haute-Vienne

| | |
|---|---|
| Tel | +33 (0)5 55 68 86 86 |
| Email | chambrehote@freesurf.fr |
| Web | www.laflambee.info |

## Limousin

### Château du Fraisse

After 800 years of family and estate symbiosis, Le Fraisse is a living history book, mainly a rustic-grand Renaissance gem by the great Serlio – pale limestone, discreetly elegant portico, Henry II staircase and an astonishing fireplace in the vast drawing room. Your cultured hosts, two generations now, will greet you with warmth, happily tell you about house and history and show you to your room: fine furniture, paintings and prints, traditional furnishings; one bathroom has a fragment of a 16th-century fresco. If you return late at night you must climb the steep old spiral stair to your room as the main door is locked.

| | |
|---|---|
| Rooms | 1 double, 1 twin: €90–€100.<br>1 suite for 3, 1 suite for 4: €130–€165. |
| Meals | Restaurants 6km. |
| Closed | Mid-December to mid-January. |

**Marquis & Marquise des Monstiers Mérinville**
Château du Fraisse,
Le Fraisse, 87330 Nouic
Haute-Vienne
Tel   +33 (0)5 55 68 32 68
Email  infos@chateau-du-fraisse.com
Web   www.chateau-du-fraisse.com

Entry 551   Map 9

## Limousin

### Château Ribagnac

Patrick and Colette are intelligent, thoughtful and enthusiastic, and their château, built in 1647, is an absolute treat. Grand fireplaces, original features, rugs on oak floors, superb new bathrooms (one loo in its turret): the conversion is authentic, not luxurious but elegantly comfortable. Ask for a lighter room with views over park and lake. Outside: a children's play area, an organic kitchen garden, a pool in the offing, an orchard you can enjoy... tranquillity and views. The local meat is succulent, there is a deep commitment. Conversation flows with the wine. *Minimum stay: 2 nights in high season.*

| | |
|---|---|
| Rooms | 4 suites for 2-5: €100–€160. |
| Meals | Dinner with wine, €45. |
| Closed | Christmas. |

**Patrick & Colette Bergot**
Château Ribagnac,
87400 St Martin Terressus
Haute-Vienne
Tel   +33 (0)5 55 39 77 91
Email  reservations@chateauribagnac.com
Web   www.chateauribagnac.com

Entry 552   Map 9

## Limousin

### Magnac

In an ancient manor of enormous personality, your live-wire hostess, once a Parisian designer, now paints porcelain, organises cultural events and struggles to renovate the family house and its wild park with deep respect for its originality. Utterly endearing in its battered aristocracy, it is one room deep: light pours in from both sides onto heavy floorboards, 18th-century panelling and a delightful tower cocktail room. The traditional-style bedroom in the main house is vast, the snugger suite in the half-timbered orangery is ideal if you'd rather be independent. *Children over 2 welcome.*

| | |
|---|---|
| Rooms | 1 twin/double: €110. |
| | 1 suite for 3: €110–€150. |
| Meals | Dinner with wine, €45. |
| Closed | Rarely. |

Catherine & Bertrand de la Bastide
Magnac,
87380 Magnac Bourg
Haute-Vienne

| | |
|---|---|
| Mobile | +33 (0)6 03 08 79 19 |
| Email | catdelabastide@gmail.com |
| Web | www.chateaumagnacbourg.fr |

Entry 553   Map 9

## Limousin

### Moulin de Marsaguet

The nicest people, they have done just enough to this proud old building so it looks as it did 200 years ago when it forged cannon balls. The farm is relaxed and natural, the bedrooms quaint, they have ducks and animals (including Lusitanian horses), three teenagers and a super potager, and make pâtés and 'confits' by the great mill pond, hanging the hams over the magnificent hearth in their big stone sitting room with its old-fashioned sofa. Relish the drive up past tree-framed lake (boating possible) and stone outbuildings and the prospect of breakfasting on home-grown ingredients. *Pets by arrangement.*

| | |
|---|---|
| Rooms | 3 twin/doubles: €60. |
| Meals | Dinner with wine, €22. |
| | Restaurant 3km. |
| Closed | November to mid-April. |

Valérie & Renaud Gizardin
Moulin de Marsaguet,
87500 Coussac Bonneval
Haute-Vienne

| | |
|---|---|
| Tel | +33 (0)5 55 75 28 29 |
| Mobile | +33 (0)6 26 16 34 47 |
| Email | renaudvalerie.gizardin@orange.fr |
| Web | www.moulindemarsaguet.com |

Entry 554   Map 9

# Limousin

## L'Arrosoir

This eccentric marvel appears at first sight to be more rusted than rustic, but the pitted walls conceal a modern interior that displays a gifted use of water and light. The ground floor is almost entirely occupied by an indoor pool which sparkles in the sunshine flooding in from the innovative half roof. The bedroom is on an island to the rear of the building, where a rise in the floor creates a natural dry spot so that the beds overlook the pool, but the en suite tube shower is often cold and can flood the whole property. You'll find it all too easy to spill out on to the terrace and just watch the garden grow.

| Rooms | 1 tin. |
| | Price: Check local water rates. |
| Meals | Free sunshine for absorption. |
| Closed | All year round – banned in summer, not needed in winter. |

**Jacques dujardin**
L'Arrosoir,
Saint Fiacre-sous-Robinet
Creuse
Tel +44 (0)117 204 7810
Email pour@plants.net
Web www.sawdays.co.uk

Entry 555   Map 9

# Limousin

## Les Drouilles Bleues

High on a granite hill, with views to swell your heart, the low stone house and its greenly rocky garden creak with age and history. As does the whole region. Paul and Maïthé, a most intelligent and attentive couple, take their hosting to heart, greeting with homemade treats, revelling in – and joining – the people who gather at their convivial and tasty dinner table. In converted outbuildings, handsome bedrooms large (the suite) and smaller, are simple, a touch old-fashioned and done with care and soft colours. All have working fireplaces, sleeping quarters on mezzanines, good shower rooms. Deeply, discreetly, welcoming.

| Rooms | 2 doubles: €70-€93. |
| | 1 suite for 5: €90-€150. |
| | Single €65-€88. |
| | Extra bed/sofabed €15 per person per night. |
| Meals | Dinner with wine, €26. |
| | Children under 12, €15. |
| Closed | Rarely. |

**Maïthé & Paul de Bettignies**
Les Drouilles Bleues,
La Drouille,
87800 St Hilaire les Places
Haute-Vienne
Tel +33 (0)5 55 58 21 26
Email lesdrouillesbleues@gmail.com
Web drouillesbleues.free.fr

Entry 556   Map 9

# Limousin

## La Pissarelle

In a green and lovely corner of France, discover the wee hamlet where Annie's family have always farmed. Here she and Wolfgang (he worked with NATO and speaks impeccable English) have returned to renovate a highly personal, treasure-filled farmhouse with a cosily simple Petite Maison for guests just across the patio. Having lived all over the world, they adore having visitors at their table in the former cattle byre or in the new veranda – and hope you might park your horses in their field. Before the vast ex-château fireplace, you will be regaled with tales of local life and exotic lands. A fascinating couple. *Extra single room available.*

| | |
|---|---|
| Rooms | 1 cottage for 4: €60–€150. |
| Meals | Dinner with wine, €28. |
| | 2-course lunch €15. |
| | Picnic €10. Restaurant 7km. |
| Closed | Rarely. |

|  |  |
|---|---|
| | Wolfgang & Annie Oelsner |
| | La Pissarelle, |
| | La Clupte, |
| | 23430 Châtelus le Marcheix |
| | Creuse |
| Tel | +33 (0)5 55 64 30 58 |
| Mobile | +33 (0)6 73 00 26 68 |
| Email | lapissarelle@gmail.com |
| Web | www.lapissarelle.com |

    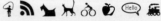

Entry 557    Map 9

# Limousin

## Maison Grandchamp

In an historic town, be welcomed by a charming, cultured couple to a 400-year-old house of fascinating origins. Thrill to Marielle's tales: her ancestors built and extended the house, their portraits hang in the panelled drawing room; find time for François' knowledge of history, geography and the environment. Up the elegant spiral stairs, bedrooms are in proper but unpompous château style, big, soft and quiet. Breakfast is in the beamy 16th-century dining room, or by the kitchen fire, or in the terraced garden overlooking jumbled rooftops, or in the luminous veranda. Then explore glorious Corrèze.

| Rooms | 2 twin/doubles; 1 twin/double with separate bathroom: €80–€90. Extra bed €25 per person per night. Overflow room for 2 available. |
|---|---|
| Meals | Dinner with aperitif & wine €29–€32. Restaurants within walking distance. |
| Closed | January – March. |

**Marielle & François Teyssier**
Maison Grandchamp,
9 place des Pénitents,
19260 Treignac
Corrèze

| | |
|---|---|
| Tel | +33 (0)5 55 98 10 69 |
| Mobile | +33 (0)6 59 05 09 46 |
| Email | teyssier.marielle@wanadoo.fr |
| Web | www.hotesgrandchamp.com |

Entry 558  Map 10

# Limousin

## Maison Numéro Neuf

Lisa and Duncan from England have embraced life in southern La Souterraine. She is the least ruffled, most contented of chefs; he serves wines with finesse; both love house, children, guests, and their secret garden with hens. Now, at last, the renovation of the former residence of the Marquis de Valady is complete. So much to enjoy: the fine proportions, the sweeping balustrade, the antique mirrors, the crystal-drop chandeliers, the pale walls, the glowing parquet... and superb breakfasts and dinners. If Lisa pops a hot water bottle into your bed it will be encased in white linen: the hospitality here is exceptional.

| Rooms | 2 doubles; 1 twin sharing shower: €65–€115. |
|---|---|
| Meals | Dinner €22–€45. Wine €18. |
| Closed | Rarely. |

**Duncan & Lisa Rowney**
Maison Numéro Neuf,
Rue Serpente,
23300 La Souterraine
Creuse

| | |
|---|---|
| Tel | +33 (0)5 55 63 43 35 |
| Email | reservations@maisonnumeroneuf.com |
| Web | www.maisonnumeroneuf.com |

Entry 559  Map 9

# Auvergne

www.sawdays.co.uk/auvergne

Photo: iStock.com/JordiRoy

## Auvergne

### Château de Clusors

Atop a hill, this small château has gazed on untouched countryside since the 14th century. Steeped in history (Henri is full of stories; Madame de Montespan once stayed here), the place is still a working farm: friendly and down-to-earth, Madame manages a herd of Charolais cows. Up the spiral stone stair are big bedrooms with fine furniture and excellent modern bathrooms; breakfast is set before family portraits and a bookcase stocked with leather-bound tomes. Outside: a large garden with orchard and pool; rest in the shade of a lime tree and admire the magnificent view. Wonderfully, authentically French.

| Rooms | 2 triples: €105. |
| --- | --- |
| | Extra bed €20 per person per night. |
| Meals | Cold meats and vegetable platter, €10. |
| | Restaurants 1km. |
| Closed | Rarely. |

**Christine & Henri Thieulin**
Château de Clusors,
03210 St Menoux
Allier

| Tel | +33 (0)4 70 43 94 69 |
| --- | --- |
| Mobile | +33 (0)6 70 79 27 75 |
| Email | henri.thieulin@orange.fr |
| Web | www.chateaudeclusors.com |

## Auvergne

*New Entry*
INSPECTED & SELECTED
A SPECIAL PLACE

### Château Neureux

With bucolic views to hills, pastures, lake and stream, a perfect little 18th-century getaway. It is now home to a Dutch film director and an American ballerina, a hospitable, delightful pair. Past deep-red walls and a beaded Deco chandelier find big elegant bedrooms that mix French classicism with Dutch sobriety, ornate wallpapers with louvered French shutters. As you tuck into breakfast's pâtisseries, gaze through tall windows to the vast estate where peacocks and donkeys roam, wild deer and foxes saunter, and a pool (shared with the gîte guests) tempts behind orchard walls. Rent bikes, stride into the hills, fish on the lake…

| Rooms | 2 doubles, 2 twin/doubles: €110–€130. |
| --- | --- |
| | 1 suite for 4: €175. |
| | Extra bed/sofabed €15 per person |
| | per night. |
| Meals | Dinner, 4 courses, €23. |
| | Child €15. Restaurant 1km. |
| Closed | Rarely. |

**Roeland Kerbosch &
Valerie Valentine**
Château Neureux,
03320 Lurcy Lévis
Allier

| Mobile | +33 (0)6 15 86 03 67 |
| --- | --- |
| Email | info@chateauneureux.com |
| Web | www.chateauneureux.com |

## Auvergne

### Domaine d'Aigrepont

Madame greets you warmly outside the original 1640s manor that her ancestors built overlooking the Allier valley. Round a grassy courtyard, the manor, chapel and handsome guest wing float in a sea of terraced gardens surging with lavender, jasmine, roses, vines and a pool. Named after family heroes, bedrooms breathe authenticity with high beams, beautiful antiques, oriental rugs, fireplaces, snow-white linen and new bathrooms, one with a bulls-eye to the courtyard. Breakfast on homemade brioche, dive into the valley for walks, gardens, vineyards and thermal baths, then off to Moulins for dinner.

| Rooms | 1 double, 1 twin/double, 1 twin: €120-€130. Singles €120. |
| --- | --- |
| Meals | Catered meals available. Restaurant 5km. |
| Closed | October – April. |

Édith de Contenson
Domaine d'Aigrepont,
Aigrepont,
03000 Bressolles
Allier

| Mobile | +33 (0)6 80 05 51 02 |
| --- | --- |
| Email | postmaster@chambres-d-hotes-en-bourbonnais.com |
| Web | www.aigrepont.com |

Entry 562  Map 10

## Auvergne

### Maison Cognet

Billowing hilly pastures wrap the hamlet in sensuality. Built in 1886 as a rich man's summer place, here is a generous, sophisticated house informed by Madame's broad cultural interests, her father's paintings and her fine Provençal furniture that looks perfect beside the beautiful original panelling and wide fireplace. Up steep shiny stairs, the guest space is a sweep of pine floor and ceiling; light floods over sitting area, big pine bed, old chest; a proud tree shades the splendid shower room. Deep rest, super breakfast and conversation, Romanesque jewels to visit, beauty sessions in Vichy – a must.

| Rooms | 1 twin/double: €70. |
| --- | --- |
| Meals | Dinner with wine, €15. Restaurants 7km. |
| Closed | November – February. |

Bénita Mourges
Maison Cognet,
03300 La Chapelle
Allier

| Tel | +33 (0)4 70 41 88 28 |
| --- | --- |
| Mobile | +33 (0)6 98 47 54 48 |
| Email | maison.cognet@free.fr |
| Web | maison.cognet.free.fr |

Entry 563  Map 10

## Château du Ludaix

Pure château with a touch of humour, Ludaix is glamorous, dramatic and utterly welcoming. David and Stephanie have boundless energy, love people (they run a training company) and lavish care on house and guests. David is exploring the archives ("Ludaix is a living history book"), and rebuilding the ancient waterworks and shady walks in the wood. Stephanie's talent cossets the rich warm rooms with English and French antiques ancient and modern, myriad hats, clocks and costumes, the odd tented ceiling. Gorgeous rooms, imaginative bathrooms, delicious food, great conversation – and lots more. *Whole house available.*

## Manoir de la Manantie

Passionate about regional gastronomy – do eat with them, it's a treat – Véronique and Guillaume quit Paris to pour their talents into this fine neoclassical manor. They've done it up to the nines, from the grand entrance with its volcanic stone stair, smart in crisp red, to the big, super-modern bathrooms. Grand, high-ceilinged bedrooms (the suite is vast), are full of light and antique furniture. The woodwork alone is worth a visit, so too is the English gentleman's room, with its head-high hog-roasting fireplace. Walk into Lezoux, stroll in the park and enjoy the Auvergne's fabulous National Parks – and cheese.

| | |
|---|---|
| Rooms | 2 suites for 2, 1 suite for 3, 1 suite for 4: €120–€180. |
| Meals | Dinner, 4 courses with wine, €40. |
| Closed | January/February. |

| | |
|---|---|
| Rooms | 2 doubles: €95–€120. 1 suite for 3: €117–€163. 1 apartment for 3: €183–€223. Singles €84–€89. Dinner, B&B €20 extra per person. Extra bed/sofabed €30 per person per night. |
| Meals | Dinner €16–€20. Children under 9, €10. Wine €15–€35. |
| Closed | Never. |

**David Morton & Stephanie Holland**
Château du Ludaix,
Rue du Ludaix,
03420 Marcillat en Combraille
Allier

Tel +33 (0)4 70 51 62 32
Mobile +44 (0)7739 431918
Email stephanie@rapport-online.com
Web www.chateauduludaix.com

**Veronique Vernat-Rossi**
Manoir de la Manantie,
Rue Georges Clémenceau,
63190 Lezoux
Puy-de-Dôme

Tel +33 (0)4 44 05 21 46
Email veronique@manoir-manantie.fr
Web www.manoir-manantie.fr

# Auvergne

## Château de Vaulx

Is it real or a fairy tale? Creak along the parquet, swan around the salon, sleep in one tower, wash in another. It's been in the family for 800 years, well-lived-in rooms have peace and romantic furnishings – worthy of the troubadours who sang here. Breakfast on home-hived honey, brioche, yogurt, eggs, cheese, get to know the four delightful young hosts who are nurturing it, as their parents did, with joy – and updating a bit. Visit the donkey, walk from quiet lawn into sweeping view, tuck into Philippe's tasty cuisine. Feeling homesick? Have a drink in Guy's cellar 'pub' with its collection of beer mats. A dream of a place. *Arrival after 5pm.*

| Rooms | 2 doubles: €80–€100. |
| | 1 family room for 3: €100–€130. |
| | Extra bed/sofabed €30 per person per night. |
| Meals | Dinner with wine, €30. |
| Closed | November – April. |

**Guy & Régine Dumas de Vaulx,**
**Philippe & Martine Vast**
Château de Vaulx,
63120 Ste Agathe
Puy-de-Dôme

| Tel | +33 (0)4 73 51 50 55 |
| Mobile | +33 (0)6 42 01 11 94 |
| Email | ph.vast@orange.fr |
| Web | www.chateaudevaulx.fr |

Entry 566   Map 10

---

# Auvergne

## Domaine de Gaudon – Le Château

Tranquil and unexpected: smart new Medici urns outside, 19th-century splendour within, glossy oak panelling, fine stucco, original glowing blue paint. Alain and Monique, generous and attentive, have created a setting of astonishing brass, gilt and quilted glamour for their polished French antiques. A fabulous wellness centre and buzzing, trilling, wooded and watery grounds. Bedrooms are extravagant; bathrooms splendidly classical. Breakfasts dazzle: Auvergne ham, baked apple, homemade nut cake, honey and jams in the Salon Bleu (coffered timber ceiling, great timber fireplace, wooden chandelier).

| Rooms | 3 doubles, 1 twin: €120. |
| | 1 suite for 2: €140. |
| | Extra bed €25 per person per night. |
| Meals | Supper trays available. |
| | Restaurant 4km. |
| Closed | Rarely. |

**Alain & Monique Bozzo**
Domaine de Gaudon – Le Château,
63520 Ceilloux
Puy-de-Dôme

| Tel | +33 (0)4 73 70 76 25 |
| Email | domainedegaudon@wanadoo.fr |
| Web | www.domainedegaudon.fr |

Entry 567   Map 10

## Auvergne

### Château Royal de Saint-Saturnin

A volcanic region is the perfect cradle for this magnificently turreted and castellated fortress, high on the forested fringes of one of France's most beautiful villages. A stone spiral, worn with age and history, leads to five swish bedrooms in the oldest wing. The Louis XIII suite, its bathroom tucked into a tower, spans the castle's width; views are to tumbling rooftops and gardens and parkland behind. The vaulted dining room, decked with gleaming coppers, is the background for relaxed breakfast spreads, and your hosts are friendly and well-travelled. Once owned by Catherine de Médici, now open to the public.

## Auvergne

### Le Chastel Montaigu

The solid reality of this magical tower is deeply moving. Michel's renovation skills (well, reconstruction from near-ruin), Anita's decorating talent and Virginie's sense of style have summoned a richly sober mood that makes the 15th-century *chastel* throb with authenticity: only 'medieval' materials; magnificent deep-tinted fabrics, many designed by Anita; antique tapestries, panelling and furniture; and a lavender-wafted south-facing garden and shaded terrace. Dozens of steps lead to spectacular bedrooms, brilliantly original bathrooms and views that stretch for ever… a very special, very generous retreat. *Minimum stay: 2 nights. Babes in arms & children over 15 welcome. Cot, high chair & all other baby equipment available.*

| | |
|---|---|
| Rooms | 2 doubles: €200–€240. |
| | 2 suites for 2-3, 1 suite for 2-5: €240–€270. |
| | Extra bed/sofabed €20–€40 per person per night. |
| Meals | Breakfast €14. |
| | Restaurant 1.5km. |
| Closed | 11 November – 20 March. |

| | |
|---|---|
| Rooms | 2 doubles, 1 twin/double with separate wcs: €145–€170. |
| | 1 family room for 3 with separate wc: €150–€180. |
| Meals | Supper with glass of wine, €25. |
| | Auberge & restaurants 1-4km. |
| Closed | October – March. |

**Emmanuel & Christine Pénicaud**
Château Royal de Saint-Saturnin,
Place de l'Ormeau,
63450 Saint Saturnin
Puy-de-Dôme

Tel +33 (0)4 73 39 39 64
Email contact@chateaudesaintsaturnin.com
Web www.chateaudesaintsaturnin.com

**Anita, Virginie & Michel Sauvadet**
Le Chastel Montaigu,
Le Château,
63320 Montaigut le Blanc
Puy-de-Dôme

Tel +33 (0)4 73 96 28 49
Mobile +33 (0)6 81 61 52 26
Email infos@lechastelmontaigu.com
Web www.lechastelmontaigu.com

Entry 568  Map 10

Entry 569  Map 10

## Les Frênes

Perched above Saint Nectaire, the old farmhouse has stupendous views from its hillside garden of the Romanesque jewel below and woods and mountains soaring beyond. Monique, chatty and knowledgeable, enthuses her guests with descriptions of the Auvergne in perfect English. She doesn't pretend to offer luxury, just the cosy comfort of a real home. You stay in an attached one-bedroom cottage with a shower and kitchen area downstairs. Breakfast is in Monique and Daniel's vaulted dining room, full of exposed beams and stone; eat copiously and enjoy the humour, zest and kindness of a couple who were born to hospitality. Astonishing value. *Parking available.*

## La Closerie de Manou

The rambling old house sits solid among the ancient volcanoes of Auvergne where great rivers rise and water is pure (it's in the taps here). There's a fine garden for games, a family-sized dining table before the great fireplace and a mixed bag of friendly armchairs guarded by a beautiful Alsatian stove in the salon. The décor is properly, comfortably rustic, bedrooms are lightly floral, no bows or furbelows, just pretty warmth and good shower rooms. Maryvonne, intelligent and chatty, knows and loves the Auvergne in depth and serves a scrumptious breakfast. A great find for walkers. *Minimum stay: 2 nights in high season. Whole house available.*

| | |
|---|---|
| Rooms | 1 cottage for 2: €58. |
| Meals | Restaurants in St Nectaire, 2km. |
| Closed | Rarely. |

| | |
|---|---|
| Rooms | 2 doubles, 1 twin/double: €85–€90. |
| | 1 suite for 3: €85–€120. |
| | 1 family room for 3: €85–€120. |
| | Extra bed €30 per person per night. |
| Meals | Restaurant within walking distance. |
| Closed | Mid-October to March. |

**Monique Deforge**
Les Frênes,
Sailles,
63710 St Nectaire
Puy-de-Dôme
Tel      +33 (0)4 73 88 40 08
Email   daniel.deforge@orange.fr
Web     pagesperso-orange.fr/deforge/lesfrenes

**Françoise & Maryvonne Larcher**
La Closerie de Manou,
Le Genestoux,
63240 Le Mont Dore
Puy-de-Dôme
Tel        +33 (0)4 73 65 26 81
Mobile   +33 (0)6 08 54 50 16
Email     lacloseriedemanou@orange.fr
Web       www.lacloseriedemanou.com

### Maison d'Hôtes de Charme
### La Fournio

The approach is mysterious and magical, the views to the Auvergne are spectacular, and your host likes nothing better than to share with you his enchanting home. Cherrywood glows with beeswax, copper pots shine, 18th-century floor boards creak and old roses grow around the door. Albert is also a passionate cook, of local sausages and Cantal cheeses, homemade jams and tasty fruit purées. Listen to birds – and cow bells – from the garden, discover lovely Argentat on the Dordogne, settle in with cards by the wood-burner, retire to delicious beds dressed in hand-embroidered linen. Exquisite!

### Château de Sédaiges

Share real château life with a delightfully energetic and sophisticated Parisienne – plus a tribe of grandchildren who occupy the attics in summer – in a historic building owned by the same family for 800 years. Open to the public and endlessly fascinating for young and old, it has a famous collection of old-fashioned toys dating back to 1860, tapestries given by Louis XVI, old parquet floors, murals, antiques, woodwork... the list is deliciously long. Expect lavish bedrooms, of course with crisp sheets, brunch in the distinctive dining room, no pomposity just cultured open-mindedness and fine things. A paradise for children. *Child's room available.*

| Rooms | 1 double: €95. |
|---|---|
| | 1 family room for 3: €70–€90. |
| | 1 cottage for 3 (wc on ground floor): €90–€110. |
| | Single €75–€120. |
| | Extra bed/sofabed €20 per person per night. |
| Meals | Dinner with wine, €23. |
| | Restaurant 2km (& 7km). |
| Closed | Rarely. |

| Rooms | 3 doubles, 3 suites for 2: €130. |
|---|---|
| | 1 family room for 4: €150–€160. |
| | Extra bed €20 per person per night. |
| Meals | Restaurant in village. |
| Closed | October – April. |

Albert Marc Charles
Maison d'Hôtes de Charme
La Fournio,
Escladines, 15700 Chaussenac
Cantal
| Tel | +33 (0)4 71 69 02 68 |
| Mobile | +33 (0)6 81 34 91 70 |
| Email | albert.charles@wanadoo.fr |
| Web | www.lafournio.fr |

Bab & Patrice de Varax
Château de Sédaiges,
15250 Marmanhac
Cantal
| Tel | +33 (0)4 71 47 30 01 |
| Email | chateau15@free.fr |
| Web | www.chateausedaiges.com |

## Auvergne

### La Roussière

Not another house in sight. Just the Cantal hills and a chattering stream. Brigitte and Christian live here with their son and have done much of the restoration themselves. Christian is a genius at woodwork: his golden staircase and panelling sit happily with mellow stone, old armoires, ancient ceiling hooks… There's an Alpine air to the place. Beds are excellent, meals 'en famille' are a delight: great food, good wine, mineral water from the spring. Be calmed by a serene, rustic elegance. There's an organic vegetable garden, green rolling hectares, a haven for wildlife; perfection. *Minimum stay: 2 nights in high season.*

| Rooms | 2 doubles: €75–€95. |
| --- | --- |
| | 1 suite for 2-3, |
| | 1 suite for 3-4: €90–€150. |
| | Extra bed/sofabed €22 per person per night. |
| Meals | Dinner with wine, €24–€28. |
| Closed | Rarely. |

**Christian Grégoir & Brigitte Renard**
La Roussière,
15800 St Clément
Cantal
Tel     +33 (0)4 71 49 67 34
Email    info@laroussiere.fr
Web     www.laroussiere.fr

Entry 574   Map 10

## Auvergne

### Château de Lescure

On the southern slope of Europe's largest extinct volcano, where nine valleys radiate, stands an atmospheric 18th-century château guarded by a medieval tower in which two rustic vaulted bedrooms soar. The twin has the right furbelowed drapery and, in the big inglenook kitchen, Sophie, a committed environmentalist, serves home-smoked ham, veg from her organic garden, fruit from her orchard. Michel's passions are heritage conservation and blazing trails across the hills straight from the door. They are bilingual hosts who may invite you to join in bread-making, cooking, visiting their medieval garden… *Minimum stay: 2 nights in high season.*

| Rooms | 1 twin; 2 doubles with separate shower rooms: €90. |
| --- | --- |
| | Extra bed €30 per person per night. |
| Meals | Dinner with wine, €20–€30. |
| | Child €10. |
| Closed | December/January. |

**Michel Couillaud &
Phoebe Sophie Verhulst**
Château de Lescure,
15230 St Martin sous Vigouroux
Cantal
Tel     +33 (0)4 71 73 40 91
Email    michel.couillaud@gmail.com

Entry 575   Map 10

# Auvergne

## Ferme des Prades

A real creaky old farmhouse – warm, atmospheric, unpretentious. A sweet, down-to-earth couple, Françoise and Philippe welcome company: their sons are away studying, and this is 'la France profonde'! The farm covers 150 hectares; walk for hours through pure air and inspiring landscapes – you need not see another soul. The house, destroyed in the French Revolution, was rebuilt by Napoleon's confessor. Within its solid walls are stripped floors and panelling, big rooms, comfortably worn sofas, fine armoires, muslin curtains – and Françoise's bedside tables fashioned from milk churns. Convivial dinners are great value. A treat.

| Rooms | 3 doubles: €75. |
| --- | --- |
| | 2 family rooms for 4-6: €95-€153. |
| | Extra bed/sofabed €22-€29 per person per night. |
| Meals | Dinner with wine, €25. |
| Closed | Rarely. |

Françoise & Philippe Vauché
Ferme des Prades,
Les Prades, Landeyrat,
15160 Allanche
Cantal
Tel +33 (0)4 71 20 48 17
Mobile +33 (0)6 88 30 79 67
Email les-prades@wanadoo.fr
Web www.fermedesprades.com

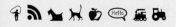

Entry 576   Map 10

# Auvergne

## La Souraïade

You dream of B&B just for two? (Though you can share with two others.) Remote rural France? Woods, wildlife and clear pure air? Above the glittering Allier (great kayaking), among a web of hiking paths, a tiny Auvergnat hamlet holds this expertly renovated cliffside house, decorated in gentle grey and taupe with finely sewn old lace (all Joëlle's work) and plenty of country antiques. Your big raftered room is pretty, cosy and private; breakfast – in the big open-fired kitchen or on the terrace – is a feast (sweet or savoury – you choose) and your hosts the easiest, most generous people you can hope for.

| Rooms | 1 family room for 2-4: €115. |
| --- | --- |
| | Extra person €20 per night. |
| | Children under 6 stay free. |
| Meals | Light dinner with wine, €15. |
| Closed | Never. |

Joëlle & Michel Gagnon
La Souraïade,
Pruneyrolles,
43380 Villeneuve d'Allier
Haute-Loire
Tel +33 (0)4 71 74 71 73
Email lasouraiade@orange.fr
Web www.emerenciane.wix.com/
la-souraiade

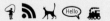

Entry 577   Map 10

# Auvergne

## Chez l'Autre

The church bells stop at 10pm and peace descends on this medieval village high in the Auvergne, and on the Jollivets' fascinating, rambling house whose features range from 8th-century to 21st. Explore steps, passages and leafy inner patios; tread flagstones under hefty beams; browse books by the fire; pop champagne from your minibar. Two traditional bedrooms, one in the house under the rafters, have terraces with village views. Your artistic and educated hosts restore antiques, are flexible on meals (charcuterie platter to gourmet table d'hôtes), and share tips on the valley's attractions: art, archaeology, the great outdoors.

| Rooms | 2 family rooms for 2-3: €120. Extra bed €15 per person per night. |
|---|---|
| Meals | Dinner with wine, from €25. Restaurants 10km. |
| Closed | Rarely. |

Armelle & Bernard Jollivet
Chez l'Autre,
43380 Chilhac
Haute-Loire
Tel +33 (0)4 71 77 49 98
Email jollivetb@free.fr
Web www.chez-lautre.com

# Auvergne

## La Jacquerolle

Built on the ramparts of the ancient town, just below the medieval abbey whose August music festival draws thousands, the big, atmospheric old house has been lined with wood and lovingly filled with flowers in every form – carpets, curtains, wallpaper, quilts. It is a soft French boudoir where mother and daughter, quietly attentive, welcome their guests to sleep in cosy bedrooms, some with wonderful views out to the hills, all with firm beds and good little bathrooms. (Ask for the largest.) French country cuisine is served on bone china with bohemian crystal before a huge stone fireplace.

| Rooms | 1 double, 1 twin, 1 family room for 4: €70-€80. Extra person €15 per night. |
|---|---|
| Meals | Dinner with wine, €25. |
| Closed | Rarely. |

Carole Chailly
La Jacquerolle,
Rue Marchédial,
43160 La Chaise Dieu
Haute-Loire
Tel +33 (0)4 43 07 60 54
Email lajacquerolle@hotmail.com
Web www.lajacquerolle.com

## Gîte du Tapissier

At the top of a twisty mineral village, the big black farmhouse is dated 1490-1575. Sensitively renovated by this welcoming, dynamic family (she does yoga, he does upholstery – superbly), any gloom wafting from the great stones vanishes before Sylvie's use of colour. The Blue room is... streaky blue, its floor like roiling magma, its superb shower done in multi-hued volcanic stone from Brazil, its big balcony a treat. The more traditional Gîte suite has a kitchen/diner and a terrace onto fields and volcanoes – whence the black stone; breakfast in the family kitchen showcases local produce. Then visit spectacular Polignac – and more.

## Château de Durianne

At the entrance to the gorges of the Loire is the House of Durianne where garrisons of soldiers once kept watch; the Chambons have poured heart and soul into rescuing the family château. Nothing had been touched for a century; in the attics was 120-year-old wallpaper which they lovingly re-used. Now the place, its portraits and antiques, feels like home. One huge bedroom overlooks a farm where they keep sheep, the double is up in the tower! The cultivated garden leads to the orchard, the village is just down the lane. Breakfast is generous (homemade tarte, juice from their apples) and you may be joined by delightful Françoise for coffee and a chat. *Child's bed available.*

| | |
|---|---|
| Rooms | 1 double with bathroom curtained off bedroom & wc on floor below: €70-€80.<br>1 family room for 3, separate wc: €105-€110.<br>1 dovecote for 2: €85-€90. |
| Meals | Auberge 15-minute walk. Choice of restaurants 10-minute drive. |
| Closed | November–March. |

| | |
|---|---|
| Rooms | 1 double, 1 family room for 2-4: €90-€140. Extra bed €20 per person per night. Dinner, B&B extra €25 per person. |
| Meals | Dinner with wine, €30. Restaurant 3km. |
| Closed | Rarely. |

|  | Philippe & Sylvie Pubellier |
|---|---|
| | Gîte du Tapissier, |
| | Cheyrac, |
| | 43000 Polignac |
| | Haute-Loire |
| Tel | +33 (0)4 71 02 56 42 |
| Mobile | +33 (0)6 26 21 59 70 |
| Email | pubellier@orange.fr |
| Web | www.pubellierphilippe.fr |

|  | Françoise du Garay |
|---|---|
| | Château de Durianne, |
| | 43700 Le Monteil |
| | Haute-Loire |
| Tel | +33 (0)4 71 02 90 36 |
| Mobile | +33 (0)6 80 70 59 32 |
| Email | info@chateaudedurianne.com |
| Web | www.chateaudedurianne.com |

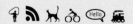

# Midi – Pyrénées

www.sawdays.co.uk/midi-pyrenees

## Midi – Pyrénées

### Manoir de Malagorse

Your passionate eager hosts, with young twins and straw-coloured retrievers that blend with the décor, offer you a refined old manor in an idyllic setting with acres of land and meals cooked by a master. Abel and Anna's restoration is caring and sophisticated, rooms and bathrooms are statements of simple luxury, and the vaulted kitchen is a dream – its fireplace massive, its cooker a wonder to behold. There is space for togetherness and privacy, your hosts are unintrusively present and Anna can offer a professional massage after Abel's demanding wine-tastings. Enjoy it to the hilt. *Minimum stay: 2 nights at weekends & in high season.*

| | |
|---|---|
| Rooms | 4 doubles: €130–€185. |
| | 2 suites for 2: €220–€310. |
| | Extra bed/sofabed €25–€40 per person per night. |
| Meals | Lunch, à la carte, from €20. |
| | Dinner €42. |
| | Wine from €20. |
| Closed | 15 December – 15 March. |

| | |
|---|---|
| | **Anna & Abel Congratel** |
| | Manoir de Malagorse, |
| | 46600 Cuzance |
| | Lot |
| Tel | +33 (0)5 65 27 14 83 |
| Mobile | +33 (0)6 76 74 86 08 |
| Email | acongratel@manoir-de-malagorse.fr |
| Web | www.manoir-de-malagorse.fr |

Entry 582   Map 9

## Midi – Pyrénées

### Moulin du Goth

The 13th-century mill – imaginatively restored by its Australian owners – guards a garden of rare peace and beauty. Find a mill pond, home to wildlife and flashing kingfishers, willows, lawns and garden sculptures. Coral is kind, dedicated, full of fun, Bill's life stories make for fascinating conversation, and big, dramatically raftered rooms have decorative iron beds and touches of old-world charm. Occasionally dinners are served in the stunning vaulted dining room (its arrow slit intact) or in the garden on the terrace within sound of the tinkling stream. Readers adore this place. *Children over 5 welcome. Pets by arrangement.*

| | |
|---|---|
| Rooms | 1 double: €80–€85. |
| | 1 triple: €80–€105. |
| Meals | Dinner with wine, €27–€31. |
| | Restaurants 3km. |
| Closed | Rarely. |

| | |
|---|---|
| | **Coral Heath-Kauffman** |
| | Moulin du Goth, |
| | 46600 Creysse |
| | Lot |
| Tel | +33 (0)5 65 32 26 04 |
| Mobile | +33 (0)6 98 63 41 80 |
| Email | coral.heath@orange.fr |
| Web | www.moulindugoth.com |

Entry 583   Map 9

## Le Moulin de Latreille

The mill is 13th century and Cistercian, the owners are talented and attentive, the setting is magical. Kingfishers and wild orchids, herons, hammocks and happy dogs… and it is just as wonderful inside. Furniture has been renovated and painted, books peep from alcoves, bathrooms are delightful, and you get a little guest sitting room with a wood-burner. Down its own bumpy track from the village, with timeless views of cliffs, woods and weir, let the chorus of birdsong and the rush of the millrace wash over you; they even generate their own electricity. Heaven in Quercy.
*Minimum stay: 2 nights.*

## Moulin de Fresquet

On the edge of Gramat, down a private drive, a gorgeous old mill and a big welcome from a hospitable couple. Cushioned loungers furnish sloping lawns down to the stream, the water flows beneath your feet and you'll relax the second you arrive. Warm inviting bedrooms, four reached down a spiral stair, and most opening to the garden, are distinguished by taffeta curtains and fine tapestries; the more private suite lies in a charming outbuilding. Gardens are a treat – a charming collection of rare ducks wander through the grounds. The region is much loved, but please note, the surroundings whilst beautiful are not suitable for small children.

| Rooms | 2 doubles: €85. |
|---|---|
| Meals | Dinner with wine, €25. |
| | Light lunch & picnic available. |
| | Restaurant in village. |
| Closed | December – February. |

| Rooms | 1 double, 2 twin/doubles: €83–€119. |
|---|---|
| | 2 suites for 2: €119–€144. |
| Meals | Restaurants 800m. |
| Closed | Mid-October to mid-April. |

FIRST EDITION VETERAN

AWARD WINNER

Old favourite

**Giles & Fi Stonor**
Le Moulin de Latreille,
Calès, 46350 Payrac
Lot

| Tel | +33 (0)5 65 41 91 83 |
| Email | gilesetfi@gmail.com |
| Web | www.moulindelatreille.com |

**Gérard & Claude Ramelot**
Moulin de Fresquet,
46500 Gramat
Lot

| Tel | +33 (0)5 65 38 70 60 |
| Email | info@moulindefresquet.com |
| Web | www.moulindefresquet.com |

## Mas Del Lum

The big airy house, with its walnut floor and chalk-painted beams, was once an auberge; take breakfast at leisure, on organic delights. Yolande is keen to share her new-found love of all things rural, and the woodland views are amazing. Rustic-chic bedrooms – each one impeccable – are spread across three little stone houses (plus a twin in the main house) linked by gravel pathways. They share a designer garden-in-the-making, a stunning outdoor kitchen (rattan sofas, barbecue, hand-carved stone sink) and an eco pool. For winter: huge estate logs and a white sofa, and a music room in the old wine press. Warm, sophisticated, enchanting. *Minimum stay: 2 nights at weekends.*

## Mas de Garrigue

Match natural Irish hospitality with the personality of a many-layered French house and you have a marriage made in heaven. Steve raises two fine black pigs in the kitchen garden each year which Sarah transforms into terrines – delicious served with their own onion or fig conserves: they care deeply about their food and its sourcing. The big, unusual house has an elegance all its own: vast rooms, supremely beamed and raftered, are furnished with quiet taste, Irish antiques and the occasional contemporary flourish; beds are the best you've ever slept in, each bathroom a poem. They are a lovely, witty couple, generous to a fault. *Minimum stay: 2 nights in high season. Minimum groups of 6 in winter.*

| Rooms | 2 twin/doubles: €85–€90. |
|---|---|
| | 1 suite for 2 with sitting room; |
| | 2 suites for 2 with single sofabeds |
| | in sitting room: €110. |
| | Extra bed €20 per person per night. |
| Meals | Dinner €25-30. |
| | Summer kitchen. |
| | Restaurants 1.5km. |
| Closed | December – February. |

| Rooms | 3 doubles, 1 twin: €100–€150. |
|---|---|
| | Singles €100–€115. |
| | Dinner, B&B €37 per person. |
| | Extra bed/sofabed €35 per person |
| | per night. |
| Meals | Dinner, 4 courses with wine, €37 |
| | (Mon, Weds & Sat only). |
| Closed | November – April. |

Yolande Skura
Mas Del Lum,
Villedieu Domain,
46100 Boussac/Figeac
Lot

| Tel | +33 (0)5 65 40 06 63 |
| Mobile | +33 (0)6 89 19 90 02 |
| Email | contact@mas-del-lum.fr |
| Web | www.mas-del-lum.fr |

Sarah Lloyd & Steven Allen
Mas de Garrigue,
La Garrigue,
46160 Calvignac
Lot

| Tel | +33 (0)5 65 53 93 31 |
| Email | info@masdegarrigue.com |
| Web | www.masdegarrigue.com |

## Midi – Pyrénées

### Domaine de Labarthe

These vital, welcoming, interesting people, who are in the wine trade and grow walnuts, have turned one wing of the handsome old family house into elegant B&B rooms, two in subtle designer colours, one in traditional cosy French style; and the two-storey pigeonnier would be perfect for a small family. Laurence's dinners alone are worth the visit, then there's the fine pool on the olive-studded terrace, the rose garden and Italianate formality rolling past walnut groves to the Lot countryside, gastronomy and wine, old villages and unmissable Cahors. Such wealth. *Minimum stay: 2 nights on weekdays & at weekends, 3 nights in high season.*

| Rooms | 1 double, 2 twin/doubles: €115–€130. 1 suite for 2-3 with kitchenette: €145–€160. |
|---|---|
| Meals | Dinner, 3 courses, €29. |
| Closed | Rarely. |

Laurence & Guillaume Bardin
Domaine de Labarthe,
46090 Espère
Lot
Tel       +33 (0)5 65 30 92 34
Email     contact@domaine-de-labarthe.com
Web       www.domainedelabarthe.com

Entry 588    Map 9

## Midi – Pyrénées

### Le Clos du Mas de Bastide

Just beyond the village of Crayssac, walled, secluded and with ravishing views, is a very old Quercynois house. From the stone courtyard off which bedrooms lie, steps ascend to a small terrace, an elegant reception and a tower with two pigeonniers. The Rouquiés are gentle and thoughtful, and Sophie's rooms are distinctive and cosy: a 'couronne' bed here, an armoire there, wallpapers stylish and flamboyant, bed linens sumptuous, shower rooms small and perfect. After delicious breakfast on the high terrace, discover Cahors (river, gardens, cathedral), a 15-minute drive. Castelfranc, with a family-run auberge for dinner, is even closer.

| Rooms | 2 doubles, 1 twin: €99–€122. |
|---|---|
| Meals | Restaurants 1.5km. |
| Closed | Rarely. |

Sophie & Jean-Paul Rouquié
Le Clos du Mas de Bastide,
Mas de Bastide,
46150 Crayssac
Lot
Tel       +33 (0)5 65 30 18 33
Mobile    +33 (0)6 60 64 72 84
Email     contact@closdumasdebastide.com
Web       www.closdumasdebastide.com

Entry 589    Map 9

## Midi – Pyrénées

### Téranga

This happy, secluded house is charged with childhood memories. Agnès, vivacious ex-English teacher, and Francis, wine-lover and retired architect, have filled the rooms with Senegalese touches and take immense pleasure in welcoming guests. Bedrooms have wooden floors and ethnic hangings, the gardens hide a delicious pool and the long vine-strewn veranda is the perfect spot for breakfast gâteaux and jams. Discover restaurants in old Pradines, history in lovely Cahors (a short drive), and the river Lot for watery adventures. *Minimum stay: 2 nights.*

| | |
|---|---|
| Rooms | 2 doubles: €74–€79. |
| | Singles €65–€69. |
| Meals | Restaurants 5-minute drive. |
| Closed | November – March. |

**Agnès & Francis Sevrin-Cance**
Téranga,
303 av Adeline Cubaynes,
46090 Pradines
Lot

| | |
|---|---|
| Tel | +33 (0)5 65 35 20 51 |
| Email | chambres.teranga@orange.fr |
| Web | www.chambresteranga.com |

Entry 590   Map 9

## Midi – Pyrénées

### Mondounet

The silvery grey Lot stone glows and the wonderful view from the breakfast terrace sweeps over mature trees. On a peaceful through road with just the postman going by, the 17th-century farmhouse has been restored to its original character, including outbuildings for B&B and gîte guests. Make friends round the fenced-in salt-purified pool, or over dinner, served before the generous fire. Zoé will charm you, see you have a good time, serve breakfast when you like. Peter plays the guitar and sings – his musical evenings are great fun. Off the lovely living room is the bedroom, simple, spacious, delightful – as is the whole place.

| | |
|---|---|
| Rooms | 1 double: €70. |
| Meals | Dinner with wine, €24. |
| Closed | Rarely. |

**Peter & Zoé Scott**
Mondounet,
46800 Fargues
Lot

| | |
|---|---|
| Tel | +33 (0)5 65 36 96 32 |
| Email | scotsprops@aol.com |
| Web | www.mondounetholidaysandhomes.com |

Entry 591   Map 14

## Midi – Pyrénées

### La Borde Neuve

Open fires for winter, rare orchids in spring, a pool in summer – and a vision of soft wooded hills and small pastures all year round. Ed and Georgi, he an artist, she a cook, long to share their discoveries. The house, fresh, light and airy, is full of art; the bedrooms, one huge and under the eaves, are serene. Wake to homemade bread and mini viennoiseries at breakfast, come home to French-inspired dinners by the great stone fireplace. You can canoe on the Lot, walk to the Compostela footpath or visit Cahors, full of history and architecture, bustling with places to eat and a great twice-weekly market. *Children over 16 welcome.*

| Rooms | 1 double, 1 twin/double with separate, private bathroom: €75–€80. |
|---|---|
| Meals | Dinner with aperitif & wine, €28. Restaurants 12km. |
| Closed | Rarely. |

**Georgi King**
La Borde Neuve,
46170 Cézac
Lot

| | |
|---|---|
| Tel | +33 (0)5 65 22 61 68 |
| Mobile | +33 (0)6 42 51 61 94 |
| Email | labordeneuve.cezac@gmail.com |
| Web | www.labordeneuve.net |

Entry 592   Map 14

## Midi – Pyrénées

### La Vayssade

Sociable foodies will love it here: Hélène and Pierre shop for local ingredients in the market every day and enjoy an ever-changing menu with their guests at a huge table, outside on the terrace on fine evenings. You'll sleep well in large bedrooms (some upstairs, some down) with masses of old beams, exposed stone, dreamy beds and generous modern bathrooms. A large living room has floor-to-ceiling arched windows at one end, wonky beams, paintings by Hélène's mother and a comfy sofa area. This is truffle country so enjoy the Saturday morning market – or stay put and wander at will through the pretty garden, or have a float in the pool.

| Rooms | 4 twin/doubles with sofabed: €87–€100. 1 suite for 4 (2 interconnecting twin/doubles): €160–€188. |
|---|---|
| Meals | Dinner with wine, €29. Restaurants 1km. |
| Closed | Rarely. |

**Famille Baysse**
La Vayssade,
205 chemin de La Vayssade,
46230 Lalbenque
Lot

| | |
|---|---|
| Tel | +33 (0)5 65 24 31 51 |
| Email | contact@lavayssade.com |
| Web | www.lavayssade.com |

Entry 593   Map 14

### Les Chimères

In a wonderful hilltop village is a big old house with a painted wrought-iron gate and matching shutters – inside and out oozes character and history. Find magazines, books, paintings, antiques, playing cards, flowers, pottery on dressers, cats on chairs and a huge fireplace in the kitchen where lovely Lisanne creates great meals and breakfasts to remember (breads, brioche, fruits, yogurts, cheese, ham and divine jams). Big bedrooms, reached via 12th-century stone stairs, are equally charming. Bathrooms are luxurious, bathrobes are colourful, there are fans, books and irons – and gorgeous views from garden and house. *Cot available.*

### Green Chambre d'Hôte

Under pollution-free skies, amid acres of meadow and woodland, a green paradise unfolds. Taking on a hunter's shack, this couple renovated their patch simply and with love and attention. Sid and Laura are a delight, as is their colourful organic garden. Landscape gardeners and experts on wildlife, they are also virtually self-sufficient; home-grown veggie cuisine for supper, solar powered everything and natural pest control. Overlooking lavender garden and vine-covered terrace is a cosy bedroom. Watch birds by day, listen to frogs sing at night, immerse yourself in unspoilt beauty. *Minimum stay: 2 nights in high season.*

| | |
|---|---|
| Rooms | 2 doubles: €65. Singles €55. Extra person €10. |
| Meals | Dinner with wine, €27. Children under 12, €12. Restaurants within walking distance. |
| Closed | Rarely. |

| | |
|---|---|
| Rooms | 1 double: €55-€75. |
| Meals | Vegetarian dinner with wine, €20. Picnic lunch available. Restaurants 10-minute drive. |
| Closed | Christmas/New Year. |

**Lisanne Ashton**
Les Chimères,
23 av Louis Bessières,
82240 Puylaroque
Tarn-et-Garonne
Tel     +33 (0)5 63 31 25 71
Email   aux-chimeres@orange.fr
Web     www.aux-chimeres.com

**Laura & Sid Havard**
Green Chambre d'Hôte,
Lausoprens,
82140 St Antonin Noble Val
Tarn-et-Garonne
Tel      +33 (0)5 63 30 53 77
Mobile   +33 (0)6 31 99 94 31
Email    green.havard@gmail.com
Web      www.greenchambredhote.com

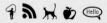

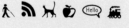

## Midi – Pyrénées

### La Résidence

Your charming hosts love being part of village life – and what a village: medieval to the core and with a famous Sunday market. It is a joy to stay in a townhouse in the heart of it all, with an atmospheric, artistic hall and a great stone staircase, rosy floor tiles and old limestone walls, and views to a sculpture-rich garden. Three of the big tranquil bedrooms overlook the garden, another has a divine terrace with rooftop views; sunlight dapples the soft colours and uncluttered spaces, modern paintings and old country pieces. Ask about their 'demi-pension packages': dinner can be arranged at a local restaurant.

### Le Mas des Anges

An exciting venture for a super couple who are squeaky-green too, running their organic vineyard. You find a very pretty house surrounded by lovely shrubs, a pool, and a separate entrance to each bedroom with terrace. These ground-floor rooms have fabulous colours, big good beds, bathrooms with thick towels, while the sitting area is airy and modern with stacks of books, magazines and interesting sculpture and art. Sophie gives you a huge breakfast with homemade bread and jams, fresh fruit, cheeses and yogurt. Mountauban is only 7km away and you are near enough to amazing Albi for a day trip.

| Rooms | 3 doubles, 2 twins: €85–€103. |
|---|---|
| Meals | Restaurants nearby. |
| Closed | Rarely. |

| Rooms | 3 doubles: €75–€80. |
|---|---|
| Meals | Restaurants 7km. |
| Closed | Rarely. |

Evert & Sabine Weijers
La Résidence,
37 rue Droite,
82140 St Antonin Noble Val
Tarn-et-Garonne
Tel     +33 (0)5 63 67 37 56
Email   info@laresidence-france.com
Web     www.laresidence-france.com

Juan & Sophie Kervyn
Le Mas des Anges,
1623 route de Verlhac Tescou,
82000 Montauban
Tarn-et-Garonne
Tel     +33 (0)5 63 24 27 05
Mobile  +33 (0)6 76 30 86 36
Email   info@lemasdesanges.com
Web     www.lemasdesanges.com

Entry 596   Map 15

Entry 597   Map 14

## Midi – Pyrénées

### Tondes

Warm country people, the Sellars left Sussex for a small farm in deepest France to run a flock of indigenous milking sheep the natural way: no pesticides, no heavy machines, animals roaming free. Their recipe for a simple rewarding life includes receiving guests happily under the beams, by the wood-burning stove, in pretty-coloured, country-furnished rooms with super walk-in showers. While Julie creates homemade marvels from her farmhouse kitchen – most of what you eat has been harvested from the garden or the farm – you can relax on the terrace with a home-brewed sun-downer and admire it all. A slice of rural bliss.

| Rooms | 1 double: €55.<br>1 family room for 4: €55–€95.<br>Extra bed/sofabed €20 per person per night. |
|---|---|
| Meals | Dinner with wine, €25. |
| Closed | Rarely. |

**Julie & Mark Sellars**
Tondes,
82400 Castelsagrat
Tarn-et-Garonne

Tel     +33 (0)5 63 94 52 13
Email   juliedsellars@gmail.com
Web     www.allezatondes.com

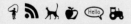

Entry 598   Map 14

## Midi – Pyrénées

### Au Château

A beguiling mix of grandeur and informality. The house is filled with light and life, thanks to this young Anglo-French family. Softly contemporary bedrooms, two in a separate building, are airy spaces that mix the best of modern with the loveliest of traditional: pale beams and white plaster walls, bold colours, luxurious silks, elegant antiques. There's a country-style breakfast room and a fully equipped kitchen so you can make your own suppers – then eat al fresco on the terrace. Visit historic towns, explore the Canal du Midi, let the kids roam free in the garden, stroll the charming village.

| Rooms | 1 double: €63–€70.<br>2 suites for 2-3: €83–€90.<br>1 family room for 4: €115–€130.<br>1 triple: €78–€105. |
|---|---|
| Meals | Restaurants within walking distance. |
| Closed | Rarely. |

**Kathrin Barker**
Au Château,
1 bd des Fossés de Raoul,
82210 St Nicolas de la Grave
Tarn-et-Garonne

Tel     +33 (0)5 63 95 96 82
Email   kathrin.barker@sfr.fr
Web     www.au-chateau-stn.com

Entry 599   Map 14

## Le Petit Feuillant

Magret de canard, beans from the garden, wines from the Côtes de Gascogne, melons from over the hill: table d'hôtes (and lots of French guests) is pure pleasure for David and Vikki. In a hilltop, out-of-the-way village, this well-restored house and barn, with its several terraces and outstanding views, has become a B&B of huge comfort and charm. Find old stone walls and tiled floors, whitewashed beams and weather-worn shutters, soft colours and uncluttered spaces, and homemade croissants for breakfast. Foodies come for the cookery courses, astronomers for the night skies. Great value. *Minimum stay: 2 nights in high season.*

| | |
|---|---|
| Rooms | 3 doubles, 1 cottage for 2 with kitchenette: €60–€90. 1 family room for 5: €70–€130. 1 triple: €80–€100. |
| Meals | Dinner with wine, €25. Auberge within walking distance. |
| Closed | Rarely. |

David & Vikki Chance
Le Petit Feuillant,
82120 Gramont
Tarn-et-Garonne
Tel      +33 (0)5 63 32 58 78
Email    david.chance@neuf.fr
Web      www.gasconcook.co.uk

## L'Arbre d'Or

How nice to find a chambre d'hôtes that offers dinner every day (do book though), and a big garden, and a pool, in the centre of bastide Beaumont. Young, friendly and fun, Chantal and Serge are enchanted with their new B&B life. Chantal's artful sense of colour and texture brings new soul to the old place, super hangings drape the beds and renovated bathrooms seduce. The lovely heart of this old town is at the door of the handsome, well-proportioned 17th-century gent's res where tall windows let in floods of light and elegant old stairs creak as they should. Superb value, and surely the finest ginkgo biloba tree in France. *Extra bed available.*

| | |
|---|---|
| Rooms | 2 doubles: €52–€78. 2 triples: €79–€90. Extra bed €21–€23 per person per night. |
| Meals | Dinner €22. Wine from €5. Restaurants 1km. |
| Closed | Rarely. |

Chantal & Serge Néger
L'Arbre d'Or,
16 rue Despeyrous,
82500 Beaumont de Lomagne
Tarn-et-Garonne
Tel      +33 (0)5 63 65 32 34
Mobile   +33 (0)7 70 08 18 86
Email    contact@maison-hote-82.com
Web      www.maison-hote-82.com

## Lacassagne

Swoop up a fine avenue of ancient oaks to land in this perfectly preserved 1750 *maison de maître*. Clever Madame cooks like a dream: an elegant table with embroidered linen is piled high with homemade delights at breakfast (bruschetta-style toasts with garden tomatoes in summer) and proper china, silver and candlelight at dinner (perhaps daube de boeuf). You'll sleep well too, in graceful, white-walled bedrooms with views over the park, gorgeous linen, plump pillows. Loll about on big sofas with good books, toast in front of the fire, take a turn through the park or stroll up the hill to the splendid village. Super.

## La Lumiane

Move into the unexpected, step off a side street and discover a delightful garden with a pool and sweet-smelling shrubs. Friendly, vivacious Mireille has just taken over this gracious house (with her charming English partner); she brims with enthusiasm for her new life and the guests it brings. In the main house, bedrooms breathe tradition and space, old fireplaces, big windows and antiques; those in the garden annexe have a contemporary feel. All have an uncluttered mix of florals and stripes and simple, spotless bathrooms. In winter, eat well on local, seasonal produce in the formal dining room, or on the terrace by candlelight.

| | |
|---|---|
| Rooms | 4 doubles: €85–€105. |
| Meals | Dinner with wine, €25. Restaurant within walking distance. |
| Closed | Never. |

| | |
|---|---|
| Rooms | 5 doubles: €68–€73. |
| Meals | Dinner with wine, €26 (not in high season). Restaurant 50m. |
| Closed | Rarely. |

Maïder Papelorey
Lacassagne,
32100 Larressingle
Gers
Tel      +33 (0)5 62 28 26 89
Email    contact@lacassagnechambresdhotes.fr
Web      www.lacassagnechambresdhotes.fr

Mireille Mabilat & Stuart Simkins
La Lumiane,
Grande Rue,
32310 St Puy
Gers
Tel      +33 (0)5 62 28 95 95
Email    info@lalumiane.com
Web      www.lalumiane.com

Entry 602   Map 14

Entry 603   Map 14

## Le Biau

Inventive artisans have done a fine job renovating the cut stone, half timbering and imposing doorways of this grand old vigneron's house (with barns), in three tranquil hectares of very gently sloping land. Your relaxed hosts left Hong Kong for Gers and welcome guests with genuine warmth. Bedrooms are lavish with oriental touches, bathrooms (half classic, half rustic) are indulging, and the salon, with wood-burner and white sofas, is the hub of the house. Fran and Ray are creating a garden full of surprising corners – an idyllic backdrop for chargrilled peppers straight from the plot, magret of duck, almond and plum tart…. delicious!

## Belliette

On a silent hill near the winding Douze river sits a 300-year-old farmhouse, serene and charming inside and out. Arum lilies run along the half-timbered façade, an ancient bread oven and rose-brick chimney stand at its core, beautifying each simple bedroom. Marie's affection for Gascon culture and armagnac shines through. Join her for an evening meal and then perhaps a peer at the night sky – totally free of light pollution. Deer roam, and there's a delightful chicken coop full of feathery inhabitants. Catch a wisp of the Pyrénées on a clear day, discover historic Eauze, summer markets and summertime jazz in Marciac. *Folding cot & baby equipment available.*

| | |
|---|---|
| Rooms | 2 doubles; 1 double with separate bathroom: €70–€110.<br>1 suite for 2 with separate sitting room: €90–€110.<br>Extra bed/sofabed €20 per person per night. |
| Meals | Dinner with wine, €27. |
| Closed | 1 November – 1 March. |

| | |
|---|---|
| Rooms | 1 double: €70.<br>1 suite for 3: €80–€100.<br>1 triple: €70–€90.<br>Children under 3 stay free. |
| Meals | Dinner with wine, €22.<br>Children under 15, €10. |
| Closed | Rarely. |

**Ray & Fran Atkinson**
Le Biau,
32190 Lannepax
Gers
Tel      +33 (0)5 62 06 47 61
Email    rayatkinson2010@hotmail.com
Web      www.lebiau.com

**Marie Cormier**
Belliette,
Cutxan,
32150 Cazaubon
Gers
Tel      +33 (0)5 62 08 18 68
Email    marie.cormier32@gmail.com
Web      www.belliette.fr

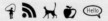

## Midi – Pyrénées

### Laouarde

In rolling Armagnac country: a former wine estate, an 1823 house with watchtower views. Simon and Catherine swapped London for warm limestone and blue shutters, beautiful sash windows and oak parquet, and 25 acres of meadows, orchards and peace. Wonderful breakfasts (compotes from the garden, delectable croissants) are taken by the open fire or on the pool terrace, and Simon's dinners are mouthwatering. Up the beeswax-polished stair are delicious bedrooms full of personality, from country-pretty to elegant Bourbon. Read, listen to music, take an aperitif in the walled courtyard, explore this amazing region.

| Rooms | 1 twin: €85–€110. |
| | 2 suites for 2: €95–€120. |
| | 1 single: €55–€65. |
| Meals | Dinner €35 (Sun-Wed). |
| | Restaurants 1km. |
| Closed | November – April, |
| | except by arrangement. |

**Simon & Catherine Butterworth**
Laouarde,
32190 Vic Fezensac
Gers
Tel    +33 (0)5 62 63 13 44
Email  info@laouarde.co.uk
Web    www.laouarde.com

Entry 606   Map 14

## Midi – Pyrénées

### Lieu dit Fitan

Complete tranquillity, beautiful gardens, charmed pool, and Dido, who loves people – an inspiration to us all. In 1999 this was just another derelict barn in the undulating Gers countryside; the restoration is a wonder. At the door, the whole superb space opens before the eyes, English antiques gleam and the fine modern kitchen sparkles (use it for a small fee). In two luscious bedrooms, one up, one down, raw stones punctuate soft white walls, patchwork cheers, books tempt. Dido paints, loves colours and cooking fresh, light food, has travelled thousands of miles and is highly cultured. A corner of paradise, it even smells heavenly.

| Rooms | 1 double, 1 twin: €70–€80. |
| Meals | Dinner with wine, €35. |
| | Use of kitchen €8. |
| Closed | Rarely. |

**Dido Streatfeild-Moore**
Lieu dit Fitan,
32230 Louslitges
Gers
Tel    +33 (0)5 62 70 81 88
Email  deedoenfrance@wanadoo.fr
Web    www.chezdeedo.com

Entry 607   Map 14

## Midi – Pyrénées

### Domaine de Peyloubère

The waterfall, the wild orchids, the pool, the painted ladies, the super food – there's no other place like it. Years ago Theresa and her late husband fell for this big romantic house, its wildlife-rich domaine and its centuries-old cedars; the enthusiasm remains undiminished, the sensitive restoration shows in every room. But the sober buildings don't prepare you for the explosion inside… late 19th-century painter Mario Cavaglieri spread his love of form and colour over ceilings and doors. Now 'his' suite has vast space, fine antiques, a dream of a bathroom, dazzling murals. Heaven for children – or an anniversary treat.

| Rooms | 2 suites for 2: €85–€120. |
|---|---|
| Meals | Dinner with wine, €30. |
| Closed | Never. |

**Theresa Martin**
Domaine de Peyloubère,
32550 Pavie – Auch
Gers
Tel    +33 (0)5 62 05 74 97
Email    martin@peyloubere.com
Web    www.peyloubere.com

Entry 608    Map 14

## Midi – Pyrénées

### Le Relais de Saux

High on a hill facing dazzling Pyrenean peaks, the house still has a few unregenerate arrow slits, left over from sterner days. You come in through the multi-coloured garden that spreads across lawns and terraces with corners for reading or painting. Bernard knows the area thoroughly and can guide you to fine walks, climbs or visits. Return to deep armchairs in the dark and timeworn salon with its garden view (some traffic hum outside). Bedrooms with carpeted bathrooms are in the same traditional, elegant mood with draped bedheads, darkish plush or flock-papered walls and an air of faded glory. Nip to Lourdes but watch the road.

| Rooms | 3 doubles, 2 twin/doubles: €96–€103. |
|---|---|
| Meals | Restaurant 2km. |
| Closed | Rarely. |

**Bernard Hères**
Le Relais de Saux,
Route de Tarbes,
Le Hameau de Saux,
65100 Lourdes
Hautes-Pyrénées
Tel    +33 (0)5 62 94 29 61
Email    contacts@lourdes-relais.com
Web    www.lourdes-relais.com

Entry 609    Map 14

## Midi – Pyrénées

### Eth Berye Petit

Beauty, harmony, tranquillity... all who stay, long to return. The grand old village *maison de maître*, in Henri's family for centuries, opens to soft green rolling meadows and the majestic Pyrénées – the finest view in all France! Basque-born Ione, graceful and gracious mother of two, ushers you up the venerable stair to wonderful warm bedrooms in pastel hues – one with a balcony – and luscious beds wrapped in antique linen. The living room, where a fire roars and a fine dinner is served on winter weekends, is a delight to come home to after a day's skiing or hiking. For summer? A dreamy garden. Exceptional.

| Rooms | 1 double; 1 twin: €75. |
| --- | --- |
| | 1 suite for 3: €75–€93. |
| | Singles €60. |
| Meals | Dinner with wine, €23. |
| | Auberge within walking distance. |
| Closed | 24 December – 2 January. |

| | Henri & Ione Vielle |
| --- | --- |
| | Eth Berye Petit, |
| | 15 route de Vielle, |
| | 65400 Beaucens |
| | Hautes-Pyrénées |
| Tel | +33 (0)5 62 97 90 02 |
| Email | contact@beryepetit.com |
| Web | www.beryepetit.com |

Entry 610   Map 14

## Midi – Pyrénées

### La Ferme du Buret

In an enchanting Heidi-esque valley in the Haute (but gently rolling) Pyrénées is a long low stone cattle stable tucked into the hills, with a barn attached. Each superb structure houses two guest bedrooms. From lofty beams to floor, interiors are lined with thick wide planks of cedar, chestnut, acacia and oak; rustic-chic fabrics and sleek bathroom fittings add to the spare, but never spartan, charm. Cathy is a champion skier and can ski-guide you, Pierre is an inspired chef of regional dinners served indoors or out at an enormous table with magnificent views. Sports and thermal spas abound, the scenery makes the heart sing.

| Rooms | 2 twin/doubles, |
| --- | --- |
| | 2 family rooms for 3: €90–€110. |
| | Extra bed €20 per person per night. |
| Meals | Dinner with wine, €25. |
| Closed | Mid-November to January |
| | (open Christmas/New Year). |

| | Pierre & Cathy Faye |
| --- | --- |
| | La Ferme du Buret, |
| | 65130 Asque |
| | Hautes-Pyrénées |
| Tel | +33 (0)5 62 39 19 26 |
| Mobile | +33 (0)6 86 77 33 71 |
| Email | info@lafermeduburet.com |
| Web | www.lafermeduburet.com |

Entry 611   Map 14

## Domaine de Jean-Pierre

Madame is gracefully down to earth and her house and garden an oasis of calm where you may share her delight in playing the piano or golf (3km) and possibly make a lifelong friend. Built in Napoleon's time, her house has an elegant hall, big airy bedrooms and great bathrooms, while fine furniture and laundered linen reflect her pride in her ancestral home – a combination of uncluttered space and character. The huge triple has space to waltz in and the smallest bathroom; the colours chosen are peaceful and harmonious; the garden is a treat; and breakfast comes with an array of honeys and civilised conversation. Great value.

| Rooms | 2 doubles: €60. |
| | 1 triple: €80. |
| Meals | Restaurants 3km. |
| Closed | Rarely. |

FIRST
EDITION
VETERAN

Marie-Sabine Colombier
Domaine de Jean-Pierre,
20 route de Villeneuve,
65300 Pinas
Hautes-Pyrénées

| Tel | +33 (0)5 62 98 15 08 |
| Mobile | +33 (0)6 84 57 15 69 |
| Email | marie@domainedejeanpierre.com |
| Web | www.domainedejeanpierre.com |

Entry 612   Map 14

## Ancienne Poste Avajan

Up the long winding mountain road to a renovated lodge with a deck for lounging and a 'secret' garden – to think the post used to be sorted here! Sojourns are packaged for sport-orientated winters and summers (hiking, biking, climbing, fishing, tennis, the list goes on…) and talented chef provides energy-charged alpine breakfasts and dinners. James, an outward bound professional par excellence, loves what he does and makes this place buzz. There's a big dining/sitting room with leather sofas, wood-burner and bar, a snug for quiet moments and six bedrooms in mountain swish style. It's inviting, comfortable and great fun.

| Rooms | 2 doubles, 1 twin, 2 triples, 1 bunk room: €256 |
| | (half-board with activity package). |
| | Ski package: €799–€899 per person per week. |
| Meals | Half-board option only (breakfast, dinner with wine & coffee). |
| Closed | Rarely. |

James Dealtry
Ancienne Poste Avajan,
65240 Avajan
Hautes-Pyrénées

| Tel | +33 (0)5 62 40 53 17 |
| Mobile | +33 (0)6 09 49 73 80 |
| Email | james@ancienneposteavajan.com |
| Web | www.ancienneposteavajan.com |

Entry 613   Map 14

## Midi – Pyrénées

### Bed in Bellongue

The village farmhouse, big and beautiful with a deep-pitch roof, stands peacefully by the side of the stream. Here live two horses, 24 chickens, one delightful dog and Marion and Xavier. full of love and life. The décor, in-your-face modern, stands in stark contrast to the big old fireplace and ancient beams and stones, and bedrooms are in similar vein, one on the ground floor, another with a balcony that runs the length of the bathroom and opens off it. Marion grows everything organically, and dinner, enjoyed at a table lined with white fabric-clothed chairs, is exactly what's wanted after serious hikes in the Haut-Couserans.

| Rooms | 1 double with separate wc: €60. |
|---|---|
| | 2 family rooms for 3: €65–€70. |
| | Singles €50. |
| | Dinner, B&B €22 extra per person. |
| | Extra bed/sofabed €15 per person per night. |
| Meals | Restaurant 5km. |
| Closed | Never. |

**Marion Dupuy**
Bed in Bellongue,
Chemin du Viellot,
09800 Aucazein
Ariège
Tel       +33 (0)5 81 15 72 55
Email    bedinbellongue@gmail.com
Web      www.bedinbellongue.fr

Entry 614   Map 14

## Midi – Pyrénées

### La Genade

Up in her beloved mountains with the wild streams splashing and an unbroken view of 13th-century Lordat, Meredith loves sharing her heaven. A passionate climber, skier and cyclist, she rebuilt a ruined auberge; old stones and new wood, craggy beams, precious furniture and a cheery fire make it rustic, warm and elegant. Under truly American care, rooms have fine linens, oriental rugs and books. The welcome is genuine, breakfast is fresh and generous, dinners are animated and delicious. Walkers and cyclists should stay a week, and there's a repair room specially for bikes. Remarkable value. *Minimum stay: 2 nights (minimum one for cyclists).*

| Rooms | 2 doubles, 1 twin: €60–€70. |
|---|---|
| | Extra bed €10 per person per night. |
| Meals | Dinner with wine, €20–€24. |
| Closed | Rarely. |

**Meredith Dickinson**
La Genade,
La route des Corniches,
09250 Axiat, Ariège
Tel       +33 (0)5 61 05 51 54
Mobile   +33 (0)7 87 45 33 26
Email    meredith.dickinson@orange.fr
Web      www.chambre-dhote-pyrenees-lagenade.com

Entry 615   Map 14

## Midi – Pyrénées

### Las Coumeilles

A Pyrenean paradise, an idyllic and remote spot for nature lovers and birdwatchers – great walks start from the door. Look out over extensive grounds, pretty lanes and glorious countryside, relax with a pre-dinner drink by the wood-burner, tuck into breakfast on a private sun terrace. Uncover rare orchids nearby, dip into the heated pool, play tennis, feast in the open-air summer kitchen. Jump at dinner if proffered – Tom is curry king and Trish the unparalleled queen of desserts. The spotless bedrooms will charm you, towels abound; nab the 'Moon Room' for superlative views. You'll love the Ariège – and its capital, Foix. *Rooms can be booked together to sleep up to 10.*

| | |
|---|---|
| Rooms | 1 double, 1 twin: €70–€80. 1 suite for 6 (3 interconnecting doubles sharing bathroom): €130–€140. Extra bed €10 per person per night. |
| Meals | Dinner, 3 courses with wine, €22. Light supper €15. Summer kitchen. Restaurants 2-3km. |
| Closed | December-January. |

Tom & Trish Littmann
Las Coumeilles,
Le Village,
09300 Leychert
Ariège

| | |
|---|---|
| Tel | +33 (0)5 61 02 61 94 |
| Mobile | +33 (0)6 72 37 16 57 |
| Email | tomlittmann@hotmail.com |
| Web | www.ariegebedandbreakfast.com |

Entry 616   Map 14

## Midi – Pyrénées

### Impasse du Temple

Breakfast among the remains of a Protestant chapel, sleep in a townhouse, one of a terrace built in 1758; John and Lee-Anne are its second owners. Delightful, humorous Australians, they have restored their elegant mansion and are very much part of the community. Graciously high ceilings, a sweeping spiral staircase, lovely great windows in an oasis of ancient, stream-kissed oaks... arrive as strangers, leave as friends. The food is fantastic and the pastel-shaded bedrooms are generous, with just enough antiques; one even has the vast original claw-footed bath. The attention to detail is exceptional and readers sing their praises.

| | |
|---|---|
| Rooms | 2 doubles: €80–€90. 1 suite for 4: €125–€130. 2 triples: €100–€105. |
| Meals | Dinner €25. Wine €9–€20. Restaurant nearby. |
| Closed | Rarely. |

John & Lee-Anne Furness
Impasse du Temple,
09600 Léran
Ariège

| | |
|---|---|
| Tel | +33 (0)5 61 01 50 02 |
| Mobile | +33 (0)6 88 19 49 22 |
| Email | john.furness@wanadoo.fr |
| Web | www.chezfurness.com |

Entry 617   Map 15

## Midi – Pyrénées

### La Ferme de Boyer

Your hosts, friendly, humorous, great fun, have filled the big rambling farmhouse with polished mahogany and family memorabilia. He was once a helicopter engineer and loves classic cars, she is a Cordon Bleu cook; both have designed furniture for first-class hotels and worked for hotels in Paris. Now they do sparkling B&B! The blue-shuttered exterior is prettier than a picture while bedrooms are sunny and charming, more English than French. The garden has pastoral views down to a rare weeping beech, and Harriet's dinners are convivial and delicious. Mirepoix, once an important cathedral town, is just down the road.

| | |
|---|---|
| Rooms | 1 double; 1 twin: €65–€80. 1 family suite for 4 with sitting room & kitchenette: €50–€80. |
| Meals | Dinner with wine, €30. |
| Closed | Rarely. |

**Robert & Harriet Stow**
La Ferme de Boyer,
09500 Coutens Mirepoix
Ariège
Tel +33 (0)5 61 68 93 41
Mobile +33 (0)6 22 04 05 84
Email ferme.boyer@gmail.com
Web www.fermeboyer.iowners.net

Entry 618   Map 15

## Midi – Pyrénées

### Gratia

Luscious texture combinations of original floor tiles discovered, virgin, in the attic along with stupendous original beams: loving hands crafted Gratia in the 1790s; flair and hard work brought it back from ruin in the 1990s. Jean-Paul's motto 'less is more' informs the wonderful uncluttered bedrooms with their pretty beds and linens; Florence, chic and charming, will do physiotherapy in the great attic studio – mats, music, massage; the breakfast is perfect, the hospitality is generous, the ethos is green. Chill out on the manicured lawn by the saltwater pool, converse delightfully, depart renewed.

| | |
|---|---|
| Rooms | 3 doubles: €100–€120. |
| Meals | Restaurants 3km. |
| Closed | Mid-September to April. |

**Florence Potey & Jean-Paul Wallaert**
Gratia,
09210 Lézat sur Lèze
Ariège
Tel +33 (0)5 61 68 64 47
Email ferme.gratia@wanadoo.fr
Web www.ariege.com/gratia

Entry 619   Map 14

## Midi – Pyrénées

### Au Delà du Temps

The owners, ex wine-growers from the Charente, love their new life in the lush Pyrénées, on the outskirts of this turn-of-the-century spa town. Outside: a small harmonious Japanese style garden with a swimming pool. Inside: three alpine suites clad in pale pine, cosy, warm with excellent bathrooms and perfect for families. A lovely breakfast of croissants, brioche, apple tart, served with candles and Scandinavian touches, sets you up for some hearty hiking and skiing: Luchon's lift whisks you to the top of the mountain. Or go shopping in Spain, or wallow in the town's spa; your friendly hosts know their patch well. *Minimum stay: 2 nights in high season.*

### La Maison du Lac

This grand 1800 Gascogne house, with its yellowy ochre façade, was saved from ruin by the Charons, then faithfully restored and now shared with you! French and English antiques meet textiles from North Africa and you can laze here all day until evening cocktails. You have the salon – once the kitchen – with its wide stone hearth and billiard table. Oak floored rooms are elegant; twin beds can be added to the open-plan suite for a family. You can breakfast on the terrace, in the summer dining room or by the pool facing the lake. Nicole is a talented cook and does noon-time grillades, and dinner on the south-facing terrace. *Minimum stay: 2 nights.*

| | |
|---|---|
| Rooms | 1 suite for 2-4; 1 suite for 2, 1 suite for 2-4 with kitchen: €80–€122. |
| Meals | Restaurants 15-minute walk. |
| Closed | Rarely. |

| | |
|---|---|
| Rooms | 1 double: €90. 1 suite for 2: €100. Extra bed/sofabed €15 per person per night. |
| Meals | Dinner with wine, €25. Restaurant 2km. |
| Closed | 1 November – 1 April. |

**Frédérique & François Roy**
Au Delà du Temps,
28 avenue de Gascogne,
31110 St Mamet
Haute-Garonne

Tel     +33 (0)5 61 89 13 53
Mobile  +33 (0)6 18 64 14 29
Email   suedcognac@wanadoo.fr
Web     www.gite-luchon.com

**Patrick & Nicole Charon**
La Maison du Lac,
Lieu-dit Michalet,
31350 Boulogne sur Gesse
Haute-Garonne

Tel     +33 (0)5 61 88 92 16
Email   nicole.charon@hotmail.fr
Web     www.lamaisondulacgascogne.com

## Les Pesques

Surrounded by rolling farmland, at the end of a quiet lane, a gorgeous old manor house in a luxuriant garden – a happy place and home. Brigitte has decorated in peaceful good taste and all is charmingly cluttered, each country antique the right one. Now the stable has been transformed into the prettiest, airiest country bedroom you have ever seen, all soft grey-blues with white linens and touches of red, and a window onto the field where the hens and horse run. It's a joyful house where Brigitte concocts delicious dinners with vegetables from the potager and has a brocante shop in the garden. All the bedrooms are dreamy.

| Rooms | 1 double, 1 twin, 1 family room for 3: €62. |
|---|---|
| Meals | Dinner with wine, €20. |
| Closed | Rarely. |

**Brigitte & Bruno Lebris**
Les Pesques,
31220 Palaminy
Haute-Garonne
Tel +33 (0)5 61 97 59 28
Email reserve@les-pesques.com
Web www.les-pesques.com

Entry 622   Map 14

## Chaumarty

Head up, up to a hilltop farmhouse with panoramic views to the Pyrénées and a lovely family who've spent 12 years fixing up their eco-friendly home. It's all hemp, lime, wood and terracotta, solar energy, a natural swimming 'bassin', horses, a donkey, a sand pit and a swing for your kids to share with theirs… such fun. Inside are two big, beamed guest rooms with country antiques, good beds and walk-in ochre showers. Sink into an easy chair by the wood-burner and browse books that reveal a passion for all things bio… as do family dinners, with Italian-Swiss Stefano and Violaine from Bordeaux. Great value, too.

| Rooms | 1 double: €60-€75. 1 family room for 4: €80-€115. |
|---|---|
| Meals | Dinner with wine, €22. Restaurant 5km. |
| Closed | Rarely. |

**Violaine & Stefano Comolli**
Chaumarty,
31550 Gaillac-Toulza
Haute-Garonne
Tel +33 (0)5 61 08 68 64
Email chaumarty@free.fr
Web www.chaumarty.com

Entry 623   Map 14

### Le Moulin Pastelier

Meals are 'en famille' – four courses and delicious – and breakfasts include homemade muffins. Donna and Chris are great hosts, love to cook, and know the best secret places to go. This fabulous house, a woad mill many centuries ago, has big windows to pull in the light and views that sail across rolling fields to the Pyrénées. Boutique bedrooms feed off a shared guest space (dining table, sofas, log-burner, books) which opens to the garden and landscaped pool. Cycle along the Canal du Midi, visit the bastide town of St Felix, return to cool colours, sophisticated bathrooms, luxurious beds, and a choice of pillows! *Children over 10 welcome. Extra bed available.*

### La Ferme d'en Pécoul

Talented Élisabeth makes jams, jellies and liqueurs, pâté, confit and foie gras, keeps hens and is wonderfully kind. Almost-retired Noël gently tends the potager as well as the fields; wrap yourself in the natural warmth of their Lauragais farmhouse. The first floor is lined with new wood, there's an airy guest sitting room and two comfy bedrooms with tiny showers. Summer meals are outside, enjoyed with your hosts. One dog, two cats, fields as far as the eye can see – and exquisite medieval Caraman (once rich from the dye cocagne) just down the road. Great value. *Minimum stay: 2 nights at weekends & summer holidays.*

| | |
|---|---|
| Rooms | 2 doubles, 2 twin/doubles: €75-€85. |
| Meals | Dinner, 4 courses with aperitif & wine, €30. |
| | Restaurants 15-minute drive. |
| Closed | Mid-November to Easter. |

| | |
|---|---|
| Rooms | 2 doubles (single child's room on request): €48. |
| Meals | Dinner with wine, €18. |
| Closed | Rarely. |

| | |
|---|---|
| | Donna Orchard |
| | Le Moulin Pastelier, |
| | Rue du Château, |
| | 31540 Bélesta en Lauragais |
| | Haute-Garonne |
| Tel | +33 (0)5 61 83 52 19 |
| Email | donna@lemoulinpastelier.com |
| Web | www.lemoulinpastelier.com |

| | |
|---|---|
| | Élisabeth & Noël Messal |
| | La Ferme d'en Pécoul, |
| | 31460 Cambiac |
| | Haute-Garonne |
| Tel | +33 (0)5 61 83 16 13 |
| Mobile | +33 (0)6 78 13 18 07 |
| Email | enpecoul@wanadoo.fr |
| Web | pagesperso-orange.fr/enpecoul |

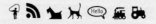

## Les Loges de St Sernin

Vast welcoming comfort lies in store behind those superb wooden doors in the heart of Toulouse – and no expense spared. Madame, living on the third floor, is a poppet: petite, delightful, up to speed with this vibrant town. Big peaceful guest bedrooms spread themselves across the floor below, each with warm colours, a huge bed, an antique mirror, luxurious linen. Breakfast is served on a balcony in good weather, as early or as late as you like it. Period detail abounds: inside shutters, marble fireplaces, sweeping parquet, tall windows beautifully dressed – Madame aims to please. Marvellous! *Minimum stay: 2 nights at weekends March-October.*

## La Villa de Mazamet & Le Petit Spa

A 'coup de foudre' caused Mark and Peter to buy this grand 1930s house in walled gardens, a few minutes' walk from the market town of Mazamet. Renovation revealed large light interiors of wood-panelled walls, parquet floors and sweeping windows. Furnished with modern elegance, the ground floor invites relaxation in comfy sofas or quiet corners. Bedrooms, with sumptuous beds and fine linen, are calmly luxurious; bathrooms are Art Deco gems. Your hosts are interesting, relaxed and well-travelled, meals in the restaurant are gastronomic. Ideal for Carcassonne, Albi and all those medieval villages. *Minimum stay: 2 nights. Children over 14 welcome.*

| | | | | |
|---|---|---|---|---|
| Rooms | 2 doubles, 2 twins: €125-€140. Singles €115-€135. Extra bed/sofabed €15-€35 per person per night. | Rooms | 3 doubles, 2 twin/doubles: €110-€190. |
| Meals | Restaurants within walking distance. | Meals | Dinner €35. Wine from €14. |
| Closed | Rarely. | Closed | November – March. |

**Sylviane Tatin**
Les Loges de St Sernin,
12 rue St Bernard,
31000 Toulouse
Haute-Garonne

Tel     +33 (0)5 61 24 44 44
Mobile   +33 (0)6 60 35 80 43
Email    logesaintsernin@live.fr
Web     www.leslogesdesaintsernin.com

**Peter Friend & Mark Barber**
La Villa de Mazamet & Le Petit Spa,
4 rue Pasteur,
81200 Mazamet
Tarn

Tel     +33 (0)5 63 97 90 33
Mobile   +33 (0)6 25 50 56 91
Email    info@villademazamet.com
Web     www.villademazamet.com

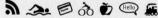

## La Terrasse de Lautrec

Le Nôtre-designed gardens backing a graceful house, with terraces overhanging the village ramparts: the beauty and the peace are restorative. Seek out the secluded shady corners and roses, the box maze, the pond brimming with waterlilies, the pool that looks over the hills. As you swan through the frescoed dining room and the drawing room with its 1810 wallpaper you feel you've stepped back into another age. Dominique, warm and intelligent, loves sharing her home with her guests. Retire to a stunning drawing room, or a large, luminous bedroom filled with ochre and gilt. *Minimum stay: 2 nights in high season.*

## Domaine d'en Naudet

Superb in every way, and such a sense of space! The domaine, surrounded by a patchwork-quilt countryside, was donated by Henri IV to a hunting crony in 1545; it was in a parlous state when Éliane and Jean fell for it. They have achieved miracles. A converted barn/stable block reveals four vast and beautiful bedrooms (two with private wicker-chaired terraces), sensuous bathrooms and a stunning open-plan breakfast/sitting room. In the grounds, masses for children and energetic adults, while the slothful may bask by the pool. Markets, history and beauty surround you, and Éliane is a lovely and attentive hostess. *Minimum stay: 2 nights in high season.*

| | | | |
|---|---|---|---|
| Rooms | 2 doubles, 1 twin: €80–€110. 1 suite for 2: €120–€130. | Rooms | 2 doubles, 2 twins: €95. |
| Meals | Restaurant within walking distance. | Meals | Guest kitchen. Restaurant 3km. |
| Closed | 1 November – 15 April. | Closed | Rarely. |

| | | | |
|---|---|---|---|
| | **Dominique Ducoudray** La Terrasse de Lautrec, 9 rue de L'Église, 81440 Lautrec Tarn | | **Éliane & Jean Barcellini** Domaine d'en Naudet, 81220 Teyssode Tarn |
| Tel | +33 (0)5 63 75 84 22 | Tel | +33 (0)5 63 70 50 59 |
| Email | d.ducoudray@wanadoo.fr | Mobile | +33 (0)6 07 17 66 08 |
| Web | www.laterrassedelautrec.com | Email | contact@domainenaudet.com |
| | | Web | www.domainenaudet.com |

### Les Buis de St Martin

The dogs are as friendly as their owner, the birds chortle in their cage, the Tarn runs at the bottom of the garden: it's a dream place. Jacqueline has lived here for 30 years and is delighted to please you and practise her English. You'll love the understated luxury of soft mushroom hues in bedrooms and bathrooms, the quilting on the excellent beds, the good paintings, the floaty muslin at the windows that look over the garden. Meals are served at one friendly table in the luminous white dining room – gleaming antiques on old tiles – or on the lovely teak-furnished patio. *Minimum stay: 2 nights in high season.*

### Domaine du Buc

Bright, smiling Brigitte is proud of her lovely 17th-century domaine, in the family for 100 years. An imposing stone staircase leads to wonderful big bedrooms with original parquet and grand mirrors, period beds, subtle paint finishes and 19th-century papers, and quirky treasures discovered in the attic: sepia photographs, antique bonnets, vintage suitcases. Showers are top-range Italian and the old arched billiards room makes a perfect salon. It's unusually, richly authentic, the breakfasts are locally sourced and delicious and you are eight miles from Albi, World Heritage Site. A huge treat. *Minimum stay: 2 nights in high season. Extra rooms available.*

| Rooms | 2 twin/doubles: €110–€120. |
|---|---|
| Meals | Dinner with wine, €30. |
| Closed | Rarely. |

| Rooms | 3 twin/doubles: €100–€120. |
|---|---|
| Meals | Guest kitchen. |
| | Restaurant 1.5km. |
| Closed | December to mid-March. |

Jacqueline Romanet
Les Buis de St Martin,
Rue St Martin,
81150 Marssac sur Tarn
Tarn

| Tel | +33 (0)5 63 55 41 23 |
| Mobile | +33 (0)6 27 86 29 48 |
| Email | jean.romanet@wanadoo.fr |
| Web | www.lesbuisdesaintmartin.com |

Brigitte Lesage
Domaine du Buc,
Route de Lagrave,
81150 Marssac sur Tarn
Tarn

| Tel | +33 (0)5 63 55 40 06 |
| Mobile | +33 (0)6 70 14 96 47 |
| Email | contact@domainedubuc.com |
| Web | www.domainedubuc.com |

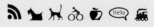

### Combettes

Come for an absolutely fabulous French bourgeois experience: a wide 16th century stone staircase deeply worn, high ceilings, southern colours, loads of stairs, interesting *objets* at every turn. Add the owners' passion for Napoleon III furniture, oil paintings and ornate mirrors and the mood, more formal than family, is unmistakably French. Bedrooms, some with rooftop views, are traditional and very comfortable; breakfast is served overlooking the old part of Gaillac. A treat to be in the heart of town, with utterly French people. Madame is a darling and it's excellent value for money.

### Le Domaine de Perches

Sheltered below the country lane, the 17th-century pale-stone building faces south, revelling in its fruitful valley. Inside: a club-like morning room, a library with a classical fireplace, a white-furnished salon in the old winery. Dip into the pool hiding below the terrace; dream under a willow by the lily pond. Bedroom moods vary: mushroom shades here, ivories and greys there; a draped bed head, a claw foot tub, immaculate lighting. Monsieur is passionate about architecture and design and his lovingly collected paintings and antiques add sparkle to the sobriety. A very beautiful place. The table d'hôtes looks outstanding. *Minimum stay: 2 nights in high season.*

| Rooms | 3 doubles, 1 twin: €60. 1 suite for 2: €75. Singles €45. |
| --- | --- |
| Meals | Restaurants within walking distance. |
| Closed | Rarely. |

| Rooms | 1 double, 1 twin/double: €155–€175. 1 suite for 2 with sitting room: €185–€215. |
| --- | --- |
| Meals | Dinner with wine, €45. Restaurants nearby. |
| Closed | Never. |

**Lucile & Marie-Pierre Pinon**
Combettes,
8 place St Michel,
81600 Gaillac
Tarn
Tel       +33 (0)5 63 57 61 48
Email   contact@combettesgaillac.com
Web     www.combettesgaillac.com

**M. Guyomarch**
Le Domaine de Perches,
Perches,
81600 Gaillac
Tarn
Tel        +33 (0)5 63 56 58 24
Mobile  +33 (0)6 08 88 19 29
Email    domainedeperches@orange.fr
Web      www.domainedeperches.com

Entry 632   Map 15

Entry 633   Map 15

## Midi – Pyrénées

### Château Cestayrols

For 400 years, this château was in the same family of wine makers. Now it is the characterful home of Murray and Jan, your Australian hosts. The inviting guest bedrooms are full of light, with painted beam ceilings, elegantly floral fabrics and the finest bed linen. Tucked off the secluded garden is a small terrace area where breakfast is served in summer, and a pretty walled pool; you are welcome to relax here as long as you wish, or sink into deep sofas inside. You're in the heart of Gaillac wine country, and stunning Albi – UNESCO heritage site – is nearby.
*Minimum stay: 2 nights*

| | |
|---|---|
| Rooms | 2 doubles: €110. |
| Meals | Restaurant 50m. |
| Closed | November–April. |

**Murray & Jan Turnbull**
Château Cestayrols,
81150 Cestayrols
Tarn

| | |
|---|---|
| Tel | +33 (0)5 63 56 95 33 |
| Email | t-bull@wanadoo.fr |
| Web | www.chateau-cestayrols.com |

Entry 633.5   Map 15

## Midi – Pyrénées

### Artichaud

Gaillac vines and Bastide villages surround this back-from-the-road, eco renovated farmhouse, which, under Liliane and Jos's expert eye, is an almost totally organic concern. Jos looks after the garden while Liliane's domain is the potager; a passionate cook, she grows produce for their table d'hôtes, including gourmet choices. Rooms are cosy with antique furniture; all look out to the garden. Breakfast on the terrace with your hosts: homemade yoghurt, preserves, croissants, and bread from their neighbours. Then laze by the pool – or curl up by the wood-burner in the reading room. Fantastic walking here – ask Jos for his tips.

| | |
|---|---|
| Rooms | 1 double, 1 twin: €75–€85. 1 suite for 2: €90–€99. Singles €75. |
| Meals | Dinner €29 (not Thurs/Fri). Restaurants 5km. |
| Closed | Rarely. |

**Liliane & Jos Delanote**
Artichaud,
Castel et Merlarié,
81140 Castelnau de Montmiral
Tarn

| | |
|---|---|
| Tel | +33 (0)5 63 57 20 42 |
| Email | liliane@artichaud.fr |
| Web | www.artichaud.fr |

Entry 634   Map 14

## Midi – Pyrénées

### La Maison au Puits

Imagine dark blue shutters and tumbling flowers, an elegant spiral staircase to spacious landings, and table d'hôtes in a stone-flagged room with candles – or in the courtyard in summer. Your generous Dutch hosts fell in love with the Tarn, then bought a house in a perfect small village at the foot of Cordes-sur-Ciel, a three-minute drive. Bedrooms and bathrooms, not huge but well designed, are on the first and second floors; beds are comfy, towels are new and paintings echo the neutral colour palette that unifies the house and creates a feeling of calm. Heaven for cyclists, walkers and history buffs. *Pets by arrangement.*

| | |
|---|---|
| Rooms | 5 doubles (2 with sofabed in adjoining room): €75–€99. Dinner, B&B €33 extra per person. |
| Meals | Dinner, 4 courses, €29. Restaurant within walking distance. |
| Closed | Christmas. |

**Christianne Zeelen**
La Maison au Puits,
20 rue Gargarides, Les Cabannes,
81170 Cordes sur Ciel
Tarn
Tel  +33 (0)5 63 60 23 05
Email  lamaisonaupuits@hotmail.com
Web  www.lamaisonaupuits.com

Entry 635   Map 15

## Midi – Pyrénées

### Aurifat

Furniture, books and paintings are thoroughly at home in this multi-stepped, history-rich house (the watchtower is 13th-century) where all is serene and inviting. Each fresh, sumptuous room has its own entrance, the twin has a cosy sitting area, the garden room a terrace for sun-drenched views – and the views are stunning. Walking distance to everything, the house is on the southern slope of Cordes (borrow a torch for a night time stroll), the pool is delicious and there's a barbecue alongside the guest kitchen. Terrace breakfasts (spot the deer) are enchanting; nothing is too much trouble for Matthew and Kay.

| | |
|---|---|
| Rooms | 4 doubles, 1 twin/double: €90. |
| Meals | Kitchen & barbecue available. Restaurants within walking distance. |
| Closed | Rarely. |

**Matthew & Kay Noble**
Aurifat,
81170 Cordes sur Ciel
Tarn
Tel  +33 (0)5 63 56 07 03
Email  aurifat@gmail.com
Web  www.aurifat.com

Entry 636   Map 15

## Midi – Pyrénées

### Hors des Brumes

In the hamlet high on the hill you can see for 20 miles. Remote but not too remote – Najac and Cordes-sur-Ciel are a 15-minute drive – this old Quercy barn in flowing gardens has been lovingly restored. From the lofty raftered living space where straw hats join plough harnesses on white lime walls to the wonky beams and pretty quilts of the bedrooms below, all feels homely and delightful – and English! Bridget, Peter and Oscar the poodle are charming hosts, offer you homemade scones at breakfast, free run of the guest kitchen, and four-course dinners. Logs for winter, a pool for summer, games, books, walks from the door – glorious. *Minimum stay: 2 nights.*

| Rooms | 1 double, 2 twins: £80. |
|---|---|
| Meals | Dinner, 4 courses, €30. |
| Closed | Rarely. |

**Bridget Wright & Peter Dixon**
Hors des Brumes,
La Maurelie,
81190 Saint Christophe
Tarn
Tel   +33 (0)5 63 76 39 87
Email   dixonwright@horsdesbrumes.com
Web   www.horsdesbrumes.com

Entry 637   Map 15

## Midi – Pyrénées

### Barbiel

You will settle quickly here. Tim and Tracy are relaxed and welcoming, all smiles and ease, the house is calming and there's a terrace for lazy breakfasts with stunning views over rolling hills. Independent ground-floor bedrooms are in the barn: aqua-washed walls, white cotton sheets, a cool mix of modern and antique furniture, zippy bathrooms with thick towels, even a tiny kitchenette for picnics or snacks. For gorgeous dinners at one big table you go to the main house where Tracy's sense of style is splashed all over a stunning art-filled sitting room. Albi is a must-see.

| Rooms | 1 double, 1 twin/double: €54–€65. |
|---|---|
| Meals | Dinner with wine, €25. Guest kitchenette. |
| Closed | Rarely. |

**Tim & Tracy Bayly**
Barbiel,
81340 Assac
Tarn
Tel   +33 (0)5 63 56 97 12
Mobile   +33 (0)6 41 69 26 06
Email   ttbayly@gmail.com
Web   www.tranquiltarn.com

Entry 638   Map 15

## Midi – Pyrénées

### La Barthe

Your Anglo-French hosts in their converted farmhouse welcome guests as friends. The pastel-painted, stencilled rooms are smallish but beds are good, the hospitality is wonderful and it's a deliciously secluded place; take a dip in the raised pool or set off into the country on foot or by bike. The Wises grow their own vegetables and summer apéritifs are hosted on the terrace overlooking the lovely Tarn valley, in a largely undiscovered part of France where birds, bees and sheep serenade you. Watch the farmers milking for roquefort and don't miss Albi, with its huge and magnificent cathedral – it's no distance at all.

| Rooms | 1 double: €55. |
| | 1 family room for 4: €80. |
| Meals | Dinner with wine, €22. |
| Closed | Rarely. |

| | Michèle & Michael Wise |
| | La Barthe, |
| | 81430 Villefranche d'Albigeois |
| | Tarn |
| Tel | +33 (0)5 63 55 96 21 |
| Email | labarthe@chezwise.com |
| Web | www.chezwise.com |

Entry 639   Map 15

## Midi – Pyrénées

### Le Gouty

A lovely old farmhouse on two levels, a terrace at the back for meals (lots of produce from sweet neighbours) and the dreamiest sunsets and views – Phillipe and Lynda, embarking on a new life in France, love the house, the community and the region. Guest bedrooms, each in a renovated farm building, have chestnut floors and reclaimed beams, the showers are super-large, and one bedroom has its own terrace – raise a glass to the view. You are in heart of the sparsely populated Aveyron – 'la France profonde.' Homemade yogurt and fig jam at breakfast, apple juice from the village and wonderful walks from the door.

| Rooms | 2 doubles: €58. |
| | Singles €55. |
| Meals | Dinner €23. |
| | Restaurant 10km. |
| Closed | Rarely. |

| | Phillipe & Lynda Denny |
| | Le Gouty, |
| | 12380 Pousthomy |
| | Aveyron |
| Tel | +33 (0)5 65 49 40 31 |
| Mobile | +33 (0)6 42 48 47 58 |
| Email | le.gouty@nordnet.fr |
| Web | legouty.webplus.net |

Entry 640   Map 15

## Quiers – Ferme Auberge

Escape to vast pastures and sensational views. This is an outdoorsy place and is brilliant for families: canoe, climb, hang-glide, spot birds, hunt orchids. The farm feels rustic, charming and somewhat shambolic – in the nicest way. Bedrooms, a short walk down a steepish track, sit snugly in the old 'bergerie'; expect shiny terracotta floors, old beams, freshly painted walls, simple pine beds. In the main house are tapestries and country antiques smelling of years of polish. Here, Véronique and her chef son, Théo, produce wonderful big meals of home-grown organic produce.

## L'Ancienne Maison du Notaire

You are in Najac, one of the most gorgeous villages in France, with an amazing mishmash of medieval streets and a castle on a hill: architectural gems at every turn. Summer hubbub does not penetrate this house's thick walls, and Hugh promises parking outside (a bonus!). He and Meg, friendly and generous, offer guests two big, airy, well-furnished bedrooms upstairs, each with a fabulous bed and a sofa to lounge on – and a little patio below, with unforgettable views. Bathe in the Aveyron river, dine at the rustic L'Oustal del Barry, tuck into figs at the Sunday market, come home to crisp linen, WiFi and books. *Double: minimum stay: 2 nights. Apartment: minimum stay: 3 nights.*

| Rooms | 2 doubles, 2 twins: €65. |
| --- | --- |
| | 1 family room for 4: €65–€102. |
| Meals | Dinner €20–€24. |
| | Wine €10–€22. |
| | Restaurants in Millau. |
| Closed | November – April. |

FIRST
EDITION
VETERAN

Véronique Lombard
Quiers – Ferme Auberge,
12520 Compeyre
Aveyron

| Tel | +33 (0)5 65 59 85 10 |
| --- | --- |
| Email | quiers@wanadoo.fr |
| Web | www.quiers.net |

Entry 641   Map 15

| Rooms | 1 double: €75–€85. |
| --- | --- |
| | 1 apartment for 2 with living area |
| | & kitchenette: €80–€90. |
| Meals | Restaurants within walking |
| | distance. |
| Closed | February. |

Meg & Hugh Macdonald
L'Ancienne Maison du Notaire,
1 rue Saint Barthélémy,
12270 Najac
Aveyron

| Tel | +33 (0)5 65 65 77 86 |
| --- | --- |
| Email | hugh@lamaisondunotaire.com |
| Web | www.lamaisondunotaire.com |

Entry 642   Map 15

### Chambres d'Hôtes Les Brunes

Swish through large wooden gates into a central courtyard and garden filled with birdsong to find lovely Monique and her 18th-century family home, complete with tower. Bedrooms are up the spiral stone tower staircase which oozes atmosphere; all are a good size ('Le Clos' is enormous) and filled with beautiful things. Antiques, beams, rugs, gilt mirrors and soft colours give an uncluttered, elegant feel; bathrooms are luxurious, views from all are lovely. You breakfast on homemade cake, farm butter and fruit salad in the handsome farmhouse kitchen. *Minimum stay: 2 nights in high season.*

| | |
|---|---|
| Rooms | 2 doubles, 2 twins: €92-€158. Extra bed/sofabed €30-€34 per person per night. |
| Meals | Guest kitchenette. Restaurant 5km. |
| Closed | Rarely. |

**Monique Philipponnat-David**
Chambres d'Hôtes Les Brunes,
Hameau les Brunes,
12340 Bozouls
Aveyron

| | |
|---|---|
| Tel | +33 (0)5 65 48 50 11 |
| Mobile | +33 (0)6 80 07 95 96 |
| Email | lesbrunes@wanadoo.fr |
| Web | www.lesbrunes.com |

Entry 643   Map 10

# Languedoc – Roussillon

www.sawdays.co.uk/languedoc-roussillon

## Languedoc – Roussillon

### Les Cessenades

Sitting snug on a hillside, surrounded by sweet chestnuts with views to hills, this huddle of dark red stone buildings soothes any weariness. You will be torn by what to do: a dip in the stream, cycle the abandoned railway track, disappear for a walk or sit on the grassy terrace and listen to the gentle wind? Within a former silk farm, spacious rooms have retained their rustic simplicity: exposed stone, wood floors, handsome chestnut furnishings, splashes of colour in rugs and throws; authentic yet comfortable. Two have fireplaces. Breakfast is a feast of local produce; dinners, too. Well-travelled Sophie and Martin are natural hosts.

| Rooms | 4 twin/doubles; sofabed available in two rooms: €70–€100. Extra room with double sofabed only, €45. Dogs €5 p.n. Child 4–8 years, €15–€25 p.n. Extra person €20–€30 p.n. |
|---|---|
| Meals | Dinner with wine, €25. Child €15. Restaurants 7-minute drive. |
| Closed | Rarely. |

|  | **Martin Waterkeyn** Les Cessenades, 48240 St Frézal de Ventalon Lozère |
|---|---|
| Tel | +33 (0)4 66 45 48 31 |
| Email | lescessenades@orange.fr |
| Web | www.lescessenades.com |

## Languedoc – Roussillon

### Transgardon en Cévennes

A light-filled valley and utter solitude. Eco-minded Pascal and Frédérique fell in love with this remote hamlet, then restored the main house and a pretty stone cottage with three, very private, bedrooms, all with their own entrance. Find gorgeous linen, gleaming antique furniture, good bathrooms. Wander up the path and over a bridge to the welcoming main house for a hunker by the stove, breakfasts of homemade brioche and honey from their bees, or a divine supper of local meat and home grown veg. Swim in the stream under the old bridge (catch a trout in the rockpool?). Hike, cycle, explore... or do nothing.

| Rooms | 3 twin/doubles (1 with extra bed on mezzanine): €110–€135. Singles €90. Under 5's free. |
|---|---|
| Meals | Dinner with wine, €25. Restaurants 6km. |
| Closed | Rarely. |

|  | **Frédérique & Pascal Mathis** Transgardon en Cévennes, Transgardon, 48240 St Privat de Vallongue Lozère |
|---|---|
| Tel | +33 (0)4 34 25 90 23 |
| Email | transgardon@transgardon.fr |
| Web | www.transgardon.fr |

## Languedoc – Roussillon

### Pont d'Ardèche

An ancestor built this fine fortified farmhouse 220 years ago; it stands by the Ardèche with its own small beach. Inside: a cavernous hall, a stone stair lined with portraits, and fresh simple bedrooms above, saved from austerity by Ghislaine's painted furniture and friezes. The glorious park – old plane trees, hidden deckchairs – invites lingerers, there's a lovely pool shared with gîte guests, and summer dinners can be enjoyed the other side of the river at their son's 'guinguette' (grilled meats, delicious salads). Pierre can accompany you on canoe trips: your sociable hosts enjoy all their guests.

| Rooms | 1 double: €70. 2 family rooms for 4: €70–€90. 1 triple: €80–€95. Child under 10, €10. Extra bed available €15 per person per night. |
|---|---|
| Meals | Dinner with wine, €25. Guest kitchen. |
| Closed | Rarely. |

FIRST
EDITION
VETERAN

Ghislaine & Pierre de Verduzan
Pont d'Ardèche,
30130 Pont St Esprit
Gard
Tel      +33 (0)4 66 39 29 80
Email    pontdardeche@orange.fr
Web      www.pont-dardeche.com

## Languedoc – Roussillon

### Le Pas de l'Âne

Sheltering under umbrella pines, an ordinary house with an extraordinary welcome. Fun for food-lovers and families; even the parrot greets you with a merry 'bonjour'. Anne, a Belgian ex-antique dealer in London, is chef; gregarious Italian Dominique is host; both are intelligent and humorous. Dinners are fabulous affairs, full of joy and fresh delights: garden strawberries, home-laid eggs, homemade spiced oils. We like the upstairs bedrooms best; the double has its own terrace. Four cats, two dogs, a pool, a big garden – heaven for kids in summer. And all those gorges and southern markets to discover.

| Rooms | 1 double, 1 twin/double, 1 twin: €75–€85. Dinner, B&B €63–€73 per person. |
|---|---|
| Meals | Dinner with wine, €23. |
| Closed | Rarely. |

Anne Le Brun
Le Pas de l'Âne,
209 chemin du Pas de l'Âne,
Combe, 30200 Sabran
Gard
Tel      +33 (0)4 66 33 14 09
Mobile   +33 (0)6 30 68 62 03
Email    pasdelane@wanadoo.fr
Web      www.pasdelane.com

### Clos de la Fontaine

The earthy colours of the south glow at every turn of this beautifully restored old house beneath the ancient fort: red-gold stone, restful white limewashed walls, terracotta tiles; the blue light filters in through garden greenery to highlight the fruit of a passion: your hosts' abundant and changing collection of modern art (works for sale) and designer furniture. She has a highly creative approach to décor; he is an excellent cook; both love opening their home to visitors, sharing the pleasure and the art. All the rooms are exquisite, with yet more original art, a lovely fireplace, old doors... Just 15 minutes from Uzès. *Minimum stay: 2 nights. Children over 12 welcome*

### La Magnanerie

This happy, artistic, relaxed couple welcome you to their light-filled former silk farm, splashed with Moroccan colour and ethnic *objets*. It has pretty ochre-coloured plates, a long wooden table on uneven flagstones, an ancient sink, beams twisting, glimpses of age-old village rooftops, a ravishing courtyard (for outdoor breakfasts in summer), big, pretty, uncluttered bedrooms and a roof terrace looking over the Cévennes foothills. Calm Michèle paints (and offers courses) and adores cooking; Michel knows his wines and the local community; their talk is cultural and enriching.

| | | | | |
|---|---|---|---|---|
| Rooms | 2 doubles, 2 twin/doubles with separate wcs: €110. Singles €90. Extra bed €30 per night. | | Rooms | 1 double: €60. 1 family room for 4: €75–€110. Children under 10 stay free. |
| Meals | Dinner, 4 courses, €25 (Mon, Weds & Sat). Wine €2–€3 a glass. Restaurant within walking distance. | | Meals | Dinner with wine, €24. |
| Closed | October – March. | | Closed | Rarely. |

| | | | | |
|---|---|---|---|---|
| | **Michel & Annick Rey** Clos de la Fontaine, 3 rue du Lavoir, 30330 St Laurent la Vernède Gard | | | **Michèle Dassonneville & Michel Genvrin** La Magnanerie, Place de l'Horloge, 30580 Fons sur Lussan Gard |
| Tel | +33 (0)4 66 72 97 85 | | | |
| Mobile | +33 (0)6 13 97 82 64 | | Tel | +33 (0)4 66 72 81 72 |
| Email | michel.rey66@orange.fr | | Email | mimi.genvrin@orange.fr |
| Web | www.closdelafontaine-provence.com | | Web | www.atelier-de-fons.com |

## Languedoc – Roussillon

### Les Marronniers

In love with their life and their 19th-century *maison de maître*, John and Michel welcome guests with exuberant gaiety. John is a joiner with a fine eye for interior design; Michel, quieter, takes care of beautiful breakfasts. From the classic tiles of the entrance hall to the art on the walls to the atmospheric lighting at night, every detail counts. Generous breakfast is elegantly served under the chestnut trees, after which you can wander off to join in with lazy village life, or visit Avignon, Uzès, Lussan – your wonderful hosts know all the best places.

| | |
|---|---|
| Rooms | 2 doubles, 2 twins: €105–€130. |
| Meals | Restaurant 5km. |
| Closed | Rarely. |

**John Karavias & Michel Comas**
Les Marronniers,
Place de la Mairie,
30580 La Bruguière
Gard
Tel   +33 (0)4 66 72 84 77
Email   info@lesmarronniers.biz
Web   www.lesmarronniers.biz

Entry 650   Map 16

## Languedoc – Roussillon

### Mas Vacquières

Thomas and Miriam have restored these lovely 18th-century buildings with pretty Dutch simplicity, white walls a perfect foil for southern-toned fabrics in outlying bedrooms reached by steep stone stairs. Mulberry trees where silkworms once fed still flower; the little vaulted room is intimate and alcoved, the big soft salon a delight. Tables on the enchantingly flowered terrace under leafy trees and a lawn sloping down to the stream make perfect spots for silent gazing; the food is superb, the table d'hôtes a delight. Enjoy the pool, sheltered in its roofless barn... it's all so relaxed you can stay all day. *Children over 12 welcome. Pets by arrangement.*

| | |
|---|---|
| Rooms | 2 doubles, 1 twin/double: €95–€140. |
| Meals | Dinner €35. |
| Closed | Rarely. |

**Thomas & Miriam van Dijke**
Mas Vacquières,
Hameau de Vacquières,
30580 St Just & Vacquières
Gard
Tel   +33 (0)4 66 83 70 75
Email   info@masvac.com
Web   www.masvac.com

Entry 651   Map 16

## Languedoc – Roussillon

### Villa Virinn

Melons and cherries in season, homemade marmalade and fig jam all year. Douglas is the chef, Geoff the greeter and gardener, both are warm hosts loving the French life. Their big new house, private and peaceful, is a short stroll from the small hilltop town: walk in for dinner and return to a candlelit garden. Inside, all is fresh, comfortable, unflashy; beds have painted headboards and matching tables, walls are blue, soft green, pale honey; those off the garden have terraces. Colourful flowers and loungers round the pool, an honesty bar, a vineyard view: the excursions are great but the temptation is to stay.

| | |
|---|---|
| Rooms | 1 double, 1 twin/double: €95. |
| Meals | Restaurants within walking distance. |
| Closed | October – April. |

**Geoff Pople & Douglas Tulloch**
Villa Virinn,
Chemin de Bercaude,
30360 Vézénobres
Gard

| | |
|---|---|
| Tel | +33 (0)4 66 83 27 30 |
| Email | geoffanddoug@villavirinn.com |
| Web | www.villavirinn.com |

Entry 652   Map 16

## Languedoc – Roussillon

### L'Espérou

Imagine a fine old house with mullioned windows in a golden hamlet five minutes from Uzès. Delight in paintings, portraits, carpets, mirrors, and a fine collection of hats up the wide stone stairs to a grandly beautiful two-bedroom suite. The rooms overlook lush lawns, white roses and southern pines: an oasis with an elegant pool and loungers awaiting aperitifs. Your hosts, passionate about baroque music, opera and treasured old things, offer you lovely lazy breakfasts on immaculate china and an indulging bathroom with Christian Dior towels. For Provençal magic, explore the shops, galleries and market of Uzès.

| | |
|---|---|
| Rooms | 2 doubles sharing bathroom (rooms interconnect to form suite): €140-€240. |
| Meals | Restaurants nearby. |
| Closed | Rarely. |

**Jacques Cauvin**
L'Espérou,
Hameau St Médiers,
30700 Montaren & St Médiers
Gard

| | |
|---|---|
| Tel | +33 (0)4 66 63 14 73 |
| Mobile | +33 (0)6 64 14 48 89 |
| Email | contact@lesperou.com |
| Web | www.lesperou.com |

Entry 653   Map 16

## Languedoc – Roussillon

## Languedoc – Roussillon

### Demeure Monte Arena

Towering over the village, by the castle, this handsome 17th-century townhouse mixes history and modernity with panache. Vaulted ceilings and flagged floors sit with modern art and black leather. Bedrooms are huge, spread between the two towers. Colours are soft, bed linen crisp, fine antiques sit happily alongside funky lights, bold rugs are spread on ancient tiles. Two rooms are duplex with stunning staircases. All have views over the courtyard garden. Breakfast – organic and homemade – is here or in the vaulted dining hall; dinners, too. Nîmes and Avignon are close or relax in the garden with its scents, secluded corners, and secret jacuzzi.

### La Claire Demeure

Surrounded by great plane trees that have never been pruned, a charming southern home. The stone vaulted salon bears witness to the days of the Knights Templar; the sofas are comfy, the fireplace glows in winter, the piano (not grand) is ready to play. Kind Claire, friendly and refined, gives you elegant bedrooms with flagged floors and high windows, fine linen, fresh flowers, a sprinkling of antiques – and simple generous family suppers enhanced by her husband's wines. He knows all about Gigondas and Châteauneuf-du-Pape so don't miss the vineyards. This is a wonderful area where markets, cafés and galleries abound.

| | |
|---|---|
| Rooms | 2 doubles: €100-€153. 2 suites for 2-3, 1 suite for 2-5: €153-€275. Extra bed/sofabed €25 per person per night. |
| Meals | Dinner, 4 courses with aperitif, wine & coffee, €50. Restaurants 10-minute walk. |
| Closed | Rarely. |

| | |
|---|---|
| Rooms | 2 doubles: €65-€88. Singles €60-€83. Extra bed/sofabed €15-€20 per person per night. |
| Meals | Dinner with wine, €15. Restaurants 10km. |
| Closed | Mid-November to mid-March. |

**Martine Julia**
Demeure Monte Arena,
6 place de la Plaine,
Montaren & St Médiers,
30700 Uzès
Gard
Tel     +33 (0)4 66 03 25 24
Email   info@monte-arena.com
Web     www.monte-arena.com

**Claire Granier**
La Claire Demeure,
1424 route de Jonquières,
30490 Montfrin
Gard
Tel      +33 (0)4 66 37 72 48
Mobile   +33 (0)6 74 50 86 84
Email    claire.tytgat@wanadoo.fr
Web      www.laclairedemeure.com

Entry 654   Map 16

Entry 655   Map 16

## Languedoc – Roussillon

### Habanera

The owners – artists, perfectionists – love nothing more than to share with guests their passion for the Camargue, and the treasures of Arles and Nîmes. Birdwatching, riding, fishing, archaeology… they can recommend the best tours and the best people. As for the house, its sleepy village façade is deceptive: in reality it is immense, with high ceilings, tall windows and a stunning courtyard garden. Walls are subtly limewashed, linen is hand monogrammed, toiletries are très chic, and the suite, spacious and serene, has its own boudoir. For breakfast? Fruit smoothies, Fougasse d'Aigle Morte pastries, homemade crème caramels. *Minimum stay: 2 nights.*

| | |
|---|---|
| Rooms | 3 doubles: €95. |
| | 1 suite for 3: €135. |
| Meals | Restaurant within walking distance. |
| Closed | Rarely. |

| | |
|---|---|
| | **Michel Joassard** |
| | Habanera, |
| | 65 rue de la Poste, |
| | 30640 Beauvoisin |
| | Gard |
| Tel | +33 (0)4 66 57 58 46 |
| Email | reservation@habanera.fr |
| Web | www.habanera.fr |

Entry 656   Map 16

## Languedoc – Roussillon

### Bed and Art

It's an old house in a little market town. Step off the narrow street to Corinne's simple, direct welcome – an unusual, interesting person – to her stone-vaulted world. Up a stone spiral lined with tapestries and smelling of waxed stone lie two attractive rooms. The patio, source of light and greenery, and the open breakfast barn are hung with Régis' paintings. Expect fine old doors and a newly-revived Bechstein: you can tell that an artist and an art historian live here, it has huge visual appeal and music is vital to them. There's a terrace on the roof, too. Don't miss Calvisson's Sunday market. *Minimum stay: 2 nights in high season.*

| | |
|---|---|
| Rooms | 1 double: €70. |
| | 1 suite for 3: €85. |
| Meals | Dinner with wine, €25. |
| | Restaurant in Calvisson. |
| Closed | Rarely. |

| | |
|---|---|
| | **Régis & Corinne Burckel de Tell** |
| | Bed and Art, |
| | 48 Grand Rue, |
| | 30420 Calvisson |
| | Gard |
| Tel | +33 (0)4 66 01 23 91 |
| Email | bedandart@gmail.com |
| Web | www.bed-and-art.com |

Entry 657   Map 16

## Languedoc – Roussillon

### Hôtel de l'Orange

Philippe receives you with warm refinement, and each hushed room is in *maison de famille* style: polished floors, warm walls and a piano that asks to be played. Stroll the magic secluded terrace garden with gasping views over the roofs of the old town, have a splash in the pool, laze with a book. Breakfast, which to Philippe is *the* moment of the day, is in the old-style dining room – or at small tables in the courtyard. Walk into the old town where the Laurence Durrell connection lives on, find good restaurants and river views. A touch of 'la vieille France'.

| Rooms | 3 doubles, 1 twin, 1 triple: €100–€160. |
|---|---|
| Meals | Dinner with wine, €40 (summer only). |
| Closed | Rarely. |

**Philippe de Frémont**
Hôtel de l'Orange,
Chemin du Château Fort,
30250 Sommières
Gard

| Tel | +33 (0)4 66 77 79 94 |
| Email | hotel.delorange@free.fr |
| Web | www.hotel-delorange.com |

Entry 658   Map 16

## Languedoc – Roussillon

### Mas de Barbut

Danielle's family home is stunning, imaginative, decorated with élan. Great travellers, the Gandons have gathered fascinating things in a strikingly harmonious way; bedrooms are Mexican, Mandarin or Provençal, outstanding bathrooms have fabulous tiles. Different food, a different table decoration every day: they love cosseting guests. The summer sitting room has a pebble floor, the stone bassin is overlooked by slatted oak loungers, there's a sweet spot for drinks by the river and the frond-shaded courtyard is bliss. Near the sea yet away from it all – and restaurants in lovely St Laurent. A treat from start to finish.

| Rooms | 2 doubles: €115–€135. 2 triples: €115–€140. 1 studio for 2: €150. |
|---|---|
| Meals | Dinner with wine, €35. |
| Closed | Rarely. |

**Danielle & Jean-Claude Gandon**
Mas de Barbut,
30220 St Laurent d'Aigouze
Gard

| Tel | +33 (0)4 66 88 12 09 |
| Mobile | +33 (0)6 64 14 28 52 |
| Email | contact@masdebarbut.com |
| Web | www.masdebarbut.com |

Entry 659   Map 16

## Languedoc – Roussillon

### Château Massal

The château façade flanks the road and the many-terraced garden rambles behind, with views across river and red-roofed town. Up a stone spiral are big beautiful bedrooms with a château feel. Walnut parquet and mosaic floors along with strong-coloured walls set off family furniture to perfection; one has a bathroom in the tower; one houses an ancient grand piano: it's enchanting. Madame, one of an old French silk family who have been here for several generations, is as elegant and charming as her house. She will show you where to have really good days out after a social breakfast round the big dining room table. *Child's bed available.*

| | |
|---|---|
| Rooms | 4 doubles: €68–€98. |
| Meals | Restaurant 5km. |
| Closed | Mid-November to March. |

**Françoise & Marie-Emmanuelle du Luc**
Château Massal,
Bez & Esparon, 30120 Le Vigan
Gard
Tel    +33 (0)4 67 81 07 60
Email   francoiseduluc@gmail.com
Web    www.cevennes-massal.com

Entry 660   Map 15

## Languedoc – Roussillon

### Au Soleil

Catherine is as elegant and welcoming as her house. Once involved in theatre PR, she now devotes her energies to guests and house; it's a treat to stay in her village-centre *maison de maître*. Behind the front door, caressed by sweet jasmine, find sunlight, space and simplicity, fine pieces of brocante and a sitting room with deep orange sofas. Bedrooms are peaceful and calm, with kilim rugs on glowing terracotta, and windows overlook the rooftops of a lush inner courtyard where cat and dog doze. Simple Mediterranean food is served with pleasure; and on Sundays in summer the bulls race through town.

| | |
|---|---|
| Rooms | 3 doubles: €65–€75. |
| Meals | Dinner with wine, €22. |
| | Restaurant within walking distance. |
| Closed | Rarely. |

**Catherine Maurel**
Au Soleil,
9 rue Pierre Brossolette,
34590 Marsillargues
Hérault
Tel    +33 (0)4 67 83 90 00
Email   catherine.maurel@ausoleil.info
Web    www.ausoleil.info

Entry 661   Map 16

## Languedoc – Roussillon

### Castle Cottage

On the edge of unspoilt woodland, in a garden full of trees and colour where 23 tortoises roam (no touching please); it's hard to believe you're a tram ride from Montpellier. The house is recent, the vegetation lush, the tempting pool (mind the alarm) set among atmospheric stone 'ruins'. In the house are small but comfortable beds in pretty rooms (shuttered in summer) full of family pieces and colour, a good shower room and doors to the terrace. Outside is a sweet little independent 'studio' for two. Your exuberant, dynamic hostess loves this place passionately, her garden is an oasis even in winter and the beach is nearby. *Minimum stay: 2 nights at weekends & in cottage.*

| Rooms | 1 double; 2 doubles sharing shower & separate wc: €92–€128. 1 studio for 2 with kitchenette: €150–€180. 1 bunk room for 2 with sofbed: €90–€120. Children under 5 stay free. Extra bed €32 p.p. per night. |
|---|---|
| Meals | For studio guests, breakfast €10. Restaurants in Montpellier, 3km. |
| Closed | Rarely. |

**Dominique Cailleau**
Castle Cottage,
289 chemin de la Rocheuse,
34170 Castelnau le Lez
Hérault
Tel     +33 (0)4 67 72 63 08
Mobile   +33 (0)6 75 50 41 50
Email   castlecottage@free.fr
Web    www.castlecottage-chambresdhotes.com

Entry 662   Map 15

---

## Languedoc – Roussillon

### Meze Maison

The welcoming aperitif sets the tone. Rob left a demanding job to turn this graceful 19th-century merchant's house into an elegant, relaxed home. Stone stairs curve to two floors of bedrooms, soft with silvery colours, chandeliers and chic bathrooms. Balconies with French windows look over the town or gardens of the nearby château. Painted in the subtle hues of Farrow & Ball and beautifully beamed, the open-plan living space is coolly stylish: antique mirrors, books, oversize table lamps. Breakfasts are served at the white dining table. Explore harbours, beaches and Meze's fish restaurants. Gentle hosts, serene surroundings.

| Rooms | 3 doubles, 1 twin/double: €95–€160. |
|---|---|
| Meals | Restaurants within walking distance. |
| Closed | November – March. |

**Rob Budden**
Meze Maison,
34140 Meze
Hérault
Mobile   +33 (0)6 05 56 46 18
Email   rob@mezemaison.com
Web    www.mezemaison.com

Entry 663   Map 15

# Languedoc – Roussillon

## Les Balcons de Molière

Like Molière, you'll discover the best thing about staying in Mèze's 16th-century auberge is you're never far from beach, wine and a pot of fresh mussels. Lap up the Old Town ambience of family bistros, rooftop views and a maze of narrow streets hung with geraniums; in summer the area fills with festivals. One bedroom is pink, silvery and small, another has a four-poster, and a feast-like breakfast is brought to all. Two rooms have their own terraces; in one, 'Belle du Seigneur', you breakfast grandly in the bathroom! Later, sink into a fireside armchair, and look forward to Corinne's excellent cooking.

| Rooms | 2 doubles; 1 twin/double with separate wc: €80–€150. |
|---|---|
| Meals | Gourmet dinner with wine, €40. Tapas with sangria, €25. Restaurants within walking distance. |
| Closed | Never. |

**Corinne Briand-Seurat**
Les Balcons de Molière,
14 rue des Trois Pigeons,
34140 Mèze
Hérault

| Tel | +33 (0)9 53 69 95 96 |
| Email | lesbalconsdemoliere@gmail.com |
| Web | www.lesbalconsdemoliere.com |

Entry 664   Map 15

# Languedoc – Roussillon

## Maison de Bacchus

Find your way to a tranquil side street in this enchanting old, twisty, stone-built Languedoc village. Knock on the door, climb the stairs from the deep dark hall, and gasp at the space and light of the living quarters. Jean and David, who've lived in Pomérols for 11 years, renovated a fine big house within ancient timbers and old stone walls and love sharing it, as well as their local knowledge. Charming, uncluttered bedrooms come with lots of storage space and pretty modern shower rooms; the generous living room and its terrace invite laziness – but your friendly hosts will inspire you to get out and explore: there's so much to see.

| Rooms | 2 doubles sharing shower room: €70–€80. 1 suite for 2-4: €85–€95. |
|---|---|
| Meals | Restaurants within walking distance. |
| Closed | Rarely. |

**David & Jean Black**
Maison de Bacchus,
12 rue des Pompes,
34810 Pomérols
Hérault

| Tel | +33 (0)4 67 01 44 15 |
| Mobile | +33 (0)7 57 50 24 45 |
| Email | jeanpomerols@gmail.com |
| Web | www.pomerols-chambres-d-hotes.com/ |

Entry 665   Map 15

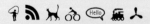

## Languedoc – Roussillon

### Chai Richard

In an old wine village, tucked behind high walls, is a tranquil, contemporary B&B. A sweet surprise to find, behind big wooden doors, a gravelled courtyard, a small pool and shady trees. Chef Richard from the Savoie cooks in colourful Provençal style, Doreen is from Mauritius, and they love to offer table d'hôtes. On the second floor of this old wine chai, up the lift or the spiralling stair, are bedrooms elegant, uncluttered and spacious, with soft colours and heated, tiled floors, and a great big roof terrace for the suite. Wild-swim in the Salagou lake, canoe on the Hérault, discover fresh seafood in the little harbour of Marsellian.

| Rooms | 1 double, 1 twin/double: €80. 1 family room for 4: €100–€140. Singles €65. |
| --- | --- |
| Meals | Dinner with wine, €30. Children under 12, €15. Restaurant 5km. |
| Closed | Rarely. |

**Richard Peillot**
Chai Richard,
1 rue Despetis,
34810 Pomérols
Hérault
Mobile    +33 (0)6 73 23 41 78
Email     lechairichard@gmail.com
Web       www.chai-richard.fr

Entry 666   Map 15

## Languedoc – Roussillon

### Le Clos de Maussanne

Surrounded by vineyards and just off the road, the unusual 17th-century house with the clock tower is smaller inside than it looks. The lovely salon, the heart of the place, looks onto a beautiful walled garden; there's a covered terrace full of tables and a super restaurant kitchen downstairs: no menu and each night a surprise. They do cookery classes, too. Bedrooms have sober cream walls, chunky modern furniture, big beds, quilted spreads. The final flourish? Élisabeth Baysset's atmospheric paintings. Visit the lovely pedestrianised old quarter of Pézenas and return to a plant-fringed pool. The motorway is so convenient.

| Rooms | 5 doubles: €120–€150. Singles €90. Extra bed/sofabed €25 per person per night. |
| --- | --- |
| Meals | Dinner from €28. Wine €17–€115. |
| Closed | Rarely. |

**Bruno Saurel &
Irwin Scott-Davidson**
Le Clos de Maussanne,
Route de Pézenas,
34500 Béziers
Hérault
Tel       +33 (0)4 67 39 31 81
Email     contact@leclosdemaussanne.com
Web       www.leclosdemaussanne.com

Entry 667   Map 15

## Languedoc – Roussillon

### Kim's House

In a posh residential area of Béziers – a short hop into town – is a generous house of glass and clean lines surrounded by high hedges and greenery. Charming Kim (brilliant at languages) gives you a peaceful minimalist bedroom with doors opening to the terrace, and buys the finest organic produce from the markets so you can enjoy delicious breakfasts. She will happily cook dinner too, served by candlelight under a cherry tree where two tortoises potter… or by the floodlit pool. In winter there's a vast living room to share, whiter than white with lovely large leather sofas just asking to be sat on.

| Rooms | 1 double: €70-€90. |
| | Singles €60-€80. |
| Meals | Dinner €25. |
| | Restaurants 2.5 km. |
| Closed | Rarely. |

Kim von Schledorn
Kim's House,
1 impasse Gustave Caillebotte,
34500 Béziers
Hérault
Tel      +33 (0)4 67 31 42 32
Email    krimhild.vonschledorn@gmail.com

## Languedoc – Roussillon

### La Bergerie de Laval

Keen cyclists and walkers, your kind hosts, Sonia and John, make unwinding easy at their traditionally dressed villa in vineyards two minutes from Pézenas. The pool, jacuzzi, lingering breakfasts (homemade jams, excellent pastries); the smell of Mediterranean plants and a hammock hung between mature pines – all help! As do the quietly decorated ground-floor rooms that come with super bedding, refreshed brocante furniture, parquet floors, good bathrooms and towels. Dine in the village or simply picnic if you've had a big day out: being sporty on Lake Salagou, eating from the Étang de Thau or marketing in medieval St Guilhem.
*Minimum stay: 2 nights.*

| Rooms | 1 double; 2 doubles with separate |
| | wc: €65-€105. |
| Meals | Restaurant within walking distance. |
| Closed | Never. |

Sonia & John Potts
La Bergerie de Laval,
21 chemin de Laval,
34120 Tourbes
Hérault
Tel      +33 (0)4 67 90 77 86
Mobile   +33 (0)6 79 25 85 52
Email    jwh.sj.potts@gmail.com
Web      www.la-bergerie-de-laval.com/

## Languedoc – Roussillon

### Villa Juliette

This house, these hosts and Pézenas itself are a treat. Gilles is French and ran the family vineyard for years – he'll give you tasting tips. Ruth is English, an interior architect and talented jam-maker – breakfasts won't disappoint. You share their lovely home in a green part of town, in a beguiling, mature garden with a curvaceous pool. All is elegantly stylish but not too grand. Rooms are quietly, comfortably attractive: softly painted, striped and parquet-floored, park and garden-viewed. Pézenas will absorb you for hours with its brocante, antique and craft shops, its market, music and theatre – and many eateries. *Minimum stay: 2 nights in high season.*

| | |
|---|---|
| Rooms | 2 twin/doubles; 2 twin/doubles with separate wc; 1 twin with separate shower & wc: €90–€120. Singles discount €10. |
| Meals | Restaurants within walking distance. |
| Closed | December/January. |

**Gilles & Ruth de Latude**
Villa Juliette,
6 chemin de la Faissine,
34120 Pézenas
Hérault
Tel      +33 (0)4 67 30 46 25
Email    ruthdelatude@wanadoo.fr
Web      www.villajuliette.fr

Entry 670   Map 15

## Languedoc – Roussillon

### 15 Grand Rue

An elegant 1880s townhouse with a flower-scented garden in the heart of an old Languedoc market town ringed by vineyards. The house has been updated by your delightful hosts (he Swedish, she English) with the utmost sensitivity. French antiques, paintings and oriental rugs glow to a backdrop of high moulded ceilings, marble fireplaces and dove-grey panelled walls. Two generous suites each have an antique bed dressed in hand-embroidered sheets, balconied views and a separate sitting area; a third ground-floor bedroom opens to the garden. Breakfast on warm croissants and Abigail's daily 'special' among the palms and acacias. *Whole house available.*

| | |
|---|---|
| Rooms | 2 twin/doubles: €135–€168. 3 suites for 2: €135–€178. Singles €125–€168. |
| Meals | Chef available when whole house rented. Restaurant 4km. |
| Closed | Christmas/New Year. |

**Abigail Turner**
15 Grand Rue,
34720 Caux
Hérault
Tel      +33 (0)4 67 37 50 61
Email    info@15grandrue.com
Web      www.15grandrue.com

Entry 671   Map 15

## Languedoc – Roussillon

### The Village House

A tall narrow house, unpretentious and spotless, run by unpushy hosts who live and work here so are always around for you. The oldest part is attached to the 14th-century ramparts of the sleepy market town which stands in a sea of Languedoc vineyards. Serene rooms are set round the charming first-floor guest terrace: the smaller one cool and light with white floor tiles, the master room splendid with its big shower room and balconies over the old fountain square. An excellent place to stay, inexpensive, stylish, discreet, it has a winter living room, too. Historic Pézenas has markets and boutiques galore, and the mountain bikes are free.
*Minimum stay: 2 nights.*

| | |
|---|---|
| Rooms | 2 doubles: €60–€65. |
| Meals | Restaurants 2km. |
| Closed | Rarely. |

John Cook & Jean-Maurice Siu
The Village House,
3 rue du Théron,
34320 Gabian
Hérault
Tel    +33 (0)4 67 24 77 27
Email  contact@thevillagehouse.info
Web    www.thevillagehouse.info

Entry 672   Map 15

## Languedoc – Roussillon

### Le Manoir

Barbara loves pampering her guests with perfect details. You have a cosy king-size room with an inspired mix of old and new furnishings – a stone basin on a chunk of wild wood and initialled pillows – and a double-aspect living room – fireplace, sofa and glass table – leading out to a big hillside garden (the free-range hens provide your breakfast eggs) and a spot in the sun in the newly-planted citrus courtyard. Enjoy this friendly, generous couple's fine art collection and travellers' tales from afar. Then set out to explore the little towns and natural wonders of the unsung Languedoc – and return to a dip in your hosts' hidden pool.
*Minimum stay: 2 nights.*

| | |
|---|---|
| Rooms | 1 suite for 2: €90–€150. |
| Meals | Dinner with aperitif & wine €35. |
| Closed | Rarely. |

Barbara Simpson-Birks
Le Manoir,
Le Grand Hermitage,
Chemin de la Faïence, Villeneuvette,
34800 Clermont l'Hérault, Hérault
Tel    +33 (0)4 67 96 62 31
Mobile +33 (0)7 71 01 48 84
Email  sunfor300days@gmail.com
Web    www.legrandhermitage.com

Entry 673   Map 15

## Languedoc – Roussillon

### Des Lits sur la Place

Right on the square of the old town, with views over rooftops and hills beyond, is a lovely old house in a rich ochre red, decorated simply and with devotion to detail. The charming young owners, former photographers from Paris, run a restaurant to the side: the menu is short, the dishes delicious. Hike in the unspoilt hills, visit vibrant Montpellier, explore the wild wooded hills, then return to big peaceful bedrooms on the second floor, painted and polished in soft earthy colours, with fine old cross beams and chic Italian showers. Breakfast at the long table will delight you: homemade yogurts, jams, pain d'épices.

| Rooms | 3 twin/doubles: €65-€75. |
| | 2 family rooms for 2-4: €96-€126. |
| Meals | Dinner from €26. |
| | Wine from €20. |
| | Lunch €19. |
| | Restaurants 10-minute drive. |
| Closed | Rarely. |

Marion & Thierry Deloulay
Des Lits sur la Place,
12 place de la Croix,
34600 Hérépian
Hérault

| Tel | +33 (0)4 67 23 16 84 |
| Mobile | +33 (0)6 41 61 43 44 |
| Email | contact@deslitssurlaplace.fr |
| Web | www.deslitssurlaplace.fr |

## Languedoc – Roussillon

### Le Saint André

You're welcomed with open arms at this old 'vigneronne' in the heart of a wine village (four shops, one lively restaurant-café). Your relaxed hosts, with young children of their own, give you four bedrooms – the brightest upstairs, all with en suite showers, one with a bath too – and a wonderful sitting/dining room with a sofa, a wood-burner and a little guest kitchen. This is where Emma prepares excellent breakfasts, served on the terrace in summer. Darren, a super cyclist, offers expert advice on routes; you can swim in the Orb river or visit charming Pézenas. Then it's back home to delicious, sociable supper. *Minimum stay: 2 nights in high season. Cot available.*

| Rooms | 2 doubles, 2 twin/doubles: €55-€75. |
| | Extra bed €20 per person per night. |
| Meals | Light dinner €15. |
| | Dinner with wine, 2 courses, €20; |
| | 3 courses, €25. |
| | Restaurants 2km. |
| Closed | Rarely. |

Darren & Emma Kennedy
Le Saint André,
27 rue Saint-André,
34480 Autignac
Hérault

| Tel | +33 (0)4 67 90 82 40 |
| Email | info@le-saint-andre.com |
| Web | www.le-saint-andre.com |

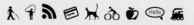

# Languedoc – Roussillon

# Languedoc – Roussillon

## Les Mimosas

The O'Rourkes love France, wine, food, their fine house in this enchanting old village and the dazzling countryside around. Enter a high cool hall with old stone stairs leading to fresh, delicately decorated bedrooms with showers and good art on the walls. Rooms at the back face south with views to the hills. You can walk, ride, climb rocks; swim, canoe in the river; visit the local market and the unusual succulent garden. Then return for drinks on the terrace with your friendly hosts, he an architect, both keen on history, art and travel. They'll readily advise on restaurants near and far. A little slice of heaven.

## La Métairie Basse

In these wild, pastoral surroundings with great walking and climbing trails, you bathe in simplicity, stream-babble and light. Your hosts, hard-working walnut and chestnut growers, have converted to 'bio' and sell delicious purées and jams. The guest barn is beautifully tended: country antiques, old lace curtains, new bedding and blue tones relax the eye; there's a fireplace and a full kitchen too. Monsieur has a big friendly handshake, Madame is gentle and welcoming, and breakfast on the shady terrace includes cheese or walnuts or honey. The wonderful Cathar city of Minerve is a 40-minute drive. Amazing value.

| | |
|---|---|
| Rooms | 4 doubles: €75. |
| | 1 apartment for 2 with kitchenette: €70. |
| Meals | Restaurants in Roquebrun. |
| Closed | November – January. |

| | |
|---|---|
| Rooms | 1 double with sofabed: €59. |
| | 1 family room for 3: €72. |
| Meals | Guest kitchen. Restaurants 3km. |
| Closed | October – March, except by arrangement. |

FIRST
EDITION
VETERAN

|  |  |
|---|---|
| | **Martin & Jacqui O'Rourke** |
| | Les Mimosas, |
| | Avenue des Orangers, |
| | 34460 Roquebrun |
| | Hérault |
| Tel | +33 (0)4 67 89 61 36 |
| Mobile | +33 (0)6 42 33 96 63 |
| Email | welcome.lesmimosas@wanadoo.fr |
| Web | www.lesmimosas.net |

|  |  |
|---|---|
| | **Éliane & Jean-Louis Lunes** |
| | La Métairie Basse, |
| | Hameau de Prouilhe, |
| | 34220 Courniou |
| | Hérault |
| Tel | +33 (0)4 67 97 21 59 |
| Mobile | +33 (0)6 11 38 07 68 |
| Email | info@metairie-basse.com |
| Web | www.metairie-basse.com |

## Languedoc – Roussillon

### Mas du Soleilla

Famous wines and wild drifting views across vineyards and pines out to the sea – of course the Romans loved it here. Reclining on the terrace with a glass of delicious estate wine, you could be one of them. A typical day begins with fresh grape juice and breakfast at a splendid great marble table, and ends, after a sumptuous meal in the nearby auberge, following the lanterns back to bed in big, cool, lime washed rooms. A dynamic Swiss couple, Christa and Peter know everything about the area, from cathedrals to markets, but the first stop is always the cellar: the wines have been famous here for 2,000 years. *Minimum stay: 2 nights. Arrival between 2pm and 6pm.*

| | |
|---|---|
| Rooms | 2 doubles, 3 twin/doubles: €115–€160. |
| Meals | Restaurant within walking distance. |
| Closed | November – March. |

**Christa Derungs & Peter Wildbolz**
Mas du Soleilla,
Route de Narbonne Plage,
11100 Narbonne
Aude

Tel +33 (0)4 68 45 24 80
Email chambres@mas-du-soleilla.com
Web www.mas-du-soleilla.com

## Languedoc – Roussillon

### La Maison des Rossignols

The village is known for its wine and Romanesque church; get up early on a clear day and you're rewarded with a Pyrenean view. This is an elegant, fresh-painted *maison de maître* whose warm, kind German owners, well integrated into French life, prepare for you a generous English breakfast (or a French one should you prefer) in a big friendly kitchen with a bright red wall. Immaculate and uncluttered bedrooms off a wide landing have sweeping wooden floors, handsome old pine doors, and space for button-back sofas. After a day out in idyllic Lagrasse or splendid Carcassonne, prepare to be spoiled by Marco's fabulous dinners.

| | |
|---|---|
| Rooms | 3 doubles, 1 twin: €80–€85. |
| Meals | Dinner with wine, €29. |
| | Restaurants 4km. |
| Closed | 1 December – 1 March. |

**Marco Raumann**
La Maison des Rossignols,
7 traverse du Mourel,
11120 Pouzols-Minervois
Aude

Mobile +33 (0)6 32 16 43 13
Email rossignols.pouzols@gmail.com
Web www.chambres-hotes-rossignols.com

# Languedoc – Roussillon

## Le Jardin d'Homps

A glorious drive through villages and vines, past the Canal du Midi, delivers you to the heart of this watery town, and a great big old house (once a hotel) with impressive panelling and Art Nouveau windows. Yours to roam: a large dining room with iron and mosaic tables, a large salon with black leather sofas, and lofty bedrooms with parquet floors. Nina, granddaughter of a pâtissier, gives you delicious fig baguettes and local honeys at breakfast, at the garden table; your hosts have five sons (just one here now) and have long done B&B. Rent bikes or a barge for the day, return to atmospheric church bells. *Child's bed & cot available.*

| Rooms | 2 doubles, 3 twin/doubles: €75–€110. Singles €62–€99. Extra bed €32 per person per night; children under 12, €19. 10% discount during April & October. |
|---|---|
| Meals | Restaurants within walking distance. |
| Closed | 1 November – 31 March. |

|  | Nina Bourdon |
|---|---|
|  | Le Jardin d'Homps, |
|  | 21 Grand rue, |
|  | 11200 Homps |
|  | Aude |
| Tel | +33 (0)4 68 91 39 50 |
| Email | ljdh@wanadoo.fr |
| Web | www.gite-chambre-hotes.com |

---

# Languedoc – Roussillon

## Le Vieux Relais

Valerie and Mike poured hearts and souls into refurbishing their 18th-century coach house. Old door hinges gleam, tiled floors sweep across the big, welcoming, fresh-faced bedrooms, each with its own sitting area and ceiling fan to keep you cool. There's a cosy guest sitting room and a flower'd courtyard garden with – joy of joys – a pool, homemade cake for tea, fabulous dinners with local wines, barbecues on a shady terrace. Your friendly English hosts have stacks of time for you and know all about local events and restaurants. Books for readers, maps for walkers: they always go the extra mile. *Minimum stay: 2 nights in high season.*

| Rooms | 1 double, 1 twin: €70–€80. 2 suites for 2: €75–€85. 1 family room for 2-5: €70–€135. |
|---|---|
| Meals | Dinner with wine, from €25. Picnic available. |
| Closed | Rarely. |

|  | Valerie & Michael Slowther |
|---|---|
|  | Le Vieux Relais, |
|  | 1 rue de l'Étang, |
|  | 11700 Pépieux |
|  | Aude |
| Tel | +33 (0)4 68 91 69 29 |
| Email | mike@levieuxrelais.net |
| Web | www.levieuxrelais.net |

## Languedoc – Roussillon

## Languedoc – Roussillon

### Château La Villatade

An enormous 19th-century wine vat (where, in times past, hundreds of tonnes of grapes were turned into wine) is the novel tasting room for the aromatic wines still made at this traditional farmhouse. Sophie and Denis invite you to share their home and their passion for wine making; their welcome is irresistible. The 'Forge' and the 'Walker' suites are charming, modern, immaculate, with lime washed walls and terracotta floors. And the grounds are idyllic: horses in the paddock, a potager, teeming trout and a natural pool, bliss for a swim on a hot day. Mountains, caves and gorges wait to be explored, Carcassonne is wonderfully close.
*Minimum stay: 2 nights in high season.*

### La Forge de Montolieu

Napoleonic cannonballs were once fashioned in this striking country forge in a secluded valley where flowers and bird-filled forests give way to waterfalls and trout-rich pools. Later, textiles emerged from its creamy walls... Now home to a charming Franco-American family, it's a wonderful renovation project with four country-pretty bedrooms, new Italian showers and a kitchenette in the guest wing. Charles' photos hint at their passion for the place, and you'll learn more over a lazy brunch, a family supper or five-course dinner – organic with seasonal veg. Walk the dogs through a pocket of woods to book-happy Montolieu.

| | |
|---|---|
| Rooms | 2 suites for 2: €95–€110. Extra bed/sofabed €20 per person per night. |
| Meals | Dinner with wine, €20. |
| Closed | January. |

| | |
|---|---|
| Rooms | 2 doubles, 1 twin: €88–€100. 1 triple: €100. Extra bed/sofabed €22 per person per night. |
| Meals | Cooked breakfast €5. Dinner €18–€30. Wine from €4–€25. Guest kitchenette. Restaurant 2km. |
| Closed | Rarely. |

| | |
|---|---|
| | **Sophie & Denis Morin** Château La Villatade, La Villatade, 11600 Sallèles Cabardès Aude |
| Tel | +33 (0)4 68 77 57 51 |
| Email | villatade@wanadoo.fr |
| Web | www.villatade.com |

| | |
|---|---|
| | **Charles Cowen** La Forge de Montolieu, Hameau de Franc, 11170 Montolieu Aude |
| Tel | +33 (0)4 68 76 60 53 |
| Email | info@forgedemontolieu.com |
| Web | www.forgedemontolieu.com |

Entry 682   Map 15

Entry 683   Map 15

## Languedoc – Roussillon

### La Rougeanne

Monique has endless energy and adores people, Paul-André is quiet and charming, together they promise you a wonderful stay. They bought the old wine-grower's estate on the edge of town in a most parlous state – but look at it now! The sitting room is stylish, restful, flooded with light and washed with pearl grey and the bedrooms are quietly luxurious; Monique has a way with interiors. Have breakfast by the lavender in summer, then discover hilltop bastides and the castles of the Cathars… monumental Carcassonne is up the road. Return to a garden within gardens and distant views, an orangery and a pool. Bliss.

| | |
|---|---|
| Rooms | 3 doubles, 1 twin: €81–€120. 1 family room for 4: €100–€170. Singles €85–€115. Extra bed/sofabed €30 per person per night. |
| Meals | Restaurants within walking distance. |
| Closed | Rarely. |

**Monique & Paul-André Glorieux**
La Rougeanne,
8 allée du Parc,
11170 Moussoulens
Aude
Tel    +33 (0)4 68 24 46 30
Mobile  +33 (0)6 61 94 69 99
Email  info@larougeanne.com
Web   www.larougeanne.com

Entry 684   Map 15

## Languedoc – Roussillon

### Villelongue Côté Jardins

Painters, poets, nature-lovers love this place, where history and romance combine. Dark 16th-century passages and uneven stone floors open into heavily beamed rooms sympathetically revived. Big, simple bedrooms, authentic in their white cotton and old armoires, the more recent on the ground floor, look out to the ancient trees of the park or the great courtyard and ruined Cistercian abbey. Sisters Renée and Claude, warm, knowledgeable, generous, were born here and provide convivial breakfasts and dinners. Wild gardens and duck ponds, lazy cats and lovely walks into the landscape.

| | |
|---|---|
| Rooms | 1 double, 1 twin: €70–€80. 1 family room for 3: €70–€83. Singles €50. Extra bed/sofabed €20. |
| Meals | Dinner with wine, €25 (not July/August). |
| Closed | Christmas. |

**Claude Antoine & Renée Marcoul**
Villelongue Côté Jardins,
Lieu-dit Villelongue,
11170 St Martin le Vieil
Aude
Tel    +33 (0)4 68 76 09 03
Email  villelongue-cote-jardins@orange.fr
Web   www.villelongue-cote-jardin.com

Entry 685   Map 15

### Domaine les Magasins

Quite a setting – on the Canal du Midi. Boats bob and Carcassonne calls. Sweep through huge gates to Luc and Marianne's beautiful home, once a hub of activity where grain was loaded on to brave little barges. Now, all is calm, and bedrooms are spacious and stylishly minimalist – nab the family room or the suite with a terrace. Have breakfast by a wonderful pool (cosy if the two gîtes are full); come evening, share colonial-style sitting and dining rooms with your gentle hosts. You can mosey along the canal for supper – or Luc will drop you 5km away and the restaurant owner will deliver you back!

### Château de la Prade

Lost among the cool shadows of tall sunlit trees beside the languid waters of the Canal du Midi is a place of understated elegance and refinement. Sitting in 12 acres, the 19th-century house is more 'domaine' than 'château' – formal hedges, fine trees, ornamental railings – though the vineyards have long gone. Swiss Roland runs the B&B, George looks after the gardens: they are kind and discreetly attentive hosts. Dinner is served on beautifully dressed tables, breakfasts are a treat, bedrooms have tall windows, polished floors and an immaculate, uncluttered charm. Half a mile from the road to Carcassonne but so peaceful.

| | |
|---|---|
| Rooms | 2 twin/doubles: €90–€95.<br>1 suite for 2: €85–€110.<br>1 family room for 4-5: €90–€170.<br>Extra bed €20–€25 per person per night. |
| Meals | Restaurants nearby. |
| Closed | Rarely. |

| | |
|---|---|
| Rooms | 4 twin/doubles: €95–€125.<br>Single €80–€105.<br>Dinner, B&B extra €18–€28 p.p.<br>Extra bed/sofabed €25 p.p per night. |
| Meals | Dinner €18–€28.<br>Wine €17–€36. |
| Closed | Mid-November to<br>mid-March. |

AWARD WINNER

Most praised breakfast

**Luc & Marianne Pringalle**
Domaine les Magasins,
Port de Bram,
11150 Bram
Aude

| | |
|---|---|
| Tel | +33 (0)4 68 79 49 18 |
| Mobile | +33 (0)6 74 53 49 07 |
| Email | zensud11@gmail.com |
| Web | www.domainelesmagasins.fr |

**Roland Kurt & René Augustin**
Château de la Prade,
11150 Bram
Aude

| | |
|---|---|
| Tel | +33 (0)4 68 78 03 99 |
| Email | chateaulaprade@wanadoo.fr |
| Web | www.chateaulaprade.fr |

Entry 686   Map 15

Entry 687   Map 15

## Languedoc – Roussillon

### Domaine St Pierre de Trapel

Coming in from the magnificent gardens, catch the scent of herbs as you walk through the house. The delightful owners, lively, educated, well-travelled, moved here from east France for a more relaxing way of life and climate. Using exquisite taste, they have combined original 18th-century elegances with new necessities in big bedrooms and bathrooms of pure luxury, each with its own soothing colour scheme. It is tranquil in all seasons, with relaxing outdoor spots for all, a superb 150-year-old cedar, olive trees, a swimming pool surrounded by roses and a lovely covered terrace. A place of beauty, elegance and space.

## Languedoc – Roussillon

### Camellas-Lloret

The streets are narrow, the approach is charming, and the house, built around a zen-like courtyard with swinging basket chairs and greenery, dates from the early 1700s. Annie is a designer, Colin a chiropractor, and the whole place exudes warmth, serenity and beauty. A wide central staircase ascends in luscious curves as subtle whites and greys create an exquisite backdrop for ornate mouldings and modernist pieces. In the light-filled suite under the eaves, you'll find lovely old tomette floors, and then there's Annie's breakfast, a treat every day, served in the greenhouse or by the little fountain. Exceptional. *Parking available.*

| | |
|---|---|
| Rooms | 3 doubles, 1 twin: €100–€145. 1 suite for 4: €95–€175. Singles €100–€175. Extra bed/sofabed €23 per person per night. |
| Meals | Restaurants 5km. |
| Closed | November – March, except by arrangement. |

| | |
|---|---|
| Rooms | 2 doubles, 1 double in garden house (summer only): €140–€200. 2 family suites for 4: €140–€180. Singles €80. Extra bed/sofabed €20 per person per night. |
| Meals | Restaurants 10km. |
| Closed | Rarely. |

| | |
|---|---|
| | **Christophe & Catherine Pariset** Domaine St Pierre de Trapel, Route de Villedubert, 11620 Villemoustaussou Aude |
| Tel | +33 (0)4 68 77 00 68 |
| Email | cpariset@trapel.com |
| Web | www.trapel.com |

| | |
|---|---|
| | **Annie Moore** Camellas-Lloret, 4 rue de l'Angle, 11290 Montréal Aude |
| Tel | +33 (0)9 67 00 40 44 |
| Email | annie@camellaslloret.com |
| Web | www.camellaslloret.com |

## Languedoc – Roussillon

### Domaine Michaud

Stylish Jolanda from Holland looks after you beautifully in ancient buildings in a pastoral setting with views of the Pyrénées and mature trees. The big living room has a fireplace, tapestries on the walls, antique furniture and a terrace for breakfast. Dinner (for locals too) is always a surprise and usually a home-grown one; and you can socialise or be private. Bright, lovely bedrooms, some with stone walls, most with views, one in romantic whites, are peaceful. The pool is just below so it may be splashy during the day and there's a self-catering studio-apartment too, in the main house with its own terrace. *Self-catering available in apartment for 2.*

| Rooms | 4 twin/doubles: €105–€135. Cot €15. |
|---|---|
| Meals | Dinner, 3 courses, €30. Restaurant 4km. |
| Closed | Rarely. |

**Jolanda Danen**
Domaine Michaud,
Route de la Malepère,
Roullens,
11290 Carcassonne
Aude
Mobile  +33 (0)6 44 29 42 30
Email  info@domainemichaud.eu
Web  www.domainemichaud.eu

Entry 690  Map 15

## Languedoc – Roussillon

### Les Marguerites

Dine deliciously and convivially at one big table – by the log fire or under the stars. On the edge of the historic little spa town of Alet les Bains is this grand old mansion and sparkling B&B – throw open elegant shutters for sunshine and views. Here live Antoinette (daughter of a renowned restaurateur) and Keith (fount of local knowledge), in love with the Languedocian life, bringing up a young family. Outside find a fabulous play area, little tables for breakfast and century-old trees. The bedrooms are big, airy, uncluttered and charming; the suite has a long sunny balcony, the village has an outdoor pool. Heaven! *Minimum stay: 2 nights in high season.*

| Rooms | 3 doubles: €65–€105. 1 suite for 4: €105–€140. |
|---|---|
| Meals | Dinner €25. Wine €12–€25. Restaurant within walking distance. |
| Closed | Rarely. |

**Keith & Antoinette Fairhurst**
Les Marguerites,
57 av Nicolas Pavillon,
11580 Alet les Bains
Aude
Tel  +33 (0)4 68 20 53 56
Email  Antoinette@les-marguerites.fr
Web  www.les-marguerites.fr

Entry 691  Map 15

## Languedoc – Roussillon

### Le Trésor

The most attractive house in the village, Le Trésor looks through green eyelids onto the sleepy town square. Inside, tall elegant windows and banistered stairs mix with white walls, crisp art and flamboyant chandeliers: ex-Londoners Will and Tilly have created a quirkily seductive B&B. Bedrooms, one with a roll top bath, have high ceilings, spare furnishings, masses of light. Tilly loves regional food so the treats continue at table, and breakfasts are superb. A hammock in the garden (kids love it!), L'Occitane oils by the shower, DVDs, snooker and super young hosts. Great for hiking or skiing or discovering Matisse's Collioure. *Minimum stay: 2 nights.*

| | |
|---|---|
| Rooms | 3 doubles, 1 suite for 2: €90–€120. |
| Meals | Dinner, 3 courses, €28. Wine €10. |
| Closed | November – March. |

**William & Tilly Howard**
Le Trésor,
20 place de l'Église,
11230 Sonnac sur l'Hers
Aude
Tel +33 (0)4 68 69 37 94
Email contact@le-tresor.com
Web www.le-tresor.com

Entry 692   Map 15

## Languedoc – Roussillon

### Le Roc sur l'Orbieu

Hélène has been renovating for 25 years. Full of life and laughter she has achieved marvels, from digging deep to find 900-year-old cobbles to creating terraces dotted with brocante and fuchsia-pink cushions – one with a counter-current swimming pool. Inside: whitewashed stone and antique terracotta, charming beds topped with vintage linen, blissful bathrooms with fluffy white towels, flowered armchairs for aperitifs by the fire. Dinner is at one table and she does it on her own – asparagus with smoked trout, chevreau in a herby crust, sorbet aux fraises. Breakfasts are divine.

| | |
|---|---|
| Rooms | 3 doubles: €102–€127. |
| | 2 family rooms for 4: €110–€142. |
| | Extra bed/sofabed €25 per person per night. |
| Meals | Dinner €24–€32. |
| | Childrens' meals available. |
| | Restaurants 5km. |
| Closed | Never. |

**Hélène Carreaud**
Le Roc sur l'Orbieu,
4 rue des Pavés,
Saint Pierre des Champs,
11220 Lagrasse
Aude
Tel +33 (0)4 68 43 39 07
Email h.carreaud@wanadoo.fr
Web www.lerocsurlorbieu.com

Entry 693   Map 15

## Languedoc – Roussillon

### La Rassada

In a corner of Corbières where wild orchids flourish and eagles soar stands Philippa's eco-friendly barn. Once used for drying rosemary and thyme, it's now a modern home, open to the rafters with massive windows and heady views. Simple, comfy, contemporary ground-floor rooms with big glass doors open to the garden, while the kitchen opens to the terrace – for breakfasts of brioche, jams, muesli and local yoghurt. Your charming host is a heavenly cook so dinners too are a treat. Perfect for nature-loving families and walkers – and the coast is close. Ask for a picnic and you can be as free as a bird all day. *Minimum stay: 2 nights; 4 nights in high season.*

| | |
|---|---|
| Rooms | 1 double, 1 twin/double sharing bathroom (let to same party only): €80–€100. Dinner, B&B €65–€75 per person. |
| Meals | Dinner with wine, €25. Restaurants 15-minute drive. |
| Closed | 1 December – 28 February. |

**Philippa Benson**
La Rassada,
Route d'Opoul,
11510 Feuilla
Aude
Tel      +33 (0)4 68 42 82 56
Email    philippa@feuillanature.com
Web      www.feuillanature.com

## Languedoc – Roussillon

### L'Orangerie

The most charming town with a bustling market, and lovely restaurants… you stay in the heart of it all. Through huge green gates enter a pretty courtyard with flowering pots, the orange tree (as announced) and a true 18th-century *maison de maître* with original terrazzo floors. Calm and relaxed, Sylvie and Claude offer a charming sitting room with a reading corner and comfy seating, and bright inviting bedrooms, one with a terrace. Breakfast in the dining room or in the courtyard brings seasonal fresh fruits, cake and homemade jams. Dinner can be served here too – in best traditional French style.

| | |
|---|---|
| Rooms | 4 doubles: €70–€95. Whole house, €2500 per week. |
| Meals | Dinner with wine, €27. |
| Closed | Rarely. |

**Sylvie & Claude Poussin**
L'Orangerie,
3T rue Ludovic Ville,
66600 Rivesaltes
Pyrénées-Orientales
Tel      +33 (0)4 68 73 74 41
Mobile   +33 (0)6 09 82 75 87
Email    maisonhoteslorangerie@wanadoo.fr
Web      www.maisonhoteslorangerie.com

## Languedoc – Roussillon

### Le Chai Catalan

Peacefully above red-roofed Ortaffa is this converted winery, a lovely sanctuary, owned by Tim and Pascale. Originally built into the medieval ramparts, the stylish house mixes ancient stones with zinc, metal and glass; all feels uplifting and inviting. There's a light-flooded sitting room in the atrium, a fridge stocked with local wines, and big bright bedrooms on the ground and first floors, with fresh white linen and huge walk-in showers. Wake to generous breakfast – served, if you're lucky, in a secret garden of palm trees and flowers, cobbles and pool. Pop into Collioure, come and go as you please.

| Rooms | 2 doubles: €90–€105. |
| --- | --- |
| | 2 family rooms for 3: €115–€130. |
| Meals | Restaurants 5km. |
| Closed | Rarely. |

Pascale Jacquot
Le Chai Catalan,
14 rue du Château,
66560 Ortaffa
Pyrénées-Orientales

Tel +33 (0)4 68 87 19 13
Email pascale.jacquot@wanadoo.fr
Web www.chai-catalan.fr

## Languedoc – Roussillon

### Clos des Aspres

Meet the guests over breakfast at the long table (Emmanuel's cakes are delicious) or by the pool with a view of Mont Canigou, and relax to the cooing of the doves. The old Catalan farmhouse is surrounded by its vineyards, there's a special building for weddings, seminars, yoga, and bedrooms and bathrooms are bright, contemporary, full of personality, with patio doors to the gardens – a delight. Visit magical Collioure by the sea, take the Little Yellow Train into the Pyrénées, return to wine cocktails as the sun goes down. An exceptional place: immaculate, uplifting, and run by the nicest people. *Minimum stay: 3 nights in high season.*

| Rooms | 3 doubles (1 with extra sofa bed): €95–€130. |
| --- | --- |
| | 1 family room for 4: €110–€180. |
| | 1 triple: €110–€155. |
| | Extra bed/sofabed €25 per person per night. |
| Meals | Dinner with wine, €25. |
| | Restaurants 2km. |
| Closed | Never. |

Pierre & Emmanuel Ortal
Clos des Aspres,
Domaine de la Camomille,
66560 Ortaffa
Pyrénées-Orientales

Tel +33 (0)4 68 95 70 74
Email contact@closdesaspres.com
Web www.closdesaspres.com

## Languedoc – Roussillon

### Château d'Ortaffa

Medieval Ortaffa sits in a pocket of sunshine between the Pyrénées and the lively port of Collioure, and this big old winemaker's château perches on its fortified walls. Breakfast on the terrace comes with a stunning tableau of mountains and sea with village rooftops tumbling below. Slip into a beautifully restored house whose elegant, pastel-shaded library and guest rooms display your hosts' love of antiques and fine art: your room may have Picasso prints, quirky graffiti, bookshelves, an antique child's bed, remnants of the former chapel... Roll down to the port for seafood, slide south along the coast to Spain. *Minimum stay: 2 nights at weekdays.*

| Rooms | 2 doubles, 1 suite for 2-3, 1 suite for 2-5: €110-€130. Extra bed/sofabed €30 per person per night. |
|---|---|
| Meals | Restaurant in village. |
| Closed | Rarely. |

**Michelle & Alain Batard**
Château d'Ortaffa,
8 rue du Château,
66560 Ortaffa
Pyrénées-Orientales

| Mobile | +33 (0)6 64 14 53 42 |
| Email | chateau.ortaffa@gmail.com |
| Web | www.chateau-ortaffa.com |

Entry 698  Map 15

## Languedoc – Roussillon

### Castell Rose

A beautiful, pink marble gentleman's house in its own parkland on the edge of a very pretty town between the sea and the mountains; the views are superb. Evelyne and Alex are both charming and give you large graceful bedrooms with calm colour schemes, good linen, tip-top bathrooms and elegant antiques. After a good breakfast, wander through the flourishing garden with its ancient olive trees to find a spot beside the lily pond, or just float in the pool. It's a five-minute stroll to village life, or take the yellow train up the mountain from Villefranche for more amazing views.

| Rooms | 3 doubles, 1 twin: €85-€99. 1 family room for 4: €119-€139. |
|---|---|
| Meals | Restaurant within walking distance. |
| Closed | Rarely. |

**Evelyne & Alex Waldvogel**
Castell Rose,
Chemin de la Litera,
66500 Prades
Pyrénées-Orientales

| Tel | +33 (0)4 68 96 07 57 |
| Email | castellroseprades@gmail.com |
| Web | www.castellrose-prades.com |

Entry 699  Map 15

# Languedoc – Roussillon

## Maison Prades

Informal, vibrant and fun is this peaceful townhouse with big sunshiney rooms. Already well-integrated into the community, the charming new owners – Robson Brazilian, Benoît Belgian – are super well-travelled and following their dream: to run a laid-back but stylish B&B. They've opened up the garden, pruned back the trees, introduced teak tables for breakfast and loungers for leisure. Original features have been restored, wooden floors uncovered, bedrooms refurbished and the whole house handsomely revived. Robson is a keen cook and table d'hôte dinners have an international flavour – as well as being fun! *Minimum stay: 2 nights in high season.*

| | |
|---|---|
| Rooms | 2 doubles, 2 twin/doubles: €65–€80. 1 triple: €80–€85. Singles €55–€80. Extra bed/sofabed €15 per person per night. |
| Meals | Dinner with wine, €30 (Mon & Wed). Restaurants 5-minute walk. |
| Closed | 5 November – 31 December & New Year. |

Robson Santana
Maison Prades,
51 av du Général de Gaulle,
66500 Prades
Pyrénées-Orientales

| | |
|---|---|
| Tel | +33 (0)4 68 05 74 27 |
| Mobile | +33 (0)6 19 01 27 86 |
| Email | info.maisonprades@gmail.com |
| Web | www.maisonprades.com |

Entry 700   Map 15

Photo: ©iStock.com/S.W.Krull

# Rhône Valley – Alps

www.sawdays.co.uk/rhone-valley-alps

## L'Evidence

Amid the terraced hills and chestnut forests of the Ardèche is a rambling multi-levelled farmhouse squirrelled away on the village edge, with mountains beyond. A pleasure to step inside and find three fresh bedrooms: Zanzibar, reached through a slick jacuzzi'd bathroom, is big and Africa-infused; Oslo, up top, is all cool blues; cosy Jaïpur (once a goat cellar) is womb-like and intimate, ideal for romancers. Breakfast in bed, or take bread and brioche to the kitchen. Suppers of seasonal bounty can be booked too, saving a drive to a restaurant – and there's a little pool. Smiley Christine, new to B&B, is a delight.

## L'Angelot

The approach is magical, winding through the gorges of the Ardèche, to lovely hilltop Antraigues and an 18th-century farmhouse full of paintings. Ilse and Fons have acres of chestnut forest, there's a circular walk to a medieval castle... and you come home to big rustic bedrooms, peaceful, private and charmingly furnished: simple natural fabrics, perhaps an old door for a bedhead. The house is on many levels, with a cool pool for aching limbs, a stream below and plenty of tranquil corners. Homemade jams and local honey for breakfast, and hosts without a whiff of pretension; walkers adore it. *Minimum stay: 2 nights.*

| Rooms | 3 doubles: €80–€120. Extra person €65 per night. |
|---|---|
| Meals | Lunch or picnic €15. Dinner with wine, €28. Restaurant 10km. |
| Closed | Rarely. |

| Rooms | 2 family rooms for 3: €80–€105. Extra person €25 per night. |
|---|---|
| Meals | Restaurants 1km. |
| Closed | Rarely. |

|  | **Christine Moser** |
|---|---|
|  | L'Evidence, Peyreplane, 07380 Prades Ardèche |
| Tel | +33 (0)4 75 94 15 89 |
| Mobile | +33 (0)6 22 62 62 82 |
| Email | christine.moser@l-evidence.com |
| Web | www.l-evidence.com |

|  | **Ilse & Fons Jaspers-Janssens** |
|---|---|
|  | L'Angelot, Ranc au Ranc, 07530 Antraigues sur Volane Ardèche |
| Tel | +33 (0)4 75 88 24 55 |
| Email | info@langelot.com |
| Web | www.langelot.com |

Entry 701 Map 11

Entry 702 Map 11

# Rhône Valley – Alps

## Château de Fontblachère

Framed by a forested valley and mountainous horizons, this 17th-century château marries Provençal peace with deep comfort and style. Bernard greets you in a courtyard whose manicured hedges and white roses dissolve into parkland: a panoramic pool, Japanese fish pond, tennis court, jacuzzi… Under vaulted ceilings are more treats: a log fire, piano, candles, art, and Turkish cushions in the orangery where you may dine on iced melon soup and quail. Sprightly Bernard cooks, serves, pours and chats all the while. Immaculate rooms have space for families and the valley cries out for walking, riding and fishing in the Rhône.

| | |
|---|---|
| Rooms | 2 family rooms for 2-3, 1 family room for 2-4, 1 family room for 2-5: €115-€165. |
| Meals | Dinner with wine, €35. Restaurants 3km. |
| Closed | 16 September – 14 June. |

**Bernard Liaudois & Eric Dussiot**
Château de Fontblachère,
07210 St Lager Bressac
Ardèche
Tel     +33 (0)4 75 65 15 02
Mobile  +33 (0)6 11 18 23 83
Email   eric.dussiot@yahoo.fr
Web     www.chateau-fontblachere.com

Entry 703   Map 11

# Rhône Valley – Alps

## Le Veyroux de Longefaye

Wonderful to wind through the cherry and apricot orchards of the Ardèche hills – especially in spring – to the peaceful old farmhouse at the end of the track, and a friendly welcome from interesting Swiss hosts. Well-travelled, they have personalised their home with eclectic paintings, prints, books and kilims. You sleep in secluded stylish quarters downstairs, then wake to a feast of pancakes, fruits, *pain au levain* and jams under the sweet linden tree – or in the huge lofty kitchen amid sleek red units and rustic wood and stone. Take a massage, slip into the pool, visit the beekeeper next door, lap up the views.

| | |
|---|---|
| Rooms | 1 double, 1 twin/double: €75-€85. |
| Meals | Restaurant 10-minute drive. |
| Closed | October – April. |

**Bernard & Dominique Betrancourt**
Le Veyroux de Longefaye,
07570 Désaignes
Ardèche
Tel    +33 (0)4 75 06 61 74
Email  leveyroux@orange.fr
Web    www.leveyrouxdelongefaye.com

Entry 704   Map 11

## Domaine du Fontenay

Huge care has been taken by these owners to make guests comfortable and well-informed. Simon's lifelong ambition was to become a wine-maker in France, now his wines are highly regarded; enjoy the tastings in the cellar. In a separate building are four super bedrooms with excellent mattresses, big showers, rugs on old terracotta tiles and astonishing views from this hilltop site; and each bedroom has an excellent folder with all the local info. In summer, breakfast is served at check-clothed tables on the big terrace. This is a great area for good-value gourmet restaurants so enjoy them – and ask about 'La Route Magique!' *Cot available.*

## Château de la Motte

The fairy-tale good looks of this Roannais château in peaceful parkland charm from the outset. Henrik and Liliane lavish it with care and sound judgement, bringing back its traditional 18th-century allure with fine furniture and art collected over decades in the business. Sophisticated Swedish francophiles, they see that you get the most out of your stay, whether you simply want to unwind by the pool or in the sauna, or take off in a hot-air balloon. Your rooms are supremely comfortable as well as stylish and you'll want to linger over brioche and homemade jams at breakfast. Dinner is a special treat and wines are good.

| | | | |
|---|---|---|---|
| Rooms | 1 suite for 2, 2 suites for 4, 1 triple: €73–€96. | Rooms | 5 doubles, 1 twin/double: €90–€150. 1 suite for 4: €166. Singles €90–€100. Extra bed/sofabed €25 per person per night. |
| Meals | Kitchen available. Restaurant nearby. | Meals | Dinner €28–€35. Wine from €15. Restaurant 5km. |
| Closed | Rarely. | Closed | Mid–December to February. |

Simon & Isabelle Hawkins
Domaine du Fontenay,
Fontenay,
42155 Villemontais
Loire
Tel      +33 (0)4 77 63 12 22
Mobile   +33 (0)6 81 03 30 33
Email    info@domainedufontenay.com
Web      www.domainedufontenay.com

Henrik & Liliane Lantz
Château de la Motte,
42640 Noailly
Loire
Tel      +33 (0)4 77 66 64 60
Email    chateaudelamotte@wanadoo.fr
Web      www.chateaudelamotte.net

### Château de Chambost

It takes little to imagine the owners' aristocratic ancestors residing in this rural, 16th-century hillside château. Traditional going on lavish, it's still fit for Lyonnais elite, its five bedrooms decked out in toile de Jouy and period furniture; one's still adorned with original 1850s parrot-flocked wallpaper. In the basement lies another gem: a striking umbrella-vaulted dining room, where vivacious hostess Véronique serves homemade aperitifs and beef reared on the château's estate. The cows have bagged most of the garden, but guests can retire to the elegant sitting room to plan countryside forays beyond.

| Rooms | 2 doubles, 2 twins: €90–€100. 1 family room for 3: €115. |
| --- | --- |
| Meals | Dinner with wine, €27.50. Restaurant 15km. |
| Closed | Rarely. |

**Vivien & Véronique de Lescure**
Château de Chambost,
69770 Chambost Longessaigne
Rhône
Tel       +33 (0)4 74 26 37 49
Mobile    +33 (0)6 30 52 04 84
Email     infos@chateaudechambost.com
Web       www.chateaudechambost.com

Entry 707   Map 11

### Les Hautes Bruyères

Once settled on this wooded hilltop in restfully subdued, country-smart comfort, you can't imagine that super-urban Lyon is ten minutes away. Karine's converted farm buildings are sophisticated yet simple – and so is she, with a genuine interest in other people and a flair for interiors. With 2,000 years of European history in its bones and a solid reputation for good food, Lyon has myriad treasures to see and taste. After a day of discovery (or work) in the city or the countryside, relax in the green and birdsung garden or by elegant Italianate pool. Tomorrow there will be delicious breakfast in the 'auberge' dayroom.

| Rooms | 2 doubles, 1 twin/double: €145–€250. 2 suites for 4 (2nd room on open mezzanine): €175–€280. Extra bed €35 per person per night. |
| --- | --- |
| Meals | Bocuse cookery school in village: weekday bookings. Lyon centre 6km. Guest kitchen. |
| Closed | Rarely. |

**Karine Laurent**
Les Hautes Bruyères,
5 chemin des Hautes Bruyères,
69130 Écully
Rhône
Tel       +33 (0)4 78 35 52 38
Mobile    +33 (0)6 08 48 69 50
Email     contact@lhb-hote.fr
Web       www.lhb-hote.fr

Entry 708   Map 11

## Rhône Valley – Alps

### La Croix de Saburin

Close to the autoroute, yet with to-die-for views – they soar over vineyards to Mounts Brouilly and Blanc. Built in regional style against the hillside is this very French, contemporary-smart house. Sociable and perfectionist, Monique and Jean-Michel began B&B when they retired; small pretty bedrooms have chalky mango-wood tables, sparkling bathrooms, glorious views. Guests are spoilt with the salon: tea-making kit and plenty of books. Rare birds, orchids and butterflies dwell in the valley below; cycling, wine tasting and Lyon are close by. Dine with the family on salade Lyonnaise and chicken in champagne. Intimate and stunning.

## Rhône Valley – Alps

### Château de Briante

This exotic-looking château in baize-green parkland – all glowing-pink stone and striking towers – is grand with a laidback touch. Rooms in the Tuscan-style wing mix original features – polished floors and wood panelling – with cool furnishings – vintage chairs and modern art. Sleek in silvers and coffees, all have green views; two have sun-drenched balconies. Breakfast on local cheese and hams, then slip through French windows to stroll the parkland – with its rose-decked orangerie – explore the vineyards or laze by the pool. Young winemakers Lauren and her husband are passionate about their estate. You will taste, learn and be charmed. *Cot available. Pets by arrangement.*

| | |
|---|---|
| Rooms | 1 double: €70.<br>1 family room for 3: €70–€88. |
| Meals | Dinner with wine, €25. |
| Closed | Rarely. |

| | |
|---|---|
| Rooms | 3 doubles: €130–€150.<br>Extra bed/sofabed €20 per person per night. |
| Meals | Restaurant 1.5km. |
| Closed | Never. |

**Jean-Michel & Monique Legat**
La Croix de Saburin,
Saburin,
69430 Quincié en Beaujolais
Rhône
Tel +33 (0)4 74 69 02 82
Mobile +33 (0)6 08 50 19 03
Email jean-michel.legat@orange.fr
Web lacroixdesaburin.free.fr

**Lauren Schneider**
Château de Briante,
810 route de Briante,
69220 Saint Lager
Rhône
Mobile +33 (0)6 83 31 28 50
Email lfaupin@gmail.com
Web www.domainedebriante.fr

## Rhône Valley – Alps

### Les Pasquiers

Come to meet Marylène and Guillaume in their beautiful home in a wine-country village. Oriental rugs and fine antiques rub shoulders with contemporary art, and gorgeous books lie around for everyone to peruse. There's a grand piano in the drawing room, heaps of CDs, bedrooms are sunny, beds have beautiful linen, new bathrooms are on their way and the garden is divine – languid terraces, organic potager, summerhouse, pool. Marylène loves to cook, and great dinners are shared 'en famille'. One of the best – and surprisingly close to the autoroute. *Whole house available on a self-catering basis.*

| | |
|---|---|
| Rooms | 1 twin/double, 1 suite for 4, 1 family room for 5: €88. Extra bed €20 per person per night. |
| Meals | Dinner with wine, €32.50. Children over 7, €12–28. Children under 7 eat free. Restaurants 6km. |
| Closed | Rarely. |

Marylène & Guillaume
Peyraverney
Les Pasquiers,
69220 Lancié
Rhône

| | |
|---|---|
| Tel | +33 (0)4 74 69 86 33 |
| Mobile | +33 (0)6 83 19 01 37 |
| Email | lespasquiers@orange.fr |
| Web | www.lespasquiers.com |

Entry 711  Map 11

## Rhône Valley – Alps

### Maison d'hôtes de La Verrière

Hugging the edge of a beautiful valley in Beaujolais, a serenely secluded family home with magnificent views. Whether waking in your quirky country bedroom, meeting guests at the breakfast table (sampling yogurt cake and nine homemade jams) or swimming in the natural salt pool among wild mountain flowers, the valley is always there, it is particularly beautiful in autumn. Grégoire's guided walks start from the house. Both he and Christine love having guests to stay, and their French cuisine is so good (never the same dish twice) there's no reason to dine anywhere else.

| | |
|---|---|
| Rooms | 3 twin/doubles: €78. 1 triple: €93. 1 quadruple: €113. Singles €63. Extra bed/sofabed €15 per person per night. |
| Meals | Dinner with wine, €28. Restaurant 15km. |
| Closed | Rarely. |

Christine Gesse & Grégoire Lamy
Maison d'hôtes de La Verrière,
69430 Les Ardillats
Rhône

| | |
|---|---|
| Tel | +33 (0)4 74 04 71 46 |
| Email | christine.gesse@orange.fr |

Entry 712  Map 11

## Le Clos du Châtelet

Sweeping gardens overlook the valley, the garden is full of sequoias, and an outbuilding is home to a collection of antique bird cages. Bedrooms are peaceful havens of elegantly muted colours: 'Joubert' in pink-ochre, its twin wrought-iron four-posters dressed in toile de Jouy; 'Lamartine' in palest aqua. All have polished wooden floors and gently sober bathrooms. There's much comfort here: an open fire in the sitting room, period furniture, prints, antlers on the wall and a delicious air of calm. Dinner is by candlelight in an atmospheric dining room with a wonderful old terracotta floor. Peace, charm and spectacular views.

## Château de Marmont

An amazing avenue of plane trees delivers you to an authentic 'time warp' château experience – and private access directly onto the second hole: bring the golf clubs! Madame, a classical historian, is a joy, and her house as colourful as she. Find polished family heirlooms, original wallpapers, a billiard room you can use. Up the grand stairs is a bedroom with books and fresh flowers, and a bathroom with a claw foot bath and trompe-l'œil walls. Breakfasts are in the orangery or by the fire: classical music plays, the candle is lit, the coffee is hot, the oranges and the squeezer are to hand and the homemade jam is delicious.

| Rooms | 3 doubles; 1 double with separate bath: €120–€125. |
|---|---|
| Meals | Restaurant 5-minute drive. |
| Closed | Rarely. |

| Rooms | 1 double: €95.<br>1 family suite for 3-5: €140. |
|---|---|
| Meals | Restaurant 3km. |
| Closed | Rarely. |

|  | **Madame Durand–Pont**<br>Le Clos du Châtelet,<br>01190 Sermoyer<br>Ain |
|---|---|
| Tel | +33 (0)3 85 51 84 37 |
| Email | leclosduchatelet@free.fr |
| Web | www.leclosduchatelet.com |

|  | **Geneviève & Henri Guido-Alhéritière**<br>Château de Marmont,<br>2043 route de Condeissiat,<br>01960 St André sur Vieux Jonc<br>Ain |
|---|---|
| Tel | +33 (0)4 74 52 79 74 |
| Web | www.chateau-marmont.info |

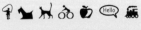

Entry 713   Map 11

Entry 714   Map 11

# Rhône Valley – Alps

## Ancienne École du Chapuy

In the rural quiet of forests, lakes and unsung villages sits this old school house, peaceful by the road. Classily converted by Marie-Christine and Alain, it has a warm, happy atmosphere. Up a winding staircase, immaculate bedrooms with fine bedding and handsome bedsteads look out to lush pastures. Bathrooms glitter in sea greens and have huge bathtubs. Pleasing contrasts of bold fabrics, striking modern pieces and antiques in the sitting room; breakfasts are superb. Make the most of the cycle tracks, then tuck into those good old French clichés, frogs' legs and snails – local specialities! Intimate, charming.

| Rooms | 1 double: €65–€130. |
| --- | --- |
| | 1 suite for 4: €65–€130. |
| Meals | Restaurant 2km. |
| Closed | November – March. |

**Alain Privel & Marie-Christine Palaysi**
Ancienne École du Chapuy,
Les Bruyères,
Châtillon sur Chalaronne,
01400 Romans, Ain

| Tel | +33 (0)4 74 55 63 30 |
| --- | --- |
| Mobile | +33 (0)6 83 86 82 68 |
| Email | ecoleduchapuy@hotmail.fr |
| Web | www.ecoleduchapuy.com |

Entry 715  Map 11

---

# Rhône Valley – Alps

## Château de Tanay

Surrounded by flat lands, a magnificent château in acres of parkland with pool. Inside is equally splendid. A sleek modern décor illuminates fine stonework and medieval beams, there's a games room for children, a grand piano for musicians and a convivial dining table; in summer, take breakfast by the moat beneath the willow. Spend the day in charming old Lyon or treat the family to the Parc des Oiseaux... return for a château tour with your hosts, trot off for dinner at the local pizzeria. Big tasteful bedrooms lie in the courtyard stables but the family room is in the château itself – with an amazing massage bath. *Extra bed available.*

| Rooms | 4 twin/doubles (in stables): €85–€135. |
| --- | --- |
| | 1 suite for 4: €160–€200. |
| Meals | Restaurant 1km. |
| Closed | 15 December – 3 January. |

**Benoît Haym**
Château de Tanay,
Chemin de Tanay,
01600 St Didier de Formans
Ain

| Tel | +33 (0)9 53 36 87 42 |
| --- | --- |
| Mobile | +33 (0)6 63 94 70 27 |
| Email | info@chateau-tanay.com |
| Web | www.chateau-tanay.com |

Entry 716  Map 11

## La Ferme du Champ Pelaz

Deeply rural is this gentle land where distant peaks tantalise and three generations of Smiths live in the big, creeper-smothered, 19th-century farmhouse. Guests have their quarters in the middle with Michael and Linda at one end, daughter Katey and her children at the other. The owners know all about the area (Michael specialises in golf breaks) and can guide you towards the best alpine walks. Bedrooms are cosy and pretty, pastel-painted, wooden floored, a good size and ideal for all. There's a pool for summer heat, and a big log fire and deep sofas in the dayroom for cool nights. *Minimum stay: 2 nights in high season.*

| Rooms | 2 doubles sharing wc on landing: €75. |
| --- | --- |
| | 2 triples: €90. |
| | Extra bed/sofabed €10 per person per night. |
| Meals | Restaurant 5-minute drive. |
| Closed | Rarely. |

**Michael & Linda Smith**
La Ferme du Champ Pelaz,
57 chemin de la Biolle, Pesey,
74150 Thusy
Haute-Savoie

| Tel | +33 (0)4 50 69 25 15 |
| --- | --- |
| Mobile | +33 (0)6 31 85 55 54 |
| Email | champ-pelaz@wanadoo.fr |
| Web | www.champ-pelaz.com |

Entry 717　Map 11

## La Thébaïde

Higgledy-piggledy gardens, chickens under the cherry trees, and a terrace shaded by vines: this is 15 minutes from Geneva yet feels like the countryside. The much-loved chalet, built in 1916, remains endearingly old-fashioned inside. Charming Susan gives you delicious breakfast (and later, lapin à la moutarde, crème brûlée…) in a cosy panelled dining room dominated by a huge ceramic stove; upstairs is a TV room lined with books. Tall windows and high ceilings distinguish first-floor bedrooms, and the family room is under the eaves. Play golf in the village, visit Switzerland for the day.

| Rooms | 1 double sharing bath/shower room; |
| --- | --- |
| | 1 twin/double with separate bath/shower room across corridor: €65. |
| | 1 family room for 3 sharing bath/shower room: €80. |
| | Extra person €25 per night. |
| | Children under 12, €15. |
| Meals | Dinner €25. Restaurant in village. |
| Closed | Christmas. |

**Susan Sirges**
La Thébaïde,
214 chemin de la Thébaïde,
74930 Esery-Reignier
Haute-Savoie

| Tel | +33 (0)4 50 94 40 52 |
| --- | --- |
| Email | sirges.susan@orange.fr |

Entry 718　Map 12

## Rhône Valley – Alps

### Chalet Châtelet

The cow-belled Vallée d'Abondance envelops this pretty pine chalet, the result of years of your hosts' creative energy. Oak floors, soft shapes and high ceilings hug reclaimed furniture and works by other members of this arty family. Warmth comes from a Finnish stove and solar panels – an eco-lover's dream and you still find bliss in the hot tub (along with spectacular views). Expect cultured chat in the intimate dining room and Suzie's range-cooked local and organic food. Bedrooms have stunning views too, and dreamy bathrooms; gaze to mountains you climbed, snow-shoed or skied that day. Heavenly. *Short breaks available.*

## Rhône Valley – Alps

*New Entry*

### Chalet Cannelle

The diffuse light of a contemporary chandelier spills onto the white walls of this stylish chalet. Circled by wintry snows or May's wild flowers, in a hamlet just outside Châtel, the lovely old farmhouse has balconies for big windows and stunning views, pine-cosy sleeping quarters, a kids' dorm with its own TV, and a toy-filled mezzanine. Delicious treats (eggs from the hens, truffled pecorino, Lake Geneva trout) flow from the kitchen or the terrace's wood-fired oven. Gather for log fires and nightcaps around the three-beam coffee table as you discuss the exploits of the day. Once in you won't want to leave. *Minimum stay: 2 nights at weekends.,*

| | |
|---|---|
| Rooms | 2 doubles, 2 triples: €90–€150. Ski package: €690–€1,140 per person per week. Winter: dinner, B&B €520–860 per person per week. |
| Meals | Dinner with wine, €30. |
| Closed | Rarely. |

| | |
|---|---|
| Rooms | 1 double, 2 twin/doubles, 1 family room for 4: €100–€150. 1 quadruple with children's den: €80–€120. Ski package: €690–€1,100 per person per week. Singles €100–€150. Dinner, B&B €80–€115 per person. |
| Meals | Dinner €29. |
| Closed | Never. |

**Pascal & Suzie Immediato**
Chalet Châtelet,
Route d'Abondance,
74360 Bonnevaux
Haute-Savoie

Tel    +33 (0)4 50 73 69 48
Email   info@chalet-chatelet.com
Web    www.chalet-chatelet.com

**Lorraine McDermott**
Chalet Cannelle,
Suvay,
74360 Châtel
Haute-Savoie

Email   info@chaletcannelle.co.uk
Web    www.chaletcannelle.co.uk

## La Ferme de Margot

A real old farmhouse on the south-facing flank of Morzine with original slates, knobbly beams, and heaps of space. Everything has been beautifully considered by generous English owners (who live downstairs), from the study/snug with its wood-burner to the fabulous living area on the top floor to the media room in between. Imagine silver reindeer heads, a sweeping crushed-velvet sofa, a long matt-white dining table, cowhide wallpaper, a wooden 'sun-beam' ceiling and tartan flourishes. Step out for beautiful mountain and lakeside walks; there's a good golf course ten minutes' away. Return to fabulous food, beers and wines. *Minimum stay: 2 nights in high season.*

| | |
|---|---|
| Rooms | 4 twin/doubles: £120-£150. 1 suite for 4: £150-£200. Ski package: £695-£725 per person per week. |
| Meals | Dinner with wine, €40. Restaurants within walking distance. |
| Closed | Rarely. |

Jane & Stephen Fenlon
La Ferme de Margot,
332 chemin Martenant,
74110 Morzine
Haute-Savoie

Tel     +33 (0)9 67 01 12 68
Email   hello@grandcruski.com
Web    www.grandcruski.com

## Chalet Amuse Bouche

On the edge of an attractive village (1.2km) and close to the resort of Morzine (3km), is a sparkling new chalet run by Lindsay and Steve. Picture windows pull in the views, three bedrooms open to the terrace, two more have private balconies, and the interiors are Alpine and contemporary. Best of all is the food, from Lindsay's breakfast bagels and buns (sticky cinnamon a favourite!) to Steve's delectable dinners (sauces a speciality). For summer: white water rafting, canoeing, climbing and biking. For winter: a free shuttle to the Ardent télécabine and access to the snow-sure Avoriaz, then home to a round of pool, a hot tub and sauna, and a river to sing you to sleep. *Minimum stay: 3 nights.*

| | |
|---|---|
| Rooms | 1 double, 1 twin/double, 1 twin: €100-€110. 2 family rooms for 4: €100-€200. Ski package: €500-€1,100 per person per week. |
| Meals | Dinner with wine, €35. Restaurants 1km. |
| Closed | Rarely. |

Lindsay Butcher
Chalet Amuse Bouche,
223 chemin sur la Char,
Montriond, 74110 Morzine
Haute-Savoie

Tel     +33 (0)9 80 87 42 02
Email   escapetothealps@aol.com
Web    www.escapetothealps.com

## Chalet Twenty26

With Morzine below and superb peaks above, the Hamblins' chalet is super-stylish and fun. On the deck: a blissful, bubbling, sunken hot tub and a barrel sauna. Indoors: an eye-catching living area with cow-hides, a sleek fireplace, designer seating, an honesty bar, a surround sound music system – downstairs a dedicated cinema. Under the rafters bedrooms are all different, everything top notch; bathrooms chic with fluffy robes. And the food is outstanding; meals on the balcony a treat. As for summer sport: great walking, a well-equipped bike store for cyclists, a nearby water park and swimming complex. A top address!

## Chalet APASSION

Perched on the mountainside above the lovely old resort of Samoëns, a luxurious, new-build pine chalet; one of four, settled quietly down a private lane. Majestic views stretch from the terraces and balcony, and a great big cedar hot tub is the perfect place to soak away the day's strain after long summer's days spent biking, hiking or climbing. Glossy bedspreads and scatter cushions finish pristine rooms, while in the open-plan sitting/dining room, plush leather sofas sit in the glow of a real fire. Breakfast is just as relaxed – simply let attentive Vicky and Rob know when you'd like it. Delightful dinners are on request. *Minimum stay: 3 nights.*

| | |
|---|---|
| Rooms | 5 twin/doubles (extra single bed in two rooms): £100–£190. Ski package: £695–£1,695 per person per week. Singles 20% reduction. Cots £5. |
| Meals | Dinner with wine, £35. Restaurants 15-minute walk. |
| Closed | Rarely. |

| | |
|---|---|
| Rooms | 5 twin/doubles: €126–€150. Ski package: €755–€1,312 per person per week. |
| Meals | Dinner with wine, 2-3 courses, €36–€47. Restaurants 1km. |
| Closed | November to mid-December. |

**Sarah & Chris Hamblin**
Chalet Twenty26,
Route de la Manche,
74110 Morzine
Haute-Savoie

Tel    +44 (0)203 582 6409
Mobile    +33 (0)6 35 41 11 02
Email    info@theboutiquechalet.com
Web    www.theboutiquechalet.com

**Rob & Vicky Tarr**
Chalet APASSION,
77 chemin du Battieu, Vercland,
74340 Samoëns
Haute-Savoie

Tel    +33 (0)4 50 18 68 33
Mobile    +33 (0)6 06 70 81 57
Email    robandvicky@apassion.com
Web    www.apassion.co.uk

## Rhône Valley – Alps

### Ferme du Ciel

High above the valley and pretty Samoëns, the huge old chalet-style farmhouse has been expertly renovated to reveal soaring beams, a great woody open-plan living space, a shiny modern kitchen and big lofty bedrooms; also, a log fire in winter, a lovely balcony-terrace in summer. The whole place oozes comfort and style in patterned rugs, stripey curtains and heated floors. Your hard-working hosts are very present for B&B guests or decently discreet if you self-cater. There's a hot tub, a sauna and a garden swimming pool. Beyond are lakes and mountains, fresh air and cowbells — and beauty galore. *Minimum stay: 3 nights.*

| Rooms | 1 double, 4 twin/doubles with sofabed: €130-€150. 1 family room for 5: €130-€150. |
|---|---|
| Meals | Catered meals available. |
| Closed | Rarely. |

**Andrew & Su Lyell**
Ferme du Ciel,
773 route Mathonex,
Mathonex, 74340 Samoëns
Haute-Savoie

| Tel | +33 (0)4 50 58 44 57 |
| Mobile | +33 (0)6 21 19 74 83 |
| Email | info@fermeduciel.com |
| Web | www.fermeduciel.com |

Entry 725   Map 12

## Rhône Valley – Alps

### La Vieille Ferme

At the foot of the soaring Alps, a lovingly renovated farmhouse decorated in charming country style. Cosy rooms in the main chalet have balconies overlooking fir-clad mountains, while the two spacious self-contained apartments will suit families on an adventure. Outside, the Grand Massif awaits — in summer try paragliding for a bird's eye view of the valley, or for explorers there are challenging walks and mountain biking. Breakfast on pastries and local Savoie ham and cheese to prepare you for the physical rigours of the day ahead. At night warm your bones in front of the traditional Haute-Savoie central fireplace. *Minimum stay: 2 nights.*

| Rooms | 3 twin/doubles; one with sofabed: €120-€140. 1 apartment for 3, 1 apartment for 6: €100-€140. Ski package: £499-£699 per person per week. |
|---|---|
| Meals | Dinner €35-€45 (min. 4). Restaurant 5-min drive. |
| Closed | Rarely. |

AWARD WINNER
Favourite newcomer

**Mitch Patching**
La Vieille Ferme,
121 route de Vallon d'en haut,
74340 Samoëns
Haute-Savoie

| Mobile | +33 (0)7 85 56 71 14 |
| Email | mitch@la-vieille-ferme.co.uk |
| Web | www.la-vieille-ferme.co.uk |

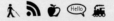

Entry 726   Map 12

# Rhône Valley – Alps

## Chalet Odysseus

The village has character; Chalet Odysseus has much besides. There's comfort in soft sofas, check curtains, bright rugs and open fire, and swishness in the sauna, and your relaxed English hosts look after you well (Kate is a fine cook, Barry is a professional sheep dog trainer and breeder, so expect dogginess.) They have the ground floor of this recently-built chalet and you live above. Cheerfully cosy and spotless bedrooms come with the requisite pine garb and balconies that catch the sun. Good for an active (dog-loving) family break with so much to do round and about, from skiing to hiking and hang-gliding. *Minimum stay: 2 nights.*

| Rooms | 2 doubles, 1 twin/double: €85. Winter: dinner, B&B €140–€200 per night (for 2). |
| --- | --- |
| Meals | Dinner with wine, €40. |
| Closed | Rarely. |

Kate & Barry Joyce
Chalet Odysseus,
210 route de Lachat,
74300 Les Carroz d'Araches
Haute-Savoie
Tel      +33 (0)4 50 90 66 00
Mobile   +33 (0)6 85 77 06 54
Email    chaletodysseus@wanadoo.fr
Web      www.chaletodysseuslachat.com

Entry 727   Map 12

# Rhône Valley – Alps

## Maison La Cerisaie

This lovely green-shuttered 1830s chalet has been part of the community for years; today it shines. No short cuts have been taken by generous hosts Sally-Anne and Simon (ex-Navy) who delight in providing the best. Start the day with breakfast at a time to suit you (fresh croissants, local jams, Nespresso coffee, Pukka teas), plunge into mountain adventures, return to a hot tub in the garden and supper at the auberge. Or eat in: the food is varied and delicious. Warm, woody, clean-cut bedrooms wait on the first floor, one with an extra sofabed, two with the views, all with bathrobes and toasty bathroom floors. *Minimum stay: 2 nights.*

| Rooms | 1 double, 2 twin/doubles, 1 family room for 2 with sofabed: €90–€110. Ski package: €540–€765 per person per week. |
| --- | --- |
| Meals | Dinner, 3 courses, with wine, €30. |
| Closed | Never. |

Simon & Sally-Anne Airey
Maison La Cerisaie,
Salvagny,
74740 Sixt Fer à Cheval
Haute-Savoie
Tel    +33 (0)4 50 89 94 78
Email  contact@maisonlacerisaie.com
Web    www.maisonlacerisaie.com

Entry 728   Map 12

### La Ferme du Soleil

The hamlet of four old wooden houses (two chalets, two farm buildings) is high up, impossibly pretty, detached from the bustling world, with views to lift spirits and a deep silence in which to contemplate such beauty. In winter, you are a stroll from the top of a chair lift and a quick slide from the bottom of several, so you can stop skiing when you're ready for a blazing log fire and a delicious bite. In summer you can wander the mountains to enjoy the flowers and the bell-ringing cows. The word 'idyll' really does apply. Big, cosy, beautiful, open and convivial – another dream realised.
*Minimum stay: 7 nights.*

| | |
|---|---|
| Rooms | 4 doubles, 1 twin; 1 double, 1 bunk sharing bathroom. Ski package: £580-£850 per person. per week. |
| Meals | Winter: half-board. Summer: self-catered. |
| Closed | May/June, November/December. |

|  | Veroni Gilbert |
|---|---|
| | La Ferme du Soleil, |
| | Les Gettiers, |
| | 74450 Le Grand Bornand |
| | Haute-Savoie |
| Tel | +33 (0)9 52 76 34 01 |
| Mobile | +44 (0)7789 947024 |
| Email | lafermefrance@gmail.com |
| Web | www.lafermedusoleil.com |

Entry 729  Map 12

---

### Proveyroz

Josette has boundless energy, is a great walker, adores her mountain retreat in this beautiful valley and cooks extremely well. Her chalet rooms, all wood-clad of course, are bright and welcoming in blue, white and orange, with high ceilings and plenty of space; the triple has its own balcony and the views are stunning. After a day on the slopes (the lifts are four miles but there's a free shuttle to get there) what bliss to come home to the great big wood-burner. In summer, huge windows open to a sun-soaked terrace and little garden... you can't help but unwind. Annecy is close, Geneva is an hour away.

| | |
|---|---|
| Rooms | 1 double with separate bathroom: €60. 1 triple with separate wc: €70. Singles €50. |
| Meals | Dinner with wine, €20. |
| Closed | Rarely. |

|  | Josette Barbaud |
|---|---|
| | Proveyroz, |
| | 74230 Manigod |
| | Haute-Savoie |
| Tel | +33 (0)4 50 44 95 25 |
| Mobile | +33 (0)6 70 55 63 60 |
| Email | josette.barbaud@sfr.fr |
| Web | josette.barbaud.free.fr |

Entry 730  Map 12

## Rhône Valley – Alps

### La Touvière

Mountains march past Mont Blanc and over into Italy, cows graze in the foreground, the place is perfect for exploring this walkers' paradise. Myriam, bubbly and easy, adores having guests with everyone joining in the lively, light-hearted family atmosphere. In the typical old unsmart farmhouse, the cosy family room is the hub of life. Marcel is part-time home improver, part-time farmer (just a few cows now). One room has a properly snowy valley view, the other overlooks the owners' second chalet, let as a gîte; both are a decent size, simple but not basic, while shower rooms are spotless. Remarkable value.

| | |
|---|---|
| Rooms | 2 doubles: €60. |
| Meals | Restaurant 3km. |
| Closed | Rarely. |

**Marcel & Myriam Marin-Cudraz**
La Touvière,
73590 Flumet
Savoie
Tel    +33 (0)4 79 31 70 11
Email  marcel.marin-cudraz@wanadoo.fr
Web    www.touviere.fr

Entry 731  Map 12

## Rhône Valley – Alps

### Château des Allues

A breathtaking setting for an atmospheric château, 13th century and facing the mountains. There's an incredible feeling of openness and space, and a house party feel if you stay. Stéphane's warm personality gives the place soul; Didier is charming; dinners are innovative and delicious and vegetables are from the potager – a glory. Inside: flowers, paintings, sculptures, quirky-chic antiques, music classical and modern, and comforting old-style suites with huge walk-in wardrobes and tip-top bathrooms. Climb snow-topped peaks, collapse by the pool, visit the Château de Miolans. Breakfast will set you up for a hearty day out. *Cot available.*

| | |
|---|---|
| Rooms | 2 doubles: €140–€165. |
| | 1 suite for 2, |
| | 2 suites for 4: €150–€240. |
| Meals | Dinner with wine, €48. |
| | Restaurants 5-minute drive. |
| Closed | 3 weeks in December. |

**Stéphane Vandeville**
Château des Allues,
73250 Saint Pierre d'Albigny
Savoie
Mobile  +33 (0)6 75 38 61 56
Email   info@chateaudesallues.com
Web    www.chateaudesallues.com

Entry 732  Map 12

## Le Petit Nid

Sitting quietly in a breathtaking Alpine panorama that lifts the spirits, the old watermill has been lovingly renovated with impressive craftsmanship and neat design, from the handmade timber staircase that runs through the heart of the house to the original millstones on the patio. Warm, attentive owner and Cordon Bleu chef Sarah lives next door and is on hand to meet your every need, leaving you free to enjoy her locally sourced food. Take in the poetic garden – complete with bubbling trout stream and the scent of wisteria, lavender and rosemary – or ski, hike and bike the mountain tracks.

## Chalet Savoie Faire

At the top of a winding road are mountains, clear skies and world-class trails and cross-country skiing – and, behind the façade of this old Savoyard farmhouse is a luxurious B&B. Friendly owners Hugh and Nikki – she runs wonderful cookery courses – have put everything into the renovation and each room has charming touches. The intimate dining room is chandelier-hung and atmospheric; the sitting room has a toasty fire and a rug to snuggle toes in; the bedrooms are a delight, especially the family suite on the first floor with chunky-chic furniture from old timbers. Bathrooms are a wow. *Minimum stay: 2 nights.*

| | |
|---|---|
| Rooms | 1 double, 1 twin: €60. |
| Meals | Dinner with wine, €20–€25. Restaurant 1km. |
| Closed | Rarely. |

| | |
|---|---|
| Rooms | 2 doubles (one links with bunk room for children), 1 twin with separate bathroom: €100–€130. Ski package: €380 p.p. per week. |
| Meals | Dinner, 3 courses with wine, €30. Restaurant 1km. |
| Closed | Rarely. |

| | |
|---|---|
| | Sarah Gill |
| | Le Petit Nid, |
| | 73220 St Alban des Hurtières |
| | Savoie |
| Tel | +33 (0)4 79 36 07 54 |
| Email | sarahgill@orange.fr |
| Web | www.lepetitnid.blogspot.fr |

| | |
|---|---|
| | Nikki Shields-Quinn |
| | Chalet Savoie Faire, |
| | Fontaines-Naves, |
| | 73260 La Léchère |
| | Savoie |
| Mobile | +33 (0)6 17 54 83 40 |
| Email | nikki@chaletsavoiefaire.com |
| Web | www.chaletsavoiefaire.com |

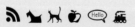

## Ferme Blanche

Up and up through forests and pastures to a hamlet-village in a supreme alpine setting. Sam and Alvaro have renovated their farmhouse with love, panache and a sympathetic eye. Bedrooms, one with a balcony, have cushioned window seats for views, fat feather duvets and fabulous bathrooms. Best of all are the meals, served on a terrace surrounded by mountain views (the spiced ginger ice cream is to die for; so are breakfast's pancakes.) What's more, the ski lifts of La Plagne are a five-minute drive. Short circular walk or hearty hiking trail? Whichever you choose, your dog will be as welcome as you are! *Children over 10 welcome.*

## Maison Coutin

In summer it's all flowers, birds and rushing streams; the balconies bloom, the garden is exuberant. Your friendly, sporty hosts have known the valley all their lives, have three children and will be helpful with yours. View-filled bedrooms are traditionally dark-beamed and attractively, imaginatively furnished. Delicious, mostly organic, food is cooked in the wood-fired oven (including the bread), the vegetables are home-grown, the eggs are from the hens, and there's a dayroom with a fridge. Great value and a deeply eco-friendly ethos.

| Rooms | 2 twin/doubles: €70-€150. Ski package: £595-£750 per person. per week. Dinner, B&B €80-€140 per person. |
| --- | --- |
| Meals | Dinner €30. |
| Closed | Rarely. |

| Rooms | 1 family room for 3, 1 family room for 4, 1 family room for 6: €62-€135. Ski package: €300-€340 per person. per week. |
| --- | --- |
| Meals | Restaurant within walking distance. |
| Closed | Rarely. |

FIRST EDITION VETERAN

AWARD WINNER

Old favourite

|  | **Sam Hinton**<br>Ferme Blanche,<br>Plagne Montalbert,<br>Montvilliers,<br>73210 Aime<br>Savoie |
| --- | --- |
| Email | info@ferme-blanche.com |
| Web | www.ferme-blanche.com |

|  | **Claude Coutin & Franck Chenal**<br>Maison Coutin,<br>Chemin de la Fruitière,<br>73210 Peisey Nancroix<br>Savoie |
| --- | --- |
| Tel | +33 (0)4 79 07 93 05 |
| Mobile | +33 (0)6 14 11 54 65 |
| Email | maison-coutin@orange.fr |
| Web | www.maison-coutin.fr |

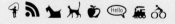

## Maison Caramel

Pancakes at breakfast and delicious table d'hôtes with veg from the sweet little garden, brought to the terrace with views: Sam and Alvaro's young chalet hosts look after you brilliantly. Little Landry is down the path, Bourg St Maurice (shops, restaurants, cafés) is a pootle away, and you are on the edge of the glorious Vanoise National Park. Skiing, rafting, hiking, biking, marmot-spotting… all yours from this sympathetic conversion of a rambling (lots of steps) farmhouse, stable and barn. Come home to vintage pieces, designer touches and a roll top tub with forest and glacier views: bliss!

## La Ferme d'Angèle

Savoyard charm oozes from this 1830s chalet. Think flagstones and furs, antlers and candles, wooden headboards and hearts, balconies and billowing window boxes. Romantic 'La Gentiane' is in the mazot, 'Edelweiss' is perfect for families. Relax in the starlit hot tub amid swaying larch; thaw in the sauna. With breakfast crêpes à l'ancienne, tartiflette, fire-smoked ham and strawberry soup for dinner, Valérie loves to spoil. Intimate tables dot an atmospheric stone-walled living room. Keen cyclists can pedal to Italy via the Petit St Bernard pass. There are watersports and masses of scope for walkers. A heart-warming place. *Minimum stay: 2 nights in school holidays.*

| Rooms | 2 doubles, 2 twins: €70–€110. 1 family room for 3: €100–€140. Ski package: €550–€750 per person per week. |
| --- | --- |
| Meals | Dinner with wine, €35. Picnic lunch €10. Restaurants within walking distance. |
| Closed | Rarely. |

| Rooms | 1 double: €160. 1 family room for 3, 3 family rooms for 4: €225–€300. Ski package: €530–€665 per person per week. Singles €90. Child €60. |
| --- | --- |
| Meals | Dinner €25. Wine €20. |
| Closed | Rarely. |

|  | Alvaro Gil |
| --- | --- |
|  | Maison Caramel, |
|  | Chemin des Glières, |
|  | 73210 Landry |
|  | Savoie |
| Mobile | +33 (0)6 26 80 77 67 |
| Email | info@maisoncaramel.com |
| Web | www.maisoncaramel.com |

|  | Valérie & Olivier Graziano |
| --- | --- |
|  | La Ferme d'Angèle, |
|  | 73700 Seez |
|  | Savoie |
| Tel | +33 (0)4 79 41 05 71 |
| Mobile | +33 (0)6 07 67 43 20 |
| Email | contact@ferme-angele.com |
| Web | www.ferme-angele.com |

## Rhône Valley – Alps

### Chalet Colinn

Mylène and Elizabeth love the outdoors, hence their five-year fight to reincarnate a fallen ruin as a luxury mountain retreat. Join them for gourmet dinner under soaring, raftered ceilings in the grand living space which hovers above Tignes dam. Or soak in the terrace hot tub under the stars; there's a sauna too. Urban rusticity, mountain chic: the place reeks Italian style yet is impossibly hidden in this tiny hamlet. For daytime adventure: the slopes at Val d'Isère, or Tignes, or the Vanoise park. Just ask Elizabeth, off-piste skier extraordinaire.

| Rooms | 3 twin/doubles, 2 triples: €190–€400 (winter), €120–€180 (summer). Winter price includes dinner, B&B for 2. |
|---|---|
| Meals | Dinner €35. Wine from €13. |
| Closed | Rarely. |

Elizabeth Chabert &
Mylène Charrière
Chalet Colinn,
Le Franchet de Tignes, BP 125,
73150 Val d'Isère
Savoie

| Tel | +33 (0)4 79 06 26 99 |
| Email | contact@chaletcolinn.com |
| Web | www.chaletcolinn.com |

Entry 739  Map 12

## Rhône Valley – Alps

### Domaine de Gorneton

The most caring of B&B owners: he, warmly humorous and humble about his excellent cooking; she, generous and outgoing. Built high on a hill as a fort in 1646, beside the spring that runs through the magnificent garden (a genuine Roman ruin, too), their superb old house is wrapped round a green-clad courtyard. Inside, levels change, vast timbers span the dining room, country antiques sprawl by the fire in the salon. In an outside single-storey building are traditional, rather sombre guest rooms with pristine bathrooms – and a bedhead from Hollywood in the best room. Family friendliness in deep country 15 minutes from Lyon.

| Rooms | 3 doubles, 1 suite for 4: €120–€180. |
|---|---|
| Meals | Dinner with wine, €40. |
| Closed | Rarely. |

M & Mme Fleitou
Domaine de Gorneton,
712 chemin de Violans,
38670 Chasse sur Rhône
Isère

| Tel | +33 (0)4 72 24 19 15 |
| Mobile | +33 (0)6 99 81 72 08 |
| Email | gorneton@wanadoo.fr |
| Web | www.gorneton.com |

Entry 740  Map 11

### Longeville

There is a gentle elegance about this house and the people who live in it, including three sleek cats and two friendly dogs. Of Scots and Irish origin, the Barrs also give you run of the pretty garden with swimming pool. Their love for this 1750s farmhouse shows in their artistic touch with decorating, their mix of old and modern furniture, their gorgeous big bedrooms done in soft pale colours that leave space for the views that rush in from the hills. A high place of comfort and civilised contact where dinner in the airy white living room is a chance to get to know your kind, laid-back hosts more fully.

| | |
|---|---|
| Rooms | 2 twin/doubles: €50–€90. |
| Meals | Dinner with wine, €25. |
| Closed | Rarely. |

**Mary & Greig Barr**
Longeville,
5 Longeville,
38300 Succieu
Isère
Tel     +33 (0)4 74 27 94 07
Mobile  +33 (0)6 87 47 59 46
Email   mary.barr@wanadoo.fr

### Le Traversoud

Rooms are named after painters; lovely 'Cézanne' lies under the eaves on the top floor. Nathalie, warm, bright and amusing, and attentive Pascal welcome you to their farmhouse, guide you up the outside stairs to colourful, comfortable bedrooms and spotless shower rooms (a sauna, too) and treat you to some of the best home cooking in France, served at a long table; even the brioche is homemade. The garden overflows with grass and trees, crickets chirrup, the Bernese Mountain dog bounds, the donkeys graze and the exuberant courtyard is a safe space for your children to join theirs. Wonderful, informal B&B.

| | |
|---|---|
| Rooms | 1 twin: €60.
1 family room for 3,
1 family room for 4: €76–€92.
Children under 10, €10. |
| Meals | Dinner with wine, €25. |
| Closed | Rarely. |

**Nathalie & Pascal Deroi**
Le Traversoud,
484 chemin Sous l'École,
38110 Faverges de la Tour
Isère
Tel     +33 (0)4 74 83 90 40
Mobile  +33 (0)6 07 11 99 42
Email   deroi.traversoud@orange.fr
Web     www.le-traversoud.com

## Rhône Valley – Alps

### Montchâteau

Views swoop across the green rolling landscape of the National Park as far as the eye can see; sit on the glazed veranda and drink it all in. High in the hills, utterly peaceful, this 19th-century hunting lodge is 15 minutes from lakes, 30 minutes from slopes, and 40 minutes from Grenoble: a special situation. Your gently attentive hosts give you large tranquil bedrooms in uncluttered French style – Rococo-repro here, Louis XV there – and super-spoiling bathrooms. Downstairs are plush leather chesterfields on a sweeping floor, a marble fireplace, English TV, and thrice-weekly meals at the big table.

| Rooms | 3 doubles: €65-€99. |
| | 1 family room for 4: €98-€143. |
| Meals | Dinner with wine, €25 |
| | (Fri, Sat & Mon only; |
| | cold supper available rest of week). |
| | Restaurant 4 km. |
| Closed | 13 December – 31 January. |

| | Hazel Watson |
| | Montchâteau, |
| | Reyssabot, |
| | 38620 Merlas |
| | Isère |
| Tel | +33 (0)4 76 66 16 82 |
| Email | hazel@montchateau.com |
| Web | www.montchateau.com |

🕴 📶 📧 🐈 🍎 Hello

Entry 743   Map 11

## Rhône Valley – Alps

### Château de Pâquier

Old, mighty, atmospheric – yet so homely. Enormous rooms, high heavy-beamed ceilings, large windows with sensational valley views; terraced gardens and animals; impressive bedrooms (handsome wardrobes, underfloor heating) up an ancient spiral staircase that sets the imagination reeling. Twice a week Hélène prepares dinner for guests in her modernised 17th-century tower kitchen (wood-fired range, stone sink, cobbled floor) where she makes her bread, honey, jams and walnut aperitif. Jacques and their daughter run an auberge next door – so do eat there too. And drink wine from the Rossis' own vineyard near Montpellier.

| Rooms | 3 twin/doubles: €82-€86. |
| | 2 family rooms for 5: €86-€146. |
| | Singles €72. |
| | Extra bed/sofabed €20 per person |
| | per night. |
| Meals | Dinner €20-€29. Wine €5. |
| | Auberge next door. |
| Closed | Rarely. |

| | Jacques & Hélène Rossi |
| | Château de Pâquier, |
| | Chemin du Château, |
| | 38650 St Martin de la Cluze |
| | Isère |
| Tel | +33 (0)4 76 72 77 33 |
| Email | chateau.de.paquier@free.fr |
| Web | chateau.de.paquier.free.fr |

🕴 📶 📧 🐈 🍎 Hello 🚂

Entry 744   Map 11

## Rhône Valley – Alps

### Clos de la Sauvagine

A modern-traditional hillside house with owners who go above and beyond for their guests; literally, a breath of fresh air. Once you've trekked and climbed all you can, come home to cosy pine-clad bedrooms with plump duvets and soft lighting – in the main house or in the chalet. The intricate, sloping garden glows with flowers, trees, vegetables, birds, little winding pathways and views to die for; sip wine on the terrace, flip open a book. Henri and Janine, both incredibly kind and generous, share their homely open-plan living area with you. An immaculate, pampering, very beautiful place – and Henri designed the house. *Children over 10 welcome.*

| Rooms | 1 double with separate wc: €120. |
| | 1 chalet for 4: €120-€180. |
| | Singles €90. |
| Meals | Dinner €30. Restaurant 10km. |
| Closed | 15 September – 30 April. |

Janine & Henri Bonneville
Clos de la Sauvagine,
La Chapelle,
38650 Château Bernard
Isère
Tel     +33 (0)4 76 34 00 84
Mobile  +33 (0)6 08 60 18 61
Email   henribonneville@orange.fr
Web     www.closdelasauvagine.com

Entry 745  Map 11

## Rhône Valley – Alps

### Les Marais

Opt for the simple country life at this friendly farm, which has been in the family for over 100 years and has returned to organic methods. A couple of horses, a few hens, and, when there's a full house, beautiful meals of regional recipes served family-style, with homemade chestnut cake and 'vin de noix' aperitif. Monsieur collects old farming artefacts and Madame, although busy, always finds time for a chat. The bedrooms are in a separate wing with varnished ceilings, antique beds, some florals; baths are old-fashioned pink, new showers delight Americans. At the foot of the Vercors range, French charm, utter peace.

| Rooms | 1 double, 1 twin: €55-€60. |
| | 1 family room for 4: €98. |
| | 1 triple: €70. |
| Meals | Dinner with wine, €18 |
| | (not Sundays). |
| Closed | Rarely. |

FIRST
EDITION
VETERAN

Christiane & Jean-Pierre Imbert
Les Marais,
285 route des Massouillards,
26300 Charpey
Drôme
Tel     +33 (0)4 75 47 03 50
Mobile  +33 (0)6 27 32 23 65
Email   imbert.jean-pierre@wanadoo.fr
Web     pagesperso-orange.fr/les-marais

Entry 746  Map 11

## Rhône Valley – Alps

### Les Péris

Here is the grandmother we all dream of, a woman who cossets her guests, puts flowers and sweets in the bedrooms and sends you off with walnuts from the farm. In the family for ten generations, the old stone house facing the mountains is a happy and delightful home. Join family, friends and guests round the long kitchen table for walnut cakes at breakfast and daughter Élisabeth's delicious 'menu curieux' that uses forgotten vegetables. Roomy, old-fashioned bedrooms with armoires breathe a comfortable, informal air. Great for kids: a garden for wild flowers and a duck pond for splashing in.

| Rooms | 1 double: €50. |
| | 1 suite for 3: €50–€70. |
| | 1 family room for 4: €50–€90. |
| Meals | Dinner with wine, €20. |
| Closed | Never. |

FIRST
EDITION
VETERAN

Madeleine Cabanes
& Élisabeth Berger
Les Péris,
D154 – Route de Combovin,
26120 Châteaudouble
Drôme
Tel  +33 (0)4 75 59 80 51

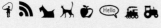

## Rhône Valley – Alps

### Chambres d'Hôtes Morin Salomé

A feast of colour and art, surrounded by breathtaking views, the Morin house is a visual treat, and is owned by a charming couple. He has created the windows and ironwork of the pergolas, she has tiled, fresco'd and frieze'd bathrooms, bedrooms and kitchen, with skill and imagination. Bedrooms are all river-side, brilliantly done, and fun. Dine on the terrace at one long table amongst a fabulous collection of pots and clambering plants, with the magnificent cliff beyond and rushing river sounds. A second terrace with ponds and goldfish almost drips over the river – the perfect solace. Tons to do nearby. Stunning.

| Rooms | 2 doubles, 1 triple: €70. |
| | 2 family rooms for 4: €70–€80. |
| Meals | Dinner with wine, €27.50. |
| | Restaurant 5-minute walk. |
| Closed | Rarely. |

Frédéric & Salomé Morin
Chambres d'Hôtes Morin Salomé,
34 rue Faubourg du Temple,
26340 Saillans
Drôme
Tel  +33 (0)4 75 21 43 95
Mobile  +33 (0)6 14 18 75 89
Email  morin-salome@orange.fr
Web  www.chambres-hotes-morin-salome.fr

## La Moutière

Surrounded by gorgeous gardens, the bastide sits large and square amid old outbuildings concealing perfectly converted gîtes. Bare stone façades and limestone trims under a Provençal roof set the tone for simple, fresh, uncluttered interiors: new limestone floors, white furniture, neutral tones and flashes of unexpected colour. Bedding is sumptuous, bathrooms fashionably funky, views from the beautiful pale blue pool glide pleasingly over rows of poplars and fields of lavender. Your wonderfully exuberant Belgian hostess gives convivial weekly dinner parties under the chestnut trees during high season. Divine.

## La Lauren

Below stretch glorious views south over the Sault plateau, west to Mont Ventoux. Here, surrounded by lavender fields, all is whisper-quiet. Warm friendly Christine has renovated her 17th-century sheep farm with extreme care and furnished it with walnut antiques and rich deep brocade – character oozes from every pore. She has a large garden, a handsome whippet, and serves six homemade jams at breakfast, under the trees or in the baronial hall. Just for guests: teal velvet armchairs, a Renaissance fireplace, and down-steps bedrooms with deep colours, splendid beds, south-facing views. Special for writers, artists, romantics. *Minimum stay: 2 nights in high season.*

| Rooms | 3 twin/doubles: €120–€130. Singles €120–€130. Extra bed/sofabed €30 per person per night. |
|---|---|
| Meals | Dinner €38. Guest kitchen. Restaurant 3km. |
| Closed | Rarely. |

| Rooms | 1 double: €95–€115. 1 family room for 4: €160. |
|---|---|
| Meals | Guest kitchenette. Restaurant 9km. |
| Closed | November – April. |

|  | Françoise Lefebvre La Moutière, Quartier Moutière, 26230 Colonzelle Drôme |
|---|---|
| Tel | +33 (0)4 75 46 26 88 |
| Mobile | +33 (0)6 76 94 90 25 |
| Email | lamoutiere@gmail.com |
| Web | www.lamoutiere.com |

|  | Christine Gourbin La Lauren, Route de Séderon, 26570 Ferrasieres Drôme |
|---|---|
| Mobile | +33 (0)6 25 79 33 56 |
| Email | kris.lauren@yahoo.fr |
| Web | www.la-lauren.com |

Provence – Alps – Riviera

www.sawdays.co.uk/provence-alps-riviera

Photo: ©iStock.com/rzdeb

## La Maison du Guil

The 16th-century stone and timber priory, the oldest house in this remote narrow hamlet, has the same glorious views as ever, out over the rooftops to the surrounding peaks. Inside is all stone and timber, too, beautifully architect-renovated and furnished with a cleancut imaginative eye. The big living room has an arched stone ceiling, a stunning foil for high-modern scarlet chairs and table cloths. Delighted with their Alpine venture, the charming new young owners can offer you big traditional bedrooms or a funkier cave-like room with stone nooks for lights and a sunken shower. Superb. *Minimum stay: 3 nights in high season.*

## Mas St Joseph

Come for the view – row upon row of peaks fading into the distance – the walking, the welcome and the Slow Food. Hélène and Olivier bought the old *mas* and its sloping terrain, restored it with love, then moved in and began taking guests. Olivier is the walker and knows all the trails; the countryside is spectacular. One bedroom has the old bread oven in the corner; another was the stable and the old manger proves it; all are rustic and charming. Delicious, delightful table d'hôtes is held on the terrace in warm weather or in the lovely old barn. Further treats: massage treatments, a hot tub and a pool. And, oh, those views!

| Rooms | 2 doubles, 2 family rooms for 3: €120–€130. Child €45. |
|---|---|
| Meals | Dinner with aperitif & coffee, €35. Wine from €5. Restaurant 3km. |
| Closed | Rarely. |

| Rooms | 1 double, 1 gypsy caravan for 2: €60–€69. 2 suites for 4: €98–€107. 1 triple: €79–€88. Singles €54–€60. Extra bed/sofabed €19 per person per night. |
|---|---|
| Meals | Dinner with wine, €17–€23. |
| Closed | Mid-November to March. |

**AWARD WINNER**

One of a kind

**Tom Van De Velde**
La Maison du Guil,
La Font,
05600 Eygliers
Hautes-Alpes
Tel   +33 (0)4 92 50 16 20
Email   info@lamaisonduguil.com
Web   www.lamaisonduguil.com

**Hélène & Olivier Lenoir**
Mas St Joseph,
04200 Châteauneuf Val St Donat
Alpes-de-Haute-Provence
Tel   +33 (0)4 92 62 47 54
Mobile   +33 (0)6 60 04 70 66
Email   contact@lemassaintjoseph.com
Web   www.lemassaintjoseph.com

### Le Jas du Bœuf

Here is Haute Provence bliss surrounded for miles by forests, vineyards and lavender and with stunning views of the Lubéron. Jérôme and Dana have restored the big 17th-century farmhouse to perfection and love having guests. Choose between traditional bedrooms in the house and two breathtakingly modern, wood-and-glass poolside lodges that pull the outside in. Star attractions are Wendy's art and design courses, yet a multitude of sports, delightful villages, gardens and markets call you. Then chill out by the infinity pool or in the exotic sunken siesta house. Exquisitely minimalist, wonderfully remote and welcoming.

### Le Clos de Rohan

Cloaked in a remote valley sweet with lavender lies an 18th-century farmhouse with ingeniously restored barns – find lavender stalks in the plaster! Lovely generous rooms have classy bathrooms, iron beds, crisp linen, a patio and terrace each, and views over valley and hills fat with bees. The chic two-storey suite comes with an open fire and a kitchenette, the other suite is more rustic, and there's a shared living room with a cosy wood-burner. In a courtyard garden heady with blooms, breakfast on homemade honey, cherries, plums, then daydream by the small pool. Provence at its bucolic best.

| | |
|---|---|
| Rooms | 2 doubles; 1 double with separate bathroom: €80–€115. 2 lodges for 2: €95–€130. Extra bed/sofabed €30 per person per night. |
| Meals | Dinner with wine, €30. Summer kitchen. Restaurants 3-8km. |
| Closed | Rarely. |

| | |
|---|---|
| Rooms | 2 suites for 2: €100–€120. Extra bed/sofabed €20–€60 per person per night. |
| Meals | Dinner with wine, €30. Guest kitchen. |
| Closed | Rarely. |

**Jérôme Mantel & Dana Silk**
Le Jas du Bœuf,
Lieu-dit Parrot,
04230 Cruis
Alpes-de-Haute-Provence
Tel +33 (0)4 92 79 01 05
Email lejasduboeuf@orange.fr
Web www.lejasduboeuf.fr

**Françoise Cavallo**
Le Clos de Rohan,
04150 Simiane la Rotonde
Alpes-de-Haute-Provence
Tel +33 (0)4 92 74 49 42
Mobile +33 (0)6 20 06 59 76
Email francoise.cavallo@terranet.fr
Web www.le-clos-de-rohan.eu

Entry 753  Map 16

Entry 754  Map 16

## La Belle Cour

The moment you enter the gorgeous big courtyard you feel at home. Angela and Rodney's welcome is second to none: cheerful and open, warm and humorous. On medieval foundations, this 18th-century staging post for pilgrims is all exposed stone and beams, its décor traditional/rustic; you'll love the embracing living rooms, the open fire, the cosy library with surround-sound music. Bedrooms overlook the courtyard and have private staircases; wallow in luscious fabrics and colours and intriguing treasures like the exquisite Japanese silk paintings. Truly special, and in a friendly village with restaurants and a public pool. *Minimum stay: 2 nights.*

## L'École Buissonnière

A stone jewel set in southern lushness and miles of green vines and purple hills. Country furniture – a particularly seductive choice of Provençal chairs – is polished with wax and time; big whitewashed bedrooms are freshly sober; birds sing to the tune of the aviary outside. One balconied bedroom, in the mezzanined old barn, has a saddle and a herdsman's hat from a spell in the Camargue; ask about John's travels. He rightly calls himself a Provençal Englishman, Monique is warmly welcoming too, theirs is a happy house, where German is also spoken. Wonderful Vaison la Romaine is four miles away.

| Rooms | 2 doubles: €90–€105. |
|---|---|
| Meals | Restaurants within walking distance. |
| Closed | November – March. |

| Rooms | 2 doubles: €68–€78. |
|---|---|
| | 1 family room for 4: €103–€108. |
| | Singles €52–€56. |
| Meals | Guest kitchen. |
| | Restaurant in village, 1km. |
| Closed | Rarely. |

**Rodney & Angela Heath**
La Belle Cour,
Place Daniel Vigouroux,
04280 Céreste
Alpes-de-Haute-Provence

Tel +33 (0)4 92 72 48 76
Email angela.heath@orange.fr
Web www.labellecour.com

**Monique Alex & John Parsons**
L'École Buissonnière,
D75,
84110 Buisson
Vaucluse

Tel +33 (0)4 90 28 95 19
Email ecole.buissonniere@wanadoo.fr
Web www.buissonniere-provence.com

## Provence – Alps – Riviera

### L'Évêché

Narrow, cobbled streets lead to this fascinating and beautifully furnished house that was once part of the 17th-century Bishop's Palace. The Verdiers are charming, relaxed, cultured hosts – he an architect/builder, she a teacher. The white walls of the guest sitting room-library are lined with modern art and framed posters, and the cosy, quilted bedrooms, all whitewashed beams and terracotta floors, have a serene Provençal feel. Views fly over beautiful terracotta rooftops from the balconied suite, and handsome breakfasts are served on the terrace, complete with exceptional views to the Roman bridge.

| Rooms | 3 twin/doubles: €85–€95. 2 suites for 2-3: €120–€145. Singles €80–€120. |
|---|---|
| Meals | Restaurants nearby. |
| Closed | Christmas, New Year. |

FIRST
EDITION
VETERAN

Aude & Jean-Loup Verdier
L'Évêché,
14 rue de l'Evêché, Cité Médiévale,
84110 Vaison la Romaine
Vaucluse

| Tel | +33 (0)4 90 36 13 46 |
| Mobile | +33 (0)6 03 03 21 42 |
| Email | eveche@aol.com |
| Web | www.eveche.com |

Entry 757   Map 16

## Provence – Alps – Riviera

### La Maison aux Volets Rouges

Step off the street into the 'red-shuttered' house to be wrapped in its warm embrace. Rooms are big with tiled floors, beams and antiques; family photographs line the stairs; there's an open fire for cool days, a courtyard for warm ones. High-beamed bedrooms have good storage and individual touches – a brass bed, an arched window, a teddy bear on the baby's bed. Garden and pool are a three-minute walk, restaurants a short stroll. Borrow a bike, stride out for wonderful walks, drop in on the glories of Avignon and Aix. Delightful, energetic Brigitte has perfect English, looks after you impeccably and does delicious breakfasts.

| Rooms | 1 double; 1 double with separate shower: €70–€90. |
|---|---|
| Meals | Restaurants within walking distance. |
| Closed | Rarely. |

Brigitte Woodward
La Maison aux Volets Rouges,
2 place de l'Église,
Les Farjons,
84100 Uchaux
Vaucluse

| Tel | +33 (0)4 90 40 62 18 |
| Email | b.woodward@hotmail.fr |
| Web | www.lamaisonauxvoletsrouges.com |

Entry 758   Map 16

## Villa Aurenjo

New guests' names are writ large on the blackboard – such is the welcome to this house. The thoughtfulness of your busy Dutch hosts extends to pancakes and smoothies at breakfasts and simple pastel-themed bedrooms with scented soaps and soft bathrobes. In the bustling suburbs of town, this grand Provençal house and its high-shaded oasis garden (tennis court, orangerie and pool) hide behind electric gates. Imagine log fires and well-worn sofas in a huge woodsmoke-patina'd salon, one sunny bedroom opening to a patio, two with roof terraces – and summer opera in the amphitheatre, a walk away. Relaxed place, friendly people. *Minimum stay: 2 nights in high season.*

## L'A Propos

Step through the looking glass into a world of refined French elegance; the smell of fresh coffee drifting through the salon, the click of a heel on polished parquet. White is softened by 19th-century features, earthy fabrics and the odd wacky touch: walls clothed in blown-up black-and-white postcards. There are three private parks for cypress shaded wanderings, a heated pool, a balneotherapy, a boules pitch, a buddha for peace and harmony. Large rooms are classic–contemporary, with ample bathrooms attached. Beyond are ancient ruins, vibrant markets, canoeing on the Ardèche, wine tasting in Châteauneuf-du-Pape.

| Rooms | 3 doubles: €95–€200.<br>1 suite for 2 with sofabed:<br>€150–€240.<br>1 family room for 4: €190–€280. |
|---|---|
| Meals | Dinner, 3 courses, €29.50.<br>Wine €15–€40.<br>Restaurants 600m. |
| Closed | Rarely. |

| Rooms | 1 double: €112–€160.<br>4 suites for 2-4: €180–€260. |
|---|---|
| Meals | Restaurants within walking distance. |
| Closed | Rarely. |

|  | **The Manager**<br>Villa Aurenjo,<br>121 rue François Chambovet,<br>84100 Orange<br>Vaucluse |
|---|---|
| Tel | +33 (0)4 90 11 10 00 |
| Email | villa-aurenjo@wanadoo.fr |
| Web | www.villaaurenjo.com |

|  | **Estelle Godefroy-Mourier**<br>L'A Propos,<br>15 avenue Frédéric Mistral,<br>84100 Orange<br>Vaucluse |
|---|---|
| Tel | +33 (0)4 90 34 54 91 |
| Mobile | +33 (0)6 10 33 06 32 |
| Email | info@lapropos.com |
| Web | www.lapropos.com |

## Provence – Alps – Riviera

### La Maison des Remparts

Built into the honey-coloured walls of this fortified village, a stylish refuge decorated with a restraint that lets the ancient walls and beams tell their own story. The house is arranged around a secluded courtyard with an azure pool at its centre, overlooked by a big bright living room. Bedrooms are a symphony of pale colours and crisp white linen, elegance and space; unashamedly gorgeous, they have bathrooms to match. Enjoy a madly indulgent breakfast around the oak table in the stone-flagged kitchen, specially set up for guests. The owners don't live here, but bubbly Ludivine makes you feel beautifully at home.

## Provence – Alps – Riviera

### Le Clos St Saourde

What a place! Outdoors turns inwards here, spectacularly: many walls, ceilings, even some furniture, are sculpted from solid rock. The décor is minimalist and luxurious with a flurry of natural materials and lots of quirky touches: the wrought-iron lamps and lanterns, the clever lighting, the solar pools. Indulge yourself in a private spa (if you have booked the treehouse) or in a breathtaking grotto bathroom. This lovely couple will tell you all about visits, vineyard tours, activities (fancy rock-climbing, a massage?) and restaurants in their exquisite area. They serve delicious gourmet platters with the right wines.

| | |
|---|---|
| Rooms | 1 double: €160. |
| | 2 suites for 2: €160–€280. |
| | 1 family room for 3, |
| | 1 family room for 4: €140–€280. |
| | Extra bed €40 per person per night. |
| Meals | Guest kitchen. |
| | Restaurants walking distance. |
| Closed | Rarely. |

| | |
|---|---|
| Rooms | 2 doubles: €180–€260. |
| | 2 suites for 2-3 with sofabeds: |
| | €220–€290. |
| | 1 treehouse for 2: €370–€470. |
| | Extra bed €40 per person per night. |
| Meals | Gourmet dinner with wine, €50. |
| | Summer kitchen. Restaurant 2km. |
| Closed | Rarely. |

| | |
|---|---|
| | **Ludivine Rivallin** |
| | La Maison des Remparts, |
| | 74 cours Louis Pasteur, |
| | 84190 Beaumes de Venise |
| | Vaucluse |
| Tel | +33 (0)4 90 62 75 49 |
| Email | contact@lamaisondesremparts.com |
| Web | www.lamaisondesremparts.com |

| | |
|---|---|
| | **Jérôme & Géraldine Thuillier** |
| | Le Clos St Saourde, |
| | Route de St Véran, |
| | 84190 Beaumes de Venise |
| | Vaucluse |
| Tel | +33 (0)4 90 37 35 20 |
| Mobile | +33 (0)6 99 41 44 19 |
| Email | contact@leclossaintsaourde.com |
| Web | www.leclossaintsaourde.com |

Entry 761  Map 16

Entry 762  Map 16

## Villa Noria

The garden sets the scene, a secluded enclave of cedars, palms, roses, lawns, and a saltwater pool with views that sweep over vineyards to mountains. Welcome to an elegant 18th-century house run by the delightful Philippe and Sylvie. Up the stone farmhouse stair are bedrooms decorated in Provençal style, the finest on the first floor. Cool tiles underfoot, beams overhead, beds swathed in white and bathrooms diagonally tiled. You breakfast in a wraparound conservatory, there's a salon with fauteuils in red and white checks, and the oval dining table waits beneath a weeping fern: don't miss the hosted dinners! Superb.

| Rooms | 3 doubles, 1 twin: €70–€120. 1 suite for 4: €140–€160. Extra bed €30 per person per night. |
|---|---|
| Meals | Dinner with wine, €35. Restaurants 3km. |
| Closed | Rarely. |

Philippe Monti
Villa Noria,
4 route de Mazan,
84330 Modène
Vaucluse
Tel      +33 (0)4 90 62 50 66
Email    post@villa-noria.com
Web      www.villa-noria.com

Entry 763   Map 16

---

## Château Juvenal

The château is lived in and loved every day, thanks to Anne-Marie and Bernard, who also produce an award-winning wine and delicious olive oil from their 600 trees. They nurture some superb specimen trees, too, out in the park. The traditional bedrooms with high ceilings and tall windows are all on the first floor and range from cosy to spacious; the sitting and dining rooms sport chandeliers and exquisite furniture. Grab your shopping basket and visit the local market, for the summer kitchen next to the pool. There are wine visits, a pony for the kids, annual tango events, a spa and two lovely apartments for longer stays. *Self-catering available in 2 apartments for 4-6.*

| Rooms | 1 double; 2 twin/doubles: €120–€155. 1 suite for 2-3: €140–€180. |
|---|---|
| Meals | Summer kitchen. Dinner with wine, €45, twice weekly. |
| Closed | Rarely. |

Anne-Marie & Bernard Forestier
Château Juvenal,
120 chemin du Long Serre,
84330 Saint Hippolyte le Graveyron
Vaucluse
Tel      +33 (0)4 90 62 31 76
Mobile   +33 (0)6 07 13 11 47
Email    chateau.juvenal@gmail.com
Web      www.chateau-juvenal-provence.com

Entry 764   Map 16

### Le Mas de la Pierre du Coq

What's especially nice about this 17th-century farmhouse is that it hasn't been over-prettified. Instead, it has the friendly, informal elegance of a house that's lived in and loved; grey-painted beams, soft stone walls, seductive bathrooms. The Lorenzes loved it the moment they saw it; it reminded gentle Stéphan of the house he grew up in. Bustling Martine starts your day with a terrific breakfast, Stéphan shows you the walks from the door. The gardens, sweet with roses, oleanders and lavender, are shaded by ancient trees and the pool and views are glorious. Stay for as long as you can; book excellent dinners in advance.

### L'Observance

You couldn't be better placed for ambling round historic Avignon than at this friendly B&B within the city's old walls. The latest incarnation of a building that has in its lifetime been part of a monastery, a barracks and a factory, there are now two light, spacious en-suite rooms in the main house and an annexe converted into a cosy apartment for four. Your lovely Dutch hosts welcome you with a glass of wine and offer generous breakfasts of pastries, ham, cheese and eggs. Though the Palais des Papes and Pont d'Avignon are only a short stroll, it's blissfully calm. Cool off in the sparkling pool after a busy day sightseeing. *Minimum stay: 2 nights in high season. Parking available.*

| Rooms | 1 double, 2 twins: €135–€150. 1 suite for 4: €230. |
|---|---|
| Meals | Dinner with wine, €40. |
| Closed | Rarely. |

| Rooms | 1 double, 1 twin/double: €95–€155. 1 apartment for 4 sharing bathroom: €140–€175. Extra bed/sofabed €20 per person per night. |
|---|---|
| Meals | Restaurants within walking distance. |
| Closed | Never. |

AWARD WINNER

Favourite newcomer

**Stéphan & Martine Lorenz**
Le Mas de la Pierre du Coq,
434 chemin de Sauzette,
84810 Aubignan
Vaucluse

| Tel | +33 (0)4 90 67 31 64 |
| Mobile | +33 (0)6 76 81 95 09 |
| Email | lorenz.stephane@wanadoo.fr |
| Web | www.masdelapierreducoq.com |

**Jacqueline & Jeroen Tutein Nolthenius**
L'Observance,
Rue de l'Observance,
84000 Avignon
Vaucluse

| Tel | +33 (0)4 13 66 05 85 |
| Email | info@lobservance.com |
| Web | www.lobservance.com |

## A l'Ombre du Palais

Gaze from the veranda, aperitif in hand, on the Palais des Papes and Notre Dame des Dômes; Sabine's house is in Avignon's old heart. Inside… a riot of russets, reds and saffrons, bright modern paintings and Louis XVI pieces, stylish orchids and tumbling cushions – a décor as generous as Sabine herself. Bedrooms, flamboyant and generous, vary greatly in size and are peaceful and private; we adored 'Kandinsky' and 'de Staël'. Sabine loves guests and house in equal measure, and gives you breakfast where and when you want it – including that veranda. Dinners are exquisite and delicious. *Minimum stay: 2 nights.*

## Le Mas de Miejour

Fred and Emma are wonderful hosts, sommeliers with a passion for wine who have escaped their city pasts. The guest bedrooms of their delightful old *mas* are all different, all serene: one on the ground floor with a painted brass bed and a white appliquéd bedcover, another with Senegalese fabrics; the family suite spreads itself over two floors. The land here is flat with a high water table so the gardens, sheltered by trees and waving maize, are ever fresh and green. It's a beautiful, artistic place to relax, your littl'uns can play with theirs, the pool is delicious and the food a delight.

| Rooms | 2 twin/doubles, 3 family rooms for 3: €130–€160. Extra bed €40 per person per night. |
|---|---|
| Meals | Dinner €40. Wine €10–€12. Restaurants within walking distance. |
| Closed | January/February. |

| Rooms | 1 double, 1 twin/double: €85–€105. 1 family room for 4: €95–€165. |
|---|---|
| Meals | Restaurants 3km. |
| Closed | November – March, except by arrangement. |

|  | Sabine Ferrand |
|---|---|
|  | A l'Ombre du Palais, |
|  | Place du Palais des Papes, |
|  | 84000 Avignon |
|  | Vaucluse |
| Mobile | +33 (0)6 23 46 50 95 |
| Email | sabine.ferrand@wanadoo.fr |
| Web | www.alombredupalais.com |

|  | Frédéric Westercamp & |
|---|---|
|  | Emmanuelle Diemont |
|  | Le Mas de Miejour, |
|  | 117 chemin du Trentin, |
|  | 84250 Le Thor, Vaucluse |
| Tel | +33 (0)4 90 02 13 79 |
| Mobile | +33 (0)6 68 25 25 06 |
| Email | contact@masdemiejour.com |
| Web | www.masdemiejour.com |

### La Bastide Rose

Once an ancient mill on the river Sourge, this pink-hued house has a relaxed but regal air. The grounds are huge, with their own island, swimming pool and an orangery where a seasonal breakfast is served. Inside, character abounds. There's a sitting room that was once an ancient kitchen and distinctive bedrooms, one with its own terrace, another with antiques and a sitting room. All have modern bathrooms. The library is stocked with books, and occasional exhibitions are held (almost more hotel than B&B!). Lovely Poppy can point you to the best walks and finest markets, or leave you to linger in this fabulous place. *Minimum stay: 2 nights in high season.*

### Mas Pichony

Summer evenings are spent beneath the ancient spreading plane tree while sunset burnishes the vines beyond the slender cypresses, and the old stones of the 17th-century *mas* breathe gold. Laetitia and Laurent have given the farmhouse style and charm, beautifying it with country antiques, books and vibrant colours. Two children, five horses and a trio of cats complete the delightful picture. Laetitia serves good Provençal food at the big, convivial table; the terracotta-roofed area by the pool is a delicious place to sit and soak up daytime views.

| Rooms | 3 twin/doubles (2 rooms can interconnect): €150-€220. 2 suites for 2: €210-€290. Extra bed €35 per person per night. Pets €10. |
|---|---|
| Meals | Breakfast €18. Lunch €25-€30. Dinner €32-€50. Wine €20-€140. Restaurant 7km. |
| Closed | Mid-January to mid-March. |

| Rooms | 3 doubles, 2 twin/doubles: €110-€122. Singles €106-€118. |
|---|---|
| Meals | Dinner with wine, €32. |
| Closed | November – March. |

**Poppy Salinger**
La Bastide Rose,
99 chemin des Croupières,
84250 Le Thor
Vaucluse

| Tel | +33 (0)4 90 02 14 33 |
| Mobile | +33 (0)6 78 43 57 33 |
| Email | contact@bastiderose.com |
| Web | www.bastiderose.com |

**Laetitia & Laurent Desbordes**
Mas Pichony,
1454 route de St Didier,
84210 Pernes les Fontaines
Vaucluse

| Tel | +33 (0)4 90 61 56 11 |
| Mobile | +33 (0)6 99 16 98 58 |
| Email | mas-pichony@wanadoo.fr |
| Web | www.maspichony.com |

## La Nesquière

The gardens alone are worth the detour: trees and greenery galore, riots of roses, all flourishing in a huge many-terraced park by a river. The 18th-century farmhouse harbours a fine collection of antiques – one of Isabelle's passions – tastefully set off by lush indoor greenery and lovely old carpets on ancient tile floors. Softly old-elegant rooms have hand-embroidered fabrics and genuine old linens, including Provençal quilts – truly exquisite – with splashes of red, orange and beige against white backgrounds. Themed weekends, too (cookery, wine, embroidery), and a warm, gracious welcome from Isabelle and her family.

## Maison Noel

Imagine a tiny Provençal village with a sun-dappled café-bar, an excellent auberge, a ruined castle, and a square off which lies Maison Noel. Enchanting, historic, and partially shaded by an old lime tree, it is the home of a charming and well-travelled hostess. The heart of the house is downstairs (open fireplace, country kitchen), the décor is stylish and soothing, and you can spill into a heavenly garden for supper (borrow the barbecue!). A perfect springboard for Provence, with a capacious bed to come home to and your own secluded patio. Artists and romantics will not wish to stir. *Minimum stay: 2 nights in high season. Self-catering available for 2.*

| Rooms | 3 twin/doubles: €115-€140. |
| | 2 family rooms for 4: €105-€125. |
| Meals | Dinner with wine, €40 (Sat & Tue). |
| Closed | Mid-December to mid-January. |

| Rooms | 1 double: €90-€110. |
| Meals | Dinner from €20. |
| | Restaurant 5-minute walk. |
| Closed | Rarely. |

|  | **Isabelle de Maintenant** |
|  | La Nesquière, |
|  | 5419 route d'Althen, |
|  | 84210 Pernes les Fontaines |
|  | Vaucluse |
| Tel | +33 (0)4 90 62 00 16 |
| Mobile | +33 (0)6 79 72 43 47 |
| Email | lanesquiere@wanadoo.fr |
| Web | www.lanesquiere.com |

|  | **Trish Michie** |
|  | Maison Noel, |
|  | 12 place du Bataillet, |
|  | 84800 Lagnes |
|  | Vaucluse |
| Mobile | +33 (0)6 72 45 36 03 |
| Email | trishmichie@gmail.com |
| Web | www.come2provence.com |

Entry 771   Map 16

Entry 772   Map 16

## Sous L'Olivier

Old stonework rules the scene, big arched openings have become dining-room windows, a stone hearth burns immense logs in winter, and all is set round a pretty courtyard. Charming young bon viveur Julien cooks for you: breakfasts are sumptuous affairs and convivial dinners are worth a serious detour; in summer, perhaps a generous barbecue. Gentle Carole is behind the very fresh, Frenchly decorated bedrooms. Agricultural land is all around, you are close to the Lubéron mountains, and the big, child-friendly, saltwater pool is arched with canvas shading and surrounded by giant pots and plants. Lovely people, fabulous food. *Extra bed available.*

## Le Domaine Saint Jean

With lovely Lubéron views over vineyards and orchards, this sturdy farm centres on a courtyard and its quenching old trough and pump. Thea and Eric came south for warmth and their Provençal project celebrates their care and flair. Thea cooks up a local feast once a week and lays on fine outdoor breakfasts too. Antique dealer Eric's finds add intrigue to calm, clean-lined rooms: white linen and beams, bursts of vibrant fabrics, good new bathrooms. There's a shared pool to plunge in and lounge by, a bar/games/sitting room to retreat to, handy access to kitchens and such a rich area to visit; visual and cultural treats all around.

| Rooms | 3 doubles: €100. | | Rooms | 1 double, 1 twin/double: €75-€140. |
|---|---|---|---|---|
| | 2 suites for 4: €138. | | | 1 family room for 3, |
| Meals | Dinner with wine, €32. | | | 1 family room for 4: €110-€200. |
| Closed | Easter; bank holidays; | | Meals | Dinner with wine, 3 courses, €30 |
| | 31 October – 1 April. | | | (once a week). |
| | | | | Tapas with wine, €15. |
| | | | | Restaurants 2km. |
| | | | Closed | December – February. |

Carole, Julien, Hugo & Clovis
Gouin
Sous L'Olivier,
997B, D900,
84800 Lagnes
Vaucluse
Tel    +33 (0)4 90 20 33 90
Email  souslolivier@orange.fr
Web    www.chambresdhotesprovence.com

Thea Hemery
Le Domaine Saint Jean,
St Jean,
84490 Saint Saturnin les Apt
Vaucluse
Tel     +33 (0)4 32 50 10 77
Mobile  +33 (0)6 82 92 56 58
Email   thea@ledomainesaintjean.com
Web     www.ledomainesaintjean.com

Entry 773   Map 16

Entry 774   Map 16

## Terrasses du Luberon

Be inspired by the views, which sweep from pool and dining terrace over vineyards, orchards and fields to breezy Mont Ventoux: plan walks or cycle rides through Provençal villages. The house sprawls in the steep Bonnieux hills, a stroll from the village, tree-wrapped in rural peace – play pétanque before dinner. New owners, back from Réunion, are busy with a veg garden, cartoon collections (Captain Haddock guards the breakfast buffet) and looking after guests; tips range from hikes to markets to Michelin-star restaurants. Rooms have private patios, space for extra beds and a shared kitchen and laundry. *Minimum stay: 3 nights in high season.*

## A Travers Champs

Which couple could resist the romance of 'La Vie en Rose' with its king-size bed and free-standing bath? Or 'La Madrague' with driftwood, sand and deck chairs; or 'Couleur Café' with coffee-coloured tiles and leather? Each fun, themed room has a private terrace, but most guests soak up the peace on giant cushions around the free-form swimming pool. There's also a sail-shaded dining terrace where Christelle, a cook, offers table d'hôtes. Breakfast is a feast of French toast, eggs and fruit from local farms. You can pop to Aix-en-Provence for city life or spend quiet days walking and cycling through the southern Lubéron. *Minimum stay: 2 nights in high season. Children over 12 welcome.*

| Rooms | 2 doubles, 3 twin/doubles: €115–€150. |
|---|---|
| Meals | Guest kitchen. |
| | Restaurants within walking distance. |
| Closed | 14 October – 27 March. |

| Rooms | 3 doubles, 1 twin: €90–€120. |
|---|---|
| | 1 suite for 2, |
| | 1 suite for 3: €120–€170. |
| | Whole house (min. stay 3 nights), €750 per night (€5,000 p.w). |
| Meals | Dinner with wine, €35 (2 nights a week). Restaurants 3km. |
| Closed | Mid-November to March. |

**Marie Laure & Jean Marc Caspar**
Terrasses du Luberon,
Quartier Les Bruillères,
84480 Bonnieux
Vaucluse

Tel    +33 (0)4 90 75 87 40
Email   information@lesterrassesduluberon.fr
Web    www.lesterrassesduluberon.fr

**Christelle Bonnet**
A Travers Champs,
Chemin de la Jaconne,
84160 Puyvert
Vaucluse

Mobile   +33 (0)6 29 68 79 84
Email    christellebonnet@sfr.fr
Web     www.a-travers-champs.com

## Maison Collongue

'Petit déjeuner' is 'grand petit déjeuner' here – local, lavish and organic. Guillaume, a graphic designer from Paris, lives with his family in two beautiful farm buildings linked by a hallway; the restoration is glorious, his energy is infectious, and you'll love every second of your stay. A ha-ha divides the garden from the fields, a pool beckons, a stream runs by, and dinner is served at tables under an ancient lime. Sunshine-streamed bedrooms, whiter than white, are dotted with French antiques and cool mid-century pieces, floors and shutters are original and walk-in showers vast. Visit the market at Lourmarin: a joy.

## Domaine La Parpaille

Recline on a cushioned lounger, book a massage by the pool, gaze across vineyards to Cucuron. The farm has been in Eve's family for generations and has never looked so dapper. Behind the house are bedrooms in barns: calm, tasteful, studiously chic. Find neutral colours, linen curtains, a country antique restored by Gilles, a Persian carpet on a polished concrete floor, and bathrooms of pure luxury, one with 'his and her' showers. Eve is a keen cook and you dine deliciously in her kitchen or on the flagged terrace. As for medieval Cucuron: Tuesday's market around the spring-fed 'bassin' is an exquisite treat.

| Rooms | 3 twin/doubles: €150–€170. |
| | 1 triple: €220. |
| Meals | Dinner €22–€37. |
| | Wine €10–€20. |
| | Restaurants 2.2km. |
| Closed | Rarely. |

| Rooms | 2 doubles: €115–€125. |
| Meals | Restaurants 2km. |
| Closed | Never. |

**Guillaume Toutain**
Maison Collongue,
Chemin de Collongue,
84160 Lourmarin
Vaucluse
Tel    +33 (0)4 90 77 44 69
Mobile  +33 (0)6 76 86 76 65
Email  guillaume.toutain.lourmarin@gmail.com
Web    www.maison-collongue.com

**Eve & Gilles Scholefield**
Domaine La Parpaille,
Campagne Blanqui,
Chemin de Blanqui,
84160 Cucuron
Vaucluse
Mobile  +33 (0)6 75 98 06 70
Email  gilles.scholefield@free.fr
Web    www.domaine-la-parpaille.com

Entry 777   Map 16

Entry 778   Map 16

## Le Moulin du Rossignol

Artistic and friendly Beatrice and Jean-Marc love sharing their serene stone giant of an ex-water mill. It's half a mile from the village in a sheltered, wooded valley and wrapped in a rambling garden with pool and ping-pong. Pretty bedrooms up the winding stairs are all about comfort, warmth and soft lighting through floaty curtains and ethnic lamps. Unwind downstairs too, where the Paranques' creativity has taken world-wide inspiration; cosy in winter, cool in summer. Breakfasts are fresh, copious-continental and you can walk into the village for dinner. Between Aix and the Lubéron – perfect for exploring inland Provence.

## Le *petit* Figuier

In a Provençal village known for its international piano festival is a grand 18th-century house with two elegant B&B rooms. Bubbly Lis welcomes you into a chequerboard-tiled hall where musical guests can try out the old family piano. On the second floor, a cosy twin room has iron beds and garden views, while a chic country-style double has cream furniture, a sunny balcony and a smart en-suite. Breakfast on delicious croissants in a tranquil garden shaded with fig and olive trees. Take a dip in the pool or hop in the car to find beautiful villages and the Abbaye de Silvacane. In the evening you can stroll to good restaurants nearby. *Minimum stay: 2 nights. Children over 14 welcome. Parking available.*

| | |
|---|---|
| Rooms | 1 double, 1 twin/double: €80–€95. 1 suite for 3: €120–€135. 1 triple: €105–€125. Extra bed/sofabed €25–€30 per person per night. |
| Meals | Restaurants within walking distance. |
| Closed | Rarely. |

| | |
|---|---|
| Rooms | 1 double, 1 twin; day beds in rooms: €110–€125. Extra bed/sofabed €35 per person per night. |
| Meals | Summer kitchen. Restaurants 5-minute walk. |
| Closed | Rarely. |

| | |
|---|---|
| | **Béatrice Paranque** Le Moulin du Rossignol, 13840 Rognes Bouches-du-Rhône |
| Tel | +33 (0)4 42 50 16 29 |
| Email | lerossignol@free.fr |
| Web | www.moulindurossignol.com |

| | |
|---|---|
| | **Lis & Graham Steeden** Le *petit* Figuier, 23 rue du Poilu, 13640 La Roque d'Anthéron Bouches-du-Rhône |
| Mobile | +33 (0)7 82 20 19 38 / +44 (0)7941 172388 |
| Email | lis.steeden@hotmail.com |
| Web | www.lepetitfiguier.com |

## Mas Val Ample

An architect-designed delight tucked away in a quiet rural setting just outside Eygalières and cleverly built in old Provençal style but with ultra modern interiors. You'll feel entirely private in the vast grounds which have a large salt treated swimming pool for proper swimmers, shady places for a good book under a mature oak or plane tree, and comfortable loungers. Both swish and elegant bedrooms have their own terrace and large glass doors to draw the garden in. Wander into the village for breakfast or hop over to the hotel next door, which charming Claudine has an arrangement with. Stylish and restful but with lots to do round and about. *Minimum stay: 2 nights.*

## Le Mas d'Arvieux

Caroline is a fabulous host, and her elegant manor house in Provence is full of colour. Big bedrooms, one in the tower wing, one with a carved mezzanine, have beams, stone walls, fine old armoires, luxurious bathrooms and long views. Arvieux' orchards drip with olives and luscious jam-worthy fruit; have afternoon tea or a delicious breakfast by the pool. Peaceful out of season, it's a great set-up for families in summer and the whole house can be booked; perfect for a wedding venue too. Cookery and art classes can be arranged, there are toys and games outside for little ones, and a boutique selling local crafts and estate produce.

| | |
|---|---|
| Rooms | 1 double, 1 twin/double: €150. |
| Meals | Breakfast available at hotel next door, €12.50. Restaurants 1km. |
| Closed | Rarely. |

| | |
|---|---|
| Rooms | 2 doubles: €105. 1 suite for 2: €135. 2 triples, 1 studio for 2: €130. |
| Meals | Dinner with wine, €35. Restaurant 3km. |
| Closed | Rarely. |

| | |
|---|---|
| | **Claudine Leclercq** Mas Val Ample, Chemin de Pestelade - Impasse Fulcrand, 13810 Eygalières Bouches-du-Rhône |
| Tel | +33 (0)4 90 95 94 33 |
| Email | claudine@valample.com |
| Web | www.valample.com |

| | |
|---|---|
| | **Caroline Villon** Le Mas d'Arvieux, Route d'Avignon, 13150 Tarascon Bouches-du-Rhône |
| Tel | +33 (0)4 90 90 78 77 |
| Mobile | +33 (0)6 11 71 91 40 |
| Email | mas@arvieux-provence.com |
| Web | www.arvieux-provence.com |

Entry 781   Map 16

Entry 782   Map 16

## 24 rue du Château

On a medieval street near one of the finest castles in France, two *maisons de maître* are joined by an ochre-hued courtyard and a continuity of taste. It's an impeccable renovation that has kept all the soft patina of stone walls and tiles. No garden, but a courtyard for candlelit evenings and immaculate breakfasts. Calming, gracious bedrooms have fine old furniture and beams, perfect bathrooms, crisp linen. While you can be totally independent, your courteous hostess is relaxed and friendly and thoroughly enjoys her guests. Deeply atmospheric. *Minimum stay: 2 nights.*

## Galerie Huit

In the ancient heart of Arles, a fascinating 17th-century mansion. Warm vibrant Julia is curator of aesthetics, cultured conversation and a gallery that combines art with hospitality. Flagstones, fireplaces and original panelling abound, homemade jams at breakfast accompany a stylish tea selection and occasional dinners are paired with wine from friends' vineyards. And staircases wind past Chinese scrolls to your suite: exquisite tommette tiles, a dreamy 'ciel de lit,' restored frescoes, marble touches and a small mosaic shower room with a gilded mirror. Explore Arles, a town ripe for discovery, and enjoy the Camargue wilds! *Minimum stay: 2 nights.*

| Rooms | 2 doubles, 2 twins: €80–€100. |
|---|---|
| Meals | Restaurants in town. |
| Closed | November – March. |

| Rooms | 1 suite for 2: €95–€150. |
|---|---|
| | Extra bed €30 per person per night. |
| Meals | Dinner with wine, €35. |
| | Restaurants nearby. |
| Closed | Rarely. |

Martine Laraison
24 rue du Château,
13150 Tarascon
Bouches-du-Rhône
Tel +33 (0)4 90 91 09 99
Email ylaraison@gmail.com
Web www.rue-du-chateau.com

Julia de Bierre
Galerie Huit,
8 rue de la Calade,
13200 Arles
Bouches-du-Rhône
Mobile +33 (0)6 82 04 39 60
Email contact@galeriehuit.com
Web www.galeriehuit.com

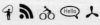

## Mas de Ravert

At last: a genuine old family-run farmhouse in Provence, close to everything but away from the crowds. Muriel discreetly welcomes you into the sitting/dining room… with its raftered ceiling, grand piano and billiard table decked in Bordeaux red felt, it's quite a conversion from the old goat barn. All is contemporary, nothing is too cluttered, not even the pièce de résistance, the Littérature suite, wonderfully private and cool. Look out for the dancing prints of Provençal artist Léo Lelée on the stairway, as you descend for breakfast on the terrace or a dip in the pool, protected from the Mistral by tall cypress trees. Charming.

## La Maison du Paradou

This charmingly converted coaching inn in the small village of Paradou has a stupendous vaulted salon with a roaring fire and books galore; in good weather you decamp onto the terrace for delicious communal breakfasts. You'll find a boules pitch, two rather swish pools, white sun loungers and a super garden. As for the rooms, expect the best: fabulous linen on the comfiest beds, delicious colours to keep you smiling (emerald, fuchsia, lemon) and bathrooms that go the whole way. A TV/computer in each room is packed with music and movies, and downstairs walls are crammed with interesting art. Special place, special people.

| Rooms | 2 doubles, 1 twin: €80–€120. 1 suite for 4: €150–€170. Extra bed €20 per person per night. |
| --- | --- |
| Meals | Restaurants 2km. |
| Closed | Christmas. |

| Rooms | 5 doubles: €225–€295. Extra bed/sofabed €30 per person per night. |
| --- | --- |
| Meals | Lunch €35. Restaurants a 5-minute walk, in Paradou. |
| Closed | Rarely. |

**Muriel Bérard**
Mas de Ravert, Chemin de la Thèze,
Route de St Rémy,
13103 St Étienne du Grès
Bouches-du-Rhône
Tel        +33 (0)4 90 49 18 11
Mobile   +33 (0)6 50 75 29 04
Email     masderavert@wanadoo.fr
Web       www.masderavert.fr

**Andrea & Nick Morris**
La Maison du Paradou,
Route de St Roch,
13520 Paradou
Bouches-du-Rhône
Tel      +33 (0)4 90 54 65 46
Email   reservations@maisonduparadou.com
Web     www.maisonduparadou.com

## Mas des Tourterelles

Let the peace and the greenery wash over you, on the residential outskirts of town; beautiful St Rémy is five minutes away. The new face of this charming old house is warm and friendly, and housekeeper Virginie prepares a fresh breakfast and knows the best places to go. Bedrooms, restful spaces of white and grey, face south over patios and decked pool; bathrooms have stylish limestone floors and Provençal toiletries. There's a cosy sitting room for guests (leather sofas, honesty bar, log fire: you can stay in winter too) and cots and child beds are available; just ask. Park here, and stroll into town. *Minimum stay: 2 nights.*

## Mas de la Croix d'Arles

St Rémy is Provence on a plate: ancient streets, artists, restaurants, the colourful weekly market, the lush valleys and the clear light which inspired Van Gogh. A short walk down the canal, a properly Provençal farmhouse distils this peace in a bubble of olives, vines and fruit trees. Tucked away in a pale stone bungalow are two light-filled B&B rooms, whose slate tiles, painted beams and fiery red splashes give a chic twist to Provençal style. You share a plunge pool with gîte guests, and breakfast on the terrace with lovely Jordane who'll spill the area's best-kept secrets – from hilltop Les Baux to the ochre-tinged Lubéron.

| | |
|---|---|
| Rooms | 2 doubles, 1 twin; 1 double with private bathroom: €110–€125. |
| Meals | Restaurants within walking distance. |
| Closed | Rarely. |

| | |
|---|---|
| Rooms | 1 double, 1 twin/double: €75–€90. |
| Meals | Restaurants 1km. |
| Closed | Rarely. |

Hervé Lepere
Mas des Tourterelles,
21 chemin de la Combette,
13210 St Rémy de Provence
Bouches-du-Rhône

Mobile +33 (0)6 16 70 65 47
Email contact@masdestourterelles.com
Web www.masdestourterelles.com

Jordane Marsot
Mas de la Croix d'Arles,
Chemin des Servières,
13210 St Rémy de Provence
Bouches-du-Rhône

Tel +33 (0)4 90 90 04 82
Mobile +33 (0)6 28 98 30 56
Email masdelacroixdarles@sfr.fr
Web www.masdelacroixdarles.com

## Provence – Alps – Riviera

### Mas du Vigueirat

High plane trees flank the drive to the dusky pink, grey-shuttered Provençal farmhouse and inside all is light, simplicity and gentle elegance. Bedrooms are uncluttered spaces of bleached colours, limed walls and terracotta floors. Views are over the beautiful garden with its small pool cascading into a larger one, or meadows, and ground-floor 'Maillane' has a private terrace. The high-beamed dining room/salon is a calm white space with a corner for sofas and books. If the weather's warm you'll take breakfast outside; after a dip in the pool or a jaunt on the bike, enjoy one of Catherine's lunches, fresh from the vegetable garden.

| Rooms | 3 doubles: €130–€155. |
| | 1 suite for 2 (July/August only): €185. |
| Meals | Picnic available. |
| | Poolside meals in summer €15–€20. |
| | Restaurants 3km. |
| Closed | Christmas. |

| | Catherine Jeanniard |
| | Mas du Vigueirat, |
| | 1977 chemin du Grand Bourbourel, |
| | Route de Maillane, |
| | 13210 Saint Rémy de Provence |
| | Bouches-du-Rhône |
| Tel | +33 (0)4 90 92 56 07 |
| Email | contact@mas-du-vigueirat.com |
| Web | www.mas-du-vigueirat.com |

Entry 789   Map 16

## Provence – Alps – Riviera

### Mas de Vincent

In peaceful rural Provence, a lovely farmhouse with spotless B&B rooms. Virginia creepers clamber up the shuttered façade and lawned gardens planted with flowering shrubs surround the property. Dive into a sparkling pool to escape the summer heat; loungers and parasols keep both sunbathers and shade-seekers happy. Terracotta-tiled bedrooms are simple and bright, with comfortable beds dressed in white linen. Breakfast is a continental spread, in the beamed dining room or by the pool. Golfers will be in heaven – Mas de Vincent is close to three courses, while the hilltop citadel of Les Baux is a just a short drive. *Minimum stay: 2 nights on weekdays & at weekends; 3 nights in high season. Pets by arrangement.*

| Rooms | 5 doubles: €80–€110. |
| | Extra bed €20 per person per night. |
| Meals | Restaurant 3km. |
| Closed | December – February. |

| | Annette Savesi |
| | Mas de Vincent, |
| | 4 Le Coussoul, |
| | 13890 Mouriès |
| | Bouches-du-Rhône |
| Tel | +33 (0)4 90 47 62 47 |
| Email | annettesavesi@hotmail.fr |
| Web | www.masdevincent.com |

Entry 790   Map 16

Provence – Alps – Riviera

Provence – Alps – Riviera

## Mas de la Rabassière

Amazing views to the coast, fanfares of lilies at the door, Haydn inside and 'mine host' smiling in his 'Cordon Bleu' chef's apron. Vintage wines and a sculpted dancer grace the terrace table. Cookery classes with house olive oil and easy airport pick-up are all part of the elegant hospitality, aided by Thévi, Michael's serene assistant from Singapore. Big bedrooms and a drawing room with a roaring fire are comfortable in English country-house style: generous beds, erudite bookshelves, a tuned piano, Provençal antiques... and tennis, croquet, a pool. A little fading around some edges but stacks of character. *Extra bed/sofabed available.*

## Les Arnauds

Come for a lovely old laid-back stone house, with pretty views of fields and hills. Here lives Sheila, with cats and ducks! You can share the family's living space or retreat to the guest sitting room, but summer evenings are usually spent outside, drinking in the scents and peace. Breakfasts with delicious fig, cherry and apricot jams set you up for the festivals and flower markets of Aix (6km). Return to comfortable beds on carpeted floors and ceiling fans to keep you cool. Time it right (July and October) and you can join in with the lavender and olive harvests: great fun. *Minimum stay: 2 nights.*

| Rooms | 2 doubles: €85-€150. |
|---|---|
| | Singles €85. |
| | Dinner, B&B €130-€140 per person. |
| Meals | Dinner with wine, €55. |
| Closed | Rarely. |

| Rooms | 2 doubles: €80-€120. |
|---|---|
| | 1 suite for 2: €115-€125. |
| Meals | Restaurant 3km. |
| Closed | Never. |

**Michael Frost**
Mas de la Rabassière,
2137 chemin de la Rabassière,
13250 Saint Chamas
Bouches-du-Rhône

Tel +33 (0)4 90 50 70 40
Email michaelfrost@wanadoo.fr
Web www.rabassiere.com

**Sheila Spencer**
Les Arnauds,
1902 chemin du Pont Rout,
13090 Aix en Provence
Bouches-du-Rhône

Tel +33 (0)4 42 20 17 96
Mobile +33 (0)6 78 90 38 85
Email shspencer@gmail.com
Web www.lesarnauds.com

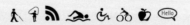

Entry 791  Map 16

Entry 792  Map 16

## Provence – Alps – Riviera

### Le Clos des Frères Gris

In through the gates of Hubert's exquisitely
tended park and well-tree'd gardens; you'd
never guess the centre of Aix en Provence
was a seven-minute drive. Polyglot Caroline
is a people person whose hospitality goes
beyond her warm welcome. A passion for
antiques is evident throughout her house, as
is a talent with fabrics and colours; bedrooms
combine comfort with cool elegance, fine
linens, thick towels, special touches. Admire
the rose and herb gardens on the way to
boules or pool, then set off to discover the
music and markets of Aix. A jewel of a
bastide, a home from home and worth every
sou. *Minimum stay: 2 nights.*

| | |
|---|---|
| Rooms | 4 doubles: €130–€190. |
| Meals | Restaurant 1km. |
| Closed | 31 October – 1 April. |

**Caroline & Hubert Lecomte**
Le Clos des Frères Gris,
2240 av Fortune Ferrini,
13080 Luynes, Aix en Provence
Bouches-du-Rhône
Tel +33 (0)4 42 24 13 37
Mobile +33 (0)6 70 26 24 80
Email freres.gris@free.fr
Web freres.gris.free.fr

Entry 793   Map 16

## Provence – Alps – Riviera

### La Bruissanne

Terraces of lavender, wisteria-covered
pergolas, breakfasts beneath mulberry trees;
Provençal living at its finest. Views from this
20th-century villa – from pool or private
patio – sweep over lawns and cypresses.
Rooms, with separate entrances, are
furnished in Provençal country-style; fresh,
uncluttered, with tiled floors, white quilts
and splashes of colour on walls and fabrics.
Choose 'Marius' for space, 'César' for
intimacy, 'Fanny' for romance. Find quiet
corners for evening aperos, a summer kitchen
for simple suppers. Stroll to Aix's museums,
markets and restaurants; warmly efficient
Sophie will advise. *Minimum stay: 2 nights.*

| | |
|---|---|
| Rooms | 2 doubles, 1 twin/double: €110–€130. Extra bed/sofabed €35 per person per night. |
| Meals | Summer kitchen. Restaurants 20-minute walk. |
| Closed | Rarely. |

**Sophie Huet Legrand**
La Bruissanne,
283 chemin du Vallon des Gardes bas,
Le Tholonet,
13100 Aix en Provence
Bouches-du-Rhône
Tel +33 (0)4 42 21 16 76
Email labruissanneaix@gmail.com
Web www.labruissanne.com

Entry 794   Map 16

## Le Moulin des Forges

Imagine copious breakfasts at little round tables, a new Provençal house with four traditional rooms, and, in the 18th-century windmill in the grounds, a romantic bolthole for two. Your hosts are interesting and fun, he a former pilot, she a lawyer, and offer you excellent dinners and colour coordinated rooms in hotelly style, not huge but très confortable, one with a balcony to sit out on. The grounds are magnificent (swimming pool, tennis court, petanque, olive trees, vines), the donkeys are adorable and the setting is spectacular, with views to the village of Fuveau and Mont St Victoire. *Minimum stay: 2 nights.*

| | |
|---|---|
| Rooms | 4 doubles, 1 twin/double: €99-€160. |
| Meals | Dinner €18. |
| | Starters & desserts €6. |
| | Restaurants 4km. |
| Closed | Rarely. |

| | |
|---|---|
| | Philippe Nicolas |
| | Le Moulin des Forges, |
| | 170 chemin du Moulin des Forges, |
| | 13710 Fuveau |
| | Bouches-du-Rhône |
| Tel | +33 (0)4 42 65 09 59 |
| Email | contact@maison-hote-provence.com |
| Web | www.maison-hote-provence.com |

Entry 795   Map 16

## La Bartavelle

French Myriam and English Alastair, kind helpful hosts, live with exceptional views across the valley and sunrises framed by oak woods in their traditionally styled modern farmhouse, a testament to deft planning. Ground-floor bedrooms spread themselves round a lovely central pool and a walled terrace loaded with pot plants while an airy sitting room provides music, mod cons and reading space. Alastair knows the history of the region off by heart and every path and trail; trek up through the woods to the ridge-perched village of Mimet, with charming restaurants and views to Marseille and the sea.

| | |
|---|---|
| Rooms | 2 doubles, 2 twins: €75-€85. |
| | 1 suite for 3: €75-€105. |
| Meals | Guest kitchen. |
| | Restaurants 3km. |
| Closed | Rarely. |

| | |
|---|---|
| | Myriam & Alastair Boyd |
| | La Bartavelle, |
| | 348 chemin des Amandiers, |
| | 13105 Mimet |
| | Bouches-du-Rhône |
| Tel | +33 (0)4 42 58 85 90 |
| Email | info@labartavelle.com |
| Web | www.labartavelle.com |

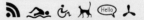

Entry 796   Map 16

## Mas Ste Anne

On its hilltop on the edge of pretty Peynier, the old *mas* stands in glory before Cézanne's Montagne Sainte Victoire: pull the cowbell, pass the wooden doors, and the red-shuttered farmhouse rises from beds of roses. Beautifully restored, it once belonged to the painter Vincent Roux and memories of his life live on, thanks to your gracious and very helpful hostess. The Roux room is the nicest, all beams, terracotta tiles, a fantastic ochre/green bathroom down the hall and a delicious garden view. The house has a wonderful old-fashioned patina and the gardens are perfectly kept. *Minimum stay: 2 nights. Older children welcome.*

## Château d'Eoures

Just outside bustling Marseilles is a haven of civilisation and tranquillity. This 18th-century bastide, in Jean-Lou's family for generations, is surrounded by dappled grounds – with peacocks, rabbits, hens, a swimming pool among the trees and irresistible wicker-furnished terraces. Music room, library, salon – the house is yours and your hosts love nothing better than to spoil you. Expect lavish breakfasts, delicious dinners and romantic rooms… a marble fireplace, a gilt mirror, a ciel-de-lit bed with beautiful linen. Don't miss Aubagne, for fêtes, festivals, fountains – and Marcel Pagnol's atmospheric house.

| | |
|---|---|
| Rooms | 1 double; 1 double with separate bathroom: €95–€115. |
| Meals | Summer kitchen. Restaurants in village. |
| Closed | Rarely. |

FIRST
EDITION
VETERAN

| | |
|---|---|
| Rooms | 1 double: €150. 1 family suite for 2-5 with separate bath: €100–€250. |
| Meals | Dinner with wine, €30. Summer kitchen. Restaurant 5km. |
| Closed | Rarely. |

Jacqueline Lambert
Mas Ste Anne,
3 rue d'Auriol,
13790 Peynier
Bouches-du-Rhône
Tel       +33 (0)4 42 53 05 32
Email    stanpeynier@yahoo.fr
Web      www.massainteanne.com

Mr & Mme Chouvet
Château d'Eoures,
53 rue Arnould,
13011 Marseille
Bouches-du-Rhône
Tel       +33 (0)4 91 44 24 53
Email    contact@chateau-eoures.com
Web      www.chateau-eoures.com

Entry 797   Map 16

Entry 798   Map 16

## Maison°9

A beautifully restored, elegant 19th-century winemaker's farmhouse on a vineyard-braided hill. Plush bedrooms, all different, are on the 'outskirts' of the main house; one is down a bamboo-screened path. Expect big beds, excellent linen, cool terracotta floors and Italianate monsoon-head showers. The delicious little garden bursts with pots of herbs, kentia palms and olive trees; the raised limestone pool is lined with canvas loungers, and views are over wooded hills to the grandiose 'Charlemagne's Crown' cliff face. Enjoy a spectacular breakfast in the main house, then stroll to the beach. Simple, chic perfection.

## La Demeure Insoupçonnée

New hosts Julie and Jean-Claude love life at their fresh, leafy oasis in juicy-sounding Cassis. Everything is beautiful: the Cap Canaille views, the pool (with dolphin detail), and the rare tranquillity in this much-visited area. Bougainvillea and sea scents are moments away as is the buzzing town centre. Spacious bedrooms are bright, one has a four-poster and mini kitchen for snacks, and the rock-hewn bathrooms make luxurious caves. Deep sleeps precede continental or charcuterie breakfasts… restful mornings merge into one. Bliss out in the pool, hammock or drive down the stunning Route des Crêtes.

| | |
|---|---|
| Rooms | 3 doubles; 1 double with sofabed: €195–€265. |
| Meals | Restaurant 2km. |
| Closed | November – March. |

| | |
|---|---|
| Rooms | 2 doubles: €130–€190. |
| | 1 suite for 6: €160–€200. |
| | Extra bed €30 per person per night. |
| Meals | Restaurant 1km. |
| Closed | Rarely. |

Cynthia Kayser-Maus
Maison°9,
9 av du Docteur Yves Bourde,
13260 Cassis
Bouches-du-Rhône
Tel      +33 (0)4 42 08 35 86
Email   contact@maison9.net
Web     www.maison9.net

Julie Kopp
La Demeure Insoupçonnée,
21 montée de la Chapelle,
13260 Cassis, Bouches-du-Rhône
Tel      +33 (0)4 42 82 35 78
Mobile  +33 (0)6 31 10 73 12
Email   lademeureinsoupconnee@gmail.com
Web     www.la-demeure-insoupconnee-cassis.com

## Bastide Ste Trinide

You'll love the simple lines and bright, airy décor of this renovated 18th-century farmhouse that once belonged to Pascale's grandparents. Prepare to be seduced by reds, whites and chocolate touches, fine linens, exposed beams, a choice of terraces for cooling breezes. One delight is the captivating chapel across the courtyard, another is the vibrant art: walls throughout are splashed with the canvasses of a family friend. You'll also love the blissful quiet up in the hills, though the beaches are minutes away. Walks, riding, golf, exotic gardens, zoo; let your charming young hosts help you explore.

## La Maison de Rocbaron

Who would not love this beautifully restored stone bergerie in a riot of greenery and flowers, with terraces dotted about gardens and pool? Jeanne and Guy's welcome is warm and easy; he keeps guests happy over an aperitif as she delivers a dinner not to be missed. The glorious black fig of Solliès is one of her specialities; both Jeanne and Guy are passionate about Slow Food. Various staircases lead to elegant rooms – symphonies in pink, white and floral – and modern bathrooms. An early dip, a feast of a breakfast, and you're ready for the day's adventures. A happy place in harmony with the world – in a peaceful Provençal village.

| | |
|---|---|
| Rooms | 1 double, 1 twin/double: €70–€90. |
| Meals | Restaurants nearby. |
| Closed | Rarely. |

| | |
|---|---|
| Rooms | 3 doubles: €98–€120. |
| | 2 suites for 2-4: €108–€130. |
| | Extra bed/sofabed €30 per person per night. |
| Meals | Dinner with wine, €40. |
| | Guest fridge & microwave. |
| | Restaurants in village. |
| Closed | Rarely. |

**Pascale Couture & Grégoire Debord**
Bastide Ste Trinide,
1671 chemin Chapelle Ste Trinide,
83110 Sanary sur Mer
Var

Tel     +33 (0)4 94 34 57 75
Email   contact@bastidesaintetrinide.com
Web    www.bastidesaintetrinide.com

**Jeanne Fischbach & Guy Laguilhemie**
La Maison de Rocbaron,
3 rue St Sauveur,
83136 Rocbaron
Var

Tel     +33 (0)4 94 04 24 03
Email   contact@maisonderocbaron.com
Web    www.maisonderocbaron.com

## Une Campagne en Provence

In spring, water gushes through myriad irrigation channels dug by the Knights Templar! Martina and Claude, proud possessors of the European Ecolabel, have planted 3,750 trees on their vast estate. The bastide keeps its fortress-like proportions and, like its owners, has bags of charm. Simple furnishings are lit by huge windows, floors are terracotta, and breakfasts and dinners put the accent on Provençal produce and their own wine. A pool with a view, a sauna, a Turkish bath, a well-stocked library, a mini cinema in the cellar... an isolated paradise for all ages, overseen by a charming young family, two geese and one dog.

## Domaine de la Blaque

The first property in the Var to be offically classified 'éco'! You are surrounded by nature at its best, and your lovely hosts have that artistic flair which puts the right things together naturally: palest pink-limed walls and white linen; old-stone courtyard walls with massed jasmine and honeysuckle; yoga groups and painters with wide open skies. Indeed, Jean-Luc is passionate about astronomy, Caroline enjoys photography, they produce olives, truffles and timber, organise courses – and love sharing their remote estate with like-minded travellers. Each pretty, independent room has its own little terrace.

| Rooms | 3 doubles: €95–€115. |
|---|---|
| | 1 suite for 2: €110–€120. |
| | 1 studio for 2 with kitchenette: €110–€130. |
| Meals | Dinner with wine, €36. Restaurant 3km. |
| Closed | January to mid-March. |

| Rooms | 1 double, |
|---|---|
| | 1 twin with kitchenette: €85–€98. |
| Meals | Restaurants 2.5km. |
| Closed | Rarely. |

|  | Martina & Claude Fussler |
|---|---|
| | Une Campagne en Provence, |
| | Domaine le Peyrourier, |
| | 83149 Bras |
| | Var |
| Tel | +33 (0)4 98 05 10 20 |
| Email | info@provence4u.com |
| Web | www.provence4u.com |

|  | Caroline & Jean-Luc Plouvier |
|---|---|
| | Domaine de la Blaque, |
| | 83670 Varages |
| | Var |
| Tel | +33 (0)4 94 77 86 91 |
| Mobile | +33 (0)6 25 32 22 81 |
| Email | la.blaque@gmail.com |
| Web | www.lablaque.com |

### Domaine de St Ferréol

Old, genuine and atmospheric are the words for this wine estate. Breakfast is the highlight of Armelle's hospitality and she's full of ideas for excursions, Monsieur happily sharing his knowledge. They are a warm, lively and cultured couple, their working vineyard has a timeless feel, their wine tastings are most civilised events. You get glorious views to Pontevès castle from first-class, authentically Provençal bedrooms; they and the breakfast room (with mini-kitchen) are in a separate wing but, weather permitting, breakfast is on the terrace. Peace and privacy in a beautiful old house, superb walking, and an outdoor pool.

| | |
|---|---|
| Rooms | 2 twin/doubles: €78–€920. 1 suite for 4: €110. |
| Meals | Guest kitchen. Restaurant 1.5km. |
| Closed | Mid-November to February. |

FIRST
EDITION
VETERAN

Guillaume & Armelle de Jerphanion
Domaine de St Ferréol,
83670 Pontevès
Var

| | |
|---|---|
| Tel | +33 (0)4 94 77 10 42 |
| Email | saint-ferreol@wanadoo.fr |
| Web | www.domaine-de-saint-ferreol.fr |

Entry 805   Map 16

---

Provence – Alps – Riviera

### Château Nestuby

Bravo, Nathalie! – in calm, friendly control of this gorgeous, well-restored 18th-century bastide. One whole wing is for guests: the light, airy, vineyard-view bedrooms, pastel-painted and Provençal-furnished with a happy mix of antique and modern (including WiFi), the big bourgeois sitting room (little used: it's too lovely outside), the spa on the roof terrace and the great spring-fed tank for swims. Stroll the lovely garden in the shade of 100-year-old plane trees; Jean-François runs the vineyard, the tastings and the wine talk at dinner with sweet-natured ease. Utterly relaxing and very close to perfection.
*Minimum stay: 3 nights in high season.*

| | |
|---|---|
| Rooms | 2 doubles, 2 twins, 1 suite for 2, 1 family room for 4, 1 triple: €90–€130. Extra bed €18 per person per night. |
| Meals | Dinner with wine, €27. |
| Closed | Mid-December to February. |

FIRST
EDITION
VETERAN

Nathalie & Jean-François Roubaud
Château Nestuby,
4540 route de Montford,
83570 Cotignac
Var

| | |
|---|---|
| Tel | +33 (0)4 94 04 60 02 |
| Mobile | +33 (0)6 86 16 27 93 |
| Email | nestuby@wanadoo.fr |
| Web | www.nestuby-provence.com |

Entry 806   Map 16

## La Bastide du Pin

It's a glamorous drive up from Nice to this gorgeous hideaway, set among gardens of lavender with views as far as the eye can see. Bedrooms are spacious and elegant with an understated feel, there's a beautiful shaded patio with only a fountain to disturb you, and billiards and books for evenings in. But best of all is Pierre, your interesting and attentive host, who gives you gorgeous breakfasts in a big dining room and holds court at dinner once a week in summer. A great spot from which to stroll into Lorgues, with its abbey, buzzing market, shops and bars; it's particularly alluring in spring.

## Villa de Lorgues

Expect the unexpected in this stately 18th-century townhouse. From the basement spa to the traditional living rooms – level with the delicious garden and terrace – to the bedrooms at the top, all is enchantment. A red lantern here, a ceiling mirror there, four-posters, fireplaces and candles where you least expect them. Bedrooms combine superb comfort with an elegant minimalist décor and smart bathrooms. Come evening, fairy lights wink along the wrought-iron balustrades from top to bottom. Claudie juggles a busy freelance career with talent, taste, a warm welcome and a fabulous sense of humour. *Minimum stay: 2 nights in high season.*

| | |
|---|---|
| Rooms | 4 doubles, 1 twin/double: €100–€175. 1 family room for 2-3: €125–€170. |
| Meals | Dinner with wine, €30–€40 (once weekly in summer). Restaurants 2km. |
| Closed | Rarely. |

| | |
|---|---|
| Rooms | 2 doubles: €135–€185. |
| Meals | Restaurants within walking distance. |
| Closed | Rarely. |

**Pierre Gissinger**
La Bastide du Pin,
1017 route de Salernes,
83510 Lorgues
Var

| | |
|---|---|
| Tel | +33 (0)4 94 73 90 38 |
| Email | contact@bastidedupin.com |
| Web | www.bastidedupin.com |

**Claudie Cais**
Villa de Lorgues,
7 rue de la Bourgade,
83510 Lorgues
Var

| | |
|---|---|
| Mobile | +33 (0)6 61 47 67 02 |
| Email | villadelorgues@gmail.com |
| Web | www.villadelorgues.com |

Entry 807  Map 16

Entry 808  Map 16

## L'Amandari

A dream of a place – but pinch yourself and the two shuttered buildings set in lush gardens will still be there. Inside, Cécile and Philippe have let East meet West, placing buddhas and Japanese prints in the sitting space and local antiques in the bedrooms. Beautiful, sometimes quirky touches abound: carved headboards, intricate crested mirrors, a wall-length wardrobe in 'La Lavande', a bamboo swan in intimate 'L'Olive'. Glean advice from your generous hosts and plan your day over a breakfast of homemade jam and cakes. Alternating between the heated pool and the jacuzzi may be as good a plan as any.

## Clos Saint Clement

This old stone house, oozing Provençal charm, was once a magnanerie where silkworms were raised. Now it's dedicated to your delight! The only hardship is choosing which bedroom to take: all are stylish and pale-hued, with high ceilings and ancient beams, and light streaming through shutters to illuminate beautiful old furniture. All have tiled bathrooms with extra towels for the pool – shimmering in the large garden amongst the fruit trees, figs and olives. Owners Suzanne and Pierre join you for convivial continental breakfasts at a long marble table on the terrace, or in the cool of the terracotta-flagged salon. Wonderful. *Minimum stay: 3 nights in high season. Children over 8 welcome.*

| | |
|---|---|
| Rooms | 1 double, 1 twin/double: €75–€140. 1 family room for 4: €145–€190. Pets €5–€10 per day. |
| Meals | Dinner with wine, €30. Restaurant within walking distance. |
| Closed | Rarely. |

| | |
|---|---|
| Rooms | 3 doubles: €115–€140. 1 triple: €125–€175. Singles €115–€130. |
| Meals | Dinner, 4 courses with wine, €35. Restaurant 1.2km. |
| Closed | Rarely. |

| | |
|---|---|
| | **Cécile & Philippe Louchard** L'Amandari, Vallat d'Emponse, 83120 Le Plan de la Tour Var |
| Tel | +33 (0)4 94 43 79 20 |
| Email | amandari-chambredhote@wanadoo.fr |
| Web | www.provence-holidays.com |

| | |
|---|---|
| | **Pierre & Suzanne Anselot** Clos Saint Clement, 83680 La Garde Freinet Var |
| Mobile | +33 (0)6 51 82 00 52 |
| Email | contact@clossaintclement.com |
| Web | www.clossaintclement.com |

Entry 809   Map 16

Entry 810   Map 16

## Le Clos du Pierredon

On the edge of charming Grimaud, in a road dotted with gated mansions, is an imposing but pretty former farmhouse, terracotta with green shutters. It stands in spacious grounds with a swimming pool lower down; take a dip, relax under the palms. Lovely Heather, gentle and stylish, serves summer breakfasts on the terrace outside; for dinner, village restaurants are a hilltop stroll. Or, out of season, nip into St Tropez (in high summer, cycling would be the faster option!). Smallish bedrooms come with their own entrances, one has a little terrace, another a balcony, and bathrooms are pristine, two with splendid new showers. *Children over 7 welcome.*

| Rooms | 3 doubles: €150. |
|---|---|
| Meals | Restaurants up in Grainaud. |
| Closed | Rarely. |

**Heather & Kevin Jennings**
Le Clos du Pierredon,
249 chemin St Joseph,
83310 Grimaud
Var
Mobile +44 (0)7889 452296
Email info@grimaudvacation.com
Web www.grimaudvacation.com

Entry 811  Map 16

## Le Pré aux Marguerites

Built in the 1950s in Provençal style, the house was the family's holiday home when Frédéric was a child; your captivating host was an interior designer in New York, now he runs this cliffside B&B. Breakfasts are convivial and copious, on the terrace or by the pool. You could spend all day here, up among the mimosas and palms, under the pines overlooking the sea…. there's even a path down to a private beach. The largest suite faces the sea, the other comes with a sloped beamed ceiling are refined with polished antiques. Don't miss hilltop villages Ramatuelle and Gassin – popular in summer but ever enchanting.

| Rooms | 2 suites for 2, each with kichenette: €150–€300. Extra single bed €60–€100 per night. |
|---|---|
| Meals | Dinner €45. Wine from €15. |
| Closed | January – March. |

**Frédéric Jochem**
Le Pré aux Marguerites,
1 av du Corail,
83240 Cavalaire
Var
Tel +33 (0)4 94 89 11 20
Email fjochem@aol.com
Web www.bonporto.com

Entry 812  Map 16

### 45 boulevard des Pêcheurs

From a private terrace atop this intriguing house, gaze past the umbrella pines and out to the sky-blue bay – what a tonic. The many-windowed parquet-floored bedroom, restfully done in soft colours, feels like a lookout tower; a good bathroom, too. Breakfast is served in the family dining room or on the main terrace; the luxuriant garden and superb pool area lie beyond while the wide, welcoming, uncluttered salon has nice old French furniture and ship's binoculars for those views. Your hosts – charming, active and attentive Claudine and Serge, who used to work in boats – are helpful and unintrusive. The centre is a 15-minute walk.
*Minimum stay: 2 nights.*

### L'Hirondelle Blanche

The beach is over the road, St Tropez a boat-trip away: charming out of season. Quite a character, Monsieur Georges enjoys painting, music, wine and old houses; he renovated this typical palmy 1900s Riviera villa himself. His paintings hang in the quirky sitting room, wines may appear for an evening tasting. Each room has a personal touch: a big red parasol over a bed, a fishing net on a wall; some have little balconies; bathrooms are basic with healthily rough eco-friendly, line-dried towels; breakfast is good. Despite the road, you don't need a car: fly in, train in, take a taxi or come by bike.

| | |
|---|---|
| Rooms | 1 double: €80–€90. |
| Meals | Restaurants 15-minute walk. |
| Closed | Rarely. |

| | |
|---|---|
| Rooms | 3 doubles, 1 triple: €99–€189. |
| Meals | Breakfast €5–€15. |
| | Restaurants within walking distance. |
| Closed | Mid-October to April. |

**Claudine & Serge Draganja**
45 boulevard des Pêcheurs,
Super-Lavandou,
83980 Le Lavandou
Var

Tel    +33 (0)4 94 71 46 02
Mobile    +33 (0)6 84 07 38 67
Email    draganja@orange.fr
Web    www.chambrehotes-draganja.com

**Georges & Florence Methout**
L'Hirondelle Blanche,
533 bd du Général de Gaulle,
83700 St Raphaël
Var

Tel    +33 (0)4 98 11 84 03
Email    kussler-methout@wanadoo.fr
Web    www.hirondelle-blanche.fr

## La Guillandonne

A very long drive, anticipation, then the house, the river, the cool forest. These lovely, civilised people, a former teacher of English and an architect, have treated their old house with delicacy and taste. Standing so Italianately red-ochre in its superb *parc* of great old trees and stream, it could have stepped out of a 19th-century novel. The interior speaks of your hosts' caring, imaginative approach (polished cement floors, rustic Salernes tiles). Bedrooms are full of personality, elegant and colourful; the living room is exquisite with vintage Italian hanging lamps and Le Corbusier chairs.

## Pantarou

Terraces of fruit, olive and magnolia trees; a stone-edged pool; a dining area with barbecue and glorious views... green-fingered owner Susanna found, and then improved, a place of peace and beauty. Inside: a bright living area with stone fireplace, lovely candelabra and a piano. There's a separate two-storey terrace studio and, upstairs, four charming, rustic-chic bedrooms, including the characterful 'Orange Room' and the 'White Suite' – a vision in white with a super smart en suite. Served on the sunny terrace, breakfast includes fresh treats from the local boulangerie. It's a five-minute drive to Grasse, perfume capital of the world, and half an hour to the Med. *Children over 8 welcome.*

| Rooms | 2 doubles, 1 twin: €90. |
|---|---|
| Meals | Restaurants 1.5km. |
| Closed | Rarely. |

| Rooms | 1 double, 1 studio for 2; 2 twin/doubles sharing bathroom: €100–€150. Singles €65. |
|---|---|
| Meals | Restaurant 3km. |
| Closed | Rarely. |

| | Marie-Joëlle Salaün |
|---|---|
| | La Guillandonne, |
| | 731a route des Tourrettes, |
| | 83440 Tourrettes |
| | Var |
| Tel | +33 (0)4 94 76 04 71 |
| Mobile | +33 (0)6 24 20 73 09 |
| Email | guillandonne@wanadoo.fr |

| | Susanna Johnston |
|---|---|
| | Pantarou, |
| | 58 route de la Vallée Verte, |
| | 06130 Grasse |
| | Alpes-Maritimes |
| Tel | +33 (0)9 88 66 44 25 |
| Email | pantarou.grasse@gmail.com |
| Web | www.pantarou.com |

Entry 815   Map 16

Entry 816   Map 16

## La Rivolte

Apricot-coloured villa, lavender-scented terraces, views to the shimmering Bay of Cannes; this is pure Provence. Rooms in the Belle Époque house, set above a spectacular garden, are light-filled and sorbet-coloured with rugs on tiled floors, wrought-iron bedsteads and charming brocante furnishings. One has a fireplace, another a private terrace, all have elegant bathrooms. Breakfast – homemade preserves – on the terrace or in the fire-warmed kitchen. Perfumed Grasse is strolling distance, the coast 25 minutes, relax by the pool with views and the heady scents of flowers and fruit trees. Housekeeper Suzie is charmingly capable. *Minimum stay: 2 nights.*

## Le Relais du Peyloubet

A hint of Tuscany seeps through this ancient farmhouse, its shutters and terracotta tiles, standing on a hillside wrapped in olive groves. Once growing flowers for Grasse perfumers, its delicious terraces and orchards are now tended by Roby while Xavier, a pâtissier, whisks up the fabulous breakfasts. Dinners are do-it-yourself in the summer kitchen overlooking the peaceful hills. Beamed and parquet-floored bedrooms, all with private terraces, are furnished in country Provençal style. There are shady seats in the woods, glorious views, boules, pool, and the coast 20 minutes. Blissfully calm, easy and welcoming.

| | |
|---|---|
| Rooms | 3 doubles, 2 twins: €105-€140. |
| Meals | Restaurants within walking distance. |
| Closed | Mid-May to mid-September. |

| | |
|---|---|
| Rooms | 1 double, 2 twin/doubles: €85-€115. 2 suites for 4: €95-€125. |
| Meals | Summer kitchen. Restaurant 3km. |
| Closed | Mid-November to mid-March. |

**Suzie Turner**
La Rivolte,
1 chemin des Lierres,
06130 Grasse
Alpes-Maritimes
Mobile +33 (0)6 50 97 33 31
Email suzie@larivolte.com
Web www.larivolte.com

**Xavier & Roby Stoeckel**
Le Relais du Peyloubet,
65 chemin de la Plâtrière,
06130 Grasse
Alpes-Maritimes
Mobile +33 (0)6 16 90 67 39
Email relais-peyloubet@wanadoo.fr
Web www.relais-peyloubet.com.fr

Entry 817  Map 16

Entry 818  Map 16

### Le Clos de St Paul

A young Provençal house on a lushly planted and screened piece of land where boundary hedging is high. In a guest wing, each pretty bedroom has its own patio, each bathroom is small and there's a summer kitchen for guests to share. Friendly energetic Madame has furnished in contemporary style – greys, yellows, painted chairs, the odd antique. She genuinely cares that you have the best, offers a welcome glass of rosé on her stunning shaded terrace and serves a very fresh breakfast in the garden. The large mosaic'd pool is a pleasure on a summer's day, and legendary St Paul de Vence is worth a trip. *Minimum stay: 2 nights.*

| | |
|---|---|
| Rooms | 1 double, 2 twin/doubles (1 with kitchenette): €75-€120. Singles €70-€85. Extra bed/sofabed €20 per person per night. Pets on request, €10 per night. |
| Meals | Summer kitchen. Restaurant 1km. |
| Closed | Rarely. |

Béatrice Ronin Pillet
Le Clos de St Paul,
71 chemin de la Rouguière,
06480 La Colle sur Loup
Alpes-Maritimes
Tel +33 (0)4 93 32 56 81
Email leclossaintpaul@hotmail.com
Web www.leclossaintpaul.com

Entry 819  Map 16

---

### Bleu Azur

Breakfast, ferried to the friendly communal table (or the elegant terrace) is a feast of croissants, fruits, jams and Jean-Yves' speciality: Breton crêpes. Nothing is too much trouble for these humorous hosts who have followed a long-held dream, to create an exceptional B&B. Their chosen patch, on the edge of a cobbled village between mountains and sea, has sumptuous gardens and shimmering views that reach to the Bay of Antibes. All six suites (including those for families) are sophisticated, spacious and on the ground floor. After a glamorous day on the Riviera, come home to a dive in the pool.

| | |
|---|---|
| Rooms | 3 twin/doubles: €128-€168. 3 apartments for 2: €168-€213. Extra bed/sofabed €32 per person per night. |
| Meals | Dinner, 3 courses with wine, €28-€35. Restaurants 800m. Kitchen available. |
| Closed | Never. |

Nadine Barrandon
Bleu Azur,
674 route des Queinières,
06140 Tourrettes sur Loup
Alpes-Maritimes
Tel +33 (0)4 93 32 58 55
Email contact@maisonhotes-bleuazur.com
Web www.maisondhotes-bleuazur.com

Entry 820  Map 16

## Villa Phoebe

This striking house wraps around its own private courtyard, an excellent spot for a dip in the pool and an afternoon siesta. The terraces above bring in the Provençal views and glass abounds to let in the light. Inside, stone floors and high ceilings keep it all cool. Bedrooms are distinguished with calming colours and fine fabrics (two share a bathroom); elsewhere the living spaces and kitchen are more modern, with brightly patterned vases, bold paintings and an open-plan design. Asa is a keen cook and will provide dinner, on request. Dine together under the lantern-lit olive trees and plan your hikes, rides and swims. Nice is a short drive away. *Parking available.*

## La Forge d'Hauterives

Discover a truly beautiful 18th-century 'bastide' basking between mountains and sea in the sunny Côte d'Azur close to St Paul de Vence and Nice. Anne, a talented designer, has converted the south-west facing village mansion impeccably. Find ornamental gates, a courtyard paved with pebbles, gorgeous bedrooms with antiques – some with private terraces – and a lounge with a warming fireplace. Stroll through the fecund garden cooled by an ancient fountain that pours into a swimming pool. Meet like-minded folk around a big, convivial table for sublime regional meals or wander into the village for craft shops by the castle. *Minimum stay: 2 nights.*

| Rooms | 3 doubles; 2 doubles with shared bathroom, separate bath: €80–€140. 2 singles: €60. Singles €60. Dinner, B&B €90–€180 per person. |
|---|---|
| Meals | Dinner, 3 courses with wine, €40. Restaurants in Vence a 20-minute walk. |
| Closed | Never. |

| Rooms | 4 doubles: €100–€180. 1 family room for 4: €230–€260. Extra bed €35 per person per night. |
|---|---|
| Meals | Dinner with wine, €40. Restaurants within walking distance. |
| Closed | Rarely. |

**Asa Hanna**
Villa Phoebe,
06140 Vence
Alpes-Maritimes

Tel +33 (0)4 93 58 04 86
Mobile +44 (0)7791 520541
Email asahanna@yahoo.co.uk

**Anne d'Hauterives**
La Forge d'Hauterives,
44 rue Yves Klein,
06480 Saint Paul de Vence
Alpes-Maritimes

Tel +33 (0)4 93 89 73 34
Mobile +33 (0)6 82 82 84 45
Email anne.dhauterives@newatoo.net
Web www.laforgedhauterives.com

## Les Orangers

Within walking distance of artistic Saint Paul de Vence, a tranquil hideaway with an enchanting garden shaded by palms and fruit trees. A slender pool is an oasis amid the abundant greenery. This was one of the village's original mas hotels, now Thomas and Marquesa have converted it into a delightful B&B. Five comfortable en-suite rooms are furnished with antiques and painted in rose, blue and ochre. Garden-level rooms have little terraces ideal for sipping rosé as the sun drops beneath the horizon. Breakfast is a delicious spread of ham, cheese, homemade jams and marmalades, and fruit, along with freshly-squeezed oranges from the garden. *Minimum stay: 2 nights. Parking available.*

## Le Mas St Antoine

On the residential outskirts of St Paul de Vence is a characterful B&B run by the effervescent Maric. An artist, she has joyfully decorated each of her guest rooms, our favourites being the two in the house: a gorgeous, spacious, Asian/Venetian suite, and 'Panoramic' that lives up to its name (and has a bath tub in its bedroom). All come with a private terrace and a summer kitchen so you can breakfast or lunch in peace, then bask around the splendid pool. The legendary hilltop village, all tourist boutiques, bars and cobble-stoned beauty, is an easy stroll. Nice and beaches are a bus ride away. *Minimum stay: 4 nights.*

| | |
|---|---|
| Rooms | 5 doubles: €140–€195. |
| Meals | Restaurants within walking distance. |
| Closed | Never. |

| | |
|---|---|
| Rooms | 2 doubles: €100–€120. |
| | 2 suites for 2: €110–€130. |
| | Extra bed €50 per person per night. |
| Meals | Private summer kitchens. |
| | Restaurants in village. |
| Closed | October – April. |

Marquesa Portela
Les Orangers,
Quartier Les Fumerates,
06570 Saint Paul de Vence
Alpes-Maritimes

| | |
|---|---|
| Tel | +33 (0)4 93 32 80 95 |
| Email | contact@lesorangers.fr |
| Web | www.lesorangers.fr |

Maric Trojani
Le Mas St Antoine,
1133 chemin St Étienne,
06570 Saint Paul de Vence
Alpes-Maritimes

| | |
|---|---|
| Tel | +33 (0)4 93 32 50 84 |
| Mobile | +33 (0)6 03 61 12 15 |
| Email | contact@lemassaintantoine.com |
| Web | www.lemassaintantoine.com |

## Le Mas du Chanoine

Wake up and smell the roses from the patio (15 varieties share the garden, along with lavender bushes, bougainvillea, fig and citrus trees), where you breakfast on Mariage Frères tea and Pascale's homemade jams and cakes in front of a striking stained-glass window. Inside, a treasure trove: Louis XVI Provençal cabinetry and marvellous stone fireplaces; oak parquet floors and marble bedside tables; a natural stone basin and a sunken bath. Explore the cobbled streets of Saint Paul de Vence, then soak tired limbs in the security pool with Opiocolor mosaic tiling. After dusk… pastis and boules on the floodlit court.

## Bastide Valmasque

The coral-coloured house is hard to miss. Friendly Philippe and Claudia met in India, and the influence of the subcontinent is everywhere. Indian canopies and daybeds are guarded by sacred stone cows amongst fruit trees, palms and lawns. Living and dining rooms have a hint of Bollywood – jewel coloured upholstery and mirrored furniture sizzle against pale walls. Bedrooms are spacious, bright and modern, each with charming decorative touches and a colour scheme that extends into the compact bathrooms. Breakfast indoors or on one of the terraces, then set off for Cap d'Antibes beaches: the road is close by.

| Rooms | 3 suites for 2: €150–€200. |
|---|---|
| Meals | Restaurants 2km. |
| Closed | Never. |

| Rooms | 3 doubles: €75–€125. |
|---|---|
| | 2 suites for 2: €115–€150. |
| | Extra bed €25 per person per night. |
| Meals | Restaurant nearby. |
| Closed | Rarely. |

AWARD
WINNER

One of a kind

Pascale Barissat
Le Mas du Chanoine,
831 chemin de la Bastide Rouge,
06570 Saint Paul de Vence
Alpes-Maritimes
Tel      +33 (0)4 93 08 81 03
Email   contact@masduchanoine.com
Web     www.masduchanoine.com

Philippe Bonan
Bastide Valmasque,
1110 route d'Antibes,
06410 Biot
Alpes-Maritimes
Tel      +33 (0)4 93 65 21 42
Email   bastidevalmasque@gmail.com
Web     www.bastidevalmasque.com

## Provence – Alps – Riviera

### Villa Castel

Up the coastal road, a seven-minute spin from the beaches of Cannes, is a gated, coded, securitised domaine in lush and lovely gardens. Up on the second floor of one of its 'résidences' is an English-owned apartment, awash with light and immaculately maintained. Carole – warm, humorous, good company – promises you a luxurious stay in Riviera style: a classy cosy bedroom (contemporary collages on cream walls, tall lamps throwing a soft glow), a stylish spacious bathroom, and a private terrace. Enjoy white sofas, white loungers, books, sunshine, flowers, and delicious viennoiseries to go with a breathtaking view.

| Rooms | 1 double: £170. |
|---|---|
| Meals | Restaurants 4km. |
| Closed | Rarely. |

Carole Castel
Villa Castel,
Parc Camille Amelie,
Residence Mayfair,
139 Ave du Maréchal Juin,
06400 Cannes
Alpes-Maritimes
Tel    +33 (0)4 92 02 06 64
Email  carole@villacastel.com

Entry 827   Map 16

---

## Provence – Alps – Riviera

### L'Air du Temps

Tucked away down a cul-de-sac, built by the hands of the Scassaus themselves and a short walk from the beaches, is this pretty Provençal house. One room has a sparkly chandelier and smoky-pink walls, another a sauna and private terrace. Outside: plenty of terrace to dine on, a kitchenette to whip up your dinner in and a chuckling green parrot, Ramón, who appreciates guests. The charming owners have lived here for years and are in love with their region; understandably so. Catch a ferry to St Tropez, visit the medieval villages, wander the lavender-perfumed mountains or come for the jazz in July. Delightful. *Minimum stay: 2 nights.*

| Rooms | 4 doubles: €120–€150. Singles €110–€150. Extra bed/sofabed €20 per person per night. |
|---|---|
| Meals | Summer kitchen. Restaurants within walking distance. |
| Closed | November – March. |

Rose-Marie Scassau
L'Air du Temps,
La Chênaie,
283 av des Eucalyptus,
06160 Juan les Pins
Alpes-Maritimes
Tel    +33 (0)4 93 61 27 43
Email  renato41@yahoo.com
Web    www.villaairdutemps.com

Entry 828   Map 16

### Villa Estelle

On one of the prettiest cobbled streets in France is the charming, multi-stepped Villa Estelle, once the old inn of the town where painters flocked and still do. Enjoy breakfast, English or continental, al fresco – the place is blessed with a big sunny terrace with views across rooftops to the sea. Chill out on comfy sofas amid books and magazines, negotiate the steep streets of the "Montmartre of the Riviera" choose a great restaurant for dinner. Moroccan-coloured bedrooms come in shabby-chic style, with pretty furniture, huge bathrooms, loads of space. Bubbly Fiona welcomes you warmly.
*Minimum stay: 2 nights in high season.*

### La Locandiera

Built for holidays and for early 20th-century entertaining, this Côte d'Azur villa is a literal stone's throw from the fishing port and beach, and charming Madame Rizzardo has forsaken Venice to restore it. Her villa exudes warmth, charm and peace – like stepping into the Riviera life of a more glamourous age – with gorgeous furnishings and, no doubt, witty conversation. Three of the cool, fresh, traditionally furnished bedrooms look straight out to sea over a walled garden whose jasmine-sweet corners are furnished for shaded retreat. Heaps of restaurants and smart places are reachable on foot.

| | |
|---|---|
| Rooms | 2 doubles: €102–€132. |
| | 3 family rooms for 4: €107–€172. |
| Meals | Restaurants within walking distance. |
| Closed | Never. |

| | |
|---|---|
| Rooms | 2 doubles, 1 twin: €120–€160. |
| | 2 suites for 2: €160–€190. |
| | Singles €120–€190. |
| | Extra bed/sofabed €35 per person per night. |
| Meals | Restaurants within walking distance. |
| Closed | Last 2 weeks in November. |

**Fiona Kennedy**
Villa Estelle,
5 montée de la Bourgade,
06800 Cagnes sur Mer
Alpes-Maritimes
Tel      +33 (0)4 92 02 89 83
Email   info@villa-estelle.com
Web     www.villa-estelle.com

**Daniela Rizzardo**
La Locandiera,
9 av Capitaine de Frégate Vial,
06800 Cagnes sur Mer
Alpes-Maritimes
Tel      +33 (0)4 97 22 25 86
Mobile  +33 (0)6 27 88 17 40
Email   daniela@lalocandieracagnes.com
Web     www.lalocandieracagnes.com

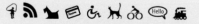

## Villa Kilauea

A grand Mediterranean villa that looks so settled in Nice's lush western hills you'd never know it was a 21st-century creation. There are balustrade-edged terraces, panoramic views and a blissful pool. Bedrooms above the pool house have a zen-like calm: wrought-iron four-posters draped in muslin, teak floors, white walls; orchids and silks hint at the exotic. The Lavender Room in the main house opens to the garden and is as feminine as the rest. Nathalie, the perfect host, kind, gentle and generous to a tee, delights in juggling family life with her B&B. Nice is a ten-minute drive down the hill.

## Villa L'Aimée

In one of the most authentic parts of Nice, a short tram ride from the city's rich culture (buses also stop virtually at the gate), Villa L'Aimée was built in 1929 and is typical of its period. Toni's decoration has restored its wonderful shapes and details to their original opulence. Warm, cultured and much-travelled – one of her lives was in the art world – she has created delightful bedrooms in subtle colours with damasks and silks, fine linen, tulle canopies and beautiful furnishings, exuding an air of old luxury. The original parquet is breathtaking, the breakfasts are superb. *Children over 10 welcome.*

| | |
|---|---|
| Rooms | 3 doubles: €130–€160. 1 suite for 2: €180–€210. |
| Meals | Restaurants in Nice. |
| Closed | Rarely. |

| | |
|---|---|
| Rooms | 2 twin/doubles, 1 twin: €110–€145. |
| Meals | Restaurants within walking distance. |
| Closed | December – March. |

**Nathalie Graffagnino**
Villa Kilauea,
6 chemin du Candeu,
06200 Nice
Alpes-Maritimes

| | |
|---|---|
| Mobile | +33 (0)6 25 37 21 44 |
| Email | nathalie@villakilauea.com |
| Web | www.villakilauea.com |

**Toni Redding**
Villa L'Aimée,
5 av Piatti,
06100 Nice
Alpes-Maritimes

| | |
|---|---|
| Tel | +33 (0)4 93 52 34 13 |
| Mobile | +33 (0)6 71 82 67 72 |
| Email | bookings@villa-aimee.co.uk |
| Web | www.villa-aimee.co.uk |

Entry 831   Map 16

Entry 832   Map 16

## La Florentine

The views from Penny and Roger's elegant 1920s villa are magnificent, stretching over the Bay of Villefranche and Cap Ferrat. Breakfasts are served on the panoramic Italianate terrace amid palms and flowers – and you can laze by the heated pool on wooden loungers. Inside are two doubles and a suite, with equally fine views and a pure, Provençal decor which gleams in the light of wide windows. Downstairs, the salon has French windows to the terrace and a roaring fire in winter. Warm and well-travelled, your hosts will point you to the best beaches, restaurants and historical sites along the Côte d'Azur. Nice is close. *Minimum stay: 3 nights.*

| Rooms | 2 doubles: €220 |
| --- | --- |
| | 1 suite for 2-3: €220-€380. |
| Meals | Restaurants 1km. |
| Closed | Rarely. |

**Penny Palmano**
La Florentine,
42 bd Settimelli Lazar,
06230 Villefranche sur Mer
Alpes-Maritimes
Mobile  +33 (0)6 40 31 73 70
Email  penny.palmano@palmano.com

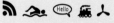

Entry 833  Map 16

## La Parare

Cradled in summer by cicada chant and the gentle wind, cocooned in winter in a romantic log-warmed bedroom, you will be bewitched by the subtle mix of clean-cut modernity and fine oriental detail that your much-travelled polyglot hosts have achieved in this craggy old house. Breakfast in bed? Bathtub for two? Elegant gourmet dinner? All of these and more: Karin from Sweden and French/Dutch Sydney love pampering people. The rough hills outside highlight the delicacy inside, the natural walled pool, the stunning bathrooms, the civilised conversation at dinner. Worth every centime. *Minimum stay: 2 nights at weekends, 4 nights in high season.*

| Rooms | 4 doubles: €140-€170. |
| --- | --- |
| Meals | Dinner with wine, €35-€50. |
| Closed | Rarely. |

**Karin & Sydney van Volen**
La Parare,
67 calade du Pastre,
06390 Châteauneuf Villevieille
Alpes-Maritimes
Tel  +33 (0)4 93 79 22 62
Email  karin@laparare.com
Web  www.laparare.com

Entry 834  Map

## Les Cyprès

Glorious views stretch over countryside and town from Frances's apricot-coloured villa. Its beautiful big garden bears olives, flowers and fruit in profusion – fig, cherry, strawberry... discover secret areas for dining or hiding away with a book. Bedrooms are traditional and minimalist with pretty bedspreads and smart bathrooms, and breakfast is scrumptious: bread, brioche, homemade jams galore. Explore the fascinating old town, tootle over to Nice, and get back in time for truly delicious four-course dinners. Whet your whistle with an apéritif in the cosy-rustic sitting room... prepare to be spoiled. *Minimum stay: 2 nights in high season.*

| | |
|---|---|
| Rooms | 3 doubles: €85–€90. |
| | Extra bed €25 per person per night. |
| Meals | Dinner, 4 courses with wine, €25. |
| | Restaurant 1km. |
| Closed | Christmas. |

**Frances Thompson**
Les Cyprès,
289 route de Châteauneuf,
06390 Contes
Alpes-Maritimes

| | |
|---|---|
| Mobile | +33 (0)6 46 27 54 95 |
| Email | contact@lescypres.fr |
| Web | www.lescypres.fr |

Entry 835   Map 16

# Corsica

## Chambres d'Hôtes à Vallecalle

Welcome to the master house in Vallecalle, on the village edge, an eagle's nest with exquisite valley views. Here live Paul Henri and Myriam, warm, witty, welcoming, living the dream, raising a family, happy to advise you on their beloved adopted land – the food, the culture – or leave you in peace to explore their home, beautiful in its simplicity. Bedrooms, two with 18th-century floorboards, are spacious and gracious. The terraced gardens have oranges, olives, a hammock, corners for shade and sun, and, below, a river to bathe in. Myriam's dishes, always delicious, can be delicate, intriguing or hearty. Stay in!

| Rooms | 1 double: €65. |
|---|---|
| | 1 suite for 2-5: €70-€136. |
| | 1 family room for 4: €70-€100. |
| | Singles €65-€70. |
| Meals | Dinner with wine, €23. |
| | Restaurant 7km. |
| Closed | Never. |

**Myriam & Paul Henri Gaucher**
Chambres d'Hôtes à Vallecalle,
Village de Vallecalle,
20232 Vallecalle
Haute-Corse

| Tel | +33 (0)4 95 37 60 60 |
|---|---|
| Email | phgaucher@sfr.fr |
| Web | www.chambresencorse.com |

Chalet Twenty26
Haute-Savoie Entry 723

Chalet Châtelet
Haute-Savoie Entry 719

La Ferme de Margot
Haute-Savoie Entry 721

La Ferme du Soleil
Haute-Savoie Entry 729

INSPECTED & SELECTED
by
Sawday's
SPECIAL PLACES

Chalet le 4
Haute-Savoie www.sawdays.co.uk/gosnow

Chalet Twenty26
Haute-Savoie Entry 723

Chalet Amuse Bouche
Haute-Savoie Entry 722

Ferme du Ciel
Haute-Savoie Entry 725

# Sawday's
# GO SNOW
## COLLECTION

It's time to hit the slopes! From the
cosy to the grand, find a chalet with
a heated pool, an underground spa
or a Michelin- starred restaurant.
With handy tips about distances to lifts,
the best places to hire equipment,
and some great après-ski pampering,
this is a superb place to start planning
your close encounter of the snowy kind.

www.sawdays.co.uk/gosnow

Alastair Sawday has been publishing books for over 20 years, finding Special Places to Stay in Britain and abroad. All our properties are inspected by us and are chosen for their charm and individuality, and with 12 titles to choose from there are plenty of places to explore. You can buy any of our books at a reader discount of 25%* on the RRP.

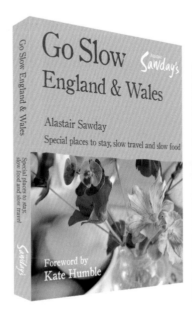
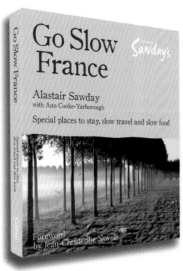

| List of titles: | RRP | Discount price |
|---|---|---|
| British Bed & Breakfast | £15.99 | £11.99 |
| Special Places to Stay in Britain for Garden Lovers | £19.99 | £14.99 |
| British Hotels and Inns | £15.99 | £11.99 |
| Pubs & Inns of England & Wales | £15.99 | £11.99 |
| Dog-friendly Breaks in Britain | £14.99 | £11.24 |
| French Bed & Breakfast | £15.99 | £11.99 |
| French Châteaux & Hotels | £15.99 | £11.99 |
| Italy | £15.99 | £11.99 |
| Portugal | £12.99 | £9.74 |
| Spain | £15.99 | £11.99 |
| Go Slow England & Wales | £19.99 | £14.99 |
| Go Slow France | £19.99 | £14.99 |

*postage and packaging is added to each order

How to order:
You can order online at: www.sawdays.co.uk/bookshop
or call: +44(0)117 204 7810

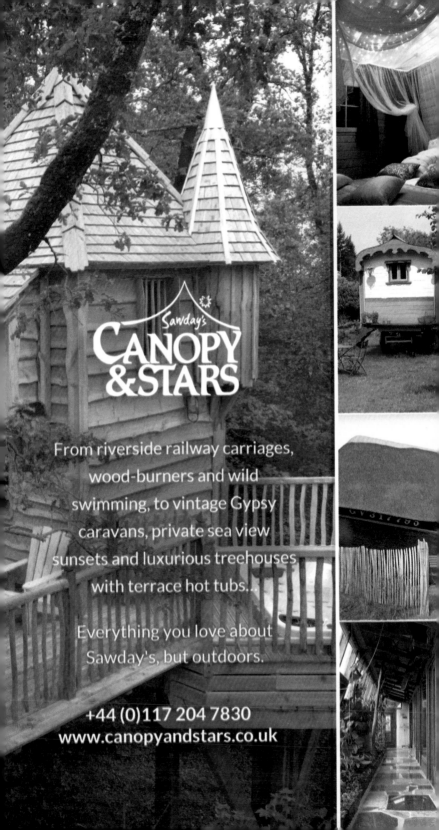

ON
WHEELS

OUT IN THE
WILDERNESS

IN THE
TREES

Château des Salles
Charente-Maritime Entry 8

Château de Pintray
Indre-et-Loire Entry 391

Peyraguey Maison Rouge
Gironde Entry 484

Château de la Vieille Chapelle
Gironde Entry 469

Domaine du Moulin de Labique
Lot-et-Garonne Entry 522

Château de Béru
Yonne Entry 124

Les Deux Chèvres
Côte-d'Or Entry 113

INSPECTED & SELECTED by Sawday's
SPECIAL PLACES

# *Vineyards*

COLLECTION

It's always a glorious time to expand your knowledge of the French grape! Stay in one of our hand picked Special Places on wine estates scattered across some of the best wine regions in France.

www.sawdays.co.uk/vineyards

These places have at least one bedroom and bathroom accessible for wheelchair users. Please contact them for further details.

The North
1 • 5 • 17 • 20

Picardy
40

Champagne – Ardenne
55 • 60 • 65 • 68 • 69 • 70

Burgundy
96 • 109 • 113 • 125

Région Parisienne
150 • 157 • 162

Normandy
172 • 180 • 182 • 185 • 187 • 191 • 193 • 200 • 201 • 210 • 238

Brittany
250 • 256 • 275 • 278

Western Loire
286 • 294 • 305 • 320 • 324 • 326

Loire Valley
371 • 375 • 380 • 384 • 389 • 400

Poitou – Charentes
415 • 422 • 438 • 439 • 444 • 450 • 452

Aquitaine
467 • 469 • 491 • 504 • 519 • 521 • 527 • 531 • 542

Limousin
556

Midi – Pyrénées
582 • 593 • 607 • 611 • 616 • 624

Languedoc – Roussillon
656 • 667 • 685 • 686 • 694

Rhône Valley – Alps
711

Provence – Alps – Riviera
762 • 769 • 782 • 791 • 796 • 799 • 804 • 810 • 811 • 819 • 820 • 830

# Join us

TIME AWAY IS FAR TOO PRECIOUS TO
SPEND IN THE WRONG PLACE. THAT'S WHY,
BACK IN 1994, WE STARTED SAWDAY'S.

Twenty years on, we're still a family concern – and still
on a crusade to stamp out the bland and predictable,
and help our guests find truly special places to stay.

If you have one, we do hope you'll decide
to take the plunge and join us.

———

ALASTAIR & TOBY SAWDAY

"Trustworthy, friendly and helpful – with a reputation
for offering wonderful places and discerning visitors."
JULIA NAISMITH, HOLLYTREE COTTAGE

"Sawday's. Is there any other?"
SONIA HODGSON, HORRY MILL

# WHY BECOME A MEMBER?

Becoming a part of our 'family' of Special Places is like being awarded a Michelin star. Our stamp of approval will tell guests that you offer a truly special experience and you will benefit from our experience, reputation and support.

### A CURATED COLLECTION

Our site presents a relatively small and careful selection of Special Places which helps us to stand out like a brilliantly shining beacon.

### INSPECT AND RE-INSPECT

Our inspectors have an eagle-eye for the special, but absolutely no check-lists. They visit every member, see every bedroom and bathroom and, on the lucky days, eat the food.

### QUALITY, NOT QUANTITY

We don't pretend (or want) to be in the same business as the sites that handle zillions of bookings a day. Using our name ensures that you attract the right kind of guests for you.

### VARIETY

From country-house hotels to city pads and funky fincas to blissful B&Bs, we genuinely delight in the individuality of our Special Places.

### LOYALTY

Nearly half of our members have been with us for five years or more. We must be doing something right!

## GET IN TOUCH WITH OUR MEMBERSHIP TEAM...

+44 (0) 117 204 7810

members@sawdays.co.uk

## ...OR APPLY ONLINE

sawdays.co.uk/joinus

*The friendly crew*

### Limousin

#### Maison Grandchamp

In an historic town, be welcomed by a charming, cultured couple to a 400-year-old house of fascinating origins. Thrill to Marielle's tales: her ancestors built and extended the house, their portraits hang in the panelled drawing room; find time for François' knowledge of history, geography and the environment. Up the elegant spiral stairs, bedrooms are in proper but unpompous château style, big, soft and quiet. Breakfast is in the beamy 16th-century dining room, or by the kitchen fire, or in the terraced garden overlooking jumbled rooftops, or in the luminous veranda. Then explore glorious Corrèze.

| Rooms | 2 twin/doubles; 1 twin/double with separate bathroom: €80–€90. Extra bed €25 per person per night. Overflow room for 2 available. |
|---|---|
| Meals | Dinner with aperitif & wine €29–€32. Restaurants within walking distance. |
| Closed | January – March. |

Marielle & François Teyssier
Maison Grandchamp,
9 place des Pénitents,
19260 Treignac
Corrèze

| Tel | +33 (0)5 55 98 10 69 |
|---|---|
| Mobile | +33 (0)6 59 05 09 46 |
| Email | teyssier.marielle@wanadoo.fr |
| Web | www.hotesgrandchamp.com |

Entry 558   Map 10

### Limousin

#### Maison Numéro Neuf

Lisa and Duncan from England have embraced life in southern La Souterraine. She is the least ruffled, most contented of chefs; he serves wines with finesse; both love house, children, guests, and their secret garden with hens. Now, at last, the renovation of the former residence of the Marquis de Valady is complete. So much to enjoy: the fine proportions, the sweeping balustrade, the antique mirrors, the crystal-drop chandeliers, the pale walls, the glowing parquet... and superb breakfasts and dinners. If Lisa pops a hot water bottle into your bed it will be encased in white linen: the hospitality here is exceptional.

| Rooms | 2 doubles; 1 twin sharing shower: €65–€115. |
|---|---|
| Meals | Dinner €22–€45. Wine €18. |
| Closed | Rarely. |

Duncan & Lisa Rowney
Maison Numéro Neuf,
Rue Serpente,
23300 La Souterraine
Creuse

| Tel | +33 (0)5 55 63 43 35 |
|---|---|
| Email | reservations@maisonnumeroneuf.com |
| Web | www.maisonnumeroneuf.com |

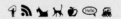

Entry 559   Map 9